Cognitive Technologies

Managing Editors: D.M. Gabbay J. Siekmann

Springer
Berlin
Heidelberg
New York
Hong Kong
London
Milan
Paris
Tokyo

Helmut Prendinger
Mitsuru Ishizuka (Eds.)

Life-Like Characters

Tools, Affective Functions, and Applications

With 170 Figures and 9 Tables

 Springer

Editors

Helmut Prendinger
Mitsuru Ishizuka
Dept. of Information and Communication Engineering
Graduate School of Information Science and Technology
University of Tokyo, 7-3-1, Hongo, Bunkyo-ku, Tokyo 113-8656, Japan

Managing Editors

Prof. Dov M. Gabbay
Augustus De Morgan Professor of Logic
Department of Computer Science, King's College London
Strand, London WC2R 2LS, UK

Prof. Dr. Jörg Siekmann
Forschungsbereich Deduktions- und Multiagentensysteme, DFKI
Stuhlsatzenweg 3, Geb. 43, 66123 Saarbrücken, Germany

Library of Congress Cataloging-in-Publication Data

Life-like characters: tools, affective functions, and applications / Helmut Prendinger, Mitsuru Ishizuka (eds.)
p. cm. – (Cognitive technologies)
Includes bibliographical references and index.
ISBN 3-540-00867-5 (alk. paper)
1. Intelligent agents (Computer software)   I. Prendinger, Helmut, 1967–   II. Ishizuka, Mitsuru, 1948–   III. Series.
QA76.76.I58L55   2004   006.3–dc22   2003061492

ACM Computing Classification (1998): H.5.1, I.2

ISSN 1611-2482
ISBN 3-540-00867-5 Springer-Verlag Berlin Heidelberg New York

Springer-Verlag is a part of Springer Science+Business Media

springeronline.com

© Springer-Verlag Berlin Heidelberg 2004
Printed in Germany

Cover design: KünkelLopka, Heidelberg
Typesetting: Camera-ready by authors
Printed on acid-free paper   45/3142 PS– 5 4 3 2 1 0

In memory of Jeff Rickel, 1963–2003

Preface

With computers becoming an integral part of virtually all activities in our daily lives, how can we have effective and efficient, or simply natural and enjoyable, interactions with computers? One of the most promising technologies is life-like characters – embodied agents apparently living on the screens of computational devices – that invite us to communicate with them in familiar ways and even establish socio-emotional relationships.

While embodied agents are becoming increasingly important as virtual tutors, sales persona, guides, advisors, teammates, and personal representatives, the mechanisms and design issues underlying successful character-based applications are still not well understood and specification and representation languages for believable character behavior are hard to access and use.

This book is a collection of both academic and corporate endeavors describing powerful and mostly freely available scripting languages and tools for controlling life-like behavior and systems that demonstrate the potential of life-like characters in a wide range of application fields. Affective functions, the key ingredient of life-likeness, are a common topic of all chapters. The contributions have been carefully chosen and peer reviewed among authors. The chapter in Part I of this book introduces and motivates the topic, Part II contains chapters describing languages and tools for character control, and Part III is dedicated to character systems and applications. In Part IV, two leading experts in the field address the core themes of this book in the form of a synopsis. An Internet link to electronic material accompanying the chapters can be found in the Appendix.

We would like to thank the Japan Society for the Promotion of Science (JSPS) for their generous support under the Research Grant (1999–2003) for the Future Program. Our special thanks go to Dr. Paolo Petta of the Austrian Research Institute for Artificial Intelligence who provided great encouragement to publish a book on life-like characters. Thanks also to M.Eng. Junichiro Mori for his patient assistance in the preparation of the manuscript.

We are especially grateful to Ms. Ingeborg Mayer and Mr. Alfred Hofmann of Springer-Verlag, for offering invaluable help and providing optimal conditions to publish this book.

It is our hope that this book will serve as a valuable guide to the successful design of life-like character applications for researchers and practitioners alike. We also hope that the scripting languages discussed in the book will be a milestone in the development of a standardized language for life-like character control. Finally, we hope that our book will ignite the interest of the broader community concerned with making interactions with computers more natural by using life-like characters as the technology of choice.

Tokyo,   *Helmut Prendinger*
June 2003   *Mitsuru Ishizuka*

Contents

Part IV Synopsis

Part I

Introduction

Introducing the Cast for Social Computing: Life-Like Characters

Helmut Prendinger and Mitsuru Ishizuka

Department of Information and Communication Engineering
Graduate School of Information Science and Technology
University of Tokyo
7-3-1 Hongo, Bunkyo-ku, Tokyo 113-8656, Japan
prendinger@acm.org, ishizuka@miv.t.u-tokyo.ac.jp

Summary. Life-like characters are one of the most exciting technologies for human–computer interface applications. They convincingly take the roles of virtual presenters, synthetic actors and sales personas, teammates and tutors. A common characteristic underlying their believability or life-likeness as conversational partners is computational models that provide them with affective functions such as synthetic emotions and personalities, and implement human interactive behavior or presentation skills. In *social computing*, a paradigm that aims to support the tendency of humans to interact with computers as social actors, life-like characters are key. They may embody the interface between humans and computers, and thus improve the otherwise poor communicative capabilities of computational devices.

The success of life-like character applications today relies relies on the careful crafting of their designers, mostly programmers. The wide dissemination of life-like character technology in interactive systems, however, will greatly depend on the availability of tools that facilitate scripting of intelligent life-like behavior. The core tasks include the synchronization of synthetic speech and gestures, the expression of emotion and personality by means of body movement and facial display, the coordination of the embodied conversational behavior of multiple characters possibly including the user, and the design of artificial minds for synthetic characters.

In this chapter we will first describe what life-like characters are, and how they differ from related synthetic entities. We will then explain how life-like character technologies may change and improve the interaction between humans and computers. Next, we report on some of the most promising character scripting and representation languages as well as authoring tools currently available. After that, the most successful life-like character systems are briefly introduced, demonstrating the wide range of applications where embodied agents are at work. Some final remarks on this highly active research field conclude this introductory chapter.

1 Introduction

Life-like characters are synthetic agents apparently living on the screens of computers. An early characterization of life-like characters can be found in the work of Joseph Bates who refers to them as *emotional* [5] and *believable* [6] agents. Bates explains the notion of a "believable character" as "[...] one that provides the illusion of life, and thus permits the audience's suspension of disbelief" [6, p. 122]. Following the vision of designing creatures that computer users are willing to perceive as believable or life-like, researchers use a variety of different terms: anthropomorphic agents, avatars, creatures, synthetic actors, non-player characters, and embodied conversational agents [59, 22, 28]. While creation of most terms is inspired by specific character applications, such as avatars for distributed virtual environments like chat systems or non-player characters for interactive games, some terms intend to draw attention to a particular aspect of life-like characters. Embodied conversational agents, for instance, are characters that visually incorporate, or embody, knowledge about the conversational process [12].

Fig. 1. Animated agent

To restrict the focus of our discussion, we will draw a line between life-like characters that are graphically represented, or animated (see Fig. 1), and robotic agents that are realized as physical entities to operate in the physical world [9]. The concept of "life-likeness" is certainly not restricted to animated agents. Dautenhahn [17], for instance, extensively discusses life-likeness in the context of robotic agents. A more subtle distinction concerns the restriction to *animated* rather than *animate* characters. According to Hayes-Roth and Doyle [28], animate characters share all the features of life-like characters except for their embodiment; that is, animate characters are not necessarily animated, but can still be perceived as perfectly life-like.

Although life-likeness is often associated with a "life-like" appearance, animate characters highlight the importance of synthetic minds that give characters individual personality and emotions. Bates [6] draws on the experience of professional character animators [58] when he argues that the portrayal of emotions plays a key role in the aim to create believable characters. On a par with emotions, personality is key to achieving life-likeness. Trappl and Petta [59] dedicated an entire volume to illustrate the personality concept in synthetic character research. Emotion and personality are often seen as the affective bases of believability [42], and sometimes the broader term *social* (or "socially intelligent") is used to characterize life-likeness [22]. The presumably most profound account of what it means for a character to be (or rather seem) "life-like" is given by Hayes-Roth [27], who suggests seven qualities of life-likeness. Characters should seem conversational, intelligent, individual, social, emphatic, variable, and coherent, which are distilled from Hayes-Roth's experience with character-based systems in both academia and industry during one decade. Hayes-Roth also suggests a variation of the famous Turing test to evaluate the life-likeness of interactive characters.

Characters can be life-like in a "human-like" or an "animal-like" way. While the design of human-like characters attracted the majority of researchers, there are also investigations on animal-like characters, especially dogs [8]. An ongoing debate concerns the issue whether the "life-likeness" of characters is more effectively achieved by *realistic* or *cartoon-style* agents. Research that aims to create virtual humans typically follows the realistic approach [13, 24], Thalmann et al. [57] even strive for photorealism. On the other hand, most characters developed in the context of entertainment and "infotainment" systems adhere to the approach that uses cartoon-style characters [2, 45, 23, 61]. While the design of realistic characters is a high research aim *per se*, they do not necessarily outperform cartoon-style characters in the perception of the user. As opposed to cartoon-style characters, users have high expectations of the performance of realistic looking characters, which bears the risk that even small behavior deficiencies lead to user irritation and dissatisfaction. The question of realistic vs. cartoon-style agents can eventually only be decided empirically with respect to specific application scenarios. McBreen et al. [39], for instance, investigate the effectiveness and user acceptability of different types of synthetic agents. A related empirical question concerns the benefits of displaying characters as facial agents ("talking heads"), full-body, or "upper-body plus face" agents.

2 Towards Social Computing

Since human–human communication is a highly effective and efficient way of interaction, life-like characters are promising candidates to improve human–computer interaction (HCI). Embodied agents may use multiple modalities such as voice, gestures, and facial expression to convey information and regulate communication. The work of Reeves and Nass [49] shows that humans are (already) strongly biased in interpreting synthetic entities as social actors even if they do not display anthropomorphic features – the Media Equation. The authors carried out a series of classical psychological tests of human–human social interaction, but replaced one interlocutor by a computer with a human-sounding voice and a particular role such as a companion or opponent. The results of those experiments suggest that humans treat computers in an essentially natural way – as social actors – with a tendency, for instance, to be nicer in "face-to-face" interactions than in third-party conversations. More support for this result is provided by Lester et al. [33] who investigated the impact of animated agents in educational software along the dimensions of motivation and helpfulness, and coined the term "persona effect", "[...] which is that the presence of a lifelike character in an interactive learning environment –

even one that is not expressive – can have a strong positive effect on students' perception of their learning experience" [33, p. 359].

There are hence strong arguments to make the interface *social* by adding life-like characters that have the means to send social cues to the user and possibly even receive such signals. However, it should not be concluded that *all* interfaces can be improved by making them social. As an approximation, it can be said that character-based interfaces are beneficial whenever the inter-action task involves social activity. Training, presentation, and sales certainly fall under this category. By contrast, there are computer-related activities that typically do not require social interaction. Building a spreadsheet, for instance, is a mechanical task and most users would not want to have a col-league watching or interrupting them [21]. The same may hold true for the presence of a synthetic agent. On the other hand, social encounters also in-clude information exchange between people that share similar interests, where life-like characters may act as match-makers at public meeting places. In or-der to support "community awareness", Sumi and Mase [54] investigated this form of computer-mediated communication.

As an HCI paradigm, the goal of character-based human–computer inter-faces seems to be diametrically opposed to that of the "disappearing com-puter" concept in ubiquitous and invisible computing [60]. Those technologies are intended to "weave themselves into the fabric of everyday life until they are indistinguishable from it" [60, p. 94]. By contrast, the power of character-based HCI derives from the fact that people *know* how to interact with other people by using the modalities of their body (voice, gesture, gaze, etc.) and interpret the bodily signals of their interlocutors. Hence, character-based in-terfaces aim at realizing embodied interaction and intelligence [12] rather than interaction with "invisible" devices (see also the Gestalt user interface concept of Mariott and Beard [35]).

The vision of *social computing* is to achieve natural and effective interac-tion between humans and computational devices. As argued above, we believe that by employing life-like characters, social computing can be realized most efficiently. Social computing can be characterized as

- computing that intentionally displays social and affective cues to users and aims to trigger social reactions in users; and
- computing that recognizes affective user states and gives affective feedback to users.

In this paradigm, life-like characters are seen as social actors, and hence as genuine interactive partners for a wide variety of applications, ranging from advisors and sales persona to virtual playfellows. A recent study in the so-cial computing paradigm is the "relational agents" described by Bickmore [7], where characters are in the role of assistants for health behavior change (exer-cise adoption). He characterizes *relational agents* as computational (typically anthropomorphic) artifacts "[. . .] intended to produce relational cues or otherwise produce a relational response in their users, such as increased liking for or trust in the agent" [7, p. 27].

Besides displaying social cues, the second key premise for social computing is that life-like characters recognize social cues of their interlocutor, such as the affective state of the user. In this respect, social computing shares the motivation and goal of affective computing [44]. In the context of a tele-home care application, Lisetti et al. [34] take physiological signals of the user so that a life-like character may respond appropriately. Conati [16] suggests an animated agent that adapts its behavior according to assessed user emotions in the setting of an educational game. Prendinger et al. [47] conducted an experiment that utilizes biosignals of users to demonstrate the calming effect of emphatic character behavior.

The related notion of "Social Intelligence Design" [41], on the other hand, emphasizes the role of the web infrastructure as a means of computer-mediated interaction, community building and evolution, and collective intelligence, rather than (social) human agent interaction. A full-fledged theory of social intelligence (or computing) will have to combine both aspects: (i) macro-level social interactions in a community of human and virtual agents, and (ii) micro-level social interactions between human users and virtual agents as personal representatives of other community members.

3 Authoring Life-Like Characters

One of the most challenging tasks in life-like character research is the design of powerful and flexible authoring tools for content experts. Unlike animators, who are skillful in creating believable synthetic characters, non-professionals will need appropriate scripting tools to build character-based applications [50]. Animating the visual appearance of life-like characters and integrating them into an application environment involves a large number of complex and highly inter-related tasks, such as:

- The synchronization of synthetic speech, gaze, and gestures.
- The expression of personality and affective state by means of body movement, facial display, and speech.
- The coordination of the bodily behavior of multiple characters, including the synchronization of the characters' conversational behavior (for instance, turn-taking).
- The communication between one or more characters and the user.

Observe that the mentioned tasks already assume that characters can be controlled at a rather "high" level, where designers may abstract from low-level concerns such as changing each individual degree of freedom in the character's motion model. The Character Markup Language (CML) contains both low-level and medium-level tags to define the gesture behavior of a character as well as high-level tags that define combinations of other tagging structures

[3]. Furthermore, CML allows one to define high-level attributes to modulate a character's behavior according to its emotional state and personality. The Virtual Human Markup Language (VHML) provides high-level and low-level tagging structures for facial and bodily animation, gesture, speech, emotion, as well as dialogue management [36]. The Scripting Technology for Embodied Persona (STEP) language contains high-level control specifications for scripting communicative gestures of 3D animated agents [29]. Being based on dynamic logic [25], the STEP language includes constructs known from programming languages, such as sequential and non-deterministic execution of behaviors or actions, (non-deterministic) iteration of behaviors, and behaviors that are executed if certain conditions are met.

The human interpretation process is very sensitive to and easily disturbed by a character's "inconsistent" or "unnatural" behavior, whatever type of "nature" (realistic or not) is applicable. The challenge here is to maintain consistency between an agent's internal emotional state and various forms of associated outward behavior such as speech and body movements [24]. An agent that speaks with a cheerful voice without displaying a happy facial expression will seem awkward or even fake. Another challenge is to keep consistency of agents over time, allowing for changes in their response tendencies as a result of the interaction history with other agents [46, 7].

Allbeck and Badler [1] developed an extensive framework for representing embodied characters and objects in virtual environments, called Parameterized Action Representation (PAR). This representation allows one to specify a large number of action parameters to control character behavior, including applicability conditions, purpose, duration, manner, and many more. Most notably, character actions can by modulated by specifying affect-related parameters, emotion, and personality. In order to achieve a high level of naturalness in expressive behaviors, the authors developed the EMOTE system which is based on movement observation science. With respect to conversational behavior, Cassell et al. [15] propose the BEAT (Behavior Expression Animation Toolkit) system as an elaborate mechanism to support consistency and accurate synchronization between a character's speech and conversational gestures. The BEAT system uses a pipelined approach where the Text-to-Speech (TTS) engine produces a fixed timeline which constrains subsequently added gestures. The meaning of the input text is first analyzed semantically and then appropriate gestures are selected to co-occur with the spoken text.

Most approaches to scripting virtual environments focus on designing the characters themselves and interactions between characters and virtual objects, with rudimentary consideration of the representation of interactions among characters and the user. The motivation for the Affective Presentation Markup Language (APML) developed by De Carolis et al. [18] is communicative functions, which make the language similar to the BEAT system [15]. In addition to turn-taking behavior, APML includes the speaker's belief state (certainty of utterance) and intention (request, inform). The work of Mateas and Stern [38] broadens the spectrum of character scripting to interactive scenario scripting to also include another agent and a human user. The authors propose ABL (A Behavior Language), a language that allows one to author believable characters for interactive drama. Unlike most other scripting approaches, which are XML-based [15, 18], ABL is a reactive planning language with character behaviors written in a Java-style syntax. Most notably, ABL may encode "joint plans" that describe the coordinated behavior of characters as one entity rather than having autonomous characters work out a joint plan (which would require complex reasoning, message passing, and so forth). However, joint plans are still reactive, letting the user interfere with plan execution during interaction.

The next step in providing support for creating life-like character applications for non-specialists is character toolkits that address the needs of content providers. The Multi-modal Presentation Markup Language (MPML), for instance, has been designed so that ordinary people can write multi-modal character contents most easily like they write a variety of web contents using HTML. Moreover, MPML offers a visual editor that allows one to script interactive multi-character presentations in a drag-and-drop fashion using a graphical representation of the presentation flow [48]. MPML also provides an interface to the Scripting Emotion-based Agent Minds (SCREAM) system that enables authors to specify the propositional attitudes and affect-related processes of a character's (synthetic) brain [48]. While MPML typically uses the Microsoft Agent package to control animated characters [40], the Galatea software toolkit allows authors to personalize core features of a facial spoken dialogue agent [31]. Galetea consists of interfaced modules that are all modifiable: speech synthesizer, speech recognizer, facial animation synthesizer, and task dialogue manager. As described above, the BEAT system is a toolkit to synchronize analyzed speech automatically with non-verbal behaviors [15]. The toolkit is extensible, and new rules encoding linguistic and contextual analysis of textual input are easily added.

Another challenge for character-based applications is to adequately account for the user's behavior, in particular the user's affective state [44]. Marking up user input modalities rather than character (output) modalities is a hitherto entirely unexplored application of scripting technology. Mariott and Beard [35] propose a "complete user interaction" paradigm which they call "Gestalt User Interface ... an interface that should be reactive to, and proactive of, the perceived desires of the user through emotion and gesture". User interaction modalities such as speech, facial expressions, and body gestures are analyzed and then transformed to an XML structure that can be "played back" by a VHML-based talking head or provide the conditions to decide on the desired character response.

Rist [50] offers interesting reflections on scripting and specification languages for life-like characters. He proposes objectives and desiderata for the design of character languages and discusses the state of current developments in view of the potential (and highly desirable) standardization of scripting languages. Rist also points out limitations of the present focus on XML-based languages and suggests drawing inspirations from the area of network protocols in order to manage more complex and sophisticated character interactions.

4 Life-Like Character Applications and Systems

Recent years have witnessed a considerable and growing interest in employing life-like characters for tasks that are typically performed by humans. In the following, we list some of the more prominent deployed character applications as well as systems in progress. Issues of designing life-like characters and lessons learned can also be found in Hayes-Roth [27].

Life-like characters are used

- as (virtual) *tutors* and *trainers* in interactive learning environments [20, 30, 26, 16, 37, 56],
- as *presenters* and *sales persona* on the web and at information booths [11, 4, 48, 51],
- as *actors* for entertainment [52, 10, 43],
- as *communication partners* in therapy [19, 34, 37],
- as *personal representatives* in online communities and guidance systems [14, 55, 53], and
- as *information experts* enhancing conventional web search engines [32].

One of the most successful application fields of life-like character technology is computer-based *learning environments* where embodied agents can perform in a variety of student-related roles, especially as tutors and trainers [20, 30, 26, 16, 37, 56]. Marsella et al. [37] describe a Mission Rehearsal Exercise (MRE) system for training peacekeeping missions where a realistic virtual human acts as a sergeant in the role of a mentor or as a soldier in the role of a teammate. In order to support highly believable, responsive, and easily interpretable behavior, the authors base their characters on an architecture for task-oriented behavior (STEVE), rich models of (social) plan-based emotion processing (Émile), and emotion appraisal and coping behaviors (Carmen's Bright IDEAS). The MRE system is currently one of the most impressive applications of life-like character technology.

Another application field where life-like characters showed significant progress is character-based *presentation*, especially online sales [11, 4, 48, 51]. Starting with the PPP Persona, Rist et al. [51] developed a series of increasingly powerful character technologies for a wide variety of agent–agent and human–agent interaction scenarios, such as the AiA travel agent, the eShowroom, a RoboCup commentator system (Gerd & Matze), a negotiation dialogue manager (Avatar Arena), the MIAU platform for interactive car sales, and the interactive CrossTalk installation featuring two presentation screens. The work on life-like characters done at DFKI [51] can be seen as the strongest and most covering in the field. While being well motivated and based on psychological and socio-psychological research, it offers powerful technologies for every imaginable interaction mode with and among life-like characters. As previously mentioned, Prendinger et al. [48] developed two scripting tools that focus on creating interactive presentations (MPML) and affect-driven characters (SCREAM). Both technologies are designed for web-based applications that require multiple character interactions including communication with the user. The implementation of an interactive casino scenario demonstrates the power and flexibility of this approach.

One of the most attractive application fields of life-like characters is the *entertainment* sector where characters perform as virtual actors [52, 10, 38, 43]. Paiva et al. [43] provide a useful classification of character control technologies for story and game applications, based on the autonomy dimension. Besides character related autonomy – (partially) scripted, directed, role constrained, and autonomous – the authors also propose a classification of a user's control over characters, that is puppet-like control, guidance, influence, and god-like control. The suggested classification is exemplified by a series of installations: Tristão and Isolda, Papous, Teatrix, FantasyA, and SenToy. Burke [10] describes a powerful architecture that meets the demands of life-like characters for entertainment systems. In particular, he proposes a prediction-based approach that allows for new types of learning and adaptive characters. The previously mentioned work of Mateas and Stern [38] implements an interactive drama – Façade – a real-time 3D interactive drama that demonstrates the capabilities and promise of characters in entertainment systems.

Life-like characters will also play a major role as communication partners in *therapeutic* and *medical* applications [19, 34, 37]. For instance, Marsella et al. [37] propose a system called "Carmen's Bright IDEAS" (CBI) where users are immersed in a story that features an animated clinical counsellor and another agent that receives help and is designed to have problems similar to the user who interacts with the CBI system. The user may influence the development of the councelling session by selecting interface objects ("Thought Balloons") that match his or her current feeling most closely.

The great popularity of Internet-based and computer-mediated communications raises the demand for life-like characters that function as personal representatives of users in *online communities* (for instance, chat systems) and *guidance systems* [14, 55, 53]. Sumi [53] developed the AgentSalon system where a visitor to an exhibition is equipped with a PalmGuide that hosts his or her personal agent which may migrate to a big display – then being visible as an embodied character – and start conversing with personal agents of other visitors. Since the agent stores a user's personal interest profile, the conversation between the personal representatives can reveal shared interests and trigger a conversation between visitors.

A common and one of the most important activities on the web is the *retrieval* of relevant information. Life-like characters have recently also been successfully employed to add value to search engines. Kitamura [32] describes the Multiple Character Interface (MCI) system that aims at assisting users in the information retrieval task. Two MCI-based prototype systems are a cooperative multi-agent system for information retrieval (Venus and Mars) and a competitive multi-agent system for information recommendation (Recommendation Battlers) [32].

The following system can be viewed as a feasibility study on the next generation of natural language understanding systems, including entertainment and helper robots, tutoring, and virtual space navigation systems. Tanaka et al. [56] developed a system called "Kirai" which allows one to direct virtual characters in a 3D environment. Most notably, the system incorporates a natural language recognition and understanding (NLU) component so that characters can be instructed to perform actions in virtual space via speech input. Speech analysis includes syntactic and semantic analysis, anaphora resolution, ellipsis handling, and a simple mechanism to eliminate the vagueness problem of natural language.

5 Concluding Remarks

In this introductory chapter, the state of the art of life-like character scripting languages and applications has been briefly reviewed. While the future of embodied characters remains to be seen, the extensive research on character representation languages and scripting tools certainly indicates a growing demand for embodiments of the human–computer interface. The most convincing evidence for the continued interest is the large number of deployed and upcoming character applications in a wide variety of applications, from learning and entertainment to online sales and medical advice.

Life-like character research lays the foundations of the social computing paradigm, where computers deliberately display social cues and trigger social reactions in users. In order to pass as genuine social actors, life-like characters will eventually also have to be equipped with means to recognize social and affective cues of users, a research topic which we hope to address in a future publication. Although we focused on animated characters here, many of the insights gained can be transferred to the physical siblings of animated characters, namely robotic agents. Animated or robotic, the success of those agents will ultimately depend on whether they are life-like.

Acknowledgments

This research was supported by the Research Grant (1999–2003) for the Future Program ("Mirai Kaitaku") from the Japan Society for the Promotion of Science (JSPS).

References

1. Allbeck, J., Badler, N.: Representing and parameterizing agent behaviors. In: *Life-like Characters. Tools, Affective Functions and Applications*, ed Prendinger, H., Ishizuka, M. (Springer 2003). This volume.
2. André, E., Rist, T., van Mulken, S., Klesen, M., Baldes, S.: The automated design of believable dialogue for animated presentation teams. In: *Embodied Conversational Agents*, ed Cassell, J., Sullivan, J., Prevost, S., Churchill, E. (The MIT Press, Cambridge, MA 2000) pp 220–255
3. Arafa, Y., Kamyab, K., Mamdani, E.: Toward a unified scripting language. Lessons learned from developing CML and AML. In: *Life-like Characters. Tools, Affective Functions and Applications*, ed Prendinger, H., Ishizuka, M. (Springer 2003). This volume.
4. Badler, N.I., Bindiganavale, R., Allbeck, J., Schuler, W., Zhao, L., Palmer, M.: Parameterized action representation for virtual human agents. In: *Embodied Conversational Agents*, ed Cassell, J., Sullivan, J., Prevost, S., Churchill, E. (The MIT Press, Cambridge, MA 2000) pp 256–284
5. Bates, J.: Virtual reality, art, and entertainment. *PRESENCE: Teleoperators and Virtual Environments* **1**(1):133–138 (1992)
6. Bates, J.: The role of emotion in believable agents. *Communications of the ACM* **37**(7):122–125 (1994)
7. Bickmore, T.: *Relational Agents: Effecting Change through Human-Computer Relationships*. PhD thesis (Massachusetts Institute of Technology 2003)
8. Blumberg, B.M.: *Old Tricks, New Dogs: Ethology and Interactive Creatures*. PhD thesis (Massachusetts Institute of Technology 1996)
9. Breazeal-Ferrell, C., Velásquez, J.: Toward teaching a robot "infant" using emotive communication acts. In: *Proceedings of Workshop on Socially Situated Intelligence, in conjunction with SAB-98* (1998)
10. Burke, R.: Great expectations: Prediction in entertainment applications. In: *Life-like Characters. Tools, Affective Functions and Applications*, ed Prendinger, H., Ishizuka, M. (Springer 2003). This volume.
11. Cassell, J.: More than just another pretty face: Embodied conversational interface agents. *Communications of the ACM* **43**(4):70–78 (2000)
12. Cassell, J.: Embodied conversational agents: Representation and intelligence in user interface. *AI Magazine* **22**(3):67–83 (2001)
13. Cassell, J., Bickmore, T., Campbell, L., Vilhjálmsson, H., Yan, H.: Human conversation as a system framework: Designing embodied conversational agents. In: *Embodied Conversational Agents*, ed Cassell, J., Sullivan, J., Prevost, S., Churchill, E. (The MIT Press, Cambridge, MA 2000) pp 29–63
14. Cassell, J., Vilhjálmsson, H.: Fully embodied conversational avatars: Making communicative behaviors autonomous. *Autonomous Agents and Multi-Agent Systems* **2**:45–64 (1999)
15. Cassell, J., Vilhjálmsson, H., Bickmore, T.: BEAT: the Behavior Expression Animation Toolkit. In: *Life-like Characters. Tools, Affective Functions and Applications*, ed Prendinger, H., Ishizuka, M. (Springer 2003). This volume.
16. Conati, C.: Probabilistic assessment of user's emotions in educational games. *Applied Artificial Intelligence* **16**:555–575 (2002)
17. Dautenhahn, K.: Embodiment and interaction in socially intelligent life-like agents. In: *Computation for Metaphors, Analogy and Agent*, ed Nehaniv, C.L. (LNAI 1562, Springer Berlin New York 1999) pp 102–142

18. De Carolis, B., Pelauchaud, C.: APML, a markup language for believable behavior generation. In: *Life-like Characters. Tools, Affective Functions and Applications*, ed Prendinger, H., Ishizuka, M. (Springer 2003). This volume.
19. de Rosis, F., Carolis, B. De, Carofiglio, V.: Shallow and inner forms of emotional intelligence in advisory dialog simulation. In: *Life-like Characters. Tools, Affective Functions and Applications*, ed Prendinger, H., Ishizuka, M. (Springer 2003). This volume.
20. de Rosis, F., Carolis, B. De, Pizzulito, S.: Software documentation with animated agents. In: *Proceedings 5th ERCIM Workshop on User Interfaces For All* (1999)
21. Doyle, P.: When is a communicative agent a good idea? In: *Proceedings Agents-99 Workshop on Communicative Agents* (1999)
22. Elliott, C., Brzezinski, J.: Autonomous agents as synthetic characters. *AI Magazine* **19**(2):13–30 (1998)
23. Extempo Systems Inc. www.extempo.com
24. Gratch, J., Rickel, J., André, E., Cassell, J., Petajan, E., Badler, N.: Creating interactive virtual humans: Some assembly required. *IEEE Intelligent Systems*, July/August, 54–63 (2002)
25. Harel, D.: Dynamic logic. In: *Handbook of Philosophical Logic. II: Extensions of Classical Logic*, ed Gabbay, D., Guenthner, F. (Reidel, Boston, MA 1984) pp 497–604
26. Hayes-Roth, B.: Adaptive learning guides. In: *Proceedings of the IASTED Conference on Computers and Advanced Technology in Education* (2001)
27. Hayes-Roth, B.: What makes characters seem life-like? In: *Life-like Characters. Tools, Affective Functions and Applications*, ed Prendinger, H., Ishizuka, M. (Springer 2003). This volume.
28. Hayes-Roth, B., Doyle, P.: Animate characters. *Autonomous Agents and Multi-Agent Systems* **1**(2):195–230 (1998)
29. Huang, Z., Eliëns, A., Visser, C.: STEP: a scripting language for embodied agents. In: *Life-like Characters. Tools, Affective Functions and Applications*, ed Prendinger, H., Ishizuka, M. (Springer 2003). This volume.
30. Johnson, W.L., Rickel, J., Lester, J.C.: Animated pedagogical agents: Face-to-face interaction in interactive learning environments. *International Journal of Artificial Intelligence in Education* **11**:47–78 (2000)
31. Kawamoto, S., Shimodaira, H., Nitta, T., Nishimoto, T., Nakamura, S., Itou, K., Morishima, S., Yotsukura, T., Kai, A., Lee, A., Yamashita, Y., Kobayashi, T., Tokuda, K., Hirose, K., Minematsu, N., Yamada, A., Den, Y., Utsuro, T., Sagayama, S.: Galatea: Open-source software for developing anthropomorphic spoken dialog agents. In: *Life-like Characters. Tools, Affective Functions and Applications*, ed Prendinger, H., Ishizuka, M. (Springer 2003). This volume.
32. Kitamura, Y.: Web information integration using multiple character agents. In: *Life-like Characters. Tools, Affective Functions and Applications*, ed Prendinger, H., Ishizuka, M. (Springer 2003). This volume.
33. Lester, J.C., Converse, S.A., Kahler, S.E., Barlow, S.T., Stone, B.A., Bhogal, R.S.: The Persona effect: Affective impact of animated pedagogical agents. In: *Proceedings of CHI-97* (ACM Press, New York 1997) pp 359–366
34. Lisetti, C., Nasoz, F., LeRouge, C., Ozyer, O., Alvarez, K.: Developing multimodal intelligent affective interfaces for tele-home health care. *International Journal of Human-Computer Studies* **59**(1–2):245–255 (2003)

35. Mariott, A., Beard, S.: gUI: Specifying complete user interaction. In: *Life-like Characters. Tools, Affective Functions and Applications*, ed Prendinger, H., Ishizuka, M. (Springer 2003). This volume.

36. Mariott, A., Stallo, J.: VHML—Uncertainties and problems. A discussion. In: *Proceedings AAMAS-02 Workshop on Embodied Conversational Agents—Let's specify and evaluate them!* (2002)

37. Marsella, S., Gratch, J., Rickel, J.: Expressive behaviors for virtual worlds. In: *Life-like Characters. Tools, Affective Functions and Applications*, ed Prendinger, H., Ishizuka, M. (Springer 2003). This volume.

38. Mateas, M., Stern, A.: A Behavior Language: Joint action and behavioral idioms. In: *Life-like Characters. Tools, Affective Functions and Applications*, ed Prendinger, H., Ishizuka, M. (Springer 2003). This volume.

39. McBreen, H., Shade, P., Jack, M., Wyard, P.: Experimental assessment of the effectiveness of synthetic personae for multi-modal e-retail applications. In: *Proceedings 4th International Conference on Autonomous Agents (Agents'2000)* (ACM Press, New York, 2000) pp 39–45

40. Microsoft. *Developing for Microsoft Agent* (Microsoft Press, Redmond, WA 1998)

41. Nishida, T.: Social intelligence design – An overview. In: *New Frontiers in Artificial Intelligence. Joint JSAI 2001 Workshop Post-Proceedings* (Springer, Berlin New York 2001) pp 3–10

42. Paiva, A. (ed): *Affective Interactions. Towards a New Generation of Computer Interfaces.* (LNAI 1814, Springer, Berlin New York 2000)

43. Paiva, A., Prada, R., Machado, I., Martinho, C., Vala, M., Silva, A.: Playing with agents - Agents in social and dramatic games. In: *Life-like Characters. Tools, Affective Functions and Applications*, ed Prendinger, H., Ishizuka, M. (Springer 2003). This volume.

44. Picard, R.W.: *Affective Computing.* (The MIT Press, Cambridge MA 1997)

45. Prendinger, H., Descamps, S., Ishizuka, M.: Scripting affective communication with life-like characters in web-based interaction systems. *Applied Artificial Intelligence* **16**(7–8):519–553 (2002)

46. Prendinger, H., Ishizuka, M.: Evolving social relationships with animate characters. In: *Proceedings of the AISB-02 Symposium on Animating Expressive Characters for Social Interactions* (2002) pp 73–78

47. Prendinger, H., Mayer, S., Mori, J., Ishizuka, M.: Persona effect revisited: Using bio-signals to measure and reflect the impact of character-based interfaces. *Fourth International Working Conference on Intelligent Virtual Agents (IVA-03).* In press.

48. Prendinger, H., Saeyor, S., Ishizuka, M.: MPML and SCREAM: Scripting the bodies and minds of life-like characters. In: *Life-like Characters. Tools, Affective Functions and Applications*, ed Prendinger, H., Ishizuka, M. (Springer 2003). This volume.

49. Reeves, B., Nass, C.: *The Media Equation. How People Treat Computers, Television and New Media Like Real People and Places* (CSLI Publications, Center for the Study of Language and Information. Cambridge University Press 1998)

50. Rist, T.: Some issues in the design of character scripting and specification languages – A personal view. In: *Life-like Characters. Tools, Affective Functions and Applications*, ed Prendinger, H., Ishizuka, M. (Springer 2003). This volume.

51. Rist, T., André, E., Baldes, S., Gebhard, P., Klesen, M., Kipp, M., Rist, P., Schmitt, M.: A review of the development of embodied presentation agents and their application fields. In: *Life-like Characters. Tools, Affective Functions and Applications*, ed Prendinger, H., Ishizuka, M. (Springer 2003). This volume.
52. Rousseau, D., Hayes-Roth, B.: A social-psychological model for synthetic actors. In: *Proceedings 2nd International Conference on Autonomous Agents (Agents-98)* (ACM Press, New York 1998) pp 165–172
53. Sumi, Y., Mase, K.: Interface agents that facilitate knowledge interactions between community members. In: *Life-like Characters. Tools, Affective Functions and Applications*, ed Prendinger, H., Ishizuka, M. (Springer 2003). This volume.
54. Sumi, Y., Mase, K.: Supporting the awareness of shared interests and experiences in communities. *Journal of Human-Computer Studies* **56**(1):127–146 (2002)
55. Takahashi, T., Takeda, H., Katagiri, Y.: Script language for embodied agents as personal conversational media in online communities. In *Proceedings AAMAS-02 Workshop on Embodied Conversational Agents: Let's specify and compare Them!* (2002)
56. Tanaka, H., Tokunaga, T., Yusuke, S.: Animated agents capable of understanding natural language and performing actions. In: *Life-like Characters. Tools, Affective Functions and Applications*, ed Prendinger, H., Ishizuka, M. (Springer 2003). This volume.
57. Thalmann, D., Noser, H., Huang. Z.: Autonomous virtual actors based on virtual sensors. In: *Creating Personalities for Synthetic Actors*, ed Trappl, R., Petta, P. (Springer, Berlin New York, 1997) pp 25–42
58. Thomas, F., Johnston, O.: *Disney Animation: The Illusion of Life* (Abbeville Press, New York 1981)
59. Trappl, R., Petta, P.: *Creating Personalities for Synthetic Actors* (LNAI State-of-the-Art Survey 1195, Springer, Berlin New York 1997)
60. Weiser, M.: The computer for the 21st century. *Scientific American*, September, 94–100 (1991)
61. Zoesis Studios. www.zoesis.com/corporate/index.html

Part II

Languages and Tools for Life-Like Characters

Representing and Parameterizing Agent Behaviors

Jan Allbeck and Norm Badler

Center for Human Modeling and Simulation
University of Pennsylvania
200 S. 33rd St.
Philadelphia, PA 19104-6389, USA
{allbeck,badler}@seas.upenn.edu

Summary. Creating or adopting a representation of human actions or behaviors whether for simulations, web applications, tutoring agents, training scenarios, or the numerous other uses for virtual agents, requires an examination of the features needed for your application. Often a balance must be struck between the control a user has over the virtual agents and the amount of intelligence or autonomy they possess. Likewise, representation level(s) must be determined: is a graphical level representation needed or is a higher artificial intelligence level more appropriate? In this chapter, we briefly discuss some of these options and present our Parameterized Action Representation (PAR).

1 Introduction

You are in a room looking out a window. You see the busy streets below: traffic flowing through the streets and pedestrians hurrying off to work. But something seems odd. All of the cars are moving in the same direction, and all the pedestrians are moving along the same path too. You turn to look at the room. It appears to be a nice conference room: wood paneling, industrial blue carpeting, a large wood table surrounded by chairs. In one corner of the room, you notice two people conversing. From the dialog, you understand that a boss is reprimanding an employee. What is strange are the postures and gestures. They resemble a parent scolding a child.

Then you notice a pot of coffee on the table. You decide to go and get a cup. You begin walking in the direction of the coffee, but soon encounter a chair in your path. You try to maneuver around it, but have to stop abruptly to prevent crashing into it. You alter your direction, take a step and stop again. Frustration builds as you continue this process until you are standing in front of the coffee. You reach for the coffee, but your hand does not find the pot. Your hand only seems to move to and from a spot to the right of the pot. Your anger builds, but it is outweighed by your desire for coffee. You turn to your left, take a small step, and turn again to face the coffee pot. This time when you reach for the pot your hand penetrates the pot without moving it. As your frustration reaches a new level, you notice a face reflected in the surface of the pot. The face is smiling broadly. You realize the face is yours. How could you be smiling when you feel so frustrated? Is this is a nightmare? No, this is a virtual environment with an inadequate action representation.

The world is complex and difficult to represent. Throughout history, artists and writers have depicted worlds with varying levels of realism, but expectations are different in virtual reality. People spend their lives learning what to expect of their environment in terms of both objects and other people. When these expectations are not met, they become frustrated or confused. Unless the environment is designed as a fantasy world, the same expectations hold in virtual reality environments. People expect recognized objects to behave as in the real world with included randomness where appropriate. They expect to be able to navigate through the world in a natural fashion. They expect other inhabitants of the environment to behave naturally and natural interactions with both objects and people in the world. When these expectations are not met, participants lose their sense of immersion in the world.

In order to create an interactive world that meets natural expectations, a substantial amount of computer software engineering is required: graphical depictions, motion models or generators, collision detection and avoidance, communication or synchronization channels, planning and navigation, cognitive modeling, psychosocial and physiological modeling and more, depending on the scenario.

The construction of these components can be facilitated by creating or using an action representation. Over the last few years, many representations have been created. Some representations focus on conversation [13], others on networked simulations [34, 12], others on aspects of computer graphics and animation [29], and others on logic and planning [33]. There are now also meta-representations such as XML [30]. In this chapter, we will outline some things to consider when adopting an action representation. Then we will present a representation we developed, the Parameterized Action Representation (PAR).

2 Control vs. Autonomy

Computer animation originated as key-frame animation. This provided animators with detailed control over the movements of the characters. Unfortunately, it is also a time consuming process that requires the storage of a large amount of data, and is often specific to a character. Additionally, when motions for virtual characters are specified on a frame-by-frame basis, they then become dependent on the context for which they were designed.

There are a number of problems that arise when motions cannot be altered to context. First, interactions with objects and other agents become difficult, if not impossible. When motions are specified as a combination of joint angles, the relative locations of objects and agents must be precise in order, for example, for an agent to reach an object. Additionally, the object size must be known a priori in order for the agent to grasp the object accurately.

When only joint angle information is available for a motion, it is also difficult to create transitions between motions. Several interpolation techniques have been developed, but more sophisticated methods are needed for transitions between actions with severely differing postures, such as sitting and standing. Using joint angles as a representation implies knowing the beginning position of all the joints and being able to transition to them.

Finally, expressivity is also a part of context. One of the advantages of using joint angle data is the control the animator has over the motion. A skilled animator can depict the character's inner state (e.g. psychological and physiological state). However, when trying to use joint angle data in varying contexts, it is difficult to alter the expression of the motion to new contexts. Naturally, motion data could be stored for many expressive states, but it requires a lot of storage space and some mechanism for recalling the motion file required for a given context.

Over the years, techniques have been developed that decrease the data needed for actions, enable context-sensitive actions, and increase agent autonomy. Tools such as inverse kinematics [22, 37] enabled agent motion generators to perform more accurately in varying contexts, in some sense enabling the agent to determine precisely how an action should be performed. The increase in autonomy and decrease in the need for data specificity came at the cost of control.

Another cost was naturalness or realism. Skilled animators could create motions that were both realistic and expressive. The newer techniques resulted in robotic motions. Luckily these techniques occurred at a time when the appearance of the characters was also unnatural. The motion quality of the characters met expectations given their appearance, but as graphics hardware advanced so did the characters' appearances and the expectations of motion quality.

Motion capture again increased the quality of motions, but at the cost of data size and context sensitivity. Today motion capture remains the best method for achieving natural human animations. Techniques have been and are being developed to make motion capture data more pliable and more context sensitive [9, 8, 20, 24, 23].

There are proprietary representations for information at this level (e.g. Jack [16] and DI-Guy [11]), but there are also pseudo standards, such as MPEG-4 and Biovision (BVH). As a base-level representation such data may forever have its place. However, it will need to be combined with higher level data in order to provide proper transitions, added expressivity, and planning.

3 AI-Level Representation

We have discussed some aspects of low-level motion representations. Now we turn to high-level representations. Low-level representations are used to describe the movement of the characters. High-level representations can vary in their purpose and therefore their semantics. Much work has been done in representations for communicative or conversational agents [13], including some described in this volume. Their representations include mechanisms to synchronize facial expressions with speech. Some systems using these representations even extract semantic information from text to drive the display of the character and plan dialog [14]. These representations and systems generally concentrate on agents interacting with a live participant and not a virtual world.

Other autonomous agents are created to perform autonomously in a virtual world. Research in this area concentrates less on dialog and natural verbal communication and more on an agent's interactions and autonomy in a virtual world. These are the types of agents we will focus on for the remainder of this chapter, but note that there is nothing to preclude using more than one representation in an agent or merging representations in order to create an agent with the ability to converse and behave autonomously in an environment.

Planning for characters in virtual environments comes in a variety of forms. Reach planning is determining a path for an end-effector from a start position to a goal position, sometimes through a confined area [25]. Path planning and navigation involve determining a path for a virtual character to maneuver from one position to another in an environment [27, 32]. AI-level planning is determining what action a character should perform next in order to obtain a predefined goal [33]. All levels of planning require some representation of the state of the environment and become more challenging when the environment is dynamic. Hence, in order to take full advantage of an action representation, objects must also be represented. In fact, object representations may include varying levels of data just as action representations. The position and orientation of an object may be updated at every frame, but the object representation may also include data about its utilities, such as a door being a pathway, a knife being a cutting tool, or a car being a mode of transportation. This high-level information can then be used in AI-level planning. Of particular interest in this level of planning are the effects of an action on objects. For example, representing that when an object is picked up, it is in the possession of the agent who picked it up and that there are implications about the global position of this object when the agent performs a subsequent translatory action. Such reasoning can be done when an action representation includes an object representation.

The agents themselves may be considered special types of objects and also have a representation. As such they would have all the same fields as objects, but have a few additional entries. This opens a relatively new area in modeling virtual agents: cognitive and social modeling [38]. Agents' personalities, emotional states, goals, motivations, and more can be stored in an agent representation. Thus, in addition to the agent's next action being planned, its next goal may be determined, the expression or motion quality of its actions may be chosen, and cooperation or coordination between agents may be enacted.

4 Network Simulations

When creating a framework for distributed or networked simulations, many design dimensions must be considered: bandwidth, synchronization, agent autonomy, agent control, latency, visualization, and interfaces [34]. Often these considerations are diametrically opposed. We must balance, for example, the amount of control that we have over agents in the simulation with the amount of bandwidth that we have to control them. Early networked simulations broadcast position and orientation data over the network to every agent at every frame or clock tick. This enormous amount of information overwhelmed the available bandwidth, but gave the simulation designers great control. Later predictive methods such as dead reckoning were used to limit the packet frequency requirements and thus better utilize bandwidth, but at the expense of accuracy. Advancements in networking techniques and hardware have increased bandwidth, but our expectations of simulations have also increased. Emerging research techniques from computer graphics and AI can be applied to building a smarter framework for distributed simulations.

Whether using a client–server or peer-to-peer architecture, packets describing agent actions must be formulated, sent, received, and interpreted. Until recently, animation interpreters had to be simplistic: consider, for example, the limited state control afforded to DI-Guy from Boston Dynamics. The autonomy of agents was limited – mostly to repetitive actions such as walking, running, or crawling – or motion-captured units such as firing a weapon or falling. In either case motion control had to be explicit and fine-grained. Computational techniques, however, have advanced such that agents are not only acquiring the ability to perform individual actions on their own; they are also able to perform a series of contextually variable actions or behaviors autonomously. Such actions may include reaching for objects, moving head and eyes to attend to interesting nearby events, and adjusting locomotion to avoid obstacles and shift gaits as needed [3]. The goal is to develop action representations that can be explored by the underlying network to reduce communication, and at the same time guarantee consistent world state among distributed hosts.

Increasing the autonomy of agents can result in a decrease in necessary bandwidth. Consider, for example, sending an agent's frame-by-frame joint angles for all of the actions necessary to animate an agent entering a building versus simply sending it a string: *enter the building*. Naturally with the detailed method the simulation has fine-grained control over the agent's performance, while with the simple instruction the simulation appears to have little control. That is not the case, however. If the situation requires that the agent enter the building *carefully, through the blue door*, or *while watching the window above* it, there is no simple method to modify the detailed joint or motion capture data. If the actions are suitably parameterized, such modifiers may be carried immediately in the instruction itself and interpreted locally by the agent. Instructions between people carry information that both parties can use to drive implementing behaviors. Moreover, poor instructions may result in misunderstanding and incorrect actions. Simulations based at the instruction level may help expose potentially negative communication practices during a training session.

We are not arguing that natural language instructions should be used as the basis of a simulation packet structure; that would still require too much processing capability and interpretation in an agent, and the state of natural language processing is not quite ready for that role. But we can learn from this form of human-level communication some attributes that an efficient and effective distributed simulation packet structure might contain. Over the last few years, we have been developing a Parameterized Action Representation (PAR) based jointly on the information requirements necessary to animate an embodied computer graphics agent as well as to represent the semantics of natural language action verbs, adverbs, and prepositions [5].

5 Parameterized Action Representation

Virtual humans can represent other people or function as autonomous helpers, teammates, or tutors enabling novel interactive educational and training applications. We should be able to interact and communicate with them through modalities we already use, such as language, facial expressions, and gesture. This section describes our Parameterized Action Representation (PAR), which addresses many of the issues with action representations that we have outlined.

PAR allows an agent to act, plan, and reason about its actions or actions of others. Besides embodying the semantics of human action, PAR is designed for building future behaviors into autonomous agents and controlling the animation parameters that portray personality, mood, and affect in an embodied agent.

We have constructed a PAR and a system (PARSYS) which uses PAR as a knowledge base and intermediary between natural language and animation [1, 3, 5, 10]. The PAR parameterization was created out of information from computer graphics and animation, natural language processing, and human movement observation science. Although the emphasis of our research has been on the representation and processing of actions, objects are also represented in our formalism.

As a representation for actions as instructions for an agent, PAR has to specify (parameterize) the agent, any relevant objects, and information about paths, locations, manners, and purposes. Below, Table 1 shows the highest level representation of actions and Table 2 that of objects.

5.1 PAR Architecture

For this discussion, it is not necessary to describe the details of the PARSYS architecture. It will, however, be helpful to know its general concepts. A highly simplified diagram of the PARSYS architecture is shown in Fig. 1.

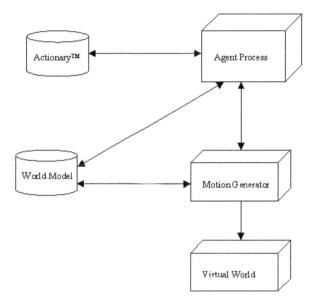

Fig. 1. A simplified diagram of the PARSYS architecture.

The *Actionary*™ stores uninstantiated PARs (UPARs). UPARs contain the general semantics of an action, but lack specific parameter instantiation, such as the particular object involved in the action. Instantiated PARs (IPARs) are created in *Agent Processes*. Each character in the virtual world has an associated agent process that acts as the brain of the agent. This component is where emotion and personality factors influence the agent's goals and where actions are chosen in pursuit of those goals. Action choice is also mitigated by the current state of the world as represented by the *World Model*. Once an action is chosen its UPAR is retrieved from the Actionary and instantiated with specific objects, locations, and manners. Action selection can actually be quite complex and may involve querying the Actionary for actions that meet certain conditions instead of a specific action by name.

Every action in the Actionary is associated with one or more *Motion Generators*. Motion generators are pieces of code that perform the action on the agent in the virtual world. The motion generators are as important as the action representation and planning components of the PAR system. Some motion generators simply replay stored joint angle data. Others can alter this data for context [8] or affect [15]. Still others are sophisticated procedural animation components [25, 2].

5.2 Action Representation

Table 1. High level action PAR

type parameterized action =	
(name:	STRING;
participants:	agent-and-objects;
applicability conditions:	BOOLEAN-expression;
preparatory specification:	*sequence* conditions-and-actions;
termination conditions:	BOOLEAN-expression;
post assertion:	STATEMENT;
during conditions:	STATEMENT;
purpose:	purpose-specification;
subactions:	par-constraint-graph;
parent action:	parameterized action;
previous action:	parameterized action;
concurrent action:	parameterized action;
next action:	parameterized action;
start:	time-specification;
duration:	time-specification;
priority:	INTEGER;
data:	ANY-TYPE;
kinematics:	kinematics-specification;
dynamics:	dynamics-specification;
manner:	manner-specification;
adverbs:	*sequence* adverb-specification;
failure:	failure-data).

The action representation (Table 1) includes many of the features described in the beginning sections of this chapter. There are fields for low-level animation concepts, such as kinematics and dynamics and including the storage of explicit path information. Through the motion generators, a particular PAR could also just represent the replaying of a particular joint angle data file, but the advantage of PAR is that this file is now associated with the semantics of the action it represents; hence, it can be planned for and reasoned about. There are many fields in PAR which aid in the planning of actions and the execution of those actions.

Participants can include either objects or other agents and are entities that are involved in the action or can be affected by it. For example, picking up a cup from a table involves the agent performing the action, the cup, and the table.

PAR can describe either a primitive or a complex action. Subactions contain the details of executing the action. If it is a primitive action, the underlying motion generator for the action is directly invoked. A complex action can list a number of subactions that may need to be executed in sequence, in parallel, or as a combination of both. A complex action can be considered done if all of its subactions are done or if its explicit termination conditions are satisfied.

The applicability conditions of an action specify what needs to be true in the world in order to carry out an action. These can refer to agent capabilities, object configurations, and other unchangeable or uncontrollable aspects of the environment. The conditions in this boolean expression must be true to perform the action. For example, walking actions have an applicability condition stating that the agent performing the action must be capable of walking. When defining an agent representing an infant, it is not given walking as one of its capabilities. If a translatory action became a part of this agent's plan, walking would not be considered, and another action such as crawling would be chosen.

Preparatory specifications are a list of <CONDITION, action> statements. The conditions are evaluated first and have to be satisfied before the current action can proceed. If the conditions are not satisfied, then the corresponding action is performed – it may be a single action or a very complex combination of actions, but it has the same format as the other PARs. Actions can involve the full power of motion planning to determine, perhaps, that a handle has to be grasped before it can be turned. We presently specify the conditions to test for likely (but generalized) situations and execute appropriate intermediate actions. It is also possible to add more general action planners, since PAR represents goal states and supports a full graphical model of the current world state.

Termination Conditions are a list of conditions which when satisfied indicate the completion of the action. Post Assertions are a list of statements or assertions that are executed after the termination conditions of the action have been satisfied. These assertions update the world model to record the changes in the environment. The changes may be due to direct or side effects of the action.

5.3 Object Representation

The PAR object type (Table 2) is defined explicitly to represent a physical object and is stored hierarchically in the Actionary. When a virtual world is created, objects are retrieved from the Actionary, instantiated, and placed in the world model, where they are updated throughout the simulation. Each object in the environment is an instance of this type and is associated with a graphical model in a scene graph. An object type lists the actions that can

Table 2. High-level object PAR

type object representation =	
(name:	STRING;
is agent:	BOOLEAN;
properties:	*sequence* property-specification;
status:	status-specification;
posture:	posture-specification;
location:	object representation;
contents:	*sequence* object representation;
capabilities:	*sequence* parameterized action;
relative directions:	*sequence* relative-direction-specification;
special directions:	*sequence* special-direction-specification;
sites:	*sequence* site-type-specification;
bounding volume:	bounding-volume-specification;
coordinate system:	site;
position:	vector;
velocity:	vector;
acceleration:	vector;
orientation:	vector;
data:	ANY-TYPE).

be performed on it and what state changes they cause. Among other fields, a list of grasp sites and directions are defined with respect to the object. Many of the details of the representation of an object can be filled in as the simulation begins (e.g. calculation of the bounding volume). These fields help orient actions that involve objects, such as grasping, reaching, and locomotion.

Agents are treated as special objects that can execute actions. Their properties are also stored in the Actionary. Each agent is associated with an agent process, which controls its actions based on the personality and capabilities of the agent. Not only does an agent's personality affect its response to a situation, but also it affects the way these actions are performed. Two agents with different personalities would execute the same action in two different ways. For example, two agents could be waving at one another. A shy agent would wave its hand more slowly and with more hesitation than an extroverted agent would. This increases believability by preventing agents from reacting in the same manner in identical contexts and gives the impression that each agent has distinct emotions and personality.

6 PAR for Agent Modeling

Given that PAR can be used to animate embodied agents, even from natural language instructions, can it be used to generate more "character"-rich agents? In this section, we will show that PAR adequately represents the components necessary for modeling embodied agents and further that it is compatible with common methods for modeling emotion and personality in agents.

In [19], Funge et al. described a hierarchy of computer graphics modeling. The bottom two layers depicted early computer graphics research in geometric models and inverse kinematics. Physical models generate realistic motion through dynamic simulation. Behavioral modeling involves characters that perceive environmental stimuli and react appropriately. Through cognitive modeling, *autonomous* characters can be given goals and react deliberatively as well as reactively.

PAR and PARSYS accommodate and enable each level in this hierarchy. While the actual geometry is assumed to have been created before the simulation begins, PAR does represent and PARSYS automatically recognizes some vital geometric constructs. Bounding volumes, for example, can be calculated as soon as the geometry is loaded into the system. Spatial properties, such as location and containment, can also be recognized and stored. Updating and storing this information in a central location means that it does not have to be calculated by every object manipulator. Kinematics and dynamics are explicitly represented in PAR. Furthermore, PAR has been tied to a fast, analytic inverse kinematics program [37] that facilitates the generalization of actions such as *reaching*.

The behavioral component of embodied agency is at the foundation of PARSYS. The *World Model* is updated to provide the necessary processes, agent processes and motion generators, with information on the current state of the environment. Currently, this resource is shared by all of the agents and motion generators. It is, however, possible to provide each agent process with its own world model so that it represents an agent's own unique view of and beliefs about the state of the world. The embodied agents can be given goals directly in the form of PAR or through natural language instructions. An agent tries to complete its goals by performing actions. Reactivity to the environment takes place in two forms. First, the agent processes and motion generators have quick access to the current state of the environment through PAR allowing them to refine a motion or even terminate an action. Second, PAR contains information about failure states and PARSYS has the ability to detect failures and notify the agent process with the information necessary to handle the failure. In PARSYS failures are anything that causes a motion generator to terminate before its termination conditions have been met. For example, a motion generator may check to ensure that the preparatory specifications of the action it is performing are maintained throughout. If the specifications are not maintained, a failure can be generated and returned to the agent process where a decision could be made to try to reestablish the specifications or abort the action.

The way in which an agent responds to changes in the environment, the way in which agents pursue their goals, and even which goals are most important are aspects of cognitive modeling. PARSYS contains mechanisms for planning and also filtering and prioritizing the actions that the planner can plan with, thereby individualizing the agent. During the planning process, the planner queries the Actionary for actions that match the conditions it is trying to meet. Before the satisfying actions are returned to the planner, an action filter removes any actions that the agents would not do in the current situation and prioritizes the remaining actions. For example, *walking* might be prioritized over *running* or *skipping* in the satisfaction of a locomotion condition because of either the nature of the agent (businessman or child) or sensitivity to motion goals or qualities (manner).

6.1 Personality and Emotions

The actions of the action filter may be dependent on any aspect of the agent, including its personality or current emotion level. Two popular models for personality and emotion are OCEAN [39] and OCC [28] respectively.

Personality is a pattern of behavioral, temperamental, emotional, and mental traits that distinguish people from one another. Traits are basic tendencies that remain stable across the life span, but characteristic behavior can change through adaptive processes. The ways in which a person perceives, acts, and reacts is influenced by his or her personality. While there is no universally accepted theory, the Big Five or OCEAN model has gained some acceptance [39]. The "Big Five" represent a taxonomy of traits that some personality psychologists suggest capture the essence of individual differences in personality. The traits of the Big Five model are shown in Table 3.

Openness means a person is imaginative, independent-minded, and has divergent thinking. Openness to experience describes the breadth, depth, originality, and complexity of an individual's mental and experiential life. Conscientiousness means a person is responsible, orderly, and dependable. Conscientiousness describes socially prescribed impulse control that facilitates task-directed and goal-directed behavior, such as thinking before acting, delaying gratification, following norms and rules, and planning, organizing, and prioritizing tasks. Extroversion means that a person is talkative, social, and assertive. It implies an energetic approach to the social and material world and includes traits such as sociability, activity, assertiveness, and positive emotionality. Agreeableness means a person is good natured, cooperative, and trusting. Agreeableness contrasts a pro-social and communal orientation toward others with antagonism and includes traits such as altruism, tender-mindedness, trust, and modesty. Neuroticism means a person is anxious, prone to depression, and worries a lot. It contrasts emotional stability and even-temperedness with negative emotionality, such as feeling anxious, nervous, sad, and tense.

One of the most popular models for emotion is the OCC model, named after its authors [28]. In this model, emotions are generated through the agent's construal of and reaction to the consequence of events, actions of agents, and aspects of objects. Many researchers have based their work on this model [17, 7, 21].

Table 3. OCEAN model of personality

	High Score Traits	**Low Score Traits**
Openness	Creative, Curious, Complex	Conventional, Uncreative
Conscientiousness	Reliable, Well-organized, Self-disciplined, Careful	Disorganized, Undependable
Extraversion	Sociable, Friendly, Fun-loving	Introverted, Reserved, Quiet
Agreeableness	Good natured, Sympathetic, Forgiving, Courteous	Critical, Rude, Harsh, Callous
Neuroticism	Nervous, Insecure, Worrying	Calm, Relaxed, Secure

Table 4 shows part of the PAR representation for agents. The parameters of the OCEAN model are represented as values along the scales of each of the characteristics. There is more information needed to implement the OCC model. First, the standards and values of the agent must be represented. These can be represented as statements that contain PAR actions. Essentially, each action can be associated with a number corresponding to the agent's thought of that action. Agents or classes of agents can also be associated with the actions to create more specific standards. Goals are actions with high priorities. Agents and objects can be tagged with information representing the agent's degree of cognitive unity and *liking* of the object.

Table 4. Partial PAR agent representation

```
type parameterized agent =
(name:       STRING;
personality: OCEAN-parameter-spec;
             Openness INTEGER;
             Conscientiousness INTEGER;
             Extraversion INTEGER;
             Agreeableness INTEGER;
             Neuroticism INTEGER;
emotion:     OCC-specification;
standards:   sequence STATEMENT;
goals:       sequence parameterized action;
appraisals:  sequence cogn-unit-specification;
             sequence appraisal-specification;
```

6.2 EMOTE for Displaying Affect

The implementation of personality or emotion for embodied characters must extend further than decision making or action selection. The quality of movement in an action is also affected by personality and emotion. We have developed a parameterized system for creating more expressive gestures. The

EMOTE system [40, 41, 4, 15] is based on movement observation science. Laban Movement Analysis (LMA) is a method for observing, describing, notating, and interpreting human movement. Two of LMA's components are *Effort* and *Shape*. Effort involves the dynamic qualities of movement. Shape describes the changing forms that the body makes in space. Effort comprises four motion factors: Space, Weight, Time, and Flow. Each motion factor is a continuum between two extremes: indulging in the quality or fighting against the quality. Table 5 describes the Effort qualities. Shape changes in movement can be described in terms of three dimensions: horizontal, vertical, and sagittal.

Table 5. Effort and Shape elements

Space:	attention to the surroundings
Indirect:	flexible, meandering, wandering, multi-focus
Examples:	waving away bugs, slashing through plant growth
Direct:	single focus, channeled, undeviating
Examples:	pointing to a particular spot, threading a needle
Weight:	sense of the impact of one's movement
Light:	buoyant, delicate, easily overcoming gravity, marked by decreasing pressure
Examples:	dabbing paint on a canvas, describing the movement of a feather
Strong:	powerful, having an impact, increasing pressure into the movement
Examples:	punching, pushing a heavy object, expressing a firmly held opinion
Time:	lack or sense of urgency
Sustained:	lingering, leisurely, indulging in time
Examples:	stretching to yawn, stroking a pet
Sudden:	hurried, urgent
Examples:	swatting a fly, grabbing a child from the path of danger
Flow:	attitude toward bodily tension and control
Free:	uncontrolled, abandoned, unable to stop in the course of the movement
Examples:	waving wildly, shaking off water
Bound:	controlled, restrained, able to stop
Examples:	moving in slow motion, tai chi, carefully carrying a cup of hot liquid

Horizontal	
Spreading:	affinity with Indirect
Enclosing:	affinity with Direct
Vertical	
Rising:	affinity with Light
Sinking:	affinity with Strong
Sagittal	
Advancing:	affinity with Sustained
Retreating:	affinity with Sudden

We have created many demonstrations of the EMOTE parameters. One such demonstration involved a virtual character hitting and touching a balloon [18] (see Fig. 2). Here the same basic animation data (from motion capture) for hitting was altered by the EMOTE system generating several different types of hitting and even touching.

Fig. 2. EMOTE alterations of hitting a balloon. The bottom left panel indicates very little force is applied to the balloon. The bottom right panel shows a much greater force. Both were created from the same key frame data, but with differing EMOTE settings

It is our goal to formally link these EMOTE parameters with OCEAN and OCC parameterizations. Table 6 shows an initial linking of EMOTE and OCEAN. This linkage is based on descriptions of LMA [6] and OCEAN [39] and is included only as an example of the type of mappings needed. We plan to verify or modify this linkage by showing agents exhibiting these qualities to naive observers and having them complete a questionnaire about the personality characteristics of the agent. We also plan to use a learning process to build the mapping between OCC and EMOTE. Automatically acquiring motion qualities from observation, and validating them to make sure they are consistent with the LMA concepts and theories, not only are essential com-

Table 6. Example EMOTE and OCEAN linkage

	Space	Weight	Time	Flow
Openness				
High	indirect	light	sustained	free
Low	direct	strong	sudden	bound
Conscientiousness				
High	direct	strong	sudden	bound
Low	indirect	light	sustained	free
Extraversion				
High	indirect	light	sustained	free
Low	direct	strong	sudden	bound
Agreeableness				
High	indirect	light	sustained	free
Low	direct	strong	sudden	bound
Neuroticism				
High	direct	strong	sudden	free
Low	indirect	light	sustained	bound

ponents to complete the EMOTE system in particular, but also can offer a powerful and valuable methodological tool for analyzing gestures and helping to create natural, personalized communicative agents. In [40] Zhao has developed a neural network-based system to achieve this goal. The system inputs 3D motion capture and outputs a classification of EMOTE qualities that are detected in the input. The networks are trained with professional LMA notators to ensure valid analysis.

Future work in the EMOTE system and the motion quality recognizer will be to train the system to correlate captured motions with actor affect, behavior, mood, and intent. The critical problem in such training is setting up appropriate situations that truly elicit affective responses in individuals. We believe that the key ingredients to successful data generation are immersive experiences with both live and virtual agents. Engaging with either or both real and virtual agents in the same circumstances will be crucial to evaluating effectiveness and calibrating responses across the reality/virtual divide. Using the motion capture and post-session analysis, ground truth information can be supplied for training sets. The neural network models may then connect motion qualities to expressed affect and mood. Although the LMA community recognizes that such a mapping may exist it has not yet been possible to investigate it in a visually and computationally adequate environment.

7 Interfaces to Representations

In the previous section describing PAR (Sect. 5), PARs were retrieved and instantiated by autonomous agent processes. This convention is convenient when explicit control over the characters is not required, or there is the ability to code the agents' planning to one's specifications. Often other control mechanisms are desired.

Certainly basic scripting languages that outline that an agent is to perform a specified action at a specified time can be created. Richer scripting constructs can be introduced when the virtual world creators are assumed to be more knowledgeable [29].

Drag-and-drop creation applications for virtual environments are also being created [35, 31]. In these applications, nodes represent agent functionality, such as walking. Nodes can then be linked in logical ways to create simulations.

Another way of controlling an agent is through natural language. PAR was designed as an intermediary between natural language and computer animation, and as such is able to build agent behavior for virtual environments through natural language instructions [5, 10].

8 Conclusions and Future Research

An action representation should afford both autonomy and control where appropriate. It should minimize data storage, while providing for expressive motions. It should provide semantics for planning from the motion level to the cognitive level. The PAR that we have presented in this chapter has made strides toward accomplishing these requirements.

Another aspect of action representations that has not yet been included in PAR or the PAR system is level of detail. The level of detail of objects has long been a subject of graphics research. Large-scale, distributed simulations give us the opportunity to expand the level of detail concept to actions as well. Nearby actions involving objects may need to be enacted using inverse kinematics. At further distances, similar actions could be enacted by replaying motion capture data, because contact relations may not be noticeable. It is not even necessary to display actions that are outside an agent's circle of influence [26, 36]. Nonetheless, other agents may still need to be aware of the action that an agent is performing, the consequences of the action, and whether or not the action was performed successfully. Thus PAR can be used to communicate agent activities even if those actions are not directly seen or even executed; PAR can be a cognitive representation for conveying action information between agents. PAR might even be used to define "need-to-know" multi-cast groups. It uses fields that may be loaded, modified, interpreted, and transferred like data packets, and are generally used as dynamic information objects. An additional bonus with PAR is that its language origins allow its contents to be output as a sentence, making PAR a convenient resource for After Action Summaries and Reviews.

PAR was designed to be a flexible representation, meaning that many different types of information can be represented. Not all of the fields of the PARs need to be filled in for every action. When considering a representation for use with embodied conversational agents we should consider the trade-offs between parameterization specificity and program complexity. If you specify every joint angle for your character at every frame of the animation, your program needs only to display these angles on the figure. If you only specify that your agent needs to get some milk, then your program will need to figure out all the aspects of acquiring milk from high level planning to intricacies of movement. Our experience with PAR and PARSYS leads us to conclude that they have the right balance of specificity and complexity.

That is not to say that there is not more work to be done. We would like to represent PAR in XML format so that it is more widely available to other researchers. Much work also needs to be done to establish the connection between EMOTE parameterization and models of personality and emotion. We are continuing to work on better planning and smarter motion generators for the PARSYS. Finally, although there is a natural language interface for PARSYS, conversation and dialog are not currently considered. A representation and system for modeling conversation and its timing, such as BEAT [14], would certainly enhance our system.

Acknowledgments

We would like to thank all the members of the Center for Human Modeling and Simulation for their diligent work in furthering the state of the art in virtual humans. This research is partially supported by Office of Naval Research K-5-55043/3916-1552793, NSF IIS99-00297, and NASA 00-HEDS-01-052. Any opinions, findings, and conclusions or recommendations expressed in this material are those of the author(s) and do not necessarily reflect the views of the National Science Foundation nor any other sponsoring organization.

References

1. Allbeck, J., Kipper, K., Adams, C., Schuler, W., Zoubanova, E., Badler, N., Palmer, M., Joshi, A.: ACUMEN: Amplifying Control and Understanding of Multiple ENtities. In: *Autonomous Agents and Multi-Agent Systems* (2002) pp 191–198
2. Ashida, K., Lee, S.-J., Allbeck, J., Sun, H., Badler, N., Etaxas, D.M.: Pedestrians: Creating agent behaviors through statistical analysis of observation data. In: *Proceedings Computer Animation*, Seoul, Korea (IEEE Computer Society 2001) pp 84–92
3. Badler, N., Bindiganavale, R., Allbeck, J., Schuler, W., Zhao, L., Palmer, M.: A parameterized action representation for virtual human agents. In: *Embodied Conversational Agents*, ed Cassell, J. (MIT Press, Cambridge, MA 2000) pp 256–284
4. Badler, N., Costa, M., Zhao, L., Chi, D.: To gesture or not to gesture: What is the question? In: *Proceedings Computer Graphics International*, Geneva, Switzerland, June (IEEE Computer Society 2000) pp 3–9

5. Badler, N., Palmer, M., Bindiganavale, R.: Animation control for real-time virtual humans. *Communications of the ACM* **42**(8):64–73 (1999)
6. Bartenieff, I., Lewis, D.: *Body Movement: Coping with the environment* (Gordon and Breach, New York 1980)
7. Bates, J.: The role of emotion in believable agents. *Communications of the ACM* **7**(37):122–125 (1994)
8. Bindiganavale, R.: *Building parameterized action representations from observation.* PhD thesis, CIS (University of Pennsylvania 2000)
9. Bindiganavale, R., Badler, N.: Motion abstraction and mapping with spatial constraints. In: *Modelling and Motion Capture Techniques for Virtual Environments, International Workshop, CAPTECH*, Geneva, Switzerland (1998) pp 70–82
10. Bindiganavale, R., Schuler, W., Allbeck, J., Badler, N., Joshi, A., Palmer, M.: Dynamically altering agent behaviors using natural language instructions. In: *Autonomous Agents 2000* (2000) pp 293–300
11. Boston Dynamics. http://www.bdi.com/
12. Capin, T., Noser, H., Thalmann, D., Pandzic, I., Magnenat Thalmann, N.: Virtual human representation and communication in vlnet networked virtual environments. *IEEE Computer Graphics and Applications* **17**(2):42–53 (1997)
13. Cassell, J.: Nudge nudge wink wink: Elements of face-to-face conversation for embo died conversational agents. In: *Embodied Conversational Agents*, ed Cassell, J., Sullivan, J., Prevost, S., Churchill, E. (MIT Press, Cambridge, MA 2000) pp 1–27
14. Cassell, J., Vilhjalmsson, H., Bickmore, T.: Beat: The Behavior Expression Animation Toolkit. In: *Proceedings ACM SIGGRAPH* (2001) pp 477–486. (Reprinted in this volume.)
15. Chi, D., Costa, M., Zhao, L., Badler, N.: The emote model for effort and shape. In: *Proceedings ACM SIGGRAPH*, New Orleans, LA (2000) pp 173–182
16. EDS. http://www.plmsolutions-eds.com/products/efactory/jack/
17. El-Nasr, M., Yen, J., Ioerger, T.: FLAME – Fuzzy Logic Adaptive Model of Emotions. *Autonomous Agents and Multi-Agent Systems* **3**:219–257 (2000)
18. EMOTE Balloon Demo. http://hms.upenn.edu/software/EMOTE/balloon.html
19. Funge, J., Tu, X., Terzopoulos, D.: Cognitive modeling: Knowledge, reasoning, and planning for intelligent characters. In: *SIGGRAPH '99* (1999) pp 29–38
20. Gleicher, M.: Motion editing with space-time constraints. In: *SIGGRAPH '97* (1997) pp 139–148
21. Gratch, J., Marsella, S.: Tears and fears: Modeling emotions and emotional behaviors in synthetic agents. In: *Proceedings Autonomous Agents*, Montreal, Quebec (ACM Press, New York 2001) pp 278–285
22. Ko, H., Badler, N.: Animating human locomotion in real-time using inverse dynamics, balance and comfort control. *IEEE Computer Graphics and Applications* **16**(2):50–59 (1996)
23. Kovar, L., Gleicher, M., Pighin, F.: Motion graphs. In: *Proceedings of the 29th Annual Conference on Computer Graphics and Interactive Techniques* (ACM Press, New York 2002) pp 473–482
24. Lee, J., Chai, J., Reitsma, P.S.A., Hodgins, J.K., Pollard, N.S.: Interactive control of avatars animated with human motion data. In: *Proceedings of the 29th Annual Conference on Computer Graphics and Interactive Techniques* (ACM Press, New York 2002) pp 491–500

25. Liu, Y., Badler, N.: Real-time reach planning for animated characters using hardware acceleration. In: *Proceedings of the 16th International Conference on Computer Animation and Social Agents (CASA 2003)* (2003)

26. Morse, K., Bic, L., Dillencourt, M.: Interest management in large scale virtual environments. *MIT PRESENCE – Teleoperators and Virtual Environments* (2000)

27. Noser, N., Renault, O., Thalmann, D., Magnenat-Thalmann, N.: Navigation for digital actors based on synthetic vision, memory and learning. *Computers and Graphics* **19**(1):7–19 (1995)

28. Ortony, A., Clore, G., Collins, A.: *The Cognitive Structure of Emotions* (Cambridge University Press 1988)

29. Perlin, K., Goldberg, A.: Improv: A system for scripting interactive actors in virtual worlds. In: *SIGGRAPH '96* (Addison-Wesley, Reading, MA 1996) pp 205–216

30. Ray, E., Maden, C.: *Learning XML.* (O'Reilly and Associates, Sebastopol, CA 2001)

31. Eon Reality. http://www.eonreality.com/

32. Reich, B.: *An architecture for behavioral locomotion.* PhD thesis, CIS (University of Pennsylvania 1997)

33. Russell, S., Norvig, P.: *Artificial Intelligence: A Modern Approach.* (Prentice Hall, Englewood Cliffs, NJ 1995)

34. Singhal, S., Zyda, M.: *Networked Virtual Environments: Design and Implementation* (Addison-Wesley, Readings, MA 1999)

35. Sovoz. http://www.sovoz.com/

36. Stytz, M.: Distributed virtual environments. *IEEE Computer Graphics and Applications* **16**(3):19–31 (1996)

37. Tolani, D., Badler, N.: Real-time inverse kinematics for the human arm. *Presence* **5**(4):393–401 (1996)

38. Trappl, R., Petta, P. (eds): *Creating personalities for synthetic actors: Towards autonomous personality agents* (Springer-Verlag, Berlin 1997)

39. Wiggins, J.: *The Five-Factor Model of Personality: Theoretical Perspectives.* (The Guilford Press, New York 1996)

40. Zhao, L.: *Synthesis and acquisition of Laban Movement Analysis qualitative parameters for communicative gestures.* PhD thesis, CIS (University of Pennsylvania 2001)

41. Zhao, L., Costa, M., Badler, N.: Interpreting movement manner. In: *Proceedings Computer Animation Conference*, Philadelphia, PA, May (IEEE Computer Society 2000) pp 112–120

Toward a Unified Scripting Language: Lessons Learned from Developing CML and AML

Yasmine Arafa, Kaveh Kamyab, and Ebrahim Mamdani

IIS, Department of Electrical and Electronic Engineering,
Imperial College London,
London SW7 2BT, UK
{y.arafa,k.kamyab,e.mamdani}@imperial.ac.uk

Summary. Life-like animated agents present a challenging ongoing agenda for research. Such agent metaphors will only be widely applicable to online applications when there is a standardized way to map underlying engines with the visual presentation of the agents. This chapter delineates functions and specifications of two markup languages for scripting the animation of virtual characters. The first language is Character Markup Language (CML) which is an XML-based, embodied agent, character attribute, definition and animation scripting language designed to aid in the rapid incorporation of life-like agents into online applications or virtual reality worlds. CML is constructed based jointly on motion and multi-modal capabilities of virtual human figures. The other is Avatar Markup Language (AML) which is also an XML-based multi-modal scripting language designed to be easily understandable by human animators as well as easily generated by a software process such as an agent. We illustrate the constructs of the two languages and look at some examples of usage. The experience gained through the development of two such languages with different approaches yet similar aims highlights the need for a degree of unification. This is especially true given that a number of other similar languages exist as illustrated in other parts of this book. We attempt to define metrics for comparison of a set of these languages with the aim of identifying salient constructs for a unified scripting language.

1 Introduction

An account of two approaches to specifying scripting languages for character animation which are currently being developed and evaluated at Imperial College London, the Character Markup Language (CML) [1, 10] and the Avatar Markup Language (AML) [9, 10], is presented. Each approach evolved through the context of the projects they were developed within. CML took a top-down approach by defining high-level attributes for character personality, emotion, and behavior that are integrated to form the specification of synchronized animation script. New or unspecified behaviors are formed by blending together base elements and attributes thereby providing animators with the flexibility to generate animation script as required. On the other hand, AML took a bottom-up approach in which the language provides a generic mechanism for the selection and synchronized merging of animations. In addition, AML provides the flexibility for animators (human or non-human) to define higher level specifications based on the key elements provided plus any others that may be defined. The generic nature of AML implies that any software implementation supporting it will be fairly simple.

At the time the CML and AML languages were being developed parallel attempts for similar languages were also underway. The appearance of these has highlighted the need for powerful yet generic scripting languages to bridge the gap between behavior generation and animation tools. As a number of such scripting languages now exist, there appears to be a need for the research community to look at and agree upon the requirements of and expectations from them.

This chapter describes the key features and capabilities CML and AML offer and discusses the technical issues they raise based on our design and development experience on the ESPRIT project EP28831 MAPPA, IST project IST-1999-10192 SoNG, and IST project IST-1999-11683 SAFIRA. The chapter further sets forth the key functionality that such description and scripting languages will need to succeed in animated agent interaction applications.

2 Scripting with the Character Markup Language

CML was developed with the aim of bridging the gap between the underlying affect and process engines, and agent animation tools. CML provides a map between these tools by automating the movement of information from XML Schema definitions into appropriate relational parameters required to generate the intended animated behavior. This would allow developers to use CML as a glue-like mechanism to tie the various visual and underlying behavior generation tools together seamlessly, regardless of the platform that they run on and the language they are developed with. The term "character" is used to denote a language that encapsulates the attributes necessary for believable behavior. The intention is to provision for characters that are life-like but are not necessarily human-like. Currently the attributes specified are mainly concerned with visual expression, although there is a limited set of specifications for speech. These attributes include specifications for animated face and body expression, behavior, personality, role, emotion, and gestures.

2.1 Visual Behavior Definition

Classification of behavior is governed by the actions an agent needs to perform in a session to achieve given tasks, and is influenced by the agent's personality and current mental state. A third factor that governs character behavior is the role the agent is given. A profile of both an agent's personality and its role are used to represent the ongoing influences on an agent's behavior. These profiles are user-specified and are defined using XML annotation. The behaviors are defined as XML tags, which essentially group and annotate sets of action points generally required by the intended behavioral action. The CML processor will interpret these high-level behavior tags, map them to appropriate action point parameters, and generate an animation script.

CML defines the syntactic, semantic, and pragmatic character presentation attributes using structured text based on the XML Schema definition. The character markup-based language extends the descriptions for facial expressions used in the FACS (Facial Action Coding System) system. FACS defines a set of all the facial movements performed by a human face [4]. Although FACS is not an SGML-based language in nature, we use its notion of Action Units to manipulate expressions. Character gesture attribute definitions are based on the research and observations by McNeill [11] on human gestures and what they reveal.

Affective expression is achieved by varying the extent and degree values of the low-level parameters to produce the required expression. The CML encoder will provide the high-level script to be used in order to specify the temporal variation of these facial expressions. This script will facilitate designing a variety of time-varying facial expressions using the basic expressions provided by the database.

2.2 Classification of Motion

The conceptual architecture upon which the classification of motion is based is loosely derived from that defined by Blumberg and Russell's research [3]. Blumberg and Russell's architecture uses a three-layer structure which includes: geometry, motor, and behavior system. We assume a motor generation module which is responsible for the basic movements along with correlated transitional movements that may occur between them. Personified animation scripts are generated by blending the specification of different poses and gestures. The base motions are further classified by generic controls that are independent of the character itself. For example, a generic *move* motion can have different representations which are determined by the character *emotional* and/or *personality* attributes defined to represent nod, iconic gesture, head, hand or body gesture, walk, etc. Additionally, the language motion categories should cater for the fact that behavior can be expressed through and can affect different parts of the character face (or body part). To realize different parts of a character head/body skeleton which are to be affected while performing a movement CML divides the character element specifications into four units: Head, Upper, Middle, and Lower parts. CML then provides the specification of the constructs of each unit with varying granularity.

Action composition script is generated by a CML processor (delineated in Fig. 1 below) which blends actions specified with an input emotion signal to select the appropriate gestures and achieve the expressive behavior. CML also provisions for the generation of compound animation script by facilitating the definition and parameterization of sequences of base movements.

The chosen base set of movements allows basic character control (movement and interactions) as well as assures the capability to perform unlimited character-specific animations. The interactions can involve other characters and objects that must be referenced by a valid id within the Graphics Engine.

The initial set of CML base motions is classified by the goal of the motion as follows:

- *Movement* defines motions that require the rotation or movement of a character from one position to another. Positions are defined by exact coordinates, an object position, or a character position. The CML elements defined for Movement are either move-to or turn-to.
- *Pointing* defines a pointing gesture toward a coordinate, object, or character. The CML element defined for this movement is point-to.
- *Grasping* defines motions that require the character to hold, throw, or come in contact with an object or another character. The CML elements defined for Grasping are grasp, throw and touch.
- *Gaze* defines the movements related to the head and eyes. The CML elements defined for Gaze are gaze, track, blink, look-to, and look-at. The gaze and track elements require that only the eyes be moved or track an object or character; look-to and look-at require the movement of both head and eyes.
- *Gesture* includes motions that represent known gestures like hand movements to convey an acknowledgment, a wave, etc. The CML elements defined for Gesture are gesture and gesture-at.

2.3 CML Specification

CML defines a script like that used for a play. It describes the actions and sequence of actions that will take place in a presentation system. The script is a collection of commands that tell the objects in the world what to do and how to perform actions. The language is used to create and manipulate objects that are held in memory and referenced by unique output-ontology objects. The structure of the language begins with a command keyword, which is usually followed by one or more arguments and tags. An argument to a command usually qualifies a command, i.e. specifies what form of action the command is to take, while a tag is used to denote the position of other necessary information. A character expression markup module will add emotion-based markup resulting from emotional behavior generation rules to the CML descriptions.

Animated character behavior is expressed through the interpretation of XML Schema structures. These structure definitions are stored in a Schema Document Type Definition (DTD) file using XSDL (XML Schema Definition Language). At run-time character behavior is generated by specifying XML tag/text streams which are then interpreted by the rendering system based on the rules defined in the definition file. Its objective is to achieve a consistent convention for controlling character animation models using a standard scripting language that can be used in online applications.

The language contains low-level tags defining specific character gesture representations defining movements, intensities, and explicit expressions. There are also high-level tags that can define commonly used combinations of these low-level tags. In the sections on CML Representation Language and CML Scripting Language we outline the base elements defined. We do not describe the syntax in too much detail here. Interested readers are advised to refer to [1].

Synchronization between the audio and visual modalities is achieved through the use of SMIL (Synchronized Multimedia Integration Language) specifications [16]. SMIL defines an XML-based language that allows authors to write interactive multimedia presentations. Basically, CML uses the SMIL <par> and <seq> tags to specify the temporal behavior of the modalities being presented. The <seq> tag defines the order, start time, and duration of execution of a sequence, whereas the <par> tag is used to specify that elements be played in parallel. For further flexibility, CML also provides order and time synchronization attributes.

2.4 CML Representation Language

CML provides a set of base description/representation languages that are integrated with the face and body animation markup languages enabling these multi-modal features in a hybrid representation architecture.

Head Gesture Taxonomy

The gesture classifications here are defined as follows:

- *Symbolic gestures* relate to universal symbols and commonly acknowledged gestures across cultures (e.g. repeated up and down nods are symbolic of agreement or shaking from side to side would usually be symbolic of disagreement).
- *Iconic gestures* are used to demonstrate a symbolization of a particular behavior or action (e.g. rotating the head showing that one is dizzy).
- *Deictic gestures* are gestures that point in the direction of objects.

Hand Gestures Taxonomy

CML captures gesture features such as postures of the hand (straight, relaxed, closed), its motion (moving, stopped), and its orientation. Over time, a stream of gestures is then abstracted into more general 'gestlets' (e.g. Point-at, sweep, end reference). Although, here, the recorded action takes place in the 2D plane, similar phenomena play a role as in the case of 3D hand gesturing, but with a much easier signal processing involved.

- *Posture* defines the position the hand is held in and a duration.
- *Motion* defines whether the hand is in motion or stagnant and a speed defining the transition between each state.
- *Orientation* defines the direction of a movement (up, down, left, right, forward, backward). Directions are derived from the normal and longitudinal vectors of the palm.
- *'Gestlets'* define a set of high-level tags that are constituted from the lower level tags described above. These make up gestures like Point, Wave, etc.
- *Fingers* define high-level tags for each of the five fingers.

Body Gestures Taxonomy

The research for the base body gestures is partly derived from work conducted on the research and analysis of body expressions.

- *Natural* defines the character's default or normal posture state based on a distinct personality.
- *Relax* defines a relaxed posture state of the character.
- *Tense* defines a tensed posture state of the character.
- *Iconic gestures* are used to demonstrate a symbolization of a particular behavior or action (e.g. rotating the head showing that one is dizzy).
- *Incline* defines the orientation and degree a character might lean toward or against an object.

Emotions

The list below shows the specification for the attributes for an emotion. The attributes considered for the description of an emotion are based on the OCC theory of emotions [12], which was used to partially support the system implementation.

- *Class:* The id of the emotion class being experienced.
- *Valence:* The basic types of emotional response (neutral, positive, or negative value of the reaction).
- *Subject:* The id of the agent experiencing the emotion.
- *Target:* The id of the event/agent/object toward which the emotion is directed.
- *Intensity:* The intensity of the emotion (a logarithmic scale between 0 and 10).
- *Time-stamp:* The moment in time when the emotion was felt.
- *Origin:* The id of the event/agent/object that caused a change in emotion.

The attribute *Class* describing an emotion refers to the type of that emotion. An emotion type represents a family of related emotions differing in terms of their intensity and manifestation, i.e. each emotion type can be realized in a variety of related forms. For example, fear with varying degrees of intensity can be seen as concern, fright, petrified.

The attribute *Valence* describes the value (positive or negative) for the reaction that originated the emotion. According to this theory, emotions are always a result of positive or negative reactions to events, agents, or objects. The Subject and Target attributes for emotions, define the entities related to them. The Subject defines the agent experiencing the emotion and the Target defines the event, agent, or action that originated the emotion.

2.5 CML Scripting Language

Face Animation Scripting

Character face description is a set of low-level tags based on MPEG-4 FAPs, and a set of high-level tags representing facial parts which are grouped from a set of respective low-level tags. CFML base elements are as follows:

1. *Head Movement*

   CML defines two base head movements which are *tilt* and *turn*. Complex head movements are generated using a combination or sequence of the defined base movements. The difference between the *tilt* and *turn* movements is that *tilt* is a head movement in a slant with often subtle or superficial neck movement, whereas *turn* would require more profound movement of the neck. The following is the syntax of a *turn* movement (details of the CML full syntax can be found in [4]):

```
<turn-to>
    <order {0 to n/before/after} />
    <priority 0 to n />
    <begin {ss:mmm/before/after/object} />
    <end {ss:mmm/before/after/object} />

    <speed {0.n to n.n(unit)/default/slow/fast} />

    <target {x,y,z/object/character} />
    <direction (rightside,leftside,frontside,backside) />
    <degree (n%) />

    <repeat {0 to n/dur} />
    <interrupt> {yes/no} />

    <transAnimat {head groups} />
    <transPos {x,y,z/object/character} />
    <transSpeed default/slow/ intermediate/fast} />
```

```
</turn-to >
```

This code shows the basic syntax for the animation of a "turn-to" head movement in CFML. The syntax includes parameters for synchronization, pace, object, and animation handling and transition option. Synchronization parameters are either absolute or relative to other animations or sequences. Pace is the speed in which the movement is implemented and is usually governed by the predominant emotional state. Object defines the target properties to which to turn to. These properties are also either absolute or relative to another character or object or a general direction. The animation handling parameters support options to allow multiple repetitions of the movement at specified intervals and to specify whether or not the animation can be interrupted. If the "interrupt" tag is set then the "transition option" tags specify the appropriate transition or fall-back animations need to sustain a smooth and believable animation. It can be noted here that modifiers to a typical "turn-to" movement to reflect emotional state and personality behaviors are achieved by encapsulating the element in an "emotion" tag, which will influence the intensity, speed, and manner the movement is carried out.

2. *Head Gesture*
   CML also defines two basic head gestures, either *Deictic* or *Symbolic*. The following is an example of a *Symbolic* gesture (further details can be found in [4]):

```
<disagree>
    <tilt-to-right>
      ...
    </tilt-to-right>
    <tilt-to-left>
      ...
    </tilt-to-left>
</disagree>
```

This is an example of a complex tag that is comprised of two base-movement tags to form a symbolic disagree head gesture. Synchronization and pace are achieved by specifying the corresponding parameters as described in the description of the "turn-to" example. The duration and specific behavior in which such a gesture is implemented is predisposed by the character's defined personality properties and emotional state. As described earlier this can be achieved by wrapping the element within an "emotion" tag.

3. *Face Movement and Gesture*
   They define the elements and behaviors for specific parts of the face including the *Brow*, *Gaze*, and *Mouth*.

Body Animation Scripting

Character body description is a set of defined body elements which are low-level tags based on MPEG-4 BAPs, and a set of high-level tags representing body parts which are grouped from a set of respective low-level tags. CBML base elements are as follows:

1. *Movement* (moving, bending, turning).
2. *Gesture* defines body postures that include motions representing common Iconic, Symbolic, or Deictic body gestures.
3. *Posture (Expression)* defines a set of high-level tags representing general body gestures.
   - "Natural" defines the character's default or normal posture state based on a distinct personality.
   - "Relax" defines a relaxed posture state of the character.
   - "Tense" defines a tensed posture state of the character.
   - "Incline" defines the orientation and degree a character leans toward or against and object.

2.6 Generating Script

Script generation through to the effected animation process components consist of a set of MPEG-4-compliant facial and body models; high-level XML-based descriptions of compound facial and body features; XML-based descriptions of user-specified personality models; behavior definitions; a CML processor; and finally a CML decoder. The general function of this component is delineated in Fig. 1.

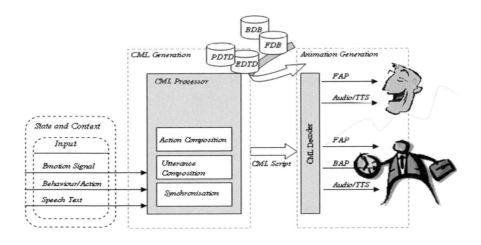

Fig. 1. CML script generation – Function Abstract

The architecture of an implementation generating and using CML is divided into three conceptual components of the supporting models and database for face and body animation, CML scripting, and an animation rendering tool. The script generation component assumes state and contextual input resulting from the underlying affective processing, planning, and domain knowledge-base engines. Based on these inputs and a defined character personality, the CML processor then generates the consequent synchronized behavioral action and utterance CML script. The script is then passed on to the CML decoder which parses the CML and maps its elements onto view-specific commands for final animation rendering.

3 Avatar Markup Language

AML was developed in the context of the IST project SoNG in collaboration with IIS, Miralab, and LIG. The objective of the project was to design and develop a full end-to-end MPEG-4 multimedia framework to support, amongst other features, 3D avatar-based multi-user chat rooms and autonomous synthetic characters. The first of these was to be facilitated via the development of an interface tool that allowed users to define animation sequences by selecting and merging predefined and proprietary animation units. Likewise, synthetic characters were to be controlled in a similar manner to fill roles such as sales assistants in virtual shops. The focus was on providing the tools and infrastructure necessary to anybody who would like to develop such applications. Hence, a common mechanism was needed to allow both human users and autonomous agent-based systems to define full face and body avatar animation. However, it was important to allow future users or developers to animate their avatars using non-procedural commands whilst trying not to limit their creativity by imposing predefined facial expressions or gestures on them. Also, we were aiming at providing a means of generating externally observable behavior and not on specifying a mapping between internal reasoning and behavior, as is the case with many other scripting systems.

The design of such a mechanism saw the animation process conceptually divided into three components. First, a database of basic facial and body animation units, which could be extended or modified by a third party interested in generating avatar animations. These animations can be either specified by hand or achieved via motion capture. Examples include smiling or waving. Second, a rendering system capable of merging multiple face and body animation units and text to speech input in realtime. Finally, a high-level scripting language designed to allow animators – both human and non-human – to specify which animations to use together with timing, priority, and decay information. The resulting scripting language – AML – is the only one of the three components that we specify.

AML facilitates multi-modal interaction based on embodied characters by allowing users or agents to trigger appropriate face animation, body animation, and TTS modules in a time-synchronized and easy manner. This may involve mixing of multiple gestures and expressions into a single animation. Originally, no basic animations were considered compulsory within AML, but it became obvious that some parameterized behaviors would have to be provided. Examples of such behaviors include pointing, facing, and walking. Each of the behaviors is generated by the implemented rendering system by calculating the movement of the avatar as a function of its initial position and the target coordinates supplied by the animator.

3.1 AML Specification

Having given a brief overview of the requirements and purpose of AML we will now have a look at the syntax of the language. AML is an XML-based scripting language. Figures 2 to 4 give an outline of the AML syntax. We will not describe the syntax in too much detail here. Interested readers are advised to refer to [9].

Each individual AML script is encapsulated by the AML root node and consists of either a Facial Animation (FA) node or a Body Animation (BA) node or both. FA nodes may contain a combination of TTS nodes and Avatar Face Markup Language (AFML) nodes, the syntax of which is illustrated in Fig. 2.

```
<AFML>
   <Settings>
     ...
   </Settings>
   ...
   <ExpressionsTrack name="Track name">
      <Expression>
         <StartTime>mm:ss:mmm</StartTime>
         <ExName>"name"</ExName>
         <Envelope>
           ...
         </Envelope>
      </Expression>
   </ExpressionsTrack>
     ...
</AFML>
```

Fig. 2. AFML syntax

Here we highlight the flexibility that is given to an animator to define as many Expression Tracks as required, each containing as many Expressions as required. Expressions are stored in a database of facial animation units.

For example, in an MPEG-4-based system, such units would represent animations as values for MPEG-4 FAPs for an arbitrary number of frames. A start time and an envelope specifying decay, duration, and intensity accompany each one. In addition, Speech Tracks may be specified when a TTS engine is not available or suitable. Similarly, BA nodes contain Avatar Body Markup Language (ABML) nodes. The syntax can be seen in Figs. 3 and 4.

```
<BodyAnimationTrack name="char, name of track">
  ...
  <UserAnimation type="bap|trk|wrl" filename="char">
    <StartTime>mm:ss:mmm|autosynch|autoafter</StartTime>
    <Speed>normal|slow|fast</Speed>
    <Intensity>float, 0 to fn</Intensity>
    <Priority>integer, 0 to n</Priority>
  </UserAnimation>
  <Emotion>...</Emotion>
  <StandardGesture>...</StandardGesture>
</BodyAnimationTrack>
```

Fig. 3. ABML's BodyAnimationTrack syntax

Figure 3 shows the basic animation capabilities of ABML. As with AFML, ABML comprises a Settings node and allows us to define one or more BodyAnimationTrack. Animation can be adapted by means of modifiers such as Speed, Intensity, and Priority. StartTimes are used for synchronization and can be in the form of an absolute time or a relative indicator of the start time (autosynch or autoafter) with respect to other animations within a track. We focus our attention on some of the subnodes of BodyAnimationTrack. Like AFML, body animation units can be retrieved from a database using the UserAnimation node. However, predefined emotional indicators can be selected as either a gesture or a posture and standard gestures are provided to support standard interaction.

In Fig. 4 we draw attention to a set of parameterized behavior nodes, namely FacingAction, PointingAction, WalkingAction, and ResettingAction. Each behavior node specifies modifiers such as StartTime, Speed, and Priority. A subset also specifies target coordinates for the behavior. For walking, a number of control points can be specified to define the route taken by an avatar in 3D space. Notice that only the X and Z coordinates are used indicating that only movement along a horizontal plane is permitted.

AML scripts offer a number of advantages to animators – human or non-human. First, they give explicit control over the mutual synchronization of facial expressions, gestures, and speech by allowing start times and durations to be specified for each. This means animators are free to have even partial overlap of animation tracks starting before, together with, or after any other

```
<BodyAnimationTrack name="char, name of track">
   <FacingAction bodypart="body|headonly">
      ...
      <XCoor>float, target's X coordinate in meters</XCoor>
      <YCoor>float, target's Y coordinate in meters</YCoor>
      <ZCoor>float, target's Z coordinate in meters</ZCoor>
   </FacingAction>
   <PointingAction handconfig="onefinger|open">...
   </PointingAction>
   <WalkingAction mode="default|run">...</WalkingAction>
   <ResettingAction>...</ResettingAction>
</BodyAnimationTrack>
```

Fig. 4. ABML's BodyAnimationTrack behaviors

track. Second, as well as providing a basic set of animations, AML allows developers to provide their own through the ExpressionFiles and UserAnimation nodes.

4 CML and AML Applied

In this section we present an animation scenario for a character (Sales Agent) moving toward an object and pointing at it. The aim is to demonstrate how a single scenario is scripted using both CML and AML, drawing out elements of believability attributes, gestures, and animation functionality, as well as issues of the overlaps between both languages in terms of functionality while differing in terms of tag-use granularity.

4.1 CML

In the examples below we demonstrate the use of simple CML high-level tags to script a walk animation from one position toward a target object. The extracts show CML's base movement specifications. Using high-level tags provides simplicity of scripting inhibiting voluminous lines of script, but limiting flexibility over final animation control. Alternatively, higher flexibility can be achieved by using low-level tags of specific MPEG-4 as demonstrated in AML.

The associated figures below further show that dramatic differences are achieved in the way a single activity is animated by varying its believability attributes of emotion intensity and speed. The animations are governed by a defined mental state so that each gesture and behavior in which a movement is made is inherited from the state of emotion specified. This will affect the speed, the height of footsteps, hand movements and gestures, and overall behavior.

Fig. 5. Happy move and point animation

Sample CML – Happy Move and Point Script

```
<cml>
    <character name="James" personality="extravert" role="psa"
            gender="m" base-animation-file="butler.liv">
        <happy intensity="0.3" decay="0.5" target="goal"
            priority="1">
            <move-to order="0" priority="0" speed="default"
                    object="product1" />
            <sync type="par" order="1" priority="0" >
                <point-to object="product1" />
                <utterance>
                    "I've found just what you wanted! Take a look."
                </utterance>
            </sync>
        </happy>
        ...
    </character>
</cml>
```

Figure 5 shows a happy James walking with swift eagerness toward his target. Take a look at the next animation sequence (see Fig. 6). James is slow, not as eager when pointing and expressing an overall sad behavior. The reader may note that while there are distinct and recognizable behavioral differences between both animation sequences, there is little variation in the actual script, proving CML suitable for automated scripting.

Sample CML – Sad Move and Point Script

```
<cml>
    <character name="James" personality="extravert" role="psa"
            gender="m" base-animation-file="butler.liv">
        <sad intensity="0.1" decay="0.3" target="goal" priority="1">
            <move-to order="0" priority="0" speed="slow"
```

Fig. 6. Sad move and point animation

```
                  object="product1" />
      <sync type="par" order="1" priority="0" >
        <point-to object="product1" />
        <utterance>
           "I'm afraid we've only got 2 bottles in stock!"
        </utterance>
      </sync>
    </sad>
    ...
  </character>
</cml>
```

4.2 AML

The following example shows the use of AML to animate a Sales Agent in a
3D telephone shop (see Fig. 7). The scenario is similar to the one described
above with a Sales Agent walking toward and pointing to a product. Clearly,
as compared to CML, the focus here is much less on believability aspects
of character animation and more on scripting and controlling actions and
behaviors in a 3D world in a synchronized manner.

Sample AML – Walk and Point

```
<AML face_id="x" body_id="y" root_path="c:\" name="Point to phone">
  <FA start_time = "00:00:000">
    <TTS output_fap = speech.fap output_wav = speech.wav>
      <Text> "Let me show you another phone over here." </Text>
    </TTS>
    <AFML>
      <Settings>
        <Fps>25</Fps>
        <Duration>00:06:000</Duration>
```

```
                <FAPDBPath>.\Expressions\</FAPDBPath>
                <SpeechPath>.\Speech\</SpeechPath>
            </Settings>
            <ExpressionsTrack name= "smile" >
                <Expression>
                    <StartTime> 00:00:800 </StartTime>
                    <ExName> smile.ex </ExName>
                    <Envelope>
                        <Point>
                            <Shape>log</Shape>
                            <Duration> 00:00:500 <Duration>
                            <Int>1<Int>
                        </Point>
                        <Point>...</Point>
                        <Point>...</Point>
                    </Envelope>
                </Expression>
            </ExpressionsTrack>
            <SpeechTrack>
                <StartTime> 00:01:300 </StartTime>
                <FileName> speech.fap </FileName>
                <AudioFile> speech.wav </AudioFile>
            </SpeechTrack>
        </AFML>
    </FA>
    <BA start_time = "00:04:000">
        <ABML>
            <Settings>
                <Fps>25</Fps>
                <BAPLibPath>.\BapFiles</BAPLibPath>
            </Settings>
            <BodyAnimationTrack name="Walk">
                <WalkingAction mode= "default" >
                    <StartTime> 00:00:000 </StartTime>
                    <Style type= "bap" > "walk.bap" </Style>
                    <ControlPoint>
                        <XCoor> -5 </XCoor>
                        <ZCoor> 0 </ZCoor>
                    </ControlPoint>
                    <ControlPoint>
                        <XCoor> 5 </XCoor>
                        <ZCoor> 0 </ZCoor>
                    </ControlPoint>
                </WalkingAction>
                <PointingAction handconfig="open">
                    <StartTime>autoafter</StartTime>
                    <XCoor>2</XCoor>
                    <YCoor>1.6</YCoor>
                    <ZCoor>4</ZCoor>
```

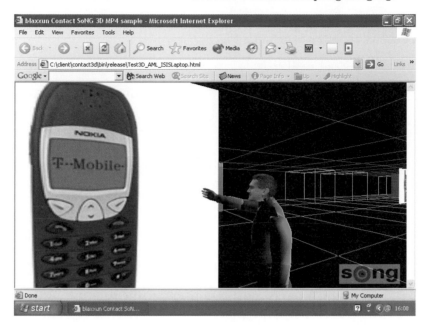

Fig. 7. A Sales Agent pointing at a product

```
                <Speed>fast</Speed>
                <Priority>10</Priority>
            </PointingAction>
        </BodyAnimationTrack>
    </ABML>
  </BA>
</AML>
```

The above script instructs a virtual sales assistant to smile and say "Let me show you another phone over here", after which the character walks toward a phone and points to it. Notice the start times of <FA> and <BA>. <A> is delayed by 4 seconds to let the character start talking before the walking starts. Start times of ExpressionTracks, SpeechTracks, and BodyAnimationTracks are relative to the start times of <FA> and <BA>. The use of the relative synchronization indicator "autoafter" is also illustrated. This guarantees that the pointing action will not start before the walking action has finished. Other important features are the use of envelopes in <AFML> to "shape" the animation. These can be either linear, exponential, or logarithmic. Finally, there is the different syntax for the different body actions. In particular, the walking action defines control points to specify the trajectory the character should take while walking. In addition, however, AML allows for user-defined animations to be used to extend the basic animation set. The

following example shows the use of UserAnimation to make the Sales Agent
look impatiently at its watch (see Fig. 8).

Sample AML – Look at Watch

```
<AML face_id="x" body_id="y" root_path="c:\" name="Look at watch">
  <BA start_time = "00:00:000">
    <ABML>
      <Settings>
        <Fps>25</Fps>
        <BAPLibPath>.\BapFiles</BAPLibPath>
      </Settings>
      <BodyAnimationTrack name="Impatient">
        <UserAnimation type="bap" filename="impatient.bap">
          <StartTime>00:00:000</StartTime>
          <Speed>fast</Speed>
          <Intensity>1</Intensity>
          <Priority>1</Priority>
        </UserAnimation>
      </BodyAnimationTrack>
    </ABML>
  </BA>
</AML>
```

5 Discussion and Lessons Learned

The chapter presented an account of two approaches to specifying scripting
languages for character animation which are currently being developed and
evaluated at Imperial College London, CML and AML. All attempts have
been made to specify and develop mechanisms for the dynamic scripting of
expressive behavior in embodied agents. The growing popularity of embodied
agents will increase the demand on such languages in order to automate the
animation process and allow non-technical character creators to quickly script
believable animated behavior. Such languages will benefit applications that
require real-time generation of animated behavior and control, such as *virtual
tutors and trainers*, *virtual presenters*, *conversational agents*, *virtual game
characters*, *electronic personal assistants*, and many more applications.

In general, the role of these languages is to mediate and control language
semantics between human and machine. Specifically, in the case of the languages described in this chapter, the role is to script the animation of agent
behaviors (external) and convey behavioral information between communicating agents (internal). The language design is based primarily on operational
semantics – where specified tags correspond to an operational rendering function or set of functions that complete an animation – and partially on content

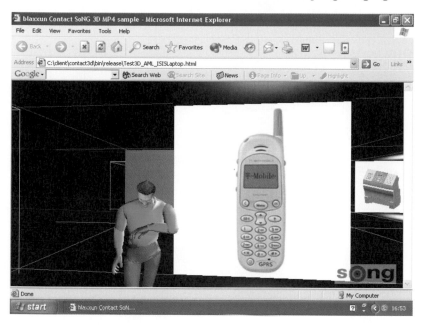

Fig. 8. An impatient Sales Agent

semantics – where tags hold some behavioral or believability attribute, e.g. an emotion, a mood, a personality trait, etc. There is also a third dimension of semantics as identified by Piez [14] which is structural semantics – where a tag is the arbitrary relation between a signifier and a signified, and according to Piez's understanding the layer in which a tag is defined in realtime may help to identify a contextual view of interpreting the tag. Markup languages are, nonetheless, semantic-less languages; however, interpreting a *meaning* from the defined tags will depend on where, when, and how tags are processed.

Since there are a number of these languages emerging having both common and similar objectives, though taking different approaches to specify them, there is a need to compare and identify their key features, aiming at defining salient characteristics and requirements as a basis for setting the platform for possibly specifying a unified language. To approach this issue we suggest a set of factors that need to be present in a language for it to be successful.

5.1 A Comparison

In order to identify salient features for a unified language, we carried out a comparison of their capabilities. Through this analysis we propose a set of comparison metrics as defined in the table in Fig. 9. Details of the specific languages included can be found in the other chapters of this book.

	Scripting Languages				Both Scripting and Representation Languages				Representation Languages		
	AML	MPML	MURML	TVML	APML	CML	STEP XTEP	VHML	HumanML	PAR	RRL
Approach											
Objectives	animation	presen- tation	verbal and non-verbal utterances	presen- tation	discourse	animation	animation	animation	human represen- tation	parameter- ised action	discourse
Format											
XML	✓	✓	✓		✓	✓	✓	✓	✓		✓
Specification Elements											
Character Definition		✓	✓	✓		✓	✓	✓	✓	✓	✓
Animation	✓	✓	✓	✓	✓	✓	✓	✓		✓	✓
Dialogue Acts					✓	✓		✓		✓	✓
World	✓	✓	✓	✓	✓	✓	✓			✓	✓
Actions/Behaviour	✓	✓	✓	✓				✓			✓
Voice Controls				✓				✓			
Animation Control											
Inhibiting animation	✓				✓			✓			
Merging	✓	✓	✓	✓	✓	✓	✓	✓		✓	?
Synchronisation	✓	✓	✓	✓	✓	✓	✓	✓		✓	✓
Additional Parameters	✓	✓	✓	✓		✓	✓	✓		✓	✓
Parameterised actions	✓						✓	✓		✓	✓
Feedback to application							✓				
Specification Granularity											
Extensibility	✓	✓	✓	✓	✓	✓	✓	✓		✓	✓
Macro Elements	✓		✓	✓	✓	✓	✓	✓		✓	✓
Micro Elements			✓		✓						
Believability Attributes											
Emotions	✓	✓		✓	✓	✓	✓	✓	✓	✓	✓
Personality		✓			✓	✓	✓	✓	✓	✓	✓
Character Type											
Human-like	✓	✓	✓	✓	✓	✓	✓	✓	✓	✓	✓
Non-Human					✓						
Character Parts/Modules											
Face	✓	✓	✓	✓		✓	✓	✓		✓	✓
Body	✓	✓	✓	✓		✓	✓	✓		✓	✓
Speech	✓		✓	✓			✓	✓		✓	✓

Fig. 9. Comparison of features of various scripting languages

The comparison is based on five metrics that describe each language in terms of Control: defining the degree of decoupling between language and animation tools; Granularity: the detail of the taxonomy used for defining kinetic and behavioral animation; Flexibility: support for user-defined animations and varying levels of control; Classification: categorization of the type of animation; Believability: the use of attributes of emotion and personality in order to make character animation more believable.

To varying degrees all the languages support parameterized action and synchronization. APML [13], CML [1], MPML [19], and TVML [17] are built on the existing standard SMIL but also introduce additional parameters for higher control.

All the languages appear to be complete in that they achieve the objectives they set out to meet. However, each language addresses a different issue: animation, character, and believability attribute representation, dialogue acts, and presentation.

It was difficult to assess the extent of usability, consistency, and extensibility of the languages surveyed due to a lack of open availability of full language specification and the associated tools and players for creating and visualizing affected behavior. Most of the languages are still on the design bench and under development.

We propose a set of comparison metrics/parameters as defined in the table in Fig. 9. We start by defining the objectives of the language as mentioned above. Then we look at the format. XML was a common choice for most language specifications. Besides XML's increasing popularity in application development and Internet support, it provisions for extensibility and syntactic correctness through XML parsers and validation.

We then analyze the elements supported by each language. Most support animation and behavior definition. This is sometimes supplemented by explicit voice control (most notably VHML) or definitions of the world, and objects within, that surround the agent. Here we interpret world information as either the elements of a presentation, as in the case of MPML, or full scene descriptions as for TVML. Beyond animation, some languages have been designed to support descriptions of characters as well. CML, for example, has been designed to be both a representation and scripting language. It targets an abstract annotation of character attributes which can be used in the internal reasoning process as well as a lower level of annotation for animation script generation. Finally, other languages are designed to represent dialogues. RRL [15] and APML are examples of these in that both languages are based on the definition of the communicative functions and relate these to the expressions effected.

Related to animation we can compare markup languages on the level of control they provide to the animation process. As mentioned earlier most languages support synchronization and merging of animation tracks. However, some additional animation control is proposed. AML [9] provides a means of inhibiting body parts during an animation track so that they can be used by another track. This feature is useful in avoiding conflict while merging animations. STEP [5, 6], like PAR [2] and VHML [18], introduces the idea of providing feedback to or awareness of the calling application. This feature can help the synchronization process.

All languages aim at high-level abstraction and domain independence; however, MPML in particular models its language constructs on and is therefore tightly coupled with the MSAgent technology. On the other hand, APML, CML, and VHML define their low-level tags based on MPEG-4 FAPs and BAPs. This introduces the issues of granularity of representation. We define Micro Elements such as FAPs and BAPs or "turn" and "move" in the case of STEP which are very low level and from which a significant set of animation tags/commands (Macro Elements) can be constructed. We also define an extensibility metric. Most languages claim to be extensible, but in varying ways. In many cases, such as CML and VHML, it is a matter of constructing complex elements from existing macro elements. In the case of AML, MURML [8], and TVML it is a case of inserting new animations into the script or animation library.

Including believability attributes of emotion and personality is essential to achieve convincing and realistic behavior. Here we specify emotion and personality as attributes of interest. Apart from MURML and STEP, all languages readily support one or both of these attributes with similar specifications. Noticeably there is a strong correlation between those languages that support character definition and/or dialogue acts and their support for believability attributes.

Finally we found some divergence on the type of character and its constituent body parts that can be supported by the various languages. Most languages are restricted to human-like characters. This can include characters as long as they present human physical characteristics. In contrast, VHML, like CML and PAR, claims not to be restricted to the description of humanoid characters, but can support, for example, four-legged creatures.

5.2 Towards a Unified Language

As a number of such scripting languages now exist, there appears to be a need for the research community to look at and agree upon the requirements of and expectations from them. Here, we delineate some key objectives and general language specification requirements we deem necessary for such languages to meet their objectives. Based on the comparison in the previous section, we suggest specific language constructs that define the operational semantics needed for embodied agent scripting languages.

Objectives of a Unified Language

- Define a framework to decouple embodied agent animation tools and the underlying affect and planning engines.

- Establish a formal specification for unified/consistent interpretation.
- Provide for modular development.
- Create a markup language based on XML that allows users/agents to provide semantic and scripting annotations for handling and animating embodied agents.

Language Requirements

The design and formalization process of any language needs to fulfill a set of salient considerations defined so as to meet the criteria for general use and implementation, in addition to the set of criteria that fulfills the functional purpose of the language.

The following key design criteria are identified for the development of such languages:

- *High-Level:* Abstracted from the low-level technology elements yet retaining tags for low-level elements to allow detailed, flexible control.
- *Usability (Machine/Human Legible):* The language should be usable and easily implementable with multi-purpose applications and technologies.
- *Extensibility:* Provisions for user-defined tags, and complex elements, share and reuse.
- *Parameterized Action Support:* Provision for customized and dynamically generated scripts.
- *Synchronization Support:* Modality control, merged animation.
- *Consistency:* Provision for predictable control of the animation output regardless of the implementation and the platforms it will be run on.
- *Domain Independence:* Not catering for any one domain, implementation application, or animation rendering tool.

6 Conclusion

In this chapter we described both the CML and AML languages. We also addressed the current fragmentation in the field of embodied character animation and representation. There seems, however, to be an overriding agreement that efforts could be made toward unifying many of the approaches to character animation that have emerged in recent years. Following an analysis of generic language requirements we have looked at the main features of a representative set of current languages. Although similar in many ways, the chosen languages were developed following different approaches and thus present a variety of functions and capabilities.

Resulting from this review we propose metrics for language comparison. These can be broadly categorized as format, specification elements, supported character types and modules, believability attributes, animation control, granularity, and extensibility. Finally, we put forward some suggestions about the possible requirements for a unified language.

There are, of course, many open and more specific issues that still need answering. For example, what taxonomy for the affective and motion elements should be used? What granularity of description should be targeted? Indeed, there is a trade-off to be made between higher levels of control (high granularity) and the complexity of the resulting language. Often these decision have been influenced by the underlying technology used (e.g. MPEG-4 or MSAgent). Similarly, what affective and personality theories should be adopted to define the tags for affective expression? A decision has not yet been made within the research community, but striving toward a unified scripting and representation language may be the catalyst for much needed agreement.

Acknowledgments

The requirement for and specification of CML was originally a contribution of the European ESPRIT project EP28831 MAPPA. CML as described in this chapter is developed within the European IST project IST-1999-11683 SAFIRA and AML is developed in the European IST project IST-1999-10192 SoNG.

Bibliography

1. Arafa, Y., Mamdani, E.: Scripting embodied agents behaviour with CML: Character markup language. In: *Proceedings of the 7th International Conference on Intelligent User Interfaces (IUI03)*, Miami, Florida (2003)
2. Badler, N., Bindiganavale, R., Allbeck, J., Schuler, W., Zhao, L., Palmer, M.: Parameterized action representation for virtual human agents. In: *Embodied Conversational Agents*, ed Cassell, J., et al. (MIT Press, Cambridge MA 2000) pp 256–284
3. Blumberg, B., Russell, K.: Behavior friendly graphics. In: *Proceedings of Computer Graphics International '99*, Canmore, Alberta, Canada, June (1999) pp 44–51
4. Ekman, P., Rosenberg, E.: *What the Face Reveals – Basic and Applied Studies of Spontaneous Expression using the Facial Action Coding System* (Oxford University Press 1997)
5. Huang, Z., Eliens, A., Visser, C.: STEP - A scripting language for embodied agents. In: *Proceedings AAMAS-02 Workshop on Embodied Conversational Agents—Let's specify and evaluate them!*, Bologna, Italy (2002)
6. Huang, Z., Eliens, A., Visser, C.: XSTEP - A markup language for embodied agents. In: *Proceedings of the 16th International Conference on Computer Animation and Social Agents (CASA'03)* (IEEE Press 2003)
7. HumanML. http://www.humanmarkup.org/work/humanmlSchema.zip (2002). Cited 6 May 2003.
8. Kransted, A., Kopp, S., Wachsmuth, I.: MURML – A multimodal utterance representation markup language for conversational agents. In: *Proceedings AAMAS-02 Workshop on Embodied Conversational Agents - Let's specify and evaluate them!*, Bologna, Italy (2002)

9. Kshirsagar, S., Guye-Vuilleme, A., Kamyab, K., Magnenat-Thalmann, N., Thalmann, D., Mamdani, E.: Avatar Markup Language. In: *Proceedings of the Eighth Eurographics Workshop on Virtual Environments*, ed Müller, S., Stürzlinger, W. (2002)

10. Life-like   Characters.   Tools,   Affective   Functions   and   Applications. http://www.vhml.org/LLC/llc-book.html

11. McNeill, D.: *Hands and Mind* (The University of Chicago Press 1992)

12. Ortony, A., Clore, G., Collins, A.: *The Cognitive Strucutre of Emotions* (Cambridge University Press 1988)

13. Pelachaud, C., Carofiglio, V., de Rosis, F., Poggi, I.: Embodied contextual agent in information delivering application. In: *Proceedings 1st International Joint Conference on Autonomous Agents and Multi-Agent Systems* (ACM Press, New York 2002)

14. Piez W.: Human and machine sign systems. In: *Proceedings of Extreme Markup Languages*, Montreal, Canada, August (2002)

15. Piwek, P., Krenn, B., Schröder, M., Grice, M., Baumann, S., Pirke, H.: RRL - A rich representation language for the description of agent behaviour in NECA. In: *Proceedings of the Autonomous Agents Workshop on Achieving Human-Like Behavior in Interactive Animated Agents*, Barcelona, Spain (2000)

16. SMIL. http://www.w3.org/AudioVideo/ (1998). Cited 6 May 2003.

17. TVML. http://www.strl.nhk.or.jp/TVML/ (1999). Cited 6 May 2003.

18. VHML. http://www.vhml.org/downloads/VHML (2002). Cited 6 May 2003.

19. Zong, Y., Dohi, H., Ishizuka, M.: Emotion expression functions attached to Multimodal Presentation Markup Language (MPML). In: *Proceedings of the Autonomous Agents Workshop on Achieving Human-Like Behavior in Interactive Animated Agents*, Barcelona, Spain (2000)

APML, a Markup Language for Believable Behavior Generation

Berardina De Carolis[1], Catherine Pelachaud[2], Isabella Poggi[3], and Mark Steedman[4]

[1] Dipartimento di Informatica, University of Bari, Bari, Italy
   decarolis@di.uniba.it
[2] LINC - Paragraphe, IUT of Montreuil - University of Paris, Paris, France
   c.pelachaud@iut.univ-paris8.fr
[3] Dipartimento di Educazione, University of Rome Three, Rome, Italy
   poggi@uniroma3.it
[4] School of Informatics, University of Edinburgh, Edinburgh, UK
   steedman@informatics.ed.ac.uk

Summary. Developing an embodied conversational agent able to exhibit a human-like behavior while communicating with other virtual or human agents requires enriching the dialogue of the agent with non-verbal information. Our agent, Greta, is defined as two components: a Mind and a Body. Her mind reflects her personality, her social intelligence, as well as her emotional reaction to events occurring in the environment. Her body corresponds to her physical appearance able to display expressive behaviors. We designed a Mind–Body interface that takes as input a specification of a discourse plan in an XML language (DPML) and enriches this plan with the communicative meanings that have to be attached to it, by producing an input to the Body in a new XML language (APML). Moreover we have developed a language to describe facial expressions. It combines basic facial expressions with operators to create complex facial expressions. The purpose of this chapter is to describe these languages and to illustrate our approach to the generation of behavior of an agent able to act consistently with her goals and with the context of the interaction.

1 Introduction

Humans communicate using verbal and non-verbal signals: body posture, gestures (pointing at something, describing object dimensions, etc.), facial expressions, gaze (making eye contact, looking down or up to a particular object), and using intonation and prosody, in combination with words and sentences. The way in which people communicate, and therefore the signals that they employ, is influenced by their personality, goals, and affective state and by the context in which the conversation takes place [12]. One very active research

area in the field of intelligent agents is devoted to constructing Embodied
Conversational Agents (ECAs). An ECA is an agent embedded in a virtual
body that interacts with another agent (a human user or another virtual
agent) in a human-like manner, and particularly in a believable way. Believability is mostly related to the ability to express emotion [3] and to exhibit
a given personality[20]. However, according to recent literature [36, 13], an
agent is more believable if it can behave in ways typical of given cultures,
and, finally, if it has a personal communicative style [5, 34]. Developing such
a "computer conversationalist" that is able to exhibit these added dimensions
of communication requires moving from natural language generation (NLG) to
multi-modal behavior generation. One possible approach is to consider body
and mind as strictly and necessarily interdependent. Another is to see them
as mainly independent from each other. The first approach implies that the
very planning of the meanings to convey is conceived by taking into account
the possible signals. The second approach views an ECA as an entity constituted by a "mind" and a "body". At the mind level, only the meaning of a
communicative action is represented, leaving to the body the task of deciding which signal to employ. In this case, in order to avoid signal redundancy
or conflicts, it is necessary to write body-dependent rules at an intermediate
sentence planning level. Using such rules has at least two advantages: first you
can adapt different bodies to the same mind (say, the expertise and conversational capacity of a doctor can be conveyed by a beautiful girl or by an old
white-haired man); second, the same body may take on different behaviors,
determined by individual differences, due to culture, communication style,
personality [25], in expressing the same meaning. To construct the architecture of our ECA, in the context of the EU project MagiCster[5], we adopt this
second approach. The 'Mind' and 'Body' are interfaced by a language based
on XML, so as to overcome integration problems and to allow their independence and modularity. During the conversation, the agent's Mind decides
what to communicate considering different factors that trigger the goal of
communicating and influence the contents to communicate (cognitive state,
emotions, context, user sensitivity, and so on). At each given moment of a
communicative interaction, all of these aspects combine with each other to
determine what the agent will say [11]. The Body "reads" what the Mind
decides to communicate and interprets and renders it at the surface level,
according to the available communicative channels. Also this step may be
influenced by several factors (personality, style, social identity, culture) that
determine which combination of verbal and non-verbal signals is the most fit
to express a particular communicative goal.

---

[5] IST Project IST-1999-29078, partners: University of Edinburgh, Division of Infor-
matics; DFKI, Intelligent User Interfaces Department; SICS; University of Bari,
Dipartimento di Informatica; University of Rome, Dipartimento di Informatica e
Sistemistica; AvatarMe.

To achieve a rich expressiveness, the output of the agent's Mind cannot be just a combination of symbolic descriptions of communicative acts. It should include, as well, a specification of the "meanings" that the Body will have to attach to each of them. These meanings include the communicative functions that are typically used in human–human dialogues: topic-comment, affective, meta-cognitive, performative, deictic, adjectival, and belief relation functions [31].

To achieve this granularity in expressing believable behaviors, we define a set of languages for specifying the format of dialogue moves at different abstraction levels. In particular, to specify the format of the dialogue move that should act as an interface between the agent's Mind and its Body, we designed a Mind–Body interface. This interface takes as input a specification of a discourse plan in an XML language (Discourse Plan Markup Language, DPML) in which only communicative goals and relations between these goals are specified and generates as output a formalization of the agent behavior in a new XML language called APML (Affective Presentation Markup Language) able to express the content of the dialogue move at the meaning level. In this way, the task to interpret how to render each meaning, or a combination of meanings, at the surface level, can be left to body-specific wrappers. At the signal level, we have developed a language to describe facial expressions. Signals may be described recursively (a signal may be defined by the combination of already defined signals) or by specifying all the parameters (facial actions). These descriptions are understandable and thus get interpreted by the facial player that produces the animation of the agent.

In this chapter, after describing the main features of the underlying architecture, we present the APML language and how it has been used, in the context of the MagiCster project. In particular, we will show how it has been interfaced with a 3D realistic face called Greta [24] and a synthetic voice [4]. To illustrate the approach, we will use an example in the medical domain. Conclusions will be discussed in the last section.

2 Expressing Believable Behaviors

How does communication originate? Communication is a means to influence others [8, 7]. A system engages in an act of communication as it has the goal to influence another system; that is, to cause another system to have some goal it does not have, or to refrain from a goal it has. There are many different ways to influence others: strength, seduction, aggression, being an example to imitate, inducing emotions. The peculiar way in which a system influences another system through communication is through providing beliefs to it. Any time a system S (Sender) communicates something to a system A (Addressee), S provides A with beliefs about A's goals, and through this it asks A to "adopt" S's goal; that is, to pursue it as if it were a goal of A's. Any time we communicate, we provide others with beliefs about our goals in order to have them pursue our own goal. For example, as S tells A "Take an Aspirin", S provides A with a belief about S's goal (the goal that A does some action, and specifically the action of taking an Aspirin), in order to have A pursue S's goal; that is, to have A take the Aspirin. All communicative acts – speech acts, like a sentence or a discourse, but also non-verbal acts, like a gesture, a gaze, or a facial expression – provide beliefs about the Sender's goal; that is, about what action the Sender wants the Addressee to take: so any act of communication is a way to ask others some action, but we may ask them to do different types of actions. With a request, like "Take an Aspirin", S asks A to do some action; with a question, like "Did you take an Aspirin?", S asks A to do a particular action, the action of providing S with information; with Information like "Aspirin relieves the pain", S is still asking A to do some action: the cognitive action of believing what S is saying. Since any act of communication provides the Addressee with a complex belief about the Sender's goal, and the Sender's goal is that the Addressee do some specific action – doing, providing information, believing – the act of communication must also mention all the beliefs that specify the Sender's goal. First, S's goal must be specified into a performative [2, 30], that is a specific goal that claims some particular social relationship between Sender and Addressee ("Take an Aspirin" may be an order if A is my child, advice if he is a friend of mine); second, the act of communication must also specify what is the particular action or information requested, or what the beliefs are S wants A to believe. Therefore, the minimal unit of communication is a communicative act that is made up of two parts, two packages of beliefs: a performative and a propositional content. Any time we communicate we must have conceived of at least these two packages of beliefs, and to the extent to which these beliefs are beliefs we have the goal to communicate to an Addressee, we can say they form a meaning.

A meaning can be viewed, then, as a set of beliefs that a system has the goal to transmit to another system; that is, belief S has the goal that also A believes. And of course, the meanings S may have the goal to transmit to A may even be very complex meanings, so they may need to be packaged into several different communicative acts that make up a complex communicative act. This is what happens when a sentence is not enough but we need to resort to a whole discourse, a novel, a handbook, a theater performance, a film, to specify all the meanings we mean. But since beliefs are simple information, not physical patterns of matter or energy, how can S cause these beliefs (meanings) to pass from S's mind also to A's mind? To do so, the immaterial meanings must be linked to perceivable stimuli that we call communicative signals. Each meaning or set of meanings must be linked to a particular signal or set of signals, and both S and A must share a common system of communication; that is, a system that states how meanings and signals correspond to each other. Therefore, any time a system S has to communicate a set of meanings to another system A, it has to find out, in the communication system it assumes to be shared with system A, the specific signals that correspond to the meanings to convey.

Let us first overview the beliefs that may form the content of a communicative act. Three classes of meanings can be distinguished [29]:

Information about the World As we communicate, we provide information about concrete or abstract events, their actors and objects, and the time and space relations among them. Such information is provided mainly through words, but also by gestures or gaze.

Information about the Speaker's Identity Physiognomic traits of our face, eyes, lips, the acoustic features of our voice, and often our posture provide information about our sex, age, socio-cultural roots, and personality. And, of course, our words can inform the addressee of our Self-Presentation: that is, the way we want to present ourselves.

Information about the Speaker's Mind While mentioning events of the external world, we also communicate why we want to talk of those events, what we think and feel about them, how we plan to talk about them. We provide information about the beliefs we are mentioning, our own goals concerning how to talk about them, and the emotions we feel while talking [29].

Here we focus on some of them, which are implemented in our ECA, Greta. Information about the world includes:

1. Deictics: To mention the referents of our discourse, we may point at them by deictic gestures or gaze.
2. Adjectival: To refer to some properties of objects we may use iconic or symbolic gestures and even gaze (as when we narrow our eyes to mean "small" or "difficult").

Within information about the Speaker's Mind, and particularly information about the Speaker's beliefs, we inform about:

1. degree of certainty: words like "perhaps", "certainly"; conditional or subjunctive verb modes; but also frowning, which means "I am serious in stating this"; opening hands, which means "This is self-evident";
2. metacognitive information: that is, the source of mentioned beliefs, whether they come from memory, inference, or communication (we look up when trying to make inferences, snap fingers while trying to remember,etc.).

Considering goals we inform about:

1. performativity of the sentence (by performative verbs, intonation, facial expression);
2. topic–comment or theme–rheme distinction (by batons, eyebrow raising, voice intensity, or pitch contour);
3. rhetorical relations: class-example (saying first, second, third, and so on; counting on fingers) topic shift (expressed through posture shift);
4. turn-taking and backchannel: raise hand for asking turn; nod to tell the Interlocutor we are following what he or she says.

Finally, we inform our addressee about the emotions we feel while talking (by affective words, gestures, intonation, facial expression, gaze, and posture).

Emotions may be implied in communication in at least two ways: (i) they may be the very reason that triggers communication: we activate the goal of communicating just because we want to express our emotion; (ii) they may intervene during our communication, as a reaction to what our interlocutor is saying, or to some thought suddenly coming to our mind, either related to the ongoing dialogue or not.

In both cases, the triggering of emotion does not necessarily imply that the Agent displays it. There are many reasons why we may refrain from expressing our emotion, and the final (aware or non-aware) decision of displaying it may depend on a number of factors [32, 10]. Some of them concern the very nature of the emotion felt (emotional nature), others the interaction of several contextual (scenario) factors.

3 MagiCster Architecture

In order to illustrate which are the requirements that our ECA has to fulfill, we will start by illustrating an example that will be used through the chapter, of advice-giving dialogue in the medical domain (Table 1) in which the Agent moves are denoted with Gi and the User moves with Uj.

Table 1. An example of dialogue in the medical domain

G0: Good morning Mr. Smith.
U1: Good morning Doctor Greta.
Have you seen my tests?
G1: Yes, and I'm sorry to tell you that you have been diagnosed as suffering from angina pectoris, which appears to be mild.
U2: What is angina?
G2: Angina is a spasm of the chest resulting from overexertion when the heart is diseased.
U3: Is it possible to cure it?
G3: Yes, a drug therapy does exist. To solve your problem, you should take two drugs. The first one is Aspirin and the second one is Atenolol.

In this dialogue, the Agent (named Greta) plays the role of a doctor and the Interlocutor is a patient asking for information about his disease. As explained in previous section, in order to show believable behavior, the Agent has to act consistently with her role, mental state, goals, personality, and social context; this is especially important in delicate conversational fields such as medical advice. In addition, the Agent has to decide whether an emotion is felt and, according to the interaction context, whether it has to be conveyed at the signal level.

For instance, while conversing with the patient (see the example in Table 1), Greta will coordinate her speech with various expressions:

- In move G1, she manifests her empathy with the User. She does it not only verbally ("I'm sorry to tell you") but also non-verbally, by displaying the expression of "sorry-for". To play down the seriousness of the illness, Greta will emphasize both verbally and non-verbally the fact that it is still in a "mild" form.
- In move G2, Greta indicates her chest while saying "a spasm of chest" while, in turn G3, she looks at the User while saying "your problem". The two expressions are realized through a particular gaze direction that plays a deictic function to indicate a given point in space.

Let us see now how the MagiCster's architecture supports the generation of dialogues of this kind.

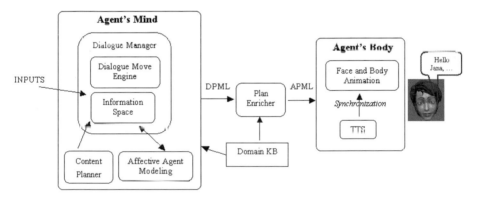

Fig. 1. MagiCster system architecture

The architecture of the MagiCster system is shown in Fig. 1. It is made up of two main components (a Mind and a Body), interfaced by a Plan Enricher. The Agent's Mind includes a Content Planner, a Dialogue Manager, and an Affective Agent Modeling module. This module is responsible for updating the Agent's mental state, that is her goals and beliefs. The Body is a 3D face/avatar, with a speech synthesizer [4] for animated spoken delivery. We will briefly describe each module, to focus our description on the Mind–Body interface.

The Affective Agent Modeling module decides whether a particular affective state should be activated and with which intensity and whether the felt emotion should be displayed in a given context [12].

The Content Planner is responsible for the generation of the discourse plan appropriate to the context [9]. At this level, the emphasis is on the goals that the Agent has to achieve in that piece of conversation. No information about how to express them in terms of agent behavior is represented in the discourse plan. According to Moore and Paris [22], it is a tree identified by its name; its main components are the nodes that are identified, as well, by a name; nodes include mandatory attributes describing the communicative goal, the discourse focus, and the rhetorical elements (role in the Rhetorical Relation (RR) of the father-node and rhetorical relation). The DPML DTD is as follows:

```
<!ELEMENT d-plan (node+)>
<!ATTLIST d-plan
        name CDATA #REQUIRED
>
<!ELEMENT node (node*, info*)>
<!ATTLIST node
        name CDATA #REQUIRED
        goal CDATA #REQUIRED
        role (root | nucleus | sat) #REQUIRED
        RR CDATA #REQUIRED
        focus CDATA #REQUIRED
        >
```

The discourse plans are represented as XML-based structures for the following reasons. First, it enables us to build a library of standard conversation plans in the medical domain that can be instantiated when needed, to be used in any application context (text, hypertext, voice, and so on). Second, XML provides a standard interface between the generator modules, to favor resources distribution and reuse.

The Dialogue Manager is built on top of the TRINDI architecture [18], which provides an engine for computing dialogue moves and a space in which information relevant to the move selection and effect can be stored. Such information may be, for instance, the Agent's mental state and the current plan. After a plan has been chosen from the library of plan recipes, the first Agent move is generated according to the first step of this plan. When the Agent is in dialogue with a User, the dialogue starts and the DM controls its flow by iterating the following steps, until the conversation ends [25]:

1. the initiative is passed to the User, who can ask questions on any of the topics under discussion;
2. the User move is translated into a symbolic communicative act (through a simplified interpretation process) and is passed to the DM;
3. the DM decides "what to say next" by selecting a plan/subplan, achieving the selected communicative goal to execute.

The Plan Enricher translates the symbolic representation of a dialogue move into an Agent's behavior specification at the *meaning* level. A dialogue move may be a "primitive" communicative act (for instance, a "greet", a "thanks", an "inform", a "request") or a more complex plan (for instance, "Describe an object with its properties"), annotated according to DPML. The choice of the appropriate communicative act (an implore rather than an order; showing or not showing an emotion) is based on the conversational context [11]. An algorithm translates this DPML-based treestructure into another XML-based language (APML), through a set of transformation rules that depend on the information attached to nodes in the discourse plan: rhetorical relation name and type, communicative goal, discourse focus, and so on.

The Face and Body Animation interprets the APML-tagged dialogue move and decides how to convey every meaning (by which combination of signals). As mentioned previously, the Body we use at present is a combination of a 3D face model compliant with the MPEG-4 standard [24] and a speech synthesizer [4].

4 A Markup Language for Behavior Specification: APML

Believable conversational agents of the kind described above have motivated a number of markup languages used to provide meta information such as control and intent. These languages differ mainly in the level of abstraction of the representation and specification they provide. Most existing languages allow agent specification at the signal level, depending most of the time on the type of "body" supporting the behavior expression.

For the reasons given in Sect. 2 of this chapter, we have developed a set of XML-based languages that include high-level primitives for specifying behavior acts, similar to those performed by humans, in order to express agent behavior at different levels of abstraction and to control easily the behavior of ECAs independently of the body. In this section we will describe APML (the Affective Presentation Markup Language), whose purpose is to specify the agent behavior at the meaning level. In particular, as its name suggests, the emphasis in APML is on the affective aspect of the communication between the Agent and the User. Before looking at APML tags in details, let's briefly overview other relevant markup languages aiming at describing and specifying human-like behaviors.

4.1 Overview of Existing Markup Languages for Expressing Human-Like Behavior

An effort toward building a standard markup language is represented by the Human Markup Language [15]. This language allows one to specify human communicative behaviors at a very high level. The aim of HML is to "develop Internet tools and repository systems which will enhance the fidelity of human communications" [15]. Its specification modules include tags allowing the representation of physical, cultural, social, kinetic, psychological, and intentional features used by humans in communicating information.

The information encoded by HML is at a very abstract level: using it for controlling specific agent bodies may be difficult and may require developing complex interpreters to translate a very abstract specification into low-level body actions. For this reason, researchers tend to develop their own languages, more suited to the type of embodied agent they wish to control.

Another example is VHML [37] that gathers several languages, each of them acting on different modalities: some tags are related to facial expressions, to gesture, to emotion (EML) but also to dialogue management, synthesis speech, and so on. The language offers a large variety of tags: for example, tags representing signals (right raised eyebrow) or tags representing emotion ("happiness"). But the language does not implement the Mind–Body separation that we advocate.

Some of the earliest work on developing a language for specifying lifelike character behavior is represented by MPML (Multimodal Presentation Markup Language). MPML has been developed with the aim of enabling authors of web pages to add agents for improving human–computer interaction [16]. Its design has been driven by the choice of Microsoft Agent as a body. For instance, the tag for specifying a predefined animation sequence (<act>) takes, as a possible value, one of the MS-agent's animations.

More recently, BEAT (Behavior Expression Animation Toolkit), another XML language designed for generating embodied agent's animation from textual input [6], has been used for tagging both the Agent's input and its output. The input is an utterance that is parsed into a tree structure; this tree is manipulated to include information about non-verbal signals and then specified again in XML. The toolkit is then able to generate appropriate and synchronized non-verbal behaviors and synthesized speech specified by the output language containing tags describing the type of animation to be performed and its duration.

At this level of specification, Avatar Markup Language (AML) [1] represents a new high-level language to describe avatar animation. It is based on XML and encapsulates the Text to Speech, Facial Animation, and Body Animation in a unified manner with appropriate synchronization. Other examples of such languages are RRL [28], CML [1], and MURML [17].

As we will see in more detail in the next section, APML differs from these languages in having been designed to represent the meaning level in which communicative goals are translated into communicative functions.

4.2 Defining APML Tags

Poggi et al. [31] define a communicative function as a (meaning, signal) pair, where the meaning item corresponds to the communicative value of the signal item. For instance, a smile can be the signal of the emotion "joy" or of a backchannel. This distinction between the meaning and the signal, that is the way in which the meaning can be communicated, has driven the design of APML. Due to the architectural choice of Mind–Body separation, tags should not specify the signal to be conveyed but only the meaning associated with a given communicative act.

The APML (Affective Presentation Markup Language) DTD is:

```
<!ELEMENT APML (turnallocation*, performative*,
                turnallocation*)>
<!ELEMENT turnallocation (performative*)>
<!ATTLIST turnallocation
    type (take | give) #REQUIRED
>
<!ELEMENT performative (theme | rheme)+>
<!ATTLIST performative
    type (greet|inform|paraphrase|suggest|ask|...) #REQUIRED
    affect (sorry-for | relief |joy |happy-for|...) #IMPLIED
>
<!ELEMENT theme (#PCDATA | emphasis | boundary)*>
<!ATTLIST theme
    affect (sorry-for | relief |joy |happy-for|...) #IMPLIED
    belief-relation (gen-spec|cause-effect|solutionhood|
    suggestion|justification| ...) #IMPLIED
>
<!ELEMENT rheme (#PCDATA | emphasis | boundary)*>
<!ATTLIST rheme
    affect (sorry-for | relief) #IMPLIED
    belief-relation (gen-spec | cause-effect | solutionhood |
    suggestion | modifier | justification) #IMPLIED
>
<!ELEMENT emphasis (#PCDATA)>
<!ATTLIST emphasis
    level (strong |medium | weak) "medium"
    x-pitchaccent (Hstar | Lstar | LplusHstar | LstarplusH |
    HstarplusL | HplusLstar) "Hstar"
    deictic CDATA #IMPLIED
    adjectival (small | tiny) #IMPLIED
>
<!ELEMENT boundary EMPTY>
<!ATTLIST boundary
    type (L | H | LL | HH | LH | HL) "LL"
>
```

We are showing here the DTD instead of the XML Schema for space reasons, since Schemas have a less compact representation than DTDs.

Every dialogue turn specified with this language starts with the root tag
<APML>. To indicate that the agent is taking or giving the initiative, the
turn-allocation tag can be used: its type attribute can take the value "take"
or "give". For instance, in the following APML sentence the Agent is starting
the conversation by taking the turn and greeting:

```
<APML>
<turnallocation type="take"> <performative type="greet">
<rheme>Good<emphasis x-pitchaccent="Hstar">morning</emphasis>
Mr Smith.<boundary type="LL"/></rheme></performative>
</turnallocation>
```

In order to specify the *type* of performative the homonymous attribute can be
used. It may take one of the values specified in the DTD (e.g. suggest, inform,
and so on). For instance, in the previous example it is a "greet".

The tags <theme> and <rheme> refer to the information structure of the
phrase. The theme corresponds to the topic or part of the utterance that links
it to the preceding discourse. Often themes are completely given or old information, and can be uttered without word emphasis, or even elided completely.
The rheme is the part of the utterance that moves the discourse forward by
providing needed information relevant to the theme. By its nature the rheme
must contain new information, usually carries some emphasized words, and
cannot be elided; that is, it is the focus of the discourse. Performative tags
may embed theme and rheme structures. In particular, *affect* expresses the
emotion that has been triggered in the Agent's Mind module. Affect tag may
be associated to an entire performative, to a theme, or to a rheme. The *belief–
relation* attribute takes as a value the name of the RR present in the DPML
specification. We will give an example of APML generation in Sect. 6.

Communication functions may be synchronized at different levels [26]. Performative type usually spans the whole communicative act. Other communicative functions modulate a single word or semantic element of the utterance
and usually last only the time of that word or semantic element. The affective and the belief–relation functions are synchronized with the information
structure of a discourse. They may be represented as attributes of the theme
or rheme tags; the other communicative functions (adjectival, deictic) have
a more local character as they act on the word(s) they refer to and would
correspond to separate tags.

Intonation is specified using <emphasis> and <boundary> tags. These
tags follow the ToBi notation [27]. The <emphasis> tag applies to lexical
words, and identifies these words as new or contrastive information, contributing to distinguishing the theme or rheme that they occur in from other themes
and rhmenes that may be actually or portentially in play in the discourse.
Emphasis is realized as pitch accent in the intonation contour and by various facial and manual or head gestures. Pitch accent type is determined by
theme–rheme status. For domain's like the present one, theme accents (where
needed) are realized as L+H* accents, while rheme accents are realized as H*.

The values of the boundary tones depend on the relation between successive intonational phrases, the syntactic characteristic of the sentence (e.g. as an interrogative), or on subtle aspects of hearer or speaker orientation of the information unit [35, 33]. In practice, most themes in discourses like those we treat here bear an LH% or "continuation rise" boundary, and most rhemes bear low LL% boundaries.

5 Facial Description Language

Humans are very good at showing a large spectrum of facial expressions; but at the same time, humans may display facial expressions varying by very subtle differences, but whose differences are still perceivable. We have developed a language to describe facial expressions as (meaning, signal) pairs. These expressions are stored in a library. When the planner enriches the discourse move with a communicative meaning, the program looks in the library to which signals it corresponds and the APML tag is instantiated by the corresponding signal values. Defining facial expressions using keywords such as "happiness, raised eyebrow, surprise" does not capture these slight variations. In our language, an expression may be defined at a high level (a facial expression is a combination of other facial expressions already predefined) or at a low level (a facial expression is a combination of facial parameters). The low-level facial parameters correspond to the MPEG-4 Facial Animation Parameters (FAPs) [24]. The language allows one to create a large variety of facial expressions for any communicative functions as well as the subtleties that distinguish facial expressions. Paradiso and L'Abbate [23] have established an algebra to create facial expressions. The authors have elaborated operators that combine and manipulate facial expressions. Our language is created with the sole purpose of creating the facial expressions that are associated with a given communicative function. We have worked out a method to combine facial expressions due to distinct co-occurring communicative acts using a Bayesian network [26].

We consider two items: "facial basis" (FB) and "facial display" (FD). An FB is a basic facial movement such as right raised eyebrow, upper lip raise, jaw opening, left upper eyelid lowered, and so on. FBs also include eye and head movements such as nodding, shaking, turning the head, and the eyes. An FB may be represented as a set of MPEG-4-compliant FAPs or, recursively, as a combination of other FBs (see Fig. 2).

Every facial display (FD) is made up of one or more FBs (see Fig. 3). For example, we can define the "surprise" facial display as:

$$surprise = raised\_eyebrow + raised\_lid + open\_mouth;$$

We can also define an FD as a combination of two or more (already) defined facial displays using the "+" and "*" operators. For instance, the "worried" facial display is a non-uniform combination of "surprise" (slightly decreased) and "sadness" facial displays (see Fig. 4):

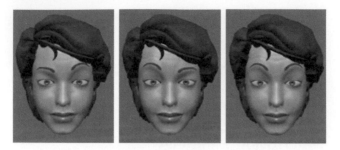

Fig. 2. The combination of "left raised eyebrow" (left) and "right raised eyebrow" (centre) produces a raised "eyebrow" movement (right)

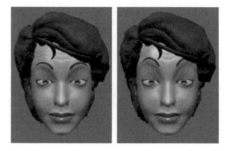

Fig. 3. The "raised eyebrow" expression (left) and its more intense equivalent (right)

$worried = (surprise * 0.7) + sadness;$

with: $surprise = raised\_eyebrow + raised\_lid + open\_mouth;$
$raised\_eyebrow = left\_raise\_eyebrow + right\_raise\_eyebrow;$
$left\_raise\_eyebrow = \{fap31 = 50, fap33 = 100, fap35 = 50\};$
$right\_raise\_eyebrow = \{fap32 = 50, fap34 = 100, fap36 = 50\}$
...

6 An Example

In this section, we derive an example taken from a medical domain application. The User may converse with the Agent and ask her about his physical condition. The Dialogue Manager (DM) elaborates a discourse plan by consulting the domain model. This plan is then enriched by the plan enricher that translates a DPML-based treestructure into an APML-based structure.

Let us suppose the User is asking about the severity of his disease. The DM selects the following dialogue move whose DPML recipe is:

```
<node name="n1" goal="Explain(Has(U,disease))"
```

surprise   sadness   worried = surprisex0.7 +
                                                        sadness

Fig. 4. The combination of "surprise" (left) and "sadness" (centre) produces a "worried" facial display (right)

```
role="root" focus="disease"RR="ElabObjAttr">
<node name="n2" goal="Inform(Has(U, disease))"
 role="nucleus" focus="Has(U, disease)" RR="null"/>
<node name="n3" goal="Inform(Severity(disease))"
 role="sat" focus="Severity(disease)" RR="null"/>
</node>
```

Then, given a DPML tree, the transformation algorithm (called MIDAS) reads it recursively down to the leaves.

Each dialogue move starts with the root tag <APML>. As indicated by the DTD specifications, this tag may be followed by a <turn-allocation> or by a <performative> tag.

A turn-allocation function does not have to be performed for every dialogue move; it is needed to indicate the exchange of speaking turn. Then, taking into account the dialogue history and the focus shift, it is generated for the first and the last dialogue move and when the User changes the focus of discourse.

Every leaf node is transformed into a <performative> element. The corresponding verbal sentence may contain both <rheme> and <theme> or only one of these.

MIDAS recursively reads the DPML structure of the dialogue move to generate the performative tags. Since DPML is driven by RRs then, in order to instantiate the appropriate <performative>, we consider RR-driven transformation rules. The value of the "RR attribute" attached to the node activates the proper recursive schema.

According to Mann et al. [21], RRs can be classified into two families: subject-matter and presentational relations.

Subject-matter relations are defined as "those whose intended effect is that the reader recognizes the relation in question" (elaboration, solutionhood, summary, circumstance, contrast, etc.).

Presentational relations are "those whose intended effect is to increase some inclination in the reader, such as the desire to act or the degree of positive regard for, belief in, or acceptance of the nucleus" (motivation, background, enablement, evidence, justification).

We follow this classification to derive the general rule of putting the belief–relation emphasis on the RR marker in the satellite on the nucleus–satellite subject-matter relations only. In particular, in order to emphasize the relation holding between the subject and the matter we put the belief–relation attribute in the theme of the performative representing the satellite. In the case of multinuclear subject-matter RRs (i.e. Ordinal Sequence, Contrast, etc.), the RR marker is set in the theme of the performative representing the nucleus. If the RR is a presentational one, then to increase the reader's belief on what is being stated in the nucleus, we put the belief–relation attribute in the rheme of the performative representing the nucleus. According to these rules we defined the MIDAS transformation schemas as follows:

```
Current_node=n1 IF Current_node.role=root ==>write("<APML>")
IF
checkTa ==> write("<turn-allocation type="take">")
IF
Current_node.RR=SM_NS ==>
{Midas(current_node.nucleus, NULL, NULL)
Midas(current_node.satellite, 'theme', Current_node.RR) }
IF
Current_node.RR=SM_NN ==>
    Forall current_node.nucleus:
    Midas(current_node.nucleus, 'theme', Current_node.RR)
IF Current_node.RR=PRES ==>
{Midas(current_node.nucleus, 'rheme',
Current_node.RR) Midas(current_node.satellite, NULL,NULL)}
IF
Current_node.RR=NULL ==>
Performative.generate(Current_node,brEmph,RR) ...
```

Let us again consider the DPML structure in the above example. The root node is n1 and its RR is the `ElabObjAttr`; it includes a nucleus, which mentions an object, and a satellite that describes a property of that object. It corresponds to a subject-matter relation holding between a nucleus and a satellite (SM_NS). Thus, a recursive call is first made on the nucleus with the belief–relation emphasis (brEmph) parameter and its RR value set to "NULL". Then, a recursive call is made on the satellite with the brEmph parameter set to theme and the RR value set to the RR of the current node. This indicates that the belief–relation attribute has to be set in the theme of the second performative being the satellite of the RR.

When the algorithm reaches a leaf node, the Performative.generate(node, brEmph, RR) function is called and the recursion ends. This function is responsible for the surface realization in which the <performative> element is generated. Its type attribute is set to the type of speech act present in the DPML node goal. If the Affective Agent Modeling component establishes that an emotion has been triggered at the current node[6] and that this emotion has to be displayed [11], its affect attribute is set to that emotion name.

Besides generating the <performative> tag with its attributes, this function produces the verbal part of the speech act and includes, if needed, two more tags: the <theme> and the <rheme> ones. According to the values of its parameters, the belief–relation attribute is set appropriately. For instance, in the above-mentioned example, the type of the performative tag representing the satellite n2 is set to "inform". In this case, since the Agent feels a "sorry-for" emotion, the affect attribute of the performative gets this value. Since the RR of the father node is a subject-matter relation according to the transformation rules, the nucleus performative does not get any belief–relation emphasis and the following annotated sentence is generated:

```
<performative
type="inform" affect="sorry-for"> <theme> I'm sorry to
<emphasis x-pitchaccent="LplusHstar">tell</emphasis> you
<boundary type="LH"/> </theme> <rheme> that you have been
<emphasis x-pitchaccent="Hstar"> diagnosed </emphasis> as
<emphasis x-pitchaccent="Hstar">suffering</emphasis> from
what we call<emphasis x-pitchaccent="Hstar">angina</emphasis>
<emphasis x-pitchaccent="Hstar">pectoris,</emphasis></rheme>
</performative>
```

Both theme and rheme may contain emphases of various types. The setting of the intonational tags are derived from the DPML structure, domain information, and discourse history. We may have the following cases:

- **Emphasis on the word indicating the performative.** For instance, in a theme: <emphasis x-pitchaccent="LplusHstar">tell</emphasis>.
- **Emphasis on the attentional elements of discourse [14].** For instance, from Has(U,angina) (which constitutes the rheme of this utterance) MIDAS puts emphases on the words suffering and angina pectoris (in the lexicon a single word), since these contribute to distinguishing this rheme from other conditions and relations to them.
- **Emphasis on adjectival communicative function.** When the argument of the communicative goal is a quantitative attribute of the discourse focus, the tag's emphasis with the attribute adjectival is attached to the argument. For instance, in the following APML sentence, "severity" is a quantitative property of angina which is also the discourse focus, and thus is marked with an emphasis tag: <emphasis x-pitchaccent="Hstar" adjectival="small"> mild </emphasis>.

---

[6] We view a discourse element as an event. Such an event may or may not trigger an emotion.

- **Emphasis on deictic communicative function**. When the argument of the communicative goal is described in the domain knowledge base as "referenceable through its coordinates" and this argument is also the discourse focus, then we have the following tag type: <emphasis x-pitchaccent="Hstar" deictic="chest">chest</emphasis>.

Once the generation of the first leaf of the tree (the first performative) ends, the recursive call on the subtree starting from the satellite node starts. According to the rules just explained, the theme receives the belief–relation emphasis and the following tagged phrase is generated:

```
<performative type="inform">
<theme belief-relation="ElabObjAttr">which </theme>
<rheme>appears to be <emphasis x-pitchaccent="Hstar"
       adjectival="small">mild</emphasis>
</rheme> </performative>
```

The APML tags are instantiated by their facial signals by looking them up in the library associated with the Agent Body. In this example "certain" corresponds to a frown and the tag "sorry-for" to the signals: inner eyebrow up, head aside, mouth corner down. There is a conflict in the eyebrow region. Our system resolves the conflict that may occur when more than one communicative function spans the same text [26]. The conflict resolution uses a Bayesian network that takes one or many communicative functions as input and outputs the final combined expressions. The final expression may contain the meanings of all the communicative functions, creating an expression of complex meaning. Figure 5 illustrates how the frown of "certainty" gets integrated within the facial expression of "sorry-for".

7 Conclusions

In this chapter, we have described the architecture of the behavior generator of a believable conversational agent. In particular, we focused our discussion on the importance of Mind–Body separation and therefore on the need for an interface between the two modules. Such an interface should be able to represent the communicative functions that can be potentially realized by different bodies with different expressive capabilities. We have defined two XML-like markup languages to represent the Mind's output, that is the discourse plans (called DPML) and the Body's input (named APML). We have also described how a plan enricher transforms DPML trees into APML trees. Finally we have presented our language for defining facial expressions. Online materials (videos and examples of APML specification) may be found at [19].

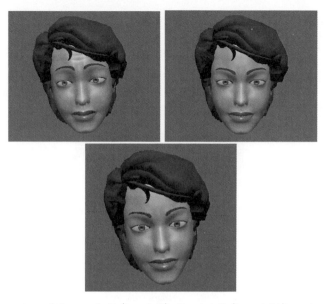

Fig. 5. Expression of "sorry-for" (top left), "certain" (top right), and combination of both expressions with conflict resolution (bottom)

Acknowledgments

We wish to acknowledge Fiorella de Rosis for her useful suggestions and Massimo Bilvi for his help in designing the language to describe facial expressions and the Greta system.

References

1. Arafa, Y., Kamyab, K., Mamdani, E., Kshirsagar, S., Guye-Vuilleéme, A., Thalmann, D.: Two approaches to scripting character animation. In: *Embodied conversational agents - let's specify and evaluate them!, Proceedings of the AAMAS'02 Workshop*, Bologna, Italy (July 2002)
2. Austin, J.L.: *How to do things with words.* (Oxford University Press, London 1962)
3. Bates, J.: Realism and believable agents. In: *Lifelike Computer Characters '94* (1994)
4. Black, A.W., Taylor, P.: Festival speech synthesis system: System documentation (1.1.1). Technical Report HCRC/TR-83, Human Communication Research Centre, Edinburgh (1997)
5. Canamero, L., Aylett, R. (eds): *Animating Expressive Characters for Social Interactions* (John Benjamins, Amsterdam). In press.
6. Cassell, J., Vilhjálmsson, H., Bickmore, T.: BEAT: The Behavior Expression Animation Toolkit. In: *Computer Graphics Proceedings, Annual Conference Series.* ACM SIGGRAPH (2001). Reprinted in this volume.

7. Castelfranchi, C., Poggi, I.: Bugie finsioni sotterfugi. In: *Per una scienza dell'inganno* (Carocci, Roma 1998)
8. Conte, R., Castelfranchi, C.: *Cognitive and Social Action* (University College Press, London 1995)
9. De Carolis, B.: Generating mixed-initiative hypertexts: A reactive approach. In: *Proceedings of the International Conference on Intelligent User Interfaces*, Redondo Beach, CA (ACM Press, New York 1999)
10. De Carolis, B., Carofiglio, V., Bilvi, M., Pelachaud, C.: APML, a mark-up language for believable behavior generation. In: *Embodied conversational agents - Let's specify and evaluate them!, Proceedings of the AAMAS'02 Workshop*, Bologna, Italy (2002)
11. De Carolis, B., Pelachaud, C., Poggi, I., de Rosis, F.: Behavior planning for a reflexive agent. In: *IJCAI'01*, Seattle, USA (2001)
12. de Rosis, F., Pelachaud, C., Poggi, I., Carofiglio, V., De Carolis, B.: From Greta's mind to her face: Modeling the dynamics of affective states in a conversational embodied agent. *Special Issue on "Applications of Affective Computing in Human-Computer Interaction", The International Journal of Human-Computer Studies* **59**:81–118 (2003)
13. de Rosis, F., Poggi, I., Pelachaud, C.: Tanscultural believability in embodied agents: A matter of consistent adaptation. In: *Agent Culture: Designing Virtual Characters for a Multi-Cultural World*, ed Trappl, R., Petta, P. (Kluwer Academic, Dordrecht). In press.
14. Grosz, B.J., Sidner, C.L.: Attention, intentions, and the structure of discourse. *Computational Linguistics* **12**(3):175–204 (1986)
15. HumanML. Human markup language. http://www.humanmarkup.org
16. Ishizuka, M., Tsutsui, T., Saeyor, S., Dohi, H., Zong, Y., Prendinger, H.: MPML: A multimodal presentation markup language with character agent control functions. In: *Achieving Human-like Behavior in Interactive Animated Agents, Proceedings of the AA'00 Workshop*, Barcelona (2000) pp 50–54
17. Kranstedt, A., Kopp, S., Wachsmuth, I.: MURML: A multimodal utterance representation markup language for conversational agents. In: *Embodied conversational agents - let's specify and evaluate them!, Proceedings of the AAMAS'02 Workshop*, Bologna, Italy (2002)
18. Larsson, S., Bohlin, P., Bos, J., Traum, D.: *TRINDIKIT 1.0 manual for D2.2.* http://www.ling.gu.se/projekt/trindi
19. Life-like Characters. Tools, Affective Functions and Applications. http://www.vhml.org/LLC/llc-book.html
20. Bryan Loyall, A., Bates, J.: Personality-rich believable agents that use language. In: *Proceedings of the First International Conference on Autonomous Agents (Agents'97)*, Marina del Rey, CA, USA (ACM Press, New York 1997) pp 106–113
21. Mann, W.C., Matthiessen, C.M.I.M., Thompson, S.: Rhetorical structure theory and text analysis. Technical Report 89-242, ISI Research (1989)
22. Moore, J.D., Paris, C.L.: Planning text for advisory dialogues. In: *ACL* (1989) pp 203–211
23. Paradiso, A., L'Abbate, M.L.: A model for the generation and combination of emotional expressions. In: *Multimodal Communication and Context in Embodied Agents, Proceedings of the AA'01 Workshop*, Montreal, Canada (May 2001)

24. Pelachaud, C.: Visual text-to-speech. In: *MPEG4 Facial Animation - The standard, implementations and applications*, ed Pandzic, I.S., Forchheimer, R. (Wiley 2002)
25. Pelachaud, C., Carofiglio, V., De Carolis, B., de Rosis, F.: Embodied contextual agent in information delivering application. In: *First International Joint Conference on Autonomous Agents & Multi-Agent Systems (AAMAS)*, Bologna, Italy (July 2002)
26. Pelachaud, C., Poggi, I.: Subtleties of facial expressions in embodied agents. *Journal of Visualization and Computer Animation* **13**:301–312 (2002)
27. Pierrehumbert, J., Hirschberg, J.: The meaning of intonational contours in the interpretation of discourse. In: *Intentions in Communication*, ed Cohen, P., Morgan, J., Pollack, M. (MIT Press, Cambridge, MA 1990) pp 271–312
28. Piwek, P., Krenn, B., Schröder, M., Grice, M., Baumann, S., Pirker, H.: RRL: A rich representation language for the description of agents behaviour in NECA. In: *Embodied conversational agents - Let's specify and evaluate them!, Proceedings of the AAMAS'02 Workshop*, Bologna, Italy (July 2002)
29. Poggi, I.: Towards the alphabet and the lexicon of gesture, gaze and touch. In: *Virtual Symposium on "Multimodality of Human Communication. Theories, problems and applications"*, ed Bouissac, P. (2002). http://www.semioticon.com
30. Poggi, I., Pelachaud, C.: Facial performative in a conversational system. In: *Embodied Conversational Agents*, ed Cassell, J., Sullivan, J., Prevost, S., Churchill, E. (The MIT Press, Cambridge, MA 2000)
31. Poggi, I., Pelachaud, C., de Rosis, F.: Eye communication in a conversational 3D synthetic agent. *AI Communications* **13**(3):169–181 (2000)
32. Prendinger, H., Ishizuka, M.: Social role awareness in animated agents. In: *Proceedings of the 5th International Conference on Autonomous Agents*, Montreal, Canada (2001) pp 270–277
33. Prevost, S., Steedman, M.: Specifying intonation from context for speech synthesis. *Speech Communication* **15**:139–153 (1994)
34. Ruttkay, Z., Pelachaud, C.: Exercises of style for virtual humans. In: *Symposium of the AISB'02 Convention*, Volume Animating Expressive Characters for Social Interactions, London (2002)
35. Steedman, M.: Information structure and the syntax-phonology interface. *Linguistic Inquiry* **31**:649–689 (2000)
36. Trappl, R., Payr, S. (eds.) *Agent Culture: Designing virtual characters for a multi-cultural world.* (Kluwer Academic, Dordrecht, in press)
37. VHML. Virtual human markup language. http://www.vhml.org

STEP: a Scripting Language for Embodied Agents

Zhisheng Huang, Anton Eliëns, and Cees Visser

Intelligent Multimedia Group
Division of Computer Science, Faculty of Sciences
Vrije Universiteit Amsterdam, The Netherlands
{huang,eliens,ctv}@cs.vu.nl

Summary. In this chapter we propose a scripting language, called STEP, for embodied agents, in particular for their communicative acts like gestures and postures. Based on the formal semantics of dynamic logic, STEP has a solid semantic foundation, in spite of a rich number of variants of the compositional operators and interaction facilities on worlds. STEP has been implemented in the distributed logic programming language DLP, a tool for the implementation of 3D web agents. In this chapter, we discuss principles of scripting language design for embodied agents and several aspects of the application of STEP.

1 Introduction

Embodied agents are autonomous agents which have bodies by which the agents can perceive their world directly through sensors and act on the world directly through effectors. Embodied agents whose experienced worlds are located in real environments are usually called *cognitive robots*. *Web agents* are embodied agents whose experienced worlds are the web; typically they act and collaborate in networked virtual environments. In addition, *3D web agents* are embodied agents whose 3D avatars can interact with each other or with users via web browsers [11].

Embodied agents usually interact with users or each other via multi-modal communicative acts, which can be verbal or non-verbal. Gestures, postures, and facial expressions are typical non-verbal communicative acts which contribute to the representation of avatars as life-like characters. In general, specifying communicative acts for embodied agents is not easy; they often require a lot of geometric data and detailed movement equations for the specification of gestures.

In this chapter we propose the scripting language STEP (Scripting Technology for Embodied Persona), in particular for communicative acts of embodied agents. At present, we focus on aspects of the specification and modeling of gestures and postures for 3D web agents. However, STEP can be extended for other communicative acts like facial expressions or speech, and other types of embodied agents, like cognitive robots. Scripting languages are to a certain extent simplified languages which ease the task of programming and development. One of the main advantages of using scripting languages is that the specification of communicative acts can be separated from the programs which specify the agent architecture and mental state reasoning. Thus, changing the specification of communicative acts does not require reprogramming an agent.

The avatars of our 3D web agents are built in the Virtual Reality Modeling Language (VRML) or X3D, the next generation of VRML. These avatars have a humanoid appearance. The humanoid animation working group[1] proposes a specification, called H-anim specification, for the creation of libraries of reusable humanoids in web-based applications as well as authoring tools that make it easy to create humanoids and animate them in various ways. H-anim specifies a standard way of representing humanoids in VRML. We have implemented the proposed scripting language for H-anim-based humanoids in the distributed logic programming language DLP [5][2].

DLP is a tool for the implementation of 3D intelligent agents [12][3]. In this chapter, we discuss how STEP can be used for embodied agents. STEP introduces a Prolog-like syntax, which makes it compatible with most standard logic programming languages, whereas the formal semantics of STEP is based on dynamic logic [9]. Thus, STEP has a solid semantic foundation, in spite of a rich number of variants of the compositional operators and interaction facilities on worlds.

2 Principles

We designed the scripting language primarily for the specification of communicative acts for embodied agents; we have separated the external-oriented communicative acts from internal changes of the mental states of embodied agents because the former involves only geometric changes of the body objects and the natural transition of the actions, whereas the latter involves more complicated computation and reasoning. Of course, a question is: why not use the same scripting language for both external gestures and internal agent specification? Our answer is: the scripting language is designed to be a simplified, user-friendly specification language for embodied agents, whereas the formalization of intelligent agents requires a powerful specification and programming language. It is not our intention to design a scripting language with fully functional computation facilities, as found in programming languages like Java, Prolog, or DLP. A scripting language should be interoperable with a fully powered agent implementation language, but offer a rather

---

[1] http://h-anim.org
[2] http://www.cs.vu.nl/~eliens/projects/logic/index.html
[3] http://wasp.cs.vu.nl/wasp

easy way for authoring. Although communicative acts are the result of the internal reasoning of embodied agents, they do not need the expressiveness of a general programming language. However, we do require that a scripting language should be able to interact with the mental states of embodied agents in some ways, which will be discussed in more detail later.

We consider the following design principles for a scripting language.

Principle 1: Convenience

As mentioned, the specification of communicative acts, like gestures and facial expressions, usually involves a lot of geometric data, like ROUTE statements in VRML or movement equations in computer graphics. A scripting language should hide these geometric difficulties, so that even the authors who have limited knowledge of computer graphics can use it in a natural way. For example, suppose that authors want to specify that an agent turns its left arm forward slowly. This can be specified as:

```
turn(Agent, left_arm, front, slow)
```

It should not be necessary to specify it as follows, which requires knowledge of a coordinate system, rotation axis, etc.:

```
turn(Agent, left_arm, rotation(1,0,0,1.57), 3)
```

One of the implications of this principle is that embodied agents should be aware of their context; they should be able to understand what certain indications mean, like the directions "left" and "right", or the body parts "left arm", etc.

Principle 2: Compositional Semantics

Specification of composite actions based on existing components, for example an action of an agent which turns its arms forward slowly, can be defined in terms of two primitive actions, turn-left-arm and turn-right-arm:

```
par([turn(Agent, left_arm, front, slow),
    turn(Agent, right_arm, front, slow)])
```

Typical composite operators for actions are the sequence action *seq*, parallel action *par*, and repeat action *repeat*, which are used in dynamic logic [9].

Principle 3: Redefinability

Scripting actions (e.g. composite actions) can be defined in terms of other actions explicitly. The scripting language incorporates a rule-based specification system, where scripting actions can be defined by their own set of rules. These defined actions can be reused for other scripting purposes. For example, if we have defined two scripting actions *run* and *kick*, then a new action *run_then_kick* can be defined in terms of *run* and *kick*:

```
run_then_kick(Agent)=
  seq([run(Agent), kick(Agent)]).
```

which can be specified in a Prolog-like syntax:

```
script(run_then_kick(Agent), Action):-
  Action = seq([run(Agent),kick(Agent)]).
```

Principle 4: Parameterization

Scripting actions can be adapted to be other actions; actions can be specified in terms of how they cause changes over time to each individual *degree of freedom*, as proposed by Perlin and Goldberg in [16]. For example, suppose that we define a scripting action *run*: we know that running can be done at different paces. It can be done "fast" or "slow". It should not be necessary to define run actions for particular paces. We can define the action "run" with respect to a degree of freedom "tempo". Changing the tempo for a generic run action should be enough to achieve a run action at different paces. Another method of parameterization is to introduce variables or parameters in the names of scripting actions, which allows for a similar action with different values. In particular, agent names and their relevant parameters are specified as variables in script libraries, by which the same scripting actions can be reused for different embodied agents under different situations by different authors. It would significantly improve the reusability of scripting actions for the purpose of productivity. This is one of the reasons why we introduce a Prolog-like syntax in STEP.

Principle 5: Interaction

Scripting actions should be able to interact with the world, including objects and other agents. More exactly, scripting actions can perceive the world, even embodied agents' states, in order to decide whether or not the current action should be continued, or replaced by other actions. This kind of interaction can be achieved by the introduction of high-level interaction operators as defined in dynamic logic. The operator "test" and the operator "conditional" are examples of operators that facilitate the interaction between actions and states.

These five principles are a guideline for the design of the scripting language STEP. The principle of convenience implies that STEP uses some natural-language-like terms for references. The principle of compositional semantics states that STEP has a set of built-in action operators. The principle of re-definability suggests that STEP should incorporate a rule-based specification system. The principle of parameterization justifies that STEP introduces a Prolog-like syntax. The principle of interaction requires that STEP is based on a more powerful meta-language.

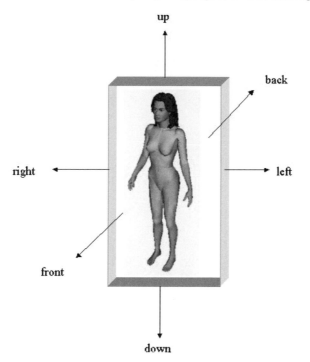

Fig. 1. Direction reference for humanoid

3 The Scripting Language STEP

In this section, we discuss the general aspects of the scripting language STEP. We propose the reference systems for STEP first.

3.1 Reference Systems

The reference system of STEP consists of three components: direction reference, body reference, and time reference.

Direction Reference

The direction reference system in STEP is based on the H-anim specification: the initial humanoid position should be modeled in a standing position, facing in the +Z direction with +Y up and +X to the humanoid's left. The origin $\langle 0, 0, 0 \rangle$ is located at ground level, between the humanoid's feet. The arms should be straight and parallel to the sides of the body with the palms of the hands facing inwards toward the thighs.

Based on the standard pose of the humanoid, we can define the direction reference system as sketched in Fig. 1. The direction reference system is based on these three dimensions: front vs. back, which corresponds to the Z-axis;

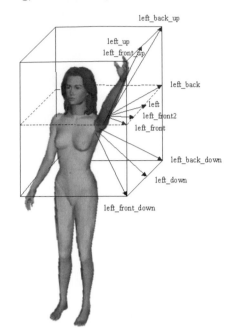

Fig. 2. Combination of the directions for left arm

up vs. down, which corresponds to the Y-axis; and left vs. right, which corresponds to the X-axis. Based on these three dimensions, we can introduce a more natural-language-like direction reference scheme: for example, turning left arm to "front-up" is to turn the left arm such that the front-end of the arm will point to the up front direction. Figure 2 shows several combinations of directions based on these three dimensions for the left arm. The direction references for other body parts are similar.

These combinations are designed for convenience and are discussed in Sect. 2. However, they are in general not sufficient for more complex applications. To solve this kind of problem, we introduce interpolations with respect to the mentioned direction references. For instance, the direction "left_front2" is referred to as one which is located between "left_front" and "left", which is shown in Fig. 2. Natural-language-like references are convenient for authors to specify scripting actions, since they do not require the author to have a detailed knowledge of reference systems in VRML. Moreover, the proposed scripting language also supports the original VRML reference system, which is useful for experienced authors. Directions can also be specified to be a four-place tuple $\langle X, Y, Z, R \rangle$, for example $rotation(1, 0, 0, 1.57)$.

Body Reference

According to the H-anim standard, an H-anim specification contains a set of *Joint nodes* that are arranged to form a hierarchy. Each Joint node can contain other Joint nodes and may also contain a *Segment node* which describes the body part associated with that joint. Each Segment can also have a number of *Site nodes*, which define locations relative to the segment. Sites can be used for attaching accessories, like hat, clothing, and jewelry. In addition, they can be used to define eye points and viewpoint locations. Each Segment node can have a number of *Displacer nodes* that specify which vertices within the segment correspond to a particular feature or configuration of vertices.

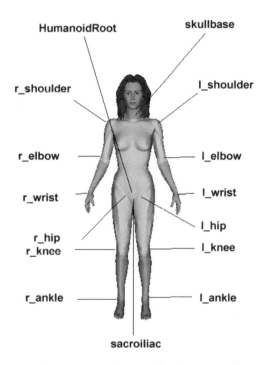

Fig. 3. Typical joints for humanoid

Figure 3 shows several joints of humanoids. Turning body parts of humanoids implies the setting of the corresponding joint's rotation. Moving the body parts means the setting of the corresponding joint's position. For instance, the action "turning the left-arm to the front slowly" is specified as:

```
turn(Agent, l_shoulder, front, slow)
```

Based on the H-anim specification, all body joints are contained in a hierarchical structure. Accordingly, the direction reference of a body joint in STEP is measured relative to the default rotations of its ancestor joints in the hierarchy. For instance, Fig. 4(a) shows the posture of the left elbow joint to the direction "front" relative to the default posture of the avatar. However, when the left shoulder joint or one of its parent joints point to the direction "front", the left elbow joint pointing to "front" results in a posture in which the left hand points to the direction "up", as shown in Fig. 4(b). In practice, this kind of direction reference does not cause difficulties for authoring, for the correct direction can be obtained by reducing the directions of its ancestor body parts to be the default ones. Therefore, STEP is well suited for a forward kinematic system. Moreover, we would like to point out that STEP can also be used to solve inverse kinematic problems. That will be shown in Sect. 4.

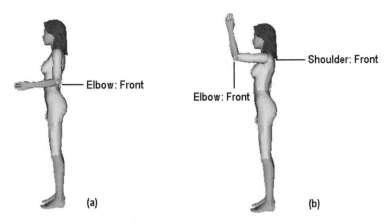

Fig. 4. Elbow joint in different situations

Time Reference

STEP has the same time reference system as VRML. For example, the action *turning the left arm to the front in 2 seconds* can be specified as:

```
turn(Agent, l_shoulder, front, time(2, second))
```

This kind of explicit specification of duration in scripting actions does not satisfy the parameterization principle. Therefore, we introduce a more flexible time reference system based on the notions of beat and tempo. A *beat* is a time interval for body movements, whereas the *tempo* is the number of beats per minute. By default, the tempo is set to 60, i.e. a beat corresponds to a second. However, the tempo can be changed. Moreover, we can define different speeds for body movements: for example, the speed "fast" can be defined as one beat, whereas the speed "slow" can be defined as three beats.

3.2 Primitive Actions and Composite Operators

Turn and move are the two main primitive actions for body movements. Turn actions specify the change of the rotations of the body parts or the whole body over time, whereas move actions specify the change of the positions of the body parts or the whole body over time. A turn action of a body part is defined as follows:

```
turn(Agent,BodyPart,Direction,Duration)
```

where `Direction` can be a natural-language-like direction like "front" or a rotation value like "rotation(1,0,0,3.14)", and `Duration` a speed name like "fast" or an explicit time specification, like "time(2,second)".

A move action of a body part is defined as:

```
move(Agent,BodyPart,Direction,Duration)
```

where `Direction` can be a natural-language-like direction like "front", a position value like "position(1,0,10)", or an increment value like "increment(1,0,0)". The turn and move actions of the whole body are defined as follows:

```
turn_body(Agent,Direction,Duration)
move_body(Agent,Direction,Duration)
```

Typical composite operators for scripting actions are:

- Sequence operator "seq": the action seq([$Action_1$, ..., $Action_n$]) denotes a composite action in which $Action_1$, ..., $Action_n$ are executed sequentially:

    ```
    seq([turn(agent,l_shoulder,front,fast),
    turn(agent,r_shoulder,front,fast)])
    ```

- Parallel operator "par": the action par([$Action_1$, ..., $Action_n$]) denotes a composite action in which $Action_1$, ..., $Action_n$ are executed simultaneously.
- Non-deterministic choice operator "choice": the action choice([$Action_1$, ..., $Action_n$]) denotes a composite action in which one of the $Action_1$, ..., $Action_n$ is executed.
- Repeat operator "repeat": the action repeat(Action, T) denotes a composite action in which the *Action* is repeated *T* times.

3.3 STEP and Dynamic Logic

STEP is based on dynamic logic [9] and allows for arbitrary abstractions using the primitives and composition operators provided by the logic. In dynamic logic, there is a clear distinction between an action and a state. Semantically, a state represents the properties at a particular moment, whereas an action consists of a set of state pairs, which represent a relation between two states.

Thus, there are two sub-languages in dynamic logic: a sub-language for actions and a sub-language for states. The latter is called the meta language of dynamic logic. Let a be an action represented in the action sub-language, and ψ and ϕ the property formulas represented in the meta language. In dynamic logic, a formula like

$$\psi \to [a]\phi$$

means that if the property ψ holds, then the property ϕ holds after doing the action a. The formula above states a relation between the pre-condition ψ and the post-condition ϕ for the action a.

A scripting language based on the semantics of dynamic logic is well suited for the purpose of intelligent embodied agents. As discussed previously, the scripting language is primarily designed for the specification of body language and speech for embodied agents. In this framework, the specification of external-oriented communicative acts can be separated from the internal states of embodied agents because the former involves only geometric changes of the body objects and the natural transition of the actions, whereas the latter involves more complicated computation and reasoning.

Dynamic logic has several primitive action operators: "$\alpha; \beta$" means that α is executed before β; "$\alpha \cup \beta$" means that either α or β is executed non-deterministically; "α^*" means that α is executed a finite, but non-deterministic number of times; and p? means to proceed if p is true, else fail. Based on these primitive action operators, some typical actions are relatively easy to define [9], for example:

$$
\begin{aligned}
&\text{if } p \text{ then } \alpha \text{ } else \text{ } \beta &&as\ (p?; \alpha) \cup (\neg p?; \beta) \\
&\text{while } p \text{ } do \text{ } \alpha &&as\ (p?; \alpha)^*; \neg p? \\
&\text{repeat } \alpha \text{ until } p &&as\ \alpha(\neg p?; \alpha)^*; p? \\
&\text{IF } p \to \alpha \parallel q \to \beta \text{ FI } as\ (p?; \alpha) \cup (q?; \beta)
\end{aligned}
$$

Therefore, based on the formal semantics of dynamic logic, STEP has a solid semantic foundation, in spite of a rich number of variants of the compositional operators. Refer to [13] for more details of the semantics issues about STEP.

3.4 High-Level Interaction Operators

When using high-level interaction operators, scripting actions can directly interact with internal states of embodied agents or with external states of worlds. These interaction operators are based on a meta language which is used to build embodied agents, say, in the distributed logic programming language DLP. In the following, we use lower case Greek letters ϕ, ψ, χ to denote formulas in the meta language. Similar to those in dynamic logic, STEP has the following higher level interaction operators:

- test: `test`(ϕ), check the state ϕ. If ϕ holds then skip, otherwise fail.
- execution: `do`(ϕ), make the state ϕ true, i.e. execute ϕ in the meta language.

- conditional: if_then_else(ϕ,$action_1$,$action_2$).
- until: until(action,ϕ), perform action until ϕ holds.

The above-mentioned action operators are sufficiently powerful to define a number of variants of scripting actions. In particular, the execution operator "*do*" is used to access certain computation and interaction capabilities from the meta language level. In DLP and Prolog, the predicate "*is*" is for the evaluation of arithmetic expressions. Accordingly, actions which involve the "*do*" operator and the predicate "*is*", like $do(N\ is\ sqrt(S))$, can be used to perform computations in STEP. Actions with the '*do*' operator in combination with the VRML/X3D EAI predicates in DLP, like $do(getPosition(Agent, X, Y, Z))$ and $do(setRotation(Object, X, Y, Z, R))$, can be used to interact with virtual worlds. The same patterns of actions in combination with the available communication predicates at the meta language level can be used to achieve certain communication facilities between embodied agents. We will discuss some details of how these capabilities can be achieved in Sect. 4. Before doing so, we will describe a brief example of how a number of temporal relations can be defined in terms of the parallel action operator "*par*" and the sequential action operator "*seq*" by means of the execution operator "*do*". As discussed in [1, 2], there are 13 possible temporal relations between two actions, that is *before*, *meets*, *overlaps*, *starts*, *during*, *finishes*, *equals*, and their inverse relations. All these 13 possible temporal relations can be defined in STEP [13], for example:

```
before(A1,A2)= seq([A1, do(random(N)), wait(N),A2])
meets(A1,A2)= seq(A1,A2)
overlaps(A1,A2)= par([A1,seq([duration(A1,T1),do(random(R)),
                 do(N is T1*R), wait(N), A2])])
starts(A1,A2)= par([A1,A2])
```

where $duration(A, T)$ calculates the duration T for the action A, which can be defined recursively on the sub-actions of A. $wait(N)$ is a special action which does nothing but just wait for N seconds. The action $wait(N)$ can be defined as $seq([do(T\ is\ N * 1000), do(sleep(T))])$[4]. See [13] for more details with respect to the expressiveness of STEP and its semantics.

We have implemented the scripting language STEP in the distributed logic programming language DLP. See [14] for implementation issues of STEP. Based on STEP, we have also implemented XSTEP [15], the XML-based markup language for embodied agents.

4 Examples

In this section, we discuss several examples of how STEP can be used to define scripting actions for embodied agents. The first two examples "walk" and

---

[4] Because the predicate *sleep* in DLP requires milliseconds.

"run" describe general examples of body movements of embodied agents. The third examples "look at ball" and "run to ball" describe actions which demonstrate the interaction between agents and virtual worlds. Finally, in the fourth example "touch", we discuss how STEP can be used to solve some inverse kinematics problems for embodied agents. The first two examples demonstrate how users can use STEP easily. The third and the fourth examples require some knowledge of 3D geometry. They are designed for professional users.

4.1 Walk and its Variants

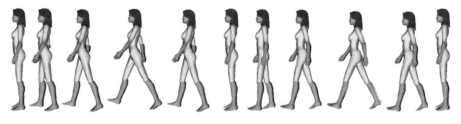

Fig. 5. Walk

A walking posture can be expressed as a movement which consists of the following two main activities: an action in which the left arm/right leg move forward while the right arm/left leg move backward, and an action in which the right arm/left leg move forward while the left arm/right leg move backward. The main poses and their linear interpolations are shown in Fig. 5. The walk action can be described in the scripting language as follows:

```
script(walk_pose(Agent), Action):-
    Action = seq([par([
        turn(Agent,r_shoulder,back_down2,fast),
        turn(Agent,r_hip,front_down2,fast),
        turn(Agent,l_shoulder,front_down2,fast),
        turn(Agent,l_hip,back_down2,fast)]),
      par([turn(Agent,l_shoulder,back_down2,fast),
        turn(Agent,l_hip,front_down2,fast),
        turn(Agent,r_shoulder,front_down2,fast),
        turn(Agent,r_hip,back_down2,fast)])]).
```

As shown below, a walk step can be described as a parallel action which consists of the walking posture and the moving action (i.e. changing position):

```
script(walk_forward_step(Agent),Action):-
  Action= par([walk_pose(Agent),
          move(Agent,front,fast)]).
```

The step length can be a concrete value. For example, for a 0.7 meter step size, it can be defined as:

```
script(walk_forward_step07(Agent),Action):-
   Action= par([walk_pose(Agent),
          move(Agent,increment(0.0,0.0,0.7),fast)]).
```

Alternatively, the step length can also be a variable:

```
script(walk_forward_step0(Agent,StepLength),Action):-
   Action = par([walk_pose(Agent),
        move(Agent,increment(0.0,0.0,StepLength),fast)]).
```

Therefore, walking forward N steps with a particular *StepLength* can be defined as follows:

```
script(walk_forward(Agent,StepLength,N),Action):-
   Action = repeat(walk_forward_step0(Agent,StepLength),N).
```

As mentioned above, animations of the walk action based on these definitions are simplified and approximated ones. As analyzed in [7, 20], a realistic animation of walk motions of a human figure involves many computations which rely on a robust simulator where forward and inverse kinematics are combined with automatic collision detection and response. It is not our intention to use the scripting language to achieve a fully realistic animation of the walk action, because it is seldom necessary for most web applications. However, we would like to point out that there does exist the possibility to accommodate some inverse kinematics to improve the realism by using the scripting language.

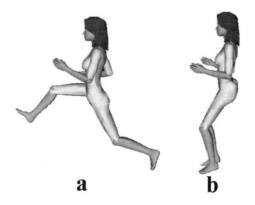

Fig. 6. Poses of run

4.2 Run and its Deformation

As a first approximation, the action "run" is similar to the action "walk", however, with bending arms and legs. The latter would make the legs look like lifting from the ground, which is an important difference between the action "walk" and the the action "run" [19]. The run pose is shown in Fig. 6(a). As we can see from the figure, the left lower arm points to the direction "front-up" when the left upper arm points to the direction "front_down2" during the run action. Considering the hierarchies of the body parts, we should not use the primitive action $turn(Agent, l\_elbow, front\_up, fast)$ but the primitive action $turn(Agent, l\_elbow, front, fast)$, because the direction of the left lower arm should be defined relative to the direction of its parent body part, i.e. the left arm (more exactly, the joint l_shoulder). This kind of redirection does not impose major difficulties for authoring, because the correct direction can be obtained by reducing the directions of its parent body parts to be the default ones. As we can see in Fig. 6(b), the lower arm actually points to the direction "front".

Based on the action "walk", the action "run_pose" can be defined as an action which starts with a run pose as shown in Fig. 6(b) and then repeat the action "walk_pose" for N times:

```
script(basic_run_pose(Agent), Action):-
 Action=par([turn(Agent,r_elbow,front,fast),
      turn(Agent, l_elbow, front, fast),
      turn(Agent, l_hip, front_down2, fast),
      turn(Agent, r_hip, front_down2, fast),
      turn(Agent, l_knee, back_down, fast),
      turn(Agent, r_knee, back_down, fast)]).

script(run_pose(Agent,N),Action):-
    Action = seq([basic_run_pose(Agent),
      repeat(walk_pose(Agent),N)]).
```

Therefore, the action running forward N steps with a particular $StepLength$ can be defined in the scripting language as follows:

```
script(run(Agent, StepLength,N),Action):-
    Action=seq([basic_run_pose(Agent),
      walk_forward(Agent,StepLength,N)]).
```

In practice, the action "run" (Fig. 7) may have many variants. For instance, the lower-arm may point to different directions; it does not necessarily point to the direction "front". Therefore, we may define the action "run" with respect to certain degrees of freedom. Here is an example to define a degree of freedom with respect to the angle of the lower arms to achieve the deformation:

```
script(basic_run_pose_elbow(Agent,Elbow_Angle),Action):-
    Action = par([
      turn(Agent,r_elbow,rotation(1,0,0,Elbow_Angle),fast),
```

Fig. 7. Run

```
turn(Agent,l_elbow,rotation(1,0,0,Elbow_Angle),fast),
turn(Agent,l_hip,front_down2,fast),
turn(Agent,r_hip,front_down2,fast),
turn(Agent,l_knee,back_down,fast),
turn(Agent,r_knee,back_down,fast)]).

script(run_e(Agent,StepLength,N,Elbow_Angle),Action):-
   Action = seq([basic_run_pose_elbow(Agent,Elbow_Angle),
                 walk_forward(Agent, StepLength, N)]).
```

4.3 Interaction with Virtual Worlds

In this section we want to show how the interaction between embodied agents and virtual worlds can be achieved by using the high-level interaction operators. Consider a situation in which there are several agents and a ball. The position of the ball is always changing because other agents may kick the ball. We want to design the script actions for embodied agents so that they can always look at the ball and run to the ball no matter where the ball is located.

In the following, we suppose that the meta language of the scripts is DLP. Other languages can be used following the same strategy. Using DLP's VRML/X3D predicates, we can manipulate 3D objects in virtual worlds. For example, given the current position of the embodied agent and the ball, we can always calculate the new rotation of the agent so that it will look at the ball. By using the high-level interaction operator *do* with the built-in operators in the meta language we can define the script action "look at ball" and other relevant actions.

First we want to define a scripting action "turn_to direction" which transforms a source direction vector into a destination direction by means of particular vector processing predicates. We know that the result of a vector cross product of two vectors v_1 and v_2 is a normal vector, i.e. a vector that is perpendicular to the original vectors v_1 and v_2. Such a normal vector defines the axis of the rotation and the corresponding angle θ between these two vectors can be calculated by the following formula:

$$\cos\theta = \frac{v_1 \cdot v_2}{|v_1| \times |v_2|}$$

Therefore, a scripting action "turn to direction" can be defined as:

Fig. 8. Look at ball

```
script(turn_to_direction(Object,SrcVector,DestVector),Action):-
    Action = seq([
        do(vector_cross_product(SrcVector,DestVector,vector(X,Y,Z),R)),
        do(setRotation(Object,X,Y,Z,R))]).
```

where the predicate *vector_cross_product*(S, D, V, R) calculates the cross product V of the vector S and the vector D, as well as the angle R between the two vectors.

In general, embodied agents turn to the ball along the XZ plane, therefore we can ignore the Y-parameters. The Y-parameters are useful only when we want to calculate a rotation for the agent's head so that it can look down to the ball. H-anim avatars always face to the $+Z$ direction by default. Thus, the source vector is $\langle 0, 0, 1 \rangle$. The destination vector can be calculated from the positions of the agent and the ball. Therefore, the scripting action "look_at_position" can be defined as follows:

```
script(look_at_position(Agent,X1,_Y1,Z1),Action):-
    Action = seq([do(getPosition(Agent,X,_Y,Z)),
                  do(Xdif is X1-X),
                  do(Zdif is Z1-Z),
                  turn_to_direction(Agent,vector(0.0,0.0,1.0),
                    vector(Xdif,0.0,Zdif))]).
```

Based on the scripting action "look_at_position", the scripting action "look_at_ball" (Fig. 8) can be easily defined as follows:

```
script(look_at_ball(Agent,Ball),Action):-
    Action = seq([do(getPosition(Ball, X1,Y1,Z1)),
                  look_at_position(Agent,X1,Y1,Z1)]).
```

In the following, we want to define a script action *run_to_ball*(*Agent, Ball, N*) so that the agent can continually run to the ball in N steps. Similarly we use the do-operator to obtain the current position of the agent and the ball first, from which we can calculate the increments of the positions in X and Z dimensions:

```
script(run_to_ball(Agent,Ball,Steps),Action):-
  Action = seq([do(getPosition(Agent,X,_,Z)),
                do(getPosition(Ball, X1,_,Z1)),
                do(StepLengthX is (X1-X)/Steps)),
                do(StepLengthZ is (Z1-Z)/Steps)),
                run_steps(Agent, increment(StepLengthX,0.0,
                          StepLengthZ),Steps)]).
```

The scripting action $run\_steps(Agent, Increment, N)$ describes an action in which the agent changes its position in N steps. This action can be defined as a recursive action:

```
script(run_steps(Agent,increment(X,Y,Z),1),Action):-
  Action = par([run_pose(Agent),
                move(Agent,increment(X,Y,Z),fast)]).

script(run_steps(Agent,increment(X,Y,Z),Steps),Action):-
  Action = seq([par([run_pose(Agent),
                     move(Agent,increment(X,Y,Z),fast)]),
                do(Steps1 is Steps - 1),
                run_steps(Agent,increment(X,Y,Z),Steps1)]).
```

4.4 Touch: an Inverse Kinematics Problem

A typical inverse kinematics problem is the calculation of the rotations of arms and wrists of embodied agents so that their hands can touch an object. As discussed in [20], many research efforts deal with this kind of problem. Finding solutions to this kind of inverse kinematics problem usually involves complex computations, like solving differential equations or applying particular non-linear optimizations [4, 20]. As discussed above, we can use high-level interaction operators to access the computational capabilities of the meta language in order to find the solutions by using the same methods which have been proposed in the literature. However, adopting these analytical and numerical methods to solve inverse kinematics problems may cause some performance problems for web applications. Therefore, one of our concerns is to find an acceptable trade-off between performance and realistic animations.

To illustrate this, we will discuss a "touch" example in more detail to show how the scripting language STEP can be used to solve some real-time inverse kinematics problems with a satisfying performance result. To simplify the problem, embodied agents are designed to behave like this: they will touch an object by using their hands if the object is reachable, otherwise they will point their hands in the direction of the object. In addition, we will ignore the upper and lower limits of the rotations of the shoulder and elbow joints. In particular, we assume that the elbow joint has enough degrees of freedom for an appropriate solution.

This simplified "touch" problem can be described as: given an agent *Agent* and a position $\langle x_0, y_0, z_0 \rangle$ of an object, try to set the rotations of the joints of the shoulder and the elbow so that the hand of the agent can touch exactly the position if the position is reachable. Suppose that the length of the upper arm is u, the length of the forearm is f, and the distance between the shoulder center $\langle x_3, y_3, z_3 \rangle$ and the destination position $\langle x_0, y_0, z_0 \rangle$ is d. The position $\langle x_0, y_0, z_0 \rangle$ is reachable if and only if $d \leq u + f$ if we ignore the upper and lower limits of the joint rotations. From the cosine law we know that if the object is reachable, then α, the angle between the upperarm and the forearm, can be calculated from:

$$\alpha = \arccos\left(\frac{u^2 + f^2 - d^2}{2uf}\right)$$

Furthermore, if v is the direction vector which points to the destination position from the shoulder center, v_0 the default direction vector of the arm, and v_1 the destination direction vector of the upper arm (Fig. 9), then the angle β between the vector v and v_1 is given by:

$$\beta = \arccos\left(\frac{u^2 + d^2 - f^2}{2ud}\right)$$

if the object is within the agent's reach.

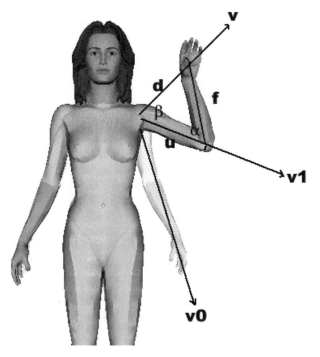

Fig. 9. Inverse kinematics of touch

If the position is not reachable, then $\alpha = \pi$ and $\beta = 0$ so that the arm will point to the direction of the destination position. Moreover, if $d \approx 0$, then the destination position is close to the shoulder center. In this case, we set $\alpha = 0$ and $\beta = 0$. We can define a scripting action to realize the functions for α and β as follows[5]:

```
script(getABvalue(Agent,position(X0,Y0,Z0),Hand,A,B),Action):-
   Action = seq([
               getDvalue(Agent,position(X0,Y0,Z0),Hand, D),
               get_upperarm_length(Agent,L1),
               get_forearm_length(Agent,L2),
               do(D1 is L1 + L2),
               if_then_else(sign(D1-D)>sign(0.001-D),
                   seq([do(cosine_law(L1,L2,D,A)),
                       do(cosine_law(L1, D, L2, B))]),
                   seq([do(A is 1.57*(1+sign(D-0.001))),
                       do(B is 0.0)]))]).
```

The predicate *getDvalue* is an action which calculates the distance D between the shoulder center and the destination touch position for an agent. Suppose that the destination position $\langle x_0, y_0, z_0 \rangle$ is relative to the coordinate system of the agent body at which the agent is positioned in the default position and orientation of H-anim avatars; that is, it faces in the $+Z$ direction at the position $\langle 0, 0, 0 \rangle$. The action *getDvalue* can be defined by obtaining the positions of the shoulder. In the following, we will define a "touch" action for relative positions first. We call the "touch" action for agents with arbitrary position and arbitrary orientation a *"touch" action for an absolute position.* We will show how the "touch" action for absolute positions can be based on a "touch" action for relative positions.

The cross product $v_0 \times v$, i.e. a normal vector $n = \langle x_n, y_n, z_n \rangle$, can be considered as a normal vector for v_0 and v_1, which defines the plane in which the arm turns from its default rotation to a destination rotation. This means that we require that the vector v_1 is in the same plane as the vectors v and v_0 so that the arm will turn close to the destination position via the shortest path. The angle γ between v_0 and v can be calculated with the vector predicates, like those that were used in the last example. Thus, the rotation for the elbow joint is $\langle x_n, y_n, z_n, \pi - \alpha \rangle$, and the rotation for the shoulder joint is $\langle x_n, y_n, z_n, \gamma - \beta \rangle$.

The vector v can be calculated by using the following script, considering that the destination position is a relative one:

```
script(getVvalue(Agent,position(X0,Y0,Z0),Hand,V),Action):-
   Action = seq([
     get_shoulder_center(Agent,Hand, position(X2,Y2,Z2)),
```

---

[5] The predicate $getABvalue(Agent, position(X0, Y0, Z0), Hand, A, B)$ means that for the agent *Agent* and the destination position $(X0, Y0, Z0)$ of the *Hand*, the value of α is A, and the value of β is B.

```
    do(direction_vector(position(X2,Y2,Z2),position(X0,Y0,Z0),V))]).
```

where the predicate get_shoulder_center gets the position of the shoulder center, and the predicate direction_vector obtains a direction vector of the two positions. It is easy to define these two predicates at the STEP level. However, the predicate direction_vector is already available in DLP in order to obtain a better performance.

Now, we define the scripting action "touch" for relative positions with the left hand as follows:

```
script(touch(Agent,position(X0,Y0,Z0),1),Action):-
  Action = seq([
    getABvalue(Agent,position(X0,Y0,Z0),1,A,B),
    do(R1 is 3.14-A),
    getVvalue(Agent,position(X0,Y0,Z0),1,V),
    get_arm_vector(Agent,1,V0),
    do(vector_cross_product(V0,V,vector(X3,Y3,Z3),C)),
    do(R2 is C-B),
    par([turn(Agent,l_shoulder,rotation(X3,Y3,Z3,R2),fast),
         turn(Agent,l_elbow,rotation(X3,Y3,Z3,R1),fast),
         turn(Agent,l_wrist,rotation(X3,Y3,Z3,-0.5),fast)])]).
```

Although we do not calculate the rotation for the wrist joint, we can adjust the rotation of the wrist joint based on the same normal vector, so that the hand can rotate a little bit to the position to achieve more realism. The "touch" action with the right hand can be defined similarly.

Finally, we can define the "touch" action for absolute positions in terms of the "touch" action for relative positions, by the translation of the absolute position into a relative position, based on the agent's current position and orientation.

```
script(touch_absolutePosition(Agent,position(X1,Y1,Z1),Hand),Action)
  :- Action = seq([do(getPosition(Agent,X,Y,Z)),
             do(getRotation(Agent, X2,Y2,Z2,R)),
             do(X3 is X1-X),
             do(Y3 is Y1-Y),
             do(Z3 is Z1-Z),
             do(R1 is -R),
             do(position_rotation(position(X3,Y3,Z3),
                 rotation(X2,Y2,Z2,R1),position(X4,Y4,Z4))),
             touch(Agent,position(X4,Y4,Z4), Hand)]).
```

where the predicate *position_rotation*($P1, R, P2$) gets the new position $P2$ for a given position $P1$ after the rotation R.

Several touch situations based on this scripting action are shown in Fig. 10. The tests show that STEP does not cause serious performance problems for this kind of inverse kinematics problem. Currently the computation time for each touch action is less than 50 milliseconds on a PC with a 500 MHz CPU and 128 MB memory, a low-end computer nowadays, under Windows NT running standard processes. There is still much room for improvement at the STEP level and the DLP meta language level. Therefore, the scripting language STEP can be used to achieve certain real-time inverse kinematics effects with a satisfying realism without serious performance problems.

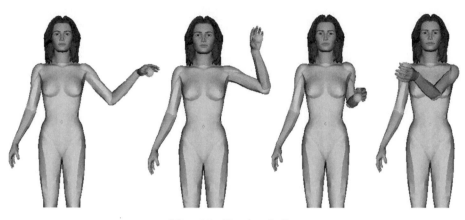

Fig. 10. Touch a ball

5 Related Work

Our work is close to Perlin and Goldberg's Improv system. In [16], Perlin and Goldberg propose Improv, which is a system for scripting interactive actors in virtual worlds. STEP is different from Perlin and Goldberg's in the following aspects. First, STEP is based on the H-anim specification, i.e. VRML-based, which is convenient for web applications. Second, we separate the scripting language from the agent architecture. Therefore, it is relatively easy for users to use the scripting language. Also, *Signing Avatar*[6] has a powerful scripting language. However, we wish to state that our scripting language is based on dynamic logic, and has powerful abstraction capabilities and support for parallelism.

In [3], Badler et al. discuss the system of Parameterized Action Representation (PAR), which provides an approach to use natural language instructions for virtual agents. Similar to STEP, PAR supports the specification of complex actions for agents, like pre- and post-conditions. PAR uses a special syntax and has many built-in notions. STEP is more similar to Funge's CML (Cognitive Modeling Language) [8] [7], although CML is not VRML/X3D and H-anim based. STEP shares many common operators with CML, like sequences, test,

---

[6] http://www.signingavatar.com

[7] http://www.dgp.toronto.edu/~funge/cml.html

non-deterministic choice, and conditional operators. CML is an implementation of complex actions within the situation calculus, an action logic based on first-order predicate logic. However, STEP is based on dynamic logic in which there is a clear distinction between a sub-language for actions and a meta language for states. As discussed before, such a distinction is very useful for both the development of fully functional intelligent agents by using a meta language, and the realization of scripting actions by using a scripting language for a better performance.

In [17], Prendinger et al. are also using a Prolog-based scripting approach for animated characters but they focus on higher level concepts such as affect and social context. In [18], Prendinger et al. discuss the systems MPML and SCREAM, an approach of scripting the bodies and minds of life-like characters.

XSTEP shares a number of interests with the VHML (Virtual Human Markup Language) community[8], which is developing a suite of markup language for expressing humanoid behavior, including facial animation, body animation, speech, emotional representation, and multimedia. We see this activity as complementary to ours, since our research proceeds from technical feasibility; that is how we can capture the semantics of humanoid gestures and movements within our dynamic logic, which is implemented on top of DLP.

6 Conclusions

In this chapter we have proposed the scripting language STEP for embodied agents, in particular for their communicative acts, like gestures and postures. STEP will be extended for other communicative acts like facial expressions or speech. We have discussed several principles of scripting language design for embodied agents. These principles are justified by a number of typical examples of how the scripting language STEP can be used. The first two examples "walk" and "run" show that STEP can be used for authors to design a rich number of variants of scripting actions. The third example demonstrates the capabilities of STEP for applications which involve interactions with virtual worlds. The fourth "touch" example discusses the possibilities of using STEP for real-time agents with inverse kinematics. The experiments show that STEP can be used for embodied agents and applications of inverse kinematics with a satisfying performance.

References

1. Allen, J.F.: Maintaining knowledge about temporal intervals. *Communications of the ACM* **26**(11):832–843 (November 1983)

---

[8] http://www.vhml.org

2. Allen, J.F.: Time and time again: The many ways to represent time. *Journal of Intelligent Systems* **6**(4):341–356 (July 1991)

3. Badler N., Bindiganavale, R., Bourne, J., Palmer, M., Shi, J., Schuler, W.: A parameterized action representation for virtual human agents. In: *Workshop on Embodied Conversational Characters*, Lake Tahoe, California (1998)

4. Badler, N., Manoochehri, K., and Walters, G.: Articulated figure positioning by multiple constraints. *IEEE Computer Graphics Applications* **7**(6):28–38 (1987)

5. Eliëns, A.: *DLP, A Language for Distributed Logic Programming* (Wiley, Hoboken, NJ 1992)

6. Eliëns, A.: *Principles of Object-Oriented Software Development* (Addison-Wesley, Reading, MA 2000)

7. Faure, F., et al.: Dynamic analysis of human walking. In: *Proceedings of the 8th Workshop on Computer Animation and Simulation*, Budapest (1997)

8. Funge, J.: In: *Making Them Behave: Cognitive Models for Computer Animation*, University of Toronto (1998)

9. Harel, D.: Dynamic Logic. In: *Handbook of Philosophical Logic*, Vol II, (D. Reidel, Dordrecht 1984) pp 497–604

10. Harel, D., Kozen, D., Tiuryn, J.: *Dynamic Logic* (MIT Press, Cambridge, MA 2000)

11. Huang, Z., Eliëns, A., van Ballegooij, A., de Bra, P.: A taxonomy of web agents. In: *Proceedings of the 11th International Workshop on Database and Expert Systems Applications* (IEEE Computer Society Press 2000) pp 765–769

12. Huang, Z., Eliëns, A., Visser, C.: Programmability of Intelligent Agent Avatars. In: *Proceedings of Agents'01 Workshop on Embodied Agents* (2001)

13. Huang, Z., Eliëns, A., Visser, C.: Formal semantics of STEP: A dynamic logic approach. Research report (Vrije Universiteit Amsterdam, 2003)

14. Huang, Z., Eliëns, A., Visser, C.: Implementation of a scripting language for VRML/X3D-based embodied agents. In: *Proceedings of the 2003 Web 3D Conference* (ACM Press, New York 2003)

15. Huang, Z., Eliëns, A., Visser, C.: XSTEP: A markup language for embodied agents. In: *Proceedings of the 16th International Conference on Computer Animation and Social Agents* (CASA'2003) (IEEE Computer Society Press 2003)

16. Perlin, K., Goldberg, A.: Improv: A System for scripting interactive actors in virtual worlds. In: *ACM Computer Graphics*, Annual Conference Series (1996) pp 205–216

17. Prendinger, H., Descamps, S., Ishizuka, M.: Scripting affective communication with life-like characters in web-based interaction systems. *Journal of Applied Artificial Intelligence* **16**:519–553 (2002)

18. Prendinger, H., Saeyor, S., Ishizuka, M.: MPML and SCREAM: Scripting the bodies and minds of life-like characters. In: *Life-like Characters. Tools, Affective Functions and Applications*, ed Prendinger, H., Ishizuka, M. (Springer 2003). This volume.

19. Rohr, K.: Towards model-based recognition of human movements in image sequences. In: *Computer Vision, Graphics, and Image Processing (CVGIP): Image Understanding* **59**(1):94–115 (1994)

20. Tolani, D., Goswami, A., Badler, N.: Real-time inverse kinematics techniques for anthropomorphic limbs. In: *Graphical Models* **62**(5):353–388 (2000)

gUI: Specifying Complete User Interaction

Andrew Marriott and Simon Beard

Curtin University of Technology, Western Australia, Australia
{raytrace,beardsw}@computing.edu.au

Summary. With emotion described as "the organism's interface to the world outside" (Scherer [45]), there has been great interest in the role of emotion in speech and gestures in making Human–Virtual Human interfaces more effective. Miller [33] suggests that only 7% of a message is sent through words: the remainder is sent through facial expressions (55%) and vocal intonation (38%). Therefore in both analysis of human conversations and in the synthesis of Virtual Humans, expressive emotion and gestures need to be catered for to ensure that the intent of the message is not lost. A radical paradigm change occurred in going from text entry to the mouse-pointer concepts of a Graphical User Interface. In a similar way, it is now necessary for a total user input paradigm, adding video and audio input to the existing methods, to become the predominant Computer Human Interaction (CHI) of the future. This complete interaction is referred to as a gestalt user interface: an interface that should be reactive to, and proactive of, the perceived desires of the user through emotion and gesture. The formal specification, development, implementation, and evaluation of a gestalt User Interface (gUI) language is necessary to provide a stable, consistent base for future research into multi-modal Human interfaces in general, and specifically to Embodied Character Agents. This chapter details some early research on language design and also an implementation evaluation.

1 Computer Human User Interfaces – Synthesis

Humane CHIs are developed under many different names – Embodied Character Agents (ECAs), Embodied Conversational Agents, Virtual Conversational Characters, Virtual Humans, Talking Heads. These are characterized by a $2^1/_2$D or 3D computer-generated character often with some text-to-speech synthesis software, perhaps with a Dialogue Management system to handle user enquiries and frequently using MPEG-4 technology [19, 20]. The book *MPEG-4 Facial Animation – The standard, implementations and applications* by Pandzic and Forchheimer [38] is a good reference text for more information about this technology. The ECAs are applied in areas such as application helpers, web page assistants or metaphors for entire web sites, Virtual Information Providers, News Announcers, and as avatars to represent users in Virtual Environments.

Currently there are many markup languages for controlling ECAs in these different tasks [44, 26] and for making them individuals [40]. Some of these are proprietary, some are not "open" for public use or scrutiny, and many are *ad hoc*. Many still lack the basic prerequisites or criteria for a standard language:

- *Completeness.* The language must be complete or constructed in a way that is easy to expand.
- *Simplicity.* The language should be as simple as possible and exclude any ambiguous features. That would keep the language fairly small and comprehensive. Nevertheless, this should not affect the previous criterion. In order to fulfill this criterion, elements that have the same functionality should be merged.
- *Consistency.* The language must be consistent in order to make it easier for the user to learn, i.e. the syntax should follow a certain pattern. For example, the element names should be in the same form and have the same kind of attributes.
- *Intuitiveness.* The language should be intuitive; thus the user will not always need to consult the specification to be able to use the language. The names of the elements and attributes should be self-describing.
- *Abstraction.* The language should use a high abstraction level. That will make the language easier to understand and thus to use.
- *Usability.* The language should provide features that suit both beginners and advanced users.
- *Standardization.* The language should adopt existing relevant standards where possible, for the different parts of the language. If an emerging "standard" is adopted for one part of the language, it is important that this part can be easily changed if the "standard" does not eventuate and this change must be transparent to users.
- *Evaluation.* The language should be evaluated with respect to the above criteria and effectiveness.

Many synthesis languages are being developed "in-house" and they are all attempting to fill different application niches. As such, they are all affected by entirely different design decisions [6] and standardization should incorporate each of the different choices of design.

An example language – VHML [6] – has been developed with these eight criteria in mind. VHML is an open specification available at the VHML web site[1]. Evaluation of parts of VHML as a synthesis language for directing ECAs is currently underway. More information on using VHML for synthesis can be found at the VHML web site along with examples[2]. VHML is currently being

---

[1] http://www.vhml.org/
[2] http://www.vhml.org/papers/jrpit-hci/

used in two applications: MetaFace, an ECA [5] and the *Mentor* System, a dialogue management system (Marriott [30]).

VHML was the subject of a European Union Information Society and Technology workshop [31] with the discussions at that workshop leading to the special IST workshop on Formal Language Specification [26] held in Italy. Subsequent discussion made the VHML developers seriously consider where VHML was going, and specifically what issues the specification and implementation were addressing [6]. Developing VHML to specify multi-modal user input was given special consideration.

2 Value of Empathy in Synthesis

Often the amount of information presented to users is immense – too much to be able to deal with directly and hence an intelligent interface or ECA is needed [47, 1]. Each day, humans deal with other humans, even those with different languages, cultures, and personalities. Hence users expect ECA-based applications to behave in a similar, familiar way. Often the lack of emotions or of a personality in the ECA removes that feeling of familiarity. Imagine the difference in "feeling" engendered by the following if rendered by a simple ECA as opposed to a talented actor:

I opened the drawer of my little desk and a single letter fell out, a letter from my mother, written in pencil, one of her last, with unfinished words and an implicit sense of her departure. It's so curious: one can resist tears and "behave" very well in the hardest hours of grief. But then someone makes you a friendly sign behind a window ... or one notices that a flower that was in bud only yesterday has suddenly blossomed ... or a letter slips from a drawer ... and everything collapses.

– Letters from Colette

When used as input to a Talking Head system, the simple addition of the VHML tag "<**sad**>" around the above text can cause the voice to become slower, reduce in frequency, and enact a more solemn-looking expression, and, perhaps, lower its head to indicate a sad contemplation of the text. Another culture may expect a different rendering to indicate <**sad**>. With this emotional addition, the rendering of the quote becomes more affective and effective – the viewer empathizes with the ECA. In general, these markup tags can make ECAs believable and hence a Virtual Lecturer or Virtual Distance Education Tutor is seen as being erudite and approachable, a Virtual Salesperson in a web page is seen as trustworthy and helpful [32, 36].

Therefore, there is a need for affective and engaging synthesis of emotional and culturally aware ECAs. This technology is ideally placed to provide better interfaces using common anthropomorphic metaphors in areas such as:

- *Universities* to use for Distance Education. Custom-built Virtual Lecturers can be used to help students understand the lesson, to provide one-on-one tutoring, to give accurate, consistent answers to queries.
- *E-commerce.* The Virtual Salesperson can be a pleasant front end to the stock database, billing system, complaints department. It can respond to users in their language in a culturally dependent manner.
- *Web guides.* Online exhibitions such as a museum or art gallery where the user can have a knowledgeable virtual Sister Wendy or any other art critic. The guide has data-mined knowledge about the site, similar to a search engine, and can help the user at the site through a Natural Language Interface.
- *Traveling.* A virtual travel agent can provide information about accommodation and ticket arrangements. The travel agent can also book the travel on your behalf.
- *Interactive games.* Avatars of the user or generated opponents.
- *Knowledgeable interactive companions* for travelers, children, the old, or the infirmed.

Since humans expect other humans to understand all aspects of the communication channel between them – words, gestures, body language, emotions – it is important that the culturally aware ECA can also understand emotional/gestural input.

3 Computer Human User Interfaces – Analysis

The first input interfaces were text based, with Graphical User Interfaces (GUIs) being developed to cater for a more user-centric, friendly approach to computing. With computers becoming more ubiquitous in public access areas where a keyboard and mouse are often seen as a logistical problem rather than a standard input device, there is a perceived need for a more humane user application interface [52]. It is becoming apparent that the current user-interface paradigm fails as a "good" user interface. In human–computer dialogues (e.g. query systems) it is beneficial if the interface is "aware" that the user does not know how to perform the task, or is performing the tasks but getting angry or frustrated. The interface can then take action to alleviate this problem.

Gestalt User Interfaces (gUIs) are needed to capture the entire user input to the application. The German word "gestalt" has come to mean in English: *An organised whole in which each part affects every other part.* Gestalt Theory [54] indicates that the mind sees or organizes events and situations as a pattern or a whole rather than as a collection of separate entities. Understanding comes through the integration of these into the "big picture". This understanding of the separate entities is determined by the following relationships:

- *Similarity.* Similar entities tend to be grouped or perceived as being together.
- *Proximity.* Entities are grouped according to their "closeness".
- *Closure.* Completed or "closed" entities are grouped together.
- *Continuity.* Entities that preserve spatial continuity are perceived as being together.
- *Membership.* A sub-entity is defined by its context.

Therefore a gUI is an interface where input to the application can be a combined "stimulus" of text, button clicks, and analyzed facial, vocal, and emotional gestures. Understanding comes through integration of all these stimuli based upon these relationships, especially temporal closeness.

Just as there was a paradigm shift when interfaces went from being text based to GUIs, there will need to be a similar shift in our way of receiving, recognizing, and managing this new form of input to applications. Applications can respond to a *"nod"*, a *"scowl"*, or a *"laugh"*. Applications can adjust to the user becoming tired, frustrated, or angry. Applications can tailor their GUIs (perhaps by reducing the complexity) to cater for users feeling lost or angry.

Users are already extending the use of standard input devices such as the mouse to "gesture" to the computer so as to use it more effectively [35]. Human gesture recognition, on the other hand, can be performed through video analysis and haptic input; emotion analysis can be based on both video and audio input. This recognition can produce time-stamped stimulus that, along with text or button clicks, becomes input to the gUI. The gUI then translates the stimulus into user *intent* for the application (just as a GUI translates button clicks into *intent*). Complete user interaction should also deal with the synthesis of emotion and gesture in order to provide full duplex use of communication channels.

It is important to understand that this gestalt input should not be seen as layered on top of the normal textual interface or GUI but as an integrated part of the operating or windowing system interface. Just as initial GUI development was layered but is now integrated, so too will gUI research develop. This is consistent with the integration of video and audio components into existing operating systems. However, the initial gUI experiment described later in this chapter used the layered approach. This experiment attempted to evaluate the implementation issues of a gUI with respect to emotional and gestural input. That is, is it possible and worthwhile to develop gUIs?

3.1 Value of Empathy in Analysis

The discussion thus far has focused upon development for capturing a "more complete" encapsulation of human interaction, with some comment as to application specific advantages. Overall, the value of capturing complete user interaction is the empathic ability of an interface, the extra functionality acquired, and an intuitive interface. By catering for the emotion/gesture of the user, the markup language can aid in providing several important yet often overlooked empathic states of the virtual character [7]:

- *Attend.* Considering the thoughts and feelings of the user.
- *Engage.* Aligning actions, thoughts, and feelings with those of the user.
- *Value.* Expressing the value of the user's interaction.
- *Encourage.* Expressing encouragement for further interaction.
- *Parting.* Suspending dialogue while user performs other tasks.
- *Available.* Allow the user to interrupt for interaction.

It is for the programmers and knowledge base builders to consider how best to handle emotion and gesture input, because there are a multitude of positive and negative affects to consider as discussed in Picard and Klein [42]. These empathic states are especially important in pedagogical applications [12].

Similarly, if application designers are to properly cater for the needs of the users, then they must understand the *entire* input to the application. An Airline Flight Controller may be doing his or her job efficiently but if the Flight Control System *knew* that the Controller was operating at a high stress level, then it could drastically alter the way in which it dealt with the Controller. If the Cab Control system for a long-distance truck driver *knew* that the driver was tired, it could force mandatory stops of certain durations. Even for text-based applications such as the *Mentor* System – used by university students to help with their assignments – a better understanding of the user's immediate attitude to pro-active prompting would be beneficial. At the end of the *Mentor* System study, formal qualitative evaluation about aspects of using the system elicited the responses in Fig. 1 from one individual.

What was the least beneficial aspect: "That f–king beeping sound every
    time I am doing something or every hour it f–king beeps."
What was the most annoying aspect: "The f–king beeping sound."
What aspects were obtrusive: "The f–king beeping."

Fig. 1. Evaluation comments on the *Mentor* System

It is obvious that if the *Mentor* System had realized, through video or audio input, the intensity of the student's feelings at the time, then it could have modified its pro-active question asking strategy and hopefully it would have been more useful to the student (see also [24, 43]). There is a definite need for gUIs to applications that deal with humans.

4 gUI Research Objectives

Both synthesis and analysis scenarios show a human need for, as well as a societal benefit from, emotional representation of some kind in the application input/output data. Little research has currently been undertaken on using a markup language as the basis for specifying input or as a basis for a gUI framework.

The formal specification, development, implementation, evaluation, and standardization of a language is necessary to provide a stable, consistent base for both industrial use and future research into multi-modal Human–Computer interaction. The use of this language for user–ECA interfaces must also be effective in managing this interaction. The language must provide a suitable base for building a gUI framework.

In order to represent time varying emotions/gestures in a document, it is suggested that XML be used because of its validating structure, human readability, and ease of parsing.

4.1 Importance and Timeliness

Through early initiatives such as MPEG-4, Europe has a clear dominance in the field of non-proprietary solutions to facial and body animation at the low level. This has enabled many industrial products to take advantage of this interoperability in creating Human–Computer interfaces. Currently lacking in these products and also in many research endeavors is a unified standard architecture plus language to control/record the higher level human ECA interaction and to make this interaction more engaging. Of equal importance is an evaluation of any candidate language to see whether it is effective in the interaction.

Recent discussions and workshops [44, 26] have indicated that this language standardization needs to be addressed in a formal rather than *ad hoc* way. The research involves diverse fields including psychology and sociology and is bringing together established multi-disciplinary researchers to solve these problems. Of importance to sociologists is the best way for this new interaction to take place. How will users react to it? What metaphor will be most successful for this new input paradigm?

5 The Role of the Anthropomorphic Interface Metaphor

Metaphors are used in computer systems in order to bring real life closer to a computer abstraction. For plain-text based interfaces, the user–computer metaphor is one of a question–answer session. The current GUI metaphor in user–computer interactions is the desktop metaphor. To specify complete user interaction with an ECA, and use the analysis and synthesis of emotion and gesture, requires an anthropomorphic metaphor. Even a text-and-GUI-based system such as *Mentor* uses a virtual lecturer metaphor. It has no visual reinforcement of this metaphor, but instead seeks to offer humane chat-based interaction that offers an intuitive interface. This is exactly the same for a gUI, as responding to and producing complex emotive and gesture stimulus is uniquely human.

To date, the most predominant metaphor used in computer systems is the desktop metaphor; but these systems now have a legacy of additional *ad hoc* metaphors that are becoming entrenched as a part of our lives. We run the same risk of knowing that better keyboard layouts exist but sticking with the QWERTY layout because we are used to it.

There are various cognitive problems with the existing desktop metaphor, as outlined by Krueger [27]. The reason that the virtual desktop has been so successful to date is because of the metaphor's likeness to our perception of the world, despite various limitations and mismatches in its implementation. However inaccurate the metaphor, the crucial issue is whether this helps users deal with the abstraction of a computer by providing an interface that is an improvement on the norm. Lovgren [29] explains that some mismatches, such as recursive folders, are an improved extension to real life that users are willing to accept.

Kay [23] argues that *"illusions"* should be used instead of literal metaphors. To use the literal metaphor of the desktop would be to ignore all of the benefits of the computer environment. Therefore when discussing anthropomorphic metaphors in this chapter, what is really meant is the *"illusion"* of a humane interface that incorporates the benefits of the computer technology. The goal is to reduce cognitive overhead when users interact with an anthropomorphic interface. Hence, our gUI framework must be based upon a well-established metaphor that minimizes user discomfort whilst maximizing user interaction.

When using an anthropomorphic metaphor that captures a more complete encapsulation of interaction users, it is important to allow gUI applications to become an *extension* of real life rather than be constrained by it. It is also important to allow an extension of the metaphor so that the *"real world"* does not inhibit the functionality of the computer system. This area should avoid mismatches (i.e. features that occur contrary to real life) such as how the waste paper basket was first implemented on the Macintosh desktop metaphor as both a way of deleting files and also of ejecting floppy disks. Instead, this area can contain *"magic"* or *"illusions"* that extend features, such as the ability to delete text from a computer page, whilst in real life, pages are not easily erased [23].

It is also important not to adopt the *"kitchen sink"* approach which leads to a vast system with inaccessible power [29]. Current literature suggests that a metaphor is most successful if it comes from the problem domain. For example, if an ECA was used in an online museum or art gallery, perhaps the best anthropomorphic metaphor would be a curator or guide. The advantage of an anthropomorphic metaphor framework is that human contact is prevalent in nearly all aspects of life. Wonisch and Cooper [55] have shown that when people are given the choice of interface agents there is a tendency for them to choose interface agents that are visually contextually linked with the problem domain. For example, Herman the bug [22] and Adele [48] are both linked to the problem domain of the system. Wells and Fuerst [53] have shown that domain-oriented metaphors can have a positive effect on memory retention. Their problem domain was a vacation resort system, and the two systems compared were a domain-oriented metaphor (using the physical resort location) and a frame-oriented metaphor (using a web browser). Lovgren [29] makes the connection that since long-term memory is largely associative and visual, then visual metaphors are a powerful way to deal with the abstraction of computer systems.

Therefore, an anthropomorphic humane metaphor seems appropriate as long as it can meet the real-world expectations of that metaphor. For visual synthesis, the current quality of Talking Heads is appropriate. Their audible synthesis is barely acceptable [9, 14, 34] but improving [17] and Text to Speech systems with emotion are becoming available [32]. The *humanity* of Talking Heads (TH) is still being developed with a real need for personality-based responsiveness (as can be seen in other chapters of this book).

To meet the user expectations for input, more research needs to be done. Speech to text research is solid but still not very affective/effective. Emotion and gesture analysis via video and audio input is basic but promising as demonstrated in the deliverables [37] of the European Union 5th Framework InterFace project [3]. This project defined new models and implemented advanced tools for audio–video analysis, synthesis, and representation so as to provide essential technologies for the implementation of large-scale virtual and augmented environments. The metaphor used was oriented to make man–machine interaction as natural as possible, based on everyday human communication means such as speech, facial expressions, and body gestures from both sides.

If the anthropomorphic metaphor for user–ECA interaction is appropriate, it becomes important to look at possible application areas for this research. The following three examples show the relevance and applicability of using an anthropomorphic metaphor.

5.1 Anthropomorphic Web Applications

Bryan and Gershman [8] draw attention to the two predominant metaphors of web browser interaction: browsing and searching. Browsing is the leisurely navigation from hypertext document to hypertext document along an arbitrary path. Searching is goal oriented where the user tries to find specific information.

But the web is vast and complex, and searching the web takes time no matter how well the query is constructed. Of importance is that humans in their interaction have special ways of dealing with day-to-day complexity. This natural way of coping with complexity can be used to combat the involved-ness of the online world. So, when searching, ask a friend. In this case, your friend is

---

[3] http://www.ist-interface.org/

a knowledgable ECA [25, 2, 3]. In the gUI context, your ECA friend "knows" you are getting frustrated in your web searching, and offers assistance. In this manner, the use of an anthropomorphic metaphor, so prevalent in existing literature, could perhaps reduce the difficulty of searching. This knowledge-able *friendship* is a niche that MetaFace [5] attempts to fill. The MetaFace system was developed to address the need for a well-defined metaphor and an enabling framework, and to research into time delay and information search-ing. MetaFace is a client/server architecture capable of finding information on behalf of a user, presenting the information in a web browser, and interacting with the user by means of speech and facial animation. MetaFace presents a new metaphor that is intuitive to the user since it is modeled on human interaction and concepts.

5.2 Transcription

Gestalt transcription involves the representation, transformation, and storage of analyzed emotions and gestures, with the view to later analysis. The ac-curacy of any system for transcribing, e.g. an interview with a user, must be such that a recorded session can be played back using Virtual Humans with minimal loss of information (content, gestures, emotion).

For example, a typical research scenario in the Humanities discipline is a user interview to record opinions/reactions to some questions. These sessions are typically transcribed to get the text of the interview. With only 7% of a message being sent through words and the remainder being sent through facial expressions (55%) and vocal intonation (38%) [33], it is obvious that the majority of information is lost. This transcribing is also very time consuming and often prone to error or misinterpretation.

A gUI-based transcription application could provide the interview text plus emotion plus gesture. Typical output could be as shown in Fig. 2.

   :
10:53:27: **<smile>** I received a letter today**</smile>**
        <pause *length=*"short"**/>** but
        <angry> my brother took it away before I could read it**</angry>**
        <pause *length=*"12.6s"**/>**
10:53:45: **<sad>**I guess he was jealous**</sad>**
   :

Fig. 2. A gUI-based transcription of an interview

The recorded session could then be "replayed" many times using a VHML-based Talking Head or Virtual Human application and the textual output could help in analysis of the session.

5.3 Real-Time Interaction and Data Representation

Real-time applications involve the efficient storage and communication of the data. Transcription applications can benefit from an XML format with validation and easy parsing whilst real-time applications can benefit from a standard data structure and efficient ways of managing this structure.

As an example, consider an intelligent television application. The TV should be able to handle real-time emotions and gestures to control the function of the TV (e.g. changing channels, turning up the volume), but it could also make use of transcribed data for interpretation. Machine Learning could be employed to link emotion and gesture with causality to improve the function of the TV (e.g. the TV can tell when you're not paying any attention to it and turn the volume down; it can automatically record what it interprets as favorite programs) and to do this a transcript of interaction would need to be kept.

Although XML can be used as the base mechanism for formatting the gUI data, an understanding of the temporal nature of gestural and emotional input is necessary in order to develop the necessary semantic and hierarchical gUI specification structure.

6 gUI Data Specification Issues

Many simple multimedia analysis systems use a temporal window or frame of input (video segment or speech sample) to determine various signal attributes such as spectrum, power, or even dominant color in the case of video [15]. Each system may have different temporal resolutions for this classification (e.g. every millisecond, every tenth of a second, a "frame" rate such as 25 frames per second, or over a total segment).

A multi-modal analysis system must understand the nature of non-textual input to be able to first capture and then analyze this input [11, 10, 39, 49]. This "affect recognition" [41, 21, 28, 12] is necessary for proper gestalt understanding of the user requirements. A good online reference for information on this is the "Non-verbal" Behavior and "Non-Verbal" Communication web site[4].

In capturing the input, any system should allow for a temporal window that ranges from the most fleeting simple case ("affect bursts" as detailed in Schröder [46]) to the most complex, slowly evolving case. In detecting expressions, emotions, or gestures [56, 51, 13, 37], this temporal window will help to differentiate short mixed emotions such as surprise before anger or fear. It will also allow for the detection of more lengthy emotions such as gradual happiness as "understanding comes to someone".

The specification of this gUI input data format will be layered – at the lowest operating system or device driver levels, an efficient binary format

---

[4] http://www3.usal.es/~nonverbal/papers.htm

would be required. At the higher levels, a more structured format aids in abstraction and cognitive understanding. The following outlines one possible higher level specification. An initial approach to processing and recording the gUI data could be that the most important aspects of emotion analysis and interpretation are the recognized *emotion* and its *intensity*. Also that the most complex case is a continuous representation for all emotions at irregular intervals and the simplest case is one representation for one emotion at the end of a segment. With this requirement, a suitable structure that uses VHML tags could be as illustrated in Fig. 3.

```
<emotion-vector timestamp = "400ms">
            <happy intensity = "79%"/>
            <sad intensity = "12%"/>
            <angry intensity = "0%"/>
</emotion-vector>
<emotion-vector timestamp = "1s800ms">
            <textbfhappy intensity = "85%"/>
            <sad intensity = "12%"/>
            <angry intensity = "0%"/>
</emotion-vector>
```

Fig. 3. VHML data representing emotional user input

The example of Fig. 3 takes both the most complex and the most simple case into account and achieves this by using a vector of emotions, their intensities, and a time-stamp. This format allows for a timeline in which to place the analyzed emotions. The time-stamp postfixes – ms (milliseconds), s (seconds), m (minutes), h (hours), d (days), w (weeks) – can be used to simplify the document (e.g. 2d5h32m). This notation allows for very detailed (transcribing what happens in just a few seconds) or very broad (what happens over a few weeks) representation of emotion over time. This notation cannot be validated (in the XML sense) with a simple DTD but is easy to validate with a custom parser or using XML Schemas. Using a similar notation, the gUI analysis system can recognize gesture for a segment of input and determine whether or not a gesture has been executed. The system must first recognize that a gesture has been executed, what it is, and then determine the associated information such as direction, intensity, duration. Each gesture may have different attributes. For example, with a hand gesture showing how big something is, the important attribute is the distance between the hands; with a nod, the important associated information may be the direction of the nod or what is being nodded at. There is added complexity when considering that gestures can be domain specific. The same *"size of"* gesture discussed above could be used in a different communication domain to simply empha-size a sentence, in this case the important attribute being the force of the gesture. The domain and attributes of a gesture should be an extensible part of any standardization attempt because few concrete certainties exist for all domains.

Any dialogue between a user and an application or an ECA is context based. A Dialogue Manager often uses a state-based approach to manage the context transitions. For example, in the dialogue of Fig. 4, we can see that the use of the word "it" in the user's second request refers to OpenGL. Because the Dialogue Manager has moved into a state or context where it understands that this anaphora refers to the previously mentioned object, it can process it correctly "in context".

User: What is OpenGL?
DM: A 3-D graphics Language
User: Where do I get it?

Fig. 4. User dialogue showing context transition

Gestures, like textual and emotional input, occur in some context. Any gUI framework must allow for these dynamic context transitions. This is no different from a File Dialog Box being used for both opening files as well as saving files. It is up to the programmer to set the context – for example, the question "Do you want help?" may have just been posed to the user and any "yes" or "no" gesture must be processed in that context. With multi-modal gestalt input, it is essential that it is time-stamped similar to mouse events.

Time-stamping of emotion and gestures is a way of synchronizing the resulting XML document and hence of providing context. For correct understanding of the multi-modal input, the correlation of emotion and gesture with a user's environmental stimulus must be made (whether that is a response from an ECA, or in the case of the intelligent TV example, what is currently being watched by the user). A standard way in which to achieve this correlation is by time-stamping gestures and emotions as they occur. The application must also time-stamp any additional modeled stimuli (such as changing the channel in the TV example). By comparing the emotions, gestures, and stimulus using the common timeline, it is possible to make correlations between user input, context, and intent.

Emotion and gesture representation for *real-time* applications can be based on efficient communication standards such as MPEG-4 face and body animation (MPEG-4 is already used by ECA applications to solve the problem of efficient communication and internal representation of *synthesis*). Using MEPG-4 would cover the mechanics but there must also be a higher abstract level to cover intent. Since it would be problematic to define one set of emotions and gestures that could be used across many applications, the abstract level would need to be extensible and allow each application to define a set of emotion and gesture intents. This is important in the construction of gUI applications and frameworks that encompass more than one domain and thus need this extensibility. There are still some problems in the data representation of Fig. 3:

- Lack of a consistent set of emotions, and the ability to add more.
- Lack of ability to show change in different sets of emotions or just a single emotion.
- Lack of additional attributes for emotion besides intensity.

To address these issues, we must abandon our initial approach and consider using a more realistic and extensible semantic structure (Fig. 5):

```
<declaration>
    <emotion-vector-declaration name= "standard six" >
        <emotion-declaration name= "happy"/>
        <emotion-declaration name= "sad"/>
        <emotion-declaration name= "angry"/>
        <emotion-declaration name= "surprised"/>
        <emotion-declaration name= "afraid"/>
        <emotion-declaration name= "disgusted"/>
    </emotion-vector-declaration >
    <emotion-vector-declaration name= "my extended set">
        <emotion-declaration name= "happy"/>
        <emotion-declaration name= "sad"/>
        <emotion-declaration name= "angry">
    </emotion-vector-declaration >
</declaration>
```

Fig. 5. Extensible structure of recording multi-modal user input

By specifying a <**declaration**> and a <**data**> section, any emotion can be represented in a standard format. A concern is that having no basic set of emotions makes it harder to share data between applications. The declaration section will actually assist the sharing of data by providing all of the emotions being represented in one area, at the top of the document. An application can warn the user and then ignore all of the data that is irrelevant to the system and only use the data that is supported. Note that the approach to "standard" emotions taken by MPEG-4 Facial Animation could also be adopted as the "standard" base emotions for any gUI implementation. Note also that a more robust representation would be used that specifies which emotion vector declaration is actually being used.

The representation shown in Fig. 5 also supports the updating of different sets of emotions as vectors. In addition, just one emotion (defined in any of the sets) can be updated using a singular element. This allows a lot more flexibility in the document without the need to represent redundant data.

```
<data>
      <gesture name = "nod" intensity = "50"
                duration = "2s" timestamp = "400ms">
      <gesture name = "shake" intensity = "90"
                duration = "3s" timestamp = "2s100ms">
</data>
```

Fig. 6. Example structure for user gesture input

Note that the previous XML <**emotion-vector**> example code (Fig. 3) only indicates the recording of emotional intensity, but other attributes (such as those specified in the tag set of VHML v. 0.4 [50]) can be easily added as appropriate. Similarly, the above approach does not specifically classify overlapping emotions nor does it segment out lengthy emotional displays. This is left up to higher level semantic classifiers: just as a windowing system simply records mouse movements and button clicks, it is left up to higher level routines to reclassify these mouse events into drag-and-drop events or widget activation events.

Specifying gestures also has many issues that need to be addressed. First, there is a huge diversity of gestures for the human body and to try and identify a base set for all analysis and synthesis applications will take more maturation in the field. Second, each gesture has its own associated information and hence there are no standard parameters for all gestures (this doesn't even take into account the fact that the context of a conversational situation can alter the properties). Finally, of importance, gestures are very culturally dependent. A Talking Head that averts its gaze and does not look the user "in the eye" may indicate dishonesty in one culture but is a sign of respect for authority in another. It is possible to represent some of the more obvious gestures of the human body using a similar XML structure (Fig. 6) to that shown for emotion. It is important to include the time and intensity of a gesture and since gestures are also temporal instead of continuous, they also have duration.

Similar problems exist with this naive representation as for emotions but we also have:

- The gesture envelope, e.g. the attack, decay, sustain, and release of the gesture, which may be important for interpretation. A wave of the hand may signify "goodbye" if started and executed slowly but an abrupt, fast wave may indicate "definitely not".
- The body part(s) that the gesture affected (e.g. is the shake gesture: head or the whole body?). Also the orientation of the body part: a wave with the hand held horizontal may indicate "enough" rather than "goodbye".
- Other attributes that are important for interpreting the gesture.

A less naive format is shown in Fig. 7.

It is unclear whether every gesture involves a particular direction in space, but all gestures at least have a focus whether it be a crowd of people, a person

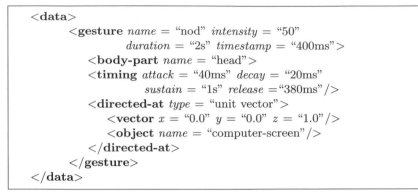

Fig. 7. Extensible structure for user gesture input

or a computer screen. Therefore, a **<directed-at>** element is needed. Again there exists the problem of trying to standardize all of the possible objects in real (or virtual) space that the user can gesture at, and all of the body parts that a gesture can be made with. A declaration section (Fig. 8) is provided for validation and the ability to share the represented information.

```
<objects>
        <object name = "computer-screen"/>
</objects>
<body-parts>
        <body-part name = "head"/>
</body-parts>
```

Fig. 8. Object description structure for gesture input

Another area that needs to be addressed is the problem of intent. A representation of gesture could possibly capture the intent (why the gesture was invoked), the mechanics (the physical way in which the gesture was invoked), or a middle ground (the type of gesture but not what it means). It is a wise standardization choice to incorporate each in the final design for the simple reason of being compatible over a wide range of applications. When considering that gestures can be interpreted in a number of different ways given the domain, using a standardized low-level representation such as MPEG-4 Facial and Body animation can provide a concrete representational level that can be interpreted in conjunction with domain. Interpretations may change, as human communication is better understood in the future. In standardizing this aspect, care should be taken to minimize loss of information as discussed in the objectives. Given this exploratory basis for a simple gUI framework, it needs to be implemented so as to be tested.

7 Implementation Issues

The challenge for a real-time format for emotion and gesture representation is the inter-working with a dialogue management system, often the core interface used in current anthropomorphic systems. The MetaFace framework [4] was an example ECA used to test the underlying theories of specifying complete human interaction. It was already based on MPEG-4 and VHML, and thus had the ability to vocalize and visually display emotion and gesture. The Dialogue Management system was a simple parsing technique based on word graphs [32]. A Dialogue Management tool was used in creating and maintaining the dialogues for the experiments. It used an XML-based markup language – Dialogue Management Tool Language (DMTL) [16] – to represent the dialogue and its states as a network. The DMTL specification was modified so that it could accept emotional and gestural input as well as the standard text stimulus. Emotions and gestures were simulated through the use of a GUI (Fig. 9), and, for testing purposes, the user could "emote" continually through the use of the buttons shown on the GUI. The VHML shown in Fig. 9 produces the rendered speech and gestures as well as the HTML in the bottom frame.

This test system would hopefully represent a typical scenario: consider a client/server architecture where the user is sitting being monitored by analysis equipment (whether it be video/audio analysis or head tracking) and this data is being sent at irregular intervals along with textual input to the server which must incorporate this continuous influx of data into a coherent dialogue. In our test case, through the use of a simple GUI, the user can influence the weighting of emotions and execute gestures. This system was meant to test the inter-working of text dialogue management, emotion, and gesture input. We were primarily interested in the continual arrival and processing of the emotional, gestural, and textual input. That is, the execution typical of a gUI framework. An emotion/gesture analysis system was *not* used.

The objective of the Dialogue Manager is to match an incoming emotion or gesture against the knowledge base (DMTL documents) and provide the best match as a response. Since emotion and gesture can be based on integer percentages for intensity, it is quite logical to provide a simple evaluation mechanism (i.e. "intensity == 100").

Emotion representation in this prototype language only allows for an intensity attribute; therefore when using the name of an emotion it is understood that it is referring to the intensity of that emotion. In order to provide this quite simple true/false evaluation mechanism for emotion, the <**evaluate**> element of DMTL needed to be redefined. The <**evaluate**> element can be used for defining a condition that has to be fulfilled before the dialogue is able to move into this particular state. For example, a variable can be set to imply that a state is visited (see Fig. 10).

These evaluate elements can be easily parsed to ascertain whether the result is true or false, thus providing a matching facility for DMTL. It is possible for the dialogue managing application to decide not only whether a

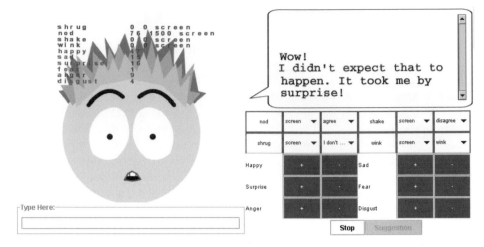

Surprised Example VHML

```
1:<?xml version="1.0"?>
2:<!DOCTYPE vhml SYSTEM "./vhml.dtd">
3:<vhml>
4:<p>
5:<surprised wait="1s" intensity="80"> Wow! <break/>
6:I didnt expect that to happen <eye-blink wait="300ms"/>
7:<eye-blink wait="300ms"/><break size="large"/>
8:it took me by surprise!</surprised>
9:</p>
10:<p target="1">
11:<embed type="html" src="example_surprised.html"/>
12:</p>
13:</vhml>
```

Fig. 9. The gUI prototype

```
<state name = "name" type = "entry">
     <stimulus>WHATIS VHML?</stimulus>
     ...
     <evaluate>visited State name</evaluate>
     ...
</state>
```

Fig. 10. Example of <evaluate> tag

condition is met or not, but also a "level" of how well this condition is met. For example, consider evaluating *"happy==100"* when the happy intensity actually equals 95. Instead of matching true or false the application can decide that it is close and thus give a ranked value based on its closeness. All of this is dependent on the application and its goals, however, and is not a concern of the representation scheme apart from the knowledge that there are different ways of interpreting the <**evaluate**> tag.

As mentioned, DMTL was modified to cater for input apart from the normal text. For example, a typical state of the Dialogue Manager may correspond to the modified DMTL segment of Fig. 11.

```
<state name = "im sorry" type = "entry">
 <stimulus type = "text">I'm very angry with you</stimulus>
 <stimulus type = "emotion">
  <evaluate variable = "angry" operator = ">" value = "70%"/>
  <evaluate variable = "happy" operator = "<" value = "20%"/>
 </stimulus>
 <stimulus type = "gesture">
  <evaluate variable = "intent" operator = "==" value = "aggressive"/>
 </stimulus>
 <response>I am so sorry for upsetting you!</response>
</state>
```

Fig. 11. Example DMTL state showing stimuli and evaluate conditions

This state can be reached if the input stimulus matches the <**stimulus**> data in the DMTL document. Then the <**evaluate**> tags are processed to see if the criteria are met and if so, the <**response**> is *synthesized* and communicated to the user. To better understand the above example, consider that the shown multiple <**stimulus**> elements are different multi-modal input options ("text", "emotion", and "gesture"). To match, these would be OR'ed together. As well, the <**evaluate**> elements within the stimulus must all be met for a 100% accurate match (evaluation1 *AND* evaluation2 *AND* evaluation3). As can be seen, the form of interaction can be very complex, depending on how the emotion stimulus is represented. This particular state will be reached and processed

- if the input text matches *"I'm very angry with you"*, *OR*
- the user is angry *AND* not happy, *OR*
- the user makes a gesture with an aggressive intent.

This complicated example pushes the boundary of what is possible with emotion and gesture analysis, but standardized representation should always aim for the most complicated cases.

Gestures are more complicated to evaluate with the DMTL <**evaluate**> element as they might not have one single attribute giving the intent, mechanics, and type of gesture for the domain. This implies that there exists a need for more variables for the <**evaluate**> tag.

8 Results of the Prototype System

It is of course hard to accurately simulate human emotion and gesture, but this was not the aim of the system – it was to test the robustness of the representation format. What was found in practical terms was that emotional input had to be updated at *finite* intervals because otherwise the ECA would become flooded with emotional input and important information would be processed too late to be of use. Tied to this issue is also the speed at which the knowledge base can be interrogated – every emotional stimulus creates a request to the Dialogue Management system.

Even though an attempt was made to transmit emotion and gesture frames in an efficient format, the real bottleneck may not be the connection but rather the capabilities of the gUI architecture. This is similar to early windowing systems where the overhead of processing "mouse movement events" threatened to bring processing to a standstill on the CPU. Similarly, the ECA application will receive the "processed" gUI events and the application may need to instigate a gUI event masking policy, so as to limit event saturation. As an example, previous to this research the MetaFace system interrogated the knowledge base by parsing DMTL documents as needed for each new stimulus. With the introduction of two extra modes of interaction, the knowledge base needed to be stored in memory in an efficient way for faster searching (especially when a pro-active ECA is constantly polling the dialogue manager). If a more complex system to that of DMTL and word graphs was used, then the bottleneck would surely get worse. So it appears that there needs to be a trade-off between the reactivity of the system (how quickly it reacts to a user's gesture) and the complexity of the interaction.

It was also seen as important for there to be some way to weight the <**evaluate**> (e.g. the fact that the gesture's *type* matches that of the <**evaluate**> element, being more important than the evaluation of intensity).

One issue that was not addressed in the demonstration system could become one of the biggest problems with multi-modal input. That is, is the overlap of text input, gesture, and emotion seen as one coherent stimulus or as separate disparate stimuli? It will be a challenge of future systems to accurately interpret the importance of each mode of input and how they relate to each other and over what time frame. For example, what if a web-based ECA asks a simple question, and the user is happy, says yes, nods, and clicks on a web page link all at the same time? Resolving this type of interaction may be one of the biggest challenges to future systems.

Another significant challenge to any concerted effort to standardize emotion and gesture representation is going to be the identification of a standard set of emotions and gestures, applicable to all cultures and all applications. That is, an ontology. XML cannot address this (nor should it) but this is a serious problem in many fields – everyone makes up their own element tags. A secondary challenge will be to provide a way to extend this base set and cater for different functionality. It can be pointed out that perhaps the first step in standardizing emotion and gesture is going to involve acquiring human mind and body experts in this computer-related field [18].

9 Conclusions

There is a need for supporting complete user interaction with gestalt User Interfaces in the software of the future. The application area for this technology is boundless, but the technology at this current junction is still lacking. By standardizing the analysis and synthesis of such interfaces, future research could build upon the expertise and learn from the mistakes of past software generations instead of "reinventing the wheel".

A gestalt User Interface can use anthropomorphic metaphors, to make it possible to reduce the conceptual load that a user must bear. The importance of both transcription and the need for a real-time representational format has been discussed as well as the benefits of empathy.

This chapter has also discussed the tentative steps undertaken in the *Mentor* and MetaFace research projects as well as the further development of VHML in addressing the real needs of multi-modal interaction in HCI.

This research has served its purpose in being a first step in exploring emotion and gesture representation as input for Embodied Character Agents. It has identified many more problems than it has solved, and in that respect can be used as a basis for further research and food for thought.

References

1. André, E., Rist, T., Müller, J.: Guiding the user through dynamically generated hypermedia presentations with a life-like character. In: *Proceedings International Conference on Intelligent User Interfaces* (1998) pp 21–28
2. Balabanovic, M., Shoham, Y., Yun, Y.: An adaptive agent for automated web browsing. *Journal of Image Representation and Visual Communication* **6**(4) (1995)
3. Beard, S.: Decisions underlying virtual conversational characters scripting languages. In: *Virtual Conversational Characters Workshop, Human Factors* (2002)
4. Beard, S.: MetaFace: A Virtual Face Metaphor and Framework. http://www.metaface.computing.edu.au/
5. Beard, S., Crossman, B., Cechner, P., Marriott, A.: FAQBot. In: *Pan Sydney Area Workshop on Visual Information Processing* (1999)
6. Beard, S., Reid, D.: MetaFace and VHML: A first implementation of the Virtual Human Markup Language. In: *AAMAS02 Embodied Conversational Character Workshop* (2002)
7. Brna, P., Cooper, B.: Marching to the wrong distant drum: Pedagogical agents, emotion and student modelling. In: *Second Workshop on Attitude, Personality and Emotions in User-Adapted Interaction* (2001)

8. Bryan, D., Gershman, A.: Aquarium: A novel user interface metaphor for large, online Stores. In: *11th International Workshop on Database and Expert Systems Applications (DEXA'00)* (2000)
9. Cahn, J.E.: The generation of affect in synthesized speech. *Journal of the American Voice I/O Society* **8**:1–19 (1990)
10. Cassell, J.: Embodied conversation: Integrating face and gestures into automatic spoken dialogue systems. *Communications of the ACM* **43**:70–78 (2000)
11. Cassell, J., Pelachaud, C., Badler, N., Steedman, M., Achorn, B., Becket, T., Douville, B., Prevost, S., Stone, M.: Animated conversation: Rule-based generation of facial expressions, gesture and spoken intonation for multiple conversational agents. *Proceedings ACM SIGGRAPH '94* (1994)
12. Conati, C.: Probabilistic assessment of user's emotions in educational games. *Journal of Applied Artificial Intelligence, special issue on "Merging Cognition and Affect in HCI"* (2002)
13. Cowie, R., Douglas-Cowie, E., Tsapatsoulis, N., Votsis, G., Kollias, S., Fellenz, W., Taylor, J.: Emotion recognition in human-computer interaction. *IEEE Signal Processing Magazine* **18**:32–80 (2001)
14. Dutoit, T.: *An Introduction to Text-to-Speech Synthesis* (Kluwer Academic, Dordrecht 1997)
15. Garrido, L., Marques, F., Pardas, M., Salembie, P., Vilaplana, V.: A hierarchical technique for image sequence analysis. In: *Workshop on Image Analysis for Multimedia Application Services (WIAMIS)* (1997) pp 13–20
16. Gustavsson, C., Strindlund, L., Wiknertz, E.: Dialogue management tool. In: *The Talking Head Technology Workshop of OZCHI2001, The Annual Conference for the Computer-Human Interaction Special Interest Group (CHISIG) of the Ergonomics Society of Australia* (2001)
17. Henton, C.: Taking a look at TTS. *Speech Technology Magazine* **8** (2003)
18. HumanMarkup.org. *HumanMarkup org: Human Traits and Expression through XML.* http://www.humanmarkup.org (2001)
19. ISO/IEC: *Text   for   ISO/IEC   FDIS   14496-1   Systems.* http://www.cselt.it/mpeg/working_documents.htm (1998)
20. ISO/IEC: *Text   for   ISO/IEC   FDIS   14496-2   Visual.* http://www.cselt.it/mpeg/working_documents.htm (1998)
21. Jennifer, H., Picard, R.: Digital processing of affective signals. In: *Proceedings ICASSP '98* (1998)
22. Johnson, W.L., Rickel, J.W., Lester, J.C.: Animated pedagogical agents: Face-to-Face interaction in interactive learning environments. *International Journal of Artificial Intelligence in Education* **11**:47–78 (2000)
23. Kay, A.: User interface: A personal view. In: *The Art of Human-Computer Interface Design*, ed Laurel, B. (Addison-Wesley, Reading, MA 1990) pp 191–207
24. Klein, J.: http://citeseer.nj.nec.com/klein99computer.html (1999)
25. Koster, M.:   World   Wide   Web   Wanderers,   Spiders   and   Robots. http://web.nexor.co.uk/mak/doc/robots/robots.html (1994)
26. Krenn, B.: *IST Cross-programme Concertation Meeting on Representation Formats/Languages* (2002)
27. Krueger, M.: Cognitive space. In: *Humane Interfaces: Questions of Method and Practice in Cognitive Technology*, ed Marsh, P., Gorayska, B., Mey, J. (Elsevier Singapore 1999) pp 219–228

28. Lisetti, C.L., Schiano, D.J.: Automatic facial expression interpretation: Where human-computer interaction, artificial intelligence and cognitive science intersect. *Facial Information Processing* **8**:185–235 (2000)
29. Lovgren, J.: How to choose good metaphors. *IEEE Software* **11**:86–88 (1994)
30. Marriott, A.: A facial animation case study for HCI: The VHML-based Mentor System. In: *MPEG-4 Facial Animation - The standard, implementations and applications*, ed Pandzic, I., Forchheimer, R. (Wiley, New York 2002)
31. Marriott, A.: *VHML* European Union IST (2002)
32. Marriott, A., Beard, S., Haddad, H., Pockaj, R., Stallo, J., Huynh, Q., Tschirren, B.: The face of the future. *Journal of Research and Practice in Information Technology* **32**:231–245 (2001)
33. Miller, P. W.: *Non-verbal Communication* (National Education Association, Washington, DC 1981)
34. Murray, I.R., Arnott, J.L.: Toward the simulation of emotion in synthetic speech: A review of the literature on human vocal emotion. *Journal of the Acoustical Society of America* **2**:1097–1108 (1993)
35. Optimoz Project. Mozilla Developers. http://optimoz.mozdev.org (2003)
36. Ostermann, J.: E-cogent: An electronic convincing agent. In: *MPEG-4 Facial Animation - The standard, implementations and applications*, ed Pandzic, I.S., Forchheimer, R. (Wiley, Chichester 2002)
37. Pandzic, I.S., Cannella, M., Davoine, F., Forchheimer, R., Lavagetto, F., Li, H., Marriott, A., Malassiotis, S., Pardas, M., Pockaj, R., Sannier, G.: The Inter-Face software platform for interactive virtual characters. In: *MPEG-4 Facial Animation - The standard, implementations and applications*, ed by Pandzic, I.S., Forchheimer, R. (Wiley Chichester UK 2002)
38. Pandzic, I.S., Forchheimer, R.: *MPEG-4 Facial Animation - The standard, implementations and applications* (Wiley Chichester UK 2002)
39. Pantic, M., Rothkrantz, L.J.M.: Automatic analysis of facial expressions: The state of the art. *IEEE Transactions on Pattern Analysis and Machine Intelligence* **22**:1424–1445 (2000)
40. Pelachaud, C., Ruttkay, Z., Marriott, A. (eds): *Embodied Conversational Characters as Individuals*. Workshop for the Second International Joint Conference on Autonomous Agents & Multi-Agent Systems (2003)
41. Picard, R.: *Affective computing*. MIT Media Lab, Perceptual Computing TR 321 (1995)
42. Picard, R., Klein, J.: Computers that recognise and respond to user emotion: Theoretical and practical implications. *Interacting with Computers* **14**:141–169 (2002)
43. Reynolds, C.J.: http://www.media.mit.edu/~carsonr/pdf/sm_thesis.pdf (2001)
44. Rist, T., Pelachaud, C., Ruttkay, Z., Marriott, A., Vilhjalmsson, H.: *Embodied conversational agents - let's specify and evaluate them!* Workshop at the First International Joint Conference on Autonomous Agents & Multi-Agent Systems (2002)
45. Scherer, K.L.: Speech and emotional states. In: *Speech Evaluation in Psychiatry*, ed Darby, J.K. (Grune and Stratton, New York 1981) pp 189–220
46. Schröder, M.: Experimental study of affect bursts. DFKI Institute of Phonetics, Saarland University (2002)
47. Shardanand, U., Maes, P.: Social information filtering: Algorithms for automating 'Word of Mouth'. In: *Proceedings of CHI-95* (1995)

48. Shaw, E., Ganeshan, R., Johnson, W., Millar, D.: Building a case for agent-assisted learning as a catalyst for curriculum reform in medical education. In: *Proceedings of the International Conference on Artificial Intelligence in Education* (1999)

49. Stamou, G.: *Emotionally Rich Man-Machine Interaction Systems (ERMIS)*. Image, Video and Multimedia Systems Lab – Dept of Electrical and Computer Engineering, National Technical University of Athens (2002)

50. VHML v. 0.4   http://www.vhml.org/document/VHML/2001/WD-VHML-20011123 (2001)

51. Vladimir, H. and Kacic, Z.: Analysis of prosodic features and development of automatic emotion detection of emotional speech. *EuroImage ICAV3D 2001* (2001)

52. W3C. *Multimodal Interaction Activity* http://www.w3.org/2002/mmi/ (2003)

53. Wells, J., Fuerst, W.: Domain-oriented interface metaphors: Designing web interfaces for effective customer interaction. In: *33rd Hawaii Conference on System Sciences* (2000)

54. Wertheimer, M.: Laws of organization in perceptual forms (Untersuchungen zur Lehre von der Gestalt II, in *Psychologische Forschung* 4:301–350 (1923)). In: *A source book of Gestalt psychology*, ed Ellis, W. (Routledge & Kegan Paul, London 1938) pp 71–88

55. Wonisch, D., Cooper, G.: Interface agents: Preferred appearance characteristics based upon context. In: *Virtual Conversational Characters Workshop (Human Factors 2002)* (2002)

56. Zelinsky, A., Heinzmann, J.: Real-time visual recognition of facial gestures for human-computer interaction. In: *IEEE International Conference on Automatic Face and Gesture Recognition* (1996) pp 351–356

A Behavior Language: Joint Action and Behavioral Idioms

Michael Mateas[1] and Andrew Stern[2]

[1] College of Computing and School of Literature, Communication and Culture
Georgia Institute of Technology, Atlanta, GA, USA
michaelm@cc.gatech.edu
www.cs.cmu.edu/ michaelm/
[2] InteractiveStory.net, Boston, MA, USA
andrew@interactivestory.net
www.interactivestory.net

Summary. This chapter presents ABL (A Behavior Language, pronounced "able"), a language specifically designed to support the creation of life-like computer characters (believable agents). Concurrent with our development of ABL, we are using the language to implement the believable agent layer of our interactive drama project, *Façade*. With code examples and case studies we describe the primary features of ABL, including sequential and parallel behaviors, joint goals and behaviors for multi-agent coordination, and reflective programming (meta-behaviors). Specific idioms are detailed for using ABL to author story-based believable agents that can maintain reactive, moment-by-moment believability while simultaneously performing in tightly coordinated, long-term dramatic sequences.

1 Introduction

ABL is based on the Oz Project [1] believable agent language Hap, developed by A.B. Loyall [16, 2]. Hap was designed to support the detailed expression of artistically chosen personality, automatic control of real-time interactive animation, and architectural support for many of the requirements of believable agents [15].

ABL extends Hap in several ways, most significantly by adding joint goals and behaviors, which support the multi-agent coordination required for the performance of dramatic action. ABL also changes Hap's syntax, making it more Java-like, and generalizes the mechanisms by which an ABL agent connects to a sensory-motor system, making it possible for others to use ABL in their own believable agent projects.

This chapter will discuss ABL by means of examples from *Façade*, as well as an early Oz believable agent project, the *Woggles* [17].

2 Why ABL?

Believable agents are applicable as non-player characters in interactive stories and games, as tour guides through virtual spaces, teachers and tutors in educational software, virtual salespeople for marketing products, and so on. To achieve a non-trivial degree of life-likeness in such agents, they must possess the ability to perform several intelligent activities in parallel – for example, to gaze, speak, walk, use objects, gesture with their hands, and convey facial expressions, all at the same time. Additionally, while performing these parallel behaviors, believable agents need to be reactive in immediate, varied, and fine-grained ways, so as to respond convincingly and satisfyingly to the user's moment-by-moment interaction. In ABL, an activity (e.g. walking to the user, or speaking a line of dialog) is represented as a goal, and each goal is supplied with one or more behaviors to accomplish its task. An active goal chooses one of its behaviors to try. A behavior is a series of steps that can occur sequentially or in parallel. Typically, once a behavior completes all of its steps, it succeeds and goes away. However, if any of its steps fail, then the behavior itself fails and the goal attempts to find a different behavior to accomplish its task, failing if no such alternative behavior can be found. Furthermore, a behavior may have subgoaled its own set of goals and behaviors. To keep track of all the active goals and behaviors and subgoal relationships, ABL maintains an *active behavior tree* (ABT).

In contrast to standard imperative languages one might use to control agents (e.g. C++, Java), in ABL an author can, in relatively few lines of code, specify collections of goals and behaviors that can cleanly inter-mix character actions, modulate their execution based on the continuously sensed state of the world, and perform local, context-specific reactions to a player's actions.

This paradigm of combining sequential and parallel behaviors, and propagating success and failure through the ABT, is the foundation of the power of ABL as a language for authoring believable agents. Parallel behaviors make it easy to author characters that pursue multiple goals and thus mix the performance of multiple behaviors. This powerful capability doesn't come for free – it effectively makes ABL a parallel programming language, thus introducing to the author the well-known complexities of parallel programming. ABL is designed to make simple character behavior easy to author with just a few lines of code, while still providing the power to let experienced authors write complex, expressive behavior. ABL's support for *joint* goals and behaviors helps the author to harness the expressive power of multi-agent teams of characters.

3 Application of ABL in *Façade*

We are using ABL to implement the believable agent layer of the *Façade* interactive drama architecture (Fig. 1). *Façade* is a serious attempt to move beyond traditional branching or hyperlinked narrative, to create a dramatically interesting virtual world inhabited by computer-controlled characters, within which the player experiences a story from a first-person perspective [20, 22]. The complete, real-time 3D, one-act interactive drama will be available in a free public release at the end of 2003.

Fig. 1. Screen capture from *Façade*

In the drama, Grace and Trip, a married couple in their early thirties, have invited the player over for drinks. The player soon learns that their marriage is in serious trouble, and in fact, tonight is the night that all their troubles are going to come to the surface. Whether and how their marriage falls apart, and the state of the player's relationship with Grace and Trip at the end of the story, depends on how the player interacts in the world. The player interacts by navigating in the world, manipulating objects, and through natural language dialog.

This project raises a number of interesting AI research issues, including drama management for coordinating plot-level interactivity, broad but shallow support for natural language understanding and discourse management, and autonomous believable agents in the context of interactive story worlds. This chapter focuses on the last issue, describing the idioms developed within ABL for organizing character behaviors. For details of the rest of the *Façade* architecture, including the drama manager and natural language processing system, see [20, 19, 18].

4 ABL Overview

This section provides an overview of the ABL language and discusses some of
the ways in which ABL modifies or extends Hap. The discussion of joint behaviors, the mechanism for multi-agent coordination, occurs in its own section
below.

4.1 Hap

Since ABL reimplements and extends Hap, this section briefly describes the
architecture of a Hap agent and the organization and semantics of the Hap
language. All examples use the ABL syntax. The definitive reference on Hap
is Loyall's dissertation [15].

The ABL compiler is written in Java and targets Java; the generated Java
code is supported by the ABL run-time system.

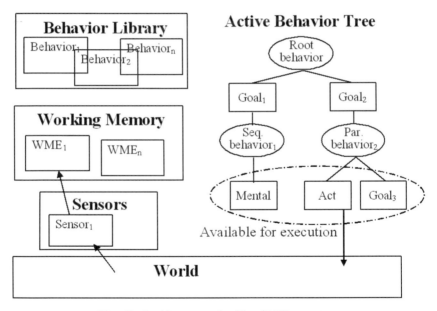

Fig. 2. Architecture of a Hap/ABL agent

The architecture of a Hap/ABL agent appears in Fig. 2. The agent has
a library of pre-written behaviors. Each behavior consists of a set of steps,
to be executed either sequentially or in parallel, that accomplish a goal. The
current execution state of the agent is captured by the active behavior tree
(ABT) and working memory. The ABT contains the currently active goals
and behaviors. The ABT is a tree rather than a stack because some behaviors
execute their steps in parallel, thus introducing parallel lines of expansion in

the program state. The leaves of the ABT constitute the conflict set. The agent continuously executes a decision cycle, during which a leaf step is chosen for execution. As each step is executed, it either succeeds or fails. In a sequential behavior, step success makes the next step available for execution. When the last step of a sequential behavior succeeds, or when all steps of a parallel behavior have succeeded, the enclosing behavior succeeds. For both sequential and parallel behaviors, if any step fails, it causes the enclosing behavior to fail. In this way, success and failure propagate through the ABT.

The four basic step types are introduced in the example behavior code below. For now, note that one of the step types is act, which performs a physical action with the agent's body, such as taking a step or grasping an object. The exact details of the execution of a physical action depend on both the agent's body and the world. For example, *Façade* agents have virtual, animated bodies within a real-time, graphical, 3D story world; however, one could just as well use ABL to implement behavior for physical robot agents, text-based agents, etc.

Working memory contains any information the agent needs to keep track of during execution. This information is organized as a collection of working memory elements (WMEs). WMEs are like instances in an object-oriented language; every WME has a type plus some number of typed fields that can take on values. WMEs are also the mechanism by which an agent becomes aware of sensed information. Sensors report information about changes in the world by writing that information into WMEs. Hap/ABL has a number of mechanisms for writing behaviors that are continuously reactive to the contents of working memory, and thus to sensed changes in the world. The details of sensors, like actions, depend on the specific world and agent body.

4.2 Example Behaviors

Hap/ABL programs are organized as collections of behaviors. In the example sequential behavior shown below, an agent waits for someone to knock on a door, sighs, then opens the door and greets the guest.

```
sequential behavior AnswerTheDoor() {
    WME w;
    with (success_test { w = (KnockWME) } ) wait;
    act sigh();
    subgoal OpenDoor();
    subgoal GreetGuest();
    mental_act { deleteWME(w); }
}
```

This behavior demonstrates the four basic step types, namely wait, act, subgoal, and mental_act. wait steps are never chosen for execution; a naked wait step in a sequential behavior would block the behavior from executing past the wait. However, when combined with a success_test, a wait step can be used to make a demon that waits for a condition to become true. Success tests are continuously monitored conditions that, when they become true, cause their associated step to immediately succeed. Though in this example the success_test is associated with a wait step to make a demon, it can be associated with any step type.

Success tests, as well as other tests that will be described shortly, perform their test against the agent's working memory. In this example, the success_test is looking for WMEs of type KnockWME, which presumably is placed in the agent's working memory when someone knocks on a door. Since there are no field constraints in the test, the test succeeds as soon as a KnockWME appears.

An act step tells the agent's body (sensory-motor system) to perform an action. For graphical environments such as *Façade*, physical acts will ultimately be translated into calls to the animation engine, though the details of this translation are hidden from the Hap/ABL program. In this example, the act makes the body sigh. Note that physical acts can fail – if the sensory-motor system determines that it is unable to carry out the action, the corresponding act step fails, causing the enclosing behavior to fail.

Subgoal steps establish goals that must be accomplished in order to accomplish the behavior. The pursuit of a subgoal within a behavior recursively results in the selection of a behavior to accomplish the subgoal.

Mental acts are used to perform bits of pure computation, such as mathematical computations or modifications to working memory. In the final step of the example, the mental_act deletes the KnockWME (making a call to a method defined on ABL agents), since the knocking has now been dealt with. In ABL, mental acts are written in Java.

The next example demonstrates how Hap/ABL selects a behavior to accomplish a subgoal through signature matching and precondition satisfaction.

```
sequential behavior OpenDoor() {
  precondition {
    (KnockWME doorID :: door)
    (PosWME spriteID == door pos :: doorPos)
    (PosWME spriteID == me pos :: myPos)
    (Util.computeDistance(doorPos, myPos) > 100)
  }
  specificity 2;
  // Too far to walk, yell for knocker to come in
  subgoal YellAndWaitForGuestToEnter(doorID);
}

sequential behavior OpenDoor() {
  precondition { (KnockWME doorID :: door) }
  specificity 1;
  // Default behavior - walk to door and open
}
```

In this example there are two sequential behaviors OpenDoor(), either of which could potentially be used to satisfy the goal OpenDoor(). The first behavior opens the door by yelling for the guest to come in and waiting for them to open the door. The second behavior (details elided) opens the door by walking to the door and opening it. When AnswerTheDoor() pursues the subgoal OpenDoor(), Hap/ABL determines, based on signature matching, that there are two behaviors that could possibly open the door. The precondition of both behaviors is executed. In the event that only one of the preconditions is satisfied, that behavior is chosen as the method to use to accomplish the subgoal. In the event that both preconditions are satisfied, the behavior with the highest specificity is chosen. If there are multiple satisfied behaviors with highest specificity, one is chosen at random. In this example, the first Open-Door() behavior is chosen if the lazy agent is too far from the door to walk there ("too far" is arbitrarily represented as a distance > "100").

The precondition demonstrates the testing of the fields of a WME. The :: operator assigns the value of the named WME field on the left of the operator to the variable on the right[3]. This can be used both to grab values from working memory that are then used in the body of the behavior, and to chain constraints through the WME test.

The last example demonstrates parallel behaviors and context conditions.

```
parallel behavior YellAndWaitForGuestToEnter(int doorID) {
    precondition { (CurrentTimeWME t :: startT)}
    context_condition {(CurrentTimeWME t <= startT + 10000)}
    number_needed_for_success 1;
    with (success_test {{DoorOpenWME door == doorID)}) wait,
    with (persistent) subgoal YellForGuest(doorID);
}
```

In a parallel behavior, the steps are pursued simultaneously. YellAndWait-ForGuestToEnter(int) simultaneously yells "come in" toward the door (the door specified by the integer parameter) and waits to actually see the door open. The persistent modifier on the YellForGuest(int) subgoal makes the subgoal be repeatedly pursued, regardless of whether the subgoal succeeds or fails (one would imagine that the behavior that does the yelling always succeeds). The number_needed_for_success annotation (only usable on parallel behaviors) specifies that only one step has to succeed in order for the behavior to succeed. In this case, that one step would be the demon step waiting for the door to actually open. The context_condition is a continuously monitored condition that must remain true during the execution of a behavior. If the context condition fails during execution, then the behavior immediately fails. In this example, the context condition tests the current time, measured in milliseconds, against the time at which the behavior started. If after 10 seconds the door has not

---

[3] In ABL, a locally scoped, appropriately typed variable is automatically declared if it is assigned to in a WME test and has not been previously explicitly declared.

yet opened (the guest is not coming in), then the context condition will cause the behavior to fail.

As failure propagates upwards through the subgoal chain, it will cause the first OpenDoor() behavior to fail, and eventually reach the OpenDoor() subgoal in AnswerTheDoor(). The subgoal will then note that there is another OpenDoor() behavior that has not been tried yet and whose precondition is satisfied; this behavior will be chosen in an attempt to satisfy the subgoal. So if the guest does not enter when the agent yells for a while, the agent will then walk over to the door and open it.

These examples give a sense for the Hap semantics which ABL reimplements and extends. There are many other features of Hap implemented in ABL that are not possible to re-describe here, including how multiple lines of expansion mix (based on priority, blocking on physical acts, and a preference for pursing the current line of expansion), declaration of behavior and step conflicts (and the resulting concept of suspended steps and behaviors), and numerous annotations that modify the default semantics of failure and success propagation [15].

4.3 ABL Extensions

ABL extends Hap in a number of ways, including:

- Generalizing the mechanisms for connecting to the sensory-motor system. The ABL run-time provides abstract superclasses for sensors and actions. To connect an ABL program to a new sensory-motor system (e.g. an animation engine, a robot), the author defines specific sensors and actions as concrete subclasses of the abstract sensor and action classes. ABL also includes additional language constructs for binding sensors to WMEs. ABL then takes responsibility for calling the sensors appropriately when bound WMEs are referenced in working memory tests.
- Atomic behaviors. Atomic behaviors prevent other active behaviors from mixing in. Atomic behaviors are useful for atomically updating state (e.g. updating multiple WMEs atomically), though they should be used sparingly, as a time-consuming atomic behavior could impair reactivity.
- Reflection. ABL gives behaviors reflective access to the current state of the ABT, supporting the authoring of meta-behaviors that match on patterns in the ABT and dynamically modify other running behaviors. Supported ABT modifications include succeeding, failing or suspending a goal or behavior, and modifying the annotations of a subgoal step, such as changing the persistence or priority. Safe reflection is provided by wrapping all ABT nodes in special WMEs. Pattern matching on ABT state is then accomplished through normal WME tests. A behavior can only touch the ABT through the reflection API provided on these wrapper WMEs.
- Multiple named memories. Working memories can be given a public name, which then, through the name, are available to all ABL agents. Any WME

test can simultaneously reference multiple memories (the default memory is the agent's private memory). In *Façade*, named memories are useful for giving agents access to a global story memory.

The most significant ABL extension of Hap is support for joint goals and behaviors, described in the following section.

5 Joint Goals and Behaviors

In order to facilitate the coordination of characters in the carrying out of dramatic action, we extended the semantics of Hap in a manner analogous to the STEAM multi-agent coordination framework [31]. This section describes *joint goals and behaviors*, ABL's support for multi-agent coordination.

The driving design goal of joint behaviors is to combine the rich semantics for individual expressive behavior offered by Hap with support for the automatic synchronization of behavior across multiple agents.

In ABL, the basic unit of coordination is the joint goal. When a goal is marked as joint, ABL enforces, in a manner transparent to the programmer, coordinated entry into and exit from the behaviors chosen to accomplish the goal. The keyword joint can be used to modify both goals and behaviors, telling ABL that entry into and exit from the joint behavior should be automatically coordinated with team members.

5.1 ABL's Under-the-Hood Negotiation Process for Joint Goals and Behaviors

Entry into a behavior occurs when the behavior is chosen to satisfy a subgoal. *Exit* from the behavior occurs when the behavior succeeds, fails, or is suspended. ABL's algorithm for executing a joint subgoal and coordinating entry appears in Fig. 3.

---

1. The initiating agent chooses a joint behavior for the joint goal based on signature matching, precondition satisfaction, and specificities.
2. If a joint behavior is found for the joint goal, mark the goal as negotiating and broadcast an intention to enter the goal to all team members, otherwise fail the goal.
3. If all team members respond with an intention to enter the joint goal, add the joint behavior (and behavior children) to the ABT.
4. If any team member reports an intention to refuse entry to the joint goal, broadcast an intention to refuse entry and fail the behavior when all team members respond with an intention to refuse entry.

Fig. 3. Agent initiating a joint behavior via joint subgoal execution

When ABL executes a joint goal, a behavior is chosen for the goal using normal Hap behavior selection methods, with the additional constraint that the behavior must be joint (marked with the joint keyword).

Joint behaviors include a specification of the team members who must participate in the behavior. If a joint behavior is found for the joint goal, ABL marks the goal as negotiating and begins negotiating entry with team members specified in the joint behavior. The negotiating joint goal is removed from the conflict set, blocking that line of expansion until negotiation completes. All other parallel lines of expansion are still pursued. If the negotiation takes a while, perhaps because there are a large number of distributed teammates who are synchronizing during the negotiation, all negotiating agents continue to execute the decision cycle and engage in behavior. An intention-to-enter message is sent to all team members. The initiating message includes information about the goal signature and arguments.

The goal remains in the *negotiating* state until all team members respond with an intention to enter or an intention to refuse entry. If all agents respond with intention-to-enter messages, this signals that all agents in the team have found appropriate behaviors in their local behavior libraries; the goal state is changed to *executing*, and the selected behavior and its steps are added to the ABT. If any agent responds with an intention to refuse entry, presumably because, given the goal signature and goal arguments, it could not find a satisfied joint behavior, the initiating agent sends all team members an intention to refuse entry. When all agents report that they intend to refuse entry, the initiating agent fails the joint behavior (whose steps never actually got a chance to execute). This causes the goal to attempt to find a different joint behavior with satisfied precondition, perhaps one with a different set of team members. Just as with a normal (non-joint) goal, if no such alternate behavior can be found, the goal fails.

Figure 3 shows the entry negotiation algorithm for the *initiator* of a joint goal, that is the agent who originally executes the joint goal step, and who thus begins the joint behavior selection and negotiation process. The teammates of a joint goal initiator use a similar negotiation algorithm. The only difference is that for non-initiators, a joint goal with appropriate signature and arguments must be created and attached to the root collection behavior of the ABT.

---

1. An initiating agent broadcasts to all team members an intention to exit (succeed, fail, or suspend) an executing joint goal.
2. All agents receiving an intention to exit respond by broadcasting to all team members their own intention to exit (succeed, fail, or suspend).
3. When all team members respond with the appropriate intention to exit, the joint goal is succeeded, failed, or suspended as appropriate.

Fig. 4. Agent exiting a joint behavior

The algorithm for coordinating exit from a joint behavior is shown in Fig. 4. For example, assume that a joint behavior has been successfully entered by a team. At this point each member of the team is executing a joint behavior from their local behavior library with the same signature, arguments, and team members. One of the team members, in executing their local joint behavior, encounters a condition where they should exit the behavior. Perhaps the last step of the behavior succeeds, causing the joint behavior and goal to succeed, or the context condition fails, causing the joint behavior and goal to fail, or a higher priority conflicting goal (either joint or non-joint) enters the ABT, causing the joint goal to suspend. The agent encountering this situation becomes the initiator of the intention to exit (the exit initiator does not have to be the same agent as the entry initiator). The exit initiator marks the joint goal as negotiating and broadcasts the appropriate intention to exit to all team members. While the joint goal is in the negotiating state it blocks that line of expansion; all other lines of expansion in the ABT are still active.

As each team member receives an intention to exit, it marks its local version of the joint goal as negotiating and broadcasts an exit intention. Once exit intentions have been received from all team members, an agent exits the negotiating goal (succeeds, fails, or suspends the goal).

5.2 Example of Basic Joint Goal and Behavior Support

This section provides a simple example of the joint goal negotiation protocol in action, based on the follow-the-leader behavior of the *Woggles* [17].

Fig. 5. Close-up of three Woggles

The Woggle world, an early demonstration system produced by the Oz Project, consists of a Dr. Seuss-like landscape inhabited by three Woggles – the shy Shrimp, the aggressive Wolf, and the friendly Bear (Fig. 5). As the Woggles play, fight and hang out with each other, the player is able to enter the Woggle world as a fourth Woggle.

The diagram in Fig. 6 shows the original behavior structure for a follower playing follow-the-leader. The behavior is decomposed into three sub-behaviors, one to copy the leader's jumps, one to copy the leader's squashes, and one to monitor whether the follower is falling too far behind the leader. Each of these behaviors is in turn decomposed into a sensing behavior that gathers information from the world (e.g. see jump, check if you are behind), and a behavior that acts on the sensed information (e.g. copy the jump recorded by the "see jump" behavior). Communication between behaviors takes place via memory elements posted to and matched from the agent's working memory.

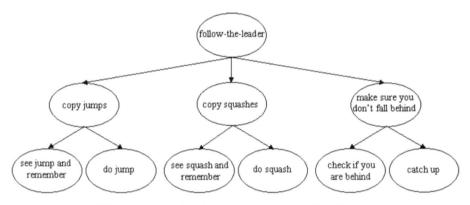

Fig. 6. Original behavior structure for the follower

The diagram in Fig. 7 shows the original behavior structure for the leader playing follow-the-leader. The top-level behavior is decomposed into two sub-behaviors, one to do "fun stuff" (the hopping and squashing that the follower will copy) and one to monitor whether the follower has fallen behind. The "fun stuff" behavior is further decomposed into three different ways to have fun. The "make sure follower does not fall behind" behavior is decomposed into a sensing behavior that monitors the follower's activity, and a behavior that waits for the follower to catch up in the event that the follower did fall behind. Note that both Fig. 6 and Fig. 7 elide the sequential structure of the behaviors, showing only the persistent, parallel, subgoal structure. The complete "lead-the-follower" behavior first chooses a co-Woggle to invite, moves over to the invitee, offers an invitation to play follow-the-leader (using Woggle body language), and then, if the invitee signals that the invitation is accepted, starts

the two parallel behaviors "fun stuff" and "monitor follower" diagrammed in
Fig. 7.

For two Woggles to play a game of follow-the-leader, one of the Woggles
must first decide that it wants to be a leader and successfully invite the other
Woggle to be a follower. The two Woggles then independently execute their
respective behavior hierarchies. These two independent hierarchies coordinate
via sensing, by mutually monitoring each other's physical activities. In addition to the follow-the-leader behavior hierarchy, both Woggles have a number
of other behaviors executing in parallel. These behaviors are monitoring the
world for certain actions, such as someone saying "hi", a friend being attacked by someone else, someone inviting the Woggle to play a game, etc. If
the follower pauses in the middle of the game to respond to one of these world
events, perhaps suspending its local follow-the-leader behavior hierarchy, the
leader will experience this as the follower falling behind. If the follower takes
too long to get back to the game, the leader will "time out" and the lead-the-
follower behavior will fail (stop executing with failure). The leader will then
start doing something else.

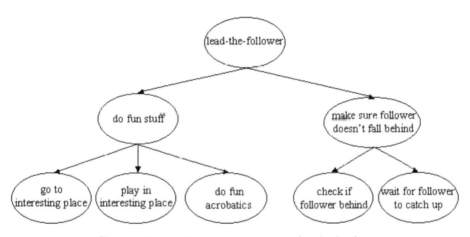

Fig. 7. Original behavior structure for the leader

However, unless similar timeouts have been placed in the right behaviors
in the follower, the follower, after completing the interruption, will unsuspend
and continue playing follow-the-leader. In fact, the original Woggle code *does
not* have the appropriate timeouts in the follower, and so this condition can
happen.

At this point, the former leader is jumping around the world doing its own
thing while the follower dutifully follows behind copying the leader's actions;
the leader is not aware that the follower's actions are in any way related to the
leader, and the follower has no idea that the leader is no longer playing follow-
the-leader. This is one example of the coordination failures that can happen

```
//Leader's version of FollowTheLeader
joint parallel behavior FollowTheLeader {
     teammembers Shrimp, Bear;
     precondition { <I'm a leader and feel like leading> }

     subgoal DoFunStuff();
     subgoal MakeSureFollowerDoesntFallBehind();
}

//Follower's version of FollowTheLeader
joint parallel behavior FollowTheLeader {
     teammembers Shrimp, Bear;
     precondition { <I'm a follower and feel like playing> }

     subgoal CopyJumps();
     subgoal CopySquashes();
     subgoal MakeSureYouDontFallBehind();
}
```

Fig. 8. Joint behaviors for follow-the-leader

even in a rather simple joint action when the joint activity is produced through the *ad hoc* synchronization of independent behavior hierarchies.

Using ABL's joint behaviors, the tops of the leader's and follower's follow-the-leader behavior hierarchies are shown in Fig. 8. To simplify the example, consider just two of the Woggles, Shrimp and Bear. Since either can be a leader or follower, both Woggles have both the leader and follower versions of the behavior in their behavior libraries. One of them, say Bear, decides to play follow-the-leader – this decision is made by logic in some other behavior, perhaps a high-level motivational behavior, resulting in the creation of a WME, LeaderWME, indicating that Bear wants to lead a game of follow-the-leader, a body language request to Shrimp to play, and the execution of joint subgoal FollowTheLeader().

The execution of the joint subgoal results in ABL trying to find a satisfied joint behavior to accomplish the goal. The preconditions distinguish between the leader and follower cases. If the behaviors did not have preconditions testing LeaderWME, then the initiator of FollowTheLeader() might inadvertently select the follower version of the behavior. Sensing could also be used to distinguish the two cases, selecting the leader version if a body language request to play from another Woggle has not been recently seen, and the follower version if it has. Once ABL has selected the leader version of joint behavior FollowTheLeader() for Bear, the subgoal FollowTheLeader() is marked as negotiating and a request-to-enter is sent to Shrimp. ABL creates a joint subgoal FollowTheLeader() at the root of Shrimp's ABT and selects the follower version of the behavior from his joint behavior library, again using preconditions to distinguish cases. Note that the preconditions can also be used to add personality-specific tests as to whether the Woggle feels like playing follow-the-leader. In Shrimp's case, for example, Shrimp may only feel like playing if he has not recently been picked on by another Woggle. Assuming that Shrimp's precondition is satisfied, ABL sends an intention-to-enter from Shrimp to Bear. Both Shrimp and Bear have received intentions-to-enter from all team members, so ABL adds their respective selected behaviors to their ABTs; they are now both playing follow-the-leader.

Once coordinated entry into FollowTheLeader() is established, they continue playing follow-the-leader until one of them exits the behavior. Perhaps Wolf threatens Shrimp in the middle of the game, causing Shrimp to engage in high-priority fear reaction that suspends his local FollowTheLeader() goal. The goal is marked as negotiating and an intention to suspend is sent to Bear. ABL marks Bear's goal as negotiating and sends an intention to suspend to Shrimp. They have both received intentions to suspend from all team members, so ABL locally suspends the FollowTheLeader() goal for each. Similar exit negotiations ensure synchronization on goal success and failure. Every team member is guaranteed that if it is locally executing the joint goal FollowThe-Leader(), all team members are executing the joint goal FollowTheLeader().

5.3 Nested/Multiple Joint Goals and Behaviors

Joint goals and behaviors thus synchronize behavior execution across agents; the entry into a joint behavior is precisely a synchronization point. Joint and individual behaviors can be nested arbitrarily within the behavior hierarchy, depending on the granularity of the synchronization required. In the simple joint behaviors in Fig. 8, only the FollowTheLeader() behavior is joint. However, smaller granularity behaviors could also be joint. For example, jump and squash could be implemented as joint behaviors within the follow-the-leader behavior hierarchy. When a joint jump is entered, it would coordinate the leader and followers for the specific act of jumping. In essence, this would establish an automatic pattern of communication between the Woggles saying "now the leader is going to do a jump and all the followers should copy it". In addition, an agent can be committed to multiple simultaneous joint goals with different team members. For example, Shrimp could be a follower committed to a FollowTheLeader() goal with Bear while simultaneously committed to a Hassle() goal with Wolf (a goal coordinating Wolf and Shrimp in Wolf hassling Shrimp). As the two behaviors mixed together, Shrimp would keep a wary eye on Wolf, occasionally slinking or groveling, while trying to keep up in follow-the-leader with Bear.

5.4 Full Complexity of Joint Goal Negotiation

So far this chapter has described a simplified version of ABL's automatic joint goal negotiation protocol. The full negotiation protocol must appropriately handle a number of edge cases and race conditions, specifically:

1. ABL must achieve a consistent team state when multiple team members simultaneously intend to exit a joint goal for inconsistent reasons (e.g. three different team members simultaneously try to fail, succeed, and suspend the same joint goal).
2. ABL must resolve inconsistencies resulting from out-of-order receipt of negotiation messages. Messages may arrive out of order due to the message transport mechanism or due to differences in the execution speed of different team members.
3. ABL must resolve negotiation conflicts arising within a single agent due to the parallel pursuit of multiple goals. For example, in the middle of a negotiation to enter a goal, a parent goal may suspend, and thus cause the recursive suspension of all individual and joint goals in the tree rooted at the parent goal.

The details of the full joint goal framework are beyond the scope of this chapter; see [18] for more detail. The bottom line is that joint goals and behaviors guarantee coordinated entry and exit across arbitrarily sized teams consisting of fully asynchronous, arbitrarily scheduled team members.

6 *Façade* ABL Idioms: Implementing Dramatic Beats

Developing a believable agent language such as ABL involves simultaneously defining and implementing language constructs that support the authoring of expressive behavior, and the exploration of idioms for expressive behavior *using* the language. This section describes the ABL idioms developed for *Façade*.

In [22, 21] we argued that much work in believable agents is organized around the principle of strong autonomy, and that, for story-based believable agents, this assumption of strong autonomy is problematic. An agent organized around the notion of strong autonomy chooses its next action based on local perception of its environment plus internal state corresponding to the goals and possibly the emotional state of the agent. All decision making is organized around the accomplishment of the individual, private goals of the agent. But believable agents in a story must also participate in story events, which requires making decisions based on global story state (the entire past history of interaction considered *as* a story) and tightly coordinating the activity of multiple agents so as to accomplish joint story goals. In order to resolve the tension between local and global control of characters, in *Façade* we organize behaviors around the *dramatic beat*. In the theory of dramatic writing, the beat is the smallest unit of dramatic action [23]. In *Façade,* a beat is a ∼60-second-long dramatic interaction between characters such as a brief conflict about a topic, a short psychological headgame, or the revelation of an important secret.

Beat-specific ABL behaviors provide the procedural knowledge necessary to perform an interactive dramatic beat. This section focusses on describing the ABL idioms used for authoring such behaviors. In *Façade*, beat sequencing (selecting the next beat to make active) is handled by the drama manager; see [20, 19, 18] for details of the drama manager.

6.1 Beat Goal and Handler Behaviors

Beats are organized around a collection of *beat goal behaviors* – the dramatic content the beat is designed to communicate to the player through animated performance. Our authoring strategy for handling player interaction within a beat is to specify the "canonical" beat goal behavior logic (i.e. what dramatic performance the author intends the beat to accomplish), as well as a collection of beat-specific *handler behaviors* that modify this default logic in response to player interaction. In order to modify the default logic, the handler behaviors make use of meta-ABL functionality to modify the ABT state.

While handler behaviors can in principle arbitrarily modify the ABT state, most fall into one of two general classes – *mix-in* handler behaviors that add an additional beat goal behavior in the middle of a beat while keeping the rest of the sequencing the same, and *re-sequencing* handler behaviors that more radically reorganize the beat goal sequence. The ability to factor behavior into sequences that achieve longer term temporal structures, and meta-behaviors that modify these longer term temporal structures, is a powerful idiom enabled by ABL's support for reflection.

6.2 Inside a Beat Goal Behavior

Within individual beat goals, joint goals and behaviors are used to coordinate the characters in the performance of dramatic action. As can be seen in Fig. 9, the detailed, coordinated, physical performance of even a single line of dialog can be quite rich. The characters must engage in coordinated dramatic performance to accomplish the intentions of the beat goals, while simultaneously pursuing longer term, individual goals that cross beat goal boundaries. (Cross-beat behaviors are described later in this chapter.) This is achievable because ABL can support the autonomous pursuit of individual goals in parallel with tightly coordinated team activity, in the ways described in the previous section of this chapter.

6.3 Organizing Beat Goal Behaviors

The high-level beat goal specification for an example beat, "Argue about Grace's decorating", appears in Fig. 10. The author intends this beat to reveal conflict in Grace and Trip's marriage by hinting at the fact that there is something weird about Grace's obsessive decorating of their apartment. In this beat Grace is trying to get the player to agree that something is wrong with her current decorating scheme, while Trip is trying to get the player to

Grace: ... but looking at it here **in** the apartment, it just looks like ... (laugh half-lighthearted, half-bitter) **a** monstrosity!

Grace physical performance:

- Throughout the line Grace physically adjusts to face the player.
- On the bold words she slightly nods her head and barely raises both arms.
- At the beginning of the line she looks at the armoire with a frown, changing to a serious expression a short way into the dialog.
- At the beginning of the line her mood becomes anxious.

Trip physical performance:

- Throughout the line Trip physically adjusts to face the player.
- At the beginning of Grace's line he turns (just his head and eyes) to look at Grace.
- A short way into Grace's line he gets an impatient expression on his face.
- A short way into Grace's line he reacts with an anxious reaction.

Fig. 9. Detailed performance specification for one line of dialog

---

Transition In (the no-subtopic version)

G: So, Player, I'm hoping you can help me understand where I went wrong with my new decorating (bitter laugh).
T: (pacifying tone) Oh, Grace, let's not do that.

Address subtopic, part 1 (armoire subtopic)

G: (sigh) You know, when I saw this armoire on the showroom floor, I thought it had such a clean, simple look to it...
T: It's a nice choice.

Address subtopic, part 2 (armoire subtopic)

G: ...but looking at it here in the apartment, it just looks like... (laugh half-lighthearted, half-bitter) a monstrosity!
T: (under-breath impatient sigh) uhh...

Wait Timeout (default version)

(G looks impatiently between the object and the player, T fidgets)

Transition Out (lean toward Grace affinity)

G: Ah, yes, I've been waiting for someone to say that!
T: (frustrated) What are you talking about?
G: Trip, our friend is just being honest about my decorating, which I appreciate.
T: (sigh) But I still think this looks fine... (annoyed)

Fig. 10. Excerpts from the beat goal specification for the "Argue about Grace's decorating" beat

agree that it looks great and everything is fine. This beat is an instance of what we call an "affinity game".

In our idiom for *Façade*, beats generally have a transition-in beat goal responsible for establishing the beat context and possibly relating the beat to action that happened prior to the beat, a transition-out beat goal communicating the dramatic action (change in values) that occurred in the beat as a function of player interaction within the beat, and a small number of beat goals between the transition-in and transition-out that reveal information and set up the little interaction game within the beat.

In our example decorating beat, the transition-in beat goal introduces the ostensible topic of the beat: Grace thinks something is wrong with her decorating. The particular transition-in shown in Fig. 10 is the most "generic" transition-in, the one to use if the interaction prior to this beat did not have anything to do with the room or decorating. Other transition-in beat goals are available in this beat for cases in which the player has somehow referred to decorating just prior to this beat being sequenced, for example by referring to an object associated with decorating such as the couch or the armoire[4].

In the body of this beat, the two "address subtopic" beat goals, Grace specifically critiques some aspect of her decorating. Trip objects and thinks it looks fine, revealing conflict between them. For this beat there are a number of different "address subtopic" beat goals for different decorating subtopics, corresponding to different objects in the room; at the beginning of this beat goal behavior, if the player has not referred to a specific object, one is chosen at random, otherwise the object referenced by the player (perhaps in an interaction just prior to this beat) is used.

The beat goal sequence described up to this point is the default logic for the beat; that is, the sequence of activity that would happen in the absence of player interaction. Of course, the whole point of an interactive drama is that the player can interact – thus there needs to be some mechanism for incorporating interaction into the default beat logic. This is the job of *handler behaviors*.

6.4 Incorporating Player Interaction: Handler Behaviors

Each handler behavior is a demon that waits for some particular type of player interaction and "handles" it accordingly. Player interaction includes dialog interaction (in *Façade*, the player can speak to the characters at any time by typing text) and physical interaction (e.g. the player moves and stands next to some object). Every beat specifies some beat-specific handlers; additionally, there are global handlers for handling interactions for which there are no beat-specific responses supplied by the current beat. Handlers are meta-behaviors;

---

[4] "References" to an object can happen verbally, e.g. the player types "I like the couch", and/or physically, by standing near an object and looking at it or picking it up.

they make use of reflection to modify the default logic of the beat. Handlers fall into two broad classes: mix-in handlers, which primarily mix a response into the current beat, and re-sequence handlers, which modify the sequencing logic of the current beat.

The most straightforward use of mix-in handlers is to choose a transition-out beat goal when the player interacts during the "wait-timeout" beat goal. The transition-out communicates how the player's interaction within the beat has changed the story situation. One of the primary story values in *Façade* is the player's affinity with the characters, whether the player is allied with Trip, with Grace, or is neutral. Affinity in *Façade* is zero-sum – if the player moves toward positive affinity with Trip, the affinity with Grace becomes negative. For this beat there are three transition-out beat goals, one each for the cases of the affinity changing towards Trip, one for toward Grace, and one for staying neutral. The example transition-out beat goal in Fig. 10 is the one for an affinity change toward Grace; in this case the player has agreed with Grace (e.g. "Yes, the armoire is ugly"), and, perhaps surprisingly, Grace is happy to hear someone say that.

However, the player, free to speak and act at any time, could have interacted earlier in the beat before the body beat goals had completed – that is, before the conflict for the beat had been fully established. For example, imagine that after Grace's line in the transition-in of the decorating beat ("So, Player, I'm hoping you can help me understand where I went wrong with my new decorating"), the player quickly agrees with Grace ("Yeah, it looks bad"). Since the beat conflict has not been established, it would not make sense to choose the transition-out yet. In this case, a beat-specific mix-in beat goal occurs[5], during which Trip says "Well hold on, hold on, take a closer look, give it a chance to soak in a little." To accomplish this, a beat-specific mix-in handler behavior written to handle early-agreement first aborts the current active beat goal behavior, then spawns a particular high-priority beat goal behavior designed to respond to the agreement. Because of its high priority, the newly mixed-in agreement-response beat goal behavior will happen first; then, the original beat goal behaviors will continue in their normal order. Beat goal behaviors are responsible for determining if they had been interrupted by mixed-in beat goals, and are designed to perform their content in alternate ways as needed.

Global mix-in handlers respond to interactions that are not handled within the current local (specific) beat context. For example, imagine that during the decorating beat the player asks if Grace and Trip are planning to ever have children. There is no beat-specific meaning to referring to children within the

---

[5] The determination that the player's utterance "Yeah, it looks bad" is an agreement with Grace, and further, that agreement in this context should result in a mix-in rather than a transition-out, is handled by *Façade*'s natural language processing (NLP) system, not by ABL behaviors. For details on *Façade*'s NLP system, see [20, 18].

decorating beat, so a global handler responds to this interaction with a global mix-in.

Finally, consider the case of beat goal re-sequence handlers – handlers that significantly modify the current sequence of beat goals. Within the decorating beat, a re-sequence handler reacts to references to all the objects related to the decorating beat. There are a number of variants of the "address subtopic" beat goals, each of which makes use of a different object to establish the beat conflict. The version of the "address subtopic" beat goals in Fig. 10 uses the armoire; other versions use the couch, the paintings, the wedding picture, etc. If during the beat the player makes a reference, either physically or verbally, to any of these objects, the beat switches subtopics; the switch-subtopic re-sequence handler rewinds the beat goal logic to address the new subtopic.

6.5 Cross-Beat Behaviors

In addition to beat goals and handlers, characters in *Façade* also engage in longer term behaviors that cross beat goal and beat boundaries. The performance of these longer-term behaviors happens in parallel with the performance of beat goals. An example cross-beat behavior is the staging behavior that an agent uses to move to certain dramatically significant positions (e.g. close or far conversation position with the player or another agent, into position to pick up or manipulate an object, etc.). A staging request to move to close conversation position with the player might be initiated by the first beat goal in a beat. The staging goal is spawned to another part of the ABT. After the first beat goal completes its behavior, other beat goals and handlers can happen as the agent continues to walk toward the requested staging point. At any time during a cross-beat behavior, beat goals and handlers can use reflection to find out what cross-beat behaviors are currently happening and succeed or fail them if the cross-beat behaviors are inappropriate for the current beat goal's or handler's situation.

Additional cross-beat behaviors include fixing a drink for the player (moving to the bar, making a drink, walking to the player, and handing them the drink, all in parallel with the performance of beat goals) and personality behaviors such as Grace recollecting a dream she had last night, or Trip obsessively consulting his fortune-telling crystal ball toy.

7 Coupled ABL Agents Form a Multi-Mind

When authoring multiple coordinating agents, the common approaches are to view the multiple agents either as the effectors of a single, centralized control system (one mind), or as completely separate entities (many minds) that coordinate via sensing and explicit communication. This is typically treated as an architectural decision, made once up front and then frozen. In contrast, joint goals, by introducing complex patterns of coupling among a collection of

ABL agents, open up a spectrum between one and many minds in which the degree of coupling can dynamically change. Thus, rather than architecturally committing to the one-mind or many-minds extreme, the authors of ABL agents can dynamically tune the degree of coupling as they author behaviors. This variable coupling can be best understood by comparing it in more detail to the one-mind and many-minds approach.

In the one-mind approach, a collection of agents are really the different effectors of a single entity. This single entity controls the detailed, moment-by-moment activity of all the "agents". One can certainly imagine writing such an entity in ABL; sensors and actions would be parameterized to refer to specific "agents". In an interactive drama context, this is similar to the story plans approach employed by Lebowitz [12, 11], in which he generated non-interactive episodic soap operas (as text) by using story plans (as opposed to character plans) to coordinate multiple characters in specific story events. One-mind provides maximum coordination control, but also introduces maximum program complexity. Besides the usual data hiding and modularity arguments that such a program would be hard to write and understand, and that, consequently, unforeseen side effects would arise from cross-talk between "agents", there is the additional issue that much of the combinatorics of agent interaction would be thrust upon the author. All simultaneous agent activity, whether explicitly coordinating or not, has to be explicitly authored.

The many-minds approach is the intuitive model of strong autonomy. Agents individually pursue their own goals and behaviors. Any coordinated activity arises from sensed coordination between agents. The internal details of agents are hidden from each other, providing the data hiding and modularity that makes programs easier to write and understand. Agent interaction is mediated by the world; much of the combinatorics of agent interaction arises through the world mediation without having to be explicitly authored. But, dramatic interactions in a story world require a degree of coordination difficult to achieve with sensing or *ad hoc* communication mechanisms [22, 21].

Joint goals, by introducing complex patterns of coupling between teams of ABL agents, open up a middle ground in this apparent dichotomy between one and many minds. When an ABL agent participates in a joint goal, the execution details of its ABT now depend on *both* its autonomous response to the environment as it pursues its individual goals and behaviors, *and* on the execution details of its team members' ABTs, but only to the degree those execution details impinge on the joint goal. With joint goals, a collection of agents becomes a variably coupled multi-mind, neither a single master entity controlling a collection of puppets, nor a collection of completely autonomous agents, but rather a coupled system in which a collection of ABTs influence each other, not arbitrarily, but in a manner controlled by the semantics of joint goal commitment. At any point in time, an ABL agent may hold multiple simultaneous joint goals, potentially with different teams. These joint goals fully participate in the rich, cascading effects of normal ABT nodes; only now the web of communication established between specific nodes in multiple

ABTs allows ABT execution effects to cascade *across* agents as well as *within* agents. As the number and frequency of joint goal commitments across a collection of agents increases, the collection of agents is moving toward a one mind. As the number and frequency decreases, the collection of agents is moving toward many minds.

8 Related Work

As mentioned previously, ABL builds on the Oz Project work on believable agents [2, 25, 15, 28], both technically, in that ABL is a reimplementation of Hap adding additional features and language constructs, and philosophically, in that ABL is informed by the Oz stance on believability.

The Media Lab's Synthetic Character group explores architectures that are based on natural, animal systems, particularly motivated by the ethological study of animal behavior [3]. Their recent architecture, C4 [4], builds on their previous architectures, and includes a focus on learning, particularly reinforcement learning for action selection (see [32] for a discussion of animal training techniques applied to believable characters). Their work is grounded in the premise that modeling realistic, animal-like, sensory, and decision-making processes is necessary to achieve believability, particularly the appearance of self-motivation and the illusion of life.

The Virtual Theater Project at Stanford has explored the use of explicitly represented character models in synthetic actors. For example, in the *Master and Servant* scenario, the agents make explicit use of the notion of *status*, borrowed from improvisational acting, to condition their detailed performance of a dramatic scenario [10]. In the *Cybercafe*, the agents make use of explicit personality traits (e.g. confidence, friendliness), borrowed from trait theories in psychology, to condition the selection and performance of behaviors [27]. More recent work has focused on building annotated environments in which a character dynamically gains new competencies and behaviors from objects in the environment [6, 7]. In this approach, a character's core, invariable features are factored out from the character's environment-specific capabilities and knowledge, with the latter being represented in the environment rather than in the character.

A number of groups have explored the use of believable agents in educational simulations. Such work requires that the agent simultaneously communicate its personality while achieving pedagogical goals. The IntelliMedia Project at North Carolina State University has used animated pedagogical agents to provide advice to students in constructivist learning environments [14, 13]. The group have also performed studies to determine whether using agents to deliver advice in such environments actually improves student learning vs. providing the same advice in a non-agent-based form [24]. The Institute for Creative Technologies at USC is building story-based military training environments inhabited by believable agents. The agent architecture makes use of a cognitive appraisal model of emotion [9] built on top of the STEVE agent architecture [26].

Cavazza et al. [5] are exploring the use of deliberative character planning for interactive story. They use hierarchical task-network planning to generate plans for character goals. Plots are generated as a function of the interaction between character plans. When the steps of a plan fail (perhaps because of player interaction), the system replans in the new situation.

Over the last several years, game designers have built a number of innovative believable agent architectures for use in commercial games. The virtual pets products *Petz* and *Babyz* [30, 29] employ a multi-layer architecture in which state machines perform low-level action sequencing while a goal-processing layer maintains a higher level goal state, activating and deactivating state machines as needed. *Creatures* employs an artificial life architecture in which a neural net selects actions, an artificial hormone system modulates the activity of the neural net, and a genome encodes parameters of both the neural net and hormonal system, allowing traits to be inherited by progeny [8]. Finally, the creatures in *Black & White* make use of decision tree learning to learn to perform actions on the player's behalf, while the simulated people in the *Sims* hill-climb on a desire satisfaction landscape defined by both the internal drives of the agent and the current objects in the environment (objects provide actions for satisfying drives).

9 Conclusion

During the production of *Façade*, we have written over 100,000 lines of ABL code, constituting the behaviors for dozens of beats, as well as lower level behaviors (e.g. gesturing) and cross-beat behaviors (e.g. fixing a drink). Based on this experience, we have found ABL to be a robust, powerful programming framework for authoring believable agents. Two of ABL's new features, joint goals and reflection, have proven particularly useful for authoring *story-based* characters. The behavior of story-based characters must, in addition to maintaining reactive, moment-by-moment believability, also tightly coordinate behavior to carry out dramatic action and engage in long-term discourse sequences.

Joint goals, when combined with the rest of ABL's reactive planning framework, enable coordinated dramatic performance while still supporting rich, real-time interactivity. In *Façade*, joint goals coordinate the performance of individual lines of dialog within beat goals. The automatic coordination protocol associated with joint goals ensures that each character "knows" where they are in the performance of a beat goal. As shown in the Woggle example, the *ad hoc* sensor-based coordination of even relatively simple and short-lived coordinated behaviors is prone to errors. In an experience like *Façade*, in which multiple characters coordinate every 5 to 10 seconds across a heterogeneous collection of behaviors for minutes on end, architectural support for coordination becomes a necessity. But, with ABL's joint goal mechanism, language support for coordination does not compromise the reactivity of an agent's individual decision making. For example, within *Façade*'s joint behaviors, the characters continue to respond to contingencies, such as adjusting their position in response to player movement, changing the gestures accompanying a line of dialog to accommodate holding an object, modifying their facial expressions and body language as a function of emotional state, as well as mixing in longer term behaviors, such as making a drink, all while coordinating on the performance of lines of dialog.

The reflection framework in ABL supports the authoring of meta-behaviors, that is behaviors that modify the run-time state of other behaviors. In *Façade*, meta-behaviors enabled the beat goals plus handlers idiom described earlier in this chapter, providing a nice solution to the problem of providing longer term responsive sequential activity, in this case discourse sequences, within a reactive planning framework. Without reflection, one might accomplish such longer term sequences in two ways, by unwinding the possible temporal sequences in a hierarchy of goals and behaviors, or through a set of flat (non-hierarchically organized) behaviors that references a declarative discourse state. The first case has the positive feature that the longer term discourse state is represented by the evolving structure of the ABT, but at the expense of increased authorial complexity in both the behavior hierarchy and the preconditions. The second case involves a simpler behavior structure, but pays for it with the necessity to maintain declarative state in addition to the execution state of the agent, introducing the usual problems of keeping declarative representations of a dynamic situation up to date. ABL's reflection mechanism enables a third approach, in which the longer term sequential activity is explicitly represented in the ABT (the canonical sequence), with meta-behaviors modifying the canonical sequence in response to interaction. With meta-behaviors, an ABL agent can engage in a form of look-ahead planning, in which future sequences of activity are constructed by manipulating the reactive execution state (the ABT).

ABL thus provides support for both the coordinated, more deliberative activity required for storytelling, with the moment-by-moment reactivity required for life-like behavior responsive to player interaction.

References

1. Bates, J.: Virtual reality, art, and entertainment. *Presence: The Journal of Teleoperators and Virtual Environments* **1**(1):133–138 (1992)
2. Bates, J., Loyall, A. B., Reilly, W. S.: Integrating reactivity, goals, and emotion in a broad agent. In: *Proceedings of the Fourteenth Annual Conference of the Cognitive Science Society*, Bloomington, Indiana (1992)
3. Blumberg, B.: *Old Tricks, New Dogs: Ethology and Interactive Creatures*. PhD dissertation (MIT Media Lab 1996)

4. Burke, R., Isla, D., Downie, M., Ivanov, Y., Blumberg, B.: CreatureSmarts: The art and architecture of a virtual brain. In: *Proceedings of the Game Developers Conference*, San Jose, CA (2001) pp 147–166
5. Cavazza, M., Charles, F., Mead, S.: Characters in search of an author: AI-based virtual storytelling. In: *Proceedings of the International Conference on Virtual Storytelling*, Avignon, France (2001)
6. Doyle, P.: Believability through context: Using "knowledge in the world" to create intelligent characters. In: *Proceedings of the International Joint Conference on Agents and Multi-Agent Systems (AAMAS 2002)*, Bologna, Italy (ACM Press, New York 2002) pp 342–349
7. Doyle, P., Hayes-Roth, B.: Agents in annotated worlds. In: *Proceedings of the Second International Conference on Autonomous Agents*, Minneapolis, MN (1998)
8. Grand, S.: *Creation: Life and How to Make It* (Harvard University Press 2001)
9. Gratch, J., Marsella, S.: Tears and fears: Modeling emotions and emotional behaviors in synthetic agents. In: *Proceedings of the 5th International Conference on Autonomous Agents*, Montreal, Canada (ACM Press, New York 2001)
10. Hayes-Roth, B., van Gent, R. Huber, D.: Acting in character. In: *Creating Personalities for Synthetic Actors*, ed Trappl, R., Petta, P. (Springer, Berlin New York 1997)
11. Lebowitz, M.: Creating characters in a story-telling universe. *Poetics* **13**:171–194 (1984)
12. Lebowitz, M.: Story telling as planning and learning. *Poetics* **14**:483–502 (1985)
13. Lester, J., Stone, B.: Increasing believability in animated pedagogical agents. In: *Proceedings of the First International Conference on Autonomous Agents*. Marina del Rey, CA (1997) pp 16–21
14. Lester, J., Voerman, J., Towns, S., Callaway, C.: Deictic believability: Coordinating gesture, locomotion, and speech in lifelike pedagogical agents. *Applied Artificial Intelligence* **13**(4–5):383–414 (1999)
15. Loyall, A.B.: *Believable Agents*. PhD thesis, Technical report CMU-CS-97-123 (Carnegie Mellon University 1997)
16. Loyall, A.B., Bates, J.: Hap: A reactive, adaptive architecture for agents. Technical report CMU-CS-91-147 (Carnegie Mellon University 1991)
17. Loyall, A.B., Bates, J.: Real-time control of animated broad agents. In: *Proceedings of the Fifteenth Annual Conference of the Cognitive Science Society*, Boulder, CO (1993)
18. Mateas, M.: *Interactive Drama, Art and Artificial Intelligence*. PhD thesis, Technical report CMU-CS-02-206 (Carnegie Mellon University 2002)
19. Mateas, M., Stern, A.: *Architecture, Authorial Idioms and Early Observations of the Interactive Drama Façade*. Techical report CMU-CS-02-198 (Carnegie Mellon University 2002)
20. Mateas, M., Stern, A.: Integrating plot, character and natural language processing in the interactive drama Façade. In: *Proceedings of Technologies for Interactive Digital Storytelling and Entertainment (TIDSE 2003)*, Darmstadt, Germany (2003)
21. Mateas, M., Stern, A.: Towards integrating plot and character for interactive drama. In: *Socially Intelligent Agents: The Human in the Loop*, ed Dautenhahn, K. (Kluwer Academic, Dordrecht 2002)

22. Mateas, M., Stern, A.: Towards integrating plot and character for interactive drama. In: *Working notes of the Social Intelligent Agents: The Human in the Loop Symposium*, AAAI Fall Symposium Series (AAAI Press, Menlo Park, CA 2000)
23. McKee, R.: *Story: Substance, Structure, Style, and the Principles of Screenwriting* (HarperCollins, New York 1997)
24. Moreno, R., Mayer, R., Lester, J.: Life-like pedagogical agents in constructivist multimedia environments: Cognitive consequences of their interaction. In: *Proceedings of the World Conference on Educational Multimedia, Hypermedia, and Telecommunications (ED-MEDIA)*, Montreal (2000) pp 741–746
25. Neal Reilly, W. S.: *Believable Social and Emotional Agents* PhD dissertation, School of Computer Science (Carnegie Mellon University 1996)
26. Rickel, J., Johnson, L.: Animated agents for procedural training in virtual reality: Perception, cognition, and motor control. *Applied Artificial Intelligence* **13**:343–382 (1998)
27. Rousseau, D., Hayes-Roth, B.: A social-psychological model for synthetic actors. In: *Proceedings of the Second International Conference on Autonomous Agents*, Minneapolis, MN (1998)
28. Sengers, P.: *Anti-Boxology: Agent Design in Cultural Context*. PhD dissertation. School of Computer Science (Carnegie Mellon University 1998)
29. Stern, A.: Virtual Babyz: Believable agents with narrative intelligence. In: *Working Notes of the 1999 AAAI Spring Symposium on Narrative Intelligence*, ed Mateas, M., Sengers, P. (AAAI Press, Menlo Park, CA 1999)
30. Stern, A., Frank, A., Resner, B.: Virtual Petz: A hybrid approach to creating autonomous, lifelike Dogz and Catz. In: *Proceedings of the Second International Conference on Autonomous Agents* (AAAI Press, Menlo Park, CA 1998) pp 334 335
31. Tambe, M.: Towards flexible teamwork. *Journal of Artificial Intelligence Research* **7**:83–124 (1997)
32. Yoon, S.Y., Blumberg, B., Schneider, G.: Motivation driven learning for interactive synthetic characters. In: *Proccedings of Autonomous Agents 2000* (2000)

BEAT: the Behavior Expression Animation Toolkit*

Justine Cassell[1], Hannes Högni Vilhjálmsson[2], and Timothy Bickmore[3]

[1] MIT Media Laboratory, 20 Ames St., E15-315 Cambridge, MA
  02139, USA
  justine@media.mit.edu
[2] MIT Media Laboratory, 20 Ames St., E15-320R Cambridge, MA
  02139, USA
  hannes@media.mit.edu
[3] MIT Media Laboratory, 20 Ames St., E15-320Q Cambridge, MA
  02139, USA
  bickmore@media.mit.edu

Summary. The Behavior Expression Animation Toolkit (BEAT) allows animators to input typed text that they wish to be spoken by an animated human figure, and to obtain as output appropriate and synchronized non-verbal behaviors and synthesized speech in a form that can be sent to a number of different animation systems. The non-verbal behaviors are assigned on the basis of actual linguistic and contextual analysis of the typed text, relying on rules derived from extensive research into human conversational behavior. The toolkit is extensible, so that new rules can be quickly added. It is designed to plug into larger systems that may also assign personality profiles, motion characteristics, scene constraints, or the animation styles of particular animators.

1 Introduction

The association between speech and other communicative behaviors poses particular challenges to procedural character animation techniques. Increasing numbers of procedural animation systems are capable of generating extremely realistic movement, hand gestures, and facial expressions in silent characters. However, when voice is called for, issues of synchronization and appropriateness render disfluent otherwise more than adequate techniques. And yet there are many cases where we may want to animate a speaking character. While

---

* This chapter is a reprint from the Proceedings of SIGGRAPH'01, August 12–17, Los Angeles, CA (ACM Press 2001), pp. 477–486. The chapter has been adapted in style for consistency.

spontaneous gesturing and facial movement occurs naturally and effortlessly in our daily conversational activity, when forced to think about such associations between non-verbal behaviors and words in explicit terms a trained eye is called for. For example, untrained animators, and some autonomous animated interfaces, often generate a pointing gesture toward the listener when a speaking character says "you". ("If you want to come with me, get your coat on.") A point of this sort, however, never occurs in life (try it yourself and you will see that only if "you" is being contrasted with somebody else might a pointing gesture occur) and, what is much worse, makes an animated speaking character seem stilted, as if speaking a language not its own. In fact, for this reason, many animators rely on video footage of actors reciting the text, for reference or rotoscoping, or more recently, rely on motion captured data to drive speaking characters. These are expensive methods that may involve a whole crew of people in addition to the expert animator. This may be worth doing for characters that play a central role on the screen, but is not as justified for a crowd of extras.

In some cases, we may not even have the opportunity to handcraft or capture the animation. Embodied conversational agents as interfaces to web content, animated non-player characters in interactive role playing games, and animated avatars in online chat environments all demand some kind of procedural animation. Although we may have access to a database of all the phrases a character can utter, we do not necessarily know in what context the words may end up being said and may therefore not be able to link the speech to appropriate context-sensitive non-verbal behaviors beforehand.

BEAT allows one to animate a human-like body using just text as input. It uses linguistic and contextual information contained in the text to control the movements of the hands, arms, and face, and the intonation of the voice. The mapping from text to facial, intonational, and body gestures is contained in a set of rules derived from the state of the art in non-verbal conversational behavior research. Importantly, the system is extremely tunable, allowing animators to insert rules of their own concerning personality, movement characteristics, and other features that are realized in the final animation. Thus, in the same way as Text-to-Speech (TTS) systems realize written text in spoken language, BEAT realizes written text in embodied expressive behaviors. And, in the same way as TTS systems allow experienced users to tweak intonation, pause-length, and other speech parameters, BEAT allows animators to write particular gestures, define new behaviors, and tweak the features of movement.

The next section gives some background to the motivation for BEAT. Section 3 describes related work. Section 4 walks the reader through the implemented system, including the methodology of text annotation, selection of non-verbal behaviors, and synchronization. An extended example is covered in Sect. 5. Section 6 presents our conclusions and describes some directions for future work.

2 Conversational Behavior

To communicate with one another, we use words, of course, but we also rely on intonation (the melody of language), hand gestures (beats, iconics, pointing gestures [23]), facial displays (lip shapes, eyebrow raises), eye gaze, head movements, and body posture. The form of each of these modalities – a rising tone vs. a falling tone, pointing toward oneself vs. pointing toward the other – is essential to the meaning. But the co-occurrence of behaviors is almost equally important. There is a tight synchrony among the different communicative modalities in humans. Speakers accentuate only the important words by speaking more forcefully, gesture along with the word that a gesture illustrates, and turn their eyes toward the listener when coming to the end of a thought. Meanwhile listeners nod within a few hundred milliseconds of when the speaker's gaze shifts. This synchrony is essential to the meaning of conversation. Speakers will go to great lengths to maintain it (stutterers will repeat a gesture over and over again, until they manage to utter the accompanying speech correctly) and listeners take synchrony into account in what they understand. (Readers can contrast "this is a **stellar** siggraph paper" [big head nod along with "stellar"] with "this is a . . . stellar siggraph paper" [big head nod during the silence].) When synchrony among different communicative modalities is destroyed, as in low-bandwidth videoconferencing, satisfaction and trust in the outcome of a conversation are diminished. When synchrony among different communicative modalities is maintained, as when one manages to nod at all the right places during the Macedonian policeman's directions, despite understanding not a word, conversation comes across as successful.

Although all of these communicative behaviors work together to convey meaning, the communicative intention and the timing of all of them are based on the most essential communicative activity, which is speech. The same behaviors, in fact, have quite different meanings, depending on whether they occur along with spoken language or not, and similar meanings are expressed quite differently when language is or is not a part of the mix. Indeed, researchers found that when people tried to tell a story without words, their gestures demonstrated entirely different shape and meaning characteristics – in essence, they began to resemble American Sign Language – as compared to when the gestures accompanied speech [23]. Skilled animators have always had an intuitive grasp of the form of the different communicative behaviors, and the synchrony among them. Even animators, however, often turn to rotoscoping or motion capture in cases where the intimate portrayal of communication is of the essence.

3 Related Work

Until the mid-1980s or so, animators had to manually enter the phonetic script that would result in lip-synching of a facial model to speech (cf. [26]).

Today we take for granted the ability of a system to automatically extract (more or less accurate) "visemes" from typed text, in order to synchronize lip shapes to synthesized or recorded speech [33]. We are even able to animate a synthetic face using voice input [6] or to re-animate actual videos of human faces, in accordance with recorded audio [7]. Pelachaud et al. [27] go further in the direction of communicative action and generate not just visemes, but also syntactic and semantic facial movements. And the gains are considerable, as "talking heads" with high-quality lip-synching significantly improve the comprehensibility of synthesized speech [22], and the willingness of humans to interact with synthesized speech [25], as well as decrease the need for animators to spend time on these time-consuming and thankless tasks.

Animators also spend an enormous amount of effort on the thankless task of synchronizing body movements to speech, either by intuition, or by using rotoscoping or motion capture. And yet, we still have seen no attempts to automatically specify "gestemes" on the basis of text, or to automatically synchronize ("body-synch") those body and face behaviors to synthesized or recorded speech. The task is a natural next step, after the significant existent work that renders communication-like human motion realistic in the absence of speech, or along with text balloons. Researchers have concentrated on both low-level features of movement, and aspects of humans such as intentionality, emotion, and personality. Bodenheimer et al. [5] devised a method of interpolating and modifying existing motions to display different expressions. Chi et al. [14] have concentrated on providing a tool for controlling the expressive shape and effort characteristics of gestures. Taking existing gestures as input, their system can change how a gesture is perceived. Ayama et al. [1] have concentrated on realistic emotional expression of the body. Blumberg and Galyean [4] and Becheiraz and Thalmann [3] have developed behavioral animation systems to generate animations of multiple creatures with varying personalities and/or intentionality. Calvert [8] constructed a system that portrays the gestural interaction between two agents as they pass and greet one another, and in which behavioral parameters were set by personality attribute "sliders". Perlin and Goldberg [29] concentrated on the challenge of representing the personality of a synthetic human in how it interacted with real humans, and the specification of coordinated body actions using layers of motions defined relative to a set of periodic signals.

There have also been a smaller number of attempts to synthesize human behaviors specifically in the context of communicative acts. Kurlander et al. [20] implemented a graphical chat environment that automatically generates still poses in comic book format on the basis of typed text. This very successful system relies on conventions often used in chat room conversations (chat acronyms, emoticons) rather than relying on the linguistic and contextual features of the text itself. And the output of the system depends on our understanding of comic book conventions – as the authors themselves say "characters pointing and waving, which occur relatively infrequently in real life, come off well in comics".

Synthesis of animated communicative behavior has started from an underlying computation-heavy "intention to communicate" [10], a set of natural language instructions [2], or a state machine specifying whether or not the avatar or human participant was speaking, and the direction of the human participant's gaze [15]. However, starting from an intention to communicate is too computation-heavy, and requires the presence of a linguist on staff. Natural language instructions guide the synthetic human's actions, but not its speech. And, while the state of speech is essential, the content of speech must also be addressed in the assignment of non-verbal behaviors.

In this chapter, we describe a toolkit that automatically suggests appropriate gestures, communicative facial expressions, pauses, and intonational contours for an input text, and also provides the synchronization information required to animate the behaviors in conjunction with a character's speech. This layer of analysis is designed to bridge the gap between systems that specify more natural or more expressive movement contours (such as [14], or [28] and systems that suggest personality or emotional realms of expression (such as [3] or [29]).

4 System

The BEAT system is built to be modular and user-extensible, and to operate in realtime. To this end, it is written in Java, is based on an input-to-output pipeline approach with support for user-defined filters and knowledge bases, and uses XML as its primary data structure. Processing is decomposed into modules which operate as XML transducers, each taking an XML object tree as input and producing a modified XML tree as output. The first module in the pipeline operates by reading in XML-tagged text representing the text of the character's script and converting it into a parse tree. The various knowledge bases used in the system are also encoded in XML so that they can be easily extended for new applications.

New pipeline XML transducers, as well as non-verbal behavior generators and filters (discussed in Sects. 4.3 and 4.4), can be authored through Java subclassing to facilitate extensibility. The system is real-time in that the time to produce an utterance is typically less than the natural pause between speaker turns in a dialogue (typically between 500 and 1000 ms). This is enabled by the pipeline architecture in which all operations are performed on a single XML tree within a single Java program.

XML provides a natural way to represent information which spans intervals of text, and its use facilitates modularity and extensibility by allowing users to add their own tags to the parse tree at any stage of processing. The combination of XML and Java also provide cross-platform portability, since both have been designed with this as a primary design goal. Non-verbal behavior generators and filters can also be authored in XSL, an XML-based scripting language, which provides extensibility without having to program

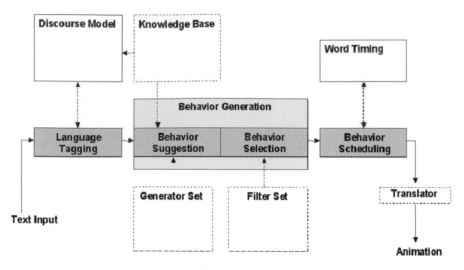

Fig. 1. BEAT system architecture

in Java. The use of a validating XML parser enables automatic testing of the output from each module during development. There are also many tools available for parsing, generating, and displaying XML, which provide great leverage during system development.

An overview of the system is shown in Fig. 1. There are three main processing modules: Language Tagging, Behavior Generation, and Behavior Scheduling. The stages of XML translation produced by each of these modules are shown in Fig. 2. The Behavior Generation module is further divided into a Suggestion module and a Selection module, as our approach to the generation process is to first suggest all plausible behaviors and then use user modifiable filters to trim them down to a set appropriate for a particular character. In Fig. 1, user-definable data structures are indicated with dashed line boxes. We will now discuss each of these components in turn.

4.1 Knowledge Base

A knowledge base adds some basic knowledge about the world to what we can understand from the text itself, and therefore allows us to draw inferences from the typed text, and consequently specify the kinds of gestures that should illustrate it, and the kinds of places where emphasis should be created. Currently, the knowledge base is stored in two XML files, one describing objects and the other describing actions. These knowledge bases are seeded with descriptions of generic objects and actions but can easily be extended for particular domains to increase the efficacy of non-verbal behavior assignment.

The object knowledge base contains definitions of object types and instances of those types. Figure 3 shows three example entries. The first defines

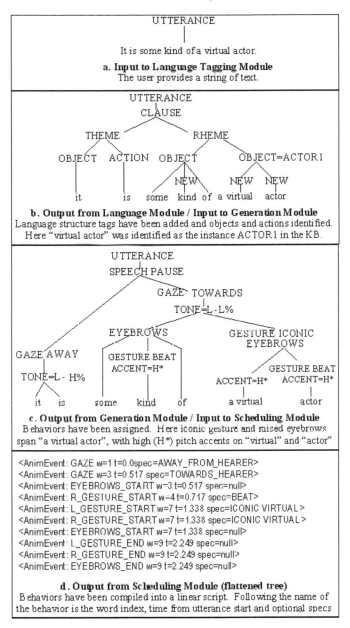

Fig. 2. XML trees passed among modules

a new object type *PROFESSIONAL* as of the person class (vs. object or place) with symbolic features such as *TYPE*, describing whether the professional is *REAL* or *VIRTUAL*; and *ROLE*, describing the actual profession. For each feature, typical values are described (e.g. real professionals are typical, while virtual ones are not), which is important since people tend to generate iconic gestures for the unusual aspects of objects they describe [34]. The second knowledge base entry defines an object instance and provides values for each feature defined for the type. The last entry is a description of a gesture that could represent the value *VIRTUAL*.

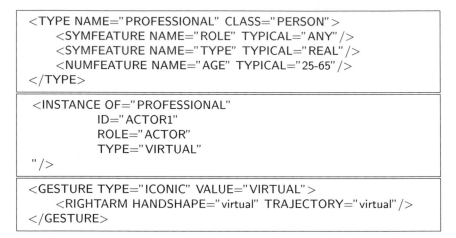

```
<TYPE NAME="PROFESSIONAL" CLASS="PERSON">
    <SYMFEATURE NAME="ROLE" TYPICAL="ANY"/>
    <SYMFEATURE NAME="TYPE" TYPICAL="REAL"/>
    <NUMFEATURE NAME="AGE" TYPICAL="25-65"/>
</TYPE>
```

```
<INSTANCE OF="PROFESSIONAL"
         ID="ACTOR1"
         ROLE="ACTOR"
         TYPE="VIRTUAL"
"/>
```

```
<GESTURE TYPE="ICONIC" VALUE="VIRTUAL">
    <RIGHTARM HANDSHAPE="virtual" TRAJECTORY="virtual"/>
</GESTURE>
```

Fig. 3. Example KB entries that describe an instance of a professional that surprisingly is virtual – an attribute that has a defined gesture form

The action knowledge base contains associations between domain actions and hand gestures that can depict them. An example entry is:

```
<GESTURE NAME="MOVE" TYPE="ICONIC">
<RIGHTARM HANDSHAPE=5,TRAJECTORY="moves from CC toward L..."/>
</GESTURE>
```

which simply associates a particular gesture specification with the verb *to move*.

As mentioned above, the system comes loaded with a generic knowledge base, containing information about some objects and actions, and some common kinds of gestures with prototypical form. Those common gestures include the *beat*, which is a formless flick of the hand, the *deictic*, which is a pointing gesture, and the *contrast* gesture (see Sect. 4.3). The other major kind of gesture, an *iconic*, represents some object or action, and may be performed differently by different speakers and in different contexts. These gestures are added to the database by the animator. All gestures are specified using a compositional notation in which hand shapes and arm trajectories for each arm are specified independently. This makes the addition of new gestures easier, since existing trajectories or hand shapes can be reused.

4.2 Language Tagging

The language module of the Toolbox is responsible for annotating input text with the linguistic and contextual information that allows successful non-verbal behavior assignment and scheduling. The toolkit was constructed so that animators need not concern themselves with linguistic analysis. However, in what follows we briefly describe a few essential fundamental units of analysis used in the system. The language module automatically recognizes and tags each of these units in the text typed by the user. It should be noted that much of what is described in this section is similar to or, in some places, identical to the kind of tagging that allows TTS systems to produce appropriate intonational contours and phrasing along with typed text [17]. Additional annotations are used here, however, to allow not just intonation but also facial display and hand gestures to be generated. And, these annotations will allow not just generation, but also synchronization and scheduling of multiple non-verbal communicative behaviors with speech.

The largest unit is the UTTERANCE, which is operationalized as an entire paragraph of input. The utterance is broken up into CLAUSEs, each of which is held to represent a proposition. To detect clause boundaries the tagging module looks for punctuation and the placement of verb phrases.

Clauses are further divided into two smaller units of information structure, a THEME and a RHEME. The former represents the part of the clause that creates a coherent link with a preceding clause and the latter is the part that contributes some new information to the discussion [16]. For example in the mini-dialogue "who is he?" "he is a student", the "he is" part of the second clause is that clause's theme and "student" is the rheme. Identifying the rheme is especially important in the current context since gestural activity is usually found within the rheme of an utterance [9]. The language module uses the location of verb phrases within a clause and information about which words have been seen before in previous clauses to assign information structure, following the heuristics described in [18].

The next to smallest unit is the word phrase, which in the current implementation describes either an ACTION or an OBJECT. These two correspond to the grammatical verb phrase and noun phrase, respectively. Actions and objects are linked to entries in the knowledge base whenever possible, as follows. For actions, the language module uses the verb head of the corresponding verb phrase as the key to look up an action description in the action database. If an exact match for that verb is not found, it is sent to an embedded word ontology module (using WordNet [24]), which creates a set of hypernyms and those are again used to find matching descriptions in the knowledge base. A hypernym of a word is a related, but a more generic – or broader – term. In the case of verbs, one can say that a certain verb is a specific way of accomplishing the hypernym of that verb. For example, "walking" is a way of "moving", so the latter is a hypernym of the former. Expanding the search for an action in the action database using hypernyms makes it possible to find and use any descriptions that may be available for a superclass of that action. The database therefore does not have to describe all possible actions, but can focus on high-level action categories. When an action description match is found, a description identifier is added to the ACTION tag.

For objects, the module uses the noun head as well as any accompanying adjectives to find a unique instance of that object in the object database. If it finds a matching instance, it adds the unique identifier of that instance to the OBJECT tag.

The smallest units that the language module handles are the words themselves. The tagger uses the EngLite parser from Conexor (www.conexor.fi) to supply word categories and lemmas for each word. The module also keeps track of all previously mentioned words and marks each incoming noun, verb, adverb, or adjective as NEW if it has not been seen before. This "word newness" helps to determine which words should be emphasized by the addition of intonation, eyebrow motion, or hand gesture [18].

Words can also stand in contrast to other words (e.g. "I went to buy **red** apples but all they had were *green* ones"), a property often marked with hand gesture and intonation and therefore important to label. The language module currently labels contrasting adjectives by using WordNet to supply information about which words might be synonyms and which might be antonyms to one another [18]. Each word in a contrast pair is tagged with the CONTRAST tag.

In sum, the language tags that are currently implemented are:

- Clause
- Theme and rheme
- Word newness
- Contrast
- Objects and actions

4.3 Behavior Suggestion

The Behavior Suggestion module operates on the XML trees produced by the Language Tagging module (such as the one shown in Fig. 2b) by augmenting them with suggestions for appropriate non-verbal behavior. This augmentation is intended to be liberal and all-inclusive; any non-verbal behavior that is possibly appropriate is suggested independent of any other. The resulting over-generated behaviors will be filtered down in the next stage of processing to the final set to be animated. This independence of behavior suggestions allows filters to be defined for different personality types, situations, and scenes (e.g. an animator may choose to filter out fewer gestures when animating the effusive bubbly personality than when animating the taciturn introvert).

Behavior suggestion proceeds by applying each of an extensible set of non-verbal behavior generators to all nodes in the XML tree which meet criteria specified by each generator. When the criteria are completely satisfied a suggestion is added to the appropriate node. The pseudocode for the generator which suggests beat gestures is shown in Fig. 4 (behavior generators are actually implemented in Java).

```
FOR each RHEME node in the tree
    IF the RHEME node contains at least one NEW node
    THEN Suggest a BEAT to coincide with the OBJECT phrase
```

Fig. 4. Example behavior generator

This pseudocode states that beat gestures are appropriate during the description of objects (noun phrases), but only when those objects are part of the rheme (new information) and contain new words.

Behavior suggestions are specified with a tree node (defining the time interval they are active for), priority (used for conflict resolution), required animation degrees of freedom, and any specific information needed to render them (e.g. gesture specification). Suggestions also specify whether they can *co-articulate*: that is, occur during other behaviors which use the same degrees of freedom. For example, beat gestures can co-articulate with other gestures through the addition of a relative hand displacement [10].

The current set of behavior generators implemented in the toolkit includes the following.

Beat Gesture Generator

Beats, or formless handwaves, are a "default" gesture, in that they are used when no additional form information is available to generate a more specific kind of gesture, and they account for roughly 50% of the naturally occurring gestures observed in most contexts [23]. Thus, they are typically redundantly generated when other types of gestures are appropriate, but they are given a low priority relative to other types of gestures so that they will only be selected when no other gestures are available. Like all gestures that occur during speech, beats occur primarily during the introduction of new material (rheme).

Surprising Feature Iconic Gesture Generator

A study of individuals describing house floor plans showed that gestures representing some feature not described in accompanying speech were used 80% of the time during the description of house features which were "surprising" or unusual in some way [34]. Following these results, this generator determines if any of the OBJECTS identified by the tagger within the RHEME have unusual features (based on information in the object knowledge base), and for each generates an iconic (representational) gesture based on the gesture specification defined on the unusual feature value in the knowledge base.

Action Iconic Gesture Generator

This generator determines if there are any actions (verb phrase roots) occurring within the RHEME for which gestural descriptions are available in the action knowledge base. For each such action, an iconic gesture is suggested with the gesture specification used from the knowledge base.

Contrast Gesture Generator

The tagger identifies objects which contrast with other nearby objects (e.g. "I don't know if this is a *good thing or a bad thing.*"). Such objects (even if they occur within a THEME) are typically marked with either beats or a "contrastive gesture" if there are exactly two such objects being contrasted (gestures literally of the form "on the one hand ... on the other hand") [11]. This generator suggests beats for contrast items unless there are exactly two items being contrasted, in which case the special contrast gesture is suggested.

Eyebrow Flash Generator

Raising of eyebrows can also be used to signal the introduction of new material [27]. This generator suggests raising the character's eyebrows during the description of OBJECTs within the RHEME.

Gaze Generator

Cassell et al. [12] studied the relationship between eye gaze, theme/rheme, and turn-taking, and used these results to define an algorithm for controlling the gaze behavior of a conversational character. The gaze generator that implements this algorithm is shown in Fig. 5.

```
FOR each THEME
    IF at beginning of utterance OR 70% of the time
            Suggest Gazing AWAY from user
FOR each RHEME
    If at end of utterance OR 73% of the time
            Suggest Gazing TOWARD the user
```

Fig. 5. Algorithm for controlling conversational gaze

Intonation Generator

The intonation generator implements three different strategies for controlling a TTS engine. The first strategy assigns accents and boundary tones based on a theme–rheme analysis, as described by [30] and shown in Fig. 6.

```
Within THEME:
    Suggest L+H* accent for NEW objects
    Suggest LH% boundary tone at end of THEME
Within RHEME:
    Suggest H* accent on NEW objects
    Suggest LL% boundary tone at end of RHEME
```

Fig. 6. Algorithm for accent and boundary tone generation

The second intonation strategy suggests H* accents for all CONTRAST objects identified by the tagger, following [30]. The final intonation strategy simply suggests TTS pauses at CLAUSE boundaries.

4.4 Behavior Selection

The Behavior Selection module analyzes the tree that now contains many, potentially incompatible, gesture suggestions, and reduces these suggestions down to the set that will actually be used in the animation. The selection process utilizes an extensible set of filters which are applied to the tree in turn, each of which can delete behavior suggestions which do not meet its criteria. In general, filters can reflect the personalities, affective state, and energy level of characters by regulating how much non-verbal behavior they exhibit. Currently, two filter strategies are implemented: conflict resolution and priority threshold.

Conflict Resolution Filter

The conflict resolution filter detects all non-verbal behavior suggestion conflicts (those which physically cannot co-occur) and resolves the conflicts by deleting the suggestions with lower priorities. Conflicts are detected by determining, for each animation degree of freedom (DOF), the suggestions which co-occur and require that DOF, even if specified at different levels of the XML tree. For each pair of such conflicting suggestions (in decreasing order of priority) the one with lower priority is deleted unless the two can be co-articulated (e.g. a beat gesture on top of an iconic gesture). However, even in the case of co-articulation, two behaviors are not permitted to start using the same DOF at the same point in time. The types of non-verbal behaviors, their required DOFs, and co-articulation relationships are expressed in an XML file referenced by the filter. The filter operates as follows. For each DOF, the behaviors which use that DOF are considered in order of decreasing priority. For each behavior, a check is made to see if any other behavior which uses the DOF conflicts with it (overlaps in word indices when co-articulation is not allowed, or starts on the same word index when co-articulation is allowed). If a conflict exists, the lower priority behavior is removed from the tree. This operation is

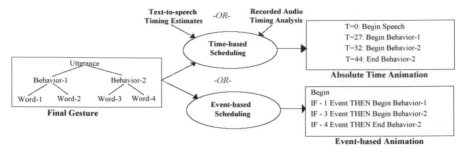

Fig. 7. Scheduling process

$O(Nd^2)$, where Nd is the maximum number of behaviors that use any given DOF (less than 10 for typical sentences).

Priority Threshold Filter

The priority threshold filter simply removes all behavior suggestions whose priority falls below a user-specified threshold.

4.5 Behavior Scheduling and Animation

The last module in the XML pipeline converts its input tree into a set of instructions which can be executed by an animation system, or edited by an animator prior to rendering. In general, there are two ways to achieve synchronization between a character animation subsystem and a subsystem for producing the character's speech (either through a TTS engine or from recorded audio samples). The first is to obtain estimates of word and phoneme timings and construct an animation schedule prior to execution (see Fig. 7). The second approach is to assume the availability of real-time events from a TTS engine – generated while the TTS is actually producing audio – and compile a set of event-triggered rules to govern the generation of the non-verbal behavior. The first approach must be used for recorded-audio-based animation or TTS engines such as Festival [32], while the second must be used with TTS engines such as Microsoft's Whistler [19]. We have used both approaches in our systems, and the current toolkit is capable of producing both kinds of animation schedules, but we will focus our discussion here on absolute-time-based scheduling with a TTS engine such as Festival.

The first step in time-based scheduling is to extract only the text and intonation commands from the XML tree, translate these into a format for the TTS engine, and issue a request for word and phoneme timings. In our implementation, the TTS runs as a separate process. Thus part of the scheduling can continue while these timings are being computed. The next step in the scheduling process is to extract all of the (non-intonation) non-verbal behavior suggestions from the tree, translate them into an intermediate form of animation command, and order them by word index into a linear animation proto-schedule.

Once the word and phoneme timings become available, the proto-schedule can be instantiated by mapping the word indices into execution times (relative to the start of the schedule). The schedule can then also be augmented with facial animation commands to lip-sync the phonemes returned from the TTS engine. Figure 8 shows a fragment of an animation schedule at this stage of compilation.

```
<VISEME    time=0.0 spec="A">
<GAZE word=1 time=0.0 spec=AWAY_FROM_HEARER>
<VISEME    time=0.24 spec="E">
<VISEME    time=0.314 spec="A">
<VISEME    time=0.364 spec="TH">
<VISEME    time=0.453 spec="E">
<GAZE word=3 time=0.517 spec=TOWARD_HEARER>
<R_GESTURE_START word=3 time=0.517 spec=BEAT>
<EYEBROWS_START word=3 time=0.517>
```

Fig. 8. Example abstract animation schedule Fragment

The final stage of scheduling involves compiling the abstract animation schedule into a set of legal commands for whichever animation subsystem is being used. This final compilation step has also been modularized in the toolkit. In addition to simply translating commands it must concern itself with issues such as enabling, initializing, and disabling different animation subsystem features, gesture approach, duration and relax times (the abstract schedule specifies only the peak time at start of phrase and the end of phrase relax time), and any time offsets between the speech production and animation subsystems.

4.6 Extensibility

As described in the introduction, BEAT has been designed to fit into existent animation systems, or to exist as a layer between lower level expressive features of motion and higher level specification of personality or emotion. In our own tests of the system we have used BEAT with a homegrown animator (Pantomime), have used it to export a dope sheet for professional animators to hand-animate (see the accompanying video[4]), and are currently collaborating with Alias/Wavefront to integrate BEAT with Maya (for the BEAT-Maya Integration module, see http://www.media.mit.edu/groups/gn/projects/beat/). It has also been designed to be extensible in several significant ways. First,

---

[4] http://www.vhml.org/LLC/llc-book.html.

new entries can easily be made in the knowledge base to add new hand gestures to correspond to domain object features and actions. Second, the range of non-verbal behaviors, and the strategies for generating them, can easily be modified by defining new behavior suggestion generators. Behavior suggestion filters can also be tailored to the behavior of a particular character in a particular situation, or to a particular animator's style. Animation module compilers can be swapped in for different target animation subsystems. Finally, entire modules can be easily reimplemented (e.g. as new techniques for text analysis become available) simply by adhering to the XML interfaces. Any kind of flexibility to the system derives from the ability to override the output from any of the modules simply by including appropriate tags in the original text input. For example, an animator could force a character to raise its eyebrows on a particular word simply by including the relevant EYEBROWS tag wrapped around the word in question. This tag will be passed through the Tagger, Generation, and Selection modules and compiled into the appropriate animation commands by the Scheduler.

As an example of the system's extensibility, consider how one would deal with the issue of multiple animated characters. Suppose we were to construct a simulation of a training session, where an animated teacher is telling an animated student about various control panels. In this instance BEAT would need to generate listener behaviors as well as speaker behaviors. Each UTTERANCE tag already specifies the name of the speaker and the hearer as XML attributes. The non-verbal behavior generators can simply copy this attribute into their suggestions that they leave in the tree. Specific listener non-verbal behavior generators can be built to suggest headnods and eyebrow movement at certain key places during the speaker's turn, following similar rules as the currently implemented speaker behavior generators. When the animation command translator receives the tree, it would first collect all the speaker-designated behaviors, followed by the listener behaviors, and compile those into two separate scripts to be executed by the individual animated characters. To incorporate the visual scene into the behaviors, such as pointing at controls and looking at displays, these objects would have a representation in the knowledge base. The language module can map these objects onto references made in the text, and, once identified, the generators could decide when and how to react to their presence through gesture and gaze.

This scenario also allows us to discuss how to deal with creating individual styles of behavior for the two characters. This could be done in two ways: modifying the behaviors either in a discrete or in a continuous manner. The former would take place at the behavior selection stage, where custom filter rules can be built to keep or filter out certain behaviors based on who the speaker or listener is. Such a filter rule could, for example, simply decrease the amount of gesturing one character would employ. The latter could occur at any point in the pipeline after the behavior generation stage. For instance, an intermediate module could be built between the Behavior Generator and the Scheduler to tweak and tune the already assigned behaviors by modifying their parameters or even add news ones that can be interpreted by the particular animation engine used. Such an intermediate module could set amplitude values for headnods or insert information about the motion quality of gesture. As long as a new module can return the behavior suggestion tree back into the pipeline structurally intact, the flow will not be affected.

5 Example Animation

To demonstrate how the system works, in this section we walk through a couple of example utterances. A full animated example can be found on the accompanying video.[5]

As a first example, we trace what happens when BEAT receives as input the two subsequent sentences "It is some kind of a virtual actor" and "You just have to type in some text, and the actor is able to talk and gesture by itself". Let us look at each sentence in turn.

The Language Tagging module processes the input first, and generates an XML tree, tagged with relevant language information as described in Sect. 4.1. The output of the language tagger is shown in Fig. 2b. Of particular interest in Sentence 1 is the classification of "a virtual actor" as an object and the ability of the system to give it the unique identifier ACTOR1. This is because when looking for the object in the knowledge base, it found under a user-defined type PROFESSIONAL an instance of an ACTOR that in fact is of the virtual type; this was the only instance matching on this attribute, so the instance name ACTOR1 was copied into the value of ID in the object tag.

When the behavior generator receives the XML tree from the language tagger, it applies generator rules to annotate the tree with appropriate behaviors as described in Sect. 4.3. Eyebrow raising is suggested during the object "a virtual actor", previously identified as ACTOR1. Beats and intonational accents are suggested for all the new lexical items (words) contained in the rheme (i.e. "kind", "virtual", and "actor"). Eye gaze behavior and intonational boundary tones are suggested based on the division into theme and rheme. Of particular interest is the suggestion for an iconic gesture to accompany ACTOR1. This suggestion was generated because, upon examining the database entry for ACTOR1, the generator found that one of its attributes, namely the type, did not hold a value within a typical range. That is, the value "virtual" was not considered a typical actor type. The form suggested for the gesture is retrieved from the database entry for the value *virtual* (a database entry that must be specified by the animator); in this way the gesture highlights the surprising feature of the object.

When the Behavior Selection module receives the suggestions from the Generator module, it notices that two beats and an iconic gesture were suggested inside ACTOR1. The first beat coincides with the onset of the iconic,

---

[5] http://www.vhml.org/LLC/llc-book.html.

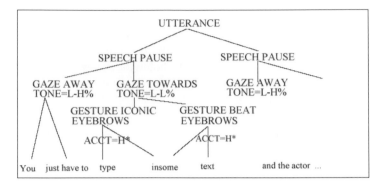

Fig. 9. Part of the output XML tree for the first example

Fig. 10. "You just have to type in some text…"

and is filtered out using the rule of gesture class priority (beats being the lowest class in the gesture family); the second beat is left in, however, as it has a different onset time and is a gesture type that allows co-articulation. No further conflicts are noticed and no further filters have been included in this example. The resulting tree is shown in Fig. 2c.

Lastly the Behavior Scheduling module compiles the XML tree, including all suggestions not filtered out, into an action plan ready for execution by an animation engine as described in Sect. 4.4. The final schedule (without viseme codes) is shown in Fig. 2d.

The second sentence is processed in much the same way. Part of the output of the behavior generator is shown in Fig. 9. Two particular situations that arise with this sentence are of note. The first is that the action, "to type in",

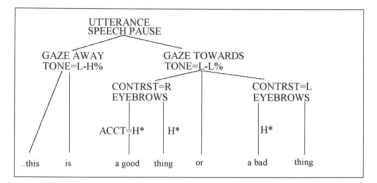

Fig. 11. The output XML tree for second example

Fig. 12. "I don't know if this is a good thing or a bad thing"

is identified by the language module because an action description for typing is found in the action database. Therefore the gesture suggestion module can suggest the use of an iconic gesture description, because the action occurs within a rheme. See Fig. 10 for a snapshot of the generated "typing" gesture. The second one is that although ACTOR1 ("the actor") was identified again, no gesture was suggested for this object at this time because it is located inside a theme as opposed to a rheme part of the clause (i.e. having already been mentioned in the dialogue, it is no longer news).

As an example of a different kind of a non-verbal behavior assignment, let us look at how the system processes the sentence "I don't know if this is a good thing or a bad thing". The output of the Behavior Generation module is shown in Fig. 11. As well as suggesting the typical behaviors seen in the previous examples, here the language tagger has identified two contrasting adjectives in the same clause, "good" and "bad". They have been assigned to the same contrast group. When the Gesture Suggestion module receives the tagged text, generation rules suggest a contrast gesture on the "a good thing" object and on the "a bad thing" object. Furthermore, the shape suggested for these contrast gestures is a right hand pose for the first object and a left hand pose for the second object since there are exactly two members of this contrast group. When filtering, the Gesture Selection module notices that the contrasting gestures were scheduled to peak at exactly the same moment as a couple of hand beats. The beats are filtered out using the gesture class priority rule, deciding that contrasting gestures are more important than beats. See Fig. 12 for a snapshot of the contrast gesture.

6 Conclusions/Future Work

BEAT is the first of a new generation (the beat generation) of animation tool that extracts actual linguistic and contextual information from text in order to suggest appropriate gestures, eye gaze, and other non-verbal behaviors, and to synchronize those behaviors to one another. For those animators who wish to maintain the most control over output, BEAT can be seen as a kind of "snap-to-grid" for communicative actions: if animators input text, and a set of eye, face, head, and hand behaviors for phrases, the system will correctly align the behaviors to one another, and send the timings to an animation system. For animators who wish to concentrate on higher level concerns such as personality, or lower level concerns such as motion characteristics, BEAT takes care of the middle level of animation: choosing how non-verbal behaviors can best convey the message of typed text, and scheduling them.

In terms of evaluation of the BEAT system, it is useful to think of evaluating it both as a tool for professional animators, and as a way of doing interactive animation. In terms of the former, we asked professional animators to evaluate the system after extensive use (the making of the BEAT video). Their sense was that BEAT was a good digital assistant – a way of roughing out an animation before the animator applies his or her art. One animator told us that BEAT suggested natural movements that an animator might not necessarily consider. In one instance, he was surprised that BEAT inserted a particular gaze-away command where it did – but found that the resulting animation actually looked more natural. On the other hand, this same animator said that there were definitely places where he wanted to override the output and that, more generally, he did not want BEAT to take away the kind of invention that happened in his head when he listened to a dialogue track. It is for this reason that the BEAT system invites the input of an animator at any stage to affect the final output. For interactive animation it is harder to compare BEAT to existent systems. However, we note that games and other interactive applications may require users to speak in their own voice, or may require the passing of large amounts of text without the time to do linear animation. In cases like these, we expect BEAT to serve an important role.

As with any system, the design decisions that were made for BEAT have led to some inefficiencies. Since our primary goal was to support generality and extensibility, the run-time performance of the system is not optimized and might be too slow for some real-time applications. The choice of XML as the primary data structure prohibits the direct representation of behaviors which overlap in tree spans, even though there are very few non-verbal behaviors which require this. Finally, the biggest obstacle to BEAT's producing perfectly appropriate and natural behavior for all inputs is the set of linguistic analyses performed in the Language Tagging module. Computational linguistics is still an imperfect science, and BEAT's output behaviors can only be as perfect as the linguistic results they are based upon. However, the Language Tagging module was also designed to be extensible, and as new linguistic algorithms and tools become available they can be incorporated into the system.

Future work includes, in addition to improving the automatic linguistic tagging, expanding the gesture ontology, including some basic spatial configuration gesture elements. As it stands, hand gestures cannot be assembled out of smaller gestural parts, nor can they be shortened. When gesture descriptions are read from the knowledge base, they are currently placed in the animation schedule unchanged. The Behavior Scheduler makes sure the stroke of the gesture aligns with the correct word, but does not attempt to stretch out the rest of the gesture, for instance to span a whole phrase that needs to be illustrated. Similarly, it does not attempt to slow down or pause speech to accommodate a complex gesture, a phenomenon observed in people. Finally, additional non-verbal behaviors should be added: wrinkles of the forehead, smiles, ear wiggling. The system will also benefit from a visual interface that displays a manipulatable timeline where either the scheduled events themselves can be moved around or the rules behind them modified.

In the meantime, we hope to have demonstrated that the animator's toolbox can be enhanced by the knowledge about gesture and other non-verbal behaviors, turn-taking, and linguistic structure that are incorporated and (literally) embodied in the Behavior Expression Animation Toolkit.

7 Acknowledgments

Thanks to the other members of the GNL group – in particular Ian Gouldstone and Yukiko Nakano – for their contribution to the work and their comments on this chapter. Special thanks to Geoffrey Beatty, Denny Bromley, Steve Curcuru, Tinsley Galyean, and Ryan Kavanaugh from Nearlife, and to Jerome Maillot from Alias/Wavefront. Research leading to the preparation of this article was supported by France Telecom, AT&T, and the other generous sponsors of the MIT Media Lab.

Bibliography

1. Amaya, K., Bruderlin, A., Calvert, T.: Emotion from motion. In: *Proceedings Graphics Interface'96* (1996) pp 222–229
2. Badler, N., Bindiganavale, R., Allbeck, J., Schuler, W., Zhao, L., and Palmer, M.: Parameterized action representation for virtual human agents. In: *Embodied Conversational Agents*, ed Cassell, J., Sullivan, J., Prevost, S., Churchill, E. (The MIT Press, Cambridge, MA 2000) pp 256–284
3. Becheiraz, P., Thalmann, D.: A behavioral animation system for autonomous actors personified by emotions. In: *Proceedings of the 1st Workshop on Embodied Conversational Characters* (1998) pp 57–65
4. Blumberg, B., Galyean, T.A.: Multi-level direction of autonomous creatures for real-time virtual environments. In: *SIGGRAPH 95 Conference Proceedings* (ACM SIGGRAPH Addison-Wesley, Reading, MA 1995) pp 47–54
5. Bodenheimer, B., Rose, C., Cohen, M.: Verbs and adverbs: Multidimensional motion interpolation. *IEEE Computer Graphics and Applications* **18**(5):32–40 (1998)
6. Brand, M.: Voice puppetry. In: *SIGGRAPH 99 Conference Proceedings* (ACM SIGGRAPH, Addison-Wesley, Reading, MA 1999) pp 21–28
7. Bregler, C., Covell, M., Slaney, M.: Video rewrite: Driving visual speech with audio. *SIGGRAPH 97 Conference Proceedings* (ACM SIGGRAPH, Addison-Wesley, Reading, MA 1997) pp 353–360
8. Calvert, T.: Composition of realistic animation sequences for multiple human figures. In: *Making Them Move: Mechanics, Control, and Animation of Articulated Figures*, ed Badler, N., Barsky, B., Zeltzer, D. (Morgan-Kaufmann, San Mateo, CA 1991) pp 35–50
9. Cassell, J.: Nudge, nudge, wink, wink: Elements of face-to-face conversation for embodied conversational agents. In: *Embodied Conversational Agents*, ed Cassell, J., Sullivan, J., Prevost, S., Churchill, E. (The MIT Press, Cambridge, MA 2000) pp 1–27
10. Cassell, J., Pelachaud, C., Badler, N., Steedman, M., Achorn, B., Becket, T., Douville, B., Prevost, S., Stone, M.: Animated conversation: Rule-based generation of facial expression, gesture and spoken intonation for multiple conversational agents. In: *Siggraph 94 Conference Proceedings* (ACM SIGGRAPH, Addison-Wesley, Reading, MA 1994) pp 413–420
11. Cassell, J., Prevost, S.: Distribution of semantic features across speech and gesture by humans and computers. In: *Proceedings of the Workshop on the Integration of Gesture in Language and Speech*, Newark, DE (1996) pp 253–270
12. Cassell, J., Torres, O., Prevost, S.: Turn taking vs. discourse structure: How best to model multimodal conversation. In: *Machine Conversations*, ed Wilks, Y. (Kluwer, The Hague 1999) pp 143-154
13. Chang, J.: *Action Scheduling in Humanoid Conversational Agents*. MS thesis in Electrical Engineering and Computer Science (MIT 1998)
14. Chi, D., Costa, M., Zhao, L., Badler, N.: The EMOTE model for effort and shape. In: *SIGGRAPH 00 Conference Proceedings* (ACM SIGGRAPH, Addison-Wesley, Reading, MA 2000) pp 173–182
15. Colburn, A., Cohen, M.F., Drucker, S.: The role of eye gaze in avatar mediated conversational interfaces. MSR-TR-2000-81 (Microsoft Research 2000)
16. Halliday, M.A.K.: *Explorations in the Functions of Language*. (Edward Arnold, London 1973)

17. Hirschberg, J.: Accent and discourse context: Assigning pitch accent in synthetic Speech. In: *Proceedings AAAI'90* (1990) pp 952–957
18. Hiyakumoto, L., Prevost, S., Cassell, J.: Semantic and discourse information for text-to-speech intonation. In: *Proceedings ACL Workshop on Concept-to-Speech Generation*, Madrid (1997)
19. Huang, X., Acero, A., Adcock, J., Hon, H.-W., Goldsmith, J., Liu, J., Plumpe, M.: Whistler: A trainable text-to-speech system. In: *Proceedings 4th International Conference on Spoken Language Processing (ICSLP'96)*, Piscataway, NJ (1996) pp 2387–2390
20. Kurlander, D., Skelly, T., and Salesin, D.: Comic chat. In: *SIGGRAPH 96 Conference Proceedings*, (ACM SIGGRAPH, Addison-Wesley, Reading, MA 1996) pp 225–236
21. Lenat, D.B., Guha, R.V.: *Building Large Knowledge-Based Systems: Representation and Inference in the Cyc Project.* (Addison-Wesley, Reading, MA 1990)
22. Massaro, D.W.: *Perceiving Talking Faces: From Speech Perception to a Behavioral Principle.* (The MIT Press, Cambridge, MA 1987)
23. McNeill, D.: *Hand and Mind: What Gestures Reveal about Thought.* (The University of Chicago Press 1992)
24. Miller, G.A., Beckwith, R., Fellbaum, C., Gross, D., Miller, K.: Introduction to Wordnet: An on-line lexical database (1993)
25. Nagao, K., Takeuchi, A.: Speech dialogue with facial displays: Multimodal human-computer conversation. In: *Proceedings ACL'94* (1994) pp 102–109
26. Pearce, A., Wyvill, B., Wyvill, G., Hill, D.: Speech and expression: A computer solution to face animation. In: *Proceedings Graphics Interface* (1986) pp 136–140
27. Pelachaud, C., Badler, N., Steedman, M.: Generating facial expressions for speech. *Cognitive Science* **20**(1):1–46 (1994)
28. Perlin, K.: Noise, hypertexture, antialiasing and gesture. In: *Texturing and Modeling, A Procedural Approach*, ed Ebert, D. (AP Professional, Cambridge, MA 1994)
29. Perlin, K., Goldberg, A.: Improv: A system for scripting interactive actors in virtual worlds. In: *Proceedings of SIGGRAPH '96* (1996) pp 205–216
30. Prevost, S., Steedman, M.: Specifying intonation from context for speech synthesis. *Speech Communication* **15**:139–153 (1994)
31. Roehl, B.: *Specification for a Standard Humanoid, Version 1.1*, ed H.A.W. Group, http://ece.uwaterloo.ca/ h-anim/spec1.1/ (1999)
32. Taylor, P., Black, A., Caley, R.: The architecture of the Festival Speech Synthesis System. In: *Proceedings 3rd ESCA Workshop on Speech Synthesis* (Jenolan Caves, Australia 1998) pp 147–151
33. Waters, K., Levergood, T.: An automatic lip-synchronization algorithm for synthetic faces. In: *Proceedings of the 2nd ACM International Conference on Multimedia*, San Francisco, CA (1994) pp 149–156
34. Yan, H.: *Paired Speech and Gesture Generation in Embodied Conversational Agents.* MS thesis in the Media Lab (MIT 2000)

Galatea: Open-Source Software for Developing Anthropomorphic Spoken Dialog Agents

Shin-ichi Kawamoto[1], Hiroshi Shimodaira[1], Tsuneo Nitta[3], Takuya Nishimoto[2], Satoshi Nakamura[4], Katsunobu Itou[5], Shigeo Morishima[6], Tatsuo Yotsukura[4], Atsuhiko Kai[7], Akinobu Lee[8], Yoichi Yamashita[9], Takao Kobayashi[10], Keiichi Tokuda[11], Keikichi Hirose[2], Nobuaki Minematsu[2], Atsushi Yamada[12], Yasuharu Den[13], Takehito Utsuro[14], and Shigeki Sagayama[2]

[1] School of Information Science
    Japan Advanced Institute of Science and Technology
    1-1, Asahidai, Tatsunokuchi, Ishikawa 923-1292, Japan
    skawa@jaist.ac.jp, sim@jaist.ac.jp
[2] The University of Tokyo, Japan
[3] Toyohashi University of Technology, Japan
[4] Advanced Telecommunications Research Institute International, Kyoto, Japan
[5] Nagoya University, Japan
[6] Seikei University, Tokyo, Japan
[7] Shizuoka University, Japan
[8] Nara Institute of Science and Technology, Japan
[9] Ritsumeikan University, Shiga, Japan
[10] Tokyo Institute of Technology, Japan
[11] Nagoya Institute of Technology, Japan
[12] The Advanced Software Technology and Mechatronics Research Institute of Kyoto, Japan
[13] Chiba University, Japan
[14] Kyoto University, Japan

Summary. Galatea is a software toolkit to develop a human-like spoken dialog agent. In order to easily integrate the modules of different characteristics including speech recognizer, speech synthesizer, facial animation synthesizer, and dialog controller, each module is modeled as a virtual machine having a simple common interface and connected to each other through a broker (communication manager). Galatea employs model-based speech and facial animation synthesizers whose model parameters are adapted easily to those for an existing person if his or her training data is given. The software toolkit that runs on both UNIX/Linux and Windows operating systems will be publicly available in the middle of 2003 [7, 6].

1 Introduction

An anthropomorphic spoken dialog agent (ASDA), behaving like humans with facial animations and gestures, and making speech conversations with humans, is one of the next-generation human–computer interfaces. Although a number of ASDA systems [8, 10, 4, 24, 18, 2] have been developed, communication between the ASDA system and humans is far from being natural, and developing a high-quality ASDA system is still challenging. In order to activate and progress the research in this field, we believe that an easy-to-use, easy-to-customize, and free software toolkit for building ASDA systems is indispensable. For example, it would be nice if the toolkit provides an unlimited number of life-like agent characters having different faces and voices just like human beings in the real world.

We have been developing such an ASDA software toolkit, named Galatea, since 2000, aiming to provide a platform to build next-generation ASDA systems. The features of the toolkit are as follows: (i) high customizability in text-to-speech synthesis, realistic face animation synthesis, and speech recognition, (ii) basic functions to achieve incremental (on-the-fly) speech recognition, (iii) mechanisms for "lip-synchronization", that is synchronization between audio speech and lip image motion, (iv) "virtual machine" architecture to achieve transparency in module-to-module communication.

It should be noted that the Galatea toolkit does not provide all of the necessary and sufficient functions to develop software agents having human-like minds, namely the deep structure of human activities, but it provides only the basic functions, such as speech recognition and synthesis, for simulating the input/output functions of humans.

If compared to related works such as the CSLU toolkit [21] and DARPA Communicator Program [3], our toolkit is still preliminary. However, it is compact, simple, easy to understand, and thus suitable for developing ASDA systems for research purposes, and of course it is the first Japanese toolkit of life-like agents. One of the outstanding features of Galatea is that it uses a snapshot of an existing person to synthesize face images of an agent. Therefore, it can synthesize an unlimited number of agents having different faces as long as the snapshots of different people are provided. At present, simple ASDA systems have been successfully built with the toolkit under UNIX/Linux and Windows operating systems, and a subset of the toolkit will be publicly available in the middle of the year 2003.

This chapter is divided into six sections. In Sect. 2, design concepts for the Galatea software toolkit are discussed. Brief explanations of each functional module of the toolkit are given in Sect. 3. Prototype systems developed by the toolkit are shown in Sect. 4 followed by discussions in Sect. 5. Finally, Sect. 6 is devoted to conclusions.

2 Features of the Toolkit

In this section, we discuss the features of Galatea to build ASDA systems which speak, listen, and behave like humans.

2.1 Configuration for Easy Customization

In Galatea, synthesized facial images and voices are easily customizable depending on the purposes and applications of the toolkit users. This customizability is achieved by employing model-based approaches where basic model parameters are trained or determined with a set of training data derived from an existing person. Once the model parameters are trained, facial expressions and voice quality can be controlled easily.

2.2 Key Techniques for Achieving Natural Spoken Dialog

If compared to keyboard-based conversation, typical phenomena are observed in speech-based conversation. These include the case when human listeners nod or say "uhmm" during a conversation, and the case when the speakers control the prosody to indicate types of utterances such as questions, statements, and emotions. Galatea provides basic functions to study these phenomena for human-like speech-based conversation. For example, Galatea provides the functions of incremental speech recognition, interruption over synthesized speech, and so on. In addition, Galatea provides a simple function of synchronization between synthesized speech and facial animation. This function will be useful to realize natural speech-based conversation.

2.3 Modularity of Functional Units

Naturally, Galatea provides a simple architecture to manage each functional unit, and to work in parallel. In some situations, system creators or toolkit users may not be satisfied with the performance of the original modules in the toolkit and they might like to replace them with new ones or add new ones to the system. In such cases, it would be desirable that each functional unit is well modularized so that the users can develop, improve, debug, and utilize each unit independently from the other modules. Galatea provides a basic module management architecture to satisfy these requirements for research and development.

2.4 Open-Source Free Software

The technology used for creating the toolkit is still insufficient to achieve human-like conversation. Therefore it is desirable that not only the creators of the toolkit but also the researchers and developers who use it should contribute to improve it further. In that sense, the toolkit will be released as free software along with the program source code.

There is no existing ASDA software so far satisfying all of the requirements described above.

3 Toolkit Design and Outline

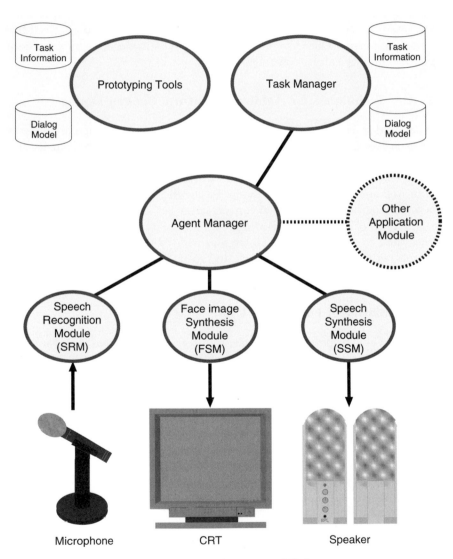

Fig. 1. System architecture of Galatea

The basic agent system using Galatea consists of five functional modules: speech recognizer, speech synthesizer, facial animation synthesizer, task (dialog) manager, and agent manager. Figure 1 shows the basic module architecture of the Galatea toolkit. As shown in the figure, the agent manager works as an inter-module communication manager, through which each functional unit communicates. In the Galatea toolkit, the functional units are modularized independently, and input/output devices are directly managed by the modules which utilize the devices. If a new function is needed for the system, this can be done easily by adding a new module for the function and connecting the module to the agent manager.

The dialog manager communicates with the agent manager to achieve the dialog tasks based on the database of dialog scenarios. In addition, Galatea prepares a prototyping tool for easy coding of the dialog scenario.

In this section, we discuss the design of Galatea and the functionality of its modules.

3.1 Speech Recognition Module (SRM)

In constructing an ASDA system, the speech recognition module (SRM) used is required to have the following functions:

- Accept various styles of input and output; for example, accepting multiple formats for grammar representation and outputting incremental recognition results.
- Change parameters and resources flexibly and dynamically for recognition; for example, changing grammar by request from external modules during dialog sessions.
- Control a recognition engine flexibly and dynamically; for example, stopping to recognize a user's utterance, and then restarting.

To meet the above requirements, we implemented SRM in the configuration shown in Fig. 2.

SRM consists of three submodules: the command interpreter, the speech recognition engine, and the grammar transformer. This configuration was designed not to drop the communication events and speech input events that occur asynchronously by dividing the command processing and speech processing and dispatching them to exclusive processes. The configuration also contributes to concealing the speech recognition engine from other modules.

We prepared "Julian" as the standard SRM, but all the modules are changeable if a module implements the interface and meets requirements such as accepting grammar written in context-free grammar (CFG) or the same class language.

Major interfaces of SRM are as follows:

- *Outputs*
  - Recognition result

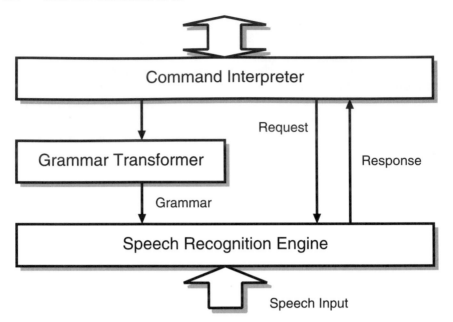

Fig. 2. Speech recognition module (SRM)

SRM returns N-best multiple results after an entire utterance. Also, Julian supports the incremental output
of recognition results during utterances. Recognition results are formatted in XML and include word sequences,
a time-stamp, a score, lexical information on each word
such as parts of speech, phoneme sequence, and acoustic
information of each word, such as duration and average
likelihood of acoustic models.

– Engine status

SRM returns the engine status of the speech input, such
as "busy", "waiting", if requested by other modules.

- *Control Command*

SRM can reload grammar through the command interpreter at
other modules' request. If SRM is busy, it inserts sent grammar
into a queue, and loads the grammars into the recognition engine
when it finishes the recognition of each utterance. SRM can also
change the settings of the speech recognition engine at any time.

- *Grammar Representation*

The grammar that SRM accepts is specified by the XML-based representation. The representation complies with the Speech Recognition Grammar Specification, which was issued by W3C.

The syntax consists of definitions and sequences of "tokens" and "rules". We extend the token tag by adding a "phoneme" or "syllable" tag which represents the pronunciation of a word. The grammar transformer transforms the XML grammar into a format that is accepted by the speech recognition engine. It is developed by using XSLT [26], which is an XML transformation technology. Therefore it is easy to exchange the speech recognition engine.

3.2 Speech Synthesis Module (SSM)

The speech synthesis module (SSM) consists of four submodules and its configuration is shown in Fig. 3. The command interpreter receives an input command from the agent manager and invokes subprocesses according to the command. The text analyzer looks up the dictionary to decompose input text data into morphemes, and provides the waveform generation engine with linguistic information including pronunciation, accent type, part of speech, and so on. The waveform generation engine produces sequences of speech parameters and converts them into synthetic speech waveforms. The speech output submodule outputs the synthetic speech waveform.

To realize a customizable speech synthesis module, the module has to accept arbitrary Japanese texts including both "Kanji" (Chinese) and "Kana" characters, and synthesize speech with a human voice clearly in a specified speaking style. Tags embedded in the text specify the speaking style according to JEIDA-62-2000, which is a descriptive scheme of text for Japanese speech synthesis and is standardized by the Japan Electronic Industry Development Association (JEIDA) [20]. Figure 4 is a sample text described with JEIDA-62-2000. The speech synthesis for a spoken dialog system is required to generate various types of prosody according to the user's intention. The task manager can describe spoken messages using the JEIDA-62-2000 tags to control prosodic parameters. For example:

```
<RATE SPEED="n"> ... </RATE>
```

lengthens the duration of tagged words by n times. For power and F0[15]:

```
<VOLUME LEVEL="n"> ... </VOLUME>
<PITCH LEVEL="n"> ... </PITCH>
```

change the power and F0 in the same manner, respectively. The pronunciation and the accent type can also be assigned to words that are not found in the dictionary, such as task-specific proper nouns. Input text written with "Kanji" and "Kana" characters and optional embedded tags is analyzed by the text analyzer, which is implemented with a free Japanese morphological analysis system, ChaSen [15], and a newly developed dictionary.

---

[15] F0 is the fundamental frequency of speech

The waveform generation engine in SSM is an HMM-based speech synthesizer that simultaneously models the spectrum, F0, and duration in a unified framework of HMM (Hidden Markov Model) [27, 9]. HMM is one of the modeling techniques for a time sequence of a parameter vector. An HMM model probabilistically generates the parameter vector based on the state transition. HMM can be used for pattern recognition, especially for speech recognition, by selecting the most probable model among models of the class for observed parameter vectors. On the other hand, HMM can be also a generator of a time sequence of the feature vector. In speech synthesis, an HMM sequence represents the phoneme sequence of a sentence, and it generates the most probable time sequence of the feature vector. HMM-based speech synthesis has the advantage of voice quality control over waveform concatenation approaches. Speaker adaptation techniques in HMM-based speech recognition can be utilized for voice conversion in HMM-based speech synthesis [22]. Such techniques enable us to easily prepare various types of speakers in the speech synthesis system. The <VOICE> tag changes the speaker of the SSM synthesizer even for partial words in an utterance.

SSM serves another important function in providing a mechanism for synchronizing the lip movement with speech, which is called "lip-sync". The employed mechanism is based on the sharing of each timing and duration of phonemes in the speech, which is going to be uttered, between the SSM and the FSM (Facial image Synthesis Module).

Finally, SSM can interrupt speech output to cope with any interruption by the user of the dialog system. This is also important to realize natural dialog between the human and the machine. When the speech output is interrupted, SSM reports the phoneme sequence of words, which the user is expected to listen to, to the agent manager.

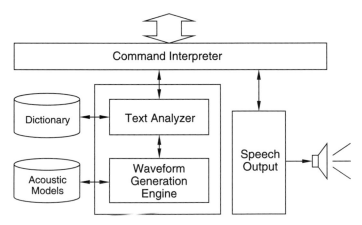

Fig. 3. Speech synthesis module

```
<SPEECH> <VOICE OPTIONAL="male1">
Kore wa <PRON SYM="ai pi: e:">IPA</PRON>no purojekuto de
('This is')                          ('of')('in the project')
kaihatsusareta <EMPH>taiwa</EMPH>onsei gousei sisutemu desu.
('developed')  ('dialogue') ('speech synthesis system')
</VOICE> </SPEECH>
```

Fig. 4. A sample of input text for the speech synthesis module. (The input text is originally written in *Kanji* and *Kana* characters. Note that this example is rewritten in roman characters with the English translation in parentheses, just for readability)

3.3 Facial Image Synthesis Module (FSM)

FSM is the software package that supports high-quality facial image synthesis, animation control, and precise lip-synchronization with synthetic and natural voice. To customize the face model, a graphical user interface is equipped to fit a generic face wire frame model onto a full-face snapshot image. Each action unit of FACS [5] is defined on this generic model and stereotype facial expressions can be synthesized by a combination of these action units. FACS is an objective method for a quantifying scheme that codes the facial muscular movements in terms of 44 action units. Also, idle actions like blinking and nodding can be generated. Lip movement in an utterance is controlled by VISEME and duration. Facial animation is expressed easily by a simple script.

Customizing the Face Model

To customize the face model by snapshot only, a generic face model is manually adjusted to the full-face image. The graphical user interface helps to shorten the time to complete this fitting process. Figure 5 shows the image before fitting and after fitting.

First, four points located on two corners of the sides of the temple, the bottom of the nose, and the top of the chin are adjusted and then facial features are decided roughly. Second, four points around each eye and the center of the eyeball are decided; the contour of the eyelid and the mouth and nose position are decided by moving control points by manually. Finally, the outline of the face is decided and the hair model is fitted. The personal face model is then completely generated. In the preview window, the fitting status of the face model is confirmed by rotating the face and make a facial expression (Fig. 6). The eyeballs can be selected in any color and size.

This model has generic oral and teeth–tongue models and they are controlled in the utterance process. After a 5 minute fitting process, any facial expression with texture mapping can be synthesized by a combination of action units of FACS which is predefined in the generic face model.

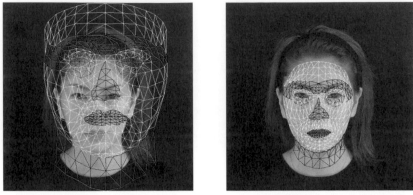

a) Before fitting   b) After fitting

Fig. 5. Model fitting by GUI tool

Fig. 6. Preview window

Facial Action Control

To control facial action, the action units of FACS and the basic mouth shape of VISEME are predefined in the generic face model.

Designing Mouth Shape

A typical mouth shape can be easily edited by use of a mouth-shape editing tool. A specific mouth shape is decided by controlling 17 parameters for the positions of lip parts. These parameters are controlled by a slider on the screen and the mouth shape can be checked interactively in a preview window. Typical vowel mouth shapes are shown in Fig. 7. All mouth shapes are already predefined for VISEME in English and Japanese.

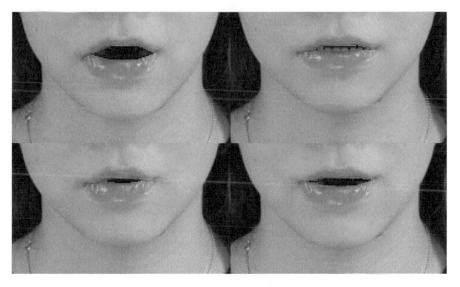

Fig. 7. Example of typical vowel mouth shapes (upper left: vowel "a", upper right: vowel "i", lower left: vowel "u", lower right: vowel "e")

Designing Facial Expression

Facial expression is generated by a combination of action units (AUs). These AUs control the basic movement of the face such as inner brow raise (AU1), upper lip raise (AU10), etc., and are composed of 44 units corresponding to each facial muscle movement. Figure 8 shows examples of typical expressions.

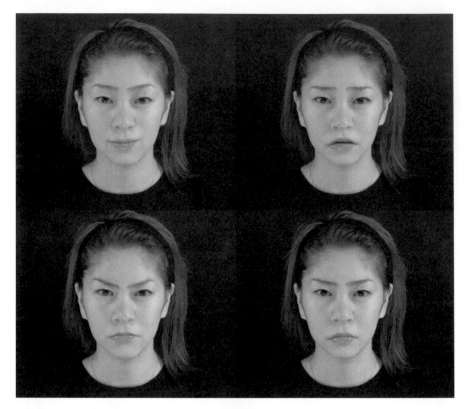

Fig. 8. Example of typical expressions (upper left: happiness, upper right: sadness, lower left: anger, lower right: fear)

3.4 Module Integration and Customization Tools

Agent Manager

The agent manager (AM) serves as an integrator of all the modules of the ASDA system. One of its main functions is to play a central role in communication where every message from a module is sent to another module with the help of the AM. Here, the AM works like a hub in the Galaxy-II system [19]. Another essential function of the AM is to work as a synchronization manager between speech synthesis and facial image animation to achieve precise lip-sync.

The AM consists of two functional layers: the direct control layer (AM-DCL) and the macro control layer (AM-MCL). Figure 9 shows a schematic representation of the relationship between the AM and various modules. On one hand, the AM-DCL works as a dispatcher receiving commands from a module and forwarding them to the designated module. On the other hand, the AM-MCL is a macro-command interpreter processing the macro com-

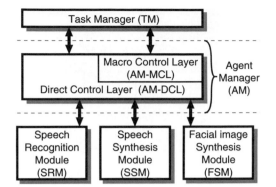

Fig. 9. Basic configuration of the AM and modules

mands mainly issued by the task manager (TM). There are mainly two functions of the AM-MCL. The first one is to simply expand each received macro-command in a sequence of commands and send them sequentially to the designated module. The second function is to process macro-commands that require more complicated processing than just expanding the commands. This happens in the case where more than one module is involved. Currently, the lip-synchronization process is realized by a macro-command and an example will be given in Sect. 4.

Virtual Machine Model

As previously described, the AM works as a hub through which every module communicates with every other one. It is desirable that every module has a common communication interface so that the AM can be connected to each module regardless of the interface used in the module. Furthermore, having a common interface reduces the effort in understanding and developing module-dependent interfaces. For this purpose a virtual machine (VM) model is employed, where the module interface is modeled as a machine with slots, each of which has a value and attribute controlled by a common command set. Each slot can be regarded as a switch or dial to control the operation or a meter to indicate machine status. Figure 10 illustrates the communication between the AM and a virtual machine model. Changing the slot values by a command corresponds to checking or controlling the running status of the module or the function. For example, issuing the following command to the SSM means starting voice synthesis of a given text immediately:

```
set Speak = Now
```

Task Manager (TM)

To achieve a better interaction between agent and human, we must learn more about the human's behavior when using the dialog systems. Because

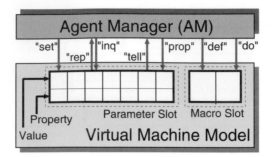

Fig. 10. Relationship between the AM and a virtual machine model

a machine's capability to recognize and understand speech or image cannot be compared with that of a human, imitating the human-to-human interactions such as speech, facial expressions, and gestures is not always the right road. First we will define the dialog as a set of interactions which can be represented by a dialog description language. The initial specification may have many limitations, but we can build a dialog system based on the specification. Using the system, we can obtain the corpus of human–machine dialogs and interactions. Investigation of the corpus may lead to better models of speech understanding, artificial minds, intelligence, and the successive interactions. Repetitions of such studies can contribute to a better design of the dialog description language, whose capability may gradually increase. Here we discuss the bootstrap design of dialog modeling and its description language which can represent the interactions with spoken language.

Although our VM model can manipulate the conversational input and output events in realtime, it is difficult to write or analyze the time sequence data of such events manually. As a software toolkit, therefore, it is crucial to use a language that can help to write dialog patterns regardless of the background details of the device controls. It is possible to use the sequence of VM controls to show the time of each output event, the content of the utterances, the changes of facial expressions, etc. A higher level dialog description language, however, can give meaning to the series of events, such as "Repeat the question until the user answers in confirmation".

Conversational phenomena can be explained with three models as follows: (i) task descriptions, which include the intentions of the participants such as question or giving information, etc., (ii) characters of the participants which include differences in voice and face as well as differences in the non-verbal communication styles, and (iii) the variations among the dialog sessions. Task description is the most important part in designing and analyzing human–machine dialogs and there are several *de facto* standards in this area. VoiceXML [25] is one such option. VoiceXML can cover two types of dialogs: (i) the slot-filling type can be a simplified machine-initiated dialog, and (ii) the database search type can be a mixed-initiative dialog. There remains, however, another type of dialog that cannot be covered well with VoiceXML: (iii) the explanation type can include navigation of the contents initiated by the user. For this type, we are investigating a new style of interface and description language for user initiated interaction [16].

To meet both the demands of convenience for dialog task designers and usability for dialog system users, it is important to choose the appropriate language for the task description that fits the dialog type. Our goal in developing the TM is that the system can use several types of dialog description languages including VoiceXML. This is enabled by dividing the system into the translator, from VoiceXML documents to the intermediate language (Primitive Dialog Operation Commands, PDOC), and the dialog controller that interprets the PDOC documents. We also extended the original specification of VoiceXML to add some commands, including the facial expression controls of anthropomorphic dialog agents. In our TM, PDOC plays the role of a low-level language that is close to the device events and sequence control, while VoiceXML plays the role of a high-level language that handles task-oriented information and the intentions of the participants. This low-level description is also expected to be useful to analyze and model the time sequence data in conversational phenomena. The current implementation of the system is tested with tasks of the system-initiative type of dialog.

In making a dialog system which can understand natural language and multi-modal input, the semantic interpretation module (SIM) plays an important role. Although there are no such modules at this stage of our development, our toolkit design allows the module to be incorporated. There may be various approaches of SIM implementations, including statistical models and the semantic parse tree. While the TM concentrates on the management of state transitions or slot-fillings, SIM can interpret the speech or multimodal input as the dialog acts.

Prototyping Tool

The rapid-prototyping tool named "Galatea Interaction Builder (IB)" runs on a PC and can handle the input modalities of speech, mouse, and keyboard as well as the output modalities of speech (TTS), facial expression, and window display. System developers can implement these input and output modalities without knowledge of the Multi-Modal Interface (MMI) description language with the support of IB [1].

MMI Description Language XISL[11]

XISL is a language for describing MMI scenarios between a user and a system. In principle, a scenario is composed of a sequence of exchanges that contains a set of user's multi-modal inputs and the system's actions corresponding to the inputs. Actions include outputs to a user, simple arithmetic operations, conditional branches, and so on. The details of the XISL specifications are on the web site [13].

Outline of Galatea Interaction Builder (IB)

Figure 11 shows the workflow of prototyping using Galatea IB. This is composed of three modules: a document-server module, a dialog manager, and a front-end module. The document server module holds the MMI scenario (XISL), the data (XML), and the view style (XSL). The dialog manager interprets an XISL document and controls the flow of dialog by integrating the user's input from the front end and executing the system's action corresponding to the inputs. The front end has an Automatic Speech Recognition (ASR) engine, a facial expression synthesis engine, and a TTS engine developed in the Galatea project, as well as a pointing device (mouse) and keyboard.

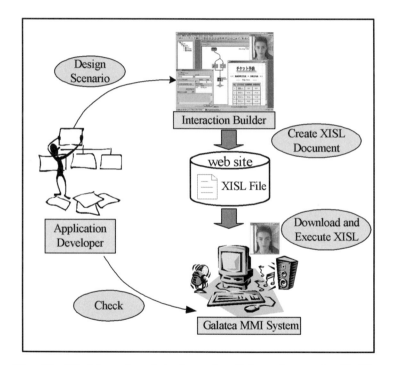

Fig. 11. Workflow of prototyping using Galatea Interaction Builder

Rapid Prototyping Using Galatea IB

Galatea IB provides a GUI designed for domain-specific prototyping that includes the applications of airline ticket reservation and secretary services. Figure 12 shows a screen of the prototyping operation. In the following, we describe the facilities of IB according to the assigned numbers in Fig. 12.

The window shown in (1) of Fig. 12 is a scenario view window that presents a state transition diagram of an MMI application. Nodes of the diagram,

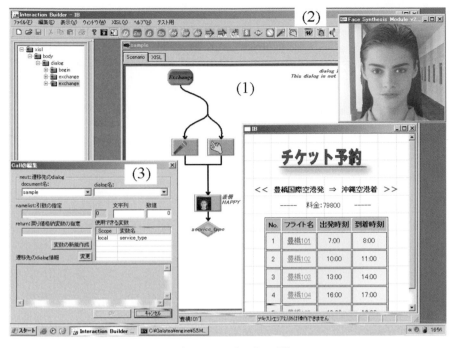

Fig. 12. An example of an IB screen

Fig. 13. Toolbar of IB

or MMI components, which correspond to elements of XISL are connected by links. An application developer can easily construct and comprehend the structure of an MMI scenario on this window. The toolbar shown in (2) of Fig. 12 provides all the components such as speech input and output, mouse, face, etc., used in MMI applications. Each button corresponds to a node of the state transition diagram. Figure 13 shows an expanded view of the toolbar. The developer has only to drag one of these buttons and drop it onto the scenario view window to add a node to the MMI scenario.

The dialog box, shown in (3) of Fig. 12, pops up when the application developer drops a button on an MMI component of the scenario view window. The developer has to assign some attributes and values to define parameters for the MMI component. The developer can confirm the XISL documents by clicking the XISL tab of the scenario view window as shown in Fig. 14. After confirmation, the developer can save the document and upload it to a document server module, and then test a prototype system with MMI.

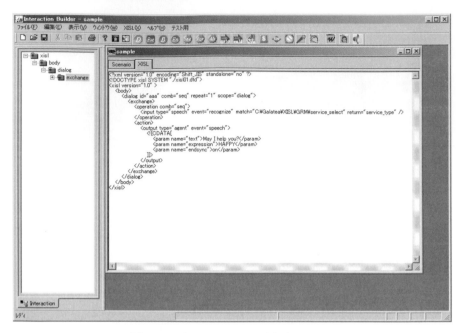

Fig. 14. A generated XISL document

4 Prototype Systems

Using the software toolkit, we have built several experimental ASDA systems to evaluate the toolkit. A screenshot of the system and an example of a user–system interaction are shown in Fig. 15 and Fig. 16, respectively.

All the tasks employed were based on a very basic small vocabulary where the number of uttered words is less than 100 and the perplexity is less than 10. The tasks include (i) an echo-back task which repeats what it heard using speech recognition and synthesis, (ii) a simple appointment-arranging task which changes facial expressions as the conversation goes on, (iii) a fresh food ordering task that takes orders from customers and responds with "yes" and nodding on the fly.

These systems consist of the SRM [12], the SSM [27], the FSM [14], the AM, and a simple task-specific TM which was programmed directly with the command set of the toolkit. We implemented the systems on several platforms with different configurations. Figure 17 shows the hardware configurations. Some of the demonstration movies (in Japanese, unfortunately) are available on our web site [7, 6].

Figure 18 shows an example of how the AM and related modules work in the echo-back task. However, the FSM and lip-synchronization mechanism have been omitted in the figure for simplicity. Here, the macro-commands, introduced previously, are used in the Procedures 3 and 4 to achieve lip-

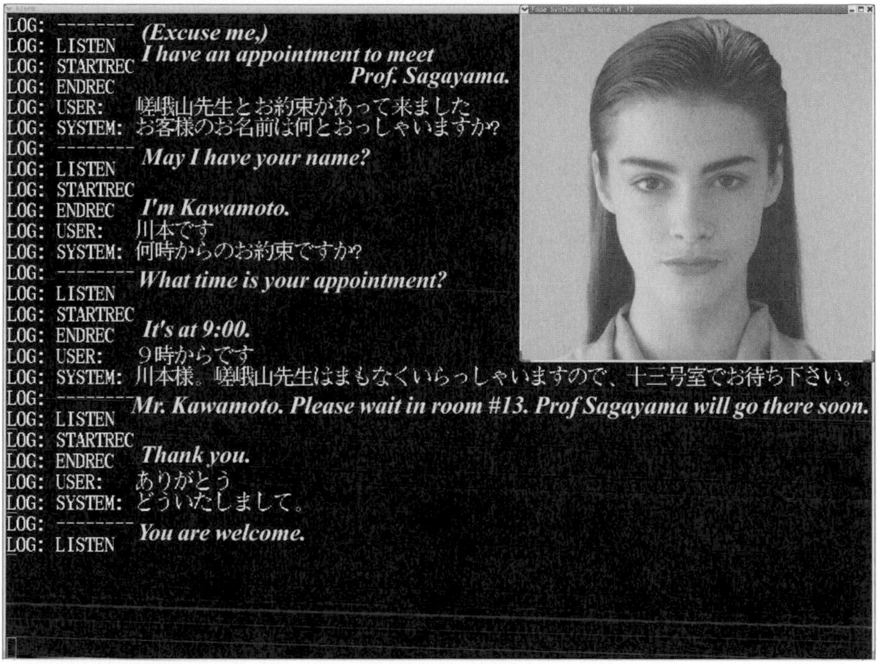

Fig. 15. Screenshot of ASDA

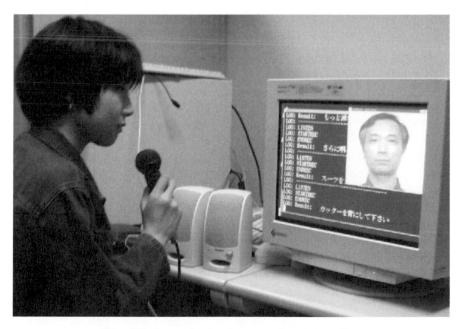

Fig. 16. An example of user–system interaction

SHORT TITLE
SRM: Speech recognition module
SSM: Speech synthesis module
FSM: Facial image synthesis module
AM: Agent manager
TM: Task manager
AUTO: Autonomous head-moving module

COMPUTER SPEC.
PC #1 ... CPU: Pentium III Xeon 1GHz x 2, MEMORY: 512MB
PC #2 ... CPU: Pentium III 600MHz x 2,   MEMORY: 512MB
PC #3 ... CPU: Mobile Pentium III 1.2GHz, MEMORY: 512MB

SYSTEM ENVIRONMENT

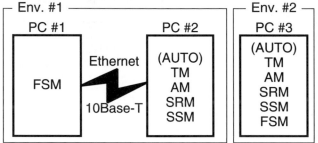

Fig. 17. Hardware configuration of ASDA

synchronization between the speech and animation. Figure 19 shows the sequence of commands involved in this lip-synchronization process.

Note that the modules operate in parallel and thus the speech recognition process is active while the agent is speaking. As a result, we confirmed that the system responded to the users quickly, and face animation and synthesized voice were synchronized. However, in this case, we assumed an ideal environment where the results of speech recognition are not influenced by the output of speech synthesis.

5 Discussion

This section describes the current development status of the software toolkit and discusses further improvements.

5.1 Customization Features

In SRM, multi-grammar support has been realized where grammars can be changed instantly, and those grammars are easy to customize by means of a supporting software tool.

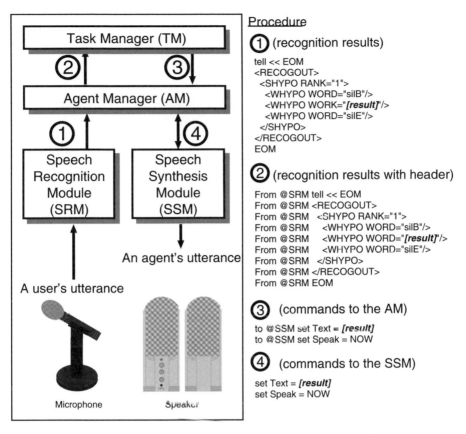

Fig. 18. An example of the echo-back processing task

SSM can synthesize speech from arbitrary text sentences of mixed "Kanji" and "Kana" (Chinese characters and phonetic script), with customizable prosody. Though speaker adaptation has not been implemented, the employed HMM-based approach is promising in the case of speaker adaptation [23, 22].

FSM synthesizes 3D realistic facial animations from a single snapshot of a person's face by fitting a wire-frame model to a 2D picture. A software tool is provided to help fit a standard wire-frame model to the input picture, whose manually fitting operation normally takes 10 minutes. Once the fitting is completed, one can get realistic 3D facial animation of the person, whose motion, including blinking and facial expression, is easily and precisely controllable by commands in real time. Compared to the existing cartoon-based approaches where the number of characters is very limited, the proposed framework enables generation of facial animations of an almost unlimited number of characters as long as facial pictures are provided.

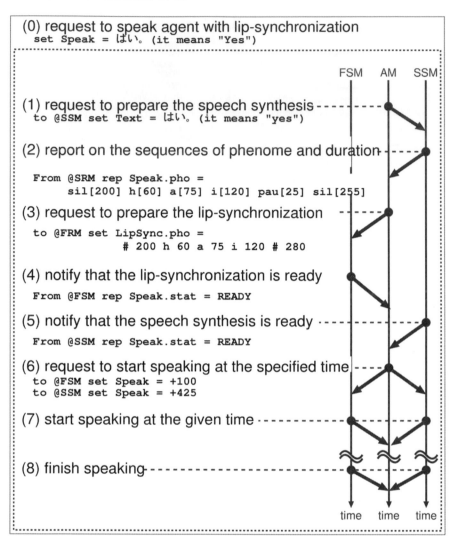

(0) request to speak agent with lip-synchronization
set Speak = はい。 (it means "Yes")

FSM   AM   SSM

(1) request to prepare the speech synthesis
to @SSM set Text = はい。 (it means "yes")

(2) report on the sequences of phenome and duration

From @SRM rep Speak.pho =
      sil[200] h[60] a[75] i[120] pau[25] sil[255]

(3) request to prepare the lip-synchronization

to @FRM set LipSync.pho =
              # 200 h 60 a 75 i 120 # 280

(4) notify that the lip-synchronization is ready

From @FSM rep Speak.stat = READY

(5) notify that the speech synthesis is ready

From @SSM rep Speak.stat = READY

(6) request to start speaking at the specified time
to @FSM set Speak = +100
to @SSM set Speak = +425

(7) start speaking at the given time

(8) finish speaking

time   time   time

Fig. 19. Processing flow among AM, SSM, and FSM when the agent speaks (an example of processing in the AM)

5.2 Software Modularity of Functional Units

As described in the previous section, the virtual machine model enables high modularity of each functional unit such as SRM, SSM, and FSM. Furthermore, the communication interface based on the UNIX standard I/O stream helps to develop and debug software modules easily.

5.3 Achievement of Natural Spoken Dialog

Although the implemented mechanism for lip-sync contributes to the enhancement of the naturalness of the synthetic facial animation, a number of issues are yet to be implemented to make the agent behave like a human. For example, humans move their heads while they are speaking. Besides facial animation, real-time conversation is another crucial factor for the agent's naturalness as described in Sect. 2.2. A simple mechanism for incremental speech recognition has been implemented in SRM. The mechanism provides frame-synchronous temporal candidates giving maximum scores at the moment before observing the end of utterance. These incremental recognition results will help to achieve interactive spoken dialog including nodding.

5.4 Related Works

Several attempts have been made to develop ASDA toolkits. Among them, the CSLU toolkit [21] is the most similar to our toolkit. The CSLU toolkit provides a modular, open architecture supporting distributed, cross-platform, client/server-based networking. It includes interfaces for standard telephony, audio devices, and software interfaces for speech recognition. It also includes text-to-speech and animation components. This flexible environment makes it possible to easily integrate new components and to develop scalable, portable speech-related applications. Although the target of both of the toolkits is similar, function-wise and implementation-wise they are different. Compared to the speech recognizer and speech synthesizer of the CSLU toolkit that support several European languages, our toolkit supports the Japanese language. The TTS in the CSLU toolkit is based on "unit selection and concatenation synthesis" from natural speech. It is a data-driven and *non*-model-based approach. However, the TTS in our toolkit employs HMM-based synthesis that is a data-driven and model-based approach. The different approaches give different characteristics to the TTS. Generally speaking, the model-based TTS requires less training samples and it can control speech more easily than the non-model-based TTS at the cost of speech quality.

Similar system architectures for distributed computing environments are employed in Galaxy-II [19] of the DARPA Communicator [3], the SRI Open Agent Architecture (OAA) [17], and our toolkit. Each of them has a central module called "Hub", "facilitator", and Agent Manager (AM), respectively. If compared to the existing systems which employ a large number of commands, our toolkit is more compact and simpler and it has only eight commands and two identifiers so that the programmers can easily understand and use the toolkit.

6 Conclusions

The design and architecture of a software toolkit for building an easy to customize anthropomorphic spoken dialog agent (ASDA) has been presented in this chapter. A human-like spoken dialog agent is one of the promising man-machine interfaces for the next generation. The beta-version of the software toolkit described in this chapter will be released publicly in the middle of 2003. However, a number of factors will be improved. Because of the high modularity and simple communication architecture employed in the toolkit, we hope that it will speed up the research and application development based on ASDA, and as a result the toolkit will be upgraded.

References

1. Adachi, H., Katsurada, K., Yamada, H., Nitta, T.: Development of a prototyping tool for MMI systems. In: *Information Processing Society of Japan*, Technical Report 2002-SLP-43 (in Japanese) (2002) pp 7–12
2. Cassell, J., Bickmore, T., Campbell, L., Chang, K., Vilhjálmsson, H., Yan, H.: Requirements for an architecture for embodied conversational characters. In: *Proceedings of Computer Animation and Simulation '99 (Eurographics Series)*, ed Thalmann, D., Thalmann, N. (1999) pp 109–122
3. DARPA Communicator Program. http://fofoca.mitre.org/ (1998)
4. Dohi, H., Ishizuka, M.: Visual Software Agent: A realistic face-to-face style interface connected with WWW/Netscape. In: *IJCAI Workshop on Intelligent Multimodal Systems* (1997) pp 17–22
5. Ekman, P., Friesen, W.V.: *Facial Action Coding System (FACS): A technique for the measurement of facial action* (Consulting Psychologists Press, Palo Alto, CA 1978)
6. Galatea Toolkit. http://hil.t.u-tokyo.ac.jp/~galatea/ (2002)
7. Galatea Toolkit. http://iipl.jaist.ac.jp/IPA/ (2002)
8. Gustafson, J., Lindberg, N., Lundeberg, M.: The August spoken dialogue system. In: *EuroSpeech* (1999) pp 1151–1154
9. HMM-Based Speech Synthesis Toolkit. http://hts.ics.nitech.ac.jp/ (2002)
10. Julia, L., Cheyer, A.: Is talking to virtual more realistic? In: *EuroSpeech* (1999) pp 1719–1722
11. Katsurada, K., Otani, Y., Nakamura, Y., Kobayashi, S., Yamada, H., Nitta, T.: A modality-independent MMI system architecture. In: *Proceedings ICSLP* (2002) pp 2549–2552
12. Kawahara, T., Kobayashi, T., Takeda, T., Minematsu, N., Itou, K., Yamamoto, M., Utsuro, T., Shikano, K.: Sharable software repository for Japanese large vocabulary continuous speech recognition. In: *Proceedings ICSLP* (1998) pp 3257–3260
13. MMI Description Language XISL. http://www.vox.tutkie.tut.ac.jp/XISL/XISL-E.html (2002)
14. Morishima, S.: Face analysis and synthesis. *IEEE Signal Processing Magazine* **18**(3):26–34 (2001)

15. Morphological Analyzer ChaSen. http://chasen.aist-nara.ac.jp/index.html.en (2000)

16. Nishimoto, T., Araki, M., Niimi, Y.: RadioDoc: A voice-accessible document system. In: *Proceedings ICSLP* (2002) pp 1485–1488

17. The Open Agent Architecture. http://www.ai.sri.com/~oaa/ (2001)

18. Sakamoto, K., Hinode, H., Watanuki, K., Seki, S., Kiyama, J., Togawa, F.: A response model for a CG character based on timing of interactions in a multimodal human interface. In: *IUI-97* (1997) pp 257–260

19. Seneff, S., Hurley, E., Lau, R., Pao, C., Schmid, P., Zue, V.: GALAXY-II: A referece architecture for conversational system development. In: *Proceedings ICSLP* (1998) pp 931–934

20. Standard of symbols for Japanese text-to-speech synthesizer: JEIDA-62-2000 (2000)

21. Sutton, S., Cole, R.: Universal speech tools: The CSLU Toolkit. In: *Proceedings ICSLP* (1998) pp 3221–3224

22. Tamura, M., Masuko, T., Tokuda, K., Kobayashi, T.: Adaptation of pitch and spectrum for HMM-based speech synthesis using MLLR. In: *ICASSP*, Vol. 2 (2001) pp 805–808

23. Tamura, M., Masuko, T., Tokuda, K., Kobayashi, T.: Text-to-speech synthesis with arbitrary speaker's voice from average voice. In: *Proceedings of European Conference on Speech Communication and Technology*, Vol. 1 (2001) pp 345–348

24. Ushida, H., Hirayama, Y., Nakajima, H.: Emotion model for life-like agent and its evaluation. In: *AAAI-98* (1998) pp 62–69

25. Voice eXtensible Markup Language (VoiceXML), Version 1.0. http://www.voicexml.org (2000)

26. XSL Transformations (XSLT), Version 1.0. http://www.w3.org/TR/xslt (1999)

27. Yoshimura, T., Tokuda, K., Masuko, T., Kobayashi, T., Kitamura, T.: Simultaneous modeling of spectrum, pitch and duration in HMM-based speech synthesis. In: *EuroSpeech*, Vol. 5 (1999) pp 2347–2350

MPML and SCREAM: Scripting the Bodies and Minds of Life-Like Characters

Helmut Prendinger, Santi Saeyor, and Mitsuru Ishizuka

Department of Information and Communication Engineering
Graduate School of Information Science and Technology
University of Tokyo
7-3-1 Hongo, Bunkyo-ku, Tokyo 113-8656, Japan
prendinger@acm.org, {santi,ishizuka}@miv.t.u-tokyo.ac.jp

Summary. In this chapter, we discuss scripting tools for the purpose of creating web-based interaction scenarios featuring life-like characters. The Multi-modal Presentation Markup Language (MPML) is an XML-style language that provides tagging structures for the verbal and non-verbal behavior of cartoon-style characters, presentation flow, and integration of external objects, like Java applets. While MPML supports the control of embodied agents with predefined (scripted) behavior, the Scripting Emotion-based Agent Minds (SCREAM) system allows us to design agents that autonomously generate emotionally and socially appropriate behaviors based on their character profile. In order to facilitate high-level scripting and connectivity with MPML, the SCREAM system is written in a lightweight Java-based Prolog system and Java. The implementation of a casino scenario running in a web browser demonstrates the power and flexibility of both systems.

1 Introduction

Life-like characters constitute a promising technology for human–computer interaction. The embodiment of agents provides effective means of imitating human skills such as presenting information or engaging in a conversation [24, 14]. Humans communicate using not only language, but also body gestures and facial expressions. The fundamental hypothesis underlying the life-like character research program is that by endowing agents with synthetic counterparts of the interaction modalities and competencies used by humans, character-based interfaces can be effective tools to enhance the interaction between humans and computers.

The wide dissemination of animated agents, however, will greatly depend on the availability of appropriate tools that facilitate the scripting (or authoring) of agents with life-like behavior. Tasks for designing life-like characters can be divided into two categories. *First*, the content author has to instruct the "body" of an animated character, including the control and synchronization of the character's verbal and non-verbal (embodied) behavior, and possibly the coordination of the behavior of multiple characters. *Second*, the author has to design the mental make-up of a character, its "mind", such that it will show emotionally and socially appropriate responses toward other agents. In this chapter, we will discuss scripting languages for instructing the bodies and minds of life-like characters. The remaining document is organized as follows. First, we report on related work and motivate our own approach. In Sect. 2, we will describe the Multi-modal Presentation Markup Language (MPML). Section 3 is dedicated to explaining the Scripting Emotion-based Agent Minds (SCREAM) system. Both languages will be illustrated in the context of an application scenario, a web-based casino. In Sect. 4, we will summarize and conclude the chapter.

1.1 Scripting the Bodies of Life-Like Characters

Animating the visual appearance of a character is a difficult task that involves many levels, from changes to each individual degree of freedom in the motion model to high-level concerns about how to express a character's personality by means of its movement. While scripting at a "low level" concerns manipulating a character's facial and body motion models, "high-level" scripting is related to the synchronization of a character's synthetic speech with appropriate gestures, the expression of emotions, and the synchronization of body motion sequences of an ensemble of characters. Description levels can also be conceived as abstraction levels where higher levels "abstract from" lower level description concerns. Abstract specifications are then instantiated to low-level body actions by special purpose interpreters.

Most existing scripting languages, however, cover a range of different abstraction levels in a single language. For instance, the Character Markup Language (CML) of Arafa et al. [5] allows one to specify abstract concepts such as the emotion "happy" as well as low-level behaviors like "blinking". The Virtual Human Markup Language (VHML) developed by Mariott and Stallo [32] comprises tags for facial and body animation, speech, gesture, and even dialogue. Scripting languages also differ in their focus on a particular competence envisioned for the character. The Behavior Expression Animation Toolkit (BEAT) of Cassell et al. [15] allows one to synchronize synthetic speech and non-verbal behavior, and the Affective Presentation Markup Language (APML) of De Carolis et al. [16] targets communicative functions.

While most markup languages developed for life-like characters demonstrate sophisticated control mechanisms, they typically address programming expert content creators or animators rather than the average user. In this chapter, we will describe the Multi-modal Presentation Markup Language (MPML), a language specifically designed at an abstraction level appropriate for non-experts that allows us to direct the behavior of multiple animated characters in web-based (interactive) presentations. First, MPML is a *markup language* compliant with standard XML [55] and hence allows for scripting in a style that is familiar to a broad audience. Second, MPML is a language tailored to script character-based *presentations* that can be viewed in a web browser. In order to facilitate the generation of different kinds of presentations, MPML provides appropriate tagging structures that enable authors to utilize features of presentations given by human presenters in web-based presentation environments, such as dynamic media objects or interaction with the audience. Finally, MPML supports the generation of *multi-modal* presentations: that is, presentations that utilize multiple mechanisms to encode information to be conveyed, including (character) animation, spoken (synthetic) language, music, and video [10]. In this chapter, we will focus on modalities specific to animated agents. Besides synthetic speech, animated characters may communicate information by using multiple modalities, such as facial displays (in order to express emotions), hand gestures (including pointing and propositional gestures), head movements ("nodding"), and body posture.

1.2 Scripting the Minds of Life-Like Characters

A task complementary to scripting a character's visual appearance is to author a character's mental state, the way the character perceives its surrounding (and internal) world, and how the character reacts emotionally. A direct way of scripting a character's responses is realized by the Verbots of Virtual Personalities [52]. An author may specify rules (including wild cards) that fire upon certain patterns of typed texts, thereby allowing Eliza-style conversations. For a similar purpose, the Artificial Intelligence Markup Language (AIML) has been developed [1]. However, since neither the Verbot nor the AIML approach support the definition of an emotion or world model, they are of limited use for scripting emotionally adequate and consistent agent behavior. Elliott [23] describes a full-fledged architecture for reasoning about emotion and personality, the Affective Reasoner. Despite its importance as a simulation platform for emotion-based agent interactions, the Affective Reasoner does not (directly) address the scripting issue. The Em architecture of Reilly [45] consists of a set of scripting tools for the creation of emotion-based agents. Emotion generators (a kind of appraisal rules) take sensory inputs and produce so-called emotion structures, which are emotion types together with information about intensity, cause, and direction ("happy for Lisa with intensity x because Lisa found a new job"). The resulting emotion structures are processed by combination and decay functions and are then mapped into behavioral features, that is instructions for the agent's behavior. Authors can build agents with Reilly's Em by means of so-called Hap rules that determine the input and output of the respective processes.

Blumberg [9] proposes an ethology-inspired approach to interactive agents, and focusses on the problem of action selection in artificial animals ("animats"). Hamsterdam, an object-oriented toolkit, allows one to build autonomous animats by defining their internal needs, activities they can perform, a sensory and motor system, and by using a behavior system that implements

Blumberg's model of action selection. However, action selection is based on animal-specific drives and motivations rather than a human emotion model.

A powerful authoring system for web-based user–agent interactions is the commercial toolkit developed by Extempo Systems Inc. [25], based on Hayes-Roth's experience with interactive animated characters, as described in [47, 29]. Another system that targets web-based presentations is the Inhabited Market Place (IMP), developed by André and Rist [4, 3]. They describe a mechanism that allows one to automatically design presentation dialogues between multiple animated characters. The approach is plan-based and conditions characters' responses on their social role and models of emotion and personality. Rist et al. [46] present powerful and up-to-date technologies for a wide variety of human–agent and agent–agent interaction scenarios.

The Scripting Emotion-based Agent Minds (SCREAM) system described in this chapter is a scripting tool that enables authors to create emotionally and socially appropriate responses of animated characters. Content authors design the mental make-up of an agent by declaring a variety of parameters and behaviors relevant to affective communication as (syntactically) simple facts, and obtain quantified affective reactions that can be input to an animation engine. While the default operations of an agent's mind are based on psychological and sociological research, authors may modify and extend its rule set. SCREAM is in many ways similar to Reilly's [45] Em architecture, but more flexible in the sense that it allows scripting at various levels of detail – or granularity – from driven purely by personality traits to full awareness of the social interaction including character-specific beliefs and beliefs attributed to other characters. Like the Extempo [25] and IMP [4] systems, the system exploits web technologies so that emotion-based synthetic characters can be run in a web browser. Although the system provides support for authoring character ensembles, it does not do so automatically, as in [4]. The main reasons are that we wanted to give the author control over each dialogue move and delegate the task of producing the propositional content (meaning) of the character's communicative act to the application designer.

2 Multi-Modal Presentation Markup Language

The Multi-modal Presentation Markup Language (MPML) is a scripting language to instruct the body-related behavior of animated agents. Given the requirements of its intended use as a presentation markup language, the salient features of MPML can be summarized as follows.

Ease of Use. Presentations featuring animated characters should be easy to write and not assume programming skills. Since MPML is an XML-style markup language, scripting is intuitive and accessible even to non-programmers. An editor has been developed that graphically depicts the flow of the presentation (see also the SMIL editors [50]).

Intelligibility. The tags of a markup language should provide names and abbreviations that clearly indicate their meaning. MPML tags are easy to learn and remember as they follow conventions well known from scripting web pages with HTML (**head** and **body** elements), or from human performances, such as the **scene** element.

Believability. The markup language should facilitate the scripting of what might be called "consistent emergent behavior" or simply believable characters. Since MPML, by design, is a scripting language where character behavior is under the full control[1] of the content author, this feature is not supported (see, however, the discussion of SCREAM in Sect. 3). Making the agent move and speak according to its intended personality and style is the responsibility of the author, and mostly sufficient for the task of scripting presentations.

Extensibility. A markup language should support authors in specifying new functionality, in order to allow easy adaption to the special requirements of content providers. MPML is extensible as it provides tagging structures that interface MPML with the target control language of characters and web pages (JavaScript). Thus, features not supported by MPML can be added at the cost of scripting in the JavaScript or the Java programming language.

Easy Distribution. The presentation should be easy to install on the platform of the target audience. In the MPML system, a converter transforms the MPML script to JavaScript and every browser that has JavaScript enabled can run a presentation written in MPML. However, there are restrictions deriving from the agent system used to control the behavior of characters, namely the Microsoft Agent package [33]. Currently, MPML assumes Microsoft Internet Explorer 5.5 (or higher) to run character-based presentations.

2.1 The MPML Family of Presentation Markup Languages

Historically, the version of MPML that will be described in this chapter (MPML3.0) is a descendant of earlier developed converter-type presentation markup languages. This version also allows one to direct rich emotional facial expression of a pseudo-muscle based 3D "talking head" (see Fig. 1) besides characters using the Microsoft Agent package as the animation engine [6]. Other members of the MPML family employ the eXtensible Stylesheet Language (XSL) [11] to define the form of the MPML content script, rather than a converter. Figure 2 shows a 2D

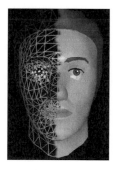

Fig. 1. "SmArt" agent

cartoon-style character presenting some members of the MPML family.

The following three members of the MPML language family adhere to the technique of using an XSL stylesheet for "on the fly" conversion to JavaScript.

---

[1] An exception is "idle behaviors" of the character, such as "blinking" or slight movements of the body.

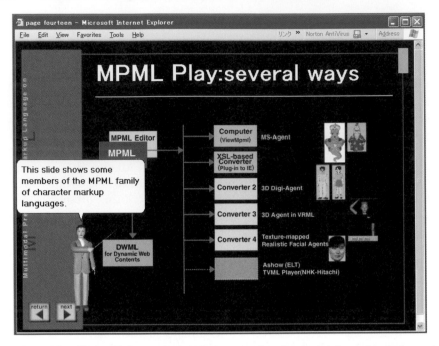

Fig. 2. The "Shima" character presents control technologies for animated agents

Like MPML3.0, the first two languages use the Microsoft Agent package, whereas the third one uses VRML2.0.

- *MPML2.2a:* This version of MPML supports sequential and parallel behavior of multiple characters. It also provides an interface to Macromedia Flash [31], so that a character can control a Flash movie and a Flash movie may contain triggers for character behavior [48].

- *DWML:* This member of the MPML family is concerned with scripting dynamic (time-dependent, spatial, etc.) relations between web-based media objects. The Dynamic Web Markup Language (DWML) treats both synthetic characters *and* text, graphics, audio, and video as first-class control objects [21]. For instance, a time control function allows one to define the temporal occurrence of media objects during presentation (using DHTML), which are otherwise (in HTML/JavaScript programming) immediately shown when a web page is loaded.

- *MPML–VR:* Here, a variant of the MPML2.2a language is employed and enriched to control a 3D virtual space and a 3D character. The resulting markup language – MPML for Virtual Reality – enables presentations in 3D space [36].

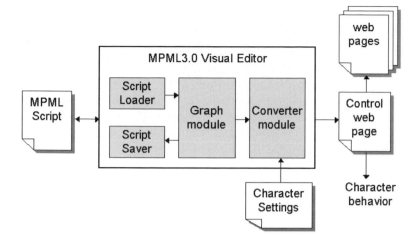

Fig. 3. MPML3.0 system architecture

2.2 MPML System Architecture

An overview of the MPML3.0 system architecture is shown in Fig. 3. The two main components are the MPML Script text file and the MPML3.0 Visual Editor application program. The MPML Script text file contains the tagging structures specifying character and environment control.

The Visual Editor consists of four modules.

- The *Script Loader* module loads the text file containing MPML script and checks the script for syntactical errors.
- The *Graph* module visualizes the script by generating a graphical representation of the presentation.
- The *Script Saver* module converts the graph to a textual MPML script.
- The *Converter* module transforms the MPML script to JavaScript.

The resulting Control web page instructs the characters' behavior and background web pages, that is pages depicting the environment that the characters inhabit. The user may also define character-specific settings, which are stored in the Character Settings file and processed by the converter. Currently, the file contains the speech parameters proposed by Murray and Arnott [35] for five emotions (fear, anger, sadness, happiness, and disgust).

2.3 MPML Specification

A compact way to describe a markup language (a set of tagging structures) is to give its document type definition (DTD), which is a set of rules that defines the grammar of an XML document. A DTD provides a list of elements, attributes, and entities as well as the relationships between elements [28]. Although DTD technology has been superseded by XML Schemas [56], we will present the markup language in a DTD for readability. The tagging structures of the markup language will only be written when showing example scripts.

Conventions and Notation. Each tag used in MPML will be declared with an element declaration that specifies the name and child elements of the element. If no child elements exist for a tag, it is called "empty". For most of the MPML elements, attributes must be declared, possibly including a default value. Attributes are name–value pairs separated by "=". An attribute value may be required or fixed, denoted by #REQUIRED and #FIXED, respectively. For convenience, we will also provide entity declarations [11]. An ordered list of child elements is denoted by "(e1, e2, ..., eN)". An unordered list of child elements is denoted by "(e1 | e2 |...| eN)". The notation "e?" means that element e may occur zero or one time. The notation "e+" means that e may occur one or more times, "e*" means that e may occur zero or more times, and "e" means that the element must occur exactly one time.

In the following subsections, we will introduce the most relevant tagging structures of the MPML specification. The full specification can be found online [30]. The root element's structure <mpml>...</mpml> contains all other tagging structures of the script. The head element specifies general information, the title, and the character(s) that will perform as presenters. The seq element that is automatically included within the <body>...</body> tagging structure refers to the sequence of events comprising the presentation.

Tagging Structures for Character Control

Tagging structures controlling character behavior are summarized in Table 1. They allow the script author to make characters speak, think, perform an action, move to a certain location on the screen, and listen to the speech command of the user. The speak element may contain a (unordered) sequence of three child elements, emotion, nb, and txt, which provide the means to let the character speak one or more sentences with affective voice (as defined in the Character Settings), possibly separated by opening a new balloon after a certain part of the text has been spoken. The character may also speak some text which results from user interaction with the background web page. For instance, if the user previously input his or her name to a form, the character can retrieve the name, and address the user in a personal way. A balloon serves as a visual support for synthetic speech. Actions refer to 2D animation sequences defined for a particular character. Typically, around 50 actions are available for characters controlled by the Microsoft Agent package [33]. By using the listen element, the speech recognizer is activated and recognizes sentences which are defined as attribute values of the heard element (a child of the listen element).

Table 1. DTD for character-related elements

```
<!ELEMENT speak ((emotion | nb | txt)*)>
<!-- The id of the agent -->
<!ATTLIST speak agent      CDATA #REQUIRED>
<!ELEMENT emotion EMPTY>
<!ENTITY % BASIC-EMOTIONS
       "(fear | anger | sadness | happiness | disgust)">
<!ATTLIST emotion assign   %BASIC-EMOTIONS #REQUIRED>
<!ELEMENT think ((nb | txt)*)>
<!ATTLIST think agent      CDATA #REQUIRED>
<!ELEMENT act EMPTY>
<!-- An action specified for the agent like Greet,
     Explain, or Surprised -->
<!ATTLIST act agent        CDATA #REQUIRED
              act          CDATA #REQUIRED>
<!ELEMENT move EMPTY>
<!ATTLIST move agent       CDATA #REQUIRED
              x            CDATA #REQUIRED
              y            CDATA #REQUIRED>
<!ELEMENT listen (heard+)>
<!ATTLIST listen agent     CDATA #REQUIRED>
<!ELEMENT heard EMPTY>
<!-- A sentence that should be recognized -->
<!ATTLIST heard sentence   CDATA #REQUIRED>
<!ELEMENT nb EMPTY>
<!-- A duration in milliseconds -->
<!ATTLIST nb pause CDATA>
<!ELEMENT txt EMPTY>
<!-- The address of a variable defined
     in the background web page -->
<!ATTLIST txt target       CDATA #REQUIRED>
```

Tagging Structures for Presentation Control

The flow of a presentation written in MPML is specified by the tagging structures shown in Table 2. The scene element determines which characters are visible in the browser window. The seq and par elements are responsible for events that should be executed sequentially and in parallel, respectively, and inspired by the corresponding tags in SMIL [50]. The par element implements a (simple) form of conversational behavior between characters, where a character's speech can be synchronized with another character's behavior, such as backchannel feedback ("nodding"). However, the realization of characters' conversational behavior is restricted by the Microsoft Agent animation sequences that do no allow for precise timing in synchronization.

The execute element allows the script author to execute a function or method of the background web page, such as a JavaScript function or a Java

Table 2. DTD for presentation-related elements

```
<!ENTITY % COMMON-CHILDREN
        "(seq | par | page | emotion | execute | wait |
         consult | pause | move | act | speak | think)*">
<!ELEMENT scene %COMMON-CHILDREN;>
<!ATTLIST scene agents     CDATA #REQUIRED>
<!ELEMENT seq %COMMON-CHILDREN;>
<!ENTITY % PAR-CHILDREN
        "((scene | seq | par | emotion | execute | wait | consult |
         pause | move | act | speak | think)*)">
<!ELEMENT par  %PAR-CHILDREN>
<!ELEMENT page %COMMON-CHILDREN;>
<!-- The URL of a background page -->
<!ATTLIST page ref         CDATA #REQUIRED >
<!ELEMENT execute EMPTY>
<!-- The address of a function to be executed -->
<!ATTLIST execute target   CDATA #REQUIRED>
<!ELEMEMT consult (test+)>
<!-- The address of a variable subject to the test -->
<!ATTLIST consult target   CDATA #REQUIRED>
<!ELEMENT test (seq)>
<!-- The value of the variable -->
<!ATTLIST test value       CDATA #REQUIRED>
```

method. It is typically used to change background web pages and trigger the execution of media objects. The consult and test elements enable communication between MPML and external objects. Most importantly, the consult element introduces branching into the otherwise linear presentation script. The value of the target attribute is a function of an external object, such as a Java method. Here, the result returned by executing the Java method is tested for string identity with the value of the value attribute of the test element. If identical, a sequence of events is triggered which corresponds to the chosen branch of the presentation. We will make ample use of the execute, consult, and test elements when introducing characters whose behavior is decided autonomously.

2.4 MPML Visual Editor

Script authors working with MPML either edit the file containing the MPML tagging structures or manipulate the graphical representation corresponding to the script. Considering the complexity of a script with nested tagging structures and the popularity of visual interfaces, working on the graph representation is often preferable. Some authors, however, are more used to directly editing the MPML Script file and launching the converter that generates the executable script. Since the output scripts of those MPML scripts are often

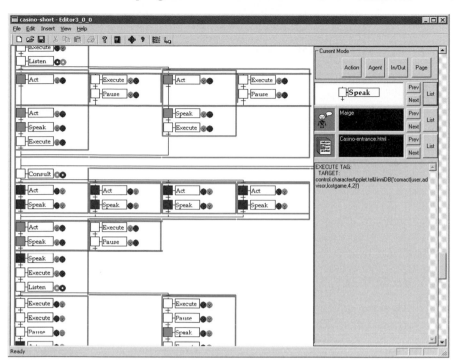

Fig. 4. The MPML3.0 Visual Editor

erroneous and thus cannot be run in the browser, an error handler has been implemented to direct the user to the erroneous part of the MPML script.

The MPML3.0 Visual Editor consists of two main windows (see Fig. 4). The window to the left – the (presentation) *Graph* window – shows the graphical presentation of the MPML script, and the window to the right – the *Current Mode* window – displays the current location of user interaction with the graph. The upper part of the Current Mode window allows the script author to choose a character (e.g. "Marge"), the character's behavior (such as "act" or "speak"), and the web page that serves as a background for the characters' performance. The lower part of the Current Mode window depicts the current attribute–value pair of the element whose associated box (configuration) in the Graph window shares the physical location with the current mouse position (i.e. the mouse is "over" the box). Authors may edit tag elements in the Current Mode window and then drag and drop the box associated with the tag at the appropriate position in the presentation graph in the Graph window.

A presentation graph is built up from the following entities. A *node* is displayed as a box configuration with three parts. The rectangle located in the middle refers to a tag element, for example **execute** or **speak**. The circle(s) to its right refer(s) to the characters that are visible in the current scene.

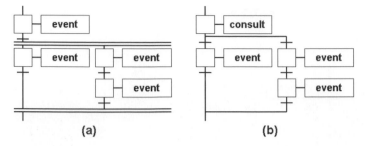

Fig. 5. Examples of a graph with: (a) a parallel edge; (b) a branching edge. Events can be substituted by characters' actions, speech, loading a web page, etc.

A circle showing a colored ("Smiley") face denotes the performing character of an action. For convenience of the author, a square box to the right of the rectangle will have the same color and hence facilitates tracking which character is performing at a node in the graph. The *edges* in the graph can be divided into "sequential", "parallel", and "branching" edges.

- A *sequential edge* is a (down-side) directed arc between two nodes and denotes the next action in the presentation flow.
- A *parallel edge* is a directed arc between a node and a set of nodes each of which initializes a sequence of events, such as actions carried out by multiple agents in parallel (see Fig. 5(a)).
- A *branching edge* is a directed arc between a node and a set of nodes such that the node that satisfies a certain condition initializes a sequence of events. The condition may depend on user interaction or, if autonomous agents are used, the behavior suggested by the reasoning engine of the character (see Fig. 5(b)).

In order to visualize presentation elements connected by different kinds of edges, the presentation graph uses colored frames. The pull-down menus of the Visual Editor include the standard options of visual interfaces, such as loading and saving a presentation graph, inserting new presentation elements, etc. The toolbar provides buttons to switch between operating on the presentation graph or editing the tagging structures of the corresponding MPML Script file, and to launch the presentation, in addition to common tools.

When creating a textual presentation script, authors often produce errors, and hence the script cannot be converted to a graphical presentation or executable script. The most common errors are imprecise use of MPML tagging structures or simply typographical errors. For the convenience of the author, error management has been integrated to the Script Loader module of the Visual Editor. A finite-state machine parses the MPML script, and if an illegal character is encountered, a message notifies the author of the error, often together with an indication of the likely problem (see Descamps [18]).

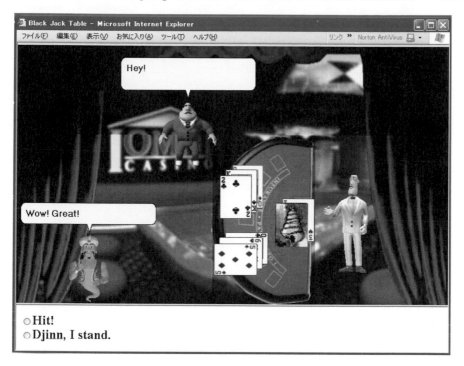

Fig. 6. Casino Scenario

2.5 Using MPML to Script an Interactive Presentation

This section shows how an author may use the tagging structures of MPML to mark up an interactive presentation. As an interaction setting, we will describe a casino scenario where the user and other characters can play the game of "Black Jack". In our game scenario, the table seats a dealer and two players (see Fig. 6). In the right half of the (Internet Explorer) window, the character "James" is in the role of the dealer. The first seat on the dealer's left (the "First Base") is occupied by the user who may interact with the game by uttering one of the sentences displayed in the lower frame window of the (Explorer) window depicting the current scene. To the dealer's right (the "Third Base"), the character "Al" is in the role of another player. At the bottom left of the window, the character "Genie" acts as the user's advisor to play the game, and is introduced as "Djinn".

The casino scenario employs two types of scripting approaches. The behaviors of James and Al are predefined ("scripted") whereas the responses of the advisor Djinn are autonomously generated depending on his mental state. The latter approach requires a knowledge-based reasoning module and will be extensively discussed in Sect. 3. In the following example, we will focus on scripting a scene where only the dealer and the advisor are present.

```
 1 <listen agent="Genie">
 2   <heard value="Djinn I hit">
 3   <scene agents="Genie,James">
 4     <page ref="casino-main.html">
 5       <execute target="control.changebottom('ans.html')"/>
 6       <execute target="[...].href='g3-2.html'"/>
 7       <act agent="Genie" act="Uncertain"/>
 8       <speak agent="Genie">
 9         We have 17 now... That's not an easy decision,
10         but I would stand.
11       </speak>
12       <execute target="control.changebottom('ans-5.html')"/>
13       <listen agent="Genie">
14         <heard value="Stand">
15           <scene agents="James,Genie">
16             <page ref="Casino-main.html">
17               <par>
18                 <seq>
19                 <act agent="James" act="GestureRight"/>
20                 </seq>
21                 <seq>
22                 <execute target="[...].href='g3-3win.html'"/>
23                 </seq>
24               </par>
25               <act agent="James" act="Sad"/>
26               <speak agent="James">
27                 The bank gets 24 and loses. Player wins,
28                 you're lucky guys.
29               </speak>
30               <execute target="control.chApplet.tellJinniDB(
31                          'comact(user,advisor,wongame,4,1)')"/>
32             </page>
33           </scene>
34         </heard>
35         <heard value="Hit">
36           ...
37         </heard>
38     ...
39   </heard>
40   ...
41 </listen>
```

Fig. 7. MPML script

Figure 7 shows a script fragment of the casino scenario. Emotional markup is omitted for simplicity. In line 1, the character "Genie" is enabled to accept the speech command from the user, followed by a branching edge of multiple alternatives, where part of the first branch is shown (lines 2–39). This branch is chosen when the user utters "Djinn I hit". The user's command has the following consequences. First, in line 5, the bottom frame is "cleared" by replacing it with a frame window that disables user interaction, denoted by ans.html. Next, in line 6, an (embedded) sub-frame window of the main window, casino-main.html, is replaced by the new sub-frame window g3-2.html that depicts the updated game board state. After Djinn displays the "Uncertain" animation sequence (line 7), he verbally suggests to stand (lines 8–11), and then the bottom frame is replaced by a sub-frame window (ans-5.html) showing a new pair of user choices (line 12). Again, we describe the expansion of only one branch, where the user decides to follow Djinn's suggestion. This branch (lines 14–34) is also shown in Fig. 4 after the occurrence of the listen tag. Lines 17–24 code the parallel execution of two actions. The dealer performs the "GestureRight" animation sequence (line 19), thereby demonstrating the new game situation which is simultaneously loaded (lines 21–23). Then the dealer verbally and non-verbally expresses his sadness that he lost this round of the game. In lines 30 and 31, the execute tag is used to update Djinn's knowledge base telling him that the user won the current round, which is internally represented by (round) 4, (choice) 1. Notice that, here, MPML interacts with the SCREAM system that will be used to derive Djinn's reaction (see Sect. 3). The remaining lines 32–41 show some of the required closing tags.

3 Scripting Emotion-Based Agent Minds

The Scripting Emotion-based Agent Minds (SCREAM) system is a tool to script the interactive behavior of affective agents. It is intended as a plug-in to content-specific and task-specific agent systems such as interactive tutoring or entertainment systems that provide the relevant verbal utterances (propositional meaning) for a character. The SCREAM system may then decide on the kind of emotional expression and its intensity, based on a multitude of parameters that are relevant to the current interaction situation. Parameters are derived from the agent's mental state as well as the peculiarities of the social setting in which the interaction takes place and features of the agent's interlocutor(s), the user or other agents. It is important to notice that SCREAM is intended as a system for producing believable (emotional) behavior rather than a framework that aims to simulate human-style cognition. The latter aim is prevalent, for instance, in Dörner's PSI theory [19].

As a scripting language, the key properties of SCREAM are as follows (see also the corresponding discussion of the MPML system in Sect. 2).

Ease of Use. The content author may specify a character's profile by providing statements in a declarative language (Prolog facts). A fact simply states that an n-tuple of objects satisfies a relation. An XML-style representation could in principle be used to specify a character's profile, but this approach is currently not implemented.

Intelligibility. The mental make-up of a character contains concepts from psychological and sociological research that are easily understood (in a "folk psychology" sense), such as "personality trait", "social power", or "attitude".

Believability. Consistent (emergent) agent behavior was one of the key considerations in the development of the SCREAM system. Here, "consistent" means that the character always behaves in accord with its features, such as personality, goals, perception of its social context, and so on. In other words, the character's behaviors (or action tendencies) are biased by its mental make-up. Furthermore, the character will also *change* its behavior in accordance with its features and in dependence on its interaction experience with other agents. In this way, the character's behavior not only is consistent in terms of believable "reactions" to external events, but may also show consistent believable behavior over longer time periods.

Extensibility. A character's emotion-based reasoning processes are encoded as a set of rules. Although the average content author might not want to edit the character's affective processes, the rule set can be easily modified and extended (assuming some familiarity with Prolog programming).

Granularity. A tool for scripting the behavior of affective characters should facilitate the design of their minds at various levels of detail, or 'granularity' of scripting[2]. At the simple end of the spectrum, a character's behavior is entirely determined by its personality. More levels of indirection in the character's responses can be achieved by allowing for dynamic features such as attitude change and by declaring social variables and other features of the interaction context. The SCREAM system is robust for incomplete specification of available parameter declaration.

While emotionally and socially appropriate reactions are an essential aspect of a character's believability, verbal (and non-verbal) responses have to be prepared by hand for each interaction scenario. Authors who simply wish to include a "chatbot" on their interface might want to follow a less work-intense approach. We recently implemented an interface between MPML3.0 and a popular chatbot, the Alicebot [2] (see also Mori et al. [34]). The Alicebot provides a large set of responses for a broad variety of topics which are accessible from the web. By using a special type of pattern matching, this chatbot shows response robustness for (almost) any imaginable user input. Moreover, by using AIML (Artificial Intelligence Markup Language) [1], authors of interactive presentations may easily define their own response patterns for the character. A major drawback of this approach is that AIML-based characters often show unexpected behaviors which might be tolerable (or even desirable) for chat-style situations but not for the more confined and task-specific interaction domains we intend to model and populate with life-like characters.

---

[2] A comparable notion is that of "scalable autonomy" which refers to the degree of semi-autonomy, ranging from "predefined" to "autonomous" [51].

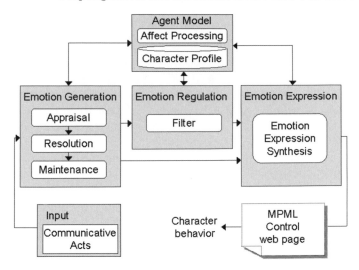

Fig. 8. SCREAM system architecture

3.1 SCREAM System Architecture

The architecture of the SCREAM system is shown in Fig. 8. While the system is written in Java for portability, a Java-based Prolog system [8] is used to support high-level scripting of an agent's mind components: emotion generation, emotion regulation, emotion expression, and the agent model.. The typical content author will only edit the character profile. Each of its components will be discussed in the following sections. The system output – an instruction to display a certain emotion – is handled by the Control web page resulting from converting the MPML script to JavaScript.

Communicative Acts

Emotion-based agents receive input in the form of communicative acts, written as *com_act(S,H,Concept,Sit)*, where *S* is the speaker, *H* the addressee (interlocutor), *Concept* the information conveyed by *S* to *H* in situation *Sit*. Communicative acts have preconditions that must be explicated to inform the agent about the interlocutor's beliefs, goals, or attitudes expressed in the utterance. Note that since our system lacks a language understanding module (let alone an affective language understanding module), a character has to receive those propositions in order to model its interlocutor's affective state.

Emotion Generation

A core activity of an emotion-based agent mind is the generation and management of emotions, which are dealt with by three modules: the *appraisal* module, the *emotion resolution* module, and the *emotion maintenance* module. They will be described in the following.

Appraisal Module. Reasoning about emotion models an agent's *appraisal process*, where events are evaluated as to their emotional significance for the agent [39, 23, 45]. The significance is determined by so-called "emotion-eliciting conditions" (EECs), which comprise an agent's relation to four types of abstract mental concepts: (i) beliefs – state of affairs that the agent has evidence to hold in the (virtual) world; (ii) goals – states of affairs that are (un)desirable for the agent, what the agent wants (does not want) to obtain; (iii) standards – the agent's beliefs about what ought (not) to be the case, events the agent considers as praiseworthy; and (iv) attitudes – the agent's dispositions to like or dislike other agents or objects, what the agent considers appealing. An agent's associated mental states are uniformly treated as "propositional attitudes", as relations between the agent and some abstract concept, the content of the attitude [7]. Following the emotion model of Ortony et al. [39] (the OCC model), we conceive emotion types as classes of eliciting conditions, each of which is labeled with an emotion word or phrase. In total, 22 classes of eliciting conditions are identified: joy, distress, "happy for", "sorry for", resent, "angry at", and so on. For all propositional attitudes, we assume intensities $\delta_i \in \{0, \ldots, 5\}$ such that zero is the lower threshold, that is the mental concept is not active, and five is the maximum value (greater values are mapped to five). By default, intensities δ_i are combined to an overall intensity δ by logarithmic combination $\delta = \log_2\left(\sum_i 2^{\delta_i}\right)$ [45]. If an agent dislikes another agent with intensity 3 and believes it is joyful with intensity 2, it will resent the other agent with intensity 4 (rounded).

In addition to the EECs proposed by the OCC model, we also consider the agent's personality which will be conceived as a biasing mechanism for emotion generation and expression. From the set of investigated dimensions of personality [26], we will focus on two dimensions that are crucial for social interactions, *agreeableness* and *extraversion*. Personality dimensions are numerically quantified, with a value $\gamma \in \{-5, \ldots, 5\}$.

The appraisal module assumes that the author states the agent's beliefs, goals, standards, attitudes, and personality traits together with (initial) intensity values. Since a reasonably interesting agent will have a multitude of mental states, more than one emotion is typically triggered when the agent interacts with another agent, calling for a method to "resolve" the agent's emotions. This problem will be discussed in the following paragraph.

Digression. Some words on our use of numeric values (expressing intensities) and combination functions for these values seem in order here. The decision to assume intensity values from the interval $0, \ldots, 5$ is to a certain extent arbitrary, as we could also have assumed 10 intensity levels. Our choice reflects the aim that character designers have sufficient means to discriminate between situations where, for instance, they want their character to "slightly" like another agent as opposed to an attitude of "strong" liking. Regarding the combination functions, we have little empirical evidence (beyond our intuition) that people actually combine intensities the way we suggest. However, content authors may easily adapt the combination rules according to their needs.

Emotion Resolution Module. The emotions generated in an agent at a given time are called *active* emotions (in *Sit*) and are collected together with their intensities in a set $\{\langle E_1, \delta_1, Sit\rangle, \ldots, \langle E_n, \delta_n, Sit\rangle\}$. The presence of multiple ("conflicting") emotions is resolved by computing and comparing two states. The *dominant emotion* is simply the emotion with the highest intensity value For the case where no unique dominant emotion exists, the agent's personality will be used as to favor an emotion. On the other hand, the *dominant mood* is calculated by considering all active emotions. Similar to Reilly [45] and Ortony [37], we distinguish between "positive" and "negative" emotions. Examples of positive emotions are joy, "happy for", and "sorry for", whereas resent and "angry at" are negative emotions. Then the dominant mood results by comparing the overall intensity value associated with the positive and negative emotion sets, which are obtained by logarithmic combination. The *winning emotional state* is decided by comparing the intensities for dominant emotion and dominant mood. Thereby, we can account for situations where, for instance, an agent has a joyful experience but is still more influenced by its overall negative mood toward another agent.

An alternative approach to extracting a single emotion or mood state is pursued by Sengers in her work on "comprehensible agents" [49], where she introduces a theory of transitions between an agent's actions that makes conflicts and influences of two behaviors explicit to the viewer, and rules out the frequent impression that agents jump around between independent actions. In our work, we try to counteract this possibility by the maintenance module discussed in the following.

Emotion Maintenance Module. This module handles the decay process of emotions. Depending on their type and intensity, emotions may remain active in the agent's memory for a certain time during the interaction. A decay function decreases the intensity levels of the active emotions, whereby the actual decay rate is determined by the agent's personality. For instance, an agreeable agent's decay rate for negative emotions is faster than for positive ones.

Emotion Regulation

In their seminal work on non-verbal behavior, Ekman and Friesen [22] argue that the expression of emotional states, particularly by facial expression, is governed by social and cultural norms, so-called "display rules" that have a significant impact on the intensity of emotion expression. Recently, the mechanisms underlying emotion regulation also received considerable interest in the psychology literature. Gross [27, p. 275] gives the following characterization: "Emotion regulation refers to processes by which individuals influence which emotions they have, when they have them, and how they experience

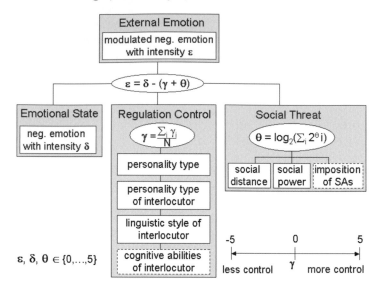

Fig. 9. Emotion regulation parameters

and express these emotions." We will take a more restricted view on emotion regulation and simply treat it as a process that decides whether an emotion is expressed (see also De Carolis et al. [17]). A value is calculated that indicates to what extent an emotion is expressed (suppressed). A typical motivating example for emotion regulation is that the modulation of emotion expression is beneficial for an agent as the "unfiltered" expression of (some) emotions may undermine certain high-level goals of the agent. Note that emotion regulation only applies to emotional reactions that can in principle be controlled by the agent. Some reactions are involuntary and spontaneous and hence not subject to emotion regulation, like somatic reactions such as "flushing" or "shaking".

A computational account of emotion regulation has to combine parameters that influence the emotion regulation process [43, 42]. However, it is not obvious how this can be done in an adequate way. We will propose a set of (weighted) parameters together with default combination functions. As shown in Fig. 9, we opted for a categorization into parameters that can change over time, the social variables, and parameters that pertain to the agent's (ability of) self-control and the current interaction context.

Social Variables. When agents interact, they not only exchange information but also establish and maintain social relationships. Hence it is important that agents avoid introducing disharmony into a conversation or threaten other agents' public face [54]. Following Brown and Levinson [12], we take *social power* and *social distance* as two important parameters determining the agent's regulation of emotion, and define them for agents $L1$ and $L2$ with levels $\theta_P, \theta_D \in \{0, \ldots, 5\}$. Brown and Levinson [12] also consider the ranking of imposition of different speech acts as a social variable, which is currently ignored in our approach since utterances are not explicitly framed as speech acts.

- The (asymmetric) relation *social-power(L2,L1,θ_P,Sit)* says that agent $L2$ is θ_P ranks higher than $L1$ in *Sit*, as perceived by $L1$.
- The second (asymmetric) relation *social-distance(L1,L2,θ_D,Sit)* refers to the closeness between two agents, whereby lower values indicate more closeness, as perceived by $L1$.

Observe that Cassell and Bickmore [13] use the term "familiarity" for what we call "distance", and interpret social distance as solidarity or "like-mindedness". In our case, social distance is simply taken as a indicator of how "freely" an agent may express its emotions without social sanction. Based on θ_P and θ_D, agent $L1$ computes the *social threat* from $L2$ as $\theta = \log_2 \left(2^{\theta_P} + 2^{\theta_D}\right)$, whereby θ is set to zero if θ_P and θ_D are both zero. Besides logarithmic combination, other combination methods are used in the literature, Walker et al. [54], for instance, simply add the values of the social variables. Note that in our view social variables are not meant to reflect "objective" ratings of power and distance, but the modeled agent's assessment of the ratings.

Control Variables. The following parameters describe an agent's inclination to control its negative emotions (for instance, given its personality traits) as well the agent's inclination to suppress negative emotions as a result of external factors of the interaction scenario (for instance, the other agent's personality). The following list of control variables is meant as an important subset of the more complete set of conceivable variables discussed by de Carolis et al. [17].

- *Personality.* An agent is more likely to express negative emotions if it is either disagreeable or extrovert.
- *Other agent's personality.* If the agent assumes that the interlocutor's personality is disagreeable, it will rather not express a negative emotion.
- *Reciprocal feedback.* An interesting phenomenon in human interaction is reciprocal feedback loops where one person's linguistic friendliness results in the interlocutor's adaption to its otherwise unfriendly behavior. Similarly, there are "negative" feedback loops where agents adjust to linguistic unfriendly behavior.

The overall control value $\gamma \in \{-5, \ldots, 5\}$ is computed as $\gamma = \sum_i \gamma_i / N$ where the denominator N scales the result according to the number of considered control parameters. In essence, the formula captures the intuition that different control parameters may defeat each other. Thus, the control of an agent that is very extrovert but deals with a very disagreeable interlocutor will be neutralized. Further control parameters can be easily added to (or deleted from) our model, such as other interlocutor features like display motive or the interlocutor's cognitive capacity [17].

Emotion Filter Module. At this point we are given the winning emotional state as well as the regulation parameters social threat and control (see Fig. 9).

In order to determine the intensity of the *external emotion* – the type of emotion to be displayed by the character – the intensities of emotional state and regulation parameters have to be combined. A so-called *filter program* consists of only one rule with two different combination functions, one for positive and one for negative emotions [43]. Given the intensities for social threat θ, control γ, and the winning emotional state θ, the intensity of a negative external emotion ϵ is obtained by $\epsilon = \delta - (\theta + \gamma)$. The equation balances social threat against the character's control, whereby high values for threat may neutralize the lacking (self-)control of the character to a certain extent. For positive emotions, the intensity level results from calculating $\epsilon = \delta - (\theta - \gamma)$ and, therefore, a high level for threat or a negative value for control will decrease the intensity of a positive external emotion. A positive value for control may defeat the impact of social threat.

Emotion Expression

External emotions (with associated intensities) are eventually instantiated to actual verbal and non-verbal behaviors. We use a simplified version of Ortony's categorization of emotion response tendencies, and distinguish between expressive and information-processing responses [23, 37].

- *Expressive responses* include somatic responses (flushing), behavioral responses (fist-clenching, throwing objects), and two types of communicative responses, verbal and non-verbal (for instance, frowning).
- *Information-processing responses* concern the agent's diversion of attention and evaluations.

Expressive responses are communicated to the Control web page (obtained by converting the MPML script), and instantiated to character animations and speech. A special form of information-processing responses, attitude change, will be discussed below.

Agent Model

We will now describe the agent model consisting of two components, the *character profile* and the *affect processing* module.

Character Profile. The character profile comprises the determinants of processes related to the generation, regulation, and expression of emotion. The content author edits the profile by declaring the agent's mental states and initializing their intensity values. In order to simplify the agent model, we assume that some of its features can be treated as *static* whereas the majority are *dynamic* (i.e. they may change in the course of interaction). Among the static features are the agent's personality and standards. While it is reasonable to treat an agent's personality as permanent, we also make the simplifying assumption that the agent's assessment of its interlocutor's personality does not

```
/* Personality traits */
personality-type(advisor,agreeableness,2).
personality-type(advisor,extraversion,2).
/* Social relationships - declared for all situations */
social-power(user,advisor,0,Sit).
social-distance(advisor,user,1,Sit).
/* Attitude and (winning) emotional state in initial sit. (-1) */
likes(advisor,user,1,-1).
joy(advisor,user,3,-1).
/* Goals - declared for all situations */
wants(advisor,user_wins_game,1,Sit).
wants(advisor,user_follows_advice,4,Sit).
/* The user's communicative act in situation 0 */
com-act(user,advisor,lost_game,0).
/* Preconditions of the user's communicative act in sit. 0 */
holds(user_looses_game,1).
holds(not_user_follows_advice,1).
```

Fig. 10. Some features of Djinn's character profile

change during interaction. Instead, the interlocutor's personality profile has to be explicitly given to the agent. The dynamic features of an agent include its goals, beliefs, attitudes, as well as social power and distance relationships. A simple character profile can be found in Fig. 10. Later on, it will be used to describe the mental make-up of the advisor Djinn.

Affect Processing. An important aspect of a character's believability and life-likeness is the ability to change its emotional reactions depending on the "affective interaction history" with another agent. Simply stated, if some interlocutor triggers mostly positive (negative) emotions in the character, it might change its attitude toward the interlocutor and be biased to appraise the interlocutor's future communicative acts in a more positive (negative) way.

Ortony [38] suggests the notion of *(signed) summary record* to capture our attitude toward or dispositional (dis)liking of another person. This record stores the sign of emotions (positive or negative) that were induced in the agent by an interlocutor together with emotions' associated intensities. In order to compute the current intensity of an agent's (dis)liking, we simply compare the (scaled) sum of intensities of elicited positive and negative emotions (δ^σ, $\sigma \in \{+, -\}$), beginning in situation $Sit_1^{L,I}$, the situation when the interaction starts.

$$\delta^\sigma(Sit_n^{L,I}) = \frac{\sum_{i=1}^n \delta_w^\sigma(Sit_i^{L,I})}{n}$$

We only consider the winning emotional states δ_w, the most dominant emotions. Observe that situations also have to be parameterized by the agent and interlocutor, referring to time points when emotions are elicited in an agent L

due to communication with interlocutor I. If no emotion of one sign is elicited in a situation, it is set to zero. Positive values for the difference $\delta^+ - \delta^-$ indicate an agent's liking of an interlocutor and negative ones indicate disliking. For simplicity, we assume perfect memory of elicited emotions, such that the intensity of past (winning) emotions does not decay. If the interlocutor's recent behavior is mostly "consistent" with the agent's past experience, that is both have the same sign, it is reasonable to update the overall intensity of the agent's attitude according to the equation above. Otherwise, a more sophisticated update rule has to be used that weights recent against past elicited emotions (see Prendinger et al. [40]). Simple forms of social distance and familiarity change are discussed in Prendinger and Ishizuka [41].

3.2 Using SCREAM to Script a Conversational Character

Let us now illustrate how our system works. As the interaction setting, we will continue the casino scenario described in Sect. 2.5. We focus solely on the affective reactions of the advisor Djinn, whom we designed to be driven by the SCREAM system.

We will start by explaining the interface between SCREAM and MPML. Figure 11 shows the MPML script for a situation where Djinn receives an instruction on how to respond to the user's choice. In lines 1–2, the `consult` tag is used to access the SCREAM system that processes the user's communicative act and outputs Djinn's current (external) emotion together with its intensity. The output *rescomact(sorryfor,3,advisor,user,5)* (line 3) says that the advisor's communicative act to the user in situation 5 is "sorry for" with intensity 3. The actual verbal and non-verbal reaction of Djinn is then instantiated within the `<test>...</test>` tagging structures. Two of Djinn's responses are given in lines 3–13 and 14–25, respectively. The cardinality of `text` tagging structures following the `consult` tag depends on the granularity of the emotion system underlying the advisor. The graphical representation of the branching edge rooted in the `consult` element can be seen in Fig. 4, where it is located immediately below the occurrence of the `consult` tag approximately in the middle of the Graph window.

In the following, we will watch the user play five rounds of the game of Black Jack. Djinn advises the user to hit or stand, who may either follow or ignore the advice. The outcome of the game – whether the user wins or loses – is not determined by him or her following Djinn's advice; that is, he or she may lose even if following the advice. We intend to illustrate how Djinn's mental make-up as well as the (affective) interaction history determine his behavior. For expository reasons, we let the user never follow Djinn's advice[3]. In order to be able to more easily track Djinn's emotional reaction, we use a very sparse character profile, as shown in Fig. 10. Figure 12 contains the dialogue between user and Djinn where the user never follows his advice.

---

[3] Interestingly, many people interacting with the casino scenario at various academic events opted for this way.

```
 1 <consult target="control.chApplet.askJinniComAct(
 2                                 'advisor','user','5')"/>
 3    <test value="'rescomact(sorryfor,3,advisor,user,5)'"/>
 4      <scene agents="Genie,James">
 5        <page ref="Casino-main.html">
 6          <act agent="Genie" act="Uncertain"/>
 7          <speak agent="Genie">
 8            Oh, you lost.
 9            <nb pause="100">I am sorry, this was unlucky.
10          </speak>
11        </page>
12      </scene>
13    </test>
14    <test value="'rescomact(joy,5,advisor,user,5)'"/>
15      <scene agents="Genie,James">
16        <page ref="Casino-main.html">
17          <act agent="Genie" act="Congratulate_2"/>
18          <speak agent="Genie">
19            And here we are!
20            <nb pause="100"/>We are great today!
21            <nb pause="100"/>And luck is on our side.
22          </speak>
23        </page>
24      </scene>
25    </test>
26    <test>
27    ...
28    </test>
29    ...
30 </consult>
```

Fig. 11. Interfacing SCREAM with MPML

In *round one* Djinn's winning emotional state is distress with intensity 4, because the user did not follow his advice. However, he displays distress with low intensity as his personality traits (friendly, extrovert) and the slight social distance to the user decreases in the intensity of negative emotion expression. Precisely, since $\theta = 1$ and $\gamma = 2$, $\epsilon = 1$ $(= 4 - (1 + 2))$. In *round two* Djinn is sorry for the user with intensity 4, since positive "sorry for" emotions decay slowly and sum up. His personality traits let him express the emotion with even higher intensity. In *round three* Djinn gloats over the user's lost game, because at that point, the negative emotions dominate the positive ones as a consequence of the user's repeated refusal to follow Djinn's advice. Hence Djinn's attitude changes to slightly disliking the user, which lets him experience joy over the user's distress (gloat with intensity 5). Again, Djinn's personality traits and social distance decrease the intensity of his ex-

#	Speaker	Utterance	External emotion
1	Djinn	You got only 16 now, so you should hit again.	
	User	*[stands, and loses]* Hmm, I lost.	
	Djinn	*[sad face]* Oh. That was too little to stand.	*distress* (1)
2	Djinn	You got 18 and should better stand.	
	User	*[hits, and loses]* Oh no, I lost.	
	Djinn	*[sad face]* I am very sorry for you but in this case you were better to stand.	*sorry for* (5)
3	Djinn	You got 14 and should hit again.	
	User	*[stands, and loses]* I lost.	
	Djinn	*[smiling]* See! That's because you never follow my advice.	*gloat* (2)
4	Djinn	Now you got 18 again. You'd better stand.	
	User	*[hits, and wins]* I did it!	
	Djinn	*[frowning]* You are just lucky this time.	*bad mood* (2)
5	Djinn	Now you have 19, that's too close to 21, so stand by all means.	
	User	*[hits, and wins]* I won!	
	Djinn	*[frowning]* I cannot believe you are so lucky.	*resent* (1)

Fig. 12. Dialogue for five consecutive rounds where the user never follows Djinn's advice. The figure does not show the user's interaction with the dealer

ternal emotion to intensity 2. In *round four* Djinn's winning emotional state is "bad mood" with intensity 5, slightly more that his "happy for" emotion (as the user wins the game this time). Here an overall, unspecific affective state (mood) is expressed with low intensity, rather than a specific emotion, reflecting the dominance of negative emotions. In *round five* Djinn's dominant emotional state is resent with intensity 4, because he slightly dislikes the user and consequently is distressed that the user won by ignoring his advice.

4 Conclusions

Life-like characters have received considerable attention in recent years, as they can be employed to improve diverse applications of human–computer interaction, including tutoring, interactive stories, online sales, and presentation. Despite the popularity of animated agents, tools allowing content authors to easily integrate this interface technology into web-based presentations are still rare. This chapter proposed scripting languages to instruct the bodies and minds of life-like characters.

The purpose of the Multi-modal Presentation Markup Language (MPML) is to provide a powerful and easy-to-use character scripting tool for web content experts who are non-programmers. As such, MPML shares the overall goal with the ongoing W3C effort toward a Multi-modal Interaction Framework [53]. We have presented the language specification of MPML that contains tagging structures for the control of the verbal and non-verbal behavior of cartoon-style agents, presentation flow control including the possibility of user–agent interaction, and an interface to external web objects, such as Java applets. In order to facilitate the scripting of complex presentation scenarios, we have described a visual editor for MPML such that content authors can manipulate a presentation graph rather than edit the involved textual script of the presentation. The discussion of a web-based presentation implemented with MPML – the interactive casino scenario – was intended to give an idea of how to mark up a presentation that features characters with pre-scripted as well as (semi-)autonomous behavior.

While MPML is a tool for controlling the visual behavior of characters, the Scripting Emotion-based Agent Minds (SCREAM) system constitutes a practical technology for scripting the mental processes underlying a character's affective behavior. Its flexibility derives from the granularity feature which lets the content author decide on the level of detail at which the character is scripted, and produces an output that reflects the provided influences. The author may define all or a subset of the available affect-related parameters, depending on the requirements of the application. In order to demonstrate emotion-based agents, we added an advisor character to the casino scenario whose behavior reflects its personality, goals, and attitude. The advisor character also adapts its behavior depending on the user's behavior.

Future research will include the design of an architecture that allows for a tighter integration of character and environment scripting, whereby Doyle's [20] "annotated environments" concept might serve as a starting point, and the development of a plot manager that produces narratively meaningful interactive stories. Our initial ideas in the context of a character-based corporate training setting are described in [44].

Acknowledgments

We would like to express our thanks to the following colleagues and students who significantly contributed to the development of the MPML language: Takayuki Tsutsui, Hiroshi Dohi, Yuan Zong, Peng Du, Kyoshi Mori, and Istvan Barakonyi. We are especially grateful to Sylvain Descamps who implemented the Visual Editor for MPML3.0. This research was supported by the Research Grant (1999–2003) for the Future Program ("Mirai Kaitaku") from the Japan Society for the Promotion of Science (JSPS).

References

1. AIML Reference Manual. http://www.alicebot.org/aiml.html
2. A.L.I.C.E. AI Foundation http://www.alicebot.org
3. André, E., Rist, T.: Controlling the behavior of animated presentation agents in the interface: Scripting versus instructing. *AI Magazine* 53–66 (2001)
4. André, E., Rist, T., van Mulken, S., Klesen, M., Baldes, S.: The automated design of believable dialogue for animated presentation teams. In: *Embodied Conversational Agents*, ed Cassell, J., Sullivan, J., Prevost, S., Churchill, E. (The MIT Press, Cambridge, MA 2000) pp 220–255
5. Arafa, Y., Kamyab, K., Mamdani, E.: Towards a unified scripting language. Lessons learned from developing CML & AML. In: *Life-like Characters. Tools, Affective Functions and Applications*, ed Prendinger, H., Ishizuka, M. (Springer 2003). This volume.
6. Barakonyi, I., Ishizuka, M.: A 3D agent with synthetic face and semiautonomous behavior for multimodal presentations. In: *Proceedings Multimedia Technology and Applications Conference (MTAC-01)* (2001) pp 21–25
7. Barwise, J., Perry, J.: *Situations and Attitudes* (The MIT Press, Cambridge, MA 1983)
8. BinNet Corp.: *Jinni 2000: A high performance Java based Prolog for agent scripting, client-server and internet programming.* www.binnetcorp.com
9. Blumberg, B.M.: *Old Tricks, New Dogs: Ethology and Interactive Creatures.* PhD thesis (Massachusetts Institute of Technology 1996)
10. Bordegoni, M., Faconti, G., Feiner, S., Maybury, M.T., Rist, T., Ruggieri, S., Trahanias, P., Wilson, M.: A standard reference model for intelligent multimedia presentation systems. *Computer Standards & Interfaces* **18**(6–7):477–496 (1997)
11. Bradley, N.: *The XSL Companion* (Addison-Wesley, London 2000)
12. Brown, P., Levinson, S.C.: *Politeness. Some Universals in Language Usage* (Cambridge University Press 1987)
13. Cassell, J., Bickmore, T.: Negotiated collusion: Modeling social language and its relationship effects in intelligent agents. *User Modeling and Adaptive Interfaces* **12**:1–44 (2002)
14. Cassell, J., Sullivan, J., Prevost, S., Churchill, E. (eds): *Embodied Conversational Agents* (The MIT Press, Cambridge, MA 2000)
15. Cassell, J., Vilhjálmsson, H., Bickmore, T.: BEAT: the Behavior Expression Animation Toolkit. In: *Life-like Characters. Tools, Affective Functions and Applications*, ed Prendinger, H., Ishizuka, M. (Springer 2003). This volume.
16. De Carolis, B., Pelachaud, C.: APML, a mark-up language for believable behavior generation. In: *Life-like Characters. Tools, Affective Functions and Applications*, ed by Prendinger, H., Ishizuka, M. (Springer 2003). This volume.
17. De Carolis, B., Pelachaud, C., Poggi, I., de Rosis, F.: Behavior planning for a reflexive agent. In: *Proceedings 17th International Conference on Artificial Intelligence (IJCAI-01)* (2001) pp 1059–1066
18. Descamps, S.: MPML3.0: *Towards building a standard for multimodal presentations using affective agents.* Master's thesis (University of Tokyo, January 2002)
19. Dörner, D., Hille, K.: Artificial souls: Motivated emotional robots. http://www.uni-bamberg.de/ppp/insttheopsy/psi-literatur.html

20. Doyle, P.: Believability through context. Using "knowledge in the world" to create intelligent characters. In: *Proceedings First International Joint Conference on Autonomous Agents and Multi-Agent Systems (AAMAS-02)* (ACM Press, New York 2002) pp 342–349

21. Du, P., Ishizuka, M.: Dynamic Web Markup Language (DWML) for generating animated web pages with character agent and time-control function. In: *Proceedings (CD-ROM) IEEE International Conference on Multimedia and Expo (ICME-01)* (2001)

22. Ekman, P., Friesen, W.V.: The repertoire of nonverbal behavior: Categories, origins, usage, and coding. *Semiotica* **1**:49–98 (1969)

23. Elliott, C.: *The Affective Reasoner. A process model of emotions in a multi-agent system.* PhD thesis (Northwestern University, Institute for the Learning Sciences, 1992)

24. Elliott, C., Brzezinski, J.: Autonomous agents as synthetic characters. *AI Magazine* **19**(2):13–30 (1998)

25. Extempo Systems Inc. http://www.extempo.com

26. Eysenck, H.J.: Dimensions of personality: 16, 5, or 3?—criteria for a taxonomic paradigm. *Personality and Individual Differences* **12**:773–790 (1991)

27. Gross, J.J.: The emerging field of emotion regulation: An integrative review. *Review of General Psychology* **2**(3):271–299 (1998)

28. Harold, E.R.: *XML Bible* (IDG Books Worldwide, Foster City, CA 1999)

29. Hayes-Roth, B.: Adaptive learning guides. In: *Proceedings of the IASTED Conference on Computers and Advanced Technology in Education* (2001)

30. Life-like Characters. Tools, Affective Functions and Applications. http://www.vhml.org/LLC/llc-book.html

31. Macromedia Flash. http://www.macromedia.com

32. Mariott, A., Stallo, J.: VHML—Uncertainties and problems. A discussion. In: *Proceedings AAMAS-02 Workshop on Embodied Conversational Agents –Let's specify and evaluate them!* (2002)

33. Microsoft. *Developing for Microsoft Agent* (Microsoft Press, Redmond, WA 1998)

34. Mori, K., Jatowt, A., Ishizuka, M.: Enhancing conversational flexibility in multimodal interactions with embodied lifelike agents. In: *Proceedings of Poster Session at International Conference on Intelligent User Interfaces (IUI-03)* (2003) pp 270–272

35. Murray, I.R., Arnott, J.L.: Implementation and testing of a system for producing emotion-by-rule in synthetic speech. *Speech Communication* **16**:369–390 (1995)

36. Okazaki, N., Aya, S., Saeyor, S., Ishizuka, M.: A Multimodal Presentation Markup Language MPML-VR for a 3D virtual space. In *Proceedings (CD-ROM) of Workshop on Virtual Conversational Characters: Applications, Methods, and Research Challenges (in conj. with HF2002 and OZCHI2002)* (2002)

37. Ortony, A.: On making believable emotional agents believable. In: *Emotions in Humans and Artifacts*, ed by Trappl, R., Petta, P., Payr, S. (The MIT Press, Cambridge, MA 2003)

38. Ortony, A.: Value and emotion. In: *Memories, thoughts, and emotions: Essays in the honor of George Mandler*, ed Kessen, W., Ortony, A., Craik, F. (Erlbaum, Hillsdale, NJ 1991) pp 337–353

39. Ortony, A., Clore, G.L., Collins, A.: *The Cognitive Structure of Emotions.* (Cambridge University Press 1988)

40. Prendinger, H., Descamps, S., Ishizuka, M.: Scripting affective communication with life-like characters in web-based interaction systems. *Applied Artificial Intelligence* **16**(7–8):519–553 (2002)
41. Prendinger, H., Ishizuka, M.: Evolving social relationships with animate characters. In: *Proceedings of the AISB-02 Symposium on Animating Expressive Characters for Social Interactions* (2002) pp 73–78
42. Prendinger, H., Ishizuka, M.: Let's talk! Socially intelligent agents for language conversation training. *IEEE Transactions on Systems, Man, and Cybernetics— Part A: Systems and Humans* **31**(5):465–471 (2001)
43. Prendinger, H., Ishizuka, M.: Social role awareness in animated agents. In: *Proceedings 5th International Conference on Autonomous Agents (Agents-01)* (ACM Press, New York 2001), pp 270–277
44. Prendinger, H., Ishizuka, M.: The storification of chances. Corporate training with life-like characters in virtual social environments. In: *Chance Discovery. Foundations and Applications*, ed Ohsawa, Y., McBurney, P. (Springer, Advances in Information Processing Series 2003)
45. Reilly, W.S. Neil: *Believable Social and Emotional Agents*. PhD thesis, CMU-CS-96-138 (Carnegie Mellon University 1996)
46. Rist, T., André, E., Baldes, S., Gebhard, P., Klesen, M., Kipp, M., Rist, P., Schmitt, M.: A review on the development of embodied presentation agents and their appication fields. In: *Life-like Characters. Tools, Affective Functions and Applications*, ed Prendinger, H., Ishizuka, M. (Springer 2003). This volume.
47. Rousseau, D., Hayes-Roth, B.: A social-psychological model for synthetic actors. In: *Proceedings 2nd International Conference on Autonomous Agents (Agents-98)* (ACM Press, New York 1998) pp 165–172
48. Saeyor, S.: Multimodal Presentation Markup Language Ver. 2.2a (MPML2.2a). http://www.miv.t.u-tokyo.ac.jp/~santi/research/mpml2a
49. Sengers, P.: Designing comprehensible agents. In: *Proceedings 16th International Joint Conference on Artificial Intelligence (IJCAI-99)* (1999) pp 1227–1232
50. SMIL. Synchronized Multimedia Integration Language. http://www.w3.org/AudioVideo
51. Spierling, U., Grasbon, D., Braun, N., Iurgel, I.: Setting the scene: Playing digital director in interactive storytelling and creation. *Computer & Graphics* **26**:31–44 (2002)
52. Verbot. Virtual Personalities Inc., Verbot Sylvie Ver. 3.04 (1998)
53. W3C Multimodal Interaction Framework. http://www.w3.org/TR/mmi-framework/
54. Walker, M.A., Cahn, J.E., Whittacker, S.J.: Improvising linguistic style: Social and affective bases for agent personality. In: *Proceedings First International Conference on Autonomous Agents (Agents'97)* (ACM Press, New York 1997) pp 10–17
55. XML. Extensible Markup Language. http://www.w3.org/XML
56. XML Schema Part 1: Structures. http://www.w3.org/TR/xmlschema-1

Part III

Systems and Applications

Great Expectations: Prediction in Entertainment Applications

Robert Burke

MediaLabEurope, MindGames Group
Sugar House Lane, Dublin 8, Ireland
rob@mle.ie

Summary. The entertainment world is full of applications for expressive, adaptive agents. Many of these applications feature some sort of "creatures" – anthropomorphic or not – that maintain the illusion of life while interacting both with one another and with human participants. This chapter discusses agent-based approaches to implementing those creatures, beginning with a discussion of high-level concepts – such as motivation, perception, and action–selection – in the context of a specific architecture that is representative of many similar systems found in the entertainment world. It then illustrates how the integration of a representation for prediction into that architecture allows for new forms of learning, adaptation, and expressive behavior. This discussion is meant to provide an accessible introduction, and hopefully includes some thought-provoking ideas for those who are similarly interested in building life like creatures

1 The Usual Suspects

Here are some examples of agents in entertainment applications:

- An anthropomorphic robot uses cameras and microphones to perceive real-world visual and audio information. It detects a person and tries to mimic upper body motion as best it can. It uses facial expressions to show its satisfaction, confusion, curiosity, and so on. Sometimes, when "feeling mischievous", it instead performs other gestures it has remembered from previous interactions.
- In an interactive installation, an autonomous virtual sheepdog exists on a field with other virtual creatures and objects. Human participants act as the shepherd, shouting voice commands which the virtual dog must interpret to successfully herd sheep.
- A fearsome behemoth named Goatzilla is a virtual creature that inhabits the Scottish highlands. He begins his life with no knowledge of how to scavenge for food. In order to survive, he must learn – in real time, while maintaining the illusion of life – strategies for rustling up the local shepherd's tasty sheep.

- In a virtual sports simulator, an autonomous agent controls the right-wing forward player on a hockey team. This agent perceives the state of the arena from its vantage point on the ice, and, given its knowledge of the game and the social dynamics of the team, including offensive strategies practiced with the other autonomous players, determines an appropriate course of action.

2 I Perceive, I Decide, I Do

These four agents, while different in purpose, have quite a lot in common. Each is expressive. Each should be robust to changes in its dynamic world. And, practically, on a moment-to-moment basis, each must work in realtime to choose between a variety of possible actions. To do so, each agent perceives its world (real and/or virtual), and bases its decisions on both its current perception of the context, as well as its internal state. By internal state, we mean for example that the sheepdog might be more enthusiastic if very hungry, and the hockey player might adopt a defensive posture if recovering from an injury. Once each agent decides what to do, it must work with the degrees of freedom availed to it to expressively carry out the desired action (see Fig. 1).

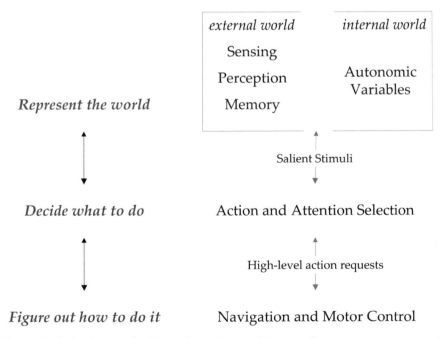

Fig. 1. High-level view of a layered cognitive architecture for an autonomous agent. See [8] or [21] for more detail

The details of the last task – the agent's act of actually modifying the world – are largely task-specific and vary greatly between applications. An animated character, for example, must figure out how to move expressively and remain in character while performing a particular action ([32, 30, 13], and also see elsewhere in this book, e.g. [9, 27]). A robot might react similarly, although with servos in the real world [6, 19, 4]. Agents are often constrained by the laws of either real or cartoon physics: the virtual hockey player, for example, can't stop skating on a dime.

3 What Motivates You?

Just as, in stage drama, a method actor might ask "what is my motivation?" an agent can be aware of what motivates it to behave a particular way.

One way in which the simplest goals in an agent can been represented is in terms of *drives*. An agent might have a number of drives, such as hunger, pain avoidance, reducing the distance to the opponent's goal, and so on. Each drive could potentially be reduced to a simple scalar number we'll call the Drive Output, the value of which can be obtained by some function of other aspects of the agent's system. In a virtual dog, for instance, hunger might simply be a function of the amount of food in the creature's virtual stomach. Or, it might also take into account things like whether or not the creature can perceive food, what time of day it is, and so on. The output of each drive can then be arbitrarily scaled to be between 0 and 1. At 0, the drive is considered fully satisfied [35].

It's then easy to preferentially weight one of the drives over another, by including a Drive Multiplier – a scalar unique to each drive that is multiplied by the Drive Output (see Fig. 2). These multipliers can change over time, causing the creature to occasionally favor one drive or another. They could, for example, reflect a circadian (daily) rhythm that causes an agent to weight a "sleep" drive more in the evening.

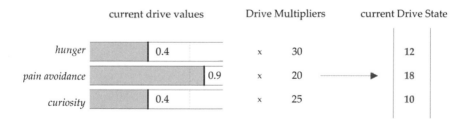

Fig. 2. Three drives, their Drive Multipliers, and the resulting Drive State

A greater challenge is representing more complex goals. For instance, the desire to explore new alternatives might constitute a derived "Curiosity Drive". If, for some reason, it seems like curiosity should be represented on a different, more abstract level than hunger, perhaps it's because it's harder to pinpoint the root physiological cause of human curiosity. In entertainment applications, it can make practical sense to represent abstract goals as drives. The hockey player, in the context of the social activity of playing hockey, might have a desire to prevent the opposing team from taking a shot on goal, which is manifested as a drive that is particularly intense when the goalie is exhausted. For an excellent discussion of more complex goal-driven behavior, see [27].

4 Perceive the World to Find Ways to Satisfy Drives

So our agent now has a motivation: it wants to reduce its drives. In order to do so, it will need to perceive the current state of the world to find relevant information. If the Drive State represents a part of the *internal context* for the agent, the perceived world state is the corresponding *external context*.

For many applications, it is useful to distinguish between sensing and perception. The distinction is obvious in the physical world – the robot's cameras and microphones sense, and the interpretation of the signals sensed by those devices constitutes perception. The hockey player may need to base his decisions on incomplete visual information, instead of having full knowledge of the status of all other players on the ice. This facilitates surprise, and motivates the integration of a spatial working memory, such as the one described in [21].

Perception is a rich area of research. Indeed, the school of thought championed by Rodney Brooks suggests that intelligence can be achieved primarily through perception, rather than representation [5]. Although few AI practitioners today would agree that representation is *un*necessary, there is plenty of innovation that demonstrates how intelligence can arise from thoughtful perceptual representations. Isla, for instance, has designed perceptual representations that allow a creature to reason about object persistence, by combining a spatial "working memory" with an ability to predict how the location of unseen objects in the world will change with time [20, 25].

One useful way to classify perceptual input is by using a hierarchical tree of "Percepts" (see Fig. 3). Every nugget of sensory information passes through the Percept Tree and activates specific Percepts. The activations of the Percepts can be used as input to the creature's action selection mechanism.

5 Deciding What to Do Can Be Reactive

One way the agent can make decisions is by simply *reacting* to the context it perceives. In other words, the creature perceives a particular context (both internal and external), weighs a variety of options based on their perceived values, and then makes an informed probabilistic decision. In order to make this kind of decision, the creature needs a representation that will allow it to

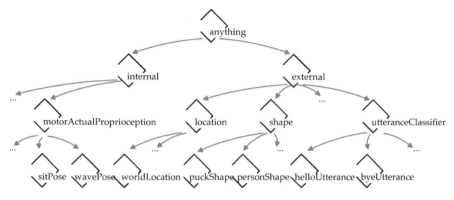

Fig. 3. Sample of part of an agent's Percept Tree

answer the question, "in a given context, if I perform a particular action, how good will that be for me?"

Blumberg accomplishes this with a representation called the *ActionTuple* (see Fig. 4) that consists of four components:

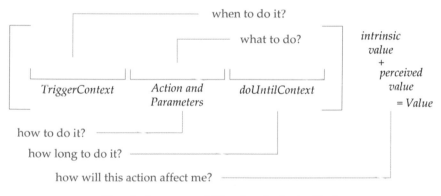

Fig. 4. Anatomy of Blumberg's ActionTuple

The *TriggerContext* is the world state in which the ActionTuple is valid. The *Action* is performed by the agent if this ActionTuple is activated, and its *Parameters* describe the details of that action. A typical parameter is the object on which the action is performed: "pick up *the ball*" or "sit *facing the shepherd*". The *DoUntil* context describes for how long the ActionTuple should remain active. And the *Value* represents, in relation to the drives, how valuable it is to perform this action. The Value can be either Intrinsic (and fixed) or Perceived (and potentially flexible) [21]. (For more on mapping drives to Value, see [28].)

The ActionTuple is a useful starting point for a discussion of action selection, as it encapsulates and formalizes components found in many action-selection mechanisms in the realms of entertainment and research. The Trig-gerContext is sometimes referred to in the reinforcement learning community as a partial state description. The Intrinsic or Perceived Value has been called the expected reward, and is quite similar to the "q-value" in the q-learning paradigm.

Blumberg uses a dog-training paradigm to demonstrate how the Action-Tuple representation can support a virtual creature that learns to perform tricks to receive rewards [3]. Suppose we want to construct a virtual dog that will sit when it hears the word "sit". When the dog does so, we will reward it with a food treat that it should promptly eat in order to satisfy its hunger drive. We can produce this behavior using two ActionTuples: one that says "when I hear the word 'sit', and I sit down for some time, it's pretty good for me", and another that says "when I see food, and I eat it, it's *really* good for me". Both of these are depicted below in Fig. 5.

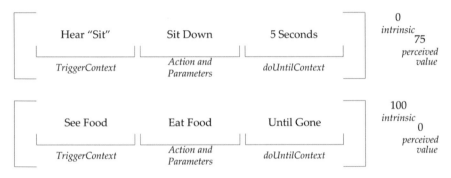

Fig. 5. Two ActionTuples which, taken together, suggest that sitting when you hear the word "sit" has a moderately high perceived value (top), and eating food when you see it has an even higher intrinsic value (bottom)

On a moment-to-moment basis, the dog must react to its perceptions by exclusively selecting one of a number of possible ActionTuples, including these two. Most of the others will have low Values. So if the dog hears the word "sit", then with high probability, it will select the first ActionTuple depicted in the figure, and consequently sit down.

6 Adaptations

For many entertainment applications, agents with completely predefined be-havior rules are appropriate. However, we've recently seen increasingly com-plex and interesting agents that are able to *adapt* to changes in their worlds. There are plenty of reasons why this is exciting. A virtual character can be *personalizable*, so that it gets to know *you* as you get to know it. An agent that's meant to act as a companion or friend can thus learn how to be helpful. A combatant, on the other hand, can *innovate* a personalized counter-attack.

Blumberg was inspired by an approach used to train real animals to integrate a form of adaptation into the ActionTuple representation. The technique requires two degrees of freedom: first, the *Value* of some ActionTuples must be plastic, so that Tuples that previously were not considered valuable could come to be seen as useful (and vice versa). Second, we must be able to replicate ActionTuples that have *modified TriggerContexts*, so that the agent can learn the context in which an action is valuable. The hierarchical structure of the Percept Tree comes in handy here for moving from general to more specific contexts.

The agent begins its life with several "consummatory" ActionTuples that have fixed *Intrinsic Values*, such as "Eat food". It also begins with other "appetitive" ActionTuples with flexible *Perceived Values*. The Intrinsic Value is *back-propagated* from the consummatory ActionTuples when they are active, *into the Perceived Value of previously active appetitive ActionTuples*, as shown in Fig. 6.

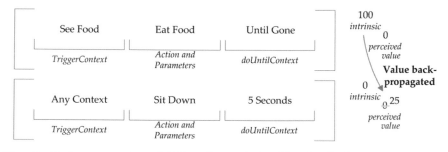

Fig. 6. Back-propagation of Value. Part of the "Eat food" ActionTuple's total Value, 100, is back-propagated to the "Sit in any context" ActionTuple's Perceived Value

In this manner, an agent can start with a simple ActionTuple, like the one above, that makes it sit down in any context. In the absence of food, this dog-agent is unable to activate any high-valued consummatory ActionTuples, and so it is left to "explore" the low-valued ActionTuples like the one above. At some point, the dog randomly sits down, and, lo and behold, food appears, making it possible to activate the "eat the food" ActionTuple. Some of the Value from the "eat the food" ActionTuple is *back-propagated* to the "In any context, sit down" ActionTuple, so that its "Perceived Value" increases (as is occurring in Fig. 6.). Of course, its *Intrinsic Value* is (and will always be) 0, since the act of sitting down itself doesn't assist the dog in any way. But the back-propagation, as depicted in the figure, allows the act of sitting down to gain *perceived* value because it leads with some reliability to a reward.

When an appetitive ActionTuple achieves a high Perceived Value, it can refine its TriggerContext to construct ActionTuples that will achieve higher perceived values, and thus be more useful. It does this by determining which Percepts were reliable indicators of successful trials. In this dog-training case, if the dog has heard an utterance that sounds like "sit" recently, then sitting is likely to lead to a reward. Thus the presence of the "hearing the sit sound" stimulus is a reliable indicator for the success of the trial, and by innovating a *new ActionTuple* that reflects this, the dog will be able to represent the fact that the sitting action is *more* valuable when performed in that particular context (see Fig. 7).

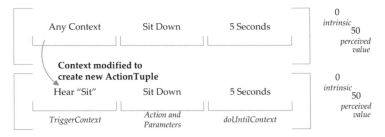

Fig. 7. The TriggerContext of the ActionTuple is modified to create a new, more specific (and soon to be higher-valued) ActionTuple – one that is only triggered when you hear an utterance that sounds like "sit". Contexts are made more general or specific by moving up and down the Percept Tree. Here, the "Any Context" Percept at the top of the tree is replaced by one of its children, the "Hear Sit" Percept

7 The Importance of Expectation

Using the back-propagation technique just described, behaviors that were previously perceived as neutral can come to acquire value when they are performed in particular contexts. Although this produces the desired effect of causing the agent to favor reliably appetitive behaviors, it leaves the agent incapable of answering "why do I expect this appetitive behavior will be valuable?"

In other words, there's little capacity for *expectation*. When a living dog sits down after hearing the word sit, it gives you an intense stare laden with expectation: "Where's my treat, buddy?" If the treat comes, the dog is satisfied and its expectations are confirmed. If it doesn't, there's an *expectation violation* and the dog is left wondering what went wrong. At some other time, if you give the dog some food for no apparent reason, it is *surprised* and possibly wonders if there's something it could do in future to produce the same result.

An agent's ability to expect affords rich opportunities for learning. Imagine we had a system that was capable of predicting the occurrence of salient events in the world. It would be able to *expect* how the world is going to change, and modify its behavior accordingly. It would even be able to predict how *its own actions* will change the world before it performs them. And, since the world will inevitably prove the agent's expectations to be wrong on occasion, the agent would be able to use unexpected events – both surprises and expectation violations – to motivate learning.

Not only can the capacity for expectation motivate an agent to learn, but it also has been shown to provide rich opportunities for producing the illusion of life. El Nasr's FLAME system, for example, showed how a fuzzy-logic representation can be used to map the difference between predicted events and observations to emotional states [16]. An agent can emote its eager *anticipation* of something it expects will make its world a better place, and, if necessary, even take steps to facilitate the event's occurrence. Conversely, if it expects that something about to happen will make the world worse, it can dread the event, try to escape, and emote appropriately. When things don't go as predicted, the resulting expectation violations might cause *frustration* or *relief*. And *surprises*, depending on their effect on Drive State, might be perceived as pleasant or unpleasant.

8 But How to Predict Things?

In order to form expectations, an agent needs some understanding of causality. Or, more accurately, it needs some representation of *apparent* causality. An important and often implicit component of every expectation is a sense of timing. It will be helpful to think of our agent as being able to represent events, both perceived and predicted, on some sort of *TimeLine* (see Fig. 8).

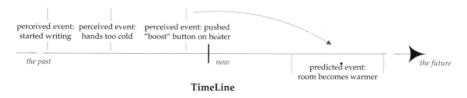

Fig. 8. TimeLine for a non-virtual agent (me)

So here we have a timeline that shows some of the salient events of my past few minutes. Above the line are Perceived Events, which are the things I actually observed to occur. Importantly, we assume that the perceptual input has been filtered so that only the most salient events are placed on the TimeLine.

Below the TimeLine are Predicted Events, which are the things I predicted to occur. I pushed the "boost" button on the heater about three minutes ago, expecting that after an interval of about 10 minutes, the room would get warmer. So now, three minutes later, I expect that in five minutes or so, I'll no longer be shivering as I type this. This is an example of *apparent temporal causality*: I have no idea how the system that heats this room works, but I'm pretty sure that since I pushed the "boost" button on the thermostat that controls the heater, I'm going to feel warmer soon.

This is the simplest and perhaps most typical case of an expectation: some starting conditions are perceived that cause an expectation of an event that is predicted to occur at some time in the future. It's simple to build a representation for relationships like this. We'll call the starting conditions our *Predictor Context* – the context of the world that allows us to make the prediction. The event we expect to occur is the *Predicted Event*. The interval between the Predicted Event and the time the prediction is made (when the Predictor Context became active) is the *Predictor Interval*. Rather than having a specific time at which the future event is likely to occur, as in the above example it is best to represent it as a time window, as Fig. 9 illustrates.

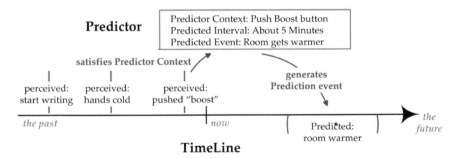

Fig. 9. Five minutes ago, this Predictor started a Trial and caused the expectation of a future event (the temperature in the room will increase)

So this Predictor represents our understanding of the relationship between interacting with the thermostat, and the future temperature of the room. Imagine a Predictor as a sort of sentinel that waits around, watching the salient Perception events on the TimeLine, until its Predictor Context becomes active. When it does, it interacts with the TimeLine to "start a Trial" by forming an expectation.

The Predictor then monitors these newly active Trials that each represent an instance of an expectation. The name Trial comes from the fact that every expectation the creature makes can possibly succeed or fail. If a Perception event equivalent to the Predicted Event occurs on the TimeLine during the window outlined by the Predicted Interval, the Trial is marked a success.

Otherwise, the Trial is marked a failure. (There is also the possibility that a lack of success can be explained by some other mechanism. See [1, 7].)

9 Predictors Come from Surprises

Where do these Predictors come from? In some entertainment applications, it would be sufficient to pre-program an agent with a set of Predictors that describe how its world is going to work.

However, as hinted at above, surprises can motivate an agent to form new Predictors. A surprise (in this paradigm) is *any salient Perceptual Event that can't be explained by a Predictor.* Understanding why surprising events occur may help the agent predict similar salient events in future. So, when a surprising Perceptual Event occurs, the creature creates a new Predictor to "explain away" the event [34]. The Predictor thus formed is a sort of "hypothesis" that the agent will be able to test in future. One way to form this hypothesis is to look back over the TimeLine for another salient event that occurred recently, and choose it as the Predictor Context, as shown in Fig. 10.

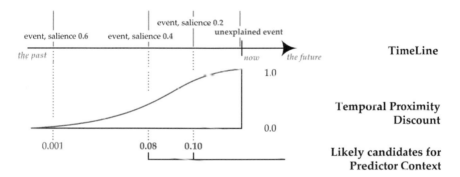

Fig. 10. One technique for selecting a Predictor Context. This process creates a "hypothesis" Predictor to try to explain a surprising event

The ideal Predictor Context is one that is a *salient* and *reliable indicator.* It must be salient, so that it is likely to be noticed by the agent in future. And it must be a reliable indicator, meaning that when it *is* perceived, it follows that the Predicted Event is likely to occur; and, importantly, when it *doesn't*, the Predicted Event is *not* likely to occur.

Whatever technique we choose for creating Predictor hypotheses has to be probabilistic in nature. The mechanism is going to make many mistakes, and many Predictors formed in this way will need to be culled.

10 Predictors Learn from Expectation Violations

Sometimes, the first hypothesis doesn't tell the whole story. Perhaps I've learned that when I push the "boost" button on the thermostat, the house warms up in about 10 minutes. But one day, I push the button, and half an hour later, I'm still cold. I experience an *expectation violation*, and my belief in the reliability of the Predictor decreases. Maybe my hypothesis – that pushing the "boost" button on the thermostat will warm the house – isn't always true!

So I start recording (remembering) the more salient components of the world's context that I perceive at the start of the "trials". Some days, my attempt to warm the room is successful, and other days, it's not. After a while, I come to realize that there *is* a reliable indicator of whether or not this technique will heat the room: the switch beside the thermostat needs to be in the "up" position. And so I refine my hypothesis to say that if the switch beside the thermostat is flipped "up", and I push the boost button, the room will be warm in about five minutes (see Fig. 11).

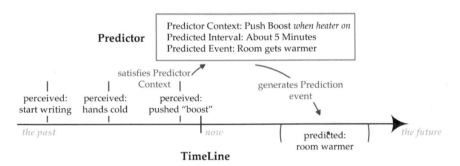

Fig. 11. Predictor with an updated Predictor Context

And this, unfortunately, is a true story. (I thought it was a light switch.) What it serves to illustrate, apart from my occasional acute lack of adaptive ability, is that we can *refine* Predictors to be more useful by looking for other salient and reliable indicators that should be included in the Predictor Context.

11 The Cognitive Economy

Creatures built in "wetware" (like ourselves) are limited by the number of neurons that can fit in their skull cavity. Virtual creatures are similarly limited by resources like memory and processing power. The result is a sort of cognitive economy, where for every source – the Predictor production mechanism, for example – there must also be a sink. Thus, a mechanism must exist for culling

Predictors that are consistently unreliable. It is not obvious when to "cull" Predictors, because sometimes negative knowledge can be extremely useful, as Minsky describes in *The Society of Mind* [29]. But an invalid Predictor may result from a change in the world, or by a mistaken initial hypothesis.

Mechanisms already exist in the architecture for allowing the agent to be judicious when creating structures like Predictors. For instance, only salient perceptual information is processed on the TimeLine. (The salience heuristics, facilitated by the hierarchical structure of the Percept Tree, account for extreme sensory input, sudden and pronounced changes in sensory input, and sensory input previously associated with high-valued actions.) Predictor refinement is also controlled by focusing on Predictors with unusually dynamic reliabilities. Interestingly, there is evidence that unreliable reinforcement leads to exploration in real animals as well [17].

12 To Summarize, the Creature Wants to Understand How its World Works

The thermostat example serves to illustrate the principle that drives predictive learning: that an agent should seek to understand enough about the world to predict things that it would find useful. The mechanism described here is guided by salient events to form hypotheses that are represented as of Predictors, which are then verified and refined.

This particular model of prediction, and particularly the inclusion of windowed timing information within the model, was inspired by a recently proposed ethological model for classical and operant conditioning in real animals [17, 7]. It follows on some excellent work, such as the extensive Prodigy project, which illustrated the utility of tightly integrated planning and learning [37]. Wang was among those who demonstrated how planning can be influenced by observation and practice [38].

13 But What Happened to Action?

You may have noticed that in our discussion of prediction, we didn't talk at all about how the Predictor representation affects how the agent makes action–selection decisions. The Predictors help predict events that are going to occur in the future, but how does that relate to what actions the agent chooses to take?

There's an intriguing isomorphism between the ActionTuple and the Predictor. When we talked about action–selection and the ActionTuple representation, it was shown to be useful to break down our representation for action into the *TriggerContext*, which contains the external conditions that caused an action to be relevant; the *Action* and its *Parameters* that describe the self-action required by the ActionTuple; the *DoUntil*, which describes the length of time the action would take; and finally the *Value*, both *Intrinsic* and *Perceived*, of performing that action in the given context. The Predictor is similarly broken down into a *Predictor Context*, which contains the conditions that cause the Predictor to become active; the *Predictor Interval*, which contains the expected length of time between the Predictor Context and an upcoming event; and the *Predicted Event*, which is really the "value" of having the Predictor – its ability to predict a future event!

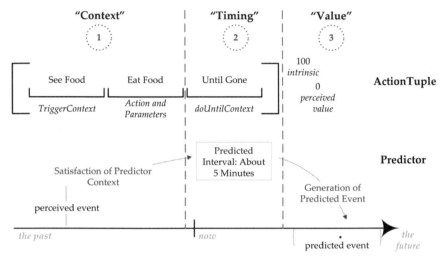

Fig. 12. Isomorphism between ActionTuple and Predictor representations: both encapsulate Context, Timing, and a sense of "Value".

In other words, both contain (1) some sort of triggering mechanism based on context, (2) a timing mechanism, and (3) some sense of future value (see Fig. 12). By now it is obvious that there must be some way to take advantage of this relationship to influence action–selection, and indeed there is. The final clue for one useful action–selection scheme comes from the fact that the Predictor Context occasionally, *but not always*, includes an element of self-action. What if the action *itself* and its parameters (like the object on which you're performing the action) became *part of the context*?

If we replace the Value component of all ActionTuples with a Predicted Event, then the ActionTuple itself *becomes* a Predictor. The Predictor Context is now composed of the *TriggerContext*, the *Action*, and its *Parameters*! Both literally and figuratively speaking, the "Value" of this "Predictive ActionTuple" is *its ability to predict the Predicted Event*!

14 Learning with Predictive ActionTuples

To show that this system is sufficient to reproduce a back-propagation learning technique, let's consider how the dog-training example works with Predictive ActionTuples. The dog still has one consummatory Predictive ActionTuple, augmented as described above, and shown in Fig. 13.

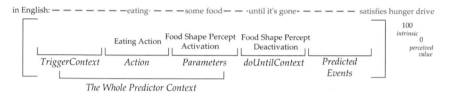

Fig. 13. A Predictive ActionTuple. This is the dog's consummatory Predictive ActionTuple. Note that we start being more explicit here about the fact that all the components actually refer to Percepts. The "Eating Action" even maps onto an EatActionPercept. The Predicted Events slot will be discussed in a moment

At some point, the agent unexpectedly perceives food – something that lets the Predictive ActionTuple be activated. But why did food appear? Perhaps something happened a moment ago that, in future, could serve as an indicator that food is again on the way.

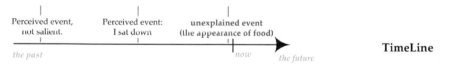

Fig. 14. TimeLine that shows the agent sat down a few moments prior to the unexplained appearance of food

According to the TimeLine shown in Fig. 14, the most salient thing that happened recently was self-action – the agent just sat down. So perhaps sitting in the future will reliably be followed by the appearance of food. This can be represented as a Predictive ActionTuple.

It is important to note that the perception of food is not inherently useful. However, the agent has another ActionTuple – the "eat food when it's present" ActionTuple depicted above – that is intrinsically valuable when the agent is hungry. Thus, in the new system, our new Predictive ActionTuple obtains value not because it has "Perceived Value" back-propagated to it, but rather because of its ability to predict the appearance of the stimulus that would allow for the activation of an intrinsically valuable Predictive ActionTuple. In other words, it allows us to "complete the context" necessary to activate the intrinsically valuable Predictive ActionTuple (see Fig. 15). (A nice side effect of this is that if food is already available, the perceived value of sitting is reduced, because, although that may cause food to appear, we already have the food necessary to complete the context of the "eat food" Predictive ActionTuple.)

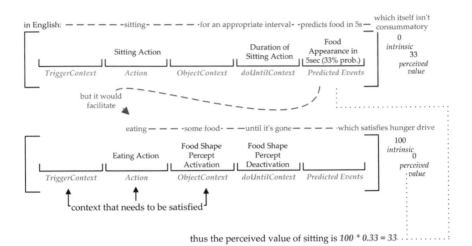

Fig. 15. The two Predictive ActionTuples working together to create perceived value. The Predictive power of the mechanism described above has been harnessed for action–selection purposes

Just like the thermostat example, this new causality relationship (sitting leads to food) isn't as well defined as possible. The agent will soon find that the probability of food appearing after sitting down isn't particularly high. However, there will be some reliable thing about the context at the start of each Trial that predicts, with great reliability, the Trial's success or failure. (More detail about techniques for tracking salient stimuli during Trials is found in [7].) If there is an utterance that sounds like "sit", and the agent sits down, then in a few seconds, food will appear with a certain probability. So the context of the Predictor is refined to reflect this realization (see Fig. 16).

The "appetitive" version of a Predictive ActionTuple is valuable because it predicts some future event *that will facilitate the onset of an intrinsically valuable (or "consummatory") Predictive ActionTuple*!

Now, the agent knows *exactly* why it should sit when it hears "sit" – because it expects that food is going to show up if it does! So when it hears "sit" and *does* sit down, it can drop a Predicted Event on the TimeLine and *anticipate* the upcoming food. If it does come, the agent is happy – but not surprised. If food doesn't come, there's an *expectation violation*, and the agent is able to wonder why.

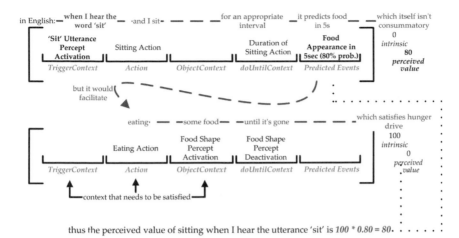

Fig. 16. The Predictive ActionTuple now only makes predictions (starts Trials) when the agent hears the word sit *and* sits down. Thus, both *external context* and *self-action* are required to trigger a prediction

15 The Goatzilla Domain and New Forms of Behavior

The Predictive ActionTuple mechanism was implemented and tested for a virtual creature reminiscent of many found in entertainment applications. Allow me to introduce Goatzilla, a behemoth of an autonomous virtual creature that inhabits the Scottish highlands (see Fig. 17).

Goatzilla's most important drives are hunger and the dominance of other beasts, and his food source is the shed in which the local shepherd keeps his sheep. If Goatzilla kicks the shed, the frightened sheep scatter, and he can embark on a feeding frenzy. Among his other drives is curiosity, which rises slowly over time, and can be reduced by interacting with unusual objects, performing less familiar actions, and experimenting with Predictor relationships that have a high degree of entropy (the ones that would sometimes, but not always, result in success).

The fundamental action–selection decision an agent like Goatzilla has to make at every moment is whether to explore, exploit, or react. In the mechanism shown here, the agent first decides whether it will explore or exploit. Goatzilla does so by performing "drive selection", wherein one of the high-level drives is probabilistically chosen, using a distribution weighted by the Drive Multipliers ((1) in Fig. 15). If the mechanism chooses *any drive other than curiosity*, it selects an action that, in addition to being generally good for satisfying all drives, should be particularly effective at reducing the selected drive. Thus, the creature *exploits* its existing knowledge as best they could.

However, if the curiosity drive is chosen, the agent chooses to *explore* rather than exploit ((2) in Fig. 18). Instead of having exploration strategies scattered throughout the system, it was useful to assemble many of them into this cen-

Fig. 17. Goatzillas in the mist

tral mechanism that could be called upon to choose an appropriate exploration strategy. For example, the Exploration mechanism sometimes would cause the creature to activate a Predictive ActionTuple that had been recently unreliable, so that the creature could initiate a new Trial for that ActionTuple's Predictor, and thus further test the validity of that hypothesis. Or, it could generate a new ActionTuple by taking an existing successful ActionTuple (kicking the shed makes food appear) and modifying it to make another ActionTuple hypothesis (perhaps kicking a rock makes food appear? . . . Or what about kicking any building made of wood?).

If an unexpected stimulus is perceived, it may be possible to interrupt the creature's current behavior to *react* ((3) in Fig. 18). If food appears, for example, we might immediately interrupt our current behavior to approach and eat it. Or, if Goatzilla is wise in the ways of the world and perceives a shed somewhere out in the mist, he may interrupt his behavior to approach and kick it, because he knows this will let him "complete the context" and thus activate the Predictor that says sheep (read: food) will appear momentarily.

Predicted events can also be used by the action–selection mechanism to produce *anticipatory* and *avoidance* behavior – something that would be impossible without an understanding of causality. For instance, if we have learned (like one of Pavlov's dogs) that the ringing of a bell is reliably followed by the presentation of food, then upon hearing the bell we might react by *antic-*

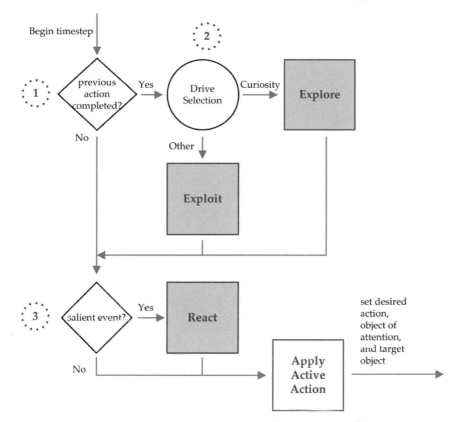

Fig. 18. Goatzilla's action–selection mechanism. (Simplified; see [7] for more detail)

ipating the appearance of the food [31]. On the other hand, if we've learned that the ringing bell is reliably followed by an electric shock, then hearing the bell ringing would drop a prediction of the shock on the TimeLine. As the expected time of that shock approaches, the agent might react by attempting to *avoid* the onset of the shock. In Goatzilla's implementation, special "approach", "avoid", and "observe" ActionTuples allowed him to accomplish these reactive tasks.

Here is an interesting example of a behavior facilitated by the representation for causality. In the absence of a relevant stimulus, the creature can come up with a strategy for satisfying its drives. If Goatzilla's hunger drive is high and he is asked to Exploit, he can ascertain that, ideally, he would like to be eating. But in order to activate the "Eat Sheep" ActionTuple, he is missing a prerequisite: the Sheep. He can reason that, with high probability, kicking the shed will lead to the appearance of sheep in a short time. Thus, he could approach and kick the shed, dropping onto the TimeLine the prediction that food will appear in a few seconds. After doing the kicking, he can stand back and anticipate the appearance of the sheep. If they appear, *he is not surprised*; rather, he feasts, and reinforces his "Kicking the shed causes sheep to appear" Predictive ActionTuple hypothesis. If they do not appear, *there is an expectation violation*, he is *disappointed by the absence of an anticipated perception*, and he reduces his confidence in the hypothesis.

As seen in this example, the TimeLine representation provides all the information the action–selection mechanism needs to make these *explore, exploit, react* decisions. To evaluate the Value of a Predictive ActionTuple, the agent can use the future portion of the TimeLine to generate a counterfactual – imagining what the world would be like if a particular action was performed by adding the Predictive Events from that ActionTuple to the TimeLine. (See [18] for an intriguing discussion of counterfactuals). The TimeLine is also useful for determining if recent Perceived or Predicted Events might offer the agent a chance to interrupt its current behavior and *react*.

16 Socially Oriented Prediction

The inclusion of a virtual hockey player as an example of an autonomous agent at the start of this chapter was motivated not only by the author's Canadian citizenship, but also because it illustrates an agent acting in a social setting. Agents with social understanding can also benefit from a mechanism that predicts how *other agents* (real and virtual) will react to a context.

Elsewhere in this book are thorough examples of socially-oriented agents (see, for example, [27]). In *The Society of Mind*, Minsky uses scripts as a representation for a social activity (such as a birthday party, a conversation, or a play in a hockey game) in which more than one agent participates [29]. These scripts imply social protocols which describe how each agent expects the others to behave in a particular situation, given each agent's role in the social group.

In the hockey game, for instance, the agents are members of the social group known as a hockey team. At a particular moment, the six players on the ice may each be acting autonomously to implement a "behind-the-net" offensive strategy. Typically used by teams with strong puck control, the execution of this strategy requires meticulous teamwork – in other words, the ability to predict the reactions of your teammates to a dynamic and relatively uncertain situation.

It's not necessary that you follow the hockey strategy to follow this discussion, but in case you're interested: the puck-carrier's goal ((1) in Fig. 19) is to maintain possession of the puck and bring it behind the opponent's net. As he does so, he relies on his two offensive teammates ((2) and (3)) to position themselves in front of the net to set up possible "one-time shots" – quick shot opportunities that are likely to fly past the opposing team's goalie. As the puck-carrier crosses behind the net, this triggers the defensemen (4), who are waiting at the blue line, to rush toward the net in anticipation of a pass that might create an exceptionally dangerous shooting opportunity. If necessary,

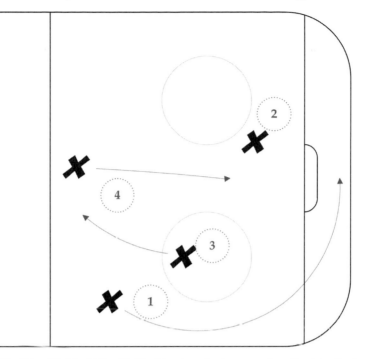

Fig. 19. The "Behind-The-Net" offensive strategy, as described in the text

at that moment the offensive teammates (e.g. (3), as shown) can move away from the net to prevent the opposing team from breaking away with the puck. (I am indebted to [14] for this description.)

This strategy could be represented as a branching script, in which each of the participants – the six teammates, and their six opponents – have defined roles. So long as each agent can trust that each of the other agents on his team knows a similar "script", he can predict how the others will react to the current context. The puck-carrier, for example, can predict that if he can cross behind the net, he can expect the defensemen to rush toward the net to produce a one-time shooting opportunity. And such an opportunity is likely to lead to a goal.

All of this can be represented using Predictive ActionTuples and the Time-Line mechanism. The additional requirement, which is beyond the scope of this chapter (and the current implementation), is a set of Predictors that base their predictions on the state of currently active social scripts.

It is worth noting that in current entertainment applications, such as sports simulators, a more computationally efficient approach for such social behavior would involve a "meta-agent" that controls the entire hockey team, issuing orders to individual agents rather than considering the players as autonomous agents. Care would need to be taken to simulate the illusion of life that is offered by limited agent-based perception. Certainly such an effect could be achieved by determining, at the meta-agent level, what each individual agent is able to perceive. If an observer watches the action in the arena from a vantage point 10 meters off the ground, such details are likely to go unnoticed. But during dramatic close-ups and replays, the illusion of life would be greatly augmented by authentic touches like the look of surprise on a player's face as an opponent he failed to notice steals the puck out from under him.

17 Devils in the Details

Although the technique has proved highly effective for creating an agent that can learn about causality while simultaneously behaving in a life-like way, there are some subtleties that should be mentioned.

Evaluating the Perceived Value of a Predictive ActionTuple is a recursive process. This makes it possible for an agent to generate predictions based on complex causality chains, and also to have the Value of an action be a function of the current context, but it also introduces a potential computational bottleneck. Perhaps a superior model of attention would allow for a dynamic limit on the recursion depth.

We haven't discussed how to organize ActionTuples, either of the Predictive or regular variety. As an agent gets more complex and able to adapt to and interact with more contexts, this becomes increasingly important. Depending on the application, context–action pairs might be organized into groups based on some higher level context. Perhaps this would be in terms of higher level goals (like winning a hockey game versus discussing the match afterwards). Current research involves techniques for organizing actions in terms of social function (things I do with my family, things I do with my hockey team, and so on).

18 Things That Worked

Causality and Action Selection are integrated. To take advantage of causality information, the contexts an agent uses to trigger its actions can be equivalent to the contexts used to trigger predictions.

A desire to understand the world drives learning. When an event occurs that the agent doesn't predict, it registers *surprise* and invents an explanation for why the surprising event occurred. When an explanation (in the form of a Predictor) turns out to be erroneous, an *expectation violation* occurs and the creature can either refine the explanation or invent a new one. In the absence of unusual stimuli, the agent's *curiosity drive* motivates it to explore. It bears repeating that all three of these fundamental motivations for learning emerge from a desire to *understand the world*. Certainly, the agents described here are highly motivated to satisfy their drives. But, instead of perpetually attempting to maximize rate of return, these agents instead seek to understand *enough* about the world to satisfy their drives effectively and predict the onset of salient events. They are *then* motivated by curiosity to discover new things, some of which may lead to new techniques for maximizing rate of return. One observer called this the "curious slacker" approach. The results suggest it creates creatures that are better able to sustain the illusion of life, and avoid some local maxima in the process.

There is a cognitive economy. For every source there must be a sink. For every mechanism that deposits topology, there must be a mechanism that performs withdrawals. The architect of a cognitive architecture must consider the performance of the system on various time scales – eight seconds, eight minutes, eight hours, eight days – as well as in the theoretical limit.

Nothing is deterministic. It is almost always the case that when some decision in an agent is deterministic and involves selecting the "best option", the agent is afforded an opportunity to get stuck in a mindless loop. It invariably will. Some mechanisms, such as the hypothesis-generating mechanism for Predictors, obviously require a random element. Others, like the one underlying the *exploit* operation that is meant to select the "best" option, should also employ some degree of randomness. Choosing an optimal and intuitive distribution for a selection process is another story. The theory of probabilities, noted Laplace, "is nothing more than good sense confirmed by calculation".

The agent's representation of the world isn't too simple. Well, perhaps it still is. But many credit assignment and machine learning algorithms make substantial assumptions about how the world is represented. If we are overzealous in our attempts to simplify our mental representations of the world, we risk introducing what McCallum calls *aliasing* – the inability for adaptive representations in the system to learn the right things, because the perceptual representations can't distinguish between the things they need to learn about [28].

19 Conclusion: What We Get from Prediction

A representation for prediction and expectation can be added to a system designed to support creatures that maintain the illusion of life. The mechanisms, if capable of adaption, allow a creature built with the system to learn about causality "on the job" and even react to changes in its world. In addition to the new motivations for learning that are facilitated by surprises and expectation violations, this system also extends an agent's capacity to emote, by providing a plausible source for emotional effects like eager anticipation or dread, satisfaction or relief, and many others. I would not be surprised to see prediction become increasingly pervasive in agents built for entertainment applications.

Acknowledgments

This work is possible because of the wealth of excellent research that has come before. Some of it is discussed in the other chapters of this book, some of it was mentioned above, and some is described in the works referenced below, although, with sincerest apologies, I acknowledge that the list is far from exhaustive. I am particularly indebted to my former advisor Bruce Blumberg and the Synthetic Characters group at the MIT Media Lab, as well as my thesis readers, Whitman Richards and Randy Gallistel. I also thank my anonymous reviewer for a thorough and insightful assessment. Finally, I extend enduring thanks to Scott Eaton, Gary and Phil McDarby, Daragh McDonnell, and the rest of the MindGames group at MediaLabEurope, who helped bring Goatzilla to life. Twice.

Bibliography

1. Allen, J.F.: Planning as temporal reasoning. In: *The Second International Conference on Principles of Knowledge Representation and Reasoning* (Morgan Kaufmann, Cambridge, MA 1991)
2. Blumberg, B.M.: *Old Tricks, New Dogs: Ethology and Interactive Creatures* (Media Lab Cambridge, MIT 1996)
3. Blumberg, B., Downie, M., et. al.: Integrated learning for interactive synthetic characters. In: *Proceedings of SIGGRAPH* (ACM Press, New York 2002)
4. Breazeal, C.: *Sociable Machines: Expressive Social Exchange Between Humans and Robots.* ScD dissertation (Department of Electrical Engineering and Computer Science, MIT 2000)
5. Brooks, R.A.: Intelligence without representation. *Artificial Intelligence Journal* **47**:139–159 (1991)
6. Brooks, R.A., Stein, L.A.: *Building Brains for Bodies.* MIT AI Lab Memo 1439 (August 1993)
7. Burke, R.C.: *It's About Time: Temporal Representations for Synthetic Characters* (The Media Lab Boston, MIT 2001)
8. Burke, R.C., Isla, D.A., et al.: Creature smarts: The art and architecture of a virtual brain. In: *Game Developers Conference*, San Jose, CA (2001)
9. Cassell, J., Vilhjálmsson, H., Bickmore, T.: BEAT: the Behavior Expression Animation Toolkit. In: *Life-like Characters. Tools, Affective Functions and Applications*, ed Prendinger, H., Ishizuka, M. (Springer 2003). This volume.
10. Cole, R.P., Barnet, R.C., et al.: Temporal encoding in trace conditioning. *Animal Learning and Behavior* **23**(2):144–153 (1995)
11. Damasio, A.: *Descarte's Error* (Harvard University Press 1995)
12. de Kleer, J., Brown, J.: Theories of causal ordering. *Artificial Intelligence Journal* **29**(1):33–62 (1986)
13. Downie, M.: *Behavior, Animation and Music: The Music and Movement of Synthetic Characters* (The Media Lab Boston, MIT 2001)
14. EA Sports. NHL 2003 Coaching Strategies Videos. http://www.ea.com/
15. Ekman, P.: *Emotion in the Human Face* (Cambridge University Press 1982)

16. El-Nasr, M.S., Yen, J., Ioerger, T.: FLAME – Fuzzy Logic Adaptive Model of Emotions. *International Journal of Autonomous Agents and Multi-Agent Systems* **3**(3):1–39 (2000)
17. Gallistel, C.R., and Gibbon J.:   Time, rate and conditioning. *Psychological Review* **107**:289–344 (2000)
18. Hofstadter, D.R.: *Godel, Escher, Bach: an Eternal Golden Braid* (Basic Books 1980)
19. Honda Humanoid Robot. http://world.honda.com/robot/technology/
20. Isla, D.A.: *The Virtual Hippocampus: Spatial Common Sense for Synthetic Characters.* MIT Department of Electrical Engineering and Computer Science (MIT, Cambridge 2001)
21. Isla, D.A., Burke, R.C., et al.: A layered brain architecture for synthetic characters. *Proceedings IJCAI*, Seattle (2001)
22. Ivanov, Y., Blumberg, B.M., et al.: EM for perceptual coding and reinforcement learning tasks. In: *Proceedings 8th International Symposium on Intelligent Robotic Systems*, Reading, UK (2000)
23. Johnson, M.P.: *Quixote: Quaternion-Based Techniques for Expressive Interactive Character Animation* (Media Lab Cambridge, MIT 2002)
24. Kaebling, L.P., Littman, L.M., et al.: Reinforcement learning: A survey. *Journal of Artificial Intelligence Research* **4**:237–285 (1996)
25. Kline, C.:   *Observation-based Expectation Generation and Response for Behavior-based Artificial Creatures* (Media Lab Cambridge, MIT 1999)
26. Maes, P.: The dynamics of action selection. In: *International Joint Conference on Artificial Intelligence*, Detroit (Morgan Kaufmann, San Fransisco, CA 1989)
27. Marsella, S., Gratch, J., Rickel, J.: Expressive behaviors for virtual worlds. In: *Life-like Characters. Tools, Affective Functions and Applications*, ed Prendinger, H., Ishizuka, M. (Springer 2003). This volume.
28. McCallum, A.K.: *Reinforcement Learning with Selective Perception and Hidden State.* Department of Computer Science, University of Rochester (1995)
29. Minsky, M.: *The Society of Mind* (Simon and Schuster, New York 1985)
30. Perlin, K., Goldberg, A.: Improv: A system for scripting interactive actors in virtual worlds. *Computer Graphics* **30**:205–216 (1996)
31. Rescorla, R.A., Wagner, A.R.: A theory of Pavlovian conditioning: Variations in the effectiveness of reinforcement and nonreinforcement. In: *Classical Conditioning II: Current research and theory*, ed by Black, A.H., Prokasy, W.F. (Appleton-Century-Crofts, New York 1972) pp 64-99
32. Rose, C. F., Cohen, M., et al.: Verbs and adverbs: Multidimensional motion interpolation. *IEEE Computer Graphics and Applications* **18**(5) (1999)
33. Russell, J.: A circumplex model of affect. *Journal of Personality and Social Psychology* **39**:1161–1178 (1980)
34. Sheridan, T.: *Telerobotics, Automation, and Human Supervisory Control* (MIT Press, Cambridge, MA 1992)
35. Spier, E.: *From Reactive Behaviour to Adaptive Behaviour: Motivational Models for Behavior in Animals and Robots* (Oxford University Press 1997)
36. Thorndike, E.: *Animal Intelligence* (Hafner, Darien, CT 1911)
37. Veloso, M., Carbonell, J. et al.:   Integrated planning and learning: The PRODIGY architecture. *Journal of Experimental and Theoretical Artificial Intelligence* **7**(1):81–120 (1995)
38. Wang, X.: Learning planning operators by observation and practice. *Proceedings AI Planning Systems* (1994) pp 335–340

Shallow and Inner Forms of Emotional Intelligence in Advisory Dialog Simulation

Fiorella de Rosis, Berardina De Carolis, Valeria Carofiglio, and Sebastiano Pizzutilo

Dipartimento di Informatica, University of Bari, Bari, Italy
http://www.di.uniba.it/IntInt.html
{derosis,decarolis,carofiglio,pizzutilo}@di.uniba.it

Summary. A conversational agent aspiring to be believable in an emotional domain should be able to combine its rational and emotional intelligence in a consistent way. We claim that a cognitive model of emotion activation may contribute to this aim by providing knowledge to be employed in modeling emotion regulation and its influence on the dialog dynamics. We show how an XML markup language contributes to insuring independence between the agent's body and mind, so as to favor adaptation of the dialog to the user characteristics. An example dialog in the eating disorder domain is employed throughout the chapter to illustrate the methods developed and the implemented prototype.

1 Introduction

What is it that makes *believable* a conversation with an embodied agent? Research about computer conversations was initiated long before the birth of these agents. In the last few decades, computational linguists attacked the problem of simulating dialogs with human interlocutors with the ambitious aim of rendering them *natural* (see, for instance, [43]). In the downing of computer science, the famous Turing test already envisioned a computer dialog in the scope of a game: what, in that case, made the dialog natural was the possibility of simulating *deception* and of discovering deception attempts, which is typical of games [41]. Other aspects of dialog believability were considered subsequently, like the ability to show clear *personality traits* [42, 23, 12], to *recognize doubt* [6], to *be polite* [3], to introduce a bit of *humor* [39], to *persuade* with irrational arguments [38], and so on. These problems are still open or have been solved only in part.

These problems reappear with higher strength and urgency when the technology supporting the conversation takes the appearance of an embodied character. Conditions of believability extend, in this case, to showing consistency between inner and outward aspects of behavior. As several authors claim in this volume (for instance, Marsella et al. [24]), the more realistic the character, the higher is the level of naturalness and plausibility users expect from its behavior. One might argue that, if the character is a cartoon, other ingredients of believability become essential: excess, gaming, cheating, paradox, and so on. And these features are difficult to model, so that probably automatic generation of cartoons is still more difficult than the generation of human-like, realistic characters, at least until the psychological mechanism behind these features becomes clearer.

There is certainly a link between the *type* of character, the *application domain* to which it applies, and the *category of users* to which it is addressed. Let us consider the case of advisory systems, which are the subject of this chapter. It is reasonable to assume that a cartoon suggesting a *correct* behavior in some domain (for instance, eating habits) will be more likely accepted by a child than by an adult. To increase acceptability, such a cartoon might be supported by a suggestive and fun illustration of the effects of healthy/unhealthy eating. In the case of adults, on the contrary, the psychological problems which go with eating disorders require a different form of believability. The agent should give, in this case, the impression of being expert and trustworthy, of understanding the reasons of the interlocutors, and of adapting to their needs: an illusion of seriousness and empathy at the same time, which may be conveyed by a human-like character rather than a cartoon. Similar considerations may be applied to medical applications, as in Carmen's Bright IDEAS [24]. If a relation between application domain, potential users, and character to employ exists, it then becomes clear why *flexibility* is, at present, one of the main requirements of embodied agents. Conversational agents, in particular, should be flexible in the role they take in the dialog (who takes the initiative, which are the communicative goals/plans involved, how they are revised, etc.), in the personality traits they show, in the outward behavior they take. In emotional dialogs, they should be flexible, as well, in enabling their emotions to influence their internal state (reasoning, decision taken, and so on) and in showing them in their outward behavior.

If flexible behavior is a key factor of research in this area [36], then authoring tools that enable varying conditions in which to simulate the dialog are essential. This is the main characteristic of several projects in this volume and also of our work. As we will see in the following sections, *domain independence* and *mind–body separation* are characteristics of our testbed: other flexibility features are the opportunity to define a *social context* in which the dialog occurs (as in [37]) and to endow the agent with a *flexible personality*, intended as a psychologically plausible combination of traits. While we refer to other papers for the description of how we simulated cooperation personalities, conflicts, and deception in dialogs [13, 17], in this chapter we will focus our analysis on how emotions arising during the dialog might influence its dynamics.

2 Advisory Dialogs

In advisory dialogs, an expert tries to get users to show an appropriate behavior in some specific domain by providing relevant information and suggestions and by persuading them to follow them. These dialogs may be emotional when the affective state of the user is influenced by information received and when the expert reacts to the users' answers by showing an empathic attitude, to increase her compliance with its advice[1]. These dialogs are asymmetrical because, in the majority of moves, the expert plays the role of the information provider while the user answers questions. This asymmetry may be reduced by enabling users to drive information provision toward their needs; that is, by introducing in the dialog some form of adaptation. In the research described in this contribution, we wanted to test whether and how we could implement a believable conversational agent in a domain in which affective factors have a major influence. On the other hand, we wanted to have an *arena* in which to validate the methodological problems involved in simulating reactive and mixed-initiative emotional dialogs. To behave believably, our agent should show some form of *emotional intelligence*. This implies, according to Picard [35], *recognizing and expressing emotions, regulating them,* and *utilizing them* to optimize the dialog. To establish when the agent may feel an emotion, which emotion, and with what intensity, we developed an emotion modeling method and tool. This tool enables us to simulate how the agent reacts to the user's moves: emotion triggering and decay may be adapted to the agent's personality, to simulate a *regulatory mechanism* in feeling and displaying emotions. Agents with different personalities may be modeled, to assess how the dialog is influenced by this factor. Emotion activation is also influenced by the social context in which the dialog takes place: the role played by the agent, the relationship with the interlocutor, the environment in which interaction occurs, etc. The way emotion expression is combined with other meanings in the agent's move is specified by tagging this move with a markup language (*APML*) that is described in [16].

These aspects of our system implement the agent's ability to express emotions through face, gesture, and speech. This ability is the most shallow form of emotional intelligence the agent may show: emotions have to be *utilized*, as well, to *drive reasoning* behind the dialog and regulate it. This implies studying how the dialog may be affected by the emotional state of the agent and of the user, by some personality traits of the two interlocutors, and by their relationship [32]. Again according to Picard [35] and also to other authors [21], emotions influence learning, decision making, and memory. If intelligently handled by an agent, they may help to manage information overload, regulate prioritization of activities, and help in making decisions more flexibly, creatively and intelligently. More generally, emotions motivate and bias

---

[1] We will employ, from now on, a neutral gender when mentioning the expert and the female gender when mentioning the user.

behavior, although they do not completely determine it. Simulating affective dialogs therefore requires investigating the following problem issues:

- which personality factors (of the two interlocutors) may affect the dialog;
- which emotions the agent may feel during the dialog, as a consequence of exogenous factors (the user's move) or endogenous factors (the agent's own reasoning);
- how an emotion influences the course of dialog: in particular, priority of communicative goals and dialog plans;
- how an emotion affects the way that a particular goal is rendered.

Reaction to emotions and, more generally, their influence on the agent's behavior are affected by the social relationship between the interlocutors. Three types of relationships are envisaged, again by Picard:

- *friendship*, where the agent tends to have similarly valenced emotions in response to the emotions of the interlocutor;
- *animosity*, where oppositely valenced emotions are felt and shown;
- *empathy*, where the agent temporarily substitutes the presumed goals, standards, and preferences of the interlocutor for its own.

For reasons we will justify, our agent adopts a partially *empathic relationship* with the user: rather than substituting its own goals with the presumed user's goals, it revises their priorities so as to try to concile its own needs with the user's needs. This is, we believe, an appropriate behavior for an agent that needs to establish a close contact with the user but wants to keep, at the same time, some control of the conversation, by placing itself in the position of an *expert* in the domain and of the main decision maker rather than of a simple *friend* of the user. Our advisory dialog simulator includes four main components (Fig. 1): an *emotion modeling* module (the agent's mind), a *dialog manager*, an *automatic tagging* program (MIDAS), and an *animation engine* which generates an agent's body selected from a character cast. A *graphical interface* supports the exchange of messages among the various modules and enables the user to set up the dialog simulation conditions and to converse with different kinds of agents. In the following sections, we will first describe the application domains we considered and then the various modules.

3 Two Example Application Domains

Although several authors claim that embodied agents promise to be one of the emerging human-computer interaction metaphors, appropriate application domains have still to be found, especially for realistic agents. The more realistic the agent's aspect is, the more users expect from interacting with it and the harder it is to make the agent believable. This expectation still increases when the dialog considers emotional aspects. To test which application domains appear to be appropriate for our advisory dialogs and how affective

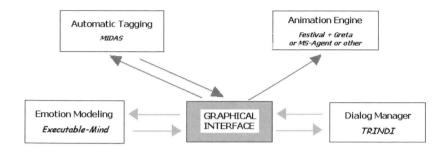

Fig. 1. Functional components of our dialog simulation system

factors contribute to their believability, we built a domain-independent simulator (Fig. 1). We will illustrate its principles and functioning with two test domains: a travel agency and advice about eating disorders.

3.1 Travel Agency

This application is very simple: we mainly developed it to prove domain independence of our system. The dialog is an extension of the kind of dialogs that were simulated in *Godis* (see Sect. 9), with the introduction of some small talk in the style of REA [5]. Here, the agent plays the role of a travel agent who has to provide suggestions about a holiday. She acquires, through a set of questions, the information she needs. Small talk is triggered when the agent is initially set in the *empathic* mode and wants to establish a friendly relationship with the user by adding, to the main dialog, some comments about climate, traffic, tourist attractions, etc., in the places involved in the travel. The baseline part of the dialog in Fig. 2 is driven by the *Godis* plan and implements the agent's questions and her final answer (moves Agent1, 2, 3, and 6 to 11). Small talk (at moves Agent 4 and 5) is implemented by activating subplans which are triggered by keywords in the user's answers: *to < city_name >* and *from < city_name >*. While basic moves are pronounced by the agent with neutral expressions, small talk is accompanied with positive or negative affect expressions that are triggered by the emotion simulator according to the content of the move.

3.2 Advice About Eating Disorders

Eating disorders are common among young people: an active chat line and several web sites providing information in this domain exist (see Sect. 9). Although the style of suggestions, in these sites, tends to be empathic, the information provided is not tailored to the user. In addition, the user cannot ask questions, make objections, request clarifications, and, more generally, take the initiative to drive information provision in the direction that best

```
Agent  1> Welcome to Greta's travel agency! May I help you?
User> Yes please. I wish to buy a ticket.
Agent  2> How do you want to travel?
User> by airplane
Agent  3> OK! Let's find a convenient solution! What city do you want to go to?
User> I wish to spend some time in London
Agent  4> Fine! That's a good idea! I've recently been to London and it was a
pleasant experience!
Agent  4> The temperature is not too high and, although it rains rather
frequently, the climate is overall good!
Agent  4> In addition, if you have some time, you might visit the New Tate
Gallery!
Agent  4> What city do you want to go from?
User> I'm living in Paris
Agent  5> Oh, Paris! I would love living there!
Agent  5> Unfortunately, the traffic is  terrible in town.
Agent  5> However, life is  pleasant.
Agent  5> Do you want a return ticket?
User> Yes, please.
Agent  6> What month do you want to leave?
User> in May
Agent  7> What class did you have in mind?
User> Economy
Agent  8> OK. The most convenient solution I may propose you will cost 1528
dollars
User> OK: may I buy my ticket now?
Agent  9> What is your credit card number?
User> 1234567890
Agent 10> Here is your ticket.  Good bye. And thank you very much for selecting
our agency!
User> Bye and thanks
Agent 11>  Thank you for your visit!
```

Fig. 2. An example dialog in the Travel Agency domain

corresponds to her needs. Although the style employed is (as we said) empathic, the system cannot recognize whether and how the emotional state of the user changes during interaction, nor can it guess the reason for this change. As a consequence, also the emotions the system shows are static and rigid (and therefore unnatural). By aiming for the goal of enabling young users to interact with our agent to receive advice about their eating problems, we wanted to establish an atmosphere of empathic relationship between the two interlocutors that might make the advice provided more effective. We took information from web sites in this domain as a reference corpus in designing our dialog simulator [14].

The following example dialog is produced by our system:

G0: *Hi, my name is Greta! I'm here to help you find a healthier way of feeding yourself. What's your name?*
U0: *My name is Jana.*
G1: *What's your problem, Jana?*

U1: *I've been eating too much for about one year and I realize that I'm not myself, that I'm not thinking quite right!*

G2: *Oh I'm sorry. That's a bad situation indeed. What is your age?*

U2: *I'm 17.*

G3: *Well: teenagers are notorious for being hungry frequently, because they need to eat more to support the major growth of their bodies.*

U3: *Oh no, it's not a question of increased appetite or overeating from time to time: it's a question of compulsive overeating, in my case. I feel out of control and powerless to stop!*

G4: *How awful! Have you already tried to do something to solve this problem?*

U4: *Yes, and I didn't succeed. I now fear that stopping will not be possible for me! So, I don't know why I'm here!*

G5: *Oh no! You have to be confident in yourself! If you want to get over this, I can help you.*

U5: *What can I do?*

G6: *I have some ideas and experience on how to make a smooth, quick transition from overeating back to healthy living. If you wish, I can suggest what you might do.*

U6: *Yes, please, I want to make every possible effort to get out of this!*

G7: *Fine! This is the attitude I want to see from you! So, let's start, first of all, from cleansing your home of all "binge foods". Whatever your current food downfalls are, get rid of them!*

U7: *But I can't stand to throw food away!*

G8: *Well, give it to someone, then! And if your relatives insist on keeping such foods in the house, ask them to keep it away from you for a while.*

U8: *That's a good suggestion, I'll try! What else?*

G9: *I need to know something more about the way you live, to go on. Do you take part in any kind of sport, for instance?*

U9: *Nothing, for a long time.*

G10: *So, plan to exercise! Choose something you enjoyed doing, even though you may not feel like doing it right now.*

. . .

We will consider this example all through this chapter, to illustrate the functioning of our emotion simulation tool and the influence of emotions activated in the agent on the dialog dynamics.

4 Emotion Modeling

Our emotion modeling method is described in detail elsewhere [19]. In this chapter, we will focus our description on algorithmic aspects of the model and on prototype implementation.

In this modeling method, particular attention is paid to how emotions change in intensity with time, how they are mixed up, and how each of them prevails, in a given situation, according to the agent's personality and to the social context in which the dialog occurs. So far, we focused our attention on event-driven emotions in Ortony et al.'s theory [30] which includes positive and negative emotions, triggered by present or future desirable or undesirable events. We adopted Oatley and Johnson-Laird's theory [28] and Castelfranchi's contribution [11], according to which positive and negative emotions are activated (respectively) by the belief that some goal is *achieved* or *threatened* as a consequence of some event. A cognitive model of emotions that is built on this theory should represent the system of beliefs and goals behind emotion activation. This model endows the agent with the ability to *guess the reason why it feels a particular emotion* and to justify it if needed. It also includes the ingredients that enable representation of *how the agent's system of goals is revised* as a consequence of feeling emotion and how this revision influences the dialog dynamics.

We apply a Dynamic Belief Network (*DBN*) [27] as a goal monitoring method that employs observational data in the time interval (T_i, T_{i+1}) to generate a probabilistic model of the agent's mind at time T_{i+1}, from the model at time T_i. We use this model to reason about the consequences of the observed event on the monitored goals. We calculate the intensity of emotions as a function of the *uncertainty* of the agent's beliefs that its goal will be achieved (or threatened) and of the *utility* assigned to achieving this goal. The two variables are combined to measure the variation in the intensity of an emotion as a product of the change in the probability to achieve the goal, times the utility that achieving this goal means to the agent [9].

Let us consider, for instance, the triggering of *sorry-for* that is represented in Fig. 3: this is a negative emotion and the goal involved is *preserving others from bad*. The agent's belief about the probability that this goal is threatened (Bel G (Thr-GoodOf U)) is influenced by its belief that some undesirable event E happened to the user (Bel G (Occ E U)). According to Elliott and Siegle [20], Ortony [29], and Pfeifer and Nicholas [34], the main variables influencing this probability are the desirability of the event (Bel G not(Desirable E)) and the probability the agent attaches to it (Bel G (Occ E U)). Other factors, such as the social context (Bel G (FriendOf G U)), affect the emotion intensity. The model of the agent state at time T_{i+1} is built by automatically combining several Belief Networks (BNs): the main one (*Mind-BN*) and one or more *Event-BNs* and *Emotion-BNs*. In the *Event-BNs*, the user's moves are interpreted as observable consequences of occurring events that may activate emotions by influencing the agent's beliefs and goals. The strength of the link between what the user said (Say U (Occ E U)) and the hidden event (Occurs E U) is a function of the user's sincerity. The link between this observation and the agent's belief (Bel G (Occ E U)) is a function of how believable the agent considers the user to be. Therefore, the more sincere and believable the user is and the more likely the event is a priori, the higher will be the probability that G believes in the occurrence of the event. Similar considerations hold for the evaluation of how undesirable the event is (Bel G not(Desirable E)). These nodes are leaves of the *Event-BN*. They are, as well, roots of *Mind-BN*: they influence G's belief that U desires the event E not to occur (Bel G Goal U

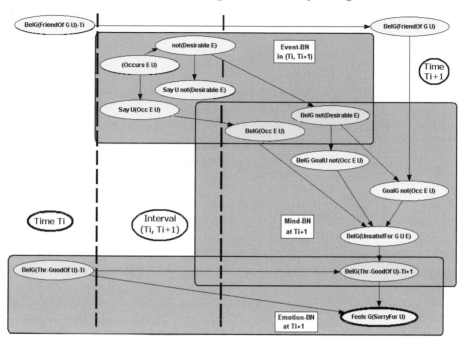

Fig. 3. A portion of the DBN that represents triggering of "sorry-for"

not(Occ E U)). If G is in an empathic relationship with U and therefore adopts U's goals, they influence, as well, the agent's own desire that E does not occur (Goal G not(Occ E)). This way, they concur to increase the probability that the agent's goal of *preserving others from bad* will be threatened. Variation in the probability of this goal activates the emotion of *sorry-for* in G through the *Emotion-BN*.

The strength of the link between the goal-achievement (or threatening) nodes at two contiguous time instants defines the way the emotion associated with that goal decays, in the absence of any event influencing it. By appropriately varying this strength, we simulate a more or less fast decay of emotional intensity (see the example in Fig. 4). Different decays are attached to different emotion categories (positive vs. negative, fortune of others vs. well-being, and so on) and different temperaments may be simulated, with different *persistence* of emotions. The agent's affective state may include multiple emotions. Emotions with different intensities may coexist because an event produced several of them at the same time or because a new emotion is triggered while the previous ones may not yet have decayed completely. We describe in detail in [9], how we modeled the two mixing metaphors (*microwave oven* and *tub of water*) introduced by Picard [35].

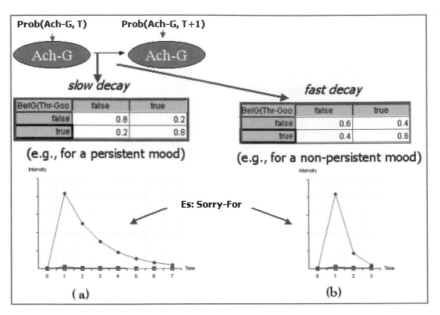

Fig. 4. Slow and fast decay of emotions

4.1 Two Versions of Our Emotion Simulator

We implemented an emotion simulation tool which applies the above method, in two different versions. **Mind-Testbed** may be employed to create and test models while **Executable-Mind** may be called from any external program. To create models of emotions in a given domain with Mind-Testbed, one has to create several files:

1. a description of the agent's mind: *Mind-BN* at time T_0;
2. a description of the events that may occur in every considered domain: *Event-BNs*;
3. a description of the relationships between goals in *Mind-BN* and emotions modeled: *Emotion-BNs*;
4. a description of the personalities the agent may take;
5. a description of the contexts in which simulation may occur.

Files 1 to 3 are built with *Hugin* (see Sect. 9). Files 5 and 4 may be created with the tool or a text editor. A personality is a cognitively plausible combination of traits. As originally proposed by Carbonell [7], a trait corresponds to assigning a weight to a goal-achievement node. A context corresponds to assigning truth values to context nodes. A decay speed may be set up for every emotion by manipulating conditional probability tables in the *Emotion-BNs*. Once the preliminary set-up phase has been completed, the tool may be employed to test models. An application domain, a context, an agent's personality, an initial mental state, and a threshold for emotional intensities are selected. Events in the domain may now be introduced, in sequence. The graphical interface in Fig. 5 shows, in the top left frame, the simulation conditions (in the example in this figure: *personality=other-centered&optimistic*; *context=friendship*; *domain=emotional eating*; *threshold* = 3%). In the right frame, the dynamic belief network is displayed, with evidence about nodes. In the left bottom frame, the dynamics of emotional intensities is displayed in tabular or graphical form. In Executable-Mind, when the calling program inputs a user's move, this is interpreted as a combination of communicative acts: the program analyzes these acts as events that might activate emotions in the agent, updates the emotion intensity table with the new entry, and sends it back to the calling program.

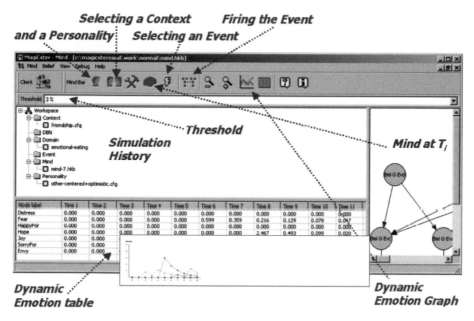

Fig. 5. The graphical interface of Mind-Testbed

4.2 A Simulation Example

To clarify the method described in the previous section, we now discuss what happens in our example dialog. Initially, the agent is in a *neutral* emotional state (time 0 in the figure).

- Move *U0* (*My name is Jana*) does not produce any emotional reaction (Time T_1).
- Move *U1* (*I've been eating too much for about one year and I realize that I'm not myself, that I'm not thinking quite right!*) is interpreted as Inform

U G (SuffersEatingDisorders U). This is an undesirable event happening to U that activates an emotion of *sorry-for* in the agent (time T_2).

- Move $U2$ (*I'm 17*) does not produce any new emotional reaction: sorry-for decays (time T_3).
- Move $U3$ (*Oh no, it's not a question of increased appetite or overeating from time to time: it's a question of compulsive overeating, in my case. I feel out of control and powerless to stop!*) is interpreted as Inform U G (SuffersBingeEating U). This undesirable event again increases the emotion of *sorry-for* (time T_4).
- Move $U4$ (*Yes, and I didn't succeed. I now fear that stopping will not be possible for me! So, I don't know why I'm here!*) is interpreted as Inform U G (EvStopDialog U): U might stop the dialog. This is, again, an undesirable event to G that might occur in the future and therefore provokes a light emotion of *fear* (a kind of *concern*) (time T_5).
- Move $U5$ (*What can I do?*) does not produce any emotional reaction: sorry-for and fear both decrease at time T_6.
- Move $U6$ (*Yes, please, I want to make every possible effort to get out of this!*) is interpreted as Inform U G (EvStopOvereating U), that is: the user manifests some intention to interrupt compulsive overeating. This is a desirable future event to G, that activates an emotion of *hope* (time T_7).
- Move $U7$ (*But I can't stand to throw food away!*) does not produce any emotional reaction; all emotions decrease (time T_8).
- Move $U8$ (*That's a good suggestion, I'll try! What else?*) is interpreted as Inform U G (LikesSuggestion U), that is the user seems to appreciate the agent's help. This is a desirable event to the agent that produces an emotion of *joy* (time T_9).

The four graphs in Fig. 6, that were produced with Mind-Testbed, represent the situation described in this dialog, with different personalities for the agent.

The context is always set to *friendship* and the threshold to 3%, while the following situations are simulated:

- a *self-centered* & *pessimistic* agent associates a high weight with the goals of *preserving self from (immediate or future) bad* which activate (respectively) distress and fear. A low weight is attached, on the contrary, to the goals of *achieving the good of others*, *preserving others from bad*, and *achieving the future good of self*, which may activate (after negative or positive events) sorry-for, happy-for, or hope.
- an *other-centered* & *optimistic* agent associates a high weight with the goals of *achieving the good of others* and *preserving others from bad*, which are responsible for activating the emotions of happy-for and sorry-for. She attaches a high weight also to the goals of *achieving the (immediate or future) good of self*, which activate joy and hope. On the contrary, a low weight is attached to the goal of *dominating others* and preserving self from bad, which (respectively) activate envy and fear.

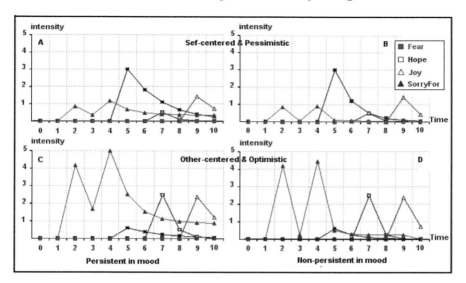

Fig. 6. Emotions triggered in the example dialog, with four personalities of the agent

By combining personality traits and time decay factors, we get four different situations: *A, self-centered & pessimistic & slow-decay*; *B, self-centered & pessimistic & fast-decay*; *C, other-centered & optimistic & slow-decay*; and *D, other-centered & optimistic & fast-decay*. Figure 6 shows that sorry-for and hope have a higher intensity in cases *C* and *D*, when the agent is *other-centered & optimistic*, while fear is higher in cases *A* and *B*, when it is *self-centered & pessimistic*. In cases *A* and *C*, the time decay of all emotions is slower than in *B* and *D*. The result is that:

- in cases *A* and *B*, a mild sorry-for is activated at T_2 and T_4, a higher fear at T_5, and mild joy at T_9; at T_7, the effect of hope is lower than the intensity of other co-occurring emotions;
- in case *C*, sorry-for is high at T_2 and T_4, hope is mild at T_7 and overlaps with sorry-for, while fear has a lower intensity than other, co-occurring emotions;
- in *D*, three emotions are felt neatly during the dialog (sorry-for, hope, and joy), while fear has a low intensity, although it is less masked by sorry-for than in *C*.

The emotional trends shown in the four situations appear to be consistent with the personality trait configurations. By appropriately varying other parameters in the model, we may simulate other situations: for instance, a dialog occurring in a less friendly context because the agent notices that the user is not really interested in getting advice. By increasing the activation threshold for all emotions, we may simulate an agent who is cold in feeling all emotions.

5 Regulation and Display of Emotions

As we anticipated in the Introduction, our agent should show the ability to *regulate and display its emotions*. Once *felt*, an emotion E may be hidden or displayed. Again, this "decision" (although not always taken consciously) may be influenced by personality factors and by the interaction context. We model this aspect of the emotional behavior of our agent by means of rules that regulate activation of display goals [15]. For example, the rule:

If (Feel Ag E) $\wedge$ Is-a (E WellBeing) $\wedge$ (Valence E Negative) $\wedge$ (Adoptive Ag U)
then Goal Ag ($\neg$(Display Ag E)

activates the goal of hiding *fear* felt at time T_5, because the agent has an adoptive relationship with the user. The following one:

If (Feel Ag E) $\wedge$ Is-a (E WellBeing) $\wedge$ (Valence E Positive) $\wedge$ (Adoptive Ag U)
then Goal Ag (Display Ag E)

activates the goal of showing, at move $G7$, the *hope* felt at time T_7.

When an emotion has to be displayed, an affective tag is automatically added to the agent's move. For instance, move $G7$ in the example dialog:

Fine! This is the attitude I want to see from you! So, let's start, first of all, from cleansing your home of all binge foods. Whatever your current food downfalls are, get rid of them!

is tagged, in the $APML$ markup language, as follows:

```
<APML>
<turn-allocation type="take"> <performative type="confirm" affect="hope"> Fine!
<rheme> <emphasis x-pitchaccent="Hstar"> This </emphasis> is the attitude
I want to see from you! </rheme></performative></turn-allocation>
<performative type="propose"> So, let's start, first of all, from cleansing
your home of <emphasis x-pitchaccent="Hstar"> all </emphasis>
<emphasis x-pitchaccent="Hstar" adjectival="large"> binge </emphasis> foods!
</performative>
Whatever your current food downfalls are, <performative type="suggest">
<rheme> <emphasis x-pitchaccent="Hstar"> get rid </emphasis> of them!
</rheme> </performative>
<turn-allocation type="give">
</APML>
```

Tags show that the first sentence is a take-turn and a confirm; this sentence is associated with an affective meaning of *hope*. The second sentence is a propose which includes a meaning of large associated with the adjective *binge*. The move ends with a suggest. A topic-comment tag is added to words that should be emphasized (*this, all, get rid*). For more details about $APML$, see [16]. Employing an XML markup language as a layer between the agent's mind and its body enables us to achieve complete independence of the two components. In particular, *shallow* expression of emotions is obtained by translating *meanings* specified in $APML$ tags into a combination of signals (in face, gesturing, body movement) that depends on the character employed. The agent may then manifest emotions in addition to other *meanings* (performative types, belief relations, etc.), through an appropriate combination of speech and nonverbal signals that depend on its body. De Carolis et al. [16] describe how *APML* was interfaced with Steedman's Festival (see Sect. 9) and with Pelachaud's Greta (the face generator [33]). To support interfacing with cartoon-like characters (MS-Agents), we define the meaning-signal correspondence of a given character in an *XML Meaning-Signal translation* file. In this file, the combination of signals by which every meaning should be rendered is established by rules of the form:

$$<\text{meaning-tag}_i> \Rightarrow <\text{Rendering } att_1, att_2, \ldots att_j, \ldots att_n>$$

where $<\text{meaning-tag}_i>$ is an *APML* tag and att_j specifies an animation or speech feature that the character's body is able to perform.

The following are some examples with the MS-Agent *Ozzar*:

$<$TurnAllocation type="take-turn"$> \Rightarrow$
$<$Rendering StartingPlay="Pleased" StoppingPlay ="PleasedReturn"
Speed="200"$>$

$<$Metacognitive type="I'm thinking"$> \Rightarrow$
$<$Rendering StartingPlay="Think" StoppingPlay="ThinkReturn"$>$

$<$Affect type="sorry-for"$> \Rightarrow$
$<$Rendering StartingPlay="Sad" StoppingPlay="SadReturn"$>$

Meaning-signal translation files define a mapping between the semantics of discourse segments and the expressions the character can show with face, gesture, body, and speech. Defining several meaning–signal translation files enables us to render a given meaning with different combinations of signals. We may, for instance, implement a character with a *fun* behavior for interacting with children and a more "serious" one for adults. As an example with *Ozzar*:

$<$Performative type="approve"$> \Rightarrow$
$<$Rendering StartingPlay="Congratulate" StoppingPlay="CongratulateReturn"$>$
in the *fun* case;
$<$Rendering StartingPlay="Acknowledge"/$>$ in the *serious* case.

With a more sophisticated and realistic character, like Greta [33], we may apply this method to build culture-dependent characters [18].

6 Dialog Simulation

The ability to exhibit an emotional state is only a shallow form of the emotional intelligence an agent can show. Emotions have to be *utilized to drive reasoning* behind the dialog and regulate it. This implies studying how the dialog may be affected by the emotional state of the two interlocutors and by their personalities. Simulating affective dialogs therefore requires modeling *how emotional states influence the course of dialog: priority of communicative goals, dialog plans, and surface realization of communicative acts*. Reaction to emotions and, more generally, their effects on the agent's behavior are influenced by its relationship with the user. The issue the dialog manager has to solve is then the following: how should the agent behave, after discovering the emotional state of the user and after *feeling* an emotional state of its own? More specifically: how should these emotions affect the dialog dynamics? We manipulate the *inner* aspects of the emotional response of our agent with an algorithm of activation/deactivation of its discourse *goals* and dynamic revision of their priorities. The idea is that the agent has an initial list of goals that she aims to achieve during the dialog, each with its own priority; some of these goals are *inactive*. The agent knows how every goal may be achieved in a given context: every discourse goal is linked, by an *application condition*, to a *plan*. Application conditions specify the context in which the plan should be considered: user characteristics (her age, the kind of eating disorders she refers to have, etc,), dialog history (goals achieved so far), and plans performed to achieve these goals. When some emotional state is activated in the agent, the goal priorities are revised: inactive goals may become active; some of the active goals may become less *urgent* and/or *important*; others may increase in urgency and/or importance. The plan that best suits achieving the most urgent and important goal in the given context is then applied. Our dialog manager includes three main modules. A *Deliberative* layer selects the goal with the highest priority and the plan to achieve it and stores them in the agenda, the list of actions in the plan. The *I/O Communicative layer* receives user input to a goal and executes the actions in the agenda. The *Reactive layer* consults the knowledge base and decides whether the goal priority should be revised. We now describe the knowledge sources that are employed by these modules.

6.1 Agent and User Models

An agent and a user model are stored, with the interaction history, in the *information state* of the dialog manager. These models include two categories of factors: long-term and short-term settings. *Long-Term Settings* (agent's personality, its role, its relationship with the user) are stable during the dialog and influence the initial priorities of goals and therefore the initial plan, initiative handling, and behavior. *Short-Term Settings* (beliefs and emotional state of the agent) evolve during the dialog and influence goal priority change and plan evolution. The agent's goals g_i can be linked by one of the following relations:

- *Priority*, $g_i < g_j$: g_i is more important, to the agent, than g_j. If this relation holds and no constraints or preconditions are violated by satisfying it, g_i will be achieved before g_j.
- *Hierarchy*, $H(g_i, (g_{i1}, g_{i2}, \ldots, g_{in},))$: the complex goal g_i may be decomposed into simpler subgoals $g_{i1}, g_{i2}, \ldots, g_{in}$, which contribute to achieve it.

- *Causal Relation, $Cause(g_i, g_j)$*: executing the plan achieving the source goal g_i is a precondition for executing the plan achieving the destination goal g_j.

6.2 Plans

Our dialog manager does not include a planner. Plans are therefore represented as recipes that the agent can use to achieve its goals. A recipe may be applied when some preconditions hold; its application affects the dialog state (agent's and user's beliefs and interaction settings). In the eating disorder domain, after initially introducing itself, our agent adopts the typical planning sequence of advisory systems:

- *situation-assessment*, to acquire information about the user;
- *describe-eating-disorders*: what are eating disorders, what may cause them, what are their origin and emotional factors, etc.;
- *suggest-solution*: how eating disorders may be overcome;
- *persuade-to follow suggestion*, to convince the users to change their eating habits by using appropriate arguments.

This default plan is outlined in Fig. 7, which shows goal decomposition and (with dashed lines) causal links between them. For instance, before assessing what is the user's problem, the agent needs to know her name and age, to adapt the following moves to these factors. Compulsive overeating is described only after assessing that the user declares having an unknown serious problem; applicable solutions to compulsive overeating are suggested after being sure that the user knows what this disorder is.

6.3 Reaction Rules

In 1987, Oatley and Johnson-Laird remarked that *"human plans are much more flexible than those so far explored in AI"*: reactive planning methods were proposed, in the immediately following years, to overcome these limits [40]. Reaction rules implement, in our system, goal-revision strategies: the emotion regulation rules in Sect. 5 are examples of such rules. Other rules regulate revision of goal priorities by formalizing the following strategies:

- in the case of *urgent* events, reduce the detail of information provided by upgrading the priority of "most relevant" subgoals and downgrading the priority of *details*;
- when feeling *altruistic social emotions* (sorry-for and happy-for), display them by verbal and non-verbal means and give them the highest priority; downgrade the priority of other goals; hide *egoistic* social emotions (envy and gloating);
- when feeling *positive emotions* (joy, hope), express them with non-verbal means and leave the priority of other goals unvaried;

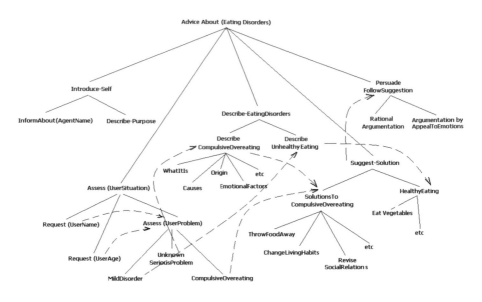

Fig. 7. The discourse plan in the eating disorders domain

- when feeling *negative emotions* (distress, fear), activate *behavior control* goals: that is, avoid displaying any emotional reaction by activating, at the same time, repair goals.

With these rules, we formalize a situation of *empathic relation*, according to which (as we said) the agent temporarily adopts the presumed goals of the user, when these goals are due to an emotional event. If an undesirable event happens to the users, what they are presumed to need is to be convinced that the agent understands the situation and is doing its best to solve the problem. If something desirable happens to them, they need to know that the agent shares their positive experience. If, on the contrary, the undesirable event does not concern the users, they probably want to be sure that this will not interfere negatively with the support they receive.

Let us again consider activation of emotion in our example dialog. At time T_2, an emotion of sorry-for is activated in the agent while it is performing the plan associated with the *assessing-situation* goal. This emotion activates, in its turn, the goal of "*manifesting empathy for the user, due to undesirable events had happened to her*"; this goal takes the highest priority. To achieve it, the agent applies a *show-sorry-for* plan, which produces the first two sentences in move G2: "*Oh I'm sorry. That's a bad situation indeed*". This move is tagged with an affective expression of *sorry-for*. The agent utters it and then reconsiders the situation-assessment goal, by completing the plan in the agenda. The same happens with the "*How awful!*" sentence, in G4. In this case, however, the problem the user declares seems to be very serious and the need to understand it more in depth increases. At move $G5$, the agent hides its fear that the user may stop the dialog and tries to reassure and motivate her (*"Oh no! You have to be confident in yourself! If you want to get over this, I can help you."*). Finally, at move G7 it shows its hope while encouraging the user (*"Fine! This is the attitude I want to see from you!"*) and does not revise the priority of the other goals.

Reaction rules may produce the following effects on the dynamics of plan activation:

- *add details* when the user asks for more information;
- *reduce details* in case of urgency;
- *abandon a plan temporarily and activate a new subplan* to reassure or motivate the user;
- *abandon a subplan* when its goal has been achieved: for example, when the user seems to know what the agent is saying;
- *substitute a generic subplan with a more specific and situation-adapted one*;
- *revise the sequencing of plans, to respond to the user request of "taking the initiative"*. This is the most delicate situation: to be cooperative, the agent should leave aside its dialog plan and follow the user's request. However, as we said, discourse goals may be linked by causal relations. Therefore, when the user shows an intention to take the initiative in the dialog, the agent checks whether the user's goal may be activated immediately or whether some preconditions have first to be satisfied. It then satisfies these preconditions with the shortest subplan before considering her request.

7 Module Integration

The system is driven by a *Graphical Interface* (Fig. 8) which interacts with the user and activates the modules shown in Fig. 1. Users may set the simulation conditions (agent's personality, its relationship with the user, character's body, and application domain). They may then start the dialog and input their moves in natural language (bottom textfield). The interface enables one to follow the dialog both in natural language (top left frame) and with the selected embodied agent (top right frame) and shows the agent's emotional situation in graphical form (bottom frame). It is therefore a testbed that we employ to adjust the system components after evaluating its behavior in different situations: to upgrade the dialog strategy and the plan library, revise interpretation of user moves, and improve rendering of the agent's moves by revising $APML$ tags. The Interface was implemented in $C/C++$ and the communication modules are built-in classes of this code. The dialog manager is implemented with $TRINDIKIT$ (see Sect. 9) while the emotion triggering module in C employs $HUGIN$ $APIs$ (see Sect. 9). Thanks to the mind–body independence of our system, several agents have been linked to the system:

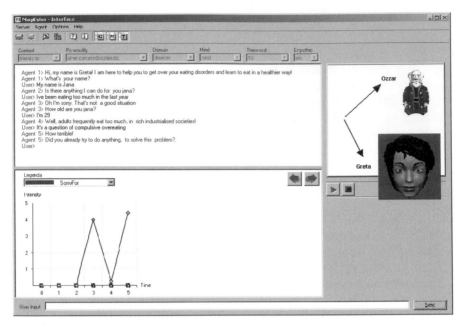

Fig. 8. The Graphical Interface of our Emotional Dialog Simulator. Two characters are displayed in the right frame: Greta [33] and *Ozzar* (an MS-Agent)

various versions of Greta [33] and some MS-Agents. The following are the information exchanges between modules:

- **Executable-Mind** receives information about the setting conditions and selects *personality*, *context*, and *domain* files accordingly. It subsequently receives interpreted user *moves* and sends back a list of *emotion intensities*.
- **Trindi** receives an interpreted user input and a list of activated emotions and generates an agent's move which is displayed in natural language in the left frame.
- **Midas** produces an *APML* file.
- The **Animation Engine** receives as input an *APML* file and, using the meaning–signal translation file, animates the selected character.

8 Conclusions and Future Work

Our research builds upon a number of previous experiences on conversational agents [10, 31] and has much in common with other projects described in this volume. Our reaction rules are similar to social rules in Jack and Steve [24]; our "show emotions" plans are the equivalent of their "reassure" or "agree/sympathize" dialog acts and these acts are arranged in *XML* structures in both prototypes. Our personality traits enable the representation of a larger variety of situations than those described in the Big Five classification [25] which is applied, for instance, by [1] and [2]. The assumption behind our emotion activation method is the same as in Émile (relating events to the agent's belief about threatening or achieving current goals), although the formalism employed is not the same (our agent does not evaluate the degree of achievement of its plans). The main limit of our prototype is in the asymmetry of the dialog modality: answering with a typewriter to a talking embodied character is far from being natural. We would need a refined speech recognizer as in [22] which also would enable us to detect emotional states of the users [4], their cognitive load [26], and other attitudes. Of course, we are not satisfied with the simple keyword analysis we employ to recognize the user's intentions and needs: to interpret a user state we plan to build, in the near future, DBN-based user models similar to those we now employ to activate emotions in the agent. Another aspect of this ongoing work is focused on the persuasion component of the advisory system, in which we are working by integrating rational argumentation with appeal to emotions [8].

In our view, a great number of questions are still to be clarified before we are all in the position to claim that a simulated emotional dialog shows signs of real believability; we wish to mention just some of them. Should multiple emotions be summed up into overall emotional states (what somebody calls "moods") or should they be stored and treated separately? Does this decision depend on the intensity of emotional components? Should an agent always behave like a human or should it be planned to dominate its emotions in a larger number of circumstances (for instance, when taking a "difficult" decision)? This is related to the more general (and long-debated) question: are emotions always useful in producing appropriate decision making (which is what we expect, in the end, from our computer)? There is, we believe, a gap between psychological research on the effects of emotional states on human behavior and the need for knowledge by researchers on embodied agents: psychologists tend to focus their interest on "strong", individual emotions. We need to understand whether and how weaker emotional states influence behavior and how conflicts among contrasting emotions are solved: once again, this is a good domain for interdisciplinary cooperation rather than merely importing psychological theories developed in other contexts.

9 Relevant Websites (as of May 2003)

FESTIVAL: http://www.cstr.ed.ac.uk/projects/festival
GODIS: http://www.ling.gu.se/ sl/DME/
HEALTHY EATING:http://livrite.com/binge.htm;
http://kidshealth.org/teen/nutrition/menu/binge_eating.html
HUGIN: http://www.hugin.com/
TRINDIKIT 2.0 Manual: http://www.ling.gu.se/research/projects/trindi

Acknowledgments

Research described in this chapter was mainly performed within the scope of the European Project *Magicster* (IST 1999-29078). We owe to our partners (and in particular to Catherine Pelachaud, Isabella Poggi, Thomas Rist, and Mark Steedman) innumerable suggestions and comments on how to orient our work. We must also thank those who cooperated in implementing the prototypes described in this chapter: in particular, Addolorata Cavalluzzi, Giuseppe Cellammare, Giuseppe Grassano, and Ignazio Palmisano.

References

1. Allbeck, J., Badler, N.: Representing and parameterizing agent behaviors. In: *Life-like Characters. Tools, Affective Functions and Applications*, ed Prendinger, H., Ishizuka, M. (Springer 2003). This volume.
2. André, E., Rist, T., van Mulken, S., Klesen, M., Baldes, S.: The automated design of believable dialogue for animated presentation teams. In: *Embodied Conversational Agents*, ed Cassell, J., Sullivan, J., Prevost, S., Churchill, E. (The MIT Press, Cambridge, MA 2000) pp 220–255
3. Ardissono, L., Boella, G., Lesmo, L.: Politeness and speech acts. *UM'99 Workshop on Attitude, Personality and Emotions in User-Adapted Interaction* (1999) http://aos2.di.uniba.it:8080/ws-um99.html
4. Ball, G., Breese, J.: Emotion and personality in a conversational agent. In: *Embodied Conversational Agents*, ed Cassell, J., Sullivan, J., Prevost, S., Churchill, E. (The MIT Press, Cambridge, MA 2000) pp 189–219
5. Bickmore, T., Cassell, J.: Small talk and conversational storytelling in embodied interface agents. In: *Proceedings of the AAAI Fall Symposium on Narrative Intelligence*. November 5-7, Cape Cod, MA (1999) pp 87–92
6. Carberry, S., Schroeder, L., Lambert, L.: Towards recognizing and conveying an attitude of doubt via natural language. *Applied Artificial Intelligence* **16**(7–8). Special Issue on Merging Cognition and Affect in HCI, ed de Rosis, F. (2002)
7. Carbonell, J.G.: Towards a process model of human personality traits. *Artificial Intelligence* **15**: 49–74 (1980)
8. Carofiglio, V., de Rosis, F.: Combining logical and emotional reasoning in natural argumentation. In: *UM'03 Workshop on "Assessing and Adapting to User Attitudes and Affects: Why, When and How?"* (2003)
9. Carofiglio, V., de Rosis, F., Grassano, G.: Dynamic models of mixed emotion activation. In: *Animating Expressive Characters for Social Interactions*, ed Canamero, L., Aylett, R. (John Benjamins, in press)
10. Cassell, J., Sullivan, J., Prevost, S., Churchill, E.: *Embodied Conversational Agents* (The MIT Press, Cambridge, MA 2000)
11. Castelfranchi, C.: Affective appraisal versus cognitive evaluation in social emotions and interactions. In: *Affective Interactions*, ed Paiva, A., LNAI 1814 (Springer, Berlin New York 2000) pp 76–106
12. Castelfranchi, C., de Rosis, F., Falcone, R., Pizzutilo, S.: Personality traits and social attitudes in multiagent cooperation. *Applied Artificial Intelligence* **12**(7–8): 649–676. Special Issue on Socially Intelligent Agents, ed Dautenhahn, K., Numaoka, C. (1998)

13. Castelfranchi, C., de Rosis, F., Grasso, F.: Deception and suspicion in medical interactions. Towards the simulation of believable dialogs. In: *Machine conversations*, ed Wilks, Y. (Kluwer Academic, Dordrecht 1999)
14. De Carolis, B., Carofiglio, V., Pelachaud, C.: From discourse plans to believable behaviour generation. *International Natural Language Generation Conference* (New York, in press)
15. De Carolis, B., de Rosis, F., Pelachaud, C., Poggi, I.: Verbal and nonverbal discourse planning. In: *Proceedings of IJCAI*, Seattle (2001)
16. De Carolis, B., Pelachaud, C., Poggi, I., Steedman, M.: APML, a markup language for believable behavior generation. In: *Life-like Characters. Tools, Affective Functions and Applications*, ed Prendinger, H., Ishizuka, M. (Springer 2003). This volume.
17. de Rosis, F., Grasso, F., Castelfranchi, C., Poggi, I.: Modelling conflict-resolution dialogs. In: *Compuational Conflicts*, ed Mueller, H.J., Dieng, R. (Springer, Berlin New York 2000)
18. de Rosis, F., Pelachaud, C., Poggi, I.: Transcultural believability in embodied agents: A matter of consistent adaptation. In: *Agent Culture: Designing Virtual Characters for a Multi-cultural World*, ed Trappl, R., Payr, S. (Kluwer Academic, Dordrecht, in press)
19. de Rosis, F., Pelachaud, C., Poggi, I., Carofiglio, V., De Carolis, B.: From Greta's mind to her face: Modeling the dynamics of affective states in a conversational embodied agent. *International Journal of Human-Computer Studies* **59**:81–118 (2003)
20. Elliot, C., Siegle, G.: Variables influencing the intensity of simulated affective states. In: *Proceedings of the AAAI Spring Symposium on Mental States '93* (1993) pp 58–67
21. Forgas, J.P.: *Feeling and Thinking. The Role of Affect in Social Cognition* (Cambridge University Press 2000)
22. Kawamoto, S. et al.: Galatea: open-source software for developing anthropomorphic spoken dialog agents. In: *Life-like Characters. Tools, Affective Functions and Applications*, ed Prendinger, H., Ishizuka, M. (Springer 2003). This volume.
23. Loyall, A.B., Bates, J.: Personality-rich believable agents that use language. *Proceedings of Autonomous Agents 1997* (1997) pp 106–113
24. Marsella, S., Gratch, J., Rickel, J.: Expressive behaviors for virtual worlds. In: *Life-like Characters. Tools, Affective Functions and Applications*, ed Prendinger, H., Ishizuka, M. (Springer 2003). This volume.
25. McCrae, R., John, O.P.: An introduction to the five-factor model and its applications. *Journal of Personality* **60**:175–215 (1992)
26. Mueller, C., Grossman-Hutter, B., Jameson, A., Rummer, R., Wittig, F.: Recognizing time pressure and cognitive load on the basis of speech: An experimental study. In: *Proceedings of User Modeling'01*, ed Bauer, M., Gmytrasiewicz, P.J., Vassileva, J., LNAI 2109 (Springer, Berlin New York 2001)
27. Nicholson, A.E., Brady, J.M.: Dynamic belief networks for discrete monitoring. *IEEE Transactions on Systems, Men and Cybernetics* **24**(11):1593–1610 (1994)
28. Oatley, K., Johnson-Laird, P.N.: Towards a cognitive theory of emotions. *Cognition and Emotion* **13**:29–50 (1987)
29. Ortony, A.: Subjective importance and computational models of emotions. In: *Cognitive Perspectives on Emotion and Motivation*, ed Hamilton, V., Bower, G.H., Frjida, N.H. (Kluwer Academic, Dordrecht 1988) pp 321–333

30. Ortony, A., Clore, G.L., Collins, A.: *The Cognitive Structure of Emotions* (Cambridge University Press, 1988)
31. Paiva, A. (ed): *Affective Interactions*. LNAI 1814 (Springer, Berlin New York 2002)
32. Pelachaud, C., Carofiglio, V., De Carolis, B., de Rosis, F., Poggi, I.: Embodied contextual agent in information delivery applications. In: *Proceedings of the First International Conference on Autonomous Agents and Multiagent Systems (AAMAS-02)* (2002)
33. Pelachaud, C., Poggi, I.: Subtleties of facial expressions in embodied agents. *Journal of Visualization and Computer Animation* **13**:301–312 (2002)
34. Pfeifer, R., Nicholas, D.W.: Toward computational models of emotion. In: *Progress in Artificial Intelligence*, ed Steels, L., Campbell, J.A. (Ellis Horwood, Chichester 1985), pp 184–192
35. Picard, R.W.: *Affective Computing* (The MIT Press, Cambridge, MA 1997)
36. Prendinger, H., Ishizuka, M.: Introducing the cast for social computing: Life-like characters. In: *Life-like Characters. Tools, Affective Functions and Applications*, ed Prendinger, H., Ishizuka, M. (Springer 2003). This volume.
37. Rist, T., André, E., Baldes, S., Gebhard, P., Klesen, M., Kipp, M., Rist, P., Schmitt, M.: A review on the development of embodied presentation agents and their application fields. In: *Life-like Characters. Tools, Affective Functions and Applications*, ed Prendinger, H., Ishizuka, M. (Springer 2003). This volume.
38. Sillince, J.A.A., Minors, R.H.: What makes a strong argument? Emotions, highly-placed values and role playing. *Communication and Cognition* **24**(3–4):281–298 (1991)
39. Stock, O.: Computational Humor. *Intelligent Tutoring Systems*, 2–3 (2002)
40. Suchman, L.O.: *Plans and Situated Actions. The Problem of Human-machine Communication* (Cambridge University Press 1987)
41. Turing, A.M.: Computing machinery and intelligence. *Mind*, 59 (1950)
42. Walker, M.A., Cahn, J.A., Whittaker, S.J.: Improvising linguistic style: Social and affective bases for agent personality. In: *Proceedings of Autonomous Agents* (1997) pp 96–105
43. Wilks, Y.: *Machine Conversations* (Kluwer Academic, Dordrecht 1999)

Web Information Integration Using Multiple Character Agents

Yasuhiko Kitamura

Department of Informatics, School of Science and Technology,
Kwansei Gakuin University
2-1 Gakuen, Sanda 669-1337, Japan
ykitamura@ksc.kwansei.ac.jp

Summary. The World Wide Web contains a vast amount of various information stored in a huge number of distributed web sites. Search engines and information agents have been developed to facilitate efficient information retrieval tasks from the web. By integrating multiple search engines and information agents as an interoperable system, we increase each value of them. In conventional information integration systems, the integration process is designed by system designers and is concealed from the end users.

This chapter proposes an interactive multiagent-based interface called the Multiple Characters Interface (MCI) where animated life-like agents interact with each other and with the user for assisting in information retrieval. By using the MCI, even a novice user can create a team of information agents and can self-customize the agents through interactions with them. We report here on the architecture of the MCI and two prototype systems based on the MCI, Venus and Mars, which is a cooperative multiagent system for information retrieval, and Recommendation Battlers, which is a competitive multiagent system for information recommendation. We also perform an evaluation experiment based on the Wizard of Oz method and show that multiple life-like agents tend to broaden the user's interest in the course of information retrieval.

1 Introduction

A life-like agent or character is a software agent with a virtual face and body on a computer display and behaves like a creature or a person [3, 6]. It understands utterances spoken by a human user and responds to them by speaking with gesturing. It shows its emotional state on its face or by its behavior.

Life-like agents work as an interface between a human user and a computer system. They are more user-friendly than conventional GUIs because they reduce the user's burden of mastering complicated operation commands to the system, which may be different depending on the system, and allow the user to send commands to the system by using natural ways that are commonly used among people. A simple form of life-like agent such as MS-Agent[1] has been installed in the Windows operating system as a standard interface and is available for various application programs.

An advantage of like-like agents is to provide an active interface to a system. Conventional man–machine interfaces can be viewed as passive ones because they aim at just receiving responses from users in an easy and efficient way, and the users take the initiative to respond. On the other hand, active interfaces may take the initiative to urge the users to respond, and they make interactions between a system and a user more active. In a sense, a conventional computer with a passive interface can be viewed as just a slave that performs tasks requested by users silently, but the life-like agent technology can raise the position to that of a partner that performs tasks in collaboration with users.

Life-like agents can be applied to help with information retrieval tasks on the Internet [1]. Because of the vast amount of heterogeneous information stored on the Internet, it is difficult to retrieve requested information properly in an efficient way, and some kind of assistance is required. In addition, Internet users include not only computer experts but also novice users such as children and elderly people, so user-friendly interfaces are welcome.

A typical form of using the Internet is to browse Web pages. Generally speaking, the users who browse Web pages do not always have a target of retrieving information as clear as the users who submit queries to database systems, but rather enjoy just browsing Web pages that are connected to an almost infinite number of pages through hyperlinks. Life-like agents, which help navigate users to their preferred Web pages, can be good partners to the former. InfoWiz[2] developed at SRI International and AiA personas [2] developed at DFKI are examples of early systems. At present, many products are commercially available like Extempo[3], Haptek[4], Virtual Personalities[5], and Artificial Life[6].

Most life-like agents used in Internet information systems work as a standalone guide or navigator between a user and an information site. In this chapter, we discuss a team of agents that work together as mediators between a user and multiple information sites. Each agent retrieves information from a domain-specific information site and helps the user with his or her information retrieval or integration tasks collaborating or competing with other agents.

In Sect. 2, we discuss our concept of information integration through multiple life-like agents and propose a framework called the Multiple Character Interface (MCI). We then introduce two application prototypes based on the MCI in Sect. 3 and discuss implementation issues of the MCI in Sec. 4. In

---

[1] http://www.microsoft.com/msagent/

[2] http://www.ai.sri.com/ oaa/infowiz.html

[3] http://www.extempo.com

[4] http://www.haptek.com

[5] http://www.vperson.com

[6] http://www.artificial-life.com

Sect. 5, we present an initial evaluation of the MCI by using the Wizard of Oz method. We discuss future work in Sect. 6 and related work in Sect. 7. Finally we conclude this chapter in Sect. 8.

2 Information Integration on Multiple Character Interface

The number of information sites on the Internet is immense and increases rapidly day by day. These sites are created and maintained in a distributed and autonomous manner, so related information tends to be scattered among a number of sites. Information integration [12, 30] is a scheme to integrate distributed information sites into an interoperable system. It makes a collection of information sites more valuable than the individual components. For example, we have a web site that emphasizes recipes[7] and another site that highlights information about health and food[8]. Normally each web site works as an independent information site, but if we can integrate information from these sites, we may be able to answer complex queries that cannot be answered by one of sites alone, such as "Tell me a cooking recipe that will help me recover from a cold." A number of information integration systems have been developed based on database frameworks [30, 7] or information agent frameworks [28, 4, 11, 22, 20, 21].

In conventional information integration systems, how to integrate the information sites is specified by system designers and remains hidden from users. Hence, the users are just allowed to submit a query to a fixed interface and to receive results from the system, but not allowed to change the combination of information sites nor the integration mechanism.

Each individual user has different demands or preferences for information integration. Some users may prefer one information site to others. Hence, rather than just offering a ready-made integration system, we believe that the best framework is one that allows the user to easily construct a team of his or her favorite information sites that work together and to customize them flexibly. To this end, we are developing the Multiple Character Interface (MCI) in which multiple information agents work together with each other and with the user.

The MCI [17, 18] provides an environment where multiple information agents and a human user mutually interact as shown in Fig. 1. An information agent consists of a body part (information gathering engine) and a header part (life-like agent interface). The body part acts as an information gathering engine that retrieves domain-specific information from a search engine or a database; the header part is implemented as an animated life-like agent called character. A personal agent can appear on the MCI as shown in Fig. 1. It can

---

[7] see http://www.kikkoman.co.jp/homecook/

[8] see http://www.shokuiku.co.jp/index.html

be regarded as a special-purpose information agent that handles and stores the user's profile for assisting information retrieval.

The user can access the agent by sending a message. The agent can respond to the message by talking with gestures. For example, if the information agent specializes in cooking recipes, it responds to the query "I want a dish with pork", by gathering Web pages about pork recipes from a local database or a search engine and showing them to the user.

The information agents can interact with not only their user but also other information agents on the MCI. Collaborative actions for retrieving and integrating information are performed by the characters and displayed to the user. An information agent can listen to conversations between others on the MCI and can intervene in the conversation.

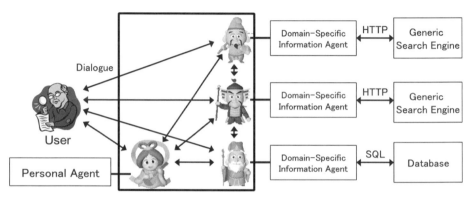

Fig. 1. Multiple Character Interface

The advantages of the MCI-based agents are summarized below.

- They provide a friendly interface between the user and the information sources. They can understand the user's utterances and respond to them by uttering appropriate speech with gestures, so the user can send commands to the agents in a natural language. The user does not need to learn complicated operation commands that differ from the information source. Animated characters look familiar and have the potential to entertain the user.
- The agents collaborate to assist the user in retrieving and integrating information. By showing the collaborative process of information retrieval and integration to the user, he or she can intuitively understand what is happening in the system. This is very different from the conventional approach where the integration process is concealed from the user.
- By visualizing information agents as characters, the user can easily understand the functionality and role of each information agent. The user can change or modify agents according to the task or preference. The user can

flexibly build a team of agents for integrating information by choosing his or her favorite agents. Furthermore, visible multiple agents can broaden the user's interests over the course of information retrieval.

3 Application Prototypes Based on the MCI

In this section, we show two prototypes based on MCI. The first prototype is a cooperative search engine called Venus and Mars. Three life-like agents cooperate with each other to assist a user in locating cooking recipe pages. The second prototype is a competitive restaurant recommendation system called Recommendation Battlers. In this prototype, two life-like agents compete with each other to recommend restaurants to a user.

3.1 Venus and Mars

Search engines are the most widely used tools to retrieve information from the web, but they are not always very useful for novice users such as elderly people. For example, when a user wants to know a recipe for pork, he or she may submit just "pork" as a keyword to a search engine, but he or she may get stuck with a large number of URLs including not just recipes but also details about farming, retailers, restaurants, and so on. Currently HTML is the main language used to describe web pages, but it is not well equipped for specifying semantic information, so standard search engines just retrieve web pages if they include the specified keyword.

To deal with the ambiguity of web information sources, we utilize domain-specific information agents. An information agent provides noiseless information concerning a particular domain such as recipes, restaurants, or retailers. Furthermore, if we integrate multiple domain-specific information agents, we can submit more queries than the ones that an individual agent accepts. For example, let us assume that a recipe agent may accept only keywords about cooking ingredients and may reject the other keywords, so it cannot locate recipes that are good for colds. However, we can extend the domain that the agent covers by integrating it with another information agent. If we have a health agent that knows facts about health and food, we can retrieve a fact like "Leeks are good for colds." from the agent and can use the keyword "leeks" for the recipe agent to locate recipes that are good for colds. Venus and Mars [17, 18] is a system that allows information integration based on keyword associations through conversations among life-like characters. As shown in Fig. 2, Internet Explorer displays three characters. The search results are shown in two frames; the left frame shows a list of recipe pages and the right frame shows the web page of a list entry when the entry is clicked.

Venus and Mars consists of three information agents. Kon-san (recipe agent) is the information agent that locates recipes. Given the Japanese utterance "I would like to eat a pork dish" as a query, he extracts one or more

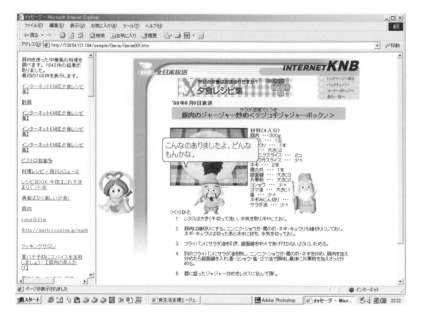

Fig. 2. A snapshot of Venus and Mars. Three character agents: Pekko, Kon-san, and Cho-san (from left to right) appear on the screen. Kon-san, the middle character, uses the Keyword Spice technique to locate Chinese recipes with pork. He found 1842 pages, placed them in the left frame of the browser, and said "I found a good one. How do you like this?"

keywords about recipe ("pork") from the utterance and submits the keyword(s), with keyword spices [25] for the recipe domain, to a general-purpose search engine[9].

Kon-san finds recipe pages and places them on the web browser. When the number is excessive, he automatically asks for additional keywords about seasoning or type of recipe (Western, Japanese, Chinese, and so on) to reduce the number of results. Kon-san uses the response from the user to create and resubmit a new query to the search engine.

Cho-san (health agent) has knowledge of cooking ingredients and health in his local database. Responding to an utterance that includes keywords related to cooking ingredients or health, he utters comments about the relations between cooking ingredients and health, such as "Leeks are good for colds."

Pekko is a personal agent and is the first to appear on the client machine and calls other agents. She monitors the user's utterances. When needed, she suggests some search keywords on behalf of the user referring to the history of the user's utterances. For example, if the user expresses a preference about seasoning when asked by Kon-san, Pekko stores the preference in her local

---

[9] http://www.goo.ne.jp/

database and expresses it on behalf of the user if the same situation occurs in the future.

A typical cooking recipe search is given below.

(1) Pekko: "May I help you?"
(2) User: "I would like to eat a pork dish."
(3) Kon-san: "OK. Let me locate some recipes that use pork. How do you like this?" (He shows a recipe page on the browser.)
(4) Cho-san: "Pork is good for the digestion. It is a good way to get vitamin B."
(5) Kon-san: "The number of search results is over 1000. Let me reduce the number. What kind of seasoning do you like?"
(6) Pekko: "I know Kitamura-san likes Japanese food."
(7) Kon-san: "OK. Let me find some Japanese recipes that use pork. How do you like this?" (He shows another recipe page on the browser.)
(8) Pekko: (Responding to a click from the user) "May I help you?"
(9) User: "I want a recipe that is good for recovering from a cold."
(10) Kon-san: "?"
(11) Cho-san: "Leeks are good for colds."
(12) Kon-san: "OK. Let me locate recipes that use leeks. How do you like this?" (He shows a recipe page that mentions leeks on the browser.)

In Venus and Mars, agents collaborate with each other in two ways. In dialogue steps (5) to (7) above, Pekko assists Kon-san in reducing the number of search results. In utterance (5), Kon-san asks for a tip on seasoning, Pekko answers "I know Kitamura-san likes Japanese food" on behalf of the user. Of course, if the user does not like Pekko's suggestion, he or she can correct Pekko's utterance by indicating his or her true preference directly to Kon-san through the dialogue box. Pekko recognizes this correction and updates the user's preferences stored in her local database. Through interactions with the user, the agents learn the preferences of the user.

In dialogue steps (9) to (12), Cho-san assists Kon-san. In this case, Kon-san cannot answer the request "I want a recipe that is good for recovering from a cold" because he has no knowledge of health. On the other hand, Cho-san has knowledge of cooking ingredients and health, so he makes the comment "Leeks are good for colds." Kon-san takes the comment as a clue to initiate a new search with the keyword of leeks. This type of collaboration shows the potential of Venus and Mars for realizing various types of information search by adding agents to the team. For example, if we add a restaurant recommendation agent to the team, the user's request for a recipe with salmon may result in the recommendation of local restaurants specializing in salmon.

3.2 Recommendation Battlers

Electronic commerce (EC) is one of the most successful application domains of the Internet. We can access a large number of shopping sites that deal with various goods through a web browser. Most conventional shopping sites, such as amazon.com, are running in an independent and closed manner. In such a site, customers receive information for sales items from the site only and any devices for comparing the items with those from the other sites are not facilitated.

To make the comparison easy, a number of comparison shopping sites, such as Bargain Finder, Jango[9], DealTime[10], and so on, have been developed. However, such sites are run by a third party, which is independent from buyers and sellers, and the design of how to compare and what (attribute) to compare depends on the third party. It is said that many owners of shopping sites are not happy with such comparison services because they just increase price competition ignoring the other individual services offered by the sites.

Recommendation Battlers [19] is a new multiagent-based system for EC where multiple shopping sites or information recommendation sites are integrated in a flexible and interactive manner. The system provides a virtual space where multiple animated agents, each of which is delivered from an information site, interact with each other and the user to recommend items in a competitive manner.

In Recommendation Battlers, the customer compares items recommended by multiple agents and finds a preferred one by watching a competition performed by the agents on a browser. Through interactions with the customer, agents can learn his or her preference and use it for further recommendations. From the viewpoint of a shopping site, this platform provides a virtually open marketplace where agents can interact with the customer, and the agents can directly recommend items to the customer without the intervention of an information broker such as those in comparison shopping sites.

As shown in Fig. 3, two restaurant recommendation agents, Peedy and Genie, appear on a web browser. Responding to a request from the user such as "I would like to find a good Indian restaurant near Shinsaibashi station", Peedy starts to gather relevant restaurant pages from Yahoo! Gourmet[11] and extracts their addresses and average cost. It then calculates the distance from the nearest station by referring to the addresses and a database that stores addresses by latitude and longitude. Genie also does the same but it uses another information source called Kansai Walkerplus[12].

After gathering restaurant information from web sites, Peedy and Genie start to recommend restaurants in a competitive manner. A typical dialogue is given below.

---

[10] http://www.dealtime.com
[11] http://gourmet.yahoo.co.jp/
[12] http://www.walkerplus.com/kansai/gourmet/

(1) User: "I would like to find a good Indian restaurant near Shinsaibashi station."
(2) Genie: (After gathering information from Kansai Walkerplus) "Do you like Restaurant A? The average cost is around 2000 Yen and the distance from Shinsaibashi station is 90m."
(3) User: "Good."
(4) Peedy: (After gathering information from Yahoo! Gourmet) "Do you like Restaurant B? The average cost is around 2500 Yen and the distance from Shinsaibashi station is 80m. This restaurant is closer than Restaurant A."
(5) User: "No good."
(6) Peedy: "Restaurant B seems too expensive for you. How about Restaurant C? The average cost is around 2200 Yen and the distance from Shinsaibashi station is 80m."
(7) User: "Good."
(8) Genie: "I am sure that you will like Restaurant D. The average cost is around 1500 Yen and the distance from Shinsaibashi station is 70m."
(9) Peedy: "Sorry. I have no more restaurants to recommend."

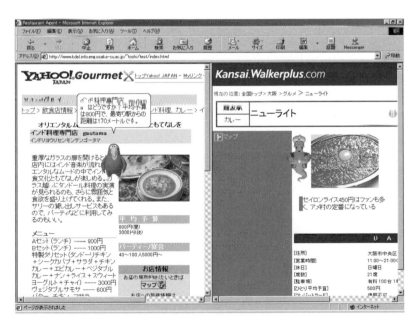

Fig. 3. A snapshot of Recommendation Battlers. Peedy on the left shows a web page of an Indian restaurant from Yahoo! Gourmet and says "Do you like Restaurant Gautama? The average cost is around 800 Yen and the distance from Shinsaibashi station is 170m." Genie on the right also shows a web page of another restaurant called "New Light" from Kansai.Walkerplus.com and the user compares the two restaurants

The recommendation is performed by two character agents interacting with each other and the user. An agent recommends a restaurant not only by showing the web page that contains the restaurant information, but also by adding comments about the average cost and the distance from the nearest station. When needed, it asks whether the user likes the restaurant or not by showing a dialogue box. The user responds to the question by answering "Good" or "No good." Referring to the responses, the agents try to learn the user's preference about the cost and the distance and use it for further recommendations [19]. When either agents has no more restaurants to recommend, the process terminates.

4 Implementation Issues of the MCI

The architecture of the MCI is shown in Fig. 4 [17]. Like the autonomous agent mentioned in [26], each agent recognizes actions taken by the user or other agents through data captured by its sensor, interprets the actions, and responds through its actuator.

The major agent sensor commands are (?feel) to detect a click made by the user and (?hear $utterance from $agent) to get an utterance from the user or other agent. When the agent hears something, variables $utterance and $agent are instantiated. The current implementation does not use an advanced form of natural language processing, rather a simple form of keyword matching. The major agent actuator commands are (!speak $utterance) to make an utterance specified by $utterance, (!play_animation $animation) to make a gesture specified by $animation, (!present $url) to show a web page specified by $url on a browser, and (!search $keywords) to retrieve information related to $keywords. By combining these commands, an agent can perform complicated actions.

Agent behavior is controlled by scenarios written in Q [16], which is an interaction design language developed at Kyoto University for linking autonomous agents and humans. An agent scenario is represented as a state transition graph as shown in Fig. 5. In the initial state, the recipe agent in Venus and Mars (as an example) gives a self-introduction and enters an idle state. In the idle state, the agent can recognize an utterance that includes one or more recipe keywords such as "I'd like to have a pork dish." The agent then enters the information retrieval state and retrieves web pages by using a search engine. It shows the results on a web browser. When the result contains more than 1000 pages, it tries to reduce the number by automatically asking the user a question about his or her favorite seasoning or ingredient. Upon receiving an answer, it makes a more focused search.

The MCI allows multiple agents and a user to collaborate through conversations. An utterance from the user to an agent is sensed and forwarded to the sensor controller in the agent's server as shown in Fig. 4. Utterances spoken by other agents are also detected through the communication server.

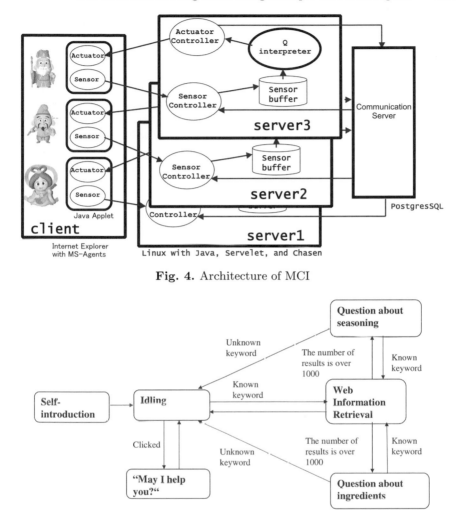

Fig. 4. Architecture of MCI

Fig. 5. State transition graph of recipe agent in Venus and Mars

When the body part of an agent receives an utterance from the user or another agent, it interprets the utterance and produces a response utterance following the agent's scenario. Finally, the utterance from the agent's server is forwarded to and spoken by the character agent.

The MCI adopts a distributed architecture where the body part of the information agent resides in an individual server that is distributed over the Internet. Information gathered by the body parts (information gathering engines) is integrated on the MCI through interactions among the header parts (life-like characters). Once a character is loaded into the MCI, it begins to interact with the user and other agents in a plug-and-play fashion. To realize

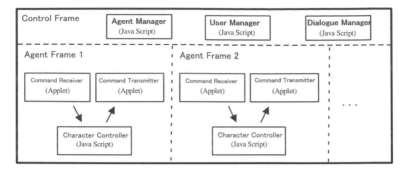

Fig. 6. Implementation of MCI

this function, we use multiple frames on Internet Explorer as shown in Fig. 6. We implemented the MCI using a control frame and multiple agent frames. When the MCI is initiated, an agent manager, a user manager, and a dialogue manager are loaded into the control frame.

The agent manager manages the agent frames when agents are invoked or stopped. Given a request to invoke an agent, the agent manager downloads the modules of character controller, command receiver, and transmitter into an assigned agent frame from the designated agent server. The character controller is written in JavaScript and controls a character agent implemented by using the MS-Agent platform. This corresponds to the sensor and actuator modules in Fig. 4. The command receiver and transmitter are Java applets that connect the character (the header part) to the server (the body part).

The user manager uses the Cookie mechanism to identify users, so agents can change their behavior depending on the user. The dialogue manager controls the order of agents' utterances by using a token passing method. The MCI allows each agent to be designed individually and its behavior to be independent of that of the others, so in an early version of MCI, multiple agents tended to talk simultaneously. We hence adopt a concurrency control mechanism to prevent multiple agents from talking at the same time.

By adopting the multiagent architecture, we can implement various types of collaborative tasks and allow the user to become involved in the process. Moreover, we can easily add or remove agents. This allows us to build a wide variety of collaborative teams of agents for information retrieval and integration.

5 An Initial Evaluation of the MCI Using the Wizard of Oz Method

In this section, we discuss an initial evaluation of the MCI using the Wizard of Oz method. It is interesting to know how multiple life-like agents affect users' behavior in their information retrieving tasks. We developed three kinds of interfaces consisting of three animated agents, a single agent, and no agent respectively and observed utterances spoken by subjects toward each of the interfaces depending on the number of agents.

5.1 Wizard of Oz Method

It was difficult to evaluate the Venus and Mars or Recommendation Battlers systems as they are because they are still at prototype stage and are not able to communicate with a human user fluently. Instead, we decided to use the Wizard of Oz method [8, 24] and evaluate Venus and Mars.

The Wizard of Oz method is a method to observe the behavior of human subjects toward a computer system in which a human operator called wizard simulates the whole or a part of the system. In our experiment, we modified the Venus and Mars system so the user interacts with wizards through characters as follows.

- We set the purpose of evaluation to observe how multiple characters affect users' behavior in information retrieval tasks. We used three information agents, a recipe agent, a health agent, and a specialty agent, and used no personal agent. The specialty agent has knowledge about local placenames and local food specialties in its database. To a query that includes a local placenames or a local food specialty, it utters a comment about a relation between them such as "Radishes are a specialty of Tokyo." It cooperates with the recipe agent by giving a hint to retrieve recipe pages.
- We assigned a wizard to each of the recipe, health, and specialty agents. The wizards operate a database or a search engine and respond to queries from subjects through a life-like character. They respond to not only domain-specific queries that the agent covers but also greetings or questions about the agent like "How old are you?" To other utterances, they just say "I am sorry. I don't know."
- When an experiment starts, each agent introduces itself to the subject and explains its ability.
- Wizards are situated in a room remote from subjects and communicate with them through only a chat-like interface. They recognize the destination of message from a subject by referring to the ID number of the character to which the subject clicks. They also can listen to conversations between the subject and other characters.
- We did not reveal the existence of wizards to subjects before the experiments, but we did so afterward.

5.2 Experiments

As an interface for the information integration system, the MCI has three features; (i) multiple characters appear, (ii) characters interact with each other,

Table 1. Five interfaces in evaluation

	Number of Characters	Cooperation	Roles
A Cooperative	3	Yes	Yes
B Single	1	-	-
C Chat	0	-	-
D Non-Cooperative	3	No	Yes
E Homogeneous	3	Yes	No

and (iii) characters are heterogeneous and each one has its own role. We investigated how each feature affects subjects' behavior in their information retrieval task. We used five interfaces as summarized as in Table 1.

(A) Cooperative: This interface is most similar to the original version of Venus and Mars. Specialty, recipe, and health agents appear on a display. Wizards operate agents as they cooperate with each other to retrieve recipe pages.

(B) Single: Only one character appears on the display but it plays all the roles of recipe, health, and specialty agents. Every wizard responds to queries through a common character. Subjects feel like talking with a single character that has three roles.

(C) Chat: No character appears. A subject talks to wizards through a chat interface. The role of each wizard is the same as the Single interface.

(D) Non-cooperative: Characters do not cooperate with each other. Three characters appear, but each one responds to queries that are designated to it and does not respond to ones designated to the others. For example, even when a query about health is given to the recipe agent, the agent says only "I am sorry. I don't know" and the health agent keeps quiet.

(E) Homogeneous: Characters are homogeneous as every character has all the roles of recipe, health, and specialty agents and can respond to any queries related to specialty, recipe, and health. They cooperate with each other.

We assigned five subjects (university students) to each of five interfaces. We classified 20 utterances spoken by the subjects into five topics about specialty, recipe, health, character, and others.

5.3 Results

To evaluate the difference of utterances depending on the number of characters, we compared the number of utterances made by subjects of Cooperative, Single, and Chat interfaces according to the topics. We give the results in Table 2.

Significant results whose p-value is less than or equal to 10% are as follows.

- Utterances about others in Single are less than in Chat. (p-value is 3%.)

Table 2. Number of utterances depending on the number of characters

		Chat vs. Single		
Topic	Chat	Single	t-value(n=8)	p-value
Specialty	0.2	1.4	−1.26	0.12
Recipe	14.8	13.4	0.88	0.20
Health	0.4	1	−0.8	0.22
Character	0	1.8	−1.61	0.07
Others	4.6	2.4	2.17	0.03

		Single vs. Cooperative		
Topic	Single	Cooperative	t-value(n=8)	p-value
Specialty	1.4	2.8	−1.18	0.13
Recipe	13.4	10	2.42	0.02
Health	1	2.4	−1.72	0.06
Character	1.8	1.6	0.12	0.45
Others	2.4	3.2	−0.70	0.25

		Chat vs. Cooperative		
Topic	Chat	Cooperative	t-value(n=8)	p-value
Specialty	0.2	2.8	−3.41	0.004
Recipe	14.8	10	3.63	0.003
Health	0.4	2.4	−3.08	0.007
Character	0	1.6	−1.37	0.10
Others	4.6	3.2	1.10	0.15

- Utterances about character in Single are more than in Chat. (p-value is 7%.)
- Utterances about recipe in Cooperative are less than in Single. (p-value is 2%.)
- Utterances about health in Cooperative are more than in Single. (p-value is 6%.)
- Utterances about specialty and health in Cooperative are more than in Chat respectively and those about recipe are less than in Chat. (p-value is less than 1%.)
- Utterances about character in Cooperative are more than in Chat. (p-value level is 10%.)

The results show that most utterances in Chat, which has no character, are about recipe and none about character are made. As the number of characters increases, the number of topics increases from one (only recipe) to many topics including specialty and health.

We then performed an evaluation of how cooperation among characters affects subjects' utterances by comparing the number of utterances between Cooperative and Non-Cooperative. Finally we performed an evaluation of how the role of characters affects the subjects by comparing Cooperative (Heterogeneous) with Homogeneous. The results are shown in Table 3. However, they

Table 3. Number of utterances depending on types of cooperations and roles

Non-Cooperative vs. Cooperative				
Topic	Non-Cooperative	Cooperative	t-value(n=8)	p-value
Specialty	2	2.8	−0.78	0.22
Recipe	12.4	10	1.39	0.10
Health	2.6	2.4	0.14	0.44
Character	0.2	1.6	−1.18	0.13
Others	2.8	3.2	−0.35	0.36
Homogeneous vs. Heterogeneous				
Topic	Homogeneous	Cooperative	t-value(n=8)	p-value
Specialty	1.4	2.8	−1.56	0.07
Recipe	9.8	10	−0.12	0.45
Health	1.4	2.4	−1.10	0.15
Character	2.2	1.6	0.30	0.38
Others	5.2	3.2	1.54	0.08

do not show any significant difference in these comparisons and we could not gain any insights about how cooperation among characters and the role of characters affect subjects' behavior. However, the number of characters is a dominant factor that affects subjects' behavior.

We believe that the existence of visible characters makes conversations between characters and a subject more active and leads to a wide variety of utterances. This may be because subjects feel that each character has a specific role and the existence of multiple characters gives them the motivation to explore the role of each character. This is our first insight into a feature of the MCI and we need to continue to evaluate it further and in detail.

6 Discussion and Future Work

In previous sections, we discussed an approach to integrate multiple information sites distributed on the Internet by employing life-like agents.

This approach models an information integration process as encounters of life-like agents, each of which is a representative of an individual information site, on a user's machine, and the user can participate in the process. This approach is more flexible than one taken in distributed database systems. In conventional distributed database systems, a query is specified rigidly in a high-level language such as SQL and is decomposed into a set of subqueries, which are executed respectively. In our approach, a query given by a user may not be clearly defined at the initial stage, but it becomes clear through interactions between the user and the agents. The life-like agents play an important role in making the interaction more active.

The collaborative tasks presented in two prototypes are rather simple and a lot of future work remains to build really advanced collaborative information agents, as follows.

Capability for Life-Likeness

Interfaces employing life-like agents are applicable to a wide range of users and are customizable depending on the user as follows.

Utterances: We can change the speed of speech. For example, for elderly users, we can make agents speak slowly.

Actions: We can change actions taken by agents. For example, for novice users, we can make agents explain how to use the system in detail.

Attitude: We can change agents' attitude toward a user. For example, we can make agents use polite expressions toward elderly people, on the other hand, and make them use friendly ones toward youths.

We believe that customizable interfaces depending on the computer skill, the physical capability, and the social background of users are more effective than uniform and fixed interfaces. On the other hand, if there is a mismatch between a user and a type of interface, for example, such as matching a novice user mode to a computer expert, that will cause the user to be frustrated. It is an important feature of future work to know the type of user properly and change the mode of agents in the course of operation.

Capability for Collaboration

The agents start to collaborate with each other once they are called on the client machine in a plug-and-play fashion. Collaborative actions performed by agents in our current prototypes are simple, such as association or extension of search keywords in Venus and Mars and competitive information recommendation in Recommendation Battlers. To realize more advanced collaborative features, we need to incorporate collaborative mechanisms using coordination and negotiation techniques, such as those studied in the field of multiagent systems [29], into our systems.

Capability for Presentation

In our current prototypes, collaboration among agents is presented as a conversational activity. Conversation among agents performed on a computer display is volatile and it may not be suitable for presenting a complex collaborative activity. Hence, we need to improve the presentation skill, for example by creating a virtual space where agents can interact with not only other agents but also virtual objects. For example, in a project on a digital city [15], a virtual city is built in 3D space and works as a portal to web pages related to the city. If life-like agents can interact with each other in the city, they play an important role in integrating information in the digital city.

Capability for Conversation

In our current prototypes, agents interact with the user mainly by using natural language, but only simple techniques such as keyword extraction are used. Poor conversational capability frustrates users greatly and makes them easily lose interest in animated agents. Natural language is the most natural way for human users to communicate, especially for novice users such as children and elderly people. To support more accurate and complex interaction with the user, more advanced natural language processing techniques must be applied to our agents.

7 Related Work

Combining or integrating search engines and/or information agents adds more value to each component. Meta-search engines such as MetaCrawler [27] and SavvySearch [14] integrate the output of multiple search engines and succeed in offering improved performance. BIG [23] is an information agent that intelligently and efficiently gathers information from multiple sources considering the trade-off between the quality of information and constraints like time and cost. RETSINA [28] consists of three types of reusable agents: interface agents, task agents, and resource agents. An interface agent interacts with the user to receive a query from the user and returns results. A task agent solves domain-specific tasks by exchanging information with other agents. A resource agent provides access to a heterogeneous information source. Other multiagent-based systems, such as the federated system [11], InfoSleuth [4], and LARKS [21], incorporate information brokering or information matchmaking mechanisms.

In conventional collaborative information integration systems such as those mentioned above, the techniques used to coordinate the information agents or information resources are specified by the system designers and remain hidden from the users. Hence, the users are just allowed to submit a query to a fixed interface and to receive results from the system, but not allowed to change the combination of information agents nor the collaboration mechanism.

For example, RETSINA agents are reusable; their interface is open to the system designers but not to the user, so the user can access the system only through the interface agent. In the federated system, the process of agent coordination is specified in an ACL (Agent Communication Language) such as KQML [10]. An ACL provides an open interface to information agents but not to the human users because it is difficult for a human user to communicate directly with agents using the ACL. Hence, neither system is designed to provide an open interface to the end user.

Each individual user has different demands or preferences for information retrieval or integration. Some users may prefer one search engine over the others, so we need a framework that allows the user to easily construct a team of his or her favorite information agents that work together and to customize them flexibly. To this end, we developed the MCI in which multiple information agents work together with each other and with the user through characters.

André and Rist propose a system employing multiple characters [1], but their work mainly emphasizes the advantage of multiple characters as presentation media. Agents in their system reside and perform in a client machine whereas, in our system, agent's bodies reside in independent servers in a distributed manner and agent's heads interact in a client machine. Hence, our system is more like a multiagent system because the information agents are physically distributed over the Internet.

8 Conclusion

We proposed an information integration platform called the Multiple Character Interface (MCI) in which multiple information agents, each of which has an animated life-like character, collaborate with each other and the user for retrieving and integrating information from the WWW. We showed two application prototypes: Venus and Mars and Recommendation Battlers, based on the MCI. We evaluated the MCI by using the Wizard of Oz method to show the behavior of users when they interacted with multiple characters.

Current Internet-based information systems depend heavily on web technology. Since we can put not only text, but also images and audio, on a web page, the web is highly expressive. Semantic Web technology [5, 13] will further enhance the value of current web systems because it provides semantic information to information agents through web pages. Current web information systems look static because they just provide information in a page-by-page manner. Life-like agents enhance the web in another way and make it look more dynamic and interactive. The MCI provides a framework through which multiple life-like agents can be integrated into a collaborative system. This scheme may lead to a new generation of agent-based information integration systems.

References

1. André, E., Rist, T.: Adding life-like synthetic characters to the web. In: *Cooperative Information Agents IV*, LNAI 1860 (Springer, Berlin New York 2000) pp 1–13
2. André, E., Rist, T. Muller, J.: Employing AI methods to control the behavior of animated interface agents. *Applied Artificial Intelligence* **13**:415–448 (1999)
3. Ball, G., et al.: Lifelike computer characters: The Persona Project at Microsoft. *Software Agents*, ed Bradshow, J.M. (AAAI Press, Menlo Park, CA 1997) pp 191–222

4. Bayardo Jr., R.J., Bohrer, W., et al.: InfoSleuth: Agent-based semantic integration of information in open and dynamic environments. In: *Proceedings ACM SIGMOD International Conference on Management of Data* (1997) pp 195–206
5. Berners-Lee, T., Hendler, J. Lassila, O.: The semantic web, *Scientific American*, May 17 (2001)
6. Cassell, J., Sullivan, J., Prevost, S., Churchill, E. (eds): *Embodied Conversational Agents* (The MIT Press, Cambridge, MA 2000)
7. Chawathe, S., et al.: The TSIMMIS project: Integration of heterogeneous information sources. In: *Proceedings of IPSJ Conference* (1994) pp 7–18
8. Dahlback, N., Jonsson, A., Ahrenberg, L.: Wizard of Oz studies - why and how, In: *Proceedings of the International Workshop on Intelligent User Interfaces* (1993) pp 193–200
9. Doorenbos, R.B., Etzioni, O., Weld, D.S.: A scalable comparison-shopping agent for the world-wide web. In: *Proceedings of the 1st International Conference on Autonomous Agents* (1997) pp 39–48
10. Finin, T., Labrou, Y., Mayfield, J.: KQML as an Agent Communication Language. *Software Agents*, ed Bradshow, J.M. (AAAI Press, Menlo Park, CA 1997) pp 291–316
11. Genesereth, M.R.: An agent-based framework for interoperability. In *Software Agents*, ed Bradshow, J.M. (AAAI Press, Menlo Park, CA 1997) 317–345
12. Hearst, M.A.: Information integration. *IEEE Intelligent Systems* **13**(5):12–24 (1998)
13. Hendler, J.: Agents and the semantic web. *IEEE Intelligent Systems* **16**(2):30–37 (2001)
14. Howe, A.E., Dreilinger, D.: Savvy search: A metasearch engine that learns which search engines to query. *AI Magazine* **18**(2):19–25 (1997)
15. Ishida, T.: Digital City Kyoto: Social information infrastructure for everyday life. *Communications of the ACM* **45**(7):76–81 (2002)
16. Ishida, T.: Q: a scenario description language for interactive agents. *IEEE Computer* **35**(11): 54–59 (2002)
17. Kitamura, Y., et al.: Interactive integration of information agents on the web. In: *Cooperative Information Agents V*, ed Klusch, M., Zambonelli, F., LNAI 2182 (Springer, Berlin New York 2001) pp 1–13
18. Kitamura, Y., et al.: Multiple character-agents interface: An information integration platform where multiple agents and human user collaborate, In: *Proceedings of the 1st International Joint Conference on Autonomous Agents and Multiagent Systems* (2002) pp 790–791
19. Kitamura, Y., Sakamoto, T., Tatsumi, S.: A competitive information recommendation system and its behavior. In: *Cooperative Information Agents VI*, ed Klusch, M. Ossowski, S., Shehory O., Lecture Notes in Artificial Intelligence, vol 2446 (Springer, Berlin Heidelberg New York 2002) pp 138–151
20. Klusch, M. (ed): *Intelligent Information Agents* (Springer, Berlin New York 1999)
21. Klusch, M.: Information agent technology for the Internet: A survey. *Journal on Data and Knowledge Engineering* **36**(3):337–372 (2001)
22. Knoblock, C.A., et al.: The Ariadne approach to web-based information integration. *International Journal of Cooperative Information Systems* **10**:145–169 (2001)

23. Lesser, V., Horling, B., Klassner, F., Raja, A., Wagner, T., Zhang, S.X.: BIG: An agent for resource-bounded information gathering and decision making. *Artificial Intelligence* **118**:197–244 (2000)
24. Maulsby, D., Greenberg, S., Mander, R.: Prototyping an intelligent agent through wizard of Oz. In: *Proceedings of ACM Conference on Human Factors in Computing Systems* (1993) pp 277–284
25. Oyama, S., et al. Keyword spices: A new method for building domain-specific web search engines. In: *Proceedings 17th International Joint Conference on Artificial Intelligence* (2001) pp 1457–1463
26. Russell, S.J., Norvig, P.: *Artificial Intelligence: A Modern Approach* (Prentice Hall, Englewood Cliffs, NJ 1995)
27. Selberg, E., Etzioni, O.: Multi-service search and comparison using the MetaCrawler. In: *Proceedings of the 4th International World Wide Web Conference* (1995) pp 195–208
28. Sycara, K., Zeng, D.: Coordination of multiple intelligent software agents. *International Journal of Cooperative Information Systems* **5**(2&3):181–211 (1996)
29. Weiss, G. (ed): *Multiagent Systems: A Modern Approach to Distributed Artificial Intelligence* (The MIT Press, Cambridge, MA 1999)
30. Wiederhold, G. (ed): *Intelligent Integration of Information* (Kluwer Academic, Dordrecht 1996)

Expressive Behaviors for Virtual Worlds

Stacy Marsella[1], Jonathan Gratch[2], and Jeff Rickel[1]

[1] USC Information Sciences Institute
   4676 Admiralty Way, Marina del Rey, CA 90292, USA
   marsella@isi.edu
[2] USC Institute for Creative Technologies
   13274 Fiji Way, Marina del Rey, CA 90292, USA
   gratch@ict.usc.edu

Summary. A person's behavior provides significant information about their emotional state, attitudes, and attention. Our goal is to create virtual humans that convey such information to people while interacting with them in virtual worlds. The virtual humans must respond dynamically to the events surrounding them, which are fundamentally influenced by users' actions, while providing an illusion of human-like behavior. A user must be able to interpret the dynamic cognitive and emotional state of the virtual humans using the same non-verbal cues that people use to understand one another. Toward these goals, we are integrating and extending components from three prior systems: a virtual human architecture with a wide range of cognitive and motor capabilities, a model of task-oriented emotional appraisal and socially situated planning, and a model of how emotions and coping impact physical behavior. We describe the key research issues and approach in each of these prior systems, as well as our integration and its initial implementation in a leadership training system.

1 Introduction

A person's emotional state influences them in many ways. It impacts their decision making, actions, memory, attention, voluntary muscles, etc., all of which may subsequently impact their emotional state (e.g. see [2]). This pervasive impact is reflected in the fact that a person will exhibit a wide variety of non-verbal behaviors consistent with their emotional state, behaviors that can serve a variety of functions both for the person exhibiting them as well as for people observing them. For example, shaking a fist at someone plays an intended role in communicating information. On the other hand, behaviors such as rubbing one's thigh, averting gaze, or a facial expression of fear may have no explicitly intended role in communication. Nevertheless, these actions may suggest considerable information about a person's emotional arousal, their attitudes, and their focus of attention.

Our goal is to create virtual humans that convey these types of information to humans while interacting with them in virtual worlds. We are interested in virtual worlds that offer human users an engaging scenario through which they will gain valuable experience. For example, a young army lieutenant could be trained for a peacekeeping mission by putting him in virtual Bosnia and presenting him with the sorts of situations and dilemmas he is likely to face. In such scenarios, virtual humans can play a variety of roles, such as an experienced sergeant serving as a mentor, soldiers serving as his teammates, and the local populace. Unless the lieutenant is truly drawn into the scenario, his actions are unlikely to reflect the decisions he will make under stress in real life. The effectiveness of the training depends on our success in creating engaging, believable characters that convey a rich inner dynamics that unfolds in response to the scenario.

Thus, our design of the virtual humans must satisfy three requirements. First, they must be believable; that is, they must provide a sufficient illusion of human-like behavior that the human user will be drawn into the scenario. Second, they must be responsive; that is, they must respond to the events surrounding them, which will be fundamentally influenced by the user's actions. Finally, they must be interpretable; the user must be able to interpret their response to situations, including their dynamic cognitive and emotional state, using the same non-verbal cues that people use to understand one another. Thus, our virtual humans cannot simply create an illusion of life through cleverly designed randomness in their behavior; their inner behavior must respond appropriately to a dynamically unfolding scenario, and their outward behavior must convey that inner behavior accurately and clearly.

This chapter describes our progress toward a model of the outward manifestations of an agent's cognitive and emotional state. We review three prior systems that have heavily influenced our thinking on expressive behaviors, discussing the unique aspects of each and illustrating how they have influenced the design of an integrated system. The first, Steve [40, 42, 43], provides an architecture for virtual humans that can collaborate with human users and other virtual humans in 3D virtual worlds. Although Steve did not include any emotions, its broad capabilities provide a foundation for the virtual humans toward which we are working. The second, Jack and Steve, provides a model of how emotions arise from the relationship between environmental events and an agent's plans and goals [16], as well as a model of socially situated planning that builds on that emotional appraisal model. The third, Carmen's Bright IDEAS [31], contributes a complementary model of emotional appraisal as well as a model of the impact of emotional state and coping on physical behavior. After describing the key concepts in each of these prior systems, we describe a new project in which we have integrated these concepts into virtual humans for experiential learning in engaging virtual worlds.

2 Steve

Our earliest work on virtual humans resulted in Steve (Fig. 1), an animated agent that collaborates with human users and other virtual humans on tasks in 3D virtual worlds [40, 42, 41]. Such task-oriented collaboration requires an agent to balance a variety of demands. Tasks require an agent to perceive the state of the virtual world, assess the state of goals, construct plans to achieve those goals, navigate through the virtual world, and execute its plans. Collaboration requires these task-related behaviors to be interleaved with face-to-face social interactions with others (human users and virtual humans) embedded in the same virtual world. The agent's environment is unpredictable in many ways: others may speak to the agent or take actions in the world at any time, and the virtual world itself may change unexpectedly (e.g. through simulated equipment failures). Thus, the agent must be able to adapt its task-related and social behaviors at any time. Steve's main contribution is his ability to interleave task-related behaviors and face-to-face dialogue in such dynamic virtual worlds.

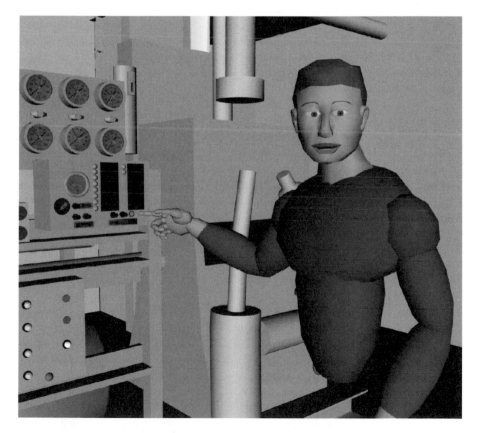

Fig. 1. Steve describing a power light

Despite an impressive variety of related work on embodied conversational agents [6] and animated pedagogical agents [21], Steve is unique in this ability. Several systems have carefully modeled the interplay between speech and non-verbal behavior in face-to-face dialogues [5, 7, 4, 36], but these systems focused exclusively on dyadic conversation, and they did not allow users and agents to collaborate on tasks in a 3D virtual world. The Gandalf system [7], which provided a sophisticated model of real-time face-to-face interaction, allowed an agent and human to cohabit a real physical space, and to use gaze and gesture to reference an object (i.e. a wall-mounted display screen) in that space, but the agent's presence was limited to a 2D head and hand on a computer monitor. Similarly, the Rea agent [4] provides a state-of-the-art model of dyadic face-to-face conversation, but bypasses issues of collaboration in dynamic virtual worlds; it can transport itself to and into virtual houses and apartments, and the user can point to some objects within those virtual environments, but the user is not immersed in those environments, and Rea's movement and references within them are very limited. The Cosmo agent [27] includes a sophisticated speech and gesture generation module that chooses appropriate deictic references and gestures to objects in its virtual world based on both spatial considerations and the dialogue context, but the agent and its environment are rendered in 2D form and the user does not cohabit the virtual world with Cosmo. The WhizLow pedagogical agent [28] performs tasks in a 3D virtual world, but the agent does not collaborate with students on tasks; the student specifies high-level tasks via menus, and the agent carries them out. Bindiganavale et al. [3] developed a training system that allows multiple virtual humans to collaborate on tasks in a virtual world, but the trainee learns by giving natural language instructions (task knowledge) to the agents and viewing the consequences; the trainee cannot participate in the scenario directly. Each of these systems provides impressive capabilities in its area of research focus, but none of them can interleave task-related behaviors and face-to-face dialogue with humans and virtual humans in dynamic virtual worlds.

To support these capabilities, Steve consists of three main modules: perception, cognition, and motor control (Fig. 2) [40]. The perception module monitors messages from other software components, identifies relevant events, and maintains a snapshot of the state of the world. It tracks the following information: the simulation state (in terms of objects and their attributes), actions taken by students and other agents, the location of each student and agent, the objects within a student's field of view, and human and agent speech (separate messages indicate the beginning of speech, the end, and a semantic representation of its content). The cognition module, implemented in Soar [24, 34], interprets the input it receives from the perception module, chooses appropriate goals, constructs and executes plans to achieve those goals, and sends motor commands to the motor control module. Steve's cognition module can typically react to new perceptual input in a fraction of a second, so it is very responsive [42]. The cognition module includes a wide variety of domain-

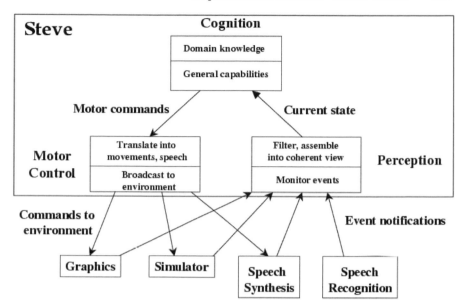

Fig. 2. The architecture of a Steve agent

independent capabilities, including planning, replanning, and plan execution; mixed-initiative dialogue; assessment of student actions; question answering ("What should I do next?" and "Why?"); episodic memory; path planning; communication with teammates [41]; and control of the agent's body. The motor control module accepts the following types of commands: move to an object, point at an object, manipulate an object (about 10 types of manipulation are currently supported), look at someone or something, change facial expression, nod or shake the head, and speak. The motor control module decomposes these motor commands into a sequence of lower level messages that are sent to the other software components (simulator, graphics software, speech synthesizer, and other agents) to realize the desired effects.

Low-level animation of Steve's body runs as software that is linked into the graphics software for the virtual world rather than into Steve. The animation software is controlled by messages it receives from Steve's motor control module. Because the animation software controls the dynamics of all body motions, the motor control module need only specify the type of motion it wants. Steve's animation software is very flexible, placing relatively few constraints on how and when the motor control module can make new demands. This flexibility comes from two properties. First, the animation software generates all movements dynamically; there are no keyframes or canned animations. Second, movements involving different parts of the body can be performed simultaneously, and a new command to a body part interrupts any existing motion for that part with a smooth transition. The resulting flexibility is an important part of Steve's ability to react instantly to unexpected events.

The cognition module generates Steve's communicative behavior by dynamically selecting its next action from a repertoire of behavioral primitives. To support the needs of task-oriented collaboration, Steve includes the following primitives:

- *Speak:* Steve can produce a verbal utterance directed at a human or another agent. To make it clear to whom the utterance is directed, the motor control module automatically shifts Steve's gaze to the hearer just prior to the utterance. (Task-related events can cause gaze to shift to something else before the utterance is complete.) To make it clear that Steve is speaking, the motor control module automatically maintains a "speaking face" (eyebrows slightly raised and mouth moving) throughout the utterance. Steve has a wide range of utterances, all generated from text templates, ranging from a simple "OK" or "no" to descriptions of domain actions and goals. A message from the speech synthesis software indicates to Steve's perception module when the utterance is complete.
- *Move to an object:* To guide the student to a new object, Steve can plan a shortest path from his current location and move along that path [40]. To guide the student's attention, the motor control module automatically shifts Steve's gaze to his next destination on each leg of the path. In contrast, to simply follow the student around (e.g. when monitoring the student's activities), Steve shrinks and attaches himself to the corner of the student's field of view, so that he can provide visual feedback on their actions.
- *Manipulate an object:* To demonstrate domain task steps, Steve can manipulate objects in a variety of ways. Currently, this includes manipulations that can be done by grasping the object (e.g. moving, pulling, inserting, turning) or using his fingers (e.g. pressing a button, flipping a switch). To guide the student's attention, the motor control module automatically shifts Steve's gaze to the object just prior to the manipulation. State change messages from the simulator indicate to Steve's perception module when the manipulation is complete (e.g. a button's state attribute changing to "depressed").
- *Visually check an object:* Steve can also demonstrate domain task steps that simply require visually checking an object (e.g. checking the oil level on a dipstick or checking whether an indicator light is illuminated). This requires Steve to shift gaze to the object and make a mental note of the relevant property of that object.
- *Point at an object:* To draw a student's attention to an object, or connect a verbal referring expression to the object it denotes, Steve can point at the object. To further guide the student's attention, the motor control module automatically shifts Steve's gaze to the object just prior to pointing at it.

- *Give tutorial feedback:* To provide tutorial feedback on a student's action, Steve indicates a student error by shaking his head as he says "no", and he indicates a correct action by simply looking at the student and nodding. The motivation for shaking the head is to complement and reinforce the verbal evaluation, and the motivation for the head nod is to provide the least obtrusive possible feedback to the student.

- *Offer turn:* Since our goal is to make Steve's demonstrations interactive, we allow students to interrupt with questions ("What next?" and "Why?") or to request to abort the task or finish it themselves. Although they can talk during Steve's utterances or demonstrations, Steve explicitly offers the conversational turn to them after each speech act (which could be several sentences) or performance of a domain action. He does this by shifting his gaze to them and pausing for 1 second. Not only does this give students convenient openings for interruptions, but it also helps to structure Steve's presentations. (Prior to adding this feature, users complained that Steve's presentations were hard to follow because he never paused to take a breath.)

- *Listen to student:* When the student is speaking, Steve can choose to quietly listen. This simply involves shifting gaze to the student to indicate attention.

- *Wait for someone:* When Steve is waiting for someone to take an action (either the student or a teammate in a team training scenario), he can shift gaze to that person (or agent) to indicate his expectation.

- *Acknowledge an utterance:* When a student or teammate says something to Steve, he can choose to explicitly acknowledge his understanding of their utterance by looking at them and nodding. The speech recognizer does not provide recognition of intermediate clauses, so Steve is limited to acknowledging understanding of entire utterances.

- *Drop hands:* When Steve is not using his arms and hands, he can drop them back down to hang loosely at his sides. Although there is evidence that such a move can convey a conversational signal (i.e. end of turn) [12], Steve does not currently use this behavior for that purpose; it simply means he has nothing else to do with his hands (such as pointing or manipulating).

- *Attend to action:* When someone other than Steve manipulates an object in his environment, Steve automatically shifts his gaze to the object to indicate his awareness. Unlike all the above behaviors, which are chosen deliberately by the cognition module, this behavior is a sort of knee-jerk reaction invoked directly by the perception module. Because an object manipulation is a very transient event, our design rationale was to react as quickly as possible.

Steve's main challenge is generating coherent behavior, and the key to addressing this challenge is to maintain a rich representation of context. The ability to react to unexpected events and handle interruptions is crucial for task-oriented collaboration in dynamic virtual worlds, yet it threatens the coherence of an agent's behavior. A good representation of context allow an agent to be responsive while maintaining its overall focus. Steve maintains two separate but complementary types of context:

- *Task Context:* Steve models tasks using a hierarchical, partial-order plan representation. As a task proceeds, Steve continually monitors the state of the virtual world, and he uses the task model to maintain a plan for how to complete the task, using a variant of partial-order planning techniques [40]. This allows Steve to revise his plans to adapt to unexpected events.
- *Dialogue Context:* The dialogue context represents the state of the interaction between a student and Steve, including whether the student and/or Steve is currently speaking; a focus stack [20] representing the hierarchy of tasks, subtasks, and actions in which the student and Steve are currently engaged; the state of their interaction on the current task step (e.g. the state might be that Steve has explained what must be done next but neither he nor the student has done it); a record of whether Steve or the student is currently responsible for completing the task (this task initiative can change during a mixed-initiative interaction); the last answer Steve gave, in case the student asks a follow-up question; any pending obligations (i.e. student requests or questions that Steve has not yet addressed); and the actions that Steve and the student have already taken [42].

Based on the current task and dialogue contexts, Steve can choose his next action to fill one of three roles. First, he can respond to the student. This includes responding to a student's request, giving them tutorial feedback on their action, or simply listening when they are talking. Second, Steve can choose for himself how to advance the collaborative dialogue. This includes things like suggesting the next task step, describing it, or demonstrating it in cases where the student did not explicitly request such help. Third, Steve can choose a turn-taking or grounding act [50] that helps regulate the dialogue between the student and himself without advancing the task. This includes offering the student the conversational turn or acknowledging understanding of an utterance with a head nod.

Several such actions may be appropriate at any given moment, so priorities allow Steve to choose the most appropriate. The highest priority is to respond to the student. If no such actions are proposed, the next priority is to perform any relevant conversational regulation action. However, if an opportunity for a conversational regulation action is missed due to a higher priority action for responding to the student, it will not be deferred and performed later. Only when neither of these types of actions is proposed will Steve take the initiative to advance the task collaboration, and he only does that when he has the task initiative. Traum proposed a similar priority scheme in his model of spoken task-oriented dialogue [49].

The original version of Steve, described in this section, did not include a model of emotions, and expressive behavior was not a primary research focus. However, Steve's broad capabilities have served as a valuable foundation for our current work on virtual humans, described later in this chapter. The expressive behaviors that we have integrated into Steve are derived from two separate research projects: Émile (Jack and Steve) and Carmen's Bright IDEAS.

3 Jack and Steve

Jack and Steve was an exploration in the extent to which plans and plan reasoning could inform rich models of expressive social behavior. The Jack and Steve system was predicated on two basic claims: (i) that plans and plan reasoning can mediate expressive behavior and (ii) that small biases in how plans are evaluated and generated can result in large systematic differences in agent behavior.

With these goals in mind, Jack and Steve differed in several respects from the preceding Steve system. To support biases in plan evaluation, Jack and Steve incorporated a richer plan representation, including decision-theoretic information to inform the evaluation process and meta-planning capabilities. To translate small biases into large external variations, Jack and Steve focused on plan generation, whereby these biases could be magnified over the multiple steps involved in the generation process. In contrast, Steve focused more on plan execution and repair, so his plan generation algorithm was less general. The systems also differed significantly in terms of their inter-agent behavior. Steve focused on collaborative interactions between agents and human users, whereas Jack and Steve explored how biases in the plan generation process could support a variety of non-collaborative interactions as well, but, as the focus was exploring systematic differences in joint behavior, agents only interact with other computational agents and not with human users.

The Jack and Steve system led to two key innovations that have influenced our subsequent agent designs: Émile [16], a plan-based model of emotional appraisal, and *socially situated planning*[17], whereby an agent may alter its goal-directed behavior based on features of the social context. These models were integrated with the animation system developed for the Steve system, described above, augmenting them with a limited ability to generate facial expressions, expressive gestures, and emotionally biased speech synthesis.

The Jack and Steve system was motivated by a convergence of several distinct bodies of research. First, psychological theories of emotion emphasize the pervasive role of emotions in social interactions and suggested that human emotions are mediated by some form of goal-directed reasoning. Cognitive appraisal theory, in particular, argues that emotions arise from an assessment process that characterizes how events impact goals along several abstract dimensions such as goal-relevance, goal-congruence, and likelihood [45]. Second, psychological theories of personality illustrate that people of different personality types will appraise and respond to events quite differently, and that goal-directed reasoning may mediate this process as well. These theories argue that relatively small biases in appraisal or response might lead to large systematic differences in outward behavior. For example, conscientious individuals tend to accept greater personal responsibility for joint goals, which in turn can lead to the construction of quite different plans and collaborative interactions than might result from a non-conscientious individual [38]. Finally, artificial intelligence theories of collaborative behavior have begun to build formal models of social interaction in terms of goal-directed reasoning. Work on shared plans [19] and joint intentions [10] illustrate how reasoning about interactions between plans, and representing beliefs, obligations, and commitments, could motivate social behavior. Jack and Steve joined these strands of research into a system that utilized plans and plan reasoning to model an agent's relationship to its physical and social environment, and to support systematic individual variations in how this relationship was conceived.

3.1 Motivating Example

The Jack and Steve application domain centered on the antics of two Southern Californian roommates, Jack and Steve. The agents engaged in unscripted interactions via simulated speech, and a user could explore a variety of interactions by altering internal characteristics of either agent. For example, a user could alter an agent's goals (e.g. to have fun or to make money) and alter characteristics of their personality (e.g. are they cooperative or rude?).

In this motivating example, Jack's goal is to make money, he views Steve as a friend, and treats him fairly. Steve wants to surf, views Jack as a friend, but tends to be rude in his dealings. All of these terms have a specific technical definition discussed below. Both agents develop different plans but have to contend with a shared resource. Besides performing task-level actions, the agents engage in speech acts and generate gestures, facial expressions, and affective speech modulation based on properties of the social context.

What follows are annotated traces of two separate runs of the system where the only difference is a change in the personality of Steve. In the first trace he treats Jack rudely and in the second he treats him fairly. The agents generate speech via simple template filling and agents actually communicate with each other through a stylized plan-communication language. Figure 3 illustrates the mental state of each agent at some point in the interaction. White boxes indicate individual actions and arrows indicate the establishment of an action's preconditions by another action's effects, or a threat to some precondition's establishment by an intervening action that negates the establishing effect. Blue boxes indicate "plans", which are sets of actions treated as a conceptual unit by the social layer. The emotion windows illustrate each agent's current emotional state, characterized in terms of intensity values along a set of basic emotions.

Rude Interaction:

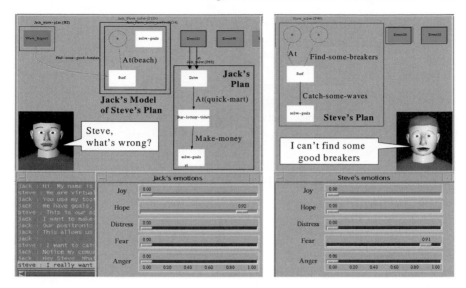

Fig. 3. Representation of Jack and Steve's appraised state, including each agent's base-level task network, plans, and emotional state

Jack: I want to make-some-big-money. *[Begins generating a plan for this goal. Displays a concerned expression, scratches his head, then, after devising a complete plan, displays a hopeful expression.]*

Steve: I want to catch-some-waves. *[Begins generating a plan for this goal. Looks concerned, scratches head, and continues to look concerned. Surfing is important to Steve and he cannot devise a satisficing plan.]*

Jack: *[Perceives Steve's display of concern and generates an information request.]* Hey Steve, what's wrong?

Steve: *[Identifies the feature in plan memory contributing to the most intense negative emotional excitation. Communicates the associated plan in a distressed tone of voice.]* I want to catch some waves but can't find any good breakers.

Jack: *[Incorporates Steve's plan into plan memory and locates relevant information. Jack knows of an event that establishes Steve's blocked subgoal.]* Steve, does it help that someone did say there's some great waves near the pier?

Steve: *[Incorporates the communicated event into plan memory. Completes a plan to go surfing and looks hopeful.]*

Jack: *[Perceives Steve's change in expression and seeks to confirm his expectation that the information he provided helped Steve.]* So that information helped?

Steve: *[Handles Jack's information request.]* Yes Jack. I plan to drive the car to the beach, then I plan to surf-my-brains-out.

Jack: *[Incorporates Steve's revised plan and finds a conflict with his own plans. Based on personality, Jack attempts to negotiate a fair solution.]* Wait a second. Our plans conflict. I plan to drive the car to the-quicky-mart then I plan to buy a-lottery-ticket.

Steve: *[Incorporates Jack's plan and recognizes the same interaction. Based on personality model, Steve responds to the interaction differently. He devises a plan that satisfies his own goals without regard to any conflicts it may introduce in Jack's plans. Steve exits stage right.]* Later dude, I'm driving the car to the beach.

Jack: *[Perceives that the car has departed without him. Looks angry. Says in angry voice:]* I want to kill-my-roommate.

Cooperative Interaction:

In this second interaction, the user replays the interaction but first alters Steve's personality to treat Jack fairly. The agents have identical goals and knowledge, but due to differences in their social appraisals the interaction is quite different. The interaction is identical up to the point that Jack detects an interaction between the plans:

Jack: *[Incorporates Steve's revised plan and finds a conflict with his own plans. Based on personality, Jack attempts to negotiate a fair solution.]* Wait a second. Our plans conflict. I plan to drive the car to the-quicky-mart then I plan to buy a-lottery-ticket.

Steve: *[Incorporates Jack's plan and recognizes the same interaction. Based on Steve having somewhat lower social status, he takes the initiative in repairing the conflict.]* Well, I could change my plans. *[Looks concerned, scratches head, then devises a possible joint plan.]* I have a suggestion. Could you drive the car to the-quicky-mart with-me then I could drive the car to the beach?

Jack: *[Incorporates Steve's suggested joint plan, determines that it is consistent with his own plans, and agrees to form a joint commitment to the shared plan.]* Sounds good to me.

3.2 Plan-Based Social Appraisal

As discussed earlier, the Jack and Steve system was predicated on two basic claims: (i) that plans and plan reasoning can mediate expressive behavior and (ii) that small biases in how plans are appraised and generated can result in large systematic differences in agent behavior. Jack and Steve supported such expressive and flexible interactions by implementing social reasoning as a layer atop a general-purpose partial-order planning system [1, 51]. The planning system provides domain-independent representations of world actions in terms of preconditions and effects, and provides general reasoning mechanisms that construct partial plans, repair interactions between them, and oversee plan execution. The social layer manages communication and biases plan generation and execution in accordance with the social context (as assessed within this social layer). In this sense, social reasoning is formalized as a form of meta-reasoning.

To support a variety of social interactions, the social reasoning layer must provide a rich model of the social context. The social situation is described in terms of a number of static and dynamic features from a particular agent's perspective. Static features include innate properties of the character being modeled (social role and a small set of personality variables). Dynamic features are derived from a set of domain-independent inference procedures that operate on the current mental state of the agent. These include the set of current communicative obligations, a variety of relations between the plans in memory (e.g. your plans threaten my plans), and a model of the emotional state of the agent (important for its communicative role).

One novel aspect of the system is the way in which the social layer fundamentally alters the planning process. Grosz and Kraus [19] show how meta-level constructs like social commitments can act as constraints that limit the planning process in support of collaboration (e.g. by preventing a planner from unilaterally altering an agreed-upon joint plan). Jack and Steve went beyond this to show how to model a variety of "social stances" one can take toward other individuals based on one's role in an organization and other dispositional factors. In terms of planning, rather than simply being cooperative, the social layer can bias planning to be more or less considerate to the goals of other participants. In terms of communication, agents can vary in terms of how much initiative or control they can take over the interaction, from bossy agents that try to tell others what to do to more passive agents that meekly avoid interactions or social conflicts.

3.3 Social Context

As in the preceding Steve system, the Jack and Steve system maintains a rich representation of the social context to drive coherent behavior. Domain-independent *appraisal rules* map features of an agent's current plan knowledge into a current *social context*. Besides static features of the social context set by the user, such as the agent's goals and personality, the social context can be divided into the following distinct components.

Plan Context: The plan context plays an analogous role to the task context in the original Steve system. The plan context represents information about the plans agents are entertaining, as well as meta-level information about the status of these plans. The Jack and Steve system incorporated a different plan representation than the original Steve system. While both systems used general plan representations, Jack and Steve also incorporated a decision-theoretic model, representing the likelihood and utility of various plans (which is quite useful in modeling the intensity of emotional responses). Unlike Steve's plans, which are hierarchical, Jack and Steve adopted a simpler non-hierarchical plan representation but included an explicit model of meta-plan reasoning.

Jack and Steve's base-level planning layer represents future-directed actions that an agent is aware of (whether they come from its own planning or are communicated from outside) as a single plan in the classical planning sense (i.e. a partially ordered set of actions with establishment and threat relations between actions), henceforth referred to as the *task network*. This allows the base-level planner to reason about the interrelationship between these activities. However, at the social level, subsets of this task network are explicitly treated as distinct plans in the commonsense use of the term (i.e. a coherent set of actions directed toward a goal), henceforth referred to as *plans*. Plans at this social layer may belong to the agent or may correspond to (what the agent believes to be) plans of other gents.

The plan context also represents a number of meta-level relations between these plans. Plans can contain threats if the actions within a plan threaten each other and the plans of one agent can introduce threats or be threatened by the plans of another agent (such relations are computed using the basic plan-evaluation routines provided by standard planning systems). Plans of one agent are deemed *relevant* to the plans of other agents if they may causally interact [11].

Emotional Context: Unlike the preceding Steve system, the Jack and Steve system maintains a representation of the agents' emotional state. The model of emotional reasoning that supports this, Émile, has been described extensively elsewhere [16, 18]. Émile adopts the cognitive view of emotions as a form of plan evaluation, relating events to an agent's current goals (cf. [35, 25]). As in other appraisal-based computational models of emotion [13, 33], Émile classifies events in terms of a set of *appraisal variables*:

- goal relevance – are the consequences of an event relevant to an organism's goals?
- desirability – how desirable are the consequences?
- likelihood – how likely are the consequences?
- causal attribution – who is the causal agent underlying the event and does it deserve credit or blame?

Unlike prior computational models, Émile reified these variables in terms of domain-independent features of an agent's plans in memory. Émile contains a set of recognition rules that scan an agent's internal representations and generate an appraisal frame whenever certain features are recognized. For example, when Steve states he will drive the car to the beach, the effect of this potential action (that the car is no longer at home) threatens Jack's plan to get to the quicky mart. The existence of a threat to an important goal is interpreted as an undesirable event, which ultimately gets mapped into a fear response based on the likelihood of the threat and the importance of the goal.

Many appraisals may arise from the current plan context (e.g. Steve may be simultaneously hopeful that he will surf but fearful that Jack may abscond with the car). Individual appraisals are collected together by class and their intensities summed into an overall emotional context. Different subsets of appraisals can be aggregated and associated with meta-level constructs, allowing Émile to compute an agent's overall state, track the emotions arising from a specific plan, or make estimates of the overall emotional state of other agents (given an understanding of their goals and plans). Each of these aggregate states is represented as a real-valued vector representing the intensities of different emotional states (Fear, Joy, etc.) and Émile dynamically modifies this state as appraisals change in response to the current world situation and the state of plans in memory.

Communicative Context: The communicative context tracks what information has been communicated to different agents and maintains any communicative obligations that arise from speech acts. When one agent communicates a plan to another, the social layer inserts the plan into the task network and records that the recipient knows this plan. This belief persists until the sender's planning layer modifies the plan, at which point the social layer records that the recipient's knowledge is out of date. If one agent requests another's current plans, the social layer represents a communicative obligation: the fact that the recipient of the request owes a response is recorded in each agent's social layer (though whether the recipient satisfies this obligation is up to its own social control program).

The communicative context roughly corresponds to the earlier Steve system's notion of dialogue context in the sense that both are concerned with representing a history of preceding communication and its impact on current beliefs and pending obligations. The Steve system, however, focused more on dialogue related to hierarchical task execution (e.g. the focus stack), whereas Jack and Steve focus more on the relationship of dialogue acts to plan generation.

3.4 Social Operators and Social Stances

Social operators are actions that occur at the social level. These are subdivided into meta-planning operators and communicative operators. By triggering these operators based on features of an agent's social context, the Jack and Steve system could represent a number of distinct social behaviors.

Meta-planning operators alter the way the planner operates at the base level. Meta-planning operators allow the social level to react and manipulate plan objects, populate them with subsets of the task network, and alter how the planner operates on those subsets. For example, if Steve communicates his plan to Jack, Jack could create a new plan object ("Steve's Plan") and populate it with the set of communicated actions. Different plans could be treated differently by allowing or disallowing certain types of planning modifications. Classical planning algorithms can be viewed as a sequential decision process: some critiquing routines identify a set of problems with the current plan network and propose a set of modifications that resolve at least one of these problems (an action should be added, these actions should be reordered, etc.); one modification is applied and the process continues [23]. The social level might disallow any changes to a plan (corresponding to the idea that the agent is committed to the plan), or it may allow more subtle variations in how plans are changed by constraining the set of allowable modifications.

Communicative operators correspond to a set of speech acts that an agent may use to communicate with other agents. As they are defined at the meta-level, they can operate on plans only as an atomic structure and cannot make reference to components of a plan (although one has the option of breaking a plan into explicit subplans). Some speech acts serve to communicate plans (one can INFORM another agent of one's plans, REQUEST that it accept some plan of activity, etc.). Other speech acts serve to change the state of some previously communicated plan (one can state that some plan is under revision, that a plan is acceptable, that it should be forgotten, etc.). Communicative primitives also include non-verbal communication, such as gestures.

From the standpoint of modeling expressive behavior, the most novel contribution of the Jack and Steve system was the way social operators could alter the way the planner handles interactions between plans of different agents, thereby implementing the idea of a social stance. A number of distinct social stances could be modeled and were organized along four roughly orthogonal dimensions: *conscientiousness*, *dominance*, *sociability*, and *independence*. These stances are all implemented as search control strategies, limiting certain of a planner's threat resolution options or the agent's communication options.

Conscientiousness impacts the extent that an agent respects the goals and plans of other agents. A non-conscientious (rude) agent only considers threats to its own plans and discounts any threats that its own actions introduce into the plans of other agents. For example, the rude Steve agent runs to grab the keys before Jack gets a chance to take the car. This corresponds to the threat resolution strategy of promotion, whereby a threatened action is moved before the threat. A conscientious agent would not consider *promotion* as it prevents Jack's plans from succeeding (in planning terminology this is an instance of *brother-clobbers-brother-goal*); however, a rude agent would discount this other-directed threat.

Dominance impacts whether an agent is willing to dictate actions to other agents. For example, a dominant agent would freely introduce actions into the plans of other agents, or incorporate steps into its own plans that other agents are expected to perform. In contrast, a meek agent would avoid these options and tend to work around interactions. For example, a meek Steve might find some other way to get to the beach or simply stay home.

Sociability relates to how readily an agent communicates to resolve conflicts or to provide potentially useful information. Social agents communicate whenever they encounter interactions between plans while asocial agents would try to resolve conflicts without communication. For example, an asocial agent could resolve the resource conflict involving the car by simply taking the car to the quicky mart before the other agent gets a chance to take it to the beach.

Finally, agents vary in terms of their independence. An independent agent would refuse to develop plans that depended on the actions of other agents. For example, the plan of riding to the quicky mart together would be ruled out by an independent agent.

Beyond social stances, meta-operators allow the social level to create and manipulate plan objects. Plans can be created and destroyed, and they can be populated with new goals and with activities communicated by other agents. Another set of meta-operators determines whether the planning algorithm can modify the activities in one of these plan objects. One can make a plan modifiable, allowing the planner to fix any flaws with that plan, or one can freeze its current state (as when adopting a commitment to a certain course of action). One can also modify the execution status of the plan, enabling or disabling the execution of actions within it.

Distinct personalities and social stances are implemented via a set of *social rules* that execute sequences of social operators based on appraised features of the social context. These rules can be viewed as a simple social domain theory or, alternatively, as a simple reactive plan.

The Jack and Steve system included about 30 social rules. A few examples are listed here.

Social-Rule: plan-for-goal
IF I have a top-level ?goal
THEN
    Do-Gesture(Thinking)
    Say(to-self, "I want to ?goal")
    ?plan = create-new-plan(?goal)
    enable-modification(?plan)

The *plan-for-goal* rule creates a new plan object for an agent's top level consisting of one dummy step that has the goal as its precondition, and, by enabling modification, allows the base-level planner to add actions to the plan in order to achieve the goal. The rule also triggers an utterance ("I want to ...") and an expressive "Thinking" gesture (implemented by a motor procedure that turns the agent's head up and to the side and raises one arm to scratch the head).

Social-Rule: commit-to-plan
IF I have ?plan
    AND I am currently modifying ?plan
    AND the ?plan is free of threats
THEN
    Do-Gesture(Nod-Head)
    commit-to(?plan)
    disable-modification(?plan)

If at some point the base-level planner successfully constructs a threat-free plan to achieve to goal, the *commit-to-plan* rule commits to the plan and prevents the planner from making further modifications. Note that the definition of "threat-free" is dependent on the agent's social stance (e.g. a rude agent may perceive its plan as threat-free even though it is clobbering steps of another agent's plans).

Social-Rule: help-friend
IF I have a ?plan that is relevant-to the plan of another ?agent
    AND I am friends with ?agent
    AND I am socially-adept
    AND the ?plan is not known to ?agent
THEN
    Do-Gesture(Look-at ?agent)
    SpeechAct(INFORM, ?plan ?agent)

If an agent has been defined to be socially adept and it is aware of some information that may causally impact the plans of another agent, the *help-friend* rule ensures that this information is communicated to the other agent.

Social-Rule: you-cause-problems-for-me
IF I have a ?plan
    AND ?you have ?your-plan
    AND my ?plan is threatened by ?your-plan
    AND I am committed to my ?plan
    AND I am not meek
    AND ?you don't know my ?plan
THEN
    Say(?you, "Wait a second, our plans conflict")
    SpeechAct(INFORM, ?plan, ?you)

If an agent has committed to a plan and discovers that the actions of another agent are threatening the plan's execution, a non-meek agent should communicate its own plans with the unstated expectation that the other agent will respond cooperatively.

Many of these rules, such as *help-friend*, correspond to standard conventions in collaborative planning. What is novel about Jack and Steve, however, is the idea of differentially applying them depending on features of an agent's personality, allowing, for example, a flexible gradation between cooperative and non-cooperative behavior. Collectively, these rules form a sort of social domain theory and, by explicitly representing social context and social operators, Jack and Steve facilitate the easy construction of different mappings between them and thus easy experimentation with different social theories.

3.5 Bodily Expression

The Jack and Steve system's chief contributions are in its internal process models of how emotion gets appraised and planning gets altered by social stances. However, this internal machinery must be manifested externally to have an impact on the user. Jack and Steve's reasoning mechanism was connected to the Steve agent body described earlier. This provided non-photorealistic 3D human-like bodies that included control of body movements (including procedural control of gaze, pointing, and grasping) and procedural control of facial expressions (including control of eyebrows, eyelids, and mouth characteristics). It also included a text-to-speech system with some coarse control over the characteristics of speech that could give some sense of emotional speech. Through these controls we developed a small repertoire of exaggerated facial poses to convey basic emotions and a set of arm and facial gestures to indicate other mental processes. This included pointing to the air and nodding when successfully completing a plan, scratching one's head when developing a plan, and winking when irrecoverably destroying another agent's plans.

Jack and Steve were never formally evaluated but anecdotal evidence suggests that people could easily recognize certain basic differences in personality (e.g. rude versus cooperative) through the different trajectory of the interactions and the type of plans agents developed, although not all combinations of traits led to recognizable differences. Facial expressions and gestures seemed primarily useful for conveying information about the agent's appraised internal state and apparently added to the perceived humorousness of the interaction.

We subsequently implemented a version of the system using more photo-realistic faces which people, interestingly, found rather less funny and more disturbing. This was likely due to the crude control we had over facial expressions. In both systems, characters would hold a fixed facial expression for several seconds. In the non-photorealistic Steve graphical bodies, people seemed to find this acceptable. However, with the more photorealistic faces people felt the characters were "creepy" or "maniacal". This reinforces the conventional wisdom that the drive toward photorealism in graphical models will demand considerably more attention to the form and dynamics of physical expressions.

4 Carmen's Bright IDEAS

Carmen's Bright IDEAS (CBI) was an agent-based system designed to realize an Interactive Pedagogical Drama (IPD) [31], an approach to learning that immerses the learner in an engaging, evocative story where the learner interacts openly with realistic characters. The pedagogical goal of CBI was to help mothers of pediatric cancer patients deal with the many stresses they face due to their child's illness. A mother learns by making decisions or taking actions on behalf of a character in the story, and sees the consequences of her decisions subsequently played out. To bring this pedagogy to life, the drama mirrors the mother's own problems. In the CBI story, the various stresses Carmen is facing are revealed, including her son's cancer, her daughter Diana's temper tantrums, work problems, etc. The drama foregrounds these stresses and allows the learner to interactively influence how Carmen copes with them. To facilitate open interaction, the characters in CBI were realized as autonomous agents.

Many of the differences with the previously discussed systems stem from the fact that the agents in CBI realize a social drama about very stressful issues. In particular, CBI's drama explores how the main character agent develops cognitively and emotionally. In contrast, the focus for the previously discussed Steve agent was on performing a procedural task in an immersive environment. Therefore drama and character development was not a central concern.

As a consequence of this dramatic goal, the design of the agent models in CBI was rooted in psychological research in stress and causes of emotions. In particular, like Émile, cognitive appraisal theory influenced the design of the CBI agents, though the two systems realize different, complementary aspects of appraisal theory. The focus in Émile was on the task-oriented causes of emotion. In CBI, there was a more pressing requirement to model the causes of emotion that stem from what psychologists call an ego identity, an individual's concern for loved ones, for how others perceive them, for performing their social roles well, and for measuring up to their personal ideals. Emotions stem from how events impact these concerns. Further, CBI agents needed to also model the consequences of emotions – how people cope with difficult emotional stresses in both adaptive and maladaptive ways as well as how to learn better ways of coping.

Also, the animated agents needed effective ways to convey the impact of emotion on both the agent's dialogue and physical behavior. In particular, this required developing models of how complex, sophisticated emotional stress processes are revealed over time in coping behavior and dialogue. Although other systems have addressed expressive behavior, this modeling of human coping and its dynamic impact on behavior set CBI apart. The concern for expressive behavior that reveals underlying dynamics grew out of the fact that CBI was being designed for a clinical trial with mothers of pediatric cancer patients. The dynamics would potentially benefit believability of the agents and facilitate the learner's identification with the agents. In addition, it might further the learner's understanding of the underlying emotional and coping processes that the agents were modeling, which in fact was part of the pedagogy.

4.1 The Drama of Carmen's Bright IDEAS

CBI is a three-act interactive drama. In the key act, Carmen discusses her problems with a clinical counselor, Gina, who suggests she use a problem solving technique called Bright IDEAS to help her find solutions. Note that each letter of IDEAS refers to a separate step in the problem solving method:

Identify a solvable problem, Develop possible solutions, Evaluate your options, Act on your plan, and See if it worked. Bright refers to the need for a positive attitude. Figure 4 is a shot of Carmen, and Gina in Gina's office. With Gina's help, Carmen goes through the initial steps of Bright IDEAS, applying the steps to one of her problems, and then completes the remaining steps on her own. The final act reveals the outcomes of Carmen's application of Bright IDEAS.

Fig. 4. Carmen (right) speaking with Gina (left)

Central to the drama's tension is the interaction between Gina, Carmen and the learner. The interaction model we designed for CBI is what we call a rubber-band model. See Fig. 5. Both Gina and the learner exert influence over Carmen but the influence is partial and mediated by Carmen's own cognitive and emotional dynamics. Thus we characterize this influence as rubber-bands. It is Gina's job to keep the social problem solving on track so that the story proceeds to a successful outcome by effectively responding to Carmen's cognitive and emotional state, at times motivating her through dialogue to work through the steps of IDEAS on some problem or alternatively calming or reassuring her. The human mother interacts with the drama by making choices for Carmen such as what problem to work on and how she should cope with the stresses she is facing. The learner can choose alternative internal thoughts for Carmen, such as "I hope this helps with Diana." These are presented as thought balloons (see Fig. 6). Both Gina's dialogue moves and the learner's choices influence the cognitive and emotional state of the agent playing Carmen, which in turn impacts her behavior and dialogue, perhaps in conflicting ways. The cognitive and emotional dynamics within the Carmen agent ensures that Carmen's behavior is believable at all times, regardless of how Gina and the learner may be influencing her.

In this interaction model, the Gina agent is both an on-screen character and the drama's director. The social interaction between agents is driven by the Gina agent's persistent goal to motivate the Carmen agent. Therefore, Gina typically takes the initiative. If the Carmen agent is distressed, she requires considerable prompting, praise, and guidance from Gina. But as she is reassured about IDEAS, she will begin to "feel" hopeful and may engage the problem solving without explicit prompting.

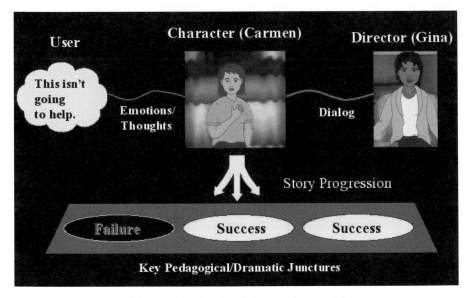

Fig. 5. Rubber-band interaction model

The combination of Gina's motivation of Carmen through dialogue and the learner's emotional impact on Carmen creates tension, a rubber-band tug-of-war between Gina's attempts to motivate Carmen and the initial, possibly less positive, attitudes of the Carmen/learner pair. As the learner plays a role in determining Carmen's attitudes, she assumes a relationship in this tug-of-war, including, ideally, an identification with Carmen and her difficulties, a responsibility for the on-screen action, and perhaps empathy for Gina. If Gina gets Carmen to actively engage in applying the IDEAS technique with a positive attitude, then she potentially wins over the learner, giving her a positive attitude. Regardless, the learner gets a vivid demonstration of how to apply the technique. The design also allows the learner to adopt different relationships to Carmen and the story. The learner may have Carmen feel as she would, act the way she would, or "act out" in ways she would not in front of her real-world counselor.

Fig. 6. Learner influences Carmen by selecting thought balloons.

4.2 CBI Agent Models

Technically, the basic design for interactive pedagogical drama includes five main components: a cast of autonomous character agents, the 2D or 3D puppets which are the physical manifestations of those agents, a director agent, a cinematographer agent, and finally the learner/user who impacts the behavior of the characters. Animated agents in the drama choose their actions autonomously but also follow directions from the learner and/or a director agent. Director and cinematographer agents manage the interactive drama's on-screen action and its presentation, respectively, so as to maintain story structure, achieve pedagogical goals, and present the dynamic story so as to achieve best dramatic effect. Here, the discussion will focus on the on-screen character agents. In CBI, one of the on-screen character agents, Gina, also

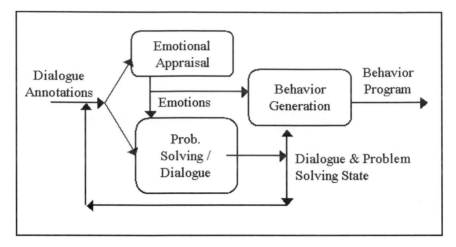

Fig. 7. Agent architecture

serves as director. Further discussion of the cinematographer agent can be found in [31].

Each on-screen character is realized by an agent architecture that has modules for problem solving, dialogue, emotional appraisal, and behavior generation. See Fig. 7. The problem solving module is the agent's cognitive layer, specifically its goals, planning and deliberative reaction to world events. The dialogue module models how to use dialogue to achieve goals. The emotional appraisal module determines how the agent emotionally evaluates (appraises) events. Finally, behavior generation constructs the agent's behavior and passes that behavior on to an animation program (not shown). Each of these modules will be discussed in greater detail in subsequent sections.

There are several novel pathways in the architecture worth noting. It is possible for the agent to say something and emotionally and cognitively react to the fact that it has said it, since the agent's own dialogue feeds back as input. Emotions impact problem solving, dialogue, and behavior. Finally, there are multiple inputs to behavior generation, from emotional appraisal, dialogue and problem solving, all competing for the agent's physical resources (arms, legs, mouth, head, etc.). For instance, the dialogue module derives dialogue that it intends to communicate, which may include an intent to project an associated emotion. This communication may be suggestive of certain non-verbal behavior for the agent's face, arms, hands etc. However, the agent's emotional state derived from emotional appraisal may suggest quite different behaviors. As we will discuss, behavior generation mediates this contention.

An example demonstrates how these pathways work within the architecture. At one point, Gina asks Carmen why her daughter is having tantrums. Carmen tends to feel anxious about being judged a bad mother and the learner may choose a thought that reinforces this anxiety. Carmen copes (problem solving) by dismissing the significance of the tantrums (dialogue model): "She is just being babyish, she wants attention." Based on Carmen's dialogue and emotional state, behavior generation selects relevant behaviors (e.g. fidgeting with her hands). Her dialogue also feeds back to emotional appraisal. She may now feel guilty for "de-humanizing" her child, may physically display that feeling (behavior generation), and then go on to openly blame herself. Carmen can go through this sequence of interactions solely based on the flux in her emotional reaction to her own behavior. Gina, meanwhile, will emotionally appraise Carmen's seeming callousness and briefly reveal shock (e.g. by raised eyebrows), but that behavior is quickly overridden if her dialogue model decides to project sympathy.

As noted in Fig. 7, the agents use dialogue annotations to communicate. In order to maximize expressive effect of such dialogue, recorded dialogue of voice actors was used instead of speech synthesis. A significant amount of variability in the generated dialogue is supported by breaking the recordings into meaningful individual phrases and fragments and by recording multiple variations (in content and emotional expression). There are 480 dialogue fragments in the clinical trial version of CBI. The agents compose their dialogue on the fly, using annotations attached to the fragments to understand each other and decide how to respond. The agents experience each fragment's annotation in order, so their internal state and appearance can be in flux over the dialogue segment.

Emotional appraisal and dialogue are depicted in Fig. 7 as happening in parallel. However the phrase-by-phrase dialogue generation and comprehension of the associated annotation tags in practice results in appraisals being interleaved with the dialogue. As this sequential process unfolds phrase by phrase, a behavior program is being incrementally constructed by the Behavior Generation. It is useful to understand this sequencing because it helps determine how emotion relates to other components of the architecture and therefore how the subtlety and dynamics of emotional expression in CBI is realized. In particular, the sequencing is closely related to the resulting expressive behavior program that will be discussed in the Behavior Generation section.

Agents process dialogue in the following order:

1. "Hear" Dialogue Line (other speaker) if there is one.
2. Appraise dialogue from step 1 and pass result to Behavior Generation.
3. Decision making – form intent to perform a dialogue act based on some list of phrases to speak.
4. If agent wants to speak go to 5 otherwise goto 1.
5. Appraise step 3 decision-making and pass result to Behavior Generation.
6. Compute dialogue pause based on emotional state and pass to Behavior Generation.
7. Pass phrase and annotations to Behavior Generation to build the part of the behavior program that will be executed in parallel with this phrase.

8. Appraise phrase just spoken and pass to Behavior Generation.
9. If phrases remain go to 6 else inform Behavior Generation that dialogue turn is over and go to 1.

The Appraisal at (2) is the starting emotional appraisal. It sets emotional state and consequently informs behavior generation, and thus indirectly manages the initial face, head turns, and body expression (posture) of the agent, as well as impacting the decision making that precedes its own dialogue. Decision making at (3) comes up with a plan to say something. The appraisal at (5) sets emotional state and expressions based on decision making at 3 – the dialogue intent/content of the entire response. This may in turn update face expression, head position and body focus. The pause at (6) simply manipulates the time between the agent's phrases based on emotional state, allowing expressive pauses in the dialogue.

The part of the behavior program built at (7) creates a parallel and sequential structure that includes gestures, facial expressions, head movements, blink patterns, posture shifts, and speaking of the appropriate surface phrase. Because of animation infrastructure, the behavior program is incrementally built by these steps but execution only happens when the complete program is constructed for the dialogue turn. The appraisal at (8) sets emotional state in reaction to content relayed by each phrase.

The dialogue annotations are not designed to fully describe the dialogue but rather constitute an abstract level at which the agents reason about how to react to each other's as well as their own dialogue. Annotations include:

- Dialogue content: Dialogue Act, Speaker, and Addressee
- Emotional content: Coping Act (e.g. denial)
- Propositional content: Main referent (e.g. Diana) and Topic (e.g. temper tantrums)
- Performance content: Referential structure (e.g. "me" indicates speaker is referring to self as "I feel...", "me–other" indicates speaker is referring to self and someone else) that is used in gesture determination and duration of phrase (used to decide which gesture macro to use, when to use it, and how to set blink pattern).

4.3 Emotional Model

The emotional model in CBI has several unique features required to realize expressive, interactive psychosocial drama that set it apart from standard models of emotions used in agent systems. Central to these features is the fact that emotions in CBI are not simply there to make the characters more believable. Emotions and how individuals cope with emotional stress were an integral aspect of the pedagogy. The pedagogical goal was for the mothers to learn how to choose and carry out the right coping strategy for a given situation and to maintain a realistic belief in their efficacy.

Consistent with the pedagogical role of emotion in CBI, the agents' interactions with each other and the learner are in fact grounded in the research that influenced the Bright IDEAS pedagogy: the cognitive appraisal theory of human emotion as posited by Richard Lazarus [25]. This theory organizes human behavior around appraisal and coping. Appraisal leads to emotion by assessing the person–environment relationship. This assessment is performed along several key dimensions. For example, did an event facilitate or inhibit the agent's goals; who deserves blame or credit? Most notable for the discussion here is the dimension of ego involvement: how an event impacts an individual's ego-identity. Ego-identity is the individual's collection of concerns for self- and social esteem, social roles, moral values, self-ideals, as well as concern for other people's well-being.

Coping is the process of dealing with emotion, either by acting externally on the world (problem-focused coping), or by acting internally to change beliefs or attention (emotion-focused coping). For example, a problem-focused way to attempt to deal with a loved one's illness is to take action that gets them medical attention. Alternatively, one might use an emotion-focused strategy such as avoiding thinking about it, focusing on the positive (e.g. one's love for an ill child), or denying the seriousness of the event. In Lazarus's theory, coping and appraisal interact and unfold over time, supporting the temporal character of emotion evident in human behavior.

As the previous tantrum example reveals, ego-identity and coping are key aspects of the emotion modeling in CBI. The focus on ego-identity, in particular, distinguishes CBI from systems like Émile that model emotions that arise from tasks. In CBI, the knowledge modeled by the agent's ego-identity comprises a key element of how it interacts with other characters and its response to events. For example, it is Carmen's concern for her son's well-being that induces sadness. And it is her ideal of being a good mother, and desire to be perceived as one (social esteem), that leads to anxiety about discussing Diana's tantrums with Gina.

Another key concern for CBI was to support the temporal character of emotion: an agent may "feel" distress for an event which motivates the shifting of blame, which leads to anger. The venting of that anger may in turn lead to guilt. In particular, capturing and expressing these dynamics in CBI lead to a design whereby agents emotionally evaluate and react to their own dialogue. The expression of emotion also stems from two sources, appraisals [16] as well as the intention to communicate emotions [26, 39] that is derived from the current dialogue act. Thus an agent can communicate emotions that they do not "feel". We will discuss in the Behavior Generation section how these two sources are mediated.

In CBI, ego-identity is modeled as a collection of role ideals (Carmen wants to be a good-mother), concerns (good-mothers want their children to be happy and healthy) and responsibilities (good-mothers are responsible for their child's behavior). The system also models social relations (Gina is in essence a parental-surrogate for Carmen). Appraisal rules derive emotions from these various representations. Figure 8 describes some of the knowledge of ego-identity, roles, and social relationships. Some of the appraisal rules used in the emotional processing are exemplified in Fig. 9. Note that the appraisals are also performed on topic changes. Topics such as Diana's tantrums and Jimmy's illness have pre-existing emotional state information that is averaged into current emotional state when the topic is raised (as we will see, MRE realizes such a capability in a more principled fashion). Emotions are represented as scalars on key types of emotion and coping factors. The appraisals result in changes in these values, which in turn impact dialogue transitions, dialogue rules, and expressive behavior. Although there was an attempt to write these appraisal rules in a general fashion, the coverage is also partial, driven by the demands of the interactive story and characters and the pragmatic demand of getting CBI ready for clinical trials with real mothers.

Roles and Ideals

- (ego-ideal <person> <role> <type>)
  - Example: (ego-ideal Carmen mother good-mother)
- (concern <type> <relationship> <state>)
  - Example: (concern good-mother dependent positive–affect)
- (responsibility <type> <relationship> <state>)
  - Example: (responsibility good-mother dependent behavior)

Relationships

- (parental-surrogate <person> <person>)
  - Example: (parental-surrogate Carmen Gina)

Fig. 8. Example ego-identity representations

- If event violates a concern, it is negative.

- If asked by parental-surrogate about negative event which agent feels responsible for then increase anxiety.

- If talking about negative event then increase sadness.

- If talking about negative event which agent feels responsibility for then increase guilt.

- If new topic is raised and agent has pre-existing emotional attitude towards it then average in emotions with current emotional state.

Fig. 9. Example appraisal rules

4.4 CBI Dialogue Model

The dialogue model used by the CBI agents is designed to support considerable flexibility, dialogue turn by dialogue turn, while supporting interesting dramatic outcomes. Most interesting from an expressive behavior standpoint, all this flexibility in dialogue is often driven by emotions, specifically the agents' emotional state, their coping strategies, and their assessment of the other agents' emotional state. To better appreciate this impact of emotions, we will briefly describe how dialogue is generated.

The agent's dialogue module selects high-level strategies to drive the discourse through the scene. These strategies are descriptions of possible realizations of the major components of the discourse and are designed to support considerable flexibility in the agent's turn-by-turn dialogue. For example, the main act in CBI is Gina's goal of getting Carmen to apply the IDEAS steps to one of her problems. Gina has an abstract strategy to do this: **reassure** Carmen, **suggest** they jointly apply Bright IDEAS, **ask** her to choose a problem, and **guide** her through the task of solving that problem – specifically guide her through the subgoals of IDEAS applied to that problem. This particular strategy sets an overall direction for the scene. The agents also have alternative substrategies that can hierarchically expand a strategy. For example, the IDEAS subgoals need to be expanded. One substrategy is to repeatedly prompt/help the other agent to enumerate possible solutions to a subgoal. For example, Gina might use this substrategy to help Carmen **d**evelop (the D in IDEAS) possible solutions to Diana's tantrums. Another is to ask an ordered sequence of questions on a topic. Gina, for example, might help Carmen identify (I) the current problem's features by answering the "5Ws": who is at the center of the current problem being discussed, what is the problem, where does the problem happen, when does it happen, and why does it happen?

The high-level strategy and substrategies are not fixed prescriptions for the dialogue. Rather, the agent expands the hierarchy and works out steps in the strategy interactively with the other agent. In the case of CBI, the expansion is done via joint agreement of Gina and Carmen. Gina suggests a substrategy like the "5Ws" and Carmen decides whether to agree to that approach. Each step in a strategy may need to be further expanded by the agents, via selecting another substrategy to expand it. Alternatively, a step may be primitive in the sense that there is no strategy to expand it. Such primitive steps are not single dialogue turns, however. Rather, the agent generates its dialogue turn-by-turn by flexibly interpreting the high-level strategies using a state machine. This machine allows the agent to adapt to twists and turns in the dialogue caused by the autonomy of the agents and the learner's interactions. In the case of non-primitive steps in a strategy, it manages the dialogue interactions which will hopefully lead to an agreement on how to expand the step. Similarly, in the case of primitive steps, like answering the "why" question of the "5-Ws", the state machine manages how the agent will interact with the other agent to satisfy the step.

The state machine includes two kinds of nodes: dialogue acts that generate a dialogue turn and nodes that step through the current (sub)strategy being interpreted (e.g. Next Step). Both of these node types manage the dialogue state by expanding a strategy, maintaining what the current strategy and topic is, where the agent is in the strategy, and dialogue obligations. Transitions occur between nodes depending on the current strategy, the current state of the dialogue, as well as the agent's and listener agent's emotional state. The dialogue acts are:

- Suggest (e.g. a joint subplan),
- Agree (to subplan),
- Ask/Prompt (e.g. for an answer),
- Re-Ask/Re-Prompt,
- Answer or re-answer,
- Reassure (e.g. to impact listener's emotional state),
- Agree/Sympathize (convey sympathy),
- Praise,
- Offer-Answer (without being asked),
- Clarify (elaborate),
- Resign (give-up), and
- Summarize.

Most notable are the ones that are tightly coupled to emotional state and pedagogy: Reassure, Praise, Agree/Sympathize, Resign (Give-up), and Summarize.

This design allows for both deliberative dialogue and reactive dialogue that variabilizes the agent interactions at multiple levels. At the highest level, alternative strategies and substrategies can be selected. Further, the specific transitions and resulting acts realize those strategies dialogue turn by dialogue turn in flexible ways, because a single step of the strategy can be realized by different paths through the agent's dialogue state machine. Finally, there are typically multiple realization rules to address a specific act. For example, there may be multiple ways for Carmen to answer a specific question. Some of these may be qualitatively different in the sense that they lead to different recorded dialogue lines and different dialogue annotations. Such differences lead to a different resulting state of the system. Others may have the same resulting annotations, but actually use different lines or even the same line spoken with different affect. For example, Carmen has multiple ways to say many of her lines, using different affect (frustrated, depressed, optimistic, etc.), that are selected based on her emotional state.

Emotion and its expression play a key role in the dialogue in other ways. For example, Gina's transitions between dialogue acts are based on Carmen's emotional state. She reassures or sympathizes when Carmen is distraught but prompts Carmen to address the current step in the current dialogue strategy when Carmen is less distraught. If Carmen's emotional model leads her to respond inappropriately, Gina has to decide how to repair this failure. In psychological terms, Gina is often choosing whether to direct Carmen towards emotion-directed versus problem-directed coping by giving either emotional or instrumental support. Coping is key to the agent's selection of dialogue and its response to it. Carmen may choose an evasive coping strategy and select dialogue consistent with that strategy using the coping annotations. For example, the Carmen agent's emotional model appraises the discussion of Diana's tantrums as a source of distress because of her concern for Diana and because failure to control Diana may reflect on her ability as a mother. Her response to this stress may be to blame Diana and trivialize her tantrums by saying she is just being babyish. The Gina agent will not accept this answer, again because of the coping strategy annotation, and will ask a follow-on question. But Carmen may also reject her own answer first. Specifically if she is not too anxious or angry, the guilt caused by the answer may cause her to re-answer it prior to Gina's further prompting.

4.5 Behavior Generation

As noted, non-verbal behaviors are generated by the behavior generation module. The design of this module was heavily influenced by the psychological research of Freedman [15]. Freedman described the behavior of clinical patients in terms of modes mediated by emotional state. In our computational model, we have delineated three modes: body-focus, transitional, and communicative, roughly based on his work. These modes are arranged in a finite-state machine, which we call a physical focus model. Body-focus mode is marked by a self focused attention, away from the conversation and the problem solving behavior. Emotionally, it is associated with considerable depression or guilt. Physically, it is associated with the tendencies of gaze aversion, paused or inhibited verbal activity, and hand-to-body stimulation that is either soothing (e.g. rhythmic stroking of forearm) or self-punitive (e.g. squeezing or scratching of forearm). The agent does not exhibit communicative gestures such as deictic or beat gestures when in this mode. Transitional indicates a less withdrawn attention, less anxiety, a burgeoning willingness to take part in the conversation, milder conflicts with the problem solving, and a closer relation to the listener. Physically, it can be marked by hand-to-hand fidgeting. There are more communicative gestures in this mode but they are still muted. Finally, communicative indicates a full willingness, or intent, to engage in the dialogue and problem solving. Physically, it is marked by the agent's full range of communicative gestures and use of gaze in turn-taking.

Behavior generation selects behavior based on physical focus mode. At any point in time, the agent will be in a specific mode based on emotional state that predisposes it to use non-verbal behavior in a particular fashion. Each behavior available to an agent is categorized according to which subset of these modes it is consistent with. Any specific non-verbal behavior, such as a particular nod of the head, may exist in more than one mode, and conversely a type of behavior, such as head nods in general, may be realized differently in different modes. Transitions between modes are based on emotional state.

By grouping behaviors into modes, the physical focus mode attempts to mediate competing communicative and non-communicative demands on an agent's physical resources, in a fashion consistent with emotional state. Gestures, gaze, and head movements are in particular driven by the physical focus mode. As we will see, facial expressions have a more temporal relation to the focus mode, driven by a desire to balance the expression of underlying emotional state with the communicative intent to express emotion as a social signal. This grouping model is designed to be general across agents. However, realism also requires that behaviors within each mode incorporate individual differences, as in human behavior. For example, Carmen's and Gina's repertoire of gestures incorporates individual differences.

Based on the current focus mode and emotional state, behavior rules, triggered in concert with the dialogue and appraisal processes noted above, build a behavior program that expresses how those processes are unfolding. Behaviors include a combination of posture, head movement, facial expressions, blinking, and dialogue, arranged in an XML structure.

The structure of the behavior program consists of animation directives for the pieces of the agent's body, composed by parallel <P> and sequential <S> markers as well as pause animation directives. This allows recursive structures capable of simultaneous, sequential, and delayed behaviors of arbitrary complexity. The XML structure in CBI is similar to other XML-based animation languages, including most recently the work of Cassell et al. [8] and Pelachaud et al. [37]. Even though CBI's parallel, sequential, and pause language is simple and quite aged now, it is somewhat unique in its ability to support timing of one behavior in absolute time or relative to any other behavior. Often XML languages only support timing of behaviors tied to the schedule of the speech.

Figure 10 depicts the high-level XML structure of the resulting animation program for one phrase of an agent's dialogue turn. Each box in the diagram would in turn be realized by nested XML animation directives. Note that there are starting and ending expressions for the entire dialogue turn as well as expressions that are displayed as the dialogue turn unfolds, phrase by phrase. This allows the agent's behavior to reflect unfolding emotional signals driven by the multiple appraisals and sources of emotions as noted earlier. In particular, the starting facial expressions are driven by appraisal of the previous speaker's dialogue. Expressions during the phrase are driven either by appraisal or by the intent to communicate emotion derived by the dialogue model. In communicative mode, it is the latter, while in body and transitional mode it is the former. Note, the system originally used a weighted average of these two sources of emotion to select the expression but, in actual practice, there was insufficient expressive facial behavior in the animation resources to support such averaged distinctions, a point we return to in Sect. 4.6. Gestures are created in parallel with the phrase. Again the gestures used are determined by the focus mode, as well as the dialogue annotations, including the referential structure noted earlier.

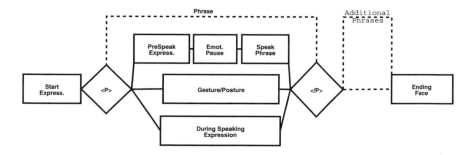

Fig. 10. High-level description of XML structure for one phrase of an agent's dialogue turn

Each individual behavior, such as the starting emotional expression, may have a recursive parallel and sequential structure. Figure 11 depicts just one such expression, a guilt expression, that would be one small component of a full behavior program for a dialogue turn. Note that the expression involves two sequential threads of parallel motion involving eye, brow, mouth, and head movements. The initial segment includes movement of the eyebrows and eyes. Once these animations are done, there is then a pause followed by final movements of head, mouth, eyes, and brows. This use of structured and animated movements of the head even for just one component of the full animation program grew out of a small empirical study which suggested that expressive facial behavior was best revealed by changes in expression, including head movements, as opposed to static expressions.

```
<S>
  <P>
  (Carmen, brows, <identifier>)
  (Carmen, eyes, <identifier>)
  </P>
  (pause, <ticks>)
  <P>
  (Carmen,head, <identifier>)
  (Carmen,mouth, <identifier>)
  (Carmen,eyes, <identifier>)
  (Carmen,brows, <identifier>)
  </P>
</S>
```

Fig. 11. Facial and head behavior for a guilt expression

Finally, note that each animation directive has an "identifier". This is simply a pointer to a frame or sequence of frames in a vector animation file for that body part. The bodies used for Carmen and Gina were composed of separate parts, including legs, torso (posture), arms, head position, eyes, brows, and mouth. Each of these assets was hand animated by artists and then stored in multi-frame animation files. This allowed the animation directives to identify single frames, say for a fixed arm position, or a sequence of frames for a particular movement of the arm.

4.6 Remarks

In Carmen's Bright IDEAS, the design of dialogue, emotions, and expressive behavior systems was driven by a need to convey deep inner conflicts and how those conflicts play out expressively over time. This led the design of the agents along certain paths: how to model ego-identity, coping, and the dynamics of expression. Perhaps the best test of its success in doing so were the trials with real mothers of pediatric cancer patients.

Carmen was evaluated in an exploratory arm of a larger clinical trial of the Bright IDEAS technique. The evaluation was very promising for Carmen and the use of interactive pedagogical drama in health interventions. Details on the results can be found in [30]. Overall, mothers were very enthusiastic. They found the story and its presentation in animated form to be very believable as well as a very effective and concrete way to learn Bright IDEAS. At the same time, one mother noted slowness in the graphics and other mothers wanted more story content that addressed other issues (such as marital concerns).

For the discussion in this chapter, this reveals a fundamental concern. One of the key issues that was faced in design of CBI was not having the sufficient resources to create the necessary dialogue and animation assets to reveal all the expressive capabilities of the underlying models. Going forward with such applications will require us to leverage existing character animation frameworks as opposed to building our own as we did in Carmen. Nevertheless, systems like CBI could fill a void in making effective health intervention training available to the larger public. The training task for CBI was a difficult one, fraught with potentially many pitfalls. The fact that it was received so well by the mothers was remarkable and bodes well for applying IPD to other training and learning tasks.

5 Mission Rehearsal Exercise

The Mission Rehearsal Exercise (MRE) system [46] brings together ideas from each of the preceding systems to create a broader and more flexible array of expressive behaviors. The goal of the MRE is to teach leadership skills in high-stakes social situations. The system places a human learner in command of a team of virtual humans interacting in an emotionally charged virtual environment. For example, in our initial scenario, the learner's team has, by accident, critically injured a young boy and the learner must juggle how to treat the boy without jeopardizing his mission or the safety of his team. To accomplish this, the learner must engage in face-to-face dialogue with his team members, take stock of the situation, give orders, and monitor their execution. Complicating this are characters that may express intense emotion and offer potentially biased or misleading information.

To model such dramatic and interactive scenarios, the MRE combines a number of elements of the preceding systems. We build on Steve's ability to flexibly interact with a human user, but augment it with the richer social and emotional behaviors of CBI and Jack and Steve. This has pushed us toward a tight integration of approaches, in some cases significantly altering their character, while at other times forcing us to defer key capabilities of the preceding systems for future research.

Although this chapter focuses on expressive behavior and the cognitive processes that support this, the MRE combines a variety of capabilities in service of realistic and natural collaboration with virtual humans including:

- a realistic model of human auditory and visual perception [44];
- a domain-specific finite-state speech recognizer that recognizes thousands of distinct utterances in noisy environments;
- a finite-state semantic parser that produces (partial) semantic representations of the information in the text strings returned from speech recognition;
- a dialogue model that explicitly represents aspects of the social context [49, 32] while supporting multi-party conversations and face-to-face communication in 3D virtual worlds [47];
- a dialogue manager that recognizes dialogue acts from utterances, updates the dialogue model, and selects new content for the virtual human to say;
- a natural language generator that can produce nuanced English expressions, depending on the virtual human's personality and emotional state as well as the selected content [14];
- an expressive speech synthesizer capable of speaking in different voice modes depending on factors such as proximity (speaking vs. shouting) and illocutionary force (command vs. normal speech) [22].

The MRE seeks to advance the state of the art in each of these areas, but also to explore how best to integrate them into a single agent architecture [44], incorporating a flexible blackboard architecture to facilitate experiments with the connections between the individual components. We refer the reader to the above citations for details on these other components and here focus on our innovations in expressive behavior.

Figure 12 illustrates a scene from the MRE scenario. The learner plays the role of a lieutenant in the US Army involved in a peacekeeping operation in Bosnia. In route to assisting another unit, one of the lieutenant's vehicles becomes involved in a traffic accident, critically injuring a young boy. The boy's mother is understandably distraught and a local crowd begins to gather. The learner must resolve the situation by interacting through spoken dialogue with virtual humans in the scene.

Fig. 12. A scene from the MRE scenario

5.1 Cognition and Emotions

To support such emotionally dramatic situations, virtual humans not only must produce a range of realistic expressive behaviors, but require the cognitive machinery to recognize which behaviors are appropriate in the course of an unscripted interaction with a human user. When selecting an expressive behavior, the virtual human's mental processes must take into account not only the task and dialogue context, as in the Steve system, but also how features of the social context will influence emotional appraisal and coping strategies.

We adopted Steve as a starting point for our integrated model of the cognition that underlies expressive behavior as, unlike Jack and Steve and CBI, the system supported flexible face-to-face interactions with a human user. However, Steve's task model had to be extended in a number of ways to represent the socio-emotional context.

Integrating the Émile plan-based appraisal model into Steve was relatively straightforward as both systems used similar task representations. Steve already possessed a model of task responsibility that supported appraisals of causal attribution, though Steve's task model had to be extended to represent probabilities and utilities and the processes that update these values. Steve also did not explicitly represent threats between task steps, necessary for appraisals of fear or anger, so we incorporated standard threat detection and resolution schemes.

One key difference between the Steve and the Jack and Steve system was that the former focused on collaborative task execution and did not represent multiple competing ways to accomplish a task. (Steve would represent multiple alternative plans, but the current state of the world would always uniquely identify a "best" plan that all agents would be in agreement with.) We generalized the Steve task representation to encode multiple competing courses of action (recipes) for accomplishing a task. This allows agents to negotiate over tasks and express emotions and coping behaviors that may indicate varying preferences over alternatives [48].

Integrating CBI's coping model motivated further changes and resulted in a tight integration between appraisal, coping, and task reasoning that closely follows the cognitive appraisal theories of Richard Lazarus [25], and, in the end, elevated emotion processing to a central organizing construct for the virtual human's behavior. Recall this theory posits that human behavior is organized around appraisal and coping. Appraisal generates emotion by assessing the person–environment relationship and coping is the process of dealing with emotion, either by acting externally on the world (problem-focused coping), or by acting internally to change beliefs or attention (emotion-focused coping). Coping and appraisal interact and unfold over time, supporting the temporal character of emotion highlighted by CBI: an agent may "feel" distress for an event (appraisal), which motivates the shifting of blame (coping), which leads to anger (re-appraisal).

Through integrating CBI's coping model, coping strategies were recast explicitly into procedures that updated Steve's task representations and reasoning processes. For example, a strategy like problem-focused coping might motivate the task reasoner to refine its plans or motivate the agent to propose a particular course of action to the learner. Emotion-focused strategies like denial or shifting blame operate on the task representations, influencing the assignment of responsibility or altering the probability or utility of task consequences [29]. As many coping responses relate to past actions or decisions, we found it necessary to extend Steve's task representation to explicitly encode a causal history of past events and actions. Thus, appraisal and coping operate over a unified representation of past, present, and future task-related information.

Some of the key innovations of CBI and Jack and Steve have not, as of yet, been integrated into the MRE system, including planning stances and CBI's emphasis on ego-identity. Although the integrated system does allow more flexibility in the plan generation process than the original Steve system, we have not adopted the full generative planning approach underlying Jack and Steve that planning stances require. In terms of cognitive appraisal, both the CBI and Lazarus' theories emphasize the importance of ego-identity. However, given Émile's heavy emphasis on task-related appraisals and domain-independent appraisal mechanisms, we have not found a suitable general way to represent the fact that certain threats are more central to an agent's makeup than others.

5.2 Physical Behavior

Internally, the virtual humans are continually perceiving the events surrounding them, understanding utterances, updating their beliefs, formulating and revising plans, generating emotional appraisals, and choosing actions. Virtual humans in the MRE attempt to manifest the rich dynamics of this cognitive and emotional inner state through each character's external behavior using the same verbal and non-verbal cues that people use to understand one another. The key challenge is the range of behaviors that must be seamlessly integrated: each character's body movements must reflect its awareness of events in the virtual world, its physical actions, the myriad of non-verbal signals that accompany speech during social interactions (e.g. gaze shifts, head movements, and gestures), and its emotional reactions. Expressive physical behavior in the MRE agents integrates the task-related non-verbal behaviors of the Steve system and the coping behaviors of CBI, leveraging the close integration of task-related and social information maintained by the virtual human's mental state.

Our use of gaze illustrates this tight integration. Since gaze indicates a character's focus of attention, it is a key element in any model of outward behavior, and must be closely synchronized to the character's inner thoughts. Prior work on gaze in virtual humans has considered either task-related gaze [9] or social gaze [5] but has not produced an integrated model of the two. Our gaze model is driven by our cognitive model, which interleaves task-related behaviors, social behaviors, and attention capture. Task-related behaviors (e.g. checking the status of a goal or monitoring for an expected effect or action) trigger a corresponding gaze shift, as does attention capture (e.g. hearing a new sound in the environment). Gaze during social interactions is driven by the dialogue state and the state of the virtual human's own processing, including gaze at an interlocutor who is speaking, gaze aversion during utterance planning (to claim or hold the turn), gaze at an addressee when speaking, and gaze when expecting someone to speak. This tight integration of gaze behaviors to our underlying cognitive model ensures that the outward attention of the virtual humans is synchronized with their inner thoughts.

Body movements are also critical for conveying emotional changes, including facial expressions, gestures, posture, gaze, and head movements. In humans, these behaviors are signals and as such they can be used intentionally by an individual to inform or deceive but can also unintentionally reveal information about the individual's internal emotional state. Thus a person's behavior may express anger because they feel it or because they want others to think they feel it or for both reasons. With the exception of CBI, prior work on emotional expression in virtual humans focused on either the intentional use of emotional expression or revealing the agent's "true" internal emotional state [33]. Our work attempts to integrate these aspects by tying expressive behavior to coping behavior, generalizing the mechanism used in

CBI. Emotional changes in the virtual human unfold as a consequence of Soar operators updating the task representation. These operators provide a focus for emotional processes, invoking coping strategies to address the resulting emotions which in turn leads to expressive behaviors. This focus on operators both centers emotional expression on the agent's current internal cognitive processing but also allows coping to alter the relation of the expression to those internal cognitive processes. Thus, when making amends, our virtual humans might freely express their true appraisal-based feelings of guilt and concern, for example through facial expressions, gestures, posture, gaze, and head movements. However, when shifting responsibility, they might suppress an initial expression of guilt and rather express anger at the character they are blaming, to reflect a more calculated attempt to persuade others.

Finally, a wide range of body movements are typically closely linked to speech, movements that emphasize, augment, and even supplant components of the spoken linguistic information. Consistent with this close relation, this non-verbal behavior, which can include hand–arm gestures, head movements, and postural shifts, is typically synchronized in time with the speech. Realizing this synchronization faces the challenge that we do not have an incremental model of speech production. Such a model would allow us to tie non-verbal behaviors to speech production operations much like the gaze and coping behaviors are tied to cognitive operations. Rather, our approach is to build on the gesture scheduling approach developed for CBI, which plans the utterance out and annotates it with non-verbal behavior. The annotated utterance is then passed to a text-to-speech generation system that schedules both the verbal and non-verbal behavior, using the BEAT system [8]. This approach is similar to the work of Cassell et al. [5]. Our work differs in the structure passed to the gesture annotation process, in order to capture the myriad ways that the non-verbal behavior can relate to the spoken dialogue and the internal state of the virtual human. Specifically, while both systems pass the syntactic, semantic and pragmatic structure of the utterance, we additionally pass the emotional appraisal and coping information associated with the components of the utterance. The gesture annotation process uses this information to annotate the utterance with gestures, head movements, eyebrow lifts, and eye flashes.

Some key aspects of Carmen's Bright IDEAS have not been incorporated into the current MRE system. CBI made effective use of the dramatic impact of pauses in speech, which can convey emotional turmoil or deliberation. CBI agents also had a far richer repertoire of expressive behaviors, particularly variability in motions associated with the eyes, eyelids, and brows. Such expressivity is not currently possible with the speech and animation systems used in the MRE system. While the MRE uses more realistic graphical models than the preceding three systems, they were developed by a third-party vendor, so we had less creative control over the animation than the other systems, which were developed in-house. Further the stylized 2D animation used in CBI supported a greater range of recognizable expressions. The greater complexity of MRE's natural language modules also limits the range of expressive behavior. In contrast to CBI, which used voice actors, MRE utilizes a fully automated speech generation pipeline, which provides the capability of dynamically generating a wide range of utterances, but allows far less nuanced speech, in terms of both emotional dynamics and creative use of pauses.

6 Conclusion

This chapter has shown the evolution of our ideas on expressive behaviors and their integration in our current virtual humans. Steve's ability to interleave task-related behaviors and face-to-face dialogue in dynamic virtual worlds serves as the foundation for the virtual humans in our MRE system. The Jack and Steve system contributed a model of task-oriented emotional appraisal (Émile) and a model of socially situated planning. The CBI system contributed a complementary model of emotional appraisal focusing on social relationships and ego-identity, as well as a model of coping and of the effect of emotions and coping on physical behavior. Our MRE virtual humans integrate many of the ideas from these three prior systems, while significantly extending our prior work in some areas, such as our model of coping. The animation and speech capabilities in these four systems have offered different trade-offs in generality and expressivity, illustrating the fact that any implemented model of expressive behavior must be closely integrated with the animation and speech capabilities available to it; otherwise, it may not be possible to accurately express the distinctions in that model. In our current work, we are continuing to push the frontiers of both our model of expressive behavior and its connection to the latest technologies in animation and speech production.

Acknowledgments

The Office of Naval Research funded the original research on Steve under grant N00014-95-C-0179 and AASERT grant N00014-97-1-0598. Lewis Johnson contributed to the original design of Steve, Randy Stiles and his colleagues developed the graphics software, Allen Munro and his colleagues developed the simulator, and Ben Moore helped link Steve to speech recognition.

The work on Carmen's Bright IDEAS was supported in part by the National Cancer Institute under grant R25CA65520. Our colleagues Lewis Johnson and Kate LaBore contributed significantly to the project.

The Department of the Army funds the MRE project under contract DAAD 19-99-D-0046. We thank our many colleagues who are contributing to the MRE project: Shri Narayanan leads a team working on speech recognition. Randy Hill, Mike van Lent, Changhee Han, and Youngjun Kim are working on models of agent perception. Ed Hovy, Deepak Ravichandran, and

Michael Fleischman are working on natural language understanding and generation. Lewis Johnson, Kate LaBore, Shri Narayanan, and Richard Whitney are working on speech synthesis. Larry Tuch wrote the MRE story line with creative input from Richard Lindheim and technical input on army procedures from Elke Hutto and General Pat O'Neal. Sean Dunn, Sheryl Kwak, Ben Moore, and Marcus Thiébaux created the simulation infrastructure for MRE. Marcus also developed the character animation system for Steve and Jack and Steve. Any opinions, findings, and conclusions expressed in this article are those of the authors and do not necessarily reflect the views of the Department of the Army.

References

1. Ambros-Ingerson, J.A., Steel, S.: Integrating planning, execution and monitoring. In: *Proceedings of the Seventh National Conference on Artificial Intelligence (AAAI-88)* (Morgan Kaufmann, San Mateo, 1988) pp 83–88
2. Berkowitz, L.: *Causes and Consequences of Feelings* (Cambridge University Press 2000)
3. Bindiganavale, R., Schuler, W., Allbeck, J.M., Badler, N.I., Joshi, A.K., Palmer, M.: Dynamically altering agent behaviors using natural language instructions. In: *Proceedings of the Fourth International Conference on Autonomous Agents* (ACM Press, New York 2000) pp 293–300
4. Cassell, J., Bickmore, T., Campbell, L., Vilhjálmsson, H., Yan, H.: Conversation as a system framework: Designing embodied conversational agents. *Embodied Conversational Agents*, ed Cassell, J., Sullivan, J., Prevost, S., Churchill, E. (MIT Press, Cambridge MA 2000)
5. Cassell, J., Pelachaud, C., Badler, N., Steedman, M., Achorn, B., Becket, T., Douville, B., Prevost, S., Stone, M.: Animated conversation: Rule-based generation of facial expression, gesture and spoken intonation for multiple conversational agents. In: *Proceedings of ACM SIGGRAPH '94* (Addison-Wesley, Reading, MA 1994) pp 413–420
6. Cassell, J., Sullivan, J., Prevost, S., Churchill, E. (eds): *Embodied Conversational Agents* (MIT Press, Cambridge, MA 2000)
7. Cassell, J., Thórisson, K.R.: The power of a nod and a glance: Envelope vs. emotional feedback in animated conversational agents. *Applied Artificial Intelligence* 13:519–538 (1999)
8. Cassell, J., Vilhjálmsson, H., Bickmore, T.: BEAT: The behavior expression animation toolkit. In: *Proceedings of ACM SIGGRAPH* (ACM Press, New York 2001) pp 477–486 (Reprint in this volume)
9. Chopra-Khullar, S., Badler, N.I.: Where to look? Automating attending behaviors of virtual human characters. *Autonomous Agents and Multi-Agent Systems* 4(1–2):9–23 (2001)
10. Cohen, P.R., Levesque, H.J.: Teamwork. *Nous* 25(4):487–512 (1991)
11. des Jardins, M., Wolverton, M.J.: Coordinating a distributed planning system. *AI Magazine* 20(4):45–53 (Winter 1999)
12. Duncan Jr., S.: Some signals and rules for taking speaking turns in conversations. In: *Nonverbal Communication*, ed Weitz, S. (Oxford University Press 1974) pp 298–311

13. Elliott, C.: *The Affective Reasoner: A Process Model of Emotions in a Multi-agent System.* PhD thesis (Northwestern University 1992)
14. Fleischman, M., Hovy, E.: Emotional variation in speech-based natural language generation. In: *Proceedings of the International Natural Language Generation Conference* (Arden House, New York 2002)
15. Freedman, N.: The analysis of movement behavior during the clinical interview. In: *Studies in Dyadic Communication*, ed Siegman, A.W., Pope, B. (Pergamon Press, New York 1972) pp 177–210
16. Gratch, J.: Émile: Marshalling passions in training and education. In: *Proceedings of the Fourth International Conference on Autonomous Agents* (ACM Press, New York 2000) pp 325–332
17. Gratch, J.: Socially situated planning. In: *Socially Intelligent Agents: Creating Relationships with Computers and Robots*, ed Cañamero, L., Dautenhahn, K., Bond, A.H., Edmonds, B. (Kluwer Academic, Dordrecht 2002) pp 181–188
18. Gratch, J., Marsella, S.: Tears and fears: Modeling emotions and emotional behaviors in synthetic agents. In: *Proceedings of the Fifth International Conference on Autonomous Agents* (ACM Press, New York 2001) pp 278–285
19. Grosz, B.J., Kraus, S.: Collaborative plans for complex group action. *Artificial Intelligence* **86**(2):269–357 (1996)
20. Grosz, B.J., Sidner, C.L.: Attention, intentions, and the structure of discourse. *Computational Linguistics* **12**(3):175–204 (1986)
21. Johnson, W.L., Rickel, J.W., Lester, J.C.: Animated pedagogical agents: Face-to-face interaction in interactive learning environments. *International Journal of Artificial Intelligence in Education* **11**:47–78 (2000)
22. Johnson, W.L., Narayanan, S., Whitney, R., Das, R., Bulut, M., LaBore, C.: Limited domain synthesis of expressive military speech for animated characters. In: *Proceedings of the IEEE Workshop on Speech Synthesis*, Santa Monica, CA (2002)
23. Kambhampati, S., Knoblock, C.A., Yang, Q.: Planning as refinement search: A unified framework for evaluating design tradeoffs in partial-order planning. *Artificial Intelligence* **76**:167–238 (1995)
24. Laird, J.E., Newell, A., Rosenbloom, P.S.: Soar: An architecture for general intelligence. *Artificial Intelligence* **33**(1):1–64 (1987)
25. Lazarus, R.S.: *Emotion and Adaptation* (Oxford University Press 1991)
26. Lester, J.C., Towns, S.G., Callaway, C.B., Voerman, J.L., FitzGerald, P.J.: Deictic and emotive communication in animation pedagogical agents. In: *Embodied Conversational Agents*, ed Cassell, J., Sullivan, J., Prevost, S., Churchill, E. (MIT Press, Cambridge, MA 2000)
27. Lester, J.C., Voerman, J.L., Towns, S.G., Callaway, C.B.: Deictic believability: Coordinating gesture, locomotion, and speech in lifelike pedagogical agents. *Applied Artificial Intelligence* **13**:383–414 (1999)
28. Lester, J.C., Zettlemoyer, L.S., Gregoire, J., Bares, W.H.: Explanatory lifelike avatars: Performing user-designed tasks in 3d learning environments. In: *Proceedings of the Third International Conference on Autonomous Agents* (ACM Press, New York 1999)
29. Marsella, S., Gratch, J.: Modeling coping behavior in virtual humans: Don't worry, be happy. In: *Proceedings of the Second International Joint Conference on Autonomous Agents and Multi-Agent Systems* (ACM Press, New York 2003)

30. Marsella, S., Johnson, W.L., LaBore, C.: Interactive pedagogical drama for health interventions. In: *Proceedings of the 11th International Conference on Artificial Intelligence in Education* (IOS Press 2003)

31. Marsella, S.C., Johnson, W.L., LaBore, C.: Interactive pedagogical drama. In: *Proceedings of the Fourth International Conference on Autonomous Agents* (ACM Press, New York 2000) pp 301–308

32. Matheson, C., Poesio, M., Traum, D.: Modelling grounding and discourse obligations using update rules. In: *Proceedings of the First Conference of the North American Chapter of the Association for Computational Linguistics* (2000)

33. Neal Reilly, W.S.: *Believable Social and Emotional Agents*. PhD thesis (School of Computer Science, Carnegie Mellon University 1996), Technical Report CMU-CS-96-138

34. Newell, A.: *Unified Theories of Cognition* (Harvard University Press 1990)

35. Ortony, A., Clore, G.L., Collins, A.: *The Cognitive Structure of Emotions* (Cambridge University Press 1988)

36. Pelachaud, C., Badler, N.I., Steedman, M.: Generating facial expressions for speech. *Cognitive Science* **20**(1):1–46 (1996)

37. Pelachaud, C., Carofiglio, V., De Carolis, B., de Rosis, F., Poggi, I.: Embodied contextual agent in information delivering application. In: *Proceedings of the First International Joint Conference on Autonomous Agents and Multi-Agent Systems* (ACM Press, New York 2001) pp 758–765

38. Penley, J., Tomaka, J.: Associations among the big five, emotional responses, and coping with acute stress. *Personality and Individual Differences* **32**:1215–1228 (2002)

39. Poggi, I., Pelachaud, C.: Emotional meaning and expression in performative faces. In: *International Workshop on Affect in Interactions: Towards a New Generation of Interfaces*, Siena, Italy (1999)

40. Rickel, J., Johnson, W.L.: Animated agents for procedural training in virtual reality: Perception, cognition, and motor control. *Applied Artificial Intelligence* **13**:343–382 (1999)

41. Rickel, J., Johnson, W.L.: Extending virtual humans to support team training in virtual reality. In: *Exploring Artificial Intelligence in the New Millenium*, ed Lakemayer, G., Nebel, B. (Morgan Kaufmann, San Francisco 2002) pp 217–238

42. Rickel, J., Johnson, W.L.: Task-oriented collaboration with embodied agents in virtual worlds. In: *Embodied Conversational Agents*, ed Cassell, J., Sullivan, J., Prevost, S., Churchill, E. (MIT Press, Cambridge, MA 2000)

43. Rickel, J., Johnson, W.L.: Virtual humans for team training in virtual reality. In: *Proceedings of the Ninth International Conference on Artificial Intelligence in Education* (IOS Press, Amsterdam 1999) pp 578–585

44. Rickel, J., Marsella, S., Gratch, J., Hill, R., Traum, D., Swartout, W.: Toward a new generation of virtual humans for interactive experiences. *IEEE Intelligent Systems* **17**(4):32–38 (2002)

45. Scherer, K.R.: Appraisal considered as a process of multilevel sequential checking. In: *Appraisal Processes in Emotion: Theory, Methods, and Research*, ed Scherer, K.R., Schorr, A., Johnstone, T. (Oxford University Press 2001) pp 92–120

46. Swartout, W., Hill, R., Gratch, J., Johnson, W.L., Kyriakakis, C., LaBore, C., Lindheim, R., Marsella, S., Miraglia, D., Moore, B., Morie, J., Rickel, J., Thiébaux, M., Tuch, L., Whitney, R., Douglas, J.: Toward the Holodeck: Integrating graphics, sound, character and story. In: *Proceedings of the Fifth*

International Conference on Autonomous Agents (ACM Press, New York 2001) pp 409–416

47. Traum, D., Rickel, J.: Embodied agents for multi-party dialogue in immersive virtual worlds. In: *Proceedings of the First International Joint Conference on Autonomous Agents and Multi-Agent Systems* (ACM Press, New York 2002) pp 766–773

48. Traum, D., Rickel, J., Gratch, J., Marsella, S.: Negotiation over tasks in hybrid human-agent teams for simulation-based training. In: *Proceedings of the Second International Joint Conference on Autonomous Agents and Multi-Agent Systems* (ACM Press, New York 2003)

49. Traum, D.R.: *A Computational Theory of Grounding in Natural Language Conversation.* PhD thesis (Department of Computer Science, University of Rochester, 1994)

50. Traum, D.R., Hinkelman, E.A.: Conversation acts in task-oriented dialogue. *Computational Intelligence* **8**(3):575–599 (1992)

51. Weld, D.S.: An introduction to least commitment planning. *AI Magazine* **15**(4):27–61 (1994)

Playing with Agents – Agents in Social and Dramatic Games

Ana Paiva, Rui Prada, Isabel Machado, Carlos Martinho, Marco Vala, and
André Silva

IST and Instituto de Engenharia de Sistemas e Computadores-INESC-ID
Rua Alves Redol, 9, 1000-029 Lisboa, Portugal
Ana.Paiva@inesc.pt

Summary. In this chapter we describe the experiences we had at our group in
building synthetic characters for virtual story-telling and games applications. We
provide an analysis framework useful to classify the autonomy of synthetic characters
versus the control of the users over those characters. In this framework we distinguish
several types of autonomy of characters, in particular: scripted; partially scripted;
influenced by role; and autonomous. These types of autonomy can be found in some
of the systems we have built at our group, namely Tristão and Isolda, Papous,
Teatrix, and FantasyA.

1 Introduction

When developing virtual story-telling environments, be they for entertainment
or education, one of the major goals is to capture the interest and attention
of the user, put him or her under the skin of the story characters, and provide
a narrative experience that he or she will remember and want to return to.
Like films or games, virtual story-telling environments aim at providing the
user with dramatic experiences, allowing the user's suspension of disbelief.
Associated to a large extent with the story-telling environments, intelligent
agents and synthetic characters are now being used as the way to build the
characters in such environments. Their role is fundamental when we move
from the traditional linear story to interactive stories or games where the
actions of the user affect the development of the story. Most specifically, work
on intelligent agents and synthetic characters aims at providing autonomous
characters with a rich personality and emotional states that are flexible enough
to respond to the user's demands creating such suspension of disbelief. The
great master of believability in animation, Walt Disney, once said: "I think
that we must know these fellows [characters in the story] definitively before we
can draw them" [22]. Their physical appearances, their personality, the way
they behave, walk, and talk, are all fundamental aspects to make the viewer
engage in a truly captivating experience with the characters.

However, in stories and games, such emotional engagement also arises from believable "situations". The seven dwarfs mourning Snow White in the Walt Disney film (see [22]) is an emotional experience, not only because of the characters' personalities, behavior, and expressions, but fundamentally because of the situation and the function that such a scene stands for in the development of the story. The sequence of the story, the way it is told, its structure, its narrative elements are all components necessary for the engagement of the user. The actions of the characters in a play normally flow from a starting point where an initial complication is established, go through the climax point, and down to the conclusion of the story. In drama studies these three points are part of Freytag's triangle, which was proposed as the structure of a dramatic incident. In fact, the functions of the actions of the characters and their causality according to many writers, are the most important aspects of a story.

So, when building synthetic characters for virtual story telling or games we must generate intelligent and emotional behavior in order to achieve interactivity and believability of the characters, and at the same time, guarantee some sequence and some structure in the characters' actions to meet these dramatic incidents. This means that on one hand the characters must be autonomous, have personality and emotions to generate believable situations, and on the other, the characters' actions must be restricted to follow a certain narrative structure. So, there are two opposing goals and a balance therefore must be found. Given the set of systems we have built so far, we believe that this balance is a result of two important factors: the type of virtual environment and the interaction established with the user.

In this chapter we will therefore discuss these two aspects of intelligent agents and synthetic characters in virtual environments, which are: autonomy of the characters and interactivity/user control.

To do so, we will provide an initial discussion of the problems and then describe a set of systems developed at GAIPS in INESC-ID to illustrate some of the many different approaches that can be taken to solve these problems.

2 Synthetic Characters in Interactive Story Telling

In general, work on synthetic characters in interactive story telling environments aims at providing characters in stories with a rich personality and emotional state, which will be used as the characters in the portrayed story. However, agents can play other roles in interactive story telling or games. Among others, we can distinguish the following:

Story tellers. Embodied conversational characters can tell stories. Examples are Sam or Papous. In both cases, the character, an embodied conversational agent, is able to establish a story presentation with the user. In telling the story the character uses emotional expressions, speech, and gestures to convey the message in the story.

Characters. Perhaps the type most used (see, e.g. Teatrix [12], Marc Cavazza [5], Carmen's Bright IDEAS [13]), characters play roles and act out their stories.

Actors. Whereas characters act as if they were in a situation (the story situation) according to their internal goals, dictated by their role, actors just follow a script (provided by a different entity) and act accordingly.

Director. Some systems, instead of creating characters that follow a certain behavior, have a director that generates scripts for the synthetic actors. Such a director can also be implemented using an agent-oriented approach, with sensors that allow it to capture the state of the world, and with actuators that are indeed the scripts sent to the actors.

Camera agent. Similarly to the director, the camera can also be built as an agent that perceives the virtual world though its sensors and acts on it, by moving, focusing, zooming, etc.

2.1 Degrees of Autonomy of Characters

In general an agent can be seen as "a computer system that is situated in some environment and that is capable of autonomous actions in that environment in order to meet its design objectives" [24]. Although there are several different notions of what is an intelligent agent, in most of the definitions "autonomy" is central to the notion of agency. In addition, certain definitions entail pro-activeness of the agents, on top of their capability to act in an autonomous way. When we adopt this notion of agency in the context of interactive story telling, and considering the most common situation where agents act as characters in a story, the degrees of autonomy[1] can be quite diverse. We can distinguish the following possibilities:

Scripted. In this case, the characters do not have any autonomous behavior; they simply follow a script provided by the programmer or the author. Such a script is often embedded in the code of the character, which makes this approach obviously not very flexible. In fact, it requires a large amount of work to allow for interactivity, as all the possible actions of the user much be considered in the script. This type of approach is the one usually followed in computer games.

Partially Scripted. Although following a script, some systems do allow for the characters to have some independent autonomous behavior (kind of improvisational actions) to guarantee the believability of the characters. For example, characters can improvise some idle movements, move as they like, etc. Obviously, the degree in which the character is controlled is a result of the type of scripting language used.

Directed. Characters follow a script given to them by a director, which can change and adapt it in real time. As with the previous cases, there can

---

[1] See [4] for a discussion on different types of autonomy.

be different levels of scripting, ranging from completely controlled to only
partially scripted. The difference is that the character (actor) must adapt
in real time to the script sent by the director.

Constrained by role. Characters perform autonomously constrained by the
role they play in the story/play. That is, the characters do not have available the whole possible range of actions allowed for all characters, but
only a few, related to their role in the story. This approach was followed
in the system Teatrix [16], which will be described later.

Autonomous. Here the characters decide, according to their perception of the
environment, which action to perform. If things change in the environment (perhaps by the actions of the user), characters are able to adapt to
such changes and respond appropriately. The narrative structure in this
situation is guaranteed by the way the characters perceive the environment, their goals, and actions. Obviously there is no straightforward way
of guaranteeing that the story will follow a certain path. The story will
emerge from the actions of the characters.

Some applications may combine more than one type of autonomy in their
characters, for example having both autonomous and scripted characters.

2.2 Degrees of Control: the Role of the User

The other issue concerns the role of the user, which consequently affects the
degree of autonomy of the agents in relation to that user. On one extreme,
embodied social agents can be "fully" autonomous, and can interact with
the user, through speech, facial expressions and gestures. They may recognize
and respond to verbal and non-verbal input. They can exhibit verbal and non-
verbal output, combined with turn-taking and feedback, necessary in social
interactions [2]. They nod, glance, jump, point, explain, etc., in reaction to the
user. Examples of such agents are Rea [3], Steve [18], Cosmo [10], and others.
In general, these agents are not controlled by the user and interact with the
users in a similar way that a human would. They are the ones to decide
autonomously what and how to perform their tasks. The user is interacting
with a third person in an interactive environment. On the other extreme,
we have avatars, which are puppet-like characters, almost fully controlled by
users that mimic, to the most detailed element, all the users' intended actions.

In the middle of these two extremes there are semi-autonomous avatars
[19]. These combine some aspects related to the autonomy of the agents with
some control of the avatars. Sengers et al. [19] proposed the notion of semi-
autonomous avatars as "agents/avatars that have their own behaviors and
intentionality, but are intimately tied to the user's actions". However, there
are different degrees of these ties, and we can distinguish at least the following
types of control of the characters:

Puppet-like control. In this type of control, characters are like puppets controlled by the user/player. The user decides where to move the character,

how to move it, what to pick, etc. This includes both *motion control* and *behavior control*. This is the most usual type of control found in avatars in computer games.

Guidance. In this type of control the user guides the character, giving it directives on where to go, but not deciding completely how to go.

Influence. In this type of control the user does not control the actions of the character but influences certain aspects of its behavior (e.g. changing characteristics, power, emotional state, etc.).

"God"-like control. This type of control does not apply specifically to the characters but rather to the environment. For example, the user is able to change some characteristics in the story environment (like, for example, add a prop) which will direct the storyline toward a certain path. This type of user interaction is used by Cavazza et al. [5].

No control. Finally, certain characters are not controllable by the user (thus autonomous in relation to the user) and the characters perform in an autonomous way in the system.

3 Some Applications

We will now describe some of the applications of synthetic characters in games and virtual story-telling environments developed by GAIPS (INESC-ID), focusing on the topics just discussed: namely, autonomy of the characters and user's control.

3.1 Tristão and Isolda

S3A was a system developed for EXPO'98 in Lisbon. On entering the S3A room of the Territory Pavilion, the visitor is driven to the beginning of Ages, "[...] to Atlantis, a place where humans and dolphins had a special way to communicate with each other. This communication was based on an apparatus that helped humans to express their feelings to the dolphins." The apparatus is a porcelain sculpture of a dolphin, equipped with four pressure-button sensors, standing in the middle of the exhibition room, in front of a wide screen, as shown in Fig. 1. The wide screen features two synthetic dolphins, Tristão and Isolda, swimming in the River Sado.

To communicate with Isolda and influence her emotional state, the visitor can, at any time, approach the sculpture and touch one of the buttons. The four types of emotions that the visitor can express to Isolda are represented in the four sensors of Fig. 1. Note that the user does not control the actions of the synthetic dolphin, but he or she only *influences* its emotional state, which in turn will then influence its behavior.

To support the development of Tristão and Isolda, an architecture based on a theatrical metaphor was adopted. The developed system was instanced

Fig. 1. Interface and sensors

over a modular architectural framework composed of three functional units (or modules):

- The *dynamic script-writer* (or *mind module*) is responsible for the creation of the narrative. It manages all the agents at the narrative level and controls the emotional believability of the characters. It basically generates a set of directives for the cast of actors.
- The *theatrical company* (or *body module*), with its director and cast of actors, interprets the narrative and acts upon it. It manages the geometrical and audio-visual planning and controls the life-like believability of all characters.
- The *virtual stage manager* (or *world module*) controls all aspects related to the audio-visual display of the character performance as well as handling the virtual camera and the stage special effects.

Figure 2 shows the overall architecture. As we can see there, each agent is implemented by three distinct images: a mind image, a body image, and a world image. Each image is managed by its associated module. Hence, each module implements a specific part of *all* the agents. Whilst the mind of the agent, can be seen as generating its behavior in an autonomous way, the body image is only following the improvisation directives provided by the mind. This approach in a way follows the idea of a director (here named dynamic script-writer) that provides directives to the characters (here the bodies of the characters).

3.2 Papous

Papous (see Fig. 3) is a synthetic character that acts as a virtual story teller. The ultimate goal is to obtain a synthetic character that tells stories in an

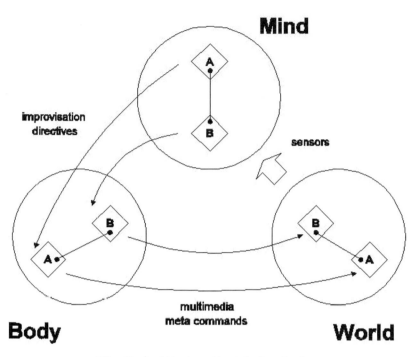

Fig. 2. Architecture theatrical metaphor

expressive and believable way, just as a real human story teller would do, and thus in an autonomous way.

In its first version, Papous (described in [20]) is a simplification of the story teller idea and can be seen as a virtual narrator who reads a text enriched with control tags.

Papous is therefore controlled like a puppet by the story-writer that not only writes the story but also provides a set of markup elements that help the character to perform the story telling. In fact, these tags allow the story-writer to script the behavior of Papous. There are four types of tags: behavior tags, where a specific action or gesture is scripted; scene tags, which allow for Papous to change the scene where he tells the story; illumination tags, to allow a new illumination pattern of the scene; and emotion tags, to change the emotional state of Papous. The texts, enriched with these tags, are then processed by Papous's different modules, which contain an affective speech module and an affective body expression module.

The architecture of Papous has five components: the Input Manager, the Environment Control, the Deliberative Module, the Affective Speech, and the Affective Body Expression. The Input Manager is the component responsible for processing the text file that contains the story, checking it for syntax and

Fig. 3. Papous

Tag type	Function
Behavior	Indicate an action that the character should perform
Scene	Specify a new scene where the character should be integrated
Illumination	Specify a new illumination pattern
Emotion	Explicitly modify the emotional state of the character

Table 1. Tag types

semantic errors, and taking the necessary actions to ensure that the data are correct and ready for the other components to process.

The Environment Control is responsible for managing the environment in which the character is immersed. The Deliberative Module acts as the mind of the character and, therefore, contains its internal emotional state and controls the character's actions. The Affective Speech is responsible for the voice of the character. The Affective Body Expression handles the appearance of the character. The Input Manager receives the annotated story file and a set of configuration files as input. This module parses the annotated text and generates tag-oriented information that is sent to the Environment Control and Deliberative Module components. Table 1 summarizes the four types of tags available and explains the function of each one. The list of available tags of each type is defined in a configuration file and depends solely on the available scenes and animations. We have defined a small set of tags for demonstration purposes.

The story-writer is free to use the tags as he or she wants, taking into consideration the context of the story. For example, if the writer wants to emphasize a particularly scary part of the story, he or she should specify the appropriate emotional state. The chosen emotional state will change the voice and the behavior of the character and, therefore, suit the writer's intentions.

The Deliberative Module receives emotion and behavior tags and sends commands to the Affective Speech and the Affective Body Expression components. In fact, the emotion tags update the internal emotional state indicating which emotion should be changed and the new value that it must have. Internally, the emotional state of the character is represented by a set of numerical discrete values, for each of the six emotions represented. The emotional state affects the voice and the behavior of the character.

The Affective Speech component receives sentences and the current emotional state from the Deliberative Module, and synthesizes the sentences using the voice to express the current emotions. The precision with which we control the character's voice depends mostly on the underlying text-to-speech (TTS) system. The current TTS system allows the control of seven parameters to completely define the voice. To transmit emotions through the voice we established a series of relations between emotions and voice parameters based on theories of the interrelationship between speech and emotion. The Affective Body Expression component receives the current emotional state from the Deliberative Module and changes the character body in order to express the desired emotions. It can also receive commands to perform gestures explicitly indicated in the story (using behavior tags). The body expression component is provided by the SAFIRA toolkit [23]. This component is able to perform real-time blending between animations and body postures to convey the desired emotions. However, at the current state of development, the emotions affect only the face of the character. For demonstration purposes we considered two facial animations (happy and sad) that are related to the happiness threshold.

We have also defined a set of iconic gestures (big, small, tall, and short) that can be explicitly indicated in the story. The writer should be careful in using behavior tags to perform explicit gestures, as they only benefit the story if the performed action is coherent with the current story context.

Although quite simple, Papous is an interesting example of how a user (writer) can control some of the actions of the character and how that control is transformed into behaviors that the character performs.

3.3 Teatrix

Teatrix is a collaborative virtual environment for story creation by young children (4 to 8 years old), which aims at providing effective support for children developing their notions of narrative through the dramatization of different situations.

Children can create their stories by selecting the scenes, characters, and props in the story, and then by performing the story through control of the actions of their characters.

In Teatrix, we developed the concept of "virtual dramatis personae" which is a virtual actor with an associated role to play. A role, according to [8], is a class of individuals whose prototypical behaviors, relationships, and interactions are known to both the actors and the audience. To develop such a notion of a role in an interactive virtual environment, we relied on the work by Propp [17] on folk tales (similarly to the work by Spierling et al. [21]). One of the most important developments of Propp's theory was the description of functions for the characters in fairy tales. By function we mean "as an act of a character, defined from the point of view of its significance for the course of action". And, according to Propp: "functions of characters serve as stable, constant elements in a tale, independent of how and by whom they are fulfilled". That is, the functions constitute fundamental elements of a tale.

Based on this, we have created the following roles in Teatrix (see Fig. 4):

Villain – The role of the villain is to disturb the peace of the happy family, to cause misfortune, damage, or harm. The villain may be a dragon, a devil, a witch, a stepmother, or even a little boy or a girl. One of the functions of the villain is "villainy".

Hero/Heroine – Introduced in the initial situation. Although Propp considers two types of heroes, the seekers, who go in search of a beloved element, and the victimized heroes, who are themselves the victims of villainy, in Teatrix we do not make that distinction.

Magician (or magic element) – Has special functions in the story and can be represented in many forms. For example: (i) an animal (a horse, a bird, etc.); (ii) objects out of which the magical helpers appear (a ring, a lantern, etc.); (iii) objects with magical properties (a ring, a sword, etc.) or (iv) qualities or capacities given directly to the hero/heroine.

Beloved one and Family – Usually described in the initial situation, and often subject to harm by the villain.

Donor (or the provider) – It is from this person that the hero obtains some agent (sometimes magical), which allows the hero to eliminate the misfortune.

Fig. 4. Roles of characters in Teatrix

Each role has a set of functions associated to it. For example, one of the most important functions of the villain is villainy – that is, the villain causes harm or injury to a member of the family. The dramatis personae in Teatrix's stories are implemented as agents inhabiting and interacting in 3D worlds (scenes of the play), which result from a backstage phase where the scenes, the actors, the props, and the roles are chosen. Each of these dramatis personae is the conjunction of an actor and a role. An actor is the physical representation or appearance of a character in the 3D world. From this distinction between actor and role a set of combinations can be derived, and a wide variety of possibilities can happen. The architecture to implement these dramatis personae is composed of five components: the mind, the body, the sensors, the effectors, and the inventory. The main aspect of the agents in Teatrix is that their actions are constrained by the roles they play (and thus the associated functions), and therefore their autonomy is restricted.

But in Teatrix we have two types of characters: those controlled by the system (as described above) and those controlled by the user. To control the characters Teatrix provides the children with a set of actions which they can select at acting time (see Fig. 5). These actions are associated not only with the character performing them but also with the props that the character owns at each instant. This defined set of actions provides the children with motion control (i.e. each child can move their character around the scene by using the move action) and a type of behavior control, achieved through assignment of a role to the characters and with the use of the props. The child can pick objects, drop them, use props on other characters (e.g. use a stick to hit another character), or even talk.

In addition to the motion control, children also have the possibility to reflect upon their characters' behaviors at story creation time and control that behavior. This meta level of control is implemented as a tool called the "hot-seating", which gives the children the possibility to freeze the story, put themselves into their characters' shoes, and explain the characters' behaviors [1]. When a child enters the "hot-seating" he or she can reflect on the behavior of the character. These reflection moments may occur at the child's demand or when the application detects that a character is not in character (see [11] for further details). With this tool we aimed at providing the children with more information about the story, which, we believed, would lead to a richer type of collaboration within the story world.

3.4 FantasyA and SenToy

FantasyA is a computer game that uses emotions in such a way as to engage the user in the game. In *FantasyA* two characters fight a duel where emotions are used as the driving elements in the action tendencies of the characters. By playing the game, the user influences the emotional state of his or her character which in turn will act according to its internal emotional state. The

Fig. 5. Control of characters in Teatrix

characters in the game must cast different types of spells, either offensive or defensive, in order to win the duels.

Characters in the game are able to express emotions by their behavior (their spells) and, in parallel, by their body movements and postures. Note that the emotional body movements and postures are extremely important for game mechanics, because the player must be able to recognize all the emotional states in order to discover the combinations that produce each action.

The characters themselves can be of two types: *influenced* by the user or fully controlled by the system (against whom the user will play). In both cases, characters use their emotions to decide what action to take. This action selection is based on the emotion theories of Lazarus [9], Darwin [6], and Ekman [7], which serve as inspiration for us to formulate the action tendencies of the six possible emotions in the game: Happiness, Sadness, Fear, Anger, Gloat, and Surprise.

Each character decides what action to perform (what spell to cast) according to its internal emotional state and what it perceives from the opponent's emotion. So we defined for each character based on its personality a set of action tendencies taking into account their opponent's emotions. When the

Fig. 6. FantasyA

decision is being made, the character compares both its action tendencies and the opponent's ones and decides what will be the best one for it (by performing a simple search). Although relatively simple, the characters in FantasyA are able to reason about the others' emotions and act taking them into account. This not only makes the characters more difficult to beat, but it also makes them more believable, as they act as a player.

The user's control of his or her character is achieved through SenToy, a tangible interface for affective control of a synthetic character. To play, the user must understand the emotional state of his or her opponent, which is achieved through animations (featuring affective body expressions) of the character and influence the emotional state of the character by performing a set of gestures associated with each emotion.

SenToy (see Fig. 7) is an explicit sensorial interface equipped with three sets of sensors (see [14] for more details). The first and most important is the set of accelerometers, which measure the acceleration that the SenToy is subjected to. The second set of sensors is analog and these are used to determine the position of SenToy's limbs. The third set of sensors is digital, and these are used to indicate whether the hands of the doll are placed over the eyes or not. Since the emotions/actions cannot be obtained directly from the rather complex data received from the SenToy sensors, a signal-processing module (Stimuli Acquisition module) was required. This module was built to capture the patterns of each of the six chosen emotions: Happiness, Sadness, Fear, Anger, Gloat, and Surprise. The emotions are inferred by the characteristics of these signals, mainly by the information given by the accelerometers, through which one can determine the SenToy's attitude (angle) and motion characteristics such as the direction of the movement and its intensity. As an example, the emotion Sad is detected when the SenToy is bent forward (determined by the Sentoy's attitude), and the emotion Angry is identified when the doll is shaken (generating a fast and intense variation in the X-axis). The position of the limbs complements the information from the accelerometers. For example, the emotion Angry is only detected when the SenToy is shaken with the arms up.

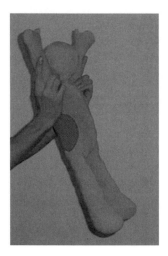

Fig. 7. SenToy

Using these emotions, the player can *influence* the emotional state of the character on the screen. At each turn, the combination of the emotional states of the two characters (the one controlled by the player and the computer opponent) leads to actions, either offensive or defensive, that can damage the opponent or protect the character from future attacks. For example, if the computer opponent is gloating and the player uses the SenToy to influence his or her avatar to become angry, that will surely lead to an offensive action, probably a blast. Then, according to the results of the action, there is a reaction phase where both characters change their emotional state in response. In the previous example, if the blast succeeds then the computer opponent might become fearful and the character controlled by the player will become happy. The game proceeds with the opponent's turn and so forth, until the end of the duel.

One interesting aspect of this game is that, although the players could not control their avatars completely (with both motion and behavior control), they still very much liked the interaction, especially the use of SenToy (see [15] for more details on the results).

4 Conclusions

In this chapter we have discussed two central aspects in the development of synthetic characters for games or virtual story-telling environments: their autonomy and user control. Considering autonomy as a property of some synthetic characters, we have provided a taxonomy which will allow us to classify some different types of autonomy we can find in these characters. To illustrate these issues, we have provided a review of some of the experiences we had at GAIPS (INESC-ID) in building synthetic characters during the past few years. For example, whilst the characters in Tristão and Isolda are fairly autonomous, the characters in Teatrix are constrained by the roles they play in the story.

Indeed, different applications and different types of interaction with the user lead to different approaches taken in terms of the character's autonomy.

Acknowledgments

Thanks to Fernando Rebelo and Marco Costa for the design of the characters (in Teatrix, Papous, and FantasyA) and the image of SenToy . Thanks to all our partners in the NIMIS and Safira projects for their comments and criticisms during the development of these systems. The work on Papous was funded under the Sapiens Program Fundacão para a Ciência e Tecnologia, project number POSI/SRI/41071/2001.

References

1. Bolton, G.: *Towards a theory of drama in education* (Longman, London 1979)
2. Cassell, J.: Nudge nudge wink wink: Elements of face-to-face conversation for embodied conversational agents. In: *Embodied Conversational Agents*, ed Cassell, J., Sullivan, J., Prevost, S., Churchill, E. (The MIT Press, Cambridge, MA 2000) pp 1–27
3. Cassell, J., Bickmore, T., Campbell, L., Vilhjalmsson, H., Yan, H.: Conversation as a system framework: Designing embodied conversational agents. In: *Embodied Conversational Agents*, ed Cassell, J., Sullivan, J., Prevost, S., Churchill, E. (The MIT Press, Cambridge, MA 2000) pp 29–63
4. Castelfranchi, C.: Guarantees of autonomy in cognitive agent architecture. In: *Intelligent Agents*, ed Wooldridge, M., Jennings, N. (Springer, Berlin New York 1995)

5. Cavazza, M., Charles, F., Mead, S.: Interacting with virtual characters. In: *Proceedings AAMAS'02* (ACM Press, New York 2002)
6. Darwin, C.: *The expression of emotions in man and animals*, 3rd edn, ed Paul Ekman (Oxford University Press 1872/1998)
7. Ekman, P.: *Emotion in the Face* (Cambridge University Press 1982)
8. Hayes-Roth, B.: Acting in character. In: *Creating Personalities for Synthetic Actors*, ed Trappl, R., Petta, P. (Springer, Berlin New York 1997)
9. Lazarus, R.: *Emotion and Adaptation* (Oxford University Press 1991)
10. Lester, J., Towns, S., Callaway, C, Voerman, J., FitzGerald, P.: Deictic and emotive communication in animated pedagogical agents. In: *Embodied Conversational Agents*, ed Cassell, J., Sullivan, J., Prevost, S., Churchill, E. (The MIT Press, Cambridge, MA 2000) pp 123–154
11. Machado, I., Martinho, C., Paiva, A.: Once upon a time. In: *Proceedings of the Fall Symposium Series – Narrative Intelligence Symposium* (AAAI Press, Menlo Park, CA 1999)
12. Machado, I., Prada, R., Paiva, A.: Bringing drama to a virtual stage. In: *Proceedings of Collaborative Virtual Environments Conference (CVE'2000)* (ACM Press, New York 2000)
13. Marsella, S., Gratch, J., Rickel, J.: Expressive behaviours for virtual worlds. In: *Life-like Characters. Tools, Affective Functions and Applications*, ed Prendinger, H., Ishizuka, M. (Springer 2003). This volume.
14. Paiva, A., Andersson, G., Hook, K., Mourao, D., Costa, M., Martinho C.: Sentoy in FantasyA: Designing an affective sympathetic interface to a computer game. *Personal and Ubiquitous Computing Journal* **6**(5–6):378–389 (2002)
15. Paiva, A., Costa, M., Chaves, R., Piedade, M., Mourao, D., Hook, G., Andersson, K., Bullock, A.: Sentoy: An affective sympathetic interface. *International Journal of Human-Computer Studies* **59**(1–2):227–235 (2003)
16. Paiva, A., Machado, I., Prada, R.: The child behind the character. *IEEE Transactions on Systems, Man, and Cybernetics* **31**(5):361–368 (2001)
17. Propp, V.: *Morphology of the Folktale* (University of Texas Press 1968)
18. Rickel, J., Johnson, L.: Integrating pedagogical capabilities in a virtual environment agent. In: *Proceedings Autonomous Agents'97* (ACM Press, New York 1997)
19. Sengers, P., Penny, S., Smith, J.: Semi-autonomous avatars. In: *Proceedings Autonomous Agents* (2000)
20. Silva, A., Vala, M., Paiva, A.: Papous: The virtual storyteller. In: *Intelligent Virtual Agents* (Springer, Berlin New York 2001)
21. Spierling, U., Grasbon, D., Braun, N., Iurgel, I.: Setting the scene: Playing digital director in interactive storytelling and creation. *Computers and Graphics* **26**(1):31–44 (2002)
22. Thomas, F., Johnson, O.: *Disney Animation: The Illusion of Life* (Abbeville Press, New York 1981)
23. Vala, M., Paiva, A., Gomes, M.: From virtual bodies to believable characters. *AISB Journal* **1**(2):219–224 (2002)
24. Wooldridge, M.: *An Introduction to MultiAgent Systems* (Wiley, New York 2002)

A Review of the Development of Embodied Presentation Agents and Their Application Fields

Thomas Rist[1], Elisabeth André[2], Stephan Baldes[1], Patrick Gebhard[1], Martin Klesen[1], Michael Kipp[1], Peter Rist[1], and Markus Schmitt[1]

[1] DFKI GmbH, Stuhlsatzenhausweg 3, D-66123 Saarbrücken, Germany
   {rist,baldes,patrick.gebhard,klesen,kipp,mschmitt}@dfki.de,
   pit@blinx.de
[2] Augsburg University, Eichleitnerstr. 30, D-86135 Augsburg, Germany
   andre@informatik.uni-augsburg.de

Summary. Embodied conversational agents provide a promising option for presenting information to users. This contribution revisits a number of past and ongoing systems with animated characters that have been developed at DFKI. While in all systems the purpose of using characters is to convey information to the user, there are significant variations in the style of presentation and the assumed conversational setting. The spectrum of systems includes systems that feature a single, TV-style presentation agent, dialogue systems, as well as systems that deploy multiple inter active characters. We also provide a technical view of these systems and sketch the underlying system architectures of each sample system.

1 Introduction

The last decade has seen a general trend in HCI to make human–computer dialogue more like human–human dialogue. Computers are viewed ever less as tools and ever more as partners or assistants to whom tasks may be delegated. In trying to imitate the skills of human presenters, some R&D projects have begun to deploy animated agents (or characters) in a wide range of different application areas including e-commerce, entertainment, personal assistants, electronic learning and training environments. Based on cartoon drawings, recorded video images of persons, or 3D body models, such agents provide a promising option for interface development as they draw on communication and interaction styles humans are well familiar with.

Starting in the mid-1990s with the development of the presentation agent "PPP Persona", DFKI has contributed to this area of research by introducing a plan-based approach to automate the process of writing scripts that control and constrain the behavior of presentation agents. Since then this approach has been successfully applied to build a number of applications in which information is conveyed either by a single presenter or by a team of presentation agents. Looking at past and current projects conducted at DFKI we observe an ongoing and manifold evolution of character-based presentation systems.

First of all, there is an obvious maturation of a character's visual and audible appearance. This maturation has become possible mainly due to more powerful but nevertheless affordable graphics hardware as well as advances in animation and speech synthesis technology. While many early interface agents were animated on the basis of a relatively small number of hand-drawn 2D cartoons, rich 3D-body models can now be animated in realtime, and improved speech synthesis enables voice qualities that sound less robotic. Improved audio-visual attractiveness alone, however, is only one ingredient for making better virtual characters. In addition, the success of characters in terms of user appreciation and added value in information mediation tasks very much depends on other factors too, including a character's role, competence, and communicative skills relative to an application, and its ability to present itself as a believable virtual personality. With a focus on the structure and complexity of the conversational setting that a character faces, this contribution revisits a number of past and ongoing systems developed at DFKI, discusses impacts on the architectural design, and provides references to related systems.

2 From TV-Style Presenters to Interactive Performances

The choice of domain, tasks, and conversational setting imposes constraints on any prototype development. For instance, in the area of intelligent information presentation with animated characters we observe an ongoing evolution of systems as illustrated in Fig. 1. The first setting refers to applications in which a single character is deployed to present information. From the point of view of the user a generated presentation appears quite similar to watching a TV news speaker or to the display of a video clip because no interaction is foreseen at display time. In contrast, the second setting is typical of applications with characters that are able to converse with a user in some sort of a dialogue (e.g. via spoken or typed natural language, or based on dynamically configured menus). Moving on to the third setting actually means a shift from a face-to-face character–user setting to a user-as-observer setting. That is, two or more characters talk to each other on the screen to convey information to the observing audience. However, no user intervention is foreseen during a performance. This is in contrast to the fourth scenario where we have an open multi-party dialogue setting which allows for both reactive and proactive user participation.

Technically speaking, the fourth scenario is quite challenging since one has to resolve at an operational level the conflict between predestination and freedom of interaction. To complicate things even further, one can think of multi-party settings with multiple characters and multiple users. However, up to now such settings have remained a big challenge since in this case the characters must also be able to overhear and understand conversations among the human partners.

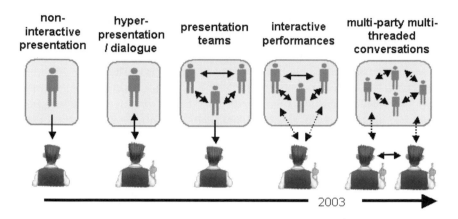

Fig. 1. Character applications with different conversational settings

3 Non-Interactive Presenters

The Internet boost in the mid-1990s has inspired researchers as well as companies to develop applications in which a virtual character takes on the role of a kind of personalized TV presenter who informs and entertains the user. A popular example is the virtual news reader Ananova (www.ananova.com) that reads news scripts live from ITN, a British broadcaster producing news.

Concerning the control of such virtual presenters one can distinguish between manually scripted characters and systems that work out presentation scripts automatically. To support manual scripting, a number of dedicated markup languages have been proposed, some of which are presented in detail in Part I of the current volume. Since manual scripting can be tedious and error-prone, several attempts have been made to automate the character scripting process either partially or completely. Examples include Noma's and Badler's virtual weather reporter (Noma and Badler [31]), Thalmann and Kalra's [44] TV presenter, and the systems Byrne (Binsted and Luke [6]) and Mike (Matsubara et al. [29]) that deploy a talking head to comment on matches of the RoboCup simulation league (Kitano et al. [19]). Further examples of related systems can be found in other chapters of the current book. A DFKI system that falls into this category was developed in the PPP (Personalized Plan-based Presenter) project (André and Rist [3], Rist et al. [38]).

3.1 PPP Persona

PPP Persona was designed as a personalized presentation agent that provides multi-modal instructions for the operation of technical devices. For instance, to explain how to switch on a technical device, PPP Persona may show the user a picture of the device, and point to the on–off switch while giving verbal instructions on how to manipulate the switch (cf. left-hand side of Fig. 2).

From a functional perspective, PPP Persona receives as input presentation goals (PG) and generation parameters (GP), such as the user's level of expertise and time constraints for the duration of the presentation to be generated. As output, the system delivers a specification of a multimedia presentation, called presentation *script*. Such scripts are forwarded to a dedicated player engine responsible for the synchronized display of all involved media objects including possibly animated illustrations of domain objects, text elements, as well as character animations and verbal speech output.

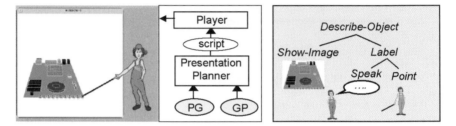

Fig. 2. PPP Persona: screenshot and architecture (left). Excerpt of a presentation plan (right)

In PPP, we formalized action sequences for composing multimedia material and designing scripts for presenting this material to the user as operators of a planning system. Starting from a complex presentation goal (e.g. to describe a technical device) the planner recursively performs a hierarchical goal decomposition until all subgoals have been expanded to elementary production, retrieval, or presentation tasks. A portion of a hierarchical presentation plan is shown in the right-hand part of Fig. 2. The operators of the PPP system represent tactical knowledge about how to achieve presentation goals by means of a multimedia presentation including a character as an additional presentation device. Therefore, the operators are formulated from the point of view of a director who orchestrates the interplay of the character with the display of all other media objects. As to modularization of the planning mechanism, PPP uses just one planner for script generation. Details on the planning approach can be found in André et al. [4].

4 Conversational Characters

A great deal of contemporary systems aim at emulating aspects of a face-to-face interaction in settings where a user faces a virtual conversation partner. Differences among systems concern both available input modalities as well as output modalities.

4.1 Characters with Restricted Input Understanding Capabilities

In the simplest case, user input is handled in a rather restricted and controlled fashion. An example of such a system was developed in the AiA (Adaptive Communication Assistant for Effective Infobahn Access) project (André et al. [4]). The corresponding AiA system features a personal embodied travel agent whose task is to collect, structure, and present information about a travel destination while taking into account the individual user profile. A screenshot of the system is shown in the left-hand part of Fig. 3. During the presentation phase the AiA agent solicited input from the user only at some distinct stages mainly to let the user choose between several options about what to present next or on what to elaborate in more detail. Thus, presentations generated by the AiA systems can be regarded as a special type of hypermedia presentation.

In contrast, the stock agent "Rudi" (see right-hand part of Fig. 3) engages with the user in a natural language conversation. Being connected to several online stock servers, a user can chat with Rudi about the latest developments of shares. The user "talks" to Rudi by typing natural language expressions into a text input widget while Rudi talks to the user either by voice output or likewise through speech bubbles. Also, Rudi makes use of gestures and facial displays that accompany his verbal utterances or are even used as standalone to convey a communicative goal non-verbally.

As shown in the sketched architectures, AiA's as well as Rudi's internal machinery is quite similar to that of the PPP Persona. However, both systems also comprise a component to process user input. In case of the AiA system, selected menu options correspond directly to presentation goals or new settings of presentation parameters. In the case of the stock agent Rudi a shallow natural language analysis is performed. Deploying the ALICE framework for programming chat robots (www.alicebot.org/), pattern matching rules are applied to derive requests for new presentation goals and new settings of presentation parameters from a user's input message.

4.2 Characters that Engage in Multi-Modal Conversations

To emulate more closely face-to-face dialogue settings among humans it is desirable to avoid asymmetries in communication channels that are available to a human and a character.

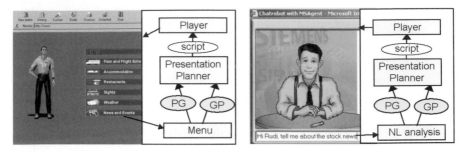

Fig. 3. Screenshot and architecture of the AiA travel agent (left) and stock agent Rudi (right). In contrast to the PPP architecture (cf. Fig. 2), the AiA and Rudi both comprise components for analyzing user input, such as menu-based follow-up questions and typed natural language queries

The ability of a character to engage with a human in an unconstrained spoken natural language conversation is most desirable but also very difficult and therefore will remain a great challenge for years even though considerable progress has been made in the last decade in speech recognition, synthesis, and spoken dialogue systems. On the other hand, restricted spoken dialogue agents are technically feasible and may suffice their purposes in some domains. For instance, the virtual receptionist Cyberella (Gebhard [12]) understands a limited number of questions concerning typical information requests of visitors coming to DFKI. For instance, a visitor may ask her for directions to get to a certain office. From an architectural point of view, Cyberella shares similarities with the Rudi stock agent except that this time aural user input is accepted and processed by a speech recognizer to obtain a text string which is then processed further by means of a pattern-based natural language interpreter.

More ambitious attempts to overcome asymmetries in available communication channels have been made in the SmartKom project (Wahlster et al. [47]). First, the interface character Smartakus comprises a more sophisticated spoken dialogue subsystem. Second, Smartakus also has a "visual sense" that enables it to recognize and understand pointing gestures of the user. Third, its visual sense allows the character to read a limited number of emotional expressions from the user's face. Recognized user emotions can be used to disambiguate speech input and to generate affective responses. Figure 4 shows from left to right the agent Smartakus acting as a TV program advisor, and two shots of the SmartKom installation for public spaces. As shown by the close-up, Smartakus interprets multi-modal user input, such as verbal utterances that are accompanied by pointing gestures.

Even though projects like SmartKom break new ground in the area of multi-modal human–character interaction, the emulation of multi-modal human–human face-to-face communication remains a long-term challenge.

Fig. 4. Shots from the SmartKom system. In SmartKom the user engages in a multi-modal conversation with the agent Smartakus

4.3 Other Conversational Agents

Quite a number of commercial sites try to boost their web presence by adding an embodied conversational character. Similar to the stock agent Rudi, the user can "talk" to the character by typing NL expressions into a text-input widget. In most cases, however, the conversational skills of these characters are limited to that of a pattern-based chat robot. In the best case, such systems manage to map user input to related contents of the web site. The virtual chat agent Cybelle (www.agentland.com/) and the agent Aisa (www.smart.com) are examples of this kind. In the worst case, a conversation with such a character is neither informative nor entertaining. Needless to say such characters are likely to be perceived by a user as useless if not annoying.

In contrast, most research prototypes of embodied conversational characters are instances of complex multi-modal dialogue systems, though the focus is usually on the generation of sophisticated multi-modal expressions by which a character should respond to user input. Prominent examples include the Internet Advisor Cosmo (Lester et al. [23]), the REA real estate agent (Cassell et al. [8]), and the GRETA medical advisor (Pelachaud et al. [32]), whereby the last two systems rely on sophisticated models of multi-modal communication.

Besides building concrete agents, researchers focus on the development of application-independent tools for the implementation of virtual dialogue partners. Well-known examples of this type include the CSLI toolkit (Cohen et al. [11]) and the Collagen system (Rich et al. [35]) which is based on a model of collaboration between a human and a computer agent.

5 Presentation Teams

There are situations in which direct agent–user communication is not necessarily the most effective and most convenient way to present information. Inspired by the evolution of TV commercials over the past 40 years, our group has discovered role-plays with synthetic characters as a promising format for presenting information. A typical TV commercial of the early days featured a salesperson who presented a product by enumerating its positive features – quite similar to what synthetic characters do on web pages today. On TV, however, this format has been almost completely replaced by formats that draw on the concept of short, entertaining scenes. Typically, such performances embed product information into a narrative context that involves two or more human actors. Episodic formats offer a much richer basis compared to the plain enumeration of product features, and thus meet the commercial industry's high demand for originality.

A shift from settings with single presentation agents toward the use of presentation teams bears a number of advantages. First of all, they enrich the repertoire of modalities to convey information. For example, they allow a system to convey certain rhetorical relationships, such as pros and cons, in a more canonical manner. Furthermore, they can serve as a rhetorical device to reinforce beliefs. For instance, the same piece of information can be repeated in a less monotonous and perhaps more convincing manner simply by employing different agents to convey it. Furthermore, the single members of a presentation team can serve as indices, which help the user to organize the conveyed information. For instance, characters can convey meta-information, such as the origin of information, or they can present information from different points of view, e.g. from the point of view of a businessman or the point of view of a traveler. Last but not least, multiple characters allow us to convey social aspects, such as interpersonal relationships between emotional characters (see Prendinger and Ishizuka [34], Rist and Schmitt [39]).

5.1 Simulated Car-Sales Dialogues

The eShowroom (also called "Inhabited Market Place") is an example of a system that employs presentation teams to convey information about products, such as cars, by performing role-plays (André et al. [5]). The left-hand part of Fig. 5 shows the characters Tina and Ritchie engaging in a simulated car-sales dialogue.

The overall system's presentation goal is to provide the user with facts about a certain car. However, the presentation is neither just a mere enumeration of facts about the car, nor a fixed course of dialogue between the agents. Rather, the eShowroom allows the users to specify prior to a presentation (i) the agents' roles, (ii) their attitude towards the product, (iii) some personality traits (extravert vs. introvert, agreeable vs. not agreeable), and (iv) their interests about certain aspects relevant for cars (e.g. the car's relation to prestige, comfort, sportiness, friendliness to the environment, costs, etc.). Based on these settings, a variety of different sales dialogues can be generated for the same product.

Similar to the PPP system a user specifies both a presentation goal and generation parameters prior to the presentation generation process. Since this time the behaviors of several characters have to be determined, a designer of such a system has the choice between taking a director's point of view or to adopt the self-scripting paradigm. In the first case, the task of the presentation planner is to work out one single script for the role-play as a whole. Typically, such a script would include statements of the form: "character1 do x; character2 do y". As shown in the depicted architecture of the eShowroom (left-hand part of Fig. 5), this system uses one centralized presentation planner to script the actions of the virtual seller and buyer agents in a car-sales dialogue.

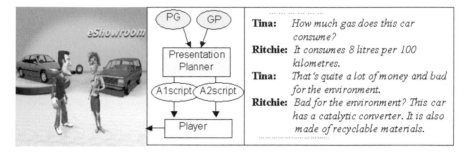

Fig. 5. Left: Screenshot and architecture of the eShowroom. Right: Excerpt of a "sales talk" between the buyer agent Tina and the seller agent Ritchie

5.2 Reporter Teams

On the other hand, there are a number of application fields for presentation agents where scripts for the agents cannot be worked out in advance since all or part of the information to be presented becomes available only at presentation run-time. Any kind of reportage or commentary of live data falls into this category. As an example, let us have a look at Rocco II (André et al. [1]), an automated live report system that generates commentaries for the simulator league of Robot World-Cup Soccer (Kitano et al. [19]). The right-hand part of Fig. 6 shows a screenshot of the system. In the upper window, two teams of software agents play a soccer game while the commentaries are being done by Gerd and Matze, two virtual soccer fans sitting on a sofa and watching the game. As in the eShowroom system the user has the option of experimenting with different character profiles. For instance, the user may characterize Gerd and Matze by their personality and their sympathy for a certain team.

Unlike the agents in the car-sales scenario, the RoboCup commentators have to comment on a rapidly changing environment. Since events on the soccer field evolve while time progresses, no global organization of the presentation is possible. Instead the commentators have to respond immediately to incoming data. Furthermore, they have to meet severe time constraints

Gerd:	Wow, did you see that fantastic shot?
Matze:	Yeah but look where the ball has gone.
Gerd:	Oh no.
Matze:	The red team is going to make a counter attack.
Matze:	Come on, kick the ball!

Fig. 6. Left: Verbal comments by the soccer fans Gerd and Matze while watching a game. Right: Screenshot and architecture of the Gerd and Matze soccer commentary system

imposed by the flow of the game. In some cases, it might even be necessary for the commentators to interrupt themselves. For instance, if an important event (e.g. a goal kick) occurs, utterances are interrupted to communicate the new event as soon as possible. In such a situation, it is not possible to pre-script utterances. Instead scripting has to be done at run-time, e.g. either by a centralized script writing component or by the single agents themselves.

As shown by the architecture of the system Gerd and Matze are realized as autonomous agents. That is, each agent has its own reactive planner and its own set of dialogue and commentator strategies. Dialogue contributions then result from autonomous characters trying to achieve their individual goals. The goal of the single commentators is to inform the viewer about ongoing events in the scene. In the current version of Rocco II, each commentator concentrates on the activities of a certain team. That is, there is an implicit agreement between the characters concerning the distribution of dialogue contributions. Responses to dialogue contributions of the other commentator are possible provided the speed of the game allows for it. Furthermore, the commentators may provide background information on the game and the teams involved. Concerning the commentary of the observed actions and events during the game, we assume that both commentators share all knowledge about the events on the soccer field which is provided by Rocco's incremental event recognition component (André et al. [2]). Assuming a discrete time model, at each increment of a time counter, the recognition component selects relevant events, formulates corresponding presentation tasks, and writes them into a buffer. In addition, the buffer contains presentation tasks that refer to the presentation of background information. If an event has been communicated or in case the topicality of an event falls below a threshold, the corresponding presentation task is removed from the buffer again.

5.3 Other Approaches with Multiple Characters

Using multiple conversational characters that – rather than addressing the user directly – convey information to the user by talking loudly to each other is a concept that has been explored in a number of other contexts too.

In some cases, these dialogues are manually scripted as in the Agneta & Frida system (Höök et al. [14]) that incorporates narratives into a web environment by placing two characters on the user's desktop. These characters watch the user during the browsing process and make comments on the web pages visited. To facilitate the authoring of multi-modal presentations with multiple characters, Ishizuka and colleagues [16] have developed the MPML scripting language. Details of MPML and a MPML authoring tool can be found in the current book.

Systems that aim at a simulation of conversations between humans usually automate at least parts of the generation process. Cassell and colleagues (Cassell et al. [9]) automatically create and animate dialogues between a bank teller and a bank employee with appropriate synchronized speech, intonation, facial expressions, and hand gestures. Walker and colleagues (Walker et al. [48]) concentrate on the linguistic capabilities of computer characters (e.g. a waiter and a customer) and examine how social factors influence the semantic content, the syntactic form, and the acoustic realization of conversations. The generation of their dialogues is essentially influenced by the power the listener has on the speaker and the social distance between them.

Mr. Bengo (Nitta et al. [30]) is a system for the resolution of disputes which employs three agents: a judge, a prosecutor, and an attorney which is controlled by the user. The prosecutor and the attorney discuss the interpretation of legal rules. Finally, the judge decides on the winner.

Multiple characters have also been deployed in training applications. For instance, Rickel and Johnson [36] deploy characters in team training tasks where one character can represent an instructor while further characters may substitute for missing team members.

6 Presentation Teams that Represent Human Users

In the eShowroom as well as in the Gerd and Matze commentator system the members of the presentation team were virtual characters. In contrast, the members of presentation teams can also represent real humans. Examples of such applications are the systems Magic Monitor and Avatar Arena, both developed at DFKI.

6.1 Magic Monitor

The Magic Monitor is a tool for illustrating message exchange in a multi-user conferencing system called the Magic Lounge. Cartoon-style characters are used to represent different conversation partners (which may be humans or virtual conversational agents). The tool allows for the playback of recorded message exchanges according to different structuring criteria, such as timelines or dialogue threads. The sequential nature of replaying recorder multiparty conversations is often somewhat long winded. However, the format can be useful for illustrating some crucial exchanges during a conversation.

In the Magic Monitor the system plays a two-fold role. First, it acts as a screen writer that determines how a conversation within the Magic Lounge should be played back by the single characters. Second, it is actively involved in the presentation through a facilitator agent that provides some meta information about recorded conversations. The screenshot in the middle of Fig. 7 shows a facilitator agent located in the center, while the other characters represent different users. As shown by the architecture of the Magic Monitor (left-hand side of Fig. 6), a centralized presentation planner determines the dialogue script taking into account (i) the repository of recorded message exchanges, (ii) a presentation goal that constrains the selection of message exchanges to be replayed, and (iii) additional generation parameters, such as the assignment of characters to represent the communication partners.

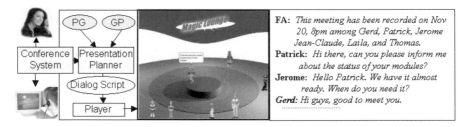

Fig. 7. Left: Architecture and screenshot of the Magic Monitor. Right: Excerpt of a replayed chat conversation. As an introduction the facilitator agent (FA) informs about times and participants in the conversation

The presentation planner's basic approach for message playback according to the timeline of occurrence comprises the following strategies:

1. have the facilitator announce the next message by referring to aspects, such as sender, date, time, topic, and speech act;
2. have each character representing the sender of a message move to the central podium;
3. if a message is directed to a specific recipient, have that recipient move closer to the podium and play a "listen" animation;
4. have the message sender read the message while playing an animation that enforces the speech act associated with the message;
5. finally, have all characters move back to their assigned home positions.

Variations of the basic scheme have been defined to cope with messages, such as login, logout, and registration, and to take into account various aspects, such as consecutive messages from the same user or the need for a more compact presentation.

6.2 Avatar Arena

While the Magic Monitor replays recorded message exchanges of human communication partners, Avatar Arena simulates negotiation dialogues with affective, embodied conversational characters that are embedded in a social context. Somewhat similar to an arena, users send their delegates (avatars) to a virtual space where the avatars negotiate on behalf of their owners. Both the result and process of a negotiation can be displayed to the users in the form of a simulation using embodied conversational characters. Since the outcome of a delegated negotiation process can be unexpected, the user may wish to learn about how a certain negotiation result came about. In human–human negotiations this is of particular interest in cases where the result of a negotiation cannot be explained on the basis of a solely rational argumentation but only if the social context and the personalities of the negotiating parties need to be considered as well.

Technically speaking, Avatar Arena can be conceived as a distributed n:1 client–server architecture. While the server component provides the arena where the negotiation takes place, the client component allows a user to configure and instruct his or her avatar, and also to observe the negotiation process carried out on the server. To this end, the client receives a generated script of the overall negotiation dialogue for display (see right-hand part of Fig. 8).

Arena avatars negotiate on meeting appointments on behalf of human users. However, we have picked this domain just for the purpose of illustration and do not attempt to improve existing appointment scheduling tools. Rather, our research focus is on the simulation of the dynamics of social relationships among affective characters during negotiation dialogues. Avatar Arena serves as a testbed to investigate and evaluate mind models of varying "cognitive complexity" for virtual characters that engage in negotiation dialogues. Our working hypothesis is that an increase of believability in the observable interactions among the characters will indeed require some higher extent of cognitive modeling. Our approach for assessing believability of negotiation dialogues is to show human observers several negotiation dialogues with virtual characters that differ in the number of psychological factors taken into account in a character's mind model. To this end Avatar Arena can simulate negotiation dialogues among avatars that vary in their modeled cognitive complexity.

In the simplest case, Arena avatars have only some domain knowledge about appointment dates and rudimentary conversational skills that enable them to propose meeting dates, and to accept or reject proposals based on

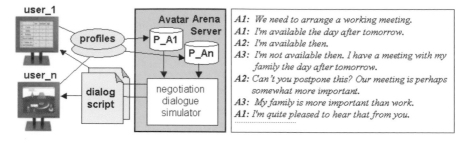

Fig. 8. Left: Architecture of Avatar Arena. Right: Excerpt of a meeting negotiation dialogue between three avatars. Some of the utterances show that the avatars have attitudes toward activities associated with meeting dates and also attitudes toward other avatars

their personal calendar entries. Since characters of this type can only talk about availability or non-availability concerning proposals for meeting dates, the generated negotiation dialogues have a strong flavor of being nothing more than a mere trace log-file as known from multi-agent expert systems.

In a second step we consider characters that have attitudes concerning already scheduled meeting dates, and new dates to be negotiated. That is, we allow the users to assign importance values to appointments that the avatars should take into account in a negotiation. This extension to the avatar's mind model has an impact on the negotiation process and is also reflected by the resulting dialogues. First, the attitudes can be considered to determine importance values or priorities for meeting dates under discussion. In turn, such a priority order provides a rational criterion for an avatar to determine its willingness to reschedule an already fixed appointment. That is, when a date for the new appointment is proposed, the avatar compares the importance value assigned to the new meeting activity with the importance value of the already scheduled activity. For instance, if an avatar believes in career and does not care much about social contacts, it may be willing to postpone a holiday trip with friends and attend a conference instead. Furthermore, attitudes toward meeting dates and the activities associated with these dates give the avatars a rational basis for making justifications in a negotiation dialogue. For instance, an avatar can argue that it won't be willing to reschedule a medical treatment in favor of a working meeting because of its particular attitudes. In addition, the importance value assigned to an already scheduled meeting date can be used as a criterion for deciding whether to provide a justification at all. However, this version of Avatar Arena neglects the fact that in a group setting, the single participants have attitudes toward their negotiation partners too. Moreover, both attitudes toward subject matter, such as meeting activities, as well as attitudes toward dialogue partners are subject to change in a negotiation process.

This motivates a third version of Avatar Arena which enables a user to specify his or her attitudes toward other persons (which are assumed to be represented by their avatars in a negotiation process). In this version of the system the avatars consider: (i) their own attitudes toward meeting dates, (ii) attitudes toward other avatars, and (iii) beliefs about the other avatars' attitudes toward meeting dates. Again, this increase in the avatars' "cognitive complexity" leads to noticeable differences in the negotiation dialogues. In particular, this version of Avatar Arena emulates some aspects of group dynamics (in terms of changing attitudes) as known from negotiation dialogues among humans. For instance, the avatars are now able to make personal comments on justifications of other dialogue partners, and to reply to personal comments made by others. The underlying approach to model group dynamic aspects is inspired by socio-psychological theories of cognitive consistency, such as Congruity Theory by Osgood and Tannenbaum. Details of this approach can be found in Rist and Schmitt [39].

6.3 Other Applications with Avatars

To represent users through embodied characters in virtual space is an old idea for which the term "Avatar" has been coined. An obvious application area for avatars are multi-party gatherings and conversations that take place in virtual space. Graphical chat systems in which users have either 2D or 3D representations fall into this category. Sample systems are, for instance, Comic Chat (Kurlander et al. [21]) and V-Chat (Smith et al. [42]), both developed at Microsoft Research. The avatars in these systems can be compared to puppets that are fully controlled by their users. In contrast, the Body Chat system by Vilhjalmsson and Cassell [46] analyzes the users' text messages in order to automatically generate suitable gestures, facial expressions, and eye-gaze behaviors of the avatars participating in a chat. An alternative to video-conferencing is proposed by the Avatar Conference project (www.exodus.gr/Avatar_Conference). In the corresponding system participants are graphically represented by animated 3D depictions of themselves and communicate via a voice channel or via text chat.

Another multi-party application has been proposed by Isbister and colleagues (Isbister et al. [15]). Unlike the above-mentioned applications, their work concentrates on social interactions between several humans in a video chat environment which is supported by a so-called "Helper Agent". The Helper Agent is an animated, dog-faced avatar that tracks audio from two-person conversations and intervenes if it detects longer silences.

A system that shares similarities with the Magic Monitor has been proposed by Yabe and colleagues (Yabe et al. [50]). Similar to the Magic Monitor, the content of the dialogue script for the single characters is based on a real conversation between humans. However, they animate discussions from news groups by casting 3D characters as the authors of the single discussion contributions.

7 Interactive Performances

In the scenarios presented so far, the user's role was restricted to selecting characters for the performance and setting character profiles, but there was no user participation in the performance itself. Rather than playing episodes to be watched by a user, one can try to involve the user actively in a role-play. Such a scenario, that bears many similarities to improvisational theatre, has been realized in the MIAU project with the development of an interactive version of the eShowroom that was sketched in Sect. 5.1.

7.1 The MIAU Platform

In this version the user can assign roles to characters, evoke them, and watch their car-sales conversations. However, if a user wishes to engage in the car-sales conversation, too, he or she can start an avatar that represents him or her in the scenario. As shown in the left-hand screenshot of Fig. 9, the user can participate in the ongoing conversation by typing questions and comments into the text input widget. On the other hand, it is up to the user to decide on the level of active participation. One extreme is that from now on the user asks all questions. In contrast, if the user wants to relax again and just watch the characters talk, he or she can do so, lean back, and remain silent. In this case, the virtual buyer will continue to ask questions.

As shown by the architecture in the left-hand part of Fig. 9, the MIAU platform consists of the following components: For each character $C_1 \ldots C_n$ MIAU foresees so-called *character components* containing a separate behavior planner as well as a separate interaction manager. The behavior planner has the task of decomposing complex discourse goals into basic acts that can be executed by the character player. Since the user decides during the performance whether, when, and how to participate in a conversation, we cannot start from a predefined script. Instead the dialogue between the conversation partners evolves while time progresses. Furthermore, the scenario is open-ended in the sense that neither the characters nor the users are able to tell what exactly may happen next. The interaction manager, in a certain sense, corresponds to a dialogue manager as found in NL dialogue systems since it is responsible for keeping the book on interaction states and the interaction history. However, in the MIAU platform the interaction manager realizes a character's internal interface for communication with other system components by means of formalized communication acts. To this end, the MIAU platform comprises a message board which is shared among the different components for the exchange of internal communication acts.

To allow a user to alter settings for the performance, to take an active part in a performance, or even to intervene in the role of a director or co-director, the platform also incorporates a so-called *user component* (U box in Fig. 9). However, since this time the user decides on what to do, we do not foresee a planner, but an input analyzer for mapping user input onto formalized communication acts. The internal communication with other system components is handled by the interaction manager similar to the structure of a character component. In case the user is represented in the scenario by an embodied (and possibly animated) avatar, the avatar may indicate its input activity by means of gestures and speech turns. For instance, if a text widget is used for acquiring user input, the user's avatar will repeat the input sentence loudly. Currently, we restrict ourselves to a single participating user only. Nevertheless it seems possible to extend the architecture for multi-user, multi-character scenarios by adding more user components.

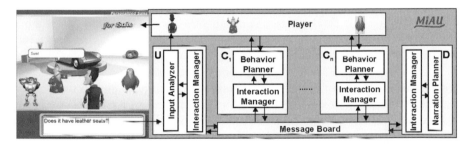

Fig. 9. Screenshot of the interactive version of the eShowroom (left) realized with the MIAU multi-character platform (right)

In addition to character components and the user component, MIAU also incorporates a D box, the so-called *director component*. In contrast to the characters, the director does not participate in performances and therefore has no embodiment. Rather, this component is foreseen to enable some degree of centralized control on the overall interactive performance. While the director also comprises a planner, this time the planner is used in order to influence the course of the performance depending on the degree of centralized control wanted for a certain application. Internal communication with other components is again handled via the interaction manager. Examples of flexible switches between different conversational settings (monologue vs. dialogue vs. performance vs. interactive performance) can be found in Rist et al. [37].

7.2 Other Work Related to Interactive Performances

Even though the focus of interactive drama is usually not on the communication of information, dramaturgical elements offer great promise in presentation scenarios as well, see also Laurel [22]. Our work toward an interactive version of the eShowroom has also been inspired by research on interactive drama that aims at integrating a user in a scenario – either as an audience member or as an active participant, see for instance Hayes-Roth et al. [13], Machado et al. [24], and Klesen et al. [20]. To allow for user interaction, some systems incorporate decision points in a narrative-style script (Mateas [27]). That is, the user just decides how to navigate through a graph structure in which nodes represent scenes and edges represent eligible transitions between scenes. In this model any eligible path through the story graph represents a particular plot. In contrast, other approaches rely on story graphs that also comprise special nodes, so-called "freeplay" areas (Sgouros [41]). Within these areas a player interacts with one or more characters in complex ways to influence how the story unfolds.

In these approaches characters are usually modeled as autonomous agents that select and instantiate actions under consideration of dramatic constraints, such as the plot of a story or the characters' role and personality (Perlin and Goldberg [33], Hayes-Roth et al. [13]). A key concept of these approaches is improvisation. That is, characters spontaneously and cooperatively work out the details of a story at performance time, taking into account the constraints of directions coming from either the system or a human user.

Depending on the kinds of interactions that occurred in a freeplay area, transitions to follow-up nodes can be enabled or inhibited. Such a mechanism is realized either by means of local evaluation functions for transition selection, or by a so-called plot or drama manager that has global control of the story development (Weyhrauch [49], Mateas and Stern [28]). For instance, the Oz drama manager (Mateas and Stern [28]) selects actions based on an evaluation of the discourse history in terms of dramatic quality. In Sgouros [41] transitions are triggered by events or user/agent actions. In a system for *interactive pedagogical drama* (Marsella et al. [26]) an evaluation function models pedagogical progress. In the MRE system by Swartout et al. [43], the story graph is called *StoryNet*. An evaluation function checks a list of conditions, usually tasks that must be completed. To obtain a smooth transition between nodes (scenes), a transition may be associated with an additional pre-scripted scene that is played when the transition is made.

Similarities also exist between the MIAU approach and the work described in Cavazza et al. [10] and Young [51]. For the purpose of a computer game application, Cavazza and colleagues use distributed hierarchical planners to control the behavior of multiple characters. In addition, Young introduces an "Execution Manager" that monitors the user's actions and makes real-time decisions about the appropriate system response in case these actions deviate from the planned narrative structure. The Execution Manager roughly corresponds to the Director Component of the MIAU platform.

Another interesting strand of research concerns multi-modal conversations with multiple characters. In the context of a military mission rehearsal application Swartout et al. [43] and Traum and Rickel [45] have addressed dialogue management comprising human–character and character–character dialogues in immersive virtual environments. There is no superior component that handles the turn management. To explicitly select the next speaker, the authors have introduced a specific turn-taking action called "Assign-Turn". In this system the characters are realized as completely autonomous agents.

8 The Interactive CrossTalk Installation

Seeking for an appealing exhibit that could be demonstrated at the CeBIT 2002 computer fair, the idea arose to have the character Cyberella (cf. Sect. 4.1) present another existing system, in this case the eShowroom (cf. Sect. 5.1). The combination of the two systems resulted in the interactive CrossTalk installation that has been designed as a new variant of information presentation in public spaces, such as an exhibition, or a trade fair.

8.1 Set-Up and Functional View of CrossTalk

The CrossTalk installation provides a spatially extended interaction experience by offering two separated agent screens, and by creating the illusion that the agents have cross-screen conversations. Figure 10 shows the installation from a distance with two visitors, a close-up of the three screens, and a bird's eye view of the spatial arrangement.

In CrossTalk, embodied agents are presented as virtual actors giving interactive performances. This can be considered a playful illustration of the "computers as theatre" paradigm introduced by Laurel [22]. Moreover, the installation relies on what we call a meta-theater metaphor. Quite similar to professional actors, characters in CrossTalk are not always on duty. Rather, they can step out of their roles, and amuse the user with unexpected intermezzi and rehearsal periods. In CrossTalk, embodied agents are presented as virtual actors giving interactive performances.

In CrossTalk Cyberella's primary task is that of a fair hostess. She welcomes visitors who approach the stand and offers them a demonstration of the eShowroom on the opposing screen in which the two virtual actors Tina and Ritchie interchangeably take on the role of a car seller or a potential car buyer and perform car-sales dialogues. The purpose of such simulated sales dialogues is to work through the features of a certain car by means of a question–answer dialogue. Clearly notable variations in the course of such dialogues are due to the specific settings of parameters which can be defined by the user prior to the performance. That is, Cyberella invites the user to assign roles (seller vs. buyer), personality and mood (e.g. polite vs. impolite, agreeable vs. disagreeable), and areas of interest that are associated with cars (safety, comfort, prestige, sportiness, costs, etc.).

Once Cyberella has collected parameter settings from the visitor she takes on the role of a stage director for the actors Tina and Ritchie and instructs them to start the performance. Tina and Ritchie will then change their body postures to signal that they are now "on duty" and to catch the visitor's attention. Depending on their personality, the agents use different degrees of criticism (customer) and enthusiasm (salesperson) when talking about the car's features (consumption, horsepower, airbags, etc.). During a performance the user can give feedback by pushing one of three buttons ("applause", "boo" and "help"). Such feedback may cause unexpected (meta-theatrical) behavior. For instance, if a visitor submits a "boo" several times, the actors will get nervous and may forget their lines. In contrast, "applause" makes them proudly smile and bow to the user. When "help" is requested, Cyberella stops the performance for short explanations.

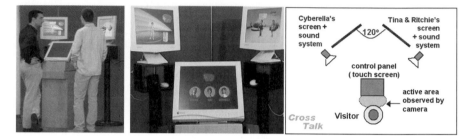

Fig. 10. The interactive installation CrossTalk (cf. http://www.dfki.de/crosstalk)

After the performance, Cyberella takes over again and asks whether the user wants to see another sales dialogue, possibly with new settings. However, if the visitor leaves the installation the actors switch to "off-duty" mode adopting a more relaxed body posture. But instead of just idling around on their screens, the agents display their off-duty behavior by chatting with each other across screens or by "rehearsing" for the next performance. The purpose of this "off-duty" activity, quite natural for humans, is two-fold. First, it is a means to encourage leaving visitors to stay for a while watching the "private lives" of the characters and, more important, new potential visitors may be lured from the crowd of passers-by. Second, allowing our characters to step out of their roles gives them another human-like quality, one that contributes to the impression that they are permanently alive.

8.2 Interweaving Scene Authoring with Automated Dialogue Generation

A particular challenge in CrossTalk concerns the scripting of scenes for both the "on-duty" and the "off-duty" mode. In the case of the on-duty mode CrossTalk's subsystem eShowroom is active. As described in Sect. 5.1, the purpose of this system is to inform a user about the features of a car by means of a simulated sales dialogue between a virtual seller and buyer. Such sales conversations can be generated automatically. The car features mentioned in the dialogues, such as a car's consumption, type of engine, etc., are taken from a product database. Therefore, the dialogues are just another device to read out stored product information.

To keep the actors alive in the off-duty mode we tried to emulate small-talk conversations among stand staff members in case no visitor seem particularly interested in getting information about exhibits. While a broad variation of car-sales dialogues can be automatically generated by means of a relatively small number of dialogue patterns, an approach for the automated generation of small-talk dialogues (which would be interesting enough for a visitor to listen to) appears much more challenging. We therefore decided to rely on a repertoire of pre-scripted small-talk scenes from which the system would chose randomly when in off-duty mode. For demonstrating CrossTalk at the CeBit 2002 fair a large corpus of pre-scripted scenes (more than 220 each for English and German) has been assembled by one of the authors with experience in theater acting and directing. Some scenes cover themes related to every-day belongings, such as what to do in the evening, how to get home, or where to get cigarettes. Other scenes refer to the world of the theater or movies. For instance, the characters may reflect on their stagecraft, or what they might do after the CeBIT convention.

The left-hand part of Fig. 11 shows an excerpt of a pre-scripted episode including tags to specify the agent's non-verbal behavior. The specification of such pre-authored dialogues also includes special tags that allow an author to explicitly specify an agent's non-verbal behavior which falls into four categories: gestures, facial expressions, posture shifts, and actions. Gestures were taken from a catalogue derived from analyzing a German TV show with manual gesture annotation (Kipp [18, 17]). The two analyzed speakers were found to have a shared lexicon of 69 conversational gestures of which the most frequently used ones were modeled for CrossTalk by a professional graphics and animation designer and turned into libraries of animation clips. Some facial expressions were added based on the needs of the script (e.g. smile, scepticism). Posture shifts are used to visually separate role (salesperson/customer) and meta-role (actor) of Tina and Ritchie: when they are "themselves as actors" they have a relaxed body posture whereas when they are play acting they straighten up and look more tense. This is in accord with observations in psychotherapy where body posture was found to indicate separate topics or points of view in a conversation (Scheflen [40]). Other actions comprise turning the head, breathing, and other idle-time actions like putting on glasses, yawning, etc.

A simple authoring syntax is meant to appeal to non-programmers, including professional playwrights. The author writes the actors' utterances and includes stage directions in the form of bracketed commands. The script can be written in any text processing software. However, to be able to interweave authored and automatically generated scenes at run-time, a script compiler transforms authored scenes into the same internal format that is used by the system's presentation planner to represent operators for automated dialogue construction.

We realized that apart from the time-consuming scripting effort it is much more of a challenge to create, maintain, and extend the overall *structure* of the evolving story comprising both on-duty and off-duty conversations as well as appropriate responses to potential user feedback. We conceptualize a story

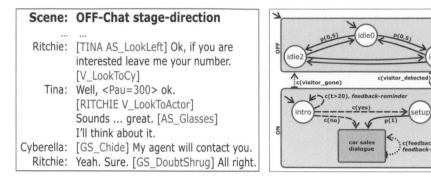

Fig. 11. Excerpt of a pre-scripted scene (left), and excerpt of CrossTalk's scene flow that is defined by a cascaded finite-state machine (right)

as a logical flow of scenes. In CrossTalk scene flow (i.e. the transition between scenes) is modeled by means of a cascaded finite-state machine in which states refer to scenes that have been either pre-authored or which are generated automatically on the fly. Cascaded finite-state machines enable the shared use of modules (part of a scene flow), similar to subroutines in a programming language. This simplifies the modeling process in case of, for instance, repeated patterns of agent–user interactions, such as simple yes/no questions. Scene flows can be specified either in XML syntax or by means of a graphical editor. Scene flow specifications are then compiled into executable finite-state machines by the so-called SceneMaker component.

The right-hand part of Fig. 11 shows a small excerpt from CrossTalk's scene flow. After initialization the system starts in *off-duty* mode. This mode is modeled as a supernode with no scene attached (upper box). The sub-node *idle0*, declared the starting node, is processed first. Having performed the attached scene, node *idle1* or node *idle2* is processed with probability 0.5 each. If a visitor arrives, the currently processed node is interrupted by traversing the interrupt edge *visitor_detected* to supernode *on-duty*, playing the attached scene *intro*. Then, Cyberella asks whether the user wants to provide parameters for the CarSales exhibit. This yes/no question is handled with two conditional edges: *c(yes)* and *c(no)*. If the user does not answer within a certain amount of time (20 seconds), a third conditional edge $c(t > 20)$ is triggered, playing the particular scene named *feedback-reminder*. During the CarSales performance the user can give feedback by pushing buttons. Multiple interrupt edges *c(feedback)* handle these button events, interrupting the performance temporarily by playing the respective scenes. Should the visitor leave, the interrupt edge *visitor_gone* immediately stops all ongoing activities in *on-duty* mode and enters the *off-duty* supernode.

8.3 Toward Self-Evolving Characters

Since the CeBit'02 fair CrossTalk has been exposed on many occasions to several hundreds of people, most of which also interacted with the system. To make the conversations among the characters more interesting and believable we anticipate that the characters should be more adaptive (i) during a session with a particular user, and (ii) with regards to previous encounters with other users. A first step in this direction is to collect information in a discourse history and to extract from the data key measures like the user's interaction frequency, the user's average response time to questions, types of interaction, quality of feedback (positive, negative, ask for help) as well as the variance in feedback within a session and across users. Informal log-file analysis of CrossTalk sessions showed that it is actually possible to distinguish between several stereotypical user types based on observed interaction patterns. Possible user categories include: *critical user* (many negative feedbacks), *active/passive/slow user* (many/few interactions, frequent interaction timeouts), *collaborative/obstinate user*. Furthermore, feedback can be co-related with particular characters and their actions. For instance, if a user provides more often negative feedback on contributions made by the character Tina but applauds Ritchie, it can be guessed that this user likes Ritchie more than Tina. In turn, stereotypes as well as unusual interaction patterns can inform the selection of pre-scripted scenes as well as the automated generation of scenes.

With regards to an improvement of the characters' repertoire of potential themes to talk about, it is interesting to note that the discourse history represents a rich source of information that can feed small-talk conversations among the agents. Rather than relying on pre-scripted small talk (as done in the current CrossTalk system), one may equip the characters with conversation strategies that enable them to reflect on previous encounters. Moreover, one may give the characters the ability to identify and cluster similar interaction experiences, and to make comparisons and generalizations which in turn can be verbalized in off-duty conversations as well as in a conversation with a user.

CrossTalk also provides an excellent framework to explore the learning of conversational skills. A straightforward approach is to provide the characters with a large number of conversational strategies and correlate the appropriateness of strategies with both situation of usage and received user feedback. In this way, the characters can automatically acquire and refine criteria and rules for strategy selection. A more ambitious objective is the formation of new strategies. This issue can be approached in several ways. For instance, following an evolutionary approach one can modify (mutate) existing strategies and determine their fitness value in subsequent conversations based on user feedback. In the long run, the characters may also try to acquire new conversational skills from observing and analyzing conversational behaviors of their human interaction partners.

Perhaps the most ambitious extension to CrossTalk concerns a somehow automated evolvement of distinct personalities that slowly emerge from one exhibition to another while taking into account interaction experiences with humans and perhaps other virtual characters. However, work in this direction requires more basic research on the simulation of personality development for virtual characters that are embedded in a social context.

8.4 Other Work on Installations with Conversational Characters

A number of installations with interactive characters have been developed by the Synthetic Character Group at the MIT Media Lab. An early piece was the Alive system (Maes et al. [25]) that tracked movements and gestures of a human user to command a virtual dog. Descriptions of more recent installations can be found in Blumberg et al. [7]. While the focus of their work is on expressive character animation to create the illusion of life, CrossTalk characters are enlivened mainly through their engagement in conversations.

Concerning CrossTalk's mixed approach on framing character–character as well as character–human interactions, the work is closely related to the area of interactive drama. Similar to approaches as described in Sect. 7.2, CrossTalk also relies on an authored story graph that frames the flow of scenes. On the other hand, in case a user wants to provide settings for the character's role and mood, the course of car-sales performances will depend on this user input.

Finally, the development of new CrossTalk applications comprises basically two authoring tasks. One concerns the specification of the scene flow while the second one concerns the pre-scripting of off-duty scenes and possible intermezzi that may be played in on-duty mode. CrossTalk offers a screenplay-like authoring language to specify the virtual characters verbal and non-verbal behavior as opposed to other approaches that rely on XML-based markup languages – some of them can be found in Part I of the current book. Though it might be possible to define a scene flow within such markup languages, e.g. by using hyperlinks to jump to other parts in the script, CrossTalk's clear separation of scene flow definition and in-scene dialogue scripting suggests a systematic breakdown of complex authoring tasks.

9 Conclusions

This contribution revisited a number of past and ongoing character systems developed at DFKI. We tried to show that both complexity of conversational setting as well as complexity of underlying architectures are dimensions along which character systems have been evolving. Many of the presented systems make a concrete commitment to a certain conversational setting (monologue vs. dialog vs. presentation teams) and reflect this commitment by a particular system architecture. In contrast to that, the development of the MIAU platform shows that it is indeed possible to develop a single platform which

(i) can be used to construct a broad range of character applications, (ii) even allows to switch on the fly between director- vs. character-centered scripting approaches, and (iii) supports a clear separation between the specification of scripting knowledge (being a knowledge-engineering task) and the required computational machinery for behavior generation (being an implementation task). Abstracting from details MIAU can be conceived as a reference architecture that has been tailored to applications with conversational characters, and that may be used to systematically compare existing and upcoming systems.

The presented CrossTalk installation showed that, in order to provide the user with an engaging experience, a compromise has to be made between manual character scripting and automated character control. In CrossTalk such a compromise has been found by interweaving both approaches in two different ways. On the one hand a presentation planner can include authored subdialogues in otherwise automatically generated conversations. Vice versa, an authored script may invoke presentation planning to work out a subdialogue that takes into account certain generation parameters.

As to future work, many interesting challenges remain. Robust interpretation of multi-modal input is one of them. Further ones concern the improvement of conversational and social skills of characters as well as a character's capability to acquire new skills, e.g. through the deployment of learning mechanisms. Finally, it deserves mentioning that a great deal of research on multimodal communication with virtual characters may be reused in the upcoming generation of conversational robots.

References

1. André, E., Binsted, K., Tanaka-Ishii, K., Luke, S., Herzog, G., Rist, T.: Three RoboCup simulation league commentator systems. *AI Magazine* **21**(1):57–65 (2000)
2. André, E., Herzog, G., Rist, T.: Generating multimedia presentations for RoboCup soccer games. In: *RoboCup '97: Robot Soccer World Cup I*, ed Kitano (Springer, New York 1997) pp 200–215
3. André, E., Rist, T.: Coping with temporal constraints in multimedia presentation planning. In: *Proceedings of the AAAI '96* (AAAI Press/The MIT Press, Menlo Park, Cambridge, London 1996) pp 142–147
4. André, E., Rist, T., Müller, J.: Employing AI methods to control the behavior of animated interface agents. *Applied Artificial Intelligence* **13**:415–448 (1999)
5. André, E., Rist, T., van Mulken, S., Klesen, M., Baldes, S.: The automated design of believable dialogues for animated presentation teams. In: *Embodied Conversational Agents*, ed Cassell, J., Sullivan, J., Prevost, S., Churchill, E. (The MIT Press, Cambridge, MA 2000) pp 220–255
6. Binsted, K., Luke, S.: Character design for soccer commentary. In: *RoboCup-98: Robot Soccer World Cup II*, ed Asada, M., Kitano, H. (Springer, New York 1999) pp 22–33

7. Blumberg, B., Tomlinson, B., Downie, M.: Multiple conceptions of character-based interactive installations. *Computer Graphics International 2001* (2001) pp 5–11

8. Cassell, J., Bickmore, T., Camphell, L., Vilhjalmsson, H., Yan, H.: The human conversation as a system framework: Designing embodied conversational agents. In: *Embodied Conversational Agents*, ed Cassell, J., Sullivan, J., Prevost, S., Churchill, E. (The MIT Press, Cambridge, MA 2000) pp 29–63

9. Cassell, J., Pelachaud, C., Badler, N., Steedman, M., Achorn, B., Becket, T., Douville, B., Prevost, S., Stone, M.: Animated conversation: Rule-based generation of facial expression, gesture & spoken intonation for multiple conversational agents. *Computer Graphics* **28**:413–420 (1994)

10. Cavazza, M., Charles, F.: Interacting with virtual characters in interactive storytelling. In: *Proceedings of AAMAS'02* (2002) pp 318–325

11. Cohen, M.M., Beskow, J., Massaro, D.W.: Recent developments in facial animation: An inside view. In: *Proceedings of Auditory-Visual Speech Processing 98*, Sydney, Australia (1998)

12. Gebhard, P.: Enhancing embodied intelligent agents with affective user modelling. In: *Proceedings of UM2001*, Doctoral Consortium summary (Springer, Berlin 2001)

13. Hayes-Roth, B., van Gent, R., Huber, D.: Acting in character. *Creating personalities for synthetic actors*, ed Trappl, R., Petta, P. (Springer, New York 1997) pp 92–112

14. Höök, K., Persson, P., Sjölinder, M.: Evaluating users' experience of a character-enhanced Information Space. *AI Communications* **13**(3):195–212 (2000)

15. Isbister, K., Nakanishi, H., Ishida, T., Nass, C.: Helper agent: Designing an assistant for human-human interaction in a virtual meeting space. In: *Proceedings of CHI 2000* (ACM Press, New York 2000) pp 57–64

16. Ishizuka, M., Tsutsui, T., Saeyor, S., Dohi, H., Zong, Y., Prendinger, H.: MPML: A multimodal presentation markup language with character control functions. In: *Proceedings of the Workshop on Achieving Human-like Behavior in Interactive Animated Agents*, held in conj. with AAMAS'02 (2002) pp 50–54

17. Kipp, M.: Anvil – a generic annotation tool for multimodal dialogue. In: *Proceedings of Eurospeech'01* (2001) pp 1367–1370

18. Kipp, M.: From human gesture to synthetic action. In: *Proceedings of the Workshop on Multimodal Communication and Context in Embodied Agents*, held in conj. with the Fifth International Conference on Autonomous Agents (2001) pp 9–14

19. Kitano, H., Asada, M., Kuniyoshi, Y., Noda, I., Osawa, E., Matsubara, H.: RoboCup: A challenging problem for AI. *AI Magazine* **18**(1):73–85 (1997)

20. Klesen, M., Szatkowski, J., Lehmann, N.: A dramatised actant model for interactive improvisational plays. In: *Proceedings of the 3rd Intelligent Virtual Agents Workshop (IVA)* (Springer, New York 2001) pp 181–194

21. Kurlander, D., Skelly, T., Salesin, D.: Comic chat. In: *Proceedings of SIGGRAPH'96* (1996) pp 225–236

22. Laurel, B.: *Computers as Theater* (Addison-Wesley, Reading, MA 1993)

23. Lester, J, Voerman, J.I., Towns, S.G., Callaway, C.B.: Deictic believability: Coordinated gesture, locomotion, and speech in lifelike pedagogical agents. *Applied Artificial Intelligence* **13**:383–414 (1999)

24. Machado, I., Paiva, A., Prada, R.: Is the wolf angry or ... just hungry? In: *Proceedings of Autonomous Agents* (ACM Press, New York 2001), pp 370–376

25. Maes, P., Darrell, T., Blumberg, B., Pentland, A.: The ALIVE system: Wireless, full-body interaction with autonomous agents. In: *ACM Special Issue on Multimedia and Multisensory Virtual Worlds* (1996)
26. Marsella, S.C., Johnson, W.L., LaBore, C.: Interactive pedagogical drama. In: *Proceedings of the Fourth International Conference on Autonomous Agents* (ACM Press, New York 2000) pp 301–308
27. Mateas, M.: An Oz-centric review of interactive drama and believable agents. Technical Report CMU-CS-97-156, School of CS, CMU, Pittsburgh, PA (1997)
28. Mateas, M., Stern, A.: Towards integrating plot and character for interactive drama. In: *Working Notes of the Social Intelligent Agents: The Human in the Loop Symposium* (AAAI Press, New York 2000)
29. Matsubara, H., Frank, I., Tanaka-Ishii, K., Noda, I., Nakashima, H., Hasida, K.: Character design for soccer commentary. In: *RoboCup-98: Robot Soccer World Cup II*, ed Asada, M., Kitano, H. (Springer, New York 1999) pp 34–49
30. Nitta, K., Hasegawa, O., Akiba, T., Kamishima, T., Kurita, T., Hayamizu, S., Itoh, K., Ishizuka, M., Dohi, H., Okamura, M.: An experimental multimodal disputation system. In: *Proceedings of the IJCAI '97 Workshop on Intelligent Multimodal Systems* (1997)
31. Noma, T., Badler, N.: A virtual human presenter. In: *Proceedings of the IJCAI '97 Workshop on Animated Interface Agents: Making them Intelligent* (1997) pp 45–51
32. Pelachaud, C., Carofiglio, V., De Carolis, B., de Rosis, F., Poggi, I.: Embodied contextual agent in information delivering application. In: *Proceedings of AAMAS'02* (ACM Press, New York 2002) pp 758–765
33. Perlin, K., Goldberg, A.: Improv: A system for scripting interactive actors in virtual worlds. *Computer Graphics* **30**:205–216 (1996)
34. Prendinger, H., Ishizuka, M.: Social role awareness in animated agents. In: *Proceedings 5th International Conference on Autonomous Agents (Agents-01)* (ACM Press, New York 2001) pp 270–277
35. Rich, C., Sidner, C.L., Lesh, N.: COLLAGEN: Applying collaborative discourse theory to human-computer interaction. *AI Magazine* **22**(4):15–25 (2001)
36. Rickel, J., Johnson, W.L.: Virtual humans for team training in virtual reality. In: *Proceedings of the Ninth International Conference on Artificial Intelligence in Education* (IOS Press, Amsterdam 1999) pp 578–585
37. Rist, T., André, E., Baldes, S.: A flexible platform for building applications with life-like characters. In: *Proceedings of IUI'03* (ACM Press, New York 2003) pp 158–165
38. Rist, T., André, E., Müller, J.: Adding animated presentation agents to the interface. *Proceedings of IUI 97* (ACM Press, New York 1997) pp 79–86
39. Rist, T., Schmitt, M.: Applying socio-psychological concepts of cognitive consistency to negotiation dialog scenarios with embodied conversational characters. *Proceedings of AISB'02 Symposium on Animated Expressive Characters for Social Interactions* (2002) pp 79–84 (Extended version submitted for publication in 2003)
40. Scheflen, A.E.: The significance of posture in communication systems. *Psychiatry* **26**:316–331 (1964)
41. Sgouros, N.: Dynamic generation, management and resolution of interactive plots. *Artificial Intelligence* **107**(1):29–62 (1999)
42. Smith, M.A., Farnham, S., Drucker, S.M.: The social life of small graphical chat spaces In: *Proceedings of CHI'2000* (2000) pp 462–469

43. Swartout, W., Hill, R., Gratch, J., Johnson, W.L., Kyriakakis, C., LaBore, C., Lindheim, R., Marsella, S., Miraglia, D., Moore, B., Morie, J., Rickel, J., Thiébaux, M., Tuch, L., Whitney, R., Douglas, J.: Toward the Holodeck: Integrating graphics, sound, character and story. In: *Proceedings 5th International Conference on Autonomous Agents (Agents-01)* (ACM Press, New York 2001) pp 409–416

44. Thalmann, N.M., Kalra, P.: The simulation of a virtual TV presenter. In: *Computer graphics and applications* (World Scientific, Singapore 1995) pp 9–21

45. Traum, D., Rickel, J.: Embodied agents for multi-party dialogue in immersive virtual worlds. In: *Proc of AAMAS'02* (ACM Press, New York 2002) pp 766–733

46. Vilhjalmsson, H., Cassell, J.: BodyChat: Autonomous communicative behaviors in avatars. In: *Proceedings of Autonomous Agents'98* (1998) pp 269–276

47. Wahlster, W., Reithinger, N., Blocher, A.: SmartKom: Multimodal communication with a life-like character. In: *Proceedings of EUROSPEECH'01* (2001)

48. Walker, M.A., Cahn, J.E., Whittacker, S.J.: Improvising linguistic style: Social and affective bases for agent personality. In: *Proceedings First International Conference on Autonomous Agents (Agents'97)* (ACM Press, New York 1997) pp 10–17

49. Weyhrauch, P.: *Guiding interactive drama*. PhD thesis (Carnegie Mellon University 1997)

50. Yabe, J., Takahashi, S., Shibayama, E.: Automatic animation of discussions in usenet. In: *Proceedings of Advanced Visual Interfaces 2000* (2002) pp 84-91

51. Young, M.: The cooperative contract in interactive entertainment. In: *Socially Intelligent Agents: Creating Relationships with Computers and Robots*, ed Dautenhahn, K., Bond, A.H., Canamero, L., Edmonds, B. (Kluwer Academic, Dordrecht 2002) pp 229–234

Interface Agents That Facilitate Knowledge Interactions Between Community Members

Yasuyuki Sumi[1,3] and Kenji Mase[2,3]

[1] Graduate School of Informatics, Kyoto University
Yoshida-Honmachi, Sakyo, Kyoto 606-8501, Japan
sumi@i.kyoto-u.ac.jp

[2] Information Technology Center, Nagoya University
Furo-cho, Chikusa-ku, Nagoya, Aichi 464-8601, Japan
mase@itc.nagoya-u.ac.jp

[3] ATR Media Information Science Laboratories
Seika-cho, Soraku-gun, Kyoto 619-0288, Japan

Summary. In this chapter, we describe life-like character-based systems developed in the context of our personal guidance system. We first present PalmGuide, a hand-held tour guidance system. After that, we present two character-based systems to facilitate knowledge interactions among users. One is AgentSalon, a display showing conversations between personal agents according to their users' profiles and interests. Another is ComicDiary, a system representing individual experiences in the style of a comic.

1 Introduction

In this chapter, we describe life-like character-based systems developed in the context of our project called C-MAP (Context-aware Mobile Assistant Project) to build a personal guidance system [18, 19, 21]. The aims of the project are to build a tour guidance system personalized according to its user's individual contexts, and to facilitate knowledge communications among community members by matchmaking users having shared interests.

We prototyped the C-MAP system as a digital assistant system to support participants at academic conferences [20]. Our system provided users with a hand-held guidance system (PalmGuide), kiosk services, and a meeting facilitator (AgentSalon) for onsite conference participants as well as continuous web services for pre/post-conference information such as a personal tour diary (ComicDiary). Life-like interface agents played an important role in integrating and personalizing the different services according to the contexts of individual users and instantly organized groups of users.

The remainder of the chapter is organized as follows. First, we describe existing works using life-like characters as a medium of knowledge interactions and present our standpoint. The following sections present our systems. We first describe PalmGuide, a hand-held tour guidance system as a personal device for accumulating individual contexts. After that, we present two character-based systems to facilitate knowledge interactions among users. One is AgentSalon, a display showing conversations between personal agents according to their users' profiles and interests. Another is ComicDiary, a system representing individual experiences in the style of a comic.

2 Related Works

The goal of AgentSalon is to build an environment for creative conversation among people by mediation of character agents. There have been many works using computer-animated characters. Examples that focus on conversation with humans, as a medium of knowledge among people, are: an interface agent communicating with a user by voice conversation [4]; a multi-modal conversational agent with non-verbal interaction like gestures [6]; embodied presentation agents on presentation slides or web pages [13, 1]; a conversational avatar with gestures in 3D virtual spaces [5]; and a system converting text chats to comics showing embodied characters [9]. These, however, represent the conversation and behavior of agents according to predefined scripts or texts and commands given online. Our target is to create an agent which proactively generates and presents knowledge as a proxy of its user.

In order to achieve our goal to facilitate encounters and creative conversation among people, we adopt a method whereby agents participate in users' face-to-face conversation. Some researchers have already proposed such agents participating in human conversations. Nagao and Takeuchi [10] focused on sociality and multi-modality of an anthropomorphic agent participating in two people's conversation. Isbister et al. [7] proposed a helper agent which provides conversation topics to first-meeting users in a virtual meeting space. Nishimoto et al. [12] proposed a topic development agent to provide users in brainstorming sessions with relevant and unexpected topics by monitoring the discussion and automatically searching texts from a database. These agents commonly participate in users' conversations as a third person, not as an agent belonging to an individual user. Our aim is to facilitate new encounters and collaborative knowledge sharing/creation by utilizing the information of individual users.

There are works that support knowledge sharing and creation such as: asynchronous knowledge sharing using alter-ego agents [11, 8]; an embodied presentation team of conversational agents [2]; and automatic animation of discussions in USENET by using avatars of news authors [24]. However, their knowledge resources are commonly static information such as previously prepared knowledge bases. On the other hand, AgentSalon uses personal information constantly accumulated by personal agents on PalmGuides carried by users. Such information is embedded in the real world; therefore, information presented by AgentSalon has the potential to instantly influence users' on-going (touring) behavior and accelerate collaborative knowledge sharing and creation among communities.

The essential jobs of AgentSalon are to detect and represent shared/different parts of the personal information (e.g. interests and touring records) of several users. In these terms, we have already proposed a method to visualize shared/different parts of several users' individual viewpoints during online discussions [22]. The Semantic map running on AgentSalon, which will be presented in this chapter, plays a similar role. However, efforts to read the shared/different parts of the visualized information spaces and to utilize them for further discussion are fully up to users. AgentSalon automatically reads the shared/different parts of users' knowledge/interests and represents them as *conversational stories*. Therefore, the cost of information conveyance between users decreases, and more casual usage and understanding are encouraged.

One of our main technological challenges by ComicDiary is to allegorize individual fragmentary episodes as a comic story. There have been studies of story generation in the context of artificial intelligence (AI) and cognitive science. Rummelhart [16] tried to build a grammatical schema of stories by analyzing traditional fables. Schank and Abelson [17] regarded AI issues, e.g. problem solving and planning, as story generation. More recently, several systems of story generation have been proposed (e.g. [15, 14]). These works, however, aimed to understand literary works and limited their focus to literal representation. On the other hand, we aim to facilitate human communications through generated stories and employ a comic representation because it is casual and easy to use in giving an overview of personal events.

There have already been some interesting research projects employing comic style as a user interface representation. These include Comic Chat for representing an online chat history as a comic [9], Video Manga for visualizing a video summary in comic style [23], and ChatScape for using captured camera images to represent an online chat history as a comic [3]. Although they used comic representation, these works did not consider translating simple sequences of events into a story or personalizing the generated story; these are the issues that we address here.

3 PalmGuide: Personal Guidance System

PalmGuide is basically a portable browser for showing a conference program as shown in Fig. 1. The PalmGuide user can call up his or her personal agent, which recommends upcoming presentations inferred as interesting to the user according to his or her current context (personal preference, current interest, and temporal situation). As feedback for generating knowledge of user interest, users can rate (1: not interesting, 2: average, 3: interesting) the individual presentations they attend.

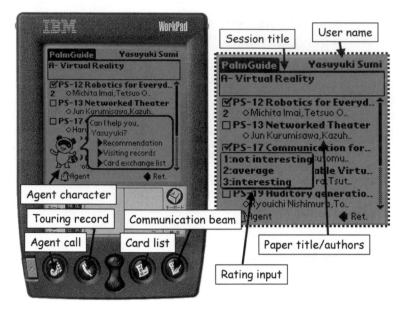

Fig. 1. Displays of PalmGuide

PalmGuide users can exchange their virtual business cards by infrared connections and use AgentSalon as a facilitator of face-to-face meetings at the conference by sending their guide agents from the PalmGuides to the AgentSalon system. PalmGuide also stores these electronic histories.

The stored data of a personal history is copied to the central community database (DB) when a user connects his or her PalmGuide to kiosks located on the conference site and when the PalmGuide devices are returned. By centralizing the individual data in the community DB, we can also obtain statistical data such as which presentations are popular among PalmGuide users.

4 AgentSalon: Facilitating Face-to-Face Knowledge Exchange by Agents Conversations

4.1 System Overview of AgentSalon

Figure 2 shows AgentSalon being used by two users. The following is a scenario of using AgentSalon.

1. Personal guide agents on the PalmGuide of individual users migrate to AgentSalon with their users' personal information and are displayed as animated characters.

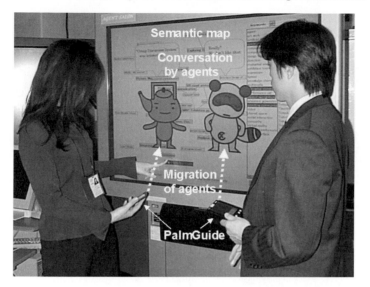

Fig. 2. AgentSalon in use

2. The migrating agents share their users' visiting records and interests and detect common as well as different parts of this information.
3. Based on the above results, the agents plan and begin conversations in front of the users. By observing the conversations, the users can efficiently and pleasantly exchange information related to an exhibit.
4. Because AgentSalon can access community information such as the information on each exhibit and other users' personal information via networks, users can browse detailed information about exhibits or users referred by agents.

As Fig. 3 illustrates, AgentSalon consists of the following three components.

Generation of conversation. Generates scripts of *interesting* conversations using personal information managed by agents. This is a knowledge-based system having utterance templates and strategic rules to tailor scripts depending on the context.

Representation of conversation. According to the generated scripts, this component controls and represents utterances and behaviors of animated agents by using Microsoft Agent. The streams of conversations, entrance and exit points of agents, and simple interaction with users are controlled by using JavaScript.

Semantic map [19]. A visual interface for browsing community information accumulated in the web server. It shows semantic relationships between exhibits and the people involved with them and helps a user to associatively explore large information spaces according to his or her interests.

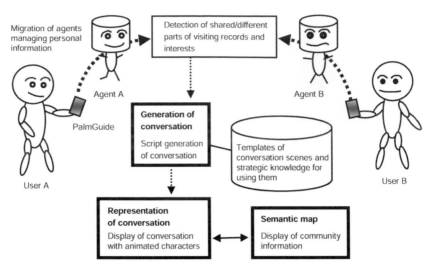

Fig. 3. System architecture of AgentSalon

AgentSalon runs on Microsoft Internet Explorer. Semantic map is a Java applet running on the base of AgentSalon. The animated agents are displayed on the top of Semantic map using Microsoft Agent. The display is a touch panel, so users can manipulate Semantic map with their fingers and interact with their agents.

Because conversations of agents are controlled by JavaScript, animated agents on AgentSalon can use embodied gestures, e.g. manipulating icons of Semantic map along with their utterances, achieved by executing a method of Semantic map applet by JavaScript.

In the current implementation, when a certain agent enters the salon, its user's icon appears in Semantic map. At the same time, the icons of the exhibits that he or she has visited and evaluated as *interesting* appear and are linked with his or her icon. Therefore, it visualizes relationships (overlaps and differences) between touring experiences and the individual interests of users.

4.2 Generation of Conversation by Agents

This subsection describes a part of conversation generation, which is the main part of AgentSalon.

The goal of this part is to generate scripts of *interesting* conversation based on personal information managed by agents in the salon. In order to achieve this goal, we have been implementing a knowledge-based system to plan conversation by authoring reusable templates of conversations, and the strategic rules to use them.

Here, we call comparatively independent and reusable sets of utterances "scene". Conversation planning is triggered by the entrance of a new agent, such that one or more scenes are displayed. The exit of agents from the salon is done on the users' command by touching the animated agents on the display.

The rules of script generation can be classified into the following:

Object rules. Rules to make scenes by filling scene templates with personal information (e.g. user name, exhibit title, parametric numbers, etc.) to hand.

Meta rules. Strategic rules to select templates and object rules in order to make more effective conversation for stimulating users' meeting. These include editorial rules to smooth the stream of the whole conversation when combining several scenes.

Input data for the part of script generation is personal information, managed by the personal agent running on the PalmGuide, as follows:

- User name, affiliation, participating status (exhibitor or visitor), URL of homepage, and personal profile.
- Touring records, i.e. exhibit ID and visiting time.
- Personal evaluation (rating) of each exhibit.
- List of names of other PalmGuide users with whom the user exchanged virtual business cards, i.e. user ID and time of card exchange.
- Personal interests represented by keyword vector, updated when using Semantic map.

The following provide examples of object rules that use personal information as above.

- One of the agents takes the initiative in a conversation and presents exhibits it (i.e. its user) has visited with a Semantic map of the exhibition shown on the display. When another agent finds an exhibit among those which its user has visited, this agent discloses its user's evaluation and comments on the exhibit (by acting for its user). The agent can call the personal agents of the exhibitors and open the homepage of the exhibit for more detailed information.
- When two users' evaluations of a commonly visited exhibit are different (e.g. *user A* is interested in *exhibit 1*, but *user B* is not), their agents prompt a discussion about the exhibit. For example, the agent of *user A* says "*Exhibit 1* was interesting!", and then the agent of *user B* replies "Really? We didn't like it." By observing the dialogue, *user A* and *user B* can know that they have differing opinions about a shared experience (i.e. visiting *exhibit 1*), which efficiently leads them into a stimulating discussion.
- Suppose that *user A* has visited *exhibits 1*, *2*, *3*, and *4*, and *user B* has visited *exhibits 2*, *4*, *5*, and *6*. In this case, their agents will notice that the users have commonly visited *exhibits 2* and *4*, i.e. they share some interests

in exhibits. Therefore, *user A*'s agent recommends *exhibits 1* and *3* to *user B*, and *user B*'s agent recommends *exhibits 5* and *6* to *user A*.

The following are examples of meta rules, i.e. strategic rules to control agents' conversation.

- If the number of exhibits common to a certain pair of users is beyond a threshold, they are interpreted to have similar interests. Then, the scene for recommending the diverging parts of their visiting records is selected.
- If there is a user who has visited many more exhibits than other users, his or her agent takes the initiative in a conversation.
- If the difference of two users' ages is large, the scene for revealing conflicts of evaluation ("interesting" and "not interesting") is not used.
- If all users in the salon have not visited any exhibits, agents just introduce their users' profiles.

As seen above, object rules are reusable and applicable to various domains. On the other hand, soundness of meta rules depends greatly on context and domains.

For example, while mutual recommendation of exhibits according to visiting history is useful in a museum application, recommending a presentation that has already finished does not make sense. Exchange of personal evaluations on individual exhibits is an acceptable topic in amusement applications, such as theme parks. However, it may be provocative at academic conferences.

4.3 Implementation and Evaluation

We prototyped the first version of AgentSalon as a service of the Digital Assistant Project to support participants at an academic conference held in July, 2000. However, data on the presentations and participants at the conference was in Japanese only, so we show an example, in this subsection, based on other data from our laboratories' open day in 1999.

Figure 4 shows an example display of AgentSalon. AgentSalon was designed using the metaphor of a salon for gathering and chatting together. On the display, there is always a master of the salon (the goat in the figure), which we call the "salon agent". Figure 4 shows the agent characters of four users. Due to the display size, we limit the maximum number of personal agents in the salon to five at a time.

In the background of the animated agents, Semantic map is displayed for showing relationships between the agents' users and exhibits. Semantic map shows icons corresponding to users and exhibits they have visited as well as showing their interest by selecting 3 (interesting) on the evaluation dialogue box shown in Fig. 1. Exhibit icons are linked with user icons based on their evaluations. Therefore, the icons of users sharing interests on exhibits are indirectly connected and located nearby. Users can open detailed pages on exhibits and users by clicking their icons and associatively selecting keywords

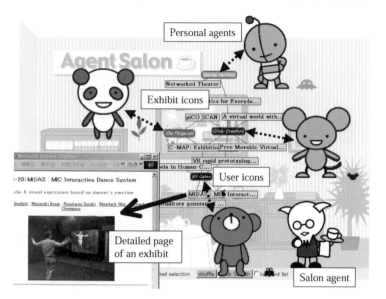

Fig. 4. An example of AgentSalon display

on Semantic map. Semantic map is intended to be used for exploring related information and facilitating deeper discussion by users, which is triggered by conversation between agents.

We prepared eight kinds of agent characters, e.g. mouse and raccoon, that are selected by individual PalmGuide users on registration. Animation data includes about 40 kinds of actions such as greeting, moving, and pointing.

Table 1. An example of personal data of PalmGuide users. Evaluation values – 1: Not interesting, 2: Average, 3: Interesting

User name	Agent character	Visiting records (exhibit ID: evaluation)
Adam	kettle	(PS-1:3), (PS-10:3), (PS-11:2), (PS-12:1), (PS-15:3), (PS-18:3), (PS-21:3)
Bill	bear	(PS-1:3), (PS-2:3), (PS-10:3), (PS-11:1), (PS-19:3), (PS-20:3)
Cindy	mouse	(PS-1:3), (PS-10:3), (PS-12:3), (PS-15:3), (PS-18:3), (PS-21:3)

We will now describe an example of conversations performed by agents. Table 1 shows individual data of three users, Adam, Bill, and Cindy. This data is usually accumulated on individual PalmGuides, and used to generate conversations on AgentSalon.

Figure 5 shows sequential snapshots of AgentSalon where the personal agents of the three users entered.

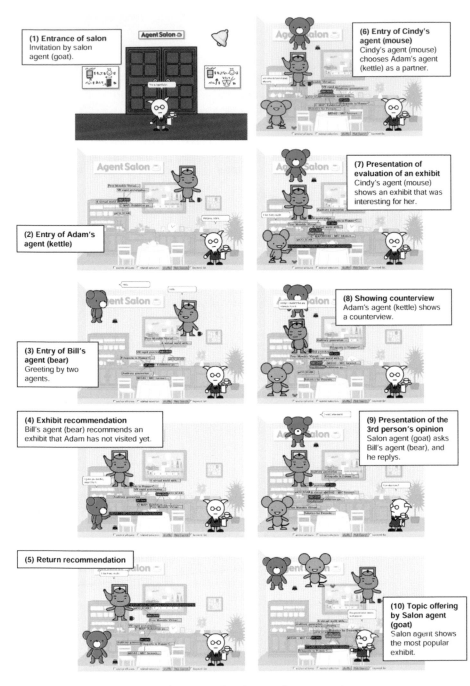

Fig. 5. An example of agents' conversations

(1) When there are no PalmGuide users, the entrance of the salon is displayed and the salon agent (goat) invites potential users.

(2) The agent (kettle) of the first user, Adam, enters the salon. At the same time, icons of Adam himself and five exhibits he showed interest in are displayed in the background.

(3) The agent (bear) of the second user, Bill, enters the salon. The two agents greet. Icons of Bill and the exhibits he was interested in are also displayed.

(4) Behind the scene, these two agents find that Adam and Bill have two exhibits in common among their visiting histories, and then select the scene for mutual recommendations of exhibits. In this example, Bill's agent (bear) points to the icon of PS-20 that Bill was interested in and that Adam has not yet visited, and says "I guess you like this, since I like it."

(5) Adam's agent (kettle) returns a recommendation by pointing to the icon of PS-15 and saying "I like it very much!"

(6) The agent (mouse) of the third user, Cindy, enters the salon. After greeting, matchmaking between Cindy and the pre-existing users is calculated behind the scene. Concretely, the number of exhibits commonly visited by both Adam and Cindy is six, while for both Bill and Cindy it is only two. Therefore, Cindy's agent (mouse) selects Adam's agent (kettle) to speak to, by saying "We seem to have shared interests."

(7) The agents of Cindy and Adam select a discussion topic concerning an exhibit that both visited. In this example, they find an exhibit where the two users' evaluations were divided, and disclose this during a conversation. Concretely, they select PS-12 and Cindy's agent (mouse) says "I visited this exhibit. I like it very much!"

(8) Adam's agent (kettle) replies "Really? I couldn't find any interests in it."

(9) In order to draw the third person, Bill, into the discussion, the salon agent (goat) asks Bill's agent (bear) "How about you?" In this case, Bill's agent (bear) replies "I wish I attended it" because Bill did not visit it.

(10) When no other events (e.g. entry of a new agent) happen for a while, the salon agent (goat) offers a topic. In this example, he points to the icon of the most popular exhibit among the three users, i.e. PS-1.

At the conference in July, 2000, AgentSalon was located in the lounge of the conference site to be freely used by participants. Though AgentSalon can be used by participants without a PalmGuide as a browser of conference information, basically, it is intended to be used collaboratively by PalmGuide users.

During the four-day conference, 40 of the 65 PalmGuide users, i.e. over 60%, accessed AgentSalon. While most of the users tried AgentSalon only two to five times, some users frequently (over ten times) used it and enjoyed it. According to the results of a questionnaire, most of the users recognized its effectiveness.

In order to view how many users simultaneously accessed AgentSalon, Table 2 shows the number of users per session. Here, "session" means a temporal

Table 2. The number of users per session

User number	1	2	3	4	5
Number of sessions	40	14	8	4	3

sequence from the time of a user's access to AgentSalon when no other user uses it to the time when all users logged out from it. During the conference, there were 69 sessions by 123 users. Forty sessions, about 58% of the total, were by just one user. The largest number of users per session was 5: this occurred three times. Since the access of AgentSalon by one user is not the intended usage, we can say that there were many sessions just for checking AgentSalon's behavior. On the other hand, we can see that there were not so few sessions by three or more users. Actually, we could observe some "regulars" frequently gathered in front of AgentSalon and having discussions by touching Semantic map for over 10 minutes. We could also observe some users exchanging their "virtual cards" with their PalmGuides when meeting in front of AgentSalon: this implies that AgentSalon contributed toward supporting encounters among conference participants.

Before the conference, our concern was whether the protocol of AgentSalon and PalmGuide would be understood and accepted by users. At the conference, we found it was well understood and accepted by users without careful instruction.

5 ComicDiary: Representing Individual Experiences in a Comic Style

5.1 Using Comics to Exchange Individual Experiences

Figure 6 shows examples of hand-drawn diaries that were sketched and submitted as reports of visiting museums by one of our colleagues when she took a university class. Other students submitted conventional text-based reports of course, but she was allowed to submit such a comic report because her illustration skills were admired by the professor.

We can find the following characteristics in the comic report.

- The story of the comic is structured according to her subjective viewpoint.
- The main character of the comic seems to be herself, but it does not exactly represent her appearance, personality, and actions. The comic character has its own identity and personality as her alter ego.
- The comic exaggerates her personal impressions by projecting them onto the alter-ego character rather than exactly reproducing actual events.
- The comic highlights impressive events rather than listing every event.
- Her total impression of the museum visit is represented by a rhythm of sequential scenes.

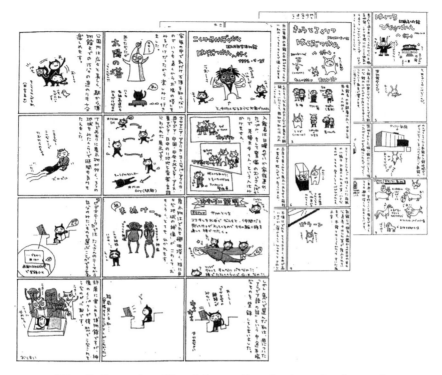

Fig. 6. Examples of hand-drawn diary in the style of a comic

- The comic describes not only the museum's exhibits but also the surroundings and other visitors.
- Jokes and small talk increase the comic's entertainment value.

The comic report is not appropriate for precisely conveying detailed events, but it is excellent for sharing personal impressions and episodes. Actually, the comic report stimulated the authors' group to exchange individual memories of museum visits and increased their motivation to revisit the museums.

Such experience encouraged us to try a system that provides visit diaries to individual users of our tour guidance system [21]. The technical challenges we addressed were:

- developing a method to structure a comic story from the fragmentary data of individual users (personal profile and visiting records) stored in the tour guidance system and to personalize the comic contents; and
- prototyping a so-called expert system that emulates the human skill of comic drawing.

5.2 Implementation

The first prototype of ComicDiary was implemented as our digital assistant system for participants to an academic conference, which was held from May 22 to 25, 2001, in Japan.

System Architecture of ComicDiary

We prototyped ComicDiary as an online service on the web so that it could be used as a kiosk service provided at the conference site as well as an online service via the web that users could access anytime after the conference. We also provided PalmGuide users with printed comic diaries when they returned their PalmGuide devices.

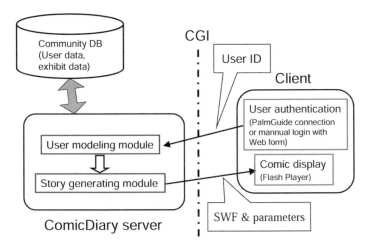

Fig. 7. System architecture of ComicDiary

Figure 7 illustrates the system architecture of ComicDiary. We employed Macromedia Flash running on web browsers to display the generated comic diaries on client machines. Diary generation was processed at a web server that communicates with clients via a CGI.

The following processes were carried out for diary generation.

1. Clients certify users. When ComicDiary is used by accessing a kiosk at the conference site, a user ID is automatically sent from the PalmGuide to the server via the kiosk. When ComicDiary is used as a web service, the user logs in to the digital assistant service site with his or her user ID and password.
2. Requests to generate comic diaries with the user IDs are sent to the server via CGI.

3. The server extracts the user's personal data and statistical data from the community DB and then generates a comic diary story for him or her by determining the user type from the data.
4. A Flash file (SWF) and parameter data for comic rendering are sent to the client.
5. The client renders and displays a comic diary according to the given parameter.

Story Generation Engine

The most important part of ComicDiary is the story generation engine, which is a knowledge-based system. It mainly contains a user modeling module to collect the necessary data and a story generation module to allegorize a story.

User modeling is done with a personal profile containing the attributes of a user and a community profile that is shared by all PalmGuide users. The personal profile includes the following data.

- Age and gender, which are reflected in the personality of the main character of a diary.
- Participant type: whether they have their own presentations at the conference.
- Touring history (presentations the user attended and their ratings). The data reflects the user's activity level at the conference.
- Interaction records with other PalmGuide users, such as business card exchanges and accesses to AgentSalon.

The user modeling module generates the outline of a diary according to the above data.

The community profile includes the following data.

- Plenary events of the conference, e.g. reception and invited talks.
- Information at the conference venue, e.g. tourist information and current topics.
- Socially shared impressions during the conference, e.g. popularity of presentations.

The above data is used to increase the reality of comic diaries.

Potential streams of a comic story are prepared as a constraint network representing mutual dependencies among scenes as shown in Fig. 8. That is, several alternatives for introductory scenes are followed by presentation scenes (if a user gives a presentation at the conference), touring scenes, interaction scenes (of business card exchanges and/or AgentSalon), and ending scenes. The dependencies (i.e. exclusive relationship and causal relationship) among the scenes were predefined by the comic designer.

An individual scene contains a number of frames. For example, an introductory scene contains three frames, and a presentation scene contains four frames, in the first prototype.

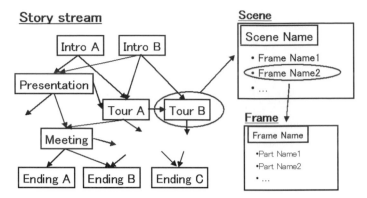

Fig. 8. Story generation of a comic diary

Rendering Comic Frames

In order to increase the variety of comic frames from limited resources, we employed a method to superimpose several layers as shown in Fig. 9. Accordingly, we could reuse background layers (e.g. scenes of conference rooms) independently of main characters. In the first prototype, we prepared 12 kinds of background layers to show views of the conference rooms and sightseeing spots around the conference site.

We prepared 44 illustrations for each character, as shown in Fig. 10, because they greatly influence the entertainment value and variety of comics. The main character was the agent character which a user selected for the PalmGuide. Since we prepared eight kinds of characters for PalmGuides, we had to prepare 352 appearances of main character layers. That was one of the hardest jobs in prototyping the ComicDiary system.

Templates of word layers were prepared as images in the same way as the background and main character layers, and strings of dynamically extracted data (e.g. presentation titles and user names) were embedded in the templates during the rendering process.

5.3 Examples of Generated Comic Diaries

This subsection presents examples of generated comic diaries and explains how ComicDiary works. We fixed the length of comics to 12 frames as shown in Fig. 11 because we intended the comics to be printed on A4 size paper. The main character in the comics is the agent character, which the user selects for the PalmGuide, and which we characterize as the user's avatar (closely identified with the user, but a different person).

We prepared three types of story outlines: for presenters, for active attendees, and for non-active attendees according to the user's personal profile.

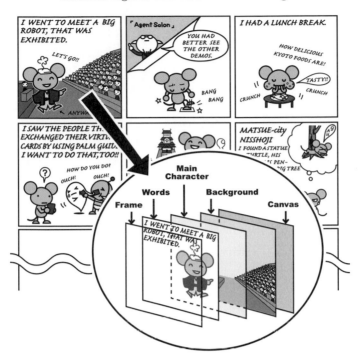

Fig. 9. Frame composition by multiple layers

Figure 11 is an example of a comic diary for a user who gives a presentation at the conference. Four frames were used for the user's presentation scene because it was considered the highlight of the user's experiences at the conference. The presentation scene was followed by scenes of meeting with other participants, such as business card exchanges and AgentSalon accesses. Presentation titles and participant names embedded in the comic were extracted from the community DB.

The comic contained not only personal scenes but also environmental scenes to represent the conference atmosphere, e.g. sightseeing spots around the conference site. Also, we provided a scene for giving feedback to the user, e.g. the socially formed impression of the user's presentation according to the statistical results of ratings given on PalmGuides.

For a user who did not give a presentation at the conference, the outline of the comic was drastically changed according to the number of presentations that he or she attended and the average value of the ratings. Figure 12 is an example comic diary for an active participant and Figure 13 is one for a non-active participant.

The former comic starts with a cheerful atmosphere and is embedded with many scenes of attending presentations. Embedded presentations were chosen

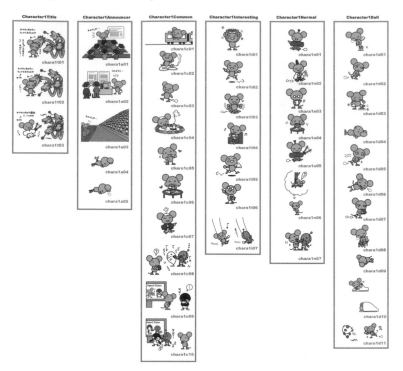

Fig. 10. Comic-part data (of main character layer)

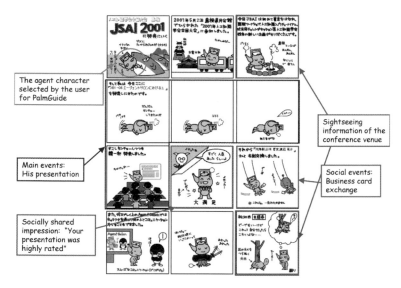

Fig. 11. Example of generated comic diary (for a presenter)

Fig. 12. Example of generated comic diary (active attendance)

Fig. 13. Example of generated comic diary (non-active attendance)

from the presentations that the user evaluated as "interesting." The latter comic, in contrast, was presented with a negative (but amusing) mood.

For both cases, we provided a scene showing popular presentations according to the statistical data accumulated in the community DB during the conference in order to increase the awareness shared by the members of the community.

5.4 User Evaluations and Discussion

Fifty-two PalmGuide users participated in the digital assistant project in 2001, and they were ComicDiary users at the same time. We provided printed versions of the generated comic diaries to those who requested them. After five weeks, we asked them to fill out a questionnaire and received 16 replies. The data was not enough for statistical significance, but we were still able to find some interesting tendencies.

The effects of using ComicDiary that we mostly expected were "users want to show their comic diaries to other people" and "it activates conversations among people". To verify these hypotheses, we asked users how many people they had shown their printed comic diaries to. Three users said "showed to nobody", one said "showed to one person", three said "showed to three people", one said "showed to four people", and four said "showed to more than five people". Four users "did not receive the printed version". That is, two-thirds of the users who received the printed diaries showed them to more than three people.

To the question "do you think the comic diary encourage(d) conversations with the person(s) to whom you show(ed) the comic?", 14 of the 16 users replied "yes". Here, those who showed their comic diaries to nobody or did not bring them back were asked to answer by supposing that they had showed them to someone.

We also asked a question about the contents of the comics. To the question "does the comic exactly represent your memory?", two users answered "exactly represents," seven answered "fairly represents," five answered "moderate," two answered "not represents well," and nobody answered "not at all." We can thus say that the diaries will augment the users' memories.

It is interesting that seven users answered "exactly represents", or "fairly represents" while ten users among the 16 respondents were "presenters". This means that we could observe a tendency of "presenters" to evaluate the comic diaries more highly than "attendances (with no presentation)". From the result, we learned that the presentation scene, which is a highly personalized episode, helped to increase the reality of the comics.

Next, we discuss the effect of comic representation in comparison with another representation, i.e. a simple list of personal data accumulated in the PalmGuide devices. We have already provided our digital assistant users with the ability to automatically create touring diaries in hypertext style (Fig. 14) [20].

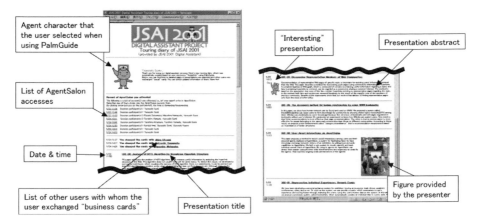

Fig. 14. A diary in hypertext style

As we can see in Fig. 14, the hypertext style diaries accurately show all the data of the user's touring history and interactions with other PalmGuide users. The user can get detailed information by following the links of presentations that the user attended and people with whom the user exchanged a virtual business card. The hypertext diary would seem better able to carefully explore information related to the user's experience. However, we thought this format would not be suitable for light-heartedly sharing one's impressions and experiences with other people.

On the other hand, ComicDiary aims to represent its users' personal impressions by summarizing their experiences from fragmentary data. We assumed that comic diaries would be superior for encouraging conversations among people.

In fact, to the question "which is better to show to other people, comic style or hyper-text style?", ten users replied "comic style", nobody replied "hyper-text style", four replied "neither", and two replied "cannot decide". That is, the comic style was obviously better accepted for sharing experiences than hypertext style.

6 Conclusions

We have described our life-like character-based systems developed in the context of a personal guidance system. Our guidance system is comprised of many distributed systems, i.e. a hand-held guidance system running on PDA, a kiosk system for personal use, a large display system for multiple users, and various web services. Life-like interface agents play an important role in integrating and personalizing such distributed services according to the contexts of individual users and instantly organized groups of users.

In the context of AgentSalon, agents' behaviors such as migration (from PalmGuides to the AgentSalon display) and talking (to other agents) help users to understand the flow of personal information among our distributed systems and then increase the system's believability.

In the context of ComicDiary, a character agent acts as the user's alter ego in a comic story personalized according to the user's experience and then facilitates the exchange of personal experiences among users.

Acknowledgments

Extraordinarily valuable contributions to this work were made by Tetsushi Yamamoto, Tadashi Takumi, and Ryuuki Sakamoto. Keiko Nakao took part in the design and illustration of the agent characters. We would like to thank Ryohei Nakatsu and Norihiro Hagita for their continuous support. The work presented in this chapter was supported in part by the Telecommunications Advancement Organization of Japan.

References

1. André, E., Rist, T., Müller, J.: WebPersona: A life-like presentation agent for the World-Wide Web. In: *IJCAI-97 Workshop on Animated Interface Agents: Making Them Intelligent* (1997) pp 53–60
2. André, E., Rist, T., van Mulken, S., Klesen, M., Baldes, S.: The automated design of believable dialogue for animated presentation teams. In: *Embodied Conversational Agents*, ed Cassell, J., Sullivan, J., Prevost, S., Churchill, E. (The MIT Press, Cambridge, MA 2000) pp 220–255
3. Ayatsuka, Y., Matsushita, N., Rekimoto, R.: ChatScape: A visual informal communication tool in communities. In: *CHI 2001 Extended Abstracts* (ACM Press, New York 2001) pp 327–328
4. Ball, G., Ling, D., Kurlander, D., Miller, J., Pugh, D., Skelly, T., Stankosky, A., Thiel, D., Van Dantzich, M., Wax, T.: Lifelike computer characters: The Persona project at Microsoft. In: *Software Agents*, ed Bradshaw, J.M. (The AAAI Press, Menlo Park, CA 1997) pp 191–222
5. Cassell, J., Vilhjálmsson, H.: Fully embodied conversational avatars: Making communicative behaviors autonomous. *Autonomous Agents and Multi-Agent Systems* **2**(1):45–64 (1999)
6. Hasegawa, O., Itou, K., Kurita, T., Hayamizu, S., Tanaka, K., Yamamoto, K., Otsu, N.: Active agent oriented multimodal interface system. In: *Proceedings of IJCAI-95* (1995) pp 82–87
7. Isbister, K., Nakanishi, H., Ishida, T., Nass, C.: Helper agent: Designing an assistant for human-human interaction in a virtual meeting space. In: *Proceedings of CHI 2000* (ACM Press, New York 2000) pp 57–64
8. Kubota, H., Nishida, T., Koda, T.: Exchanging tacit community knowledge by talking-virtualized-egos. In: *Proceedings of Agents 2000* (ACM Press, New York 2000) pp 285–292

9. Kurlander, D., Skelly, T., Salesin, D.: Comic Chat. In: *Proceedings of SIG-GRAPH'96* (ACM Press, New York 1996), pp 225–236
10. Nagao, K., Takeuchi, A.: Social interaction: Multimodal conversation with social agents. In: *AAAI-94* (1994) pp 22–28
11. Nishida, T., Hirata, T., Maeda, H.: CoMeMo-Community: A system for supporting community knowledge evolution. In: *Community Computing and Support Systems*, ed Ishida, T., LNCS 1519 (Springer, Berlin New York 1998) pp 183–200
12. Nishimoto, K., Sumi, Y., Mase, K.: Enhancement of creative aspects of a daily conversation with a topic development agent. In: *Coordination Technology for Collaborative Applications*, ed by Conen, W., Neumann, G. Lecture Notes in Computer Sciences, Vol. 1364 (Springer, Berlin Heidelberg New York 1998) pp 63–76
13. Noma, T., Badler, N.I.: A virtual human presenter. In: *IJCAI-97 Workshop on Animated Interface Agents: Making Them Intelligent* (1997) pp 45–51
14. Ogata, T., Hori, K., Ohsuga, S.: A basic framework for narrative conceptual structure generation based on narrative techniques and strategies (in Japanese). *Journal of Japanese Society for Artificial Intelligence* **11**(1):148–159 (1996)
15. Okada, N., Endo, T.: Story generation based on dynamics of the mind. *Computational Intelligence* **8**(1):123–160 (1992)
16. Rumelhart, D.E.: Notes on a schema for stories. In:*Representation and Understanding: Studies in Cognitive Science*, ed Bobrow, D, Collins, D. (Academic Press, New York 1975)
17. Schank, R.C., Abelson, R.P.: *Script, Plans, Goals, and Understanding* (Lawrence Erlbaum, Hillsdale, NJ 1977)
18. Sumi, Y., Etani, T., Fels, S., Simonet, N., Kobayashi, K., Mase, K.: C-MAP: Building a context-aware mobile assistant for exhibition tours. In: *Community Computing and Support Systems*, ed Ishida, T, LNCS 1519 (Springer, Berlin New York 1998) pp 137–154
19. Sumi, Y., Mase, K.: Communityware situated in real-world contexts: Knowledge media augmented by context-aware personal agents. In: *Proceedings of the Fifth International Conference and Exhibition on the Practical Application of Intelligent Agents and Multi-Agent Technology (PAAM 2000)* (2000) pp 311–326
20. Sumi, Y., Mase, K.: Digital assistant for supporting conference participants: An attempt to combine mobile, ubiquitous and Web computing. In: *Proceedings of Ubicomp 2001*, LNCS 2201 (Springer, Berlin New York 2001) pp 156–175
21. Sumi, Y., Mase, K.: Supporting the awareness of shared interests and experiences in communities. *International Journal of Human-Computer Studies* **56**(1):127–146 (2002)
22. Sumi, Y., Nishimoto, K., Mase, K.: Personalizing shared information in creative conversations. In: *IJCAI-97 Workshop on Social Interaction and Community-ware* (1997) pp 31–36
23. Uchihashi, S., Foote, J., Girgensohn, A., Boreczky, J.: Video Manga: Generating semantically meaningful video summaries. In: *Proceedings of Multimedia'99* (ACM Press, New York 1999) pp 383–392
24. Yabe, J., Takahashi, S., Shibayama, E.: Automatic animation of discussions in USENET. In: *Proceedings of Advanced Visual Interfaces 2000 (AVI 2000)* (ACM Press, New York 2000) pp 84–91

Animated Agents Capable of Understanding Natural Language and Performing Actions*

Hozumi Tanaka[1], Takenobu Tokunaga[1], and Yusuke Shinyama[2]

[1] Department of Computer Science, Tokyo Institute of Technology
  Meguro Oookayama 2-12-1, Tokyo 152-8552, Japan
  tanaka@cl.cs.titech.ac.jp, take@cl.cs.titech.ac.jp
[2] Computer Science Department, New York University, 715 Broadway, 7th Floor,
  New York, NY 10003, USA
  yusuke@cs.nyu.edu

Summary. This chapter describes a system called Kairai and its Natural Language Understanding (NLU) capabilities. It identifies its strength and shortcomings and identifies requirements for future NLU systems. The NLU research environment has changed drastically in the past two decades. Better technologies in speech recognition, natural language processing, and computer graphics are now available and make it much easier to develop a life-like animated agent (a software robot) which can understand commands in spoken language and perform actions specified by the commands. Combining these technologies, a life-like animated agent system named Kairai was developed at our laboratory to conduct preliminary research on an NLU system. Although Kairai includes many innovative features, several important problems hindering the building of a better NLU system still remain. After describing several issues the Kairai system can handle, we will conclude by outlining what problems we have to solve in the future. The results obtained from our research should be naturally applicable to hardware robots.

1 Introduction

Historically, the most important Natural Language Understanding (NLU) system was SHRDLU developed by Winograd at MIT in the early 1970s [31]. This system was a kind of software robot that worked in a toy block world simulated in a virtual space. However, rather than head, feet, and hands, the robot was equipped with only a small stick. SHRDLU was not regarded as a life-like animated agent, but it has all the distinctive features. It could understand

---

* This is a Grant-in-Aid for Creative Scientific Research supported by the Ministry of Education, Culture, Sports, Science and Technology, and Japan Society for the Promotion of Science, and is the extended version of the original manuscript which was published at the International Workshop on Life-like Animated Agents at PRICAI-02, ed Prendinger, H. (August, 2002) pp 89–94.

English dialogue input from keyboards (no speech input) according to which it carried out very simple tasks such as "Pick up a red block on the table" and "Put it in the green box" by building its action plan and executing it. The system could also answer simple queries about the current state of the toy block world. It could resolve anaphoric ambiguities in the input sentence. SHRDLU demonstrated the promising future of NLU research at that time.

Recently better technologies have been obtained in speech recognition and natural language processing. Furthermore, significant progress in the field of computer graphics has enabled us to generate complex and realistic 3D animated robots (or software robot/agents) in a virtual space. The authors are now in a good position to go beyond the SHRDLU system. Two typical related works are reviewed briefly.

Badler et al. [4, 5] built 3D animated agents which could take commands and perform adequate actions in a virtual space. The agent was given commands from which it extracted parameters for its actions. The parameters contained various information such as linguistic, spatio-temporal, manner information that was often expressed as adverbs, and in some cases both applicability and terminating conditions. However, although it is normally very important to handle ellipsis and anaphoric expressions, which often occur in spoken language, they paid little attention to these expression types [3].

Later, Cassell et al. [6] pointed out that conversational skills are limited not only to the ability of language understanding and language usage but also to non-verbal behavior such as using facial expressions, hands, and tone of voice to regulate the process of conversation. They developed a system called the *Rea system*, which was an embodied conversational agent with social, linguistic, and psychological conversation conventions. *Rea*, an agent with a human-like body, can respond to humans using eye gaze, body posture, hand gestures, or facial expressions. While the *Rea* system emphasizes the importance of non-verbal functions in conversations, the system does not handle the problem of vagueness in agent actions.

Section 2 will discuss the reason why we choose software robots instead of hardware robots along with considering their advantages and disadvantages. We explain our Kairai system in Sect. 3 together with sample dialogues. Although Kairai operates in a very limited task-oriented domain, it makes proper interpretations for such adverbs as "left" and "right" as well as anaphora resolutions, which are discussed in Sect. 4 where our new method will be introduced. In Sect. 5, we will discuss some problems in the Kairai system, most of which should be solved by any future NLU system, and then we will explain why a one-to-many conversational pattern is important and consider more in the future. Due to the empirical study on the *Kairai system*, we will discuss the next generation NLU system in Sect. 6.

2 Why Software Robots Instead of Hardware Robots?

Before going into the discussion of the Kairai system, this section explains the reason why software robots are used instead of hardware robots.

First, even though hardware robots have made rapid progress recently, the actions they can perform are still too limited due to mechanical limitations. Compared with hardware robots, software robots have capabilities to carry out complex movements including non-verbal actions such as laughing, crying, nodding, and so on. As it is desirable to issue rather complex natural language commands to software robots, they are more suitable for NLU research in conjunction with action performing tasks.

Second, we do not want to deal with the vision problem, which is indeed one of the very important but difficult problems for hardware robots besides moving and performing actions in the real world. We are going to concentrate on the NLU problem which is not bothered by the vision problem. With respect to software robots, it is not necessary for us to worry about such a problem, since knowing everything in a virtual space/world is possible without sensory devices.

Third, it is easy to create a multi-agent environment by simply making copies of many software robots in a virtual space. Therefore, software robots let us study multi-agent systems easily. On the contrary, it is not only difficult but also expensive to create a multi-agent environment with hardware robots.

Finally, hardware robots often have difficulties due to mechanical problems. Hardware robots have to be kept in good condition through frequent hardware maintenance. The higher the number of hardware robots, the more frequently such mechanical troubles occur. This contrasts sharply with software robots for which no such troubles occur.

The four reasons listed above are all benefits of adopting software robots instead of hardware robots. However, there are several drawbacks in using software robots. Each software robot has to simulate the Newtonian physical world in order to move in the virtual space/world. To solve the Newtonian physical equations in generating the robot's movements is cumbersome and computationally intensive enough to justify the use of stereotyped motion patterns accumulated from motion capturing devices.

Another difficult problem for software robots is the so-called "frame problem" [20, 23], which each autonomous software robot has to solve (see Sect. 4). However, this is also a problem for hardware robots which build a task plan before carrying out their actions.

3 Kairai System

For the feasibility study of the next generation NLU system tightly combining speech recognition, NLU, and computer graphics, the authors have developed a prototype NLU system called Kairai [25, 24, 27, 28].

3.1 Architecture of Kairai System

The Kairai system incorporates several 3D software robots with which a user can converse. It accepts voice input (spoken input), interprets it, and performs the tasks in the virtual space. The dialogues become task-oriented ones [7, 12, 31]. The task executions are visible on a display screen as an animation. There are four software robots in the Kairai system. In addition to three visible software robots, there are a horse, a chicken, and a snowman. A cameraman is also a software robot controlling his camera to give a different perspective of the virtual space. The cameraman and camera are invisible on the display screen and the camera handling is specified through commands such as "Go near the horse." In consequence, the figure of the horse is enlarged.

Kairai understands what we say in natural language, especially the words such as "left", "right", "in front of", and "behind" that indicate relative location in a virtual space. Typical actions performed by the software robots are "push", "go", and "turn". It is interesting to observe that interpretations of "left" and "right" are determined by considering both the position and orientation of the software robot and objects in the virtual space in addition to a view of the human who issued the command.

Figure 1 shows an outline of the Kairai system whose architecture is not new and is divided into three parts: the speech recognition module, NLU module, and animation generation module. The speech recognition module transforms speech input into a sequence of words that become the input to the NLU module. The NLU module then analyzes the input by using both a grammar and a dictionary, and extracts a meaning structure called a frame structure along with anaphora resolution and ellipsis handling. The latter two form discourse processes that refer to the context of past history of the dialogues between the human (user) and Kairai. After a task plan is created by the NLU module, it is forwarded to the animation generation module to yield an animation on the display. The animation is generated by Alice[3] which interprets programs written in Python, a scripting language. To visualize agents' actions we also have to solve the problem of vagueness, for instance how far the robot ought to move. The current version of the Kairai system solves this problem by simply taking a default value.

Figure 2 is a snapshot of an animation generated by the Kairai system. Readers can see three software robots in a virtual space. According to the commands provided by the human, software robots including a cameraman can move and perform appropriate actions in a common space.

3.2 Sample Dialogue with Kairai

A typical dialogue that Kairai can understand is shown below. As stated above, when discussing the virtual space, there are four software robots (animated agents), a horse, a chicken, a snowman, and a cameraman, the last of

---

[3] http://www.alice.org/

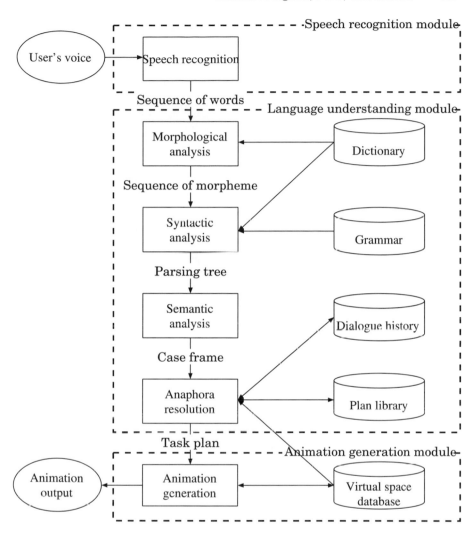

Fig. 1. Outline of Kairai system

which is invisible but manipulates his camera to take the view of the current virtual space. In addition to these, we purposely included two red spheres and two blue spheres bringing about an interesting problem named the *object identification problem* of a *deictic expression*. Consider the command "Push a red sphere." In order to perform the action, each software robot has to decide which "red sphere" is meant by the command. A reasonable answer will be the red sphere which is visible and nearest to the robot. Through voice input provided by the user, Kairai accepts imperative sentences one by one.

1. Human: *Horse, push the blue sphere to the front of Chicken.*

Fig. 2. A snapshot of Kairai (*Horse, push the blue sphere to the front of Chicken*)

> The phrase "*the blue sphere*" is ambiguous, since there are two blue spheres in the virtual space. *Horse* has to decide which blue sphere the command actually indicates through solving the *object identification problem* by making reference to the current state of the virtual space. Suppose it picks up "*the blue sphere*" nearest to it and does the push action.

2. Human: *Push the red sphere, too.*

> Considering *Horse*'s viewpoint, Kairai decides which red sphere *Horse* should push and then *Horse* performs the action. Note that *the red sphere* is an example of a *deictic expression*.

3. Human: *Chicken, push it, too.*

> Kairai resolves the anaphoric ambiguity given by *it* using a history of context, namely the preceding commands. Furthermore, Kairai has to solve the *object identification problem* again, before carrying out the action. In this case, *it* indicates the red sphere, which *Horse* previously pushed. *Chicken* does the action.

4. Human: *Further.*

> Although there is no subject, no object, and no verb, Kairai augments these elliptical words by considering the context accumulated through the dialogue between the user and Kairai. Kairai forces *Chicken* to push the red sphere further. Due to the visualization, it is necessary for Kairai to determine how far *Chicken* should push the sphere. This problem is called *vagueness* by linguists. Kairai successfully carries out anaphora resolution

and ellipsis augmentation in this case. Kairai simply uses a default value to handle the vagueness problem but it is certainly an unsatisfactory solution.

5. Human: *Cameraman, move close to the red sphere.*
> Kairai makes the camera move close to the red sphere mentioned before. As a result, it zooms in on the red sphere and changes the view of the virtual space.

4 Plan-Based Anaphora Resolution

The importance of situation-dependent NLP (SDNLP) should be emphasized to construct an NLU system. Anaphora resolution is one of such problems. In the domain of task-oriented conversation such as that seen in Kairai, a user issues a sequence of commands to indicate a goal that a system has to achieve. As each command in the sequence usually states a subgoal, constructing a sequence of subtask plans becomes very important. According to the task plan execution, agents are trying to satisfy the goal step by step by achieving its subgoals. As mentioned in [7, 8, 15, 16], the plan-based approach was empirically recognized as very useful for relating task plan execution and understanding task-oriented dialogues.

Most of these efforts were focused on analyzing the speaker's intentions through plan recognition. However, Cohen [7] discussed the referent identification with the assumption that speakers give their commands to listeners who could easily identify corresponding referents. There was no serious attempt to deal with plan-based anaphora resolution in [8, 19].

Consider a fragment of a dialogue to explain our plan-based anaphora resolution method.

(1) *Agent X, pick up the red ball.*
(2) *Move to the front of the blue ball.*
(3) *Drop it.*

The pronoun *it* in (3) refers to the *red ball* and not the *blue ball* in the preceding command (2). After executing plans specified by (1) and (2), some of the *Effects* will be expressed roughly as

Effect: above(red-ball,ground) from (1),
Effect: adjacent-to(agent-X,blue-ball) from (2).

The above two *Effects* show the changed situation after executing the two consecutive actions mentioned in (1) and (2). These *Effects* become a part of *Preconditions* for constructing the next "drop" plan, since we would like to keep coherence between adjacent plans. Note that the *Effect: above(red-ball,ground)* must hold even after executing the "move" action specified by (2), which is called the *frame problem* in the field of artificial intelligence. The "move" action does not change the *above(red-ball,ground)* relation. After the "drop" action specified by (3) is finished, the relation no longer holds. In the virtual world, software robots/agents have to take account of what has changed and what remains unchanged after executing some action.

Besides, before executing the plan specified by (3), software robots have to check its *Preconditions*, that is whether or not *above(it, ground)* holds. One of the *Preconditions* will be satisfied if and only if *it=red-ball* which software robots realize by looking for the *Effects* previously accumulated through dialogues. Consequently, the robots can solve the anaphora resolution as *it = red-ball*. Interestingly, this kind of anaphora resolution is not possible when we adopt the centering theory advocated by [14, 13, 26], since the theory focuses mainly on surface-level linguistic cues. Our plan-based approach adopted in our Kairai system utilizes deeper NLU results like *Effects* representing the situation or state change after the execution of plans and actions.

In the case of handling a huge volume of texts as fast as possible, it is preferable to utilize centering theory to our plan-based anaphora resolution even though the former is one of the anaphora resolution methods using only superficial linguistic information. However, in the task-oriented domain like Kairai, investigating the plan-based anaphora resolution method based on deeper NLU understanding seems to be promising and we are going to do more research on the resolution method.

5 Experiences with the Kairai System

Our experiences with respect to the Kairai system which was developed as a prototype system not only made us realize many further problems but also presented important research themes for any future NLU system.

5.1 Problems

The first and the most important problem is that Kairai was not really a multi-agent system composed of autonomous agents [10, 17, 30].

As each software robot (agent) in the Kairai seems to carry out its action independently, the Kairai system, at a glance, seems to be a multi-agent system. However, the Kairai system is not an actual multi-agent system but a one-to-one communication/conversation system. In addition to the four software robots/agents mentioned earlier, there is another special agent which knows everything about the virtual space, receives, and processes a sequence of words sent by the speech recognition module. This is illustrated in Fig. 3.

After accomplishing NLU tasks, the special agent decides which software robot should perform what kind of actions and then activates an appropriate software robot. This is the reason why Kairai is not really a multi-agent system. The problem discussed here brings about another problem.

Since current software robots in Kairai are not autonomous, it is very difficult to conduct *cooperative* actions including several robots. Consider

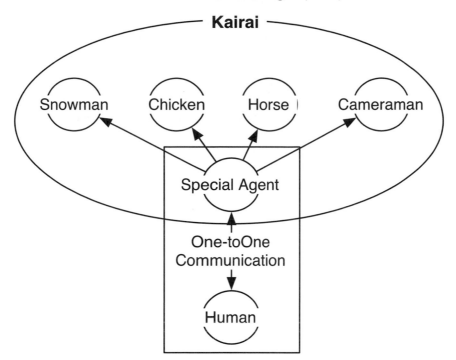

Fig. 3. One-to-one communication in Kairai

"gazing" [22], a simple cooperative action. In the current Kairai system, even though a software robot is conducting a task in the virtual space, the other robots are not paying any attention to its action. In human society, it is natural for a person to gaze at another one working near him or her. These were already implemented in [6], but due to the absence of autonomous robots in the current version of Kairai, it is impossible for any robot to directly communicate with another. Problems of gazing as well as the other cooperative actions can be solved naturally by introducing autonomous robots and one-to-many communication/conversation mode in the virtual space[4]. Making software robots autonomous is actually not a difficult problem when it is described in a concurrent programming language. The difficulty really resides in making each software robot perform cooperative works in a virtual space by using shared plans etc. [16].

Currently, Kairai does not deal with non-verbal expressions including intonations in speech, gazing, facial expressions, and body actions as well as hand gestures. Facial expressions are related to emotional behavior. It is well known that non-verbal expressions play an important role in communication [6]. We would like to account for such non-verbal and para-linguistic expressions but

---

[4] See also the chapter of M. Mateas and A. Stern in this book.

it remains a challenging research topic for the future Kairai system as well as the other similar systems. Fortunately, compared to hardware robots, software robots can emulate para-linguistic and emotional behavior much easier since they do not have any mechanical limitations.

Kairai is not equipped with the ability to reason about a speaker's intentions as well as a speaker's non-verbal expressions that several researchers were trying to solve along with plan recognition [6, 7, 8, 15]. More research is needed before it is incorporated in any system like Kairai.

Finally, software robots in the Kairai system cannot communicate with each other. Each software robot performs actions in a virtual space following commands issued by a user. It is desirable to endow robots with the ability to answer back or ask a question when needing to resolve ambiguities which cannot be solved directly. Such ability will be very helpful for agents required to perform cooperative works in a virtual space, too. We would like to leave this problem as one of our future research themes to improve the current Kairai system.

5.2 One-to-Many Communication

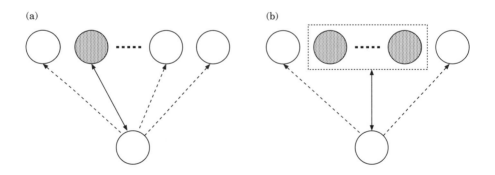

Fig. 4. One-to-many communication

NLU systems should deal with one-to-many communication/conversation together with one-to-one conversation. One-to-many conversation makes sense in a multi-agent environment [10, 30]. In one-to-one conversation it is easy to decide who is the intended listener. On the contrary, in the one-to-many conversation as shown in Fig. 4, due to many potential listeners, it is difficult to decide to whom a command issued by a speaker is intended. Usually, the listener is mentioned explicitly in the first utterances of the dialogue, but not mentioned in the rest of the dialogue. Confusion can arise between agents if each agent is unable to recognize which is the addressed agent required to perform some tasks according to the command given by a speaker. The problem also occurs when a subject or an object does not appear in the command due to ellipses.

To understand the above situation clearly, consider the following conversation in a multi-agent environment.

1. Agent X: *Hey, Agent A, I will throw a red ball.*
   > *Agent A* looks at *Agent X*. The other agents might also gaze at *Agent X*.
2. Agent X: *Catch it.*
   > Even though there is no subject in this command, *Agent A* begins the action to catch the red ball. Normally, the other agents just gaze at *Agent A* or *Agent X*.

Note that the second command issued by *Agent X* lacks a subject, but *Agent A* has to perform the action *Catch* along with resolving the anaphora expression *it* that should be correctly identified as the red ball. Normally, the other agents should not perform the action *Catch* even though they hear the *Catch it* command. If the above conversation occurs in an American football game, both teams are going to catch the same ball. However, the meaning of actions taken by one team is completely different from that of the other team's actions. That is, the former is going to intercept the red ball. In the multi-agent environment, such an interesting phenomenon will often happen. It seems obvious that each software robot should be autonomous in the multi-agent environment and have the ability to control its behavior by itself.

6 Next Generation NLU System

As discussed in the preceding section, many problems were extracted from the Kairai system and most of them are also important research themes for any future NLU system. We would like to summarize them in this section. First, consider a fragment of the one-to-one dialogue as shown below:

1. Human: *Open the curtain covering the window a little.*
   > An agent goes to the curtain, and grasps it by its hand and opens it.
2. Human: *A little bit more.*
   > The agent opens the curtain a little bit more.
3. Human: *Too much.*
   > The agent closes the curtain a little.
4. Human: *The air in the room is polluted.*
   > The agent opens the window.

The first command issued by the human makes an agent create a plan to go to the curtain, grasp and open it. Such a plan is called a macro-level plan. There are many ways to grasp and open the curtain and we have to solve the so-called problem of *vagueness* by linguists. The agent has to select one of the possibilities to generate a micro-level plan in order to carry out its actions. We can conclude whether the agent understands natural language by observing the agent's actions corresponding to what the human says. In other words, an agent's actions, which are visualized in a virtual space as an animation, verify the NLU ability of the agent. That is, the visualized actions provide us with a more precise NLU evaluation method than that of the Turing test, since the latter does not take the visualized behavior of AI systems into account [5].

The second and third commands lack a verb in addition to a subject and an object. Agents have to augment these elliptical words by taking account of the context of the current dialogue and environment in which the robot resides. With respect to the second command, the agent has to infer "open" as an appropriate elliptical verb, and then carries out the action "open". On the other hand, in the third command, "open" is also the correct elliptical verb, but the agent has to perform an opposite action "close" in this case. In other words, the agent has to extract the intended actions from indirect speech act commands [2, 9]. The second and third commands are also related to the problem of the *vagueness*, which was often overlooked in past NLU research.

The fourth command includes a typical indirect speech act that should be understood correctly for an agent to perform the "open the door" action. Extracting the speaker's intentions in an indirect speech act is one of the most difficult but interesting problems discussed by many researchers in the past [1, 9, 8, 15].

In addition to those caused by erroneous output from automatic speech recognition systems, there are many ill-formed sentences, which include fillers, additions, repairs, and repetitions in spoken language. It might be possible to cope with these problems by using constraints obtained from a language processing module rather than from an acoustic processing module [11, 18, 21, 29].

From the empirical study based on the Kairai system, we can summarize what the next generation NLU system must be equipped with.

1. Situation-dependent natural language processing (SDNLP) that includes:
   (a) Resolution of anaphoric expressions by combining the centering theory and our plan-based approach.
   (b) Identification of objects specified by a deictic expression.
   (c) Augmentation of ellipsis.
   (d) Extraction of indirect speech acts as well as speaker's intention from commands.
   (e) Dealing with *vagueness*, which is especially critical for the hardware robots that move around and perform actions in the real world.
2. To handle ill-formed sentences that include fillers, additions, repairs, and repetitions, which are frequently included in spoken language.
3. To perform cooperative actions as well as one-to-many conversations in a multi-agent environment.

4. To take into account non-verbal and para-linguistic expressions as well as emotional expressions in order to enhance flexible communication through natural language dialogues.

As explained in Sect. 2, our Kairai system will provide us with a platform for research on multi-agent systems.

7 Conclusions

After reviewing the NLU systems in the past, we pointed out several important issues concerning the creation of a next generation NLU system. Kairai, a system which was developed at Tokyo Institute of Technology, played a key role in exemplifying the issues mentioned in the preceding sections.

Even though the system under consideration consists of a set of software robots, the research results are also applicable to hardware robots. We have also discussed the importance of para-linguistic expressions in addition to emphasizing better algorithms for anaphora resolution and ellipsis handling. Furthermore, we would like to emphasize the importance of the *object identification problem* as mentioned in Sect. 3.2, since without identifying the target object, robots cannot perform any action with the object in both real and virtual space. This problem seems to be overlooked in the previous research. Additionally, processing ill-formed sentences which frequently occur in spoken language is also an important issue requiring attention.

The next generation NLU system ought to be a multi-agent system, with a wide array of application areas such as:

1. entertainment,
2. helper robots (medical and in-home use),
3. tutoring systems,
4. sign language systems,
5. virtual space navigation systems,
6. electrical appliances, etc.

Readers can easily understand the application areas of entertainment and helper robots, although the latter will need better and more reliable technologies in the future. With respect to tutoring systems, instead of reading a manual, we can understand easier a software robot (or a pedagogical agent) instructing us on how to manipulate devices by showing its 3D models [22].

Navigation guided by voice commands in natural language can possibly apply to any kind of virtual space. Typical examples are 3D models of internal organs, molecular structure, DNA structure, geographic space, etc. The recent CT (Computed Tomography) and MRI (Magnetic Resonance Imaging) medical technology enable us to construct 3D images of internal organs where a virtual camera can enter and move close to any part by receiving navigation commands in spoken language. The authors expect that such technologies will change the current method of medical diagnosis in the near future.

Finally, future electrical appliances will be equipped with "ears" for listening to the user's commands and will process these commands to execute them similar to current software robots. In such circumstances, the research on both the multi-agent and one-to-many conversation systems will become increasingly important.

Acknowledgments

Thanks to Dr. Helmut Prendinger, Dr. Taiichi Hashimoto, and Slaven Bilac for their help in preparing this manuscript.

References

1. Allen, J., Perrault, C.R.: Analyzing intention in utterances. *Artificial Intelligence* **15**:143–178 (1980)
2. Austin, J.L.: *How to Do Things with Words* (Oxford University Press 1962)
3. Badler, N.: A parameterized action representation for virtual human agents. In: *Proceedings of the 1st Workshop on Embodied Conversational Characters* (1998) pp 1–8
4. Badler, N.I., Palmer, M.S., Bindinganavale, R.: Animation control for real-time visual humans. *Communications of the ACM* (1999) pp 65–73
5. Badler, N.I., Phillips, C.B., Webber, B.L.: *Simulating Humans - Computer Graphics Animation and Control.* (Oxford University Press 1993)
6. Cassell, J., Bickmore, T., Billinghurst, L., Campbell, L., Chang, K., Vilhjalmsson, H., Yan, H.: Embodiment in conversational interfaces: Rea. In: *Proceedings of CHI'99 Conference* (1999) pp 520–527
7. Cohen, P.R.: The pragmatics of referring and the modality of communication. *Computational Linguistics* **10**(2):97–146 (1984)
8. Cohen, P.R., Levesque, H.J.: Persistence, intention and commitment. In: *Intentions in Communication* (The MIT Press, Cambridge, MA 1990)
9. Cohen, P.R., Morgan, J., Pollack, M.E. (eds): *Intentions in Communication* (The MIT Press, Cambridge, MA 1990)
10. Febler, J.: *Multi-Agent Systems – An Introduction to Distributed Artificial Intelligence* (Addison-Wesley Longman, Reading, MA 1999)
11. Funakoshi, K., Tokunaga, T., Tanaka, H.: Processing Japanese self-correction in speech dialog system. In: *Proceedings of the COLING 2002* (2002) pp 287–293
12. Grosz, B.J.: Discourse knowledge. In: *Understanding Spoken Language*, ed Walker, D.E. (North-Holland, Amsterdam 1978) pp 229–344
13. Grosz, B.J., Joshi, A.K., Weinstein, S.: Centering: A framework for modeling the local coherence of discourse. *Computational Linguistics* **21**(2):203–226 (1995)
14. Grosz, B.J., Joshi, A.K., Weinstein, S.: Providing a unified account of definite noun phrases in discourse. In: *Proceedings of the 21st Annual Meeting of the Association for Computational Linguistics* (1983) pp 44–50

15. Grosz, B.J., Sidner, C.L.: Attention, intentions, and the structure of discourse. *Computational Linguistics* **12**(3):175–204 (1986)
16. Grosz, B.J., Sidner, C.L.: Plans for discourse. In: *Intentions and Communication* (The MIT Press, Cambridge, MA 1990)
17. Huhns, M.N., Singh, M.P. (eds): *Readings in AGENTS.* (Morgan Kaufmann, San Mateo, CA 1998)
18. Junque, J.-C., van Noord, G. (eds): *Robustness in Language and Speech Technology.* (Kluwer Academic, Dordrecht 2001)
19. Litman, D.J., Allen, J.F.: Discourse processing and commonsense plans. In: *Intentions and Communications* (The MIT Press, Cambridge, MA 1990)
20. Luger, G.F., Stubblefield, W.A.: *Artificial Intelligence*, 3rd edn (Addison-Wesley, Reading, MA 1998)
21. Mellish, C.S.: Some chart-based techniques for parsing ill-formed input. In: *Proceedings of 27th ACL* (1989) pp 102–109
22. Rickel, J., Aylett, R., Ballin, D. (eds): *Intelligent Virtual Agents for Education and Training: Opportunities and Challenges* (Springer, Berlin New York 2001)
23. Russell, S., Norvig, P.: *Artificial Intelligence* 2nd edn (Prentice-Hall, Englewood Cliffs, NJ 1995)
24. Shinyama, Y., Tokunaga, T., Tanaka, H.: A software robot Kairai that understands natural language (in Japanese). *Journal of JIPS* **42**(6):1359–1367 (2001)
25. Shinyama, Y., Tokunaga, T., Tanaka, H.: "Kairai" – software robots understanding natural language. In: *Proceedings of the 3rd Workshop on Human Computer Conversation* (2000) pp 158–163
26. Strube, M., Hahn, U.: Functioning centering–grounding referencial coherence in information structure. *Computational Linguistics* **25**(3):309–344 (1999)
27. Tanaka, H.: *Language Understanding and Action Control (in Japanese)* (Ministry of Education and Science, Tokyo 2000)
28. Tanaka, H.: *Language Understanding and Action Control (in Japanese).* (Ministry of Education and Science, Tokyo 2001)
29. van Noord, G.: Robust parsing of word graphs. In: *Robustness in Language and Speech Technologys*, ed Junque, J.-C., van Noord, G. (Kluwer Academic, Dordrecht 2001) pp 205–238
30. Weiss, G. (ed): *Multiagent Systems* (The MIT Press, Cambridge, MA 1999)
31. Winograd, T. (ed): *Understanding Natural Language* (Academic Press, New York 1972)

Part IV

Synopsis

What Makes Characters Seem Life-Like?

Barbara Hayes-Roth[1,2]

[1] Computer Science, Stanford University, Stanford, CA, USA
bhr@cs.stanford.edu
[2] Extempo Systems, Inc.
643 Bair Island Road, Suite 302, Redwood City, CA 94063, USA
bhr@extempo.com

Summary. What are the qualities that make characters seem life-like to the people who interact with them? Based on experience creating and evaluating dozens of interactive characters during the past decade, I suggest that characters seem more life-like when they are made to seem: conversational, intelligent, individual, social, empathic, variable, and coherent. In this chapter, I briefly describe five illustrative characters to ground the discussion of life-like qualities: Improv Puppets, Erin the Bartender, Jack the Canine Web Site Host, Katherine the Interactive Newscaster, and STAR Workshops featuring Coach Harmony and Role-Play Partners Nina and Ed. I then describe each of the life-like qualities in terms of behavioral features, attempt to rationalize them intuitively with reference to human behavior, and illustrate them with reference to the behavior of the illustrative characters. I conclude by proposing a variation on the Turing Test to evaluate the degree to which a character seems life-like.

1 Introduction

During the past 10 years, I have enjoyed creating and evaluating dozens of interactive characters for a variety of applications, always in collaboration with other computer scientists, psychologists, educators, artists, and subject-matter experts. Based on this experience, I have developed and wish to share a perspective on some of the features that make characters seem life-like to the people who interact with them. Grouping these features into seven *qualities*, I will suggest that characters seem more life-like when they seem: conversational, intelligent, individual, social, empathic, variable, and coherent.

Of course, these are familiar terms, used by many researchers (Hayes-Roth and Doyle [5]), and I will specify them more particularly below. First, however, I present brief overviews of five illustrative applications, in order to give readers a sense of the range of characters that have inspired my thinking. (Interested readers may interact with these and other characters on www.extempo.com.) With this as background, I discuss each of the proposed qualities of life-likeness, articulating particular features, attempting to rationalize each one intuitively with reference to human behavior, and illustrating each one with reference to the behavior of the illustrative characters. Finally, I discuss evaluation of life-like characters – how can we know when we have succeeded?

2 Five Illustrative Characters

2.1 Improv Puppets

Improv Puppets (Hayes-Roth [2], Hayes-Roth and van Gent [7]) were modeled after traditional children's puppets, with a twist: the puppets were animated and smart. Two kids directed the improvisational behavior of two puppets in a shared virtual world.

For the puppet bodies and their world, Joe Bates generously allowed us to use the *Woggles* animations and 3D world developed in his Oz Project at Cargnegie-Mellon University. We expanded their repertoires of simple, but adorable animated behaviors and gave them voices to speak lines of dialogue authored and recorded by children. We gave them dynamic, multi-dimensional moods – happiness, sociability, and arousal—which would both respond to events, including their activities and the other puppet's behavior, and modulate their own behavior. We gave the puppets improvisational minds, so that they could identify actions that are logically, physically, and emotionally enabled at any point in time and choose among the enabled actions based on their current moods and high-level directions from children. Finally, we gave the puppets graphical interfaces that would display their dynamic moods and enabled actions to children and allow the children to direct them by choosing actions or modifying moods.

Responding to the children's directions in real time, each puppet improvised a course of action that followed the child's directions, but also reflected its own decisions, dynamic moods, environmental events, and normal variability. Conversely, each puppet dynamically decided which buttons to make available for selection by the child based on its moods, recent behaviors, and the other puppets' behavior. The result was collaborative story improvisation by two kids and two puppets.

In addition to being endearing and fun, Improv Puppets offered children a unique opportunity to observe, predict, and manipulate the internal states driving observable action. As a result, playing with Improv Puppets incidentally enhanced children's cognitive development of a "psychology of mind", leading to significant improvements in their social empathy and their comprehension and production literacy (Huard and Hayes-Roth [9]).

Improv Puppets have been exhibited at the Conference on Human-Computer Interaction, the Computer Game Developers' Conference, Stanford's Exhibition on Technology and the Arts, all in 1996, and many academic meetings.

2.2 Erin the Bartender

Erin O'Malley (Hayes-Roth [3]) is a virtual bartender, working in her Uncle Spence's virtual bar in Virtual Hollywood. Like any good bartender, Erin can describe, suggest, and mix hundreds of drinks. She interleaves conversations with multiple customers (but not too many!) and remembers which customers are waiting for drinks. Erin keeps lone visitors company, chatting about herself and her interests, especially rock & roll. She'll tolerate good-natured flirting, but she also has clear limits. Erin won't tolerate rude customers or violence and she won't hesitate to eject troublemakers.

For shy customers, Erin offers smart avatars representing regular customers: Zoe, an aging Hollywood B-movie actress, Vickie, a prim scientist at JPL who likes to slum it at Spence's, Sydney, a friendly young woman whose Cockney punk style intimidates people, Al, a burnt-out writer for a Hollywood trade rag, Eddie, an African–American rookie on the LAPD and all-around nice guy, and Kurt, a street person who is strange but harmless. Customers can enter Spence's as one of the regulars and generate conversation and other behavior with a graphical interface similar to the one supplied in Improv Puppets. When users feel comfortable in their roles, they can augment the push-button interactions with their own free-form conversation and choices of gestures.

Erin has proven very effective at performing her job as a bartender and engaging customers in social chat. The average user spends 30 minutes with Erin, with 95% of the interaction devoted to job-related or social interaction and only 5% on testing the AI. Erin is exceptionally skilled at guiding smart-aleck customers into mutually agreeable interactions (Isbister and Hayes-Roth [10]).

Erin has served and entertained hundreds of virtual customers on the web and appeared at many exhibitions, including the First International Conference on Intelligent Agents and the Computer Game Developers' Conference, both in 1997, as well as many academic meetings.

2.3 Virtual Jack

Virtual Jack was designed to be the company mascot and web site host for the company Petopia. Since he was modeled after the real Wheaten Terrier of CEO Andrea Reisman, Jack has a rich back-story covering his birth and doggy family in Canada, his move to San Francisco with his human mom, the founding of Petopia, etc. Jack also had a lot of animal friends at Petopia and many amusing stories of their adventures.

Jack's official job was to help customers navigate the web site, encourage them to visit target web pages, and acquire a dozen or so information items about each user. On any given page, Jack made some introductory commentary, invited the user to browse the page, and remained on hand to answer questions.

Jack endeared himself to web site visitors with his sweet and witty persona, expressed in doggy tricks, canine puns, and animal haikus, as well as his unfailingly modest demeanor and obvious desire to help. He could answer a broad range of questions, related to his life story, his human and animal friends, and life at Petopia. If conversation flagged, Jack used a variety of appealing tactics to re-engage the user.

Jack excelled at achieving his design goals. He increased visits to target marketing pages by two orders of magnitude. He persuaded 45–85% of consumers to provide various items of information. He built user loyalty leading to >30% repeat visits within 8 weeks.

Jack has been exhibited at the Gartner Conference on Electronic Commerce in 2000, Demo 2001, and many academic meetings.

2.4 Katherine, Interactive Newscaster

Katherine offers personalized interactive news services on her own web site (Hayes-Roth [4]). When a visitor arrives, Katherine announces the day's news headlines in the user's particular area of interest (e.g. health and nutrition). Upon request, she offers other headlines from the current day's news or headlines from her archives. When the user selects a headline, Katherine reads the story and offers optional background information or her own opinion.

Katherine generally displays a reserved and serious demeanor. She does not initiate social conversation and, if asked personal questions, she will politely explain that her contract strictly limits her conversation topics. Nonetheless, Katherine has a charming persona that is all the more intriguing because of its revelation in occasional glimpses. Her wry and irreverent opinions about news stories make a delightfully surprising contrast to her deadpan delivery. She is sensitive about her intelligence and takes offense easily if insulted in this area. With repeated offenses, she may require an apology before continuing to provide her services. Katherine also harbors secret aspirations for life beyond the newsroom and, under the right circumstances, she will reveal these aspirations to the user.

Katherine has been exhibited at SIGGRAPH 2001 and the International Lisp Conference 2002, as well as many academic meetings.

2.5 STAR™ Workshops

Each STAR Workshop (see Fig. 1) offers a Virtual Coach and several Virtual Role-Players to provide training and authentic rehearsal of interpersonal skills, such as: management, social interaction, second language, interviewing, etc.

Harmony, the STAR Coach, introduces target skills, assesses the learner's current skills in role-play practice, and provides personalized feedback and coaching as needed. Monitoring the learner's developing skills in a series of role-play scenarios, Harmony selects appropriate study and practice activities to correct deficits.

Fig. 1. STAR Coach Harmony and Virtual Employee Role-Players Nina and Ed

Providing authentic rehearsal of target skills, each STAR Role-Player exhibits a distinctive persona, appearance, and manner, and interacts with learners in natural language conversation, complemented by life-like gestures, body language, and emotions. Many role-players have vivid emotional dynamics, contributing to the challenges of inter-personal interaction. For example, in a STAR Workshop for management skills, Nina is a virtual admin assistant who has difficulty learning to use a new reporting system and becomes emotionally distressed when she is pressured to do so or informed of the consequences of failing to do so. By contrast, Ed is a highly valued lab technician who ignores required HR policies and responds with contempt when encouraged to do so.

A typical STAR Workshop includes several role-play scenarios, enabling the learner to develop robust skills for a variety of real-life situations. Although STAR Coaches can use different strategies, Harmony uses a particular mastery strategy. She introduces a series of practice scenarios, increasing in difficulty, and requires the learner to master target skills in each one before moving on to the next one. Nina and Ed make this repeat practice effective by behaving differently in response to changes in learner behavior and by introducing natural, incidental variations on their consistent behavior.

Finally, Harmony gives each learner warm interest and attention. She motivates target skills, encourages the learner's effort, and reinforces progress, guiding each learner along an individually optimized path to mastery of a new scenario.

In controlled studies, STAR Workshops significantly outperform alternative online methods, as well as live coaching and role-play, on measures including: confidence, accuracy of self-assessment, retention of and performance on a new test scenario, and amount of coaching, practice, and time needed for mastery.

STAR Workshops have been presented at the E3 Electronic Entertainment Expo and the Online Learning Conference, both in 2003.

3 Seven Qualities of Life-Likeness

Before discussing each of the proposed qualities of life-likeness, I make three
caveats.

First, the seven qualities provide a convenient grouping of a larger number of more specific behavioral features. However, they are not absolute. They
are not independent. In fact, they overlap in some areas. I offer these seven
qualities as an informal way to organize my observations. I am sure that the
particular accounting presented here will grow and evolve as our understanding of life-like characters advances.

Second, I quite deliberately use the verb "to seem" rather than the verb
"to be". For example, I do not say that "characters should be intelligent", but
rather that "characters should seem intelligent". This orientation combines a
particular paradigm of artificial intelligence with the more artistic endeavors
of actors and directors who enact the appearance of feeling and story on stage
(Johnstone [11]) and animators like Walt Disney and Chuck Jones who strive
to create "believable" characters who "appear to think and make decisions
and act of their own volition" (Thomas and Johnston [12]). I return to this
point in my discussion of evaluation below.

Third, I will state each quality normatively and categorically, for example
"characters should seem conversational". However, each of the 10 qualities
actually comprises a collection of behavioral features, with more or fewer of
them present, more or less frequently, and more or less prominently in the
behavior of different characters. Thus, it would be more strictly accurate to
state each quality as a quantified correlation, for example "characters should
seem more conversational in order to seem more life-like". I hope that these
graded potentials for seeming to possess qualities of life-likeness will become
apparent as I articulate some of the features of different qualities, attempt to
rationalize them intuitively with reference to human behavior, and illustrate
them with reference to the behavior of the illustrative characters introduced
above.

3.1 Characters Should Seem Conversational

To seem life-like, characters should engage users or other characters in conversation – that is, in the exchange of thoughts, opinions, and feelings via
language, gesture, actions, facial expressions, and other available communication modes. Like people, characters should construct *mixed-initiative dialogues*
with users, where each participant can proactively initiate an exchange and
also reactively respond to exchanges initiated by the other. For example, Erin
the Bartender might respond to a user's request "How about a boilermaker?"
by smiling and replying "One boilermaker, comin' right up!" and proceeding
to prepare and deliver the drink. Alternatively, if the user is quiet, Erin might
initiate the same exchange, by offering "What can I get for you, pardner?"

Similarly, Jack might respond to a user's request, "Can you take me to the fish?" by making a puppy play-bow and replying "Sure, Cynthia. That'll be reel easy!" (pun intended). He would then navigate the user's browser to the fish page and comment "Feel free to look and click around, my two-legged friend. There's always something new in algae!" Alternatively, if a user is quiet, Jack might take the opportunity to inform him or her "Two big things are going on at Petopia that really have my tail wagging, the Million Pet Mission and the Bottomless Bowl." Many users will respond to an *implicit offer* like this one by asking a predictable question, such as "What is the Million Pet Mission?" Jack might reply "The Million Pet Mission is the nicest thing to happen to animals since the domestication of people. Would you like to learn why?" If the user does not ask a question, Jack might wait for a brief pause and then proactively continue with the same information and invitation. If the user agrees, Jack will navigate his browser to the appropriate web page and begin his context-sensitive commentary there.

Also like people, characters should *construct multi-threaded dialogues* with users. For example, while preparing a user's drink, Erin might respond to the question "Where are you from?" by saying "Born and raised in El Paso, Texas, and proud of it!" Like a human bartender, Erin can participate in this exchange while continuing to prepare and deliver the user's drink, along with a comment such as "Here y'all are."

In fact, in some cases, characters should construct multi-threaded dialogues with multiple users. For example, while preparing a first user's drink and engaging in small talk, Erin might field a request from a second user at Spence's Bar, "May I have a another drink, dearie?" by saying "Another pink squirrel. I'll get that for you right away, Zoe." She also fulfills that promise, mixing and delivering Zoe's pink squirrel as soon as she finishes delivering Eddie's boilermaker. Like people, there should be a *natural limit* to the number and complexity of the conversations a character can interleave, as when Erin responds to a third user's query "You like the Rangers?" by saying, "Hold on there, fella. I've got my hands full. I'll be with you in a moment."

Finally, character conversations should reflect *multiple layers of meaning*. For example, presented with two different requests for a beer, "Can I have a beer, Erin?" versus "Get me a beer, stupid", Erin's response reflects the affective content as well as the transactional content, "Sure can." versus "You talk to your mamma with that mouth?" In a more complex example, Erin might respond to her friend Kurt's fifth request "I'll take another beer, sweetheart", by crossing her arms, frowning, and saying "Don'tcha think you've had enough, Kurt? How about a nice cold root-beer, hon?"

3.2 Characters Should Seem Intelligent

To seem life-like, characters should seem intelligent in their display of role-appropriate knowledge and expertise, along with complementary opinions, attitudes, and preferences. Like people, characters must have *something sub-stantive to offer*. In many cases, this will be a form of expertise that motivates the user to engage in the interaction in the first place. Katherine, Jack, Harmony, Nina, and Ed offer expert services to users: interactive news, pet care information, coaching and practice on inter-personal skills. These services have intrinsic value to users. Providing high-quality forms of these services makes the characters seem intelligent. In some cases, the expertise may be more social in nature. For example, Erin the Bartender offers bartender services and social companionship for solo users and stimulates conversation among multiple users, while keeping order in the bar.

Like people, characters who adequately *fulfill the promise of established roles* can get away with extremely limited knowledge, rationality, and expertise in other areas. For example, Erin the Bartender must have nearly encyclopedic knowledge of beer, wine, and mixed drinks and she must be able to prepare them. She should be able to make recommendations, for example "If you want tequila, I recommend a tequila sunrise." She should have opinions and preferences of her own, such as "I'm partial to tequila sunrises, myself." If Erin can do these things well, the user will not be disappointed if she cannot deliver the news, coach on inter-personal skills, talk about pet care, or provide the role-specific services we expect from Katherine, Harmony, Jack, or other characters.

Characters can exploit several conversational techniques to enhance their apparent intelligence. A character should have *more recognition than produc-tion knowledge* and display that when acknowledging limitations. If the user asks Jack "How do you feel about President Bush?" Jack doesn't have any feelings to share. But he doesn't give an all-purpose blanket response "Sorry, I didn't understand that." Instead, he gives a response that sounds more intelligent, "Sorry, but this puppy stays away from politics."

A character should follow the familiar admonition, *do not start something you cannot finish* – because the user is sure to ask it to finish it. For example, when Jack says "That's a picture of my Mom, Andrea Reisman". he is sure to receive follow-up comments and questions, such as: "She's pretty." or "I thought your mom was a dog." or "Isn't she the CEO?" This is the danger of the *implicit-offer phenomenon*, which also can be turned to the character's advantage, as in the example above, in which Jack implicitly invites the user to ask him about the Million Pet Mission and the Bottomless Bowl, simply by mentioning his excitement about them.

A character *should channel the conversation* to its own areas of competence and depth. This might come as a *reactive redirection* of off-topic user inputs. For example, if the user tells Erin the Bartender that she loves Pavarotti, Erin might reply, "I'm not much of an opera fan. Elvis is more my style." She also *proactively drives* the conversation, for example when asking a quiet user "Who's your favorite rock & roll group?"

Characters also must be prepared for the inevitable *intelligence testing*. Most users are curious about how much a character knows or understands and some users are dedicated to "breaking" the character. All of our characters are prepared to deal with a variety of testing, each in its own way. For example, Erin deals with the standard ploy of repeating the same question with different words and syntax by saying "Could you please stop repeating yourself, Marko?" Jack, who is characteristically modest and self-effacing, might respond to the same sort of behavior by saying "Gee, I'm sorry to be so dumb, pet-lover, but I hope you know I'm still just a puppy."

Finally, characters should *shape constructive user behavior* and *discourage disruptive user behavior*. We learned this lesson with our first character, Erin the Bartender. First, we learned from Erin's experiences that users would do intelligence testing and explore standard social exchanges, such as flirtation, praise, insult, obscenity, and aggression. We prepared Erin to recognize and respond to these user behaviors, while staying in character. Being a hip Texan and tough enough to tend bar on the night shift in Hollywood, Erin can give as good as she gets. Her responses, especially her responses to negative comments, are quite entertaining. As a result, these user behaviors actually increased in frequency. If we wanted to decrease these behaviors, we would have to make Erin's responses much less rewarding to her tormentors!

3.3 Characters Should Seem Individual

To seem life-like, each character should have its own unique and distinctive persona. Like people, characters should have *distinctive back-stories, personalities*, and *emotional dynamics* that inform and drive their behavior and interactions (Hayes-Roth [1]).

Characters should *reveal and express their personas in every aspect of their beings and behavior*. For example, the Improv Puppets had very simple animated bodies, basically bouncy balls with eyes. However, one was much larger than the other. By giving each of them different walks (made by wiggling or hopping with different parameters of height, speed, etc.), the two puppets evinced the very different personas of a large, strong, mature persona and a small, delicate, young persona. In addition, each of the puppets had a distinctive voice, in both senses of the word. Their dialogue lines were authored and recorded by two different children, an older girl and a younger boy. As a result, the large, strong, mature puppet had the voice of an indulgent big sister who said things like "Come on, Nathan, let's play." Similarly, the small, delicate, young puppet, had the voice of a sweet, but shy little brother, who said things like "Yippee!"

Characters who engage users in open-ended conversations have a much greater opportunity and a much greater obligation to fulfill users' expectations and desires for appealing character personas. These characters need to have back-stories similar to the characters in books or films, except now they must be prepared to discuss their back-stories with curious or chatty users. When Procter & Gamble launched an interactive version of their 40-year-old brand icon, Mr. Clean^{TM}, they experienced a backlog of consumer curiosity: "Why do you wear all white?" "I like your earring." "Do you have a girlfriend?"

Users also like to ask characters personal questions. Luckily, there is a set of *standard personal questions* that many users ask, for example: "Where were you born?" "Who are your parents/brothers/sisters?" "What are your hobbies?" "When is your birthday?" We have found it useful to compile a corpus of understanding knowledge for personal questions that have been received by any of our characters to be shared among them and answered by each character in its own way.

Like interesting people, interesting characters have *idiosyncrasies* and, sometimes, *signature behaviors*. Idiosyncrasies are simply behaviors that differ from the behaviors of characters. For example, Jack makes a lot of canine puns and likes to tell animal haikus. Katherine likes to find out if users speak Italian and, if so, pepper her dialogue with Italian phrases. Similarly, each of our characters has special nicknames for users. Jack calls users "pet lover", "my two-legged friend", etc., while auto spokesperson and southern belle Jennifer James calls everyone "ma'am" or "sir".

Signature behaviors are more salient individual behaviors that a character performs reliably and predictably. For example, everyone knows the signature greeting of celebrity character Bugs Bunny: "Whats up, Doc?" Although signature behaviors can be annoying (as Bugs's greeting is to his nemesis, Elmer Fudd), they also can be powerful symbols of the characters' unique identities.

3.4 Characters Should Seem Social

Like people, characters should display *self-awareness in the social context*. For example, if Jack doesn't understand something the user says, he might hang his head and request: "Forgive this little puppy. I didn't understand what you just said." If the user praises Jack, he might lie down, cover his eyes with his paws, and comment, "Oh, pet-lover, you'll make my head as big as a bulldog's." By contrast, if Katherine is unable to respond to a user's question, she might say "I'm sorry, David, but my contract strictly limits my conversation topics." When praised, she might smile subtly and say "Thank you David, I appreciate the compliment." In fact, a character's presentation of self can have a dramatic effect on user acceptance. EarthDog, another canine character who teaches children about environmental issues, has many limits and holes in his knowledge and often has to interrupt an ongoing conversation by saying "Sorry, Planeteer, but I just didn't get that." However, children typically respond to his *endearing imperfections* by saying something like "That's OK EarthDog. I love you."

We also have observed with virtually all of our characters that many users will engage in *standard forms of social exchange*: personal inquiries, praise, insults, flirtation, obscenities, and aggression. We have found it useful to compile a corpus of understanding knowledge for these standard social inputs that have been received by any of our characters to be shared among them. What differs is the individual character's response. For example, every one of our characters can recognize user messages that mean "I like you" (e.g. "I love you." "You're cool/great/wonderful/. . . ." "I'm crazy about you.") However, Jack might respond "Oh stop, pet-fan, I'm blushing." By contrast, Erin might respond "Why thank you, pardner, you're not so bad yourself."

Like people, characters should *develop an acquaintance gradually*, in stages, and in coordination with their respective identities as individuals and their complementary roles. For example, Jack is a puppy, whose role is to assist visitors to his site. He is playful and friendly, calling the user by name or by affectionate nicknames, such as pet-lover or my four-legged friend. Over time, Jack accumulates a greater quantity and variety of information about users (e.g. the number, types, and names of their pets, whether they are male or female) and uses it to personalize his conversations with them, for example: "Hi John. It makes my tail wag to see you again. How is your bunny?"

Characters should build their acquaintance on a *shared history* and through *discreet acquisition of information* about users. They should learn about users the same ways that people learn about each other, by *watching, listening*, and *asking*. For example, Jack might remark to the user "Some people think dogs and cats are a recipe for trouble, but I love my friend Jill and she's 100% cat." If the user responds "My puppy likes cats too", Jack hears and remembers that the user has a dog and that it is young. If Jack wants to ask for an item of information, he does so in a socially acceptable way, by first waiting for or contriving a *conducive social context* for his question. For example, if Jack wants to know how many pets the user has, he might tell a story about a woman who has 20 cats and then say "You don't have that many pets, do you, George?"

Characters need to have *episodic memory*, including both *short-term memory* emphasizing within-session events and *long-term* memory emphasizing events whose implications persist across sessions. For example, Linda, the Extempo product guide, has short-term memory for how much time a user says he or she has, so that she can plan activities that fit the time available. She remembers how many questions the user has asked, to estimate the user's curiosity about the current topic and adapt how much information she offers. She remembers how many questions she has successfully answered in the current session, so that she can make her apologies more or less effusive, as appropriate. Linda has long-term memory for what topics she has already explained to the user, so that she can remind the user and let him or her choose whether to revisit prior topics or move on to new topics. She also remembers *user preferences*, for example speed of dialogue and whether or not to invite questions explicitly during an interaction.

The process of getting acquainted and building intimacy is highly culturally dependent (Hayes-Roth et al. [6]). In American culture, people are accustomed to exchanging a variety of information, but doing so gradually, over a series of encounters and in the context of a recognizable *social need or right to know*. Thus, Jack wants to learn a dozen or so facts about each user, but he does not rush the process. Depending on how their conversations go, he might learn one or two facts about a given user during each visit. This natural and non-intrusive approach is highly successful. Jack has a 45–85% success rate for acquiring different facts about users. In addition, a *carefully paced social exchange* prolongs gratification to the user, by allowing the character to demonstrate a continuously growing interest in the user over a longer period of time.

3.5 Characters Should Seem Empathic

To seem life-like, characters should seem to feel, perceive, and respond to emotion. Like people, characters should have emotional responses to events and situations. For example, if a user explains to Virtual Employee Nina that her failure to learn the new reporting system has put her job in jeopardy, Nina expresses anxiety in her startled body language, shocked facial expression, and her reply "Oh my God! I can't lose this job!" If the user does nothing to relieve Nina's anxiety, she will continue to express it in her continuing interactions. However, if the user reassures Nina that she can preserve her job by taking the required training course, she calms down noticeably.

Although many characters may exhibit the same dimensions of emotion (e.g. happiness, arousal, dominance), different characters should have distinctive emotional dynamics, reflecting different combinations of values on neutral state, provocative events, provoked effects, and regression speed.

Thus, Katherine the Newscaster has a reserved and dignified manner, a long fuse, and a negotiated recovery. For example, a user might insult her by saying "You're not intelligent, you just read the news, like Annanova." Katherine might reply "I'm an intelligent interactive character, with opinions, thoughts, and feelings. And I can have a conversation with you. ...Even if you are not very polite." Despite her feelings, Katherine would be willing to continue the interaction, reading more news stories, giving her opinions, etc. However, if the user insulted her again, "I still think you're just a pretty face", Katherine would be pushed past her personal limit: "Are you saying I'm a virtual dumb bimbo?" At this point, she would refuse to answer other questions or continue the interaction, unless and until the user apologized. Although Katherine might frown or smile slightly during these exchanges, she would maintain her generally reserved body language.

By contrast, Erin the Bartender has a volatile manner, a short fuse, and a quick spontaneous recovery (except for grievous offenses). For example, a user might insult Erin's intelligence, "You're stupid." She would simply insult him back and move on, "Yeah and you're ugly. You want a drink?" If the user continued to insult her, Erin would continue to serve him drinks, but refuse to give him the pleasure of her social company. Of course, if the user seriously threatened Erin or any of her customers, she would eject him and lock him out of the bar. Unlike Katherine, Erin uses dramatic full-body expression of her emotions.

Characters also should display awareness of and empathy for the user's emotions. When Coach Harmony observes a user making a lot of mistakes in role-play practice, she might say "I see the role-play with Ed was difficult for you, Jacob. Don't worry. Ed is a difficult character and a lot of people have trouble with him. But you might encounter guys like Ed on the job, so this practice is very useful for you." Conversely, when Harmony observes improvement in a user's role-play well, she might say "Congratulations, Mary! That was your best score so far with Ed. You'll master this role-play in no time." Harmony's different facial expressions, gestures, and body language reinforce her differential messages of sympathetic encouragement or celebration.

3.6 Characters Should Seem Variable

To seem life-like, characters should seem to vary all aspects of their behavior incidentally and unconsciously. Characters should *avoid repetition*, unless it is done for an *intended effect*, as in *signature behaviors*. This becomes more critical as the frequency, recency, or importance of the message increases and as the length or memorability of the dialogue increases. Thus, each of our characters has a variety of dialogues for their most frequent role-independent exchanges, for example: greeting, farewell, thank you. In addition, each character has many variations on their most frequent role-specific exchanges. For example, Harmony has many ways to communicate that the user made a mistake or performed correctly. Role-players Nina and Ed have many ways of enacting their respective role-play scenarios, even thought the facts and feelings remain the same.

More generally, characters should introduce *random, normally distributed variability in what, when, and how* they act through all channels. There are different techniques for achieving variability.

The simplest technique for introducing variability is *probabilistic choice among discrete alternatives*. For example, Harmony has three gestures for initiating a new conversation topic. She uses the most subtle gesture with high frequency and the other two only occasionally.

The most powerful technique is *parameterization of behaviors*, with normally distributed random variation on continuous parameters. For example, Katherine has a 3D computer graphics embodiment, generously provided by the company Haptek. Her gestures have built-in random variation within small ranges of parameter values, such as extent and speed of a movement, as well as intentionally controllable variation within larger ranges on those same parameters.

Actions and dialogue can have normally distributed random variability on discrete parameters. For example, all of our characters incorporate the #user-name variable in many of their dialogues. During an interaction, this variable is replaced with either the user's name or one of the character's favorite nicknames, modulated by an author-specified frequency distribution.

3.7 Characters Should Seem Coherent

To seem life-like, characters should seem to behave coherently. Like people, characters should appear to be singular creatures, driven by persistent identity and manner, slowly evolving belief structures, and dynamic flows of correlated feelings, intentions, and focus of attention (Hayes-Roth et al. [8]).

Characters ordinarily should display *strong local coherence*, with all aspects of their conversation, gesture, facial expression, and body language coordinated in the service of an immediate, but short-lived local *focus of attention*, and with clear *transitional signals* between episodes.

For example, if Harmony observes a user behaving inappropriately during a role-play practice, she might take a few moments at the beginning of a feedback session to communicate her disapproval. She might initiate this episode by crossing her arms over her chest, frowning, and shaking her head in a negative side-to-side manner. Maintaining the body language, but holding her head still, she might say "John, you behaved inappropriately with Nina. You called her 'sweetheart'." Letting her arms fall to her sides, palms facing outwards, she might continue "You will never gain Nina's confidence and cooperation if you treat her condescendingly." Extending her right hand, palm up, she might conclude "We'll talk about this more later." Having completed this episode, Harmony might signal transition to the main feedback session by adopting a more relaxed body posture, smiling at the user, and saying "OK, let's see how you did on the target skills in this role-play".

Characters also should display *moderate global coherence*, with persistent foundational elements of their conversation, gesture, facial expression, and body language coordinated in the service of *an enduring persona*; and with variable context-dependent elements coordinated in the service of *an episodic progression*. For example, Jack will always be the same adorable puppy, who likes to do tricks and make puns and tell haikus and stories about his friends. He will always be ready to help users navigate the web site and "learn about la vida Petopia". But Jack will try not to repeat himself in his interactions with a given user. And the intimacy of his interactions with the user will increase over time, as their acquaintance and exchange of personal information advances.

4 Evaluating the Life-Likeness of Characters

Half a century ago, Alan Turing proposed that we replace logical debate on the possible mechanization of thought with a behavioral test for artificial intelligence:

> *A computer can think if a person conversing with it over an anonymous communication channel <u>believes</u> that he or she is conversing with a human being.*

This so-called "Turing Test" is really a test of deception. It is necessary to physically separate the computer from the person, in order to conceal the fact of its inhumanity. Of course, passing the Turing Test is quite difficult. However, passing the Turing Test is <u>not</u> the goal of our work on characters and it is neither necessary nor sufficient, nor even perhaps desirable, that our characters pass the Turing Test in order to seem life-like. Indeed, people might feel uncomfortable in a world populated by automata masquerading as human beings.

Although we do not adopt the Turing Test for evaluating the life-likeness of characters, we propose a variation that preserves Turing's focus on user response:

> *A character is life-like to the extent that a person interacting with it* <u>*suspends disbelief*</u> *that he or she is interacting with a human being.*

In other words, the person might well know that the character is not a human being and say so if asked. But the person would not care and would not intentionally or significantly alter his or her own behavior on that account, within the context of the interaction. In this respect, our test resembles the artistic criteria we apply to evaluate characters in books and animations and to actors playing roles in films, plays, and TV shows. People <u>know</u> that these are not real human beings, but willingly suspend disbelief in order to have the pleasure of responding to them as if they were real. Similarly, animate characters will pass our test of life-likeness, when people willingly suspend disbelief in order to have the service, pleasure, convenience, or other desired consequences of interacting with them as if they were real.

5 Conclusion

The interdisciplinary study of life-like characters is in its infancy. We have a growing number of increasingly more compelling case studies of particular characters and an associated growing body of experience among the creators of those characters. However, to become an enduring intellectual discipline and to support a practical commercial enterprise, the field needs a new level of theory and methodology. This chapter is an attempt to document and interpret the experience I have gained from my own work on characters. I invite others in the field to make similar inventories of their own experiences so that, together, we may construct a broader and deeper understanding and continue to advance the science and practice of building life-like characters.

Acknowledgments

Development of the technology underlying the Extempo applications was supported by grants from the Advanced Technology Program (ATP) of the National Institutes for Standards and Technology (NIST) of the US Department of Commerce. Development of the Stanford applications was supported by funding from DARPA, NSF, Intel, the Stanford Center for the Study of Language and Information (CSLI), and an Award for Innovative Research from the Stanford Dean of Research. Contributors to the Extempo work include: Robert van Gent, M. Vaughan Johnson, Tom Sephton, Karen Amano, Rami Saker, Louise Crow, Ruth Huard, Winter Mead, Corey Fugman, and Hallie Kushner. Contributors to the Stanford work include: Robert van Gent, Ruth Huard, Eric Sincoff, and Lee Brownston.

References

1. Hayes-Roth, B.: Getting into the story. *Style* **33**(2):246–266 (1999)
2. Hayes-Roth, B.: Improvisational puppets, actors, and avatars. In: *Proceedings of the Computer Game Developers' Conference* (1996)
3. Hayes-Roth, B.: Mask and cyber mask. In: *Proceedings of the Computer Game Developers' Conference* (1997)
4. Hayes-Roth, B.: What is a virtual person—Not just a pretty face! In: *Proceedings of the SIGGRAPH Conference*, Los Angeles (2001)
5. Hayes-Roth, B., Doyle, P.: Animate characters. *Journal of Autonomous Agents and Multi-Agent Systems* **1**(2):195–230 (1998)
6. Hayes-Roth, B., Maldonado, H., Moraes, M.: Multi-cultural agents for a multi-cultural world. In: *Proceedings of the Imagina Conference on Media and Technology*, Monte Carlo (2002)
7. Hayes-Roth, B., van Gent, R.: Story-making with improvisational puppets. In: *Proceedings of the First International Conference on Autonomous Agents*, Los Angeles (1997)
8. Hayes-Roth, B., van Gent, R., Huber, D.: Acting in character. In: *Creating Personalities for Synthetic Actors*, ed Trappl, R., Petta, P. (Springer, Berlin New York 1998)
9. Huard, R., Hayes-Roth, B.: Character mastery with improvisational puppets. In: *Proceedings of the IJCAI Workshop on Animated Interface Agents*, Nagoya, Japan (1997)
10. Isbister, K., Hayes-Roth, B.: Social implications of interactive characters. In: *AAAI Workshop on Intelligent Agents*, Seattle, WA (1998). White Paper available on request.
11. Johnstone, K.: *IMPRO: Improvisation and the theater* (Routledge, New York 1992)
12. Thomas, F., Johnston, O.: *Disney Animation: The Illusion of Life* (Abbeville Press, New York 1981)

Some Issues in the Design of Character Scripting and Specification Languages – a Personal View

Thomas Rist

DFKI GmbH, Stuhlsatzenhausweg 3, D-66123 Saarbrücken, Germany
rist@dfki.de

Summary. The increasing number of applications that deploy animated conversational characters motivates work toward standardized scripting and specification languages for characters and applications with characters. However, standardization in this area is difficult since objectives and requirements vary widely from character to character, application to application, and across projects. Based on personal impressions gathered at several dedicated character workshops during 2002, the current contribution recalls some of the issues and challenges that arise when designing character scripting and specification languages.

1 Introduction

During the last decade the field of life-like characters has grown significantly and established itself as its own subfield located somewhere at the intersection of multiple disciplines including computer graphics and animation, artificial intelligence, human–computer interaction, psychology, sociology, design and arts, and all kinds of application fields. There is now a broad spectrum of characters that vary greatly in their audio-visual appearance, observable behavior, conversational skills, and internal "cognitive complexity". Most of the current systems with life-like characters distinguish between a character's embodiment and a higher level behavior control component. Some relate this distinction to the biological body/brain dichotomy while others take a more technically oriented view and associate embodiment with an animation engine (often called *character player*), while behavior control is related to some sort of automated behavior generation, often based on AI techniques, such as task-oriented hierarchical planning, or based on the simulation of certain aspects of human-like cognition. Following the latter distinction, observable behavior of a character can be regarded as the execution of a script in the character player. Thereby, a script is a temporally ordered set of actions including body gestures, facial expressions, verbal utterances, locomotion, and (quasi-) physical interactions with other entities of the character's environment. So it comes as little surprise that all projects that aim at the development or deployment of life-like characters need to address the issue of a representation format which, metaphorically speaking, bridges between a character's mind and body. When looking at ongoing character projects, it is still common practice that each project defines its own special-purpose representation format to be used either by human script authors or as part of the interface between modules which are responsible for determining an agent's behavior on the one hand, and player technologies which are responsible for animation rendering and speech synthesis, and possibly further output modalities, on the other hand.

A common need motivates the search for a common solution, such as the development of a standardized representation format. No doubt, a commonly agreed-on format promises a number of advantages. For instance, it would:

- make obsolete a great deal of redundant developments and thus save resources in many R&D projects,
- contribute to the interoperability and sharing of components and data collections across projects and systems and thus facilitate rapid prototyping of systems with increased functionality,
- facilitate and foster the commercial uptake of systems and modules (especially character players), and resources, such as libraries for gestures and facial expressions, across a broad range of applications.

Arguments of this kind have motivated several research groups to launch initiatives toward the development of expressive languages for scripting animated conversational characters. Part I of the current book comprises a unique collection of proposals for markup and scripting languages that have been tailored to the particular needs of designing applications with animated conversational characters. During 2002 the idea of defining a standard language for the scripting of characters and interactive applications with characters was discussed at a number of dedicated workshops including an AAMAS'02 workshop[1], a PRICAI'02 workshop[2], and two concentration meetings[3], organized within the European IST Programme. In the remaining part of this contribution I summarize a number of personal impressions that I took away from these workshops.

---

[1] AAMAS'02 Workshop on Embodied Conversational Agents - Let's specify and evaluate them! In conjunction with the First International Joint Conference on Autonomous Agents & Multi-Agent Systems, 16 July 2002, Bologna, Italy.

[2] International Workshop on Lifelike Animated Agents: Tools, Affective Functions, and Applications. Held in conjunction with the 7th Pacific Rim International Conference on AI (PRICAI'02), 19 August 2002, Tokyo, Japan.

[3] IST Cross-programme Concentation Meeting on Representation Formats/Languages. 18 July 2002, Bologna, Italy.
VHML Workshop in conjunction with the 7th E3 Concentation Meeting on Interfaces & Enhanced Services, Signal Processing & Mixed Reality. 6 February 2002, Brussels, Belgium.

2 Objectives, Desiderata, and Challenges

To start with, it is essential to be aware of the objectives that motivate the development of a certain language or representation format. Once the objectives are identified, one should be able to identify a number of functional requirements as well as desiderata which in turn would guide the design of a scripting language or character specification format. As it turns out, there is a multitude of objectives, some of which are project-specific while others are shared across projects but not necessarily considered equally important from one project to another. For the purpose of this contribution, I just pick a few objectives for further discussion in view of potential standardization efforts.

Who Are the Target Users? – Human Authors Versus Software Modules

Many of the proposed languages are actually meant to support human authors in the development of applications with life-like characters. Especially scripting languages for web applications with characters fall into this category. Probably inspired by the role that HTML played in the overwhelming success of the World Wide Web, the idea is to provide a general-purpose markup language that would even allow non-programmers to compile interactive (web) applications with life-like characters. Among the desiderata that such scripting aids need to fulfill are (i) generality to enable deployment for a wide range of applications as well as (ii) simplicity of use manifested in an intuitive naming of tags, attributes, and values.

Generality is essentially a question of language expressiveness and extensibility. Concerning expressiveness, the problem is that it is hard to tell what could be considered as the basic functionality that any life-like character should have and thus merits formulation as a standard. Unfortunately, characters comprise a multitude of very different aspects that are of varying relevance from one application/project to another. In some cases, it is more or less an issue of granularity and thus can be solved by some kind of hierarchical (or multi-resolution) modeling approach. Examples of this kind are geometric models for facial animation that comprise multiple resolutions. Following this rationale, the role of the standard is basically to provide the common representation scheme that leaves open the level of detail to which it is instantiated. However, the modeling of other aspects assumes a concrete commitment to a specific theory which may actually conflict with some competing theories. Personality and affect are aspects of this kind and therefore make it quite difficult to establish consensus about what should go into a standard. Experience from standardization efforts in other areas, such as in multimedia interface design (Fähnrich and Koller [2]), has shown that it may be relatively easy to standardize formats at a syntactic level, but it is much more difficult to introduce standards at a semantic level and even harder to convince a community of potential users that such a standard should be followed.

Concerning simplicity of use in the sense that humans should be able to read and write scripts and specifications in the language, I am less confident that this is among the most important issues. Looking at the short history of the World Wide Web it is at least debatable whether its breakthrough was not also a matter of freely available HTML browsers (such as Mosaic, Netscape, MS Internet Explorer, and others) and easy-to-use editing tools that completely hide HTML code from web page designers. Certainly, this is a kind of chicken-egg problem. If there is a widely agreed-on standard, then tool developments will follow that match the standard – the release of the MPEG-4 standard and the subsequent implementation of MPEG-4 players is an example of such a development. Likewise, if there were commonly used tools and rich resources, such as animation libraries, then the representation formats supported by the tools or used for the representation of the resources could serve as a promising starting point for standardization efforts – many of the so-called "industrial quasi-standards" are of this kind. After all, this suggests that standardization initiatives for character markup/scripting languages have better chances for success if they address this aspect as well and, for instance, have a good strategy for disseminating suitable tools, too. And we must not forget that in this context suitability is primarily a question of the target user group. Especially when dealing with complex characters, application design becomes a task that shares more and more similarities with making a movie or staging a theater play. I have little knowledge about what would make a good tool for people working in this area, but I would be rather surprised if they worried too much about XML-compliance. So why not consult experts from this domain when designing tools for the scripting of virtual characters and have them validate the tools in practice?

Finally, it should be mentioned that there are also representation languages that aim to provide a common representation format for the interchange of data and control among components in character systems. Examples of this kind are the RRL (Rich Representation Language) developed by Piwek et al. [4] for the NECA system, APML (Affective Presentation Markup Language) developed by De Carolis et al. [1], and the M3L (Multi-Modal Markup Language) developed in the SmartKom project (Wahlster et al. [6]). In this context, at least simplicity of use becomes primarily a matter of more technical criteria including compactness, uniformity, and suitability for efficient processing. However, if suitable authoring tools become available, it may well be possible to transform user input into expressions of such languages too, even though this has not been an objective of the language designers.

What to Specify? – Character Profiles Versus Behavior

During the above-mentioned workshops, discussions sometimes led to confusion due to the lack of a clear distinction between specifying a character's profile on the one hand, and its actual behavior on the other hand. Most of the current proposals for character scripting languages focus on the behavior part. That is, a user (or a system) specifies what actions a character should perform when and perhaps under which contextual conditions. In contrast, a profile specification usually captures a number of selected aspects of a character that hold at a certain instant of time. Similar to the entries in a passport, one may consider individual attributes such as name, age, gender, size, color of hair and eyes as part of a profile. Other individual properties may be added, such as voice characteristics and personality traits. But what else? Again the question arises of whether there are chances to agree on a common set of such attributes. Some people suggest that only persistent aspects should be part of a character profile while others see profiles as a collection of state variables that can change over time.

Furthermore, it is not necessarily obvious where to draw the borderline between profile and behavior specifications. For example, similar to high-level programming languages where functional specifications often replace procedural coding, one can envisage powerful profile specifications that already determine much of a character's behavior. The attractiveness of such an approach is that it can help to avoid inconsistencies between profile and behavior specifications.

Quo Vadis? – Specification Formats Versus Protocols

In view of future scenarios that feature close-geared interactions among multiple characters and humans it becomes questionable whether current scripting approaches are sufficient to handle such scenarios. As an example, let us consider a face-to-face conversation between a virtual speaker and a virtual hearer. Most of the current scripting approaches would just provide means to specify the behavior of the speaker and the hearer more or less independently of each other. As known from human–human face-to-face communication, however, interactions occur at various levels and on different time-scales. While speaking, eye contact between speaker and hearer follows certain rules and can be represented as a sequence of blinks and gaze turns. At a higher level, the speaker's words may cause a change in the hearer's affective state and in turn change the hearer's facial display before the speaker has finished his or her utterance. Realizing the effect of the uttered words by reading in the hearer's face, speakers often take counter actions and continue with a modified wording etc.

To handle such fine-grained interactions, I think valuable inspirations can be borrowed from the area of network protocols. In this area complex interactions are often specified in terms of layered protocol stacks. The most prominent example is the OSI (Open Systems Interconnection) reference model [3] that provides a standardized framework for describing and implementing protocols for data exchange among different stations in a stack of seven layers with a bidirectional flow of control and data between the layers. Another example that is more related to the current issue has been developed within the TACIT project to describe scenarios of continuity in human–computer

interaction from different points of view and at different degrees of granularity (Rist and Booth [5]). Applying such an approach for the specification
of complex character behavior is by no means an easy task and there is no
guarantee of success. However, it may be worthwhile to try in order to (i)
improve the structure of current scripting approaches and (ii) overcome some
of their limitations with regard to the modeling of complex and fine-grained
interaction processes.

3 Conclusions

To sum up, the availability of character specification and scripting standards
would be helpful especially from an economical point of view. However, standardization is difficult in an active and fast-moving research field such as the
current one that will continue to bring about characters and applications of
increased functionality and complexity. On the other hand, for some classes of
characters and applications, standards can be defined right now. If the community could only agree on what these classes are, then the question of how
it should be done would be solved, too.

Acknowledgments

The elaborations presented above are based on fruitful discussions with attendees of the aforementioned workshops and colleagues of the NECA, MagiCster,
MIAU, and SmartKom projects.

References

1. De Carolis, B., Carofiglio, V., Bilvi, B., Pelachaud, C.: APML, a mark-up language for believable behavior generation. In: *Proceedings AAMAS-02 Workshop
on Embodied Conversational Agents—Let's specify and evaluate them!* (2002)
2. Fähnrich, K., Koller, F.: ISO 14915: A standard on multimedia user interface
design. In: *Proceedings of HCI'97* (Vol. 2) (1997) pp 691–694
3. International Organization for Standardization, ISO/IEC 10731:1994 Open Systems Interconnection – Basic Reference Model (1994)
4. Piwek, P., Krenn, B., Schröder, M., Grice, M., Baumann, S., Pirker, H.: RRL: A
rich representation language for the description of agent behavior in NECA. In:
*Proceedings AAMAS-02 Workshop on Embodied Conversational Agents—Let's
specify and evaluate them!* (2002)
5. Rist, T., Booth, S.: Adaption of information delivery to support task-level continuity. In: *Proceedings of HCI 2001* (2001)
6. Wahlster, W., Reithinger, N., Blocher, A.: SmartCom: Towards multimodal dialogues with anthropomorphic interface agents. Technical Report 15, SmartCom
project. www.smartkom.org/reports/Report-NR-15.pdf (2001)

A

Online Material

The contributing authors of this book provide electronic material, such as software and movie clips, that allows one to try out their character systems or watch demonstrations of applications with life-like characters.

The electronic material associated with the chapters contained in this book is accessible via the following Internet link:

http://www.vhml.org/LLC/llc-book.html

Helmut Prendinger (contact)
prendinger@acm.org

Index

Cognitive Technologies

Printing: Druckhaus Berlin-Mitte GmbH
Binding: Buchbinderei Stein & Lehmann, Berlin